AF573382

NatWest PLAYFAIR CRICKET ANNUAL 1996

49th edition

EDITED BY BILL FRINDALL

All statistics by the Editor unless otherwise credited

PLAYFAIR CRICKET COMPETITION 1996

TEST CRICKET QUIZ

£1500 TO BE WON

PLUS NATWEST FINAL TICKETS AND HOSPITALITY
PLUS 25 CONSOLATION PRIZES

First Prize £500 + overnight accommodation (B and B) at the Regents Park Hilton Hotel (opposite Lord's) on 6 and 7 September + TWO tickets to the 1996 NatWest Trophy Final + NatWest hospitality

Second Prize £400 + TWO tickets to the 1996 NatWest Trophy Final

Third Prize £300 + TWO tickets to the 1996 NatWest Trophy Final

Fourth Prize £200

Fifth Prize £100

Consolation prizes

Senders of the next 25 correct entries will each receive a signed copy of ATHERS – THE AUTHORISED BIOGRAPHY OF MIKE ATHERTON by David Norrie, published by Headline at £17.99.

Closing date for entries
is 12.00 noon on 23 July 1996

Winning entries will be drawn by the Man of the Match Adjudicator at one of the NatWest semi-finals on Tuesday 13 August.

PLAYFAIR CRICKET COMPETITION 1996

CRICKET QUIZ

ENTRY FORM

Please PRINT your answers in the spaces provided and answer every question.

The answers to all ten questions can be found within this Annual

1 Which team was first admitted to the County Championship in 1905? ....

2 On which ground did Andrew Symonds break the world six-hitting records? ....

3 Which bowler last season achieved a hat-trick in which all three victims were lbw? ....

4 Who is the only batsman to score 400 in a first-class innings on more than one occasion? ....

5 In which town could you have watched a Test match at the Arbab Niaz Stadium in 1995? ....

6 Who is the only batsman to score 8000 runs in Limited-Overs Internationals? ....

7 Which team will stage a home first-class match at Boghall Cricket Club this season? ....

8 Who was the last bowler to take 100 first-class wickets in a season? ....

9 Who was the last bowler to take 200 first-class wickets in a season? ....

10 Which substitute fielder achieved two stumpings during a first-class match last season? ....

Your name and address:

....

....

....

Your daytime telephone number: ....

Post to: PLAYFAIR CRICKET COMPETITION, Special Events, The Gibson Hall, Bishopsgate, London EC2M 4BQ.

Entries must be received before noon on 23 July 1996. All-correct entries will go into the prize-winning draw on 13 August and an announcement detailing all prize-winners will appear in the October edition of *The Cricketer* magazine. A list of winners is available on request by writing to Mrs B.J.Quinn at the above address and enclosing a stamped addressed envelope.

Rules: All entries must be on this official form. Proof of posting is not proof of entry. The decision of the editor regarding the answers to this quiz shall be final and binding; no correspondence may be entered into.

1995 PLAYFAIR CRICKET COMPETITION

CARIBBEAN CRICKET QUIZ ANSWERS

1	Who was the first West Indian to score 8000 runs in Test cricket?	G.St A. (Garfield) SOBERS
2	Who prior to 1994 was the only visiting captain to win a Test in Barbados?	R.E.S. (Bob) WYATT
3	Who first shared in two partnerships of over 500 runs in first-class matches?	F.M.M. (Frank) WORRELL
4	Who were the first holders of the Red Stripe Cup?	JAMAICA
5	Who is the only batsman to score five hundreds in successive Test innings?	E.de C. (Everton) WEEKES
6	Who established a world record by bowling 588 balls in a Test innings?	Sonny RAMADHIN
7	Who achieved the first hat-trick in Tests between England and West Indies?	P.J. (Peter) LOADER
8	On which island is first-class cricket played at Windsor Park?	DOMINICA
9	Name the first bowler to take all ten wickets in a first-class match in the West Indies?	E.E. (Eddie) HEMMINGS
10	Who scored a record aggregate of 1765 first-class runs in a Caribbean season?	E.H. (Patsy) HENDREN

There were 270 sets of correct answers out of a total of 631 entries. The winners were drawn by John Lever MBE (Essex and England) and Mr John Melbourne CBE, Deputy Group Chief Executive, National Westminster Bank at the 1995 semi-final between Yorkshire and Northamptonshire at Headingley on 15 August.

First Prize:	£500 + two nights' accommodation + two tickets to include hospitality at the 1995 NatWest Trophy Final	Mr S. BEDFORD (Hereford)
Second Prize:	£400 + two tickets to the 1995 NatWest Trophy Final	Rev P.J. WILLIAMS (Maldon)
Third Prize:	£300 + two tickets to the 1995 NatWest Trophy Final	Mr D.A.W. DIAPER (Wivenhoe)
Fourth Prize:	£200	Mr E. BOURNE (Chelmsley Wood)
Fifth Prize:	£100	Mr M.J. LISZKA (Washington)

25 Runners-up: *THE WISDEN BOOK OF CRICKET RECORDS* by Bill Frindall:

Mr B.F.Adams (Sheffield)
Mr A.M.Alpe (Chatham)
Mr B.K.Anderson (Newton-upon-Raxcliffe)
Mr J.M.Brown (Rolleston-on-Dove)
Mr P.Buckley (Newby)
Mr S.Clee (Liss)
Mrs H.A.Cording (Taunton)
Dr N.Goodwin (Farnham Common)
Ms S.Harrison (Scarborough)
Mr N.E.Hendricks (Ruislip)
Mr L.W.Isaac (Gilwern)
Mr N.Jones (Acocks Green)
Mr A.S.Kelly (Winterton)
Mr U.O'Brien (North Kensington)
Mr A.Parker (Blackpool)
Mr R.A.Parrish (Langley)
Mr P.A.Rodgers (Chesterfield)
Mr P.Sillis (Ealing)
Mr D.Spencer (Measham)
Mr G.D.Springett (Brondesbury)
Mr R.T.Tarleton (Oakham)
Mr W.E.Thorpe (Cottingham)
Mr R.Thurston (Stockton-on-Tees)
Mr A.Wainwright (Walsgrave)
Mr G.R.H.West (Barnsley)

SPONSOR'S MESSAGE FROM

NatWest

DEVELOPING EXCELLENCE

Plus ça change, plus c'est la même chose. The truth of those words, penned nearly 150 years ago, remains. The more things change, the more they stay the same. Cricket may be undergoing change with a new board structure, it may even be in crisis with its top players no longer rated as even second best in the world. But the 1996 *NatWest Playfair Cricket Annual*, the 49th in its unbeaten innings, is unchanged. It is as it always has been . . . a pocket bible full of cricketing statistics and information.

So, too, does NatWest's dedication to the game and the community remain the same. In reality, in fact, it is even stronger. This is the 15th year of our sponsorship of this annual and we are delighted to be associated with something that is so warmly welcomed every spring. However, 1996 sees an even greater commitment to cricket. The renewal of the NatWest Trophy contract means that it runs until the new millennium, and sponsorship has been widened to take in English cricket's Development of Excellence. With so many wondering after England's winter campaigns just where our next successful Test side is coming from, it is clear that the answer can be found in this programme, together of course with the Under-19 side. Let's face it, Tendulkar was playing for India at 16. Pakistan had Aqib Javed in their side at the same age and Waqar was only 17 when he made his debut. Lara made his debut for West Indies at 21 and three years later scored 375 against England. Shaun Pollock was just 22 when he burst on to the scene with such success last winter. Clearly, there is a need for us to discover and foster our young talent.

NatWest are focused on developing people. Staff training helps them as employees, building a team spirit preparing them for the day-to-day pressures of life. As with NatWest so then with cricket . . . helping to ensure that the best of our young cricketers become the best in the world. 'Supporting the Development of Excellence programme fits NatWest's philosophy perfectly,' says Martin Gray, Chief Executive of NatWest UK. 'Everything we do is about striving for excellence. Now we have created an exciting partnership which hopefully will help cricket. We wish to be able to look back and say "Thank goodness we did that".'

EDITORIAL PREFACE

First, let me pay tribute to our sponsors for extending their contract both in terms of time and in degree of support. Now that they have renewed their association with our national 60-over competition, it is fitting that this edition, the fifteenth to bear their logo, should be the first to include the name of NatWest in its title.

Secondly, I must thank Headline and in particular Ian Marshall, their senior non-fiction editor, for delaying deadlines so that we can feature the scorecard and report of yesterday's World Cup final. Sri Lanka's historic triumph over their much-vaunted and highly professional adversaries should refresh world cricket. Aravinda de Silva demonstrated the range and power of his strokeplay during his scintillating hundred in last season's Benson and Hedges Cup final as well as in many other outstanding innings for Kent. His displays against India and Australia elevated him to the highest rank of batsmanship and it is very sad that, unless the TCCB changes its hosting schedule, we are unlikely to see him or any other members of Sri Lanka's highly entertaining team in England this century.

Playfair's later typesetting has also enabled me to update all Test match and limited-overs international career records to the eve of the World Cup (13 February). With the winter season now virtually over and just the two-match Test series between West Indies and New Zealand to be played, this means that the Test records for the other seven teams will be up to date when India visit Edgbaston in June for the first of this summer's Cornhill Test matches. We offer a warm welcome to Mohammed Azharuddin's team and look forward to seeing their many gifted players, particularly Sachin Tendulkar, Anil Kumble and Javagal Srinath, during the first half of the season. Although, sadly, Lavinia, Duchess of Norfolk, passed away during the winter, the traditional Arundel tourists' pipe-opener has been preserved and India will be playing the Duke of Norfolk's XI on Sunday, 5 May. The Friends of Arundel Castle Cricket Club have safeguarded the future of cricket in that incomparable setting by electing as their president The Earl of Arundel, heir to the Norfolk title.

Later in the season we will have the additional delight of welcoming Wasim Akram's Pakistan team with its rich array of varied talent. The captain's exceptional all-round skills will be supplemented by those fine left-handed opening batsmen, Aamir Sohail and Saeed Anwar, the disdainful strokeplay of the massive Inzaman-ul-Haq, lethal pace and late swing of Waqar Younis, and the spinning wizadry of Mushtaq Ahmed. Watch out too for their exciting young off-spinner, Saqlain Mushtaq, who regrettably was given only one match in the World Cup.

Our delayed deadline has also allowed the inclusion of a brief register of prospective members of those two touring teams. For those who would like the bare bones of those statistics fleshed out, may I recommend *World Cricketers: A Biographical Dictionary*, an illuminating addition to your cricket library recently compiled by my *TMS* colleague (and father of Sussex's latest all-rounder), Christopher Martin-Jenkins.

The TCCB has fine-tuned two of our domestic competitions for the coming season. The introduction of three points for drawing a Britannic Assurance Championship match makes sound sense in preparing players mentally for Test cricket. One suspects that England's epic rearguard action at Johannesburg may have influenced this move. Even more laudable is the decision to rework the 1997 fixture list to facilitate Wednesday starts in most matches thus avoiding the absurd Sunday interruption. The second change involves reducing Benson and Hedges Cup games by five overs per innings. With 50 overs now the legal limit for all limited-overs internationals, it is a relief that at least one of our instant competitions should be of the required length.

Last year, Darren Gough's injuries and loss of form did nothing to expel the growing belief in the powers of the jinx imposed by being portrayed on the cover of this annual. Last October, one cricket writer asked me to reveal the identity of this year's victim so that he could prepare a suitable article summarising a promising career about to meet an untimely end. My choice had been Graham Thorpe, but despite his savaging my bowling during a pre-lunch century for Farnham against my Maltamaniacs a decade ago, I bear him no grudge and have decided to test the power of the infamous *Playfair* hex by awarding this dubious accolade to Wasim Akram.

For the tenth time, assembly of this wee tome has been greatly assisted by many kind providers of information, particularly by the county clubs' administrators, scorers and statisticians; by Tony Brown, Tim Lamb and Kate Jenkins at the TCCB; by Clive Hitchcock of the ICC; and by David Armstrong of the MCCA. I am again indebted to Phillip Bailey for compiling the first-class career records; to my wife Debbie for researching, dogsbodying and proof-checking despite the January arrival of Alice Katharine; to Barbara Quinn and her NatWest Special Events team for their highly efficient administration of our competition; and especially to Chris Leggett and his typesetting team at Letterpart for coping with a late avalanche of material.

BILL FRINDALL
Urchfont
18 March 1996

SRI LANKA COMES OF AGE

Defying some bookmakers' odds of 66-1 and transforming the standard format of limited-overs cricket, Sri Lanka most deservedly became the first host nation to win the World Cup. Totally underrated, they emerged as the only unbeaten team in the competition, defeating favourites Australia in the final by the overwhelming margin of seven wickets and with 22 balls in hand.

Arjuna Ranatunga's team had given ample warning of their coming of age by defeating Pakistan on their own soil 2-1 both in the Test series and in the one-day rubber a few months earlier. Then came their traumatic visit to Australia where they overcame hostility from all sides to reach the World Series finals ahead of West Indies. The horrendous bomb explosion in the heart of their capital almost ended their participation in the World Cup and denied them practice matches against Australia and West Indies when those Boards refused to allow their teams to visit. Ironically for Australia, Sri Lanka's transformation was masterminded by one of their former Test players, Colombo-born Dav Whatmore, currently their national coach and mentor. Limited-overs cricket had become increasingly stereotyped, with games following a predictable format – limited cricket in fact. Instead of delaying their batting onslaught to the last ten overs, Sri Lanka took full advantage of the fielding restrictions applicable to the first 15 overs by launching each innings with whirlwind strokeplay. Against India they scored a phenomenal 71 off the first seven overs and they savaged poor Kenya, still on Cloud Nine after their historic victory against West Indies, to the extent of a record total of 398.

Watched by a capacity crowd of 28,500, the final, Lahore's first floodlit international, featured the two best limited-overs teams and the Cup's two outstanding captains. Ranatunga challenged history by opting to field when no team batting second had previously won a World Cup final and demonstrated his flexibility when his pace bowlers conceded 68 off 13 overs by employing spin for the remainder of the innings. Mark Taylor, once considered unsuitable for this form of cricket and who would have chosen to bat anyway, registered a highly unexpected record when his score of 74 was found to be the highest by an Australian captain (Ian Chappell, Allan Border, *et al*) in all World Cup matches. When his partnership of 101 with the emergent Ricky Ponting took Australia to 137-1 in the 27th over, a total of 300 was in prospect. Aravinda de Silva had other ideas and from the moment he lured Taylor into a miscued sweep, he embarked on an exceptional performance which brought him three wickets, two catches, the third century in World Cup finals (after those by Clive Lloyd in 1975 and Viv Richards four years later), and, inevitably, the Player of the Match award.

With its flawed format devoting three weeks and 30 matches to a ridiculous preamble which not only allowed eight of the original dozen teams to qualify for the final seven games but also compelled the players to spend more time travelling than playing, and the organisers' abysmal handling of the Colombo crisis, this will not go on record as the most successful or enjoyable World Cup tournament. The matches were poorly attended in Pakistan, where cricket followers are totally partisan, while crowd control in Calcutta was so ineffectual that the match had to be abandoned. The opening ceremony bordered on farce and, inexplicably staged in Calcutta, added hundreds of miles to every team's itinerary. Those criticisms apart, it did produce much memorable cricket and a chance to see all the game's leading players, apart from the sadly injured and absent Davids, Houghton (Zimbabwe) and Richardson (South Africa). While pluperfect batting pitches proved a nightmare for the faster bowlers and led to that fine exponent, Allan Donald, being omitted from the semi-final, they did allow spin to play a major role and put an added emphasis on the importance of high-class fielding. Hopefully the seventh tournament, to be staged in Britain in 1999, will feature traditional clothing, be organised by the ICC and reward the players with a more generous share of the vast proceeds.

WILLS WORLD CUP FINAL

AUSTRALIA v SRI LANKA

At Gaddafi Stadium, Lahore, on 17 March 1996.
Toss: Sri Lanka. Result: SRI LANKA won by 7 wickets.
Debuts: None. Match Award: P.A.de Silva.

AUSTRALIA		**Runs**	**Balls**	**6s**	**4s**	**Fall**
*M.A.Taylor	c Jayasuriya b De Silva	74	83	1	8	2-137
M.E.Waugh	c Jayasuriya b Vaas	12	15	–	1	1- 36
R.T.Ponting	b De Silva	45	73	–	2	3-152
S.R.Waugh	c De Silva b Dharmasena	13	25	–	–	5-170
S.K.Warne	st Kaluwitharana b Muralitharan	2	5	–	–	4-156
S.G.Law	c De Silva b Jayasuriya	22	30	1	–	6-202
M.G.Bevan	not out	36	49	–	2	
†I.A.Healy	b De Silva	2	3	–	–	7-205
P.R.Reiffel	not out	13	18	–	–	
D.W.Fleming						
G.D.McGrath						
Extras (LB10, W11, NB1)		22				
Total (7 wickets; 50 overs; 205 minutes)		241				

SRI LANKA		**Runs**	**Balls**	**6s**	**4s**	**Fall**
S.T.Jayasuriya	run out (McGrath/Healy)	9	7	–	1	1- 12
†R.S.Kaluwitharana	c Bevan b Fleming	6	13	–	–	2- 23
A.P.Gurusinha	b Reiffel	65	99	1	6	3-148
P.A.de Silva	not out	107	124	–	13	
*A.Ranatunga	not out	47	37	1	4	
R.S.Mahanama						
H.P.Tillekeratne						
H.D.P.K.Dharmasena						
W.P.U.C.J.Vaas						
G.P.Wickremasinghe						
M.Muralitharan						
Extras (B1, LB4, W5, NB1)		11				
Total (3 wickets; 46.2 overs; 206 minutes)		245				

SRI LANKA	*O*	*M*	*R*	*W*	**AUSTRALIA**	*O*	*M*	*R*	*W*
Wickremasinghe	7	0	38	0	McGrath	8.2	1	28	0
Vaas	6	1	30	1	Fleming	6	0	43	1
Muralitharan	10	0	31	1	Warne	10	0	58	0
Dharmasena	10	0	47	1	Reiffel	10	0	49	1
Jayasuriya	8	0	43	1	M.E.Waugh	6	0	35	0
De Silva	9	0	42	3	S.R.Waugh	3	0	15	0
					Bevan	3	0	12	0

Umpires: S.A.Bucknor (31) and D.R.Shepherd (62). **Referee:** C.H.Lloyd.

WORLD CUP MATCH RESULTS

GROUP A MATCHES

Feb	*Venue*	*Batted First*	*Score*	*Batted Second*	*Score*	*Winners*	*Match Award*
16	Hyderabad (I)	Zimbabwe	151-9	West Indies	155-4	WI	C.E.L.Ambrose
17	Colombo (RPS)	Sri Lanka	–	Australia	–	SL*	–
18	Cuttack	Kenya	199-6	India	203-3	IND	S.R.Tendulkar
21	Gwalior	West Indies	173	India	174-5	IND	S.R.Tendulkar
21	Colombo (SSC)	Zimbabwe	228-6	Sri Lanka	229-4	SL	P.A.de Silva
23	Vishakhapatnam	Australia	304-7	Kenya	207-7	AUS	M.E.Waugh
25	Colombo (RPS)	Sri Lanka	–	West Indies	–	SL*	–
26, 27	Patna	Kenya	134	Zimbabwe	137-5	ZIM	P.A.Strang
27	Bombay	Australia	258	India	242	AUS	M.E.Waugh
29	Poona	Kenya	166	West Indies	93	KEN	M.Odumbe
Mar							
1	Nagpur	Zimbabwe	154	Australia	158-2	AUS	S.K.Warne
2	Delhi	India	271-3	Sri Lanka	272-4	SL	S.T.Jayasuriya
4	Jaipur	Australia	229-6	West Indies	232-6	WI	R.B.Richardson
6	Kanpur	India	247-5	Zimbabwe	207	IND	A.D.Jadeja
6	Kandy	Sri Lanka	398-5	Kenya	254-7	SL	P.A.de Silva

** Match forfeited by Sri Lanka's opponents*

GROUP A RESULTS TABLE

	P	*W*	*L*	*Points*
Sri Lanka	5	5	–	10
Australia	5	3	2	6
India	5	3	2	6
West Indies	5	2	3	4
Zimbabwe	5	1	4	2
Kenya	5	1	4	2

Hundreds

Batsman	*Score*
S.R.Tendulkar	127*
M.E.Waugh	130
M.E.Waugh	126
S.R.Tendulkar	137
R.T.Ponting	102
V.G.Kambli	106
P.A.de Silva	145

Four or More Wickets

Bowler	*Analysis*
P.A.Strang	4-40
P.A.Strang	5-21
D.W.Fleming	5-36
S.K.Warne	4-34

QUARTER-FINALS

Mar	*Venue*	*Country*	*Score*	*Country*	*Score*	*Winners*	*Match Award*
9	Faisalabad	England	235-8	Sri Lanka	236-5	SL	S.T.Jayasuriya
9	Bangalore	India	287-8	Pakistan	248-9	PAK	N.S.Sidhu
11	Karachi	West Indies	264-8	South Africa	245	WI	B.C.Lara
11	Madras	New Zealand	286-9	Australia	289-4	AUS	M.E.Waugh

Hundreds

Batsman	*Score*
B.C.Lara	111
C.Z.Harris	130
M.E.Waugh	110

Four or More Wickets

Bowler	*Analysis*
R.A.Harper	4-47

WORLD CUP MATCH RESULTS

GROUP B MATCHES

Feb	*Venue*		*Score*		*Score*	*Winners*	*Match Award*
14	Ahmedabad	New Zealand	239-6	England	228-9	NZ	N.J.Astle
15, 16	Rawalpindi	South Africa	321-2	UAE	152-8	SA	G.Kirsten
17	Baroda	New Zealand	307-8	Holland	188-7	NZ	C.M.Spearman
18	Peshawar	UAE	136	England	140-2	ENG	N.M.K.Smith
20	Faisalabad	New Zealand	177-9	South Africa	178-5	SA	W.J.Cronje
22	Peshawar	England	279-4	Holland	230-6	ENG	G.A.Hick
24	Gujranwala	UAE	109-9	Pakistan	112-1	PAK	Mushtaq Ahmed
25	Rawalpindi	South Africa	230	England	152	SA	J.N.Rhodes
26	Lahore	Holland	145-7	Pakistan	151-2	PAK	Waqar Younis
27	Faisalabad	New Zealand	276-8	UAE	167-9	NZ	R.G.Twose
29	Karachi	Pakistan	242-6	South Africa	243-5	SA	W.J.Cronje
Mar							
1	Lahore	Holland	216-9	UAE	220-3	UAE	Salim Raza/ S.Dukanwala
3	Karachi	England	249-9	Pakistan	250-3	PAK	Aamir Sohail
5	Rawalpindi	South Africa	328-3	Holland	168-8	SA	A.C.Hudson
6	Lahore	Pakistan	281-5	New Zealand	235	PAK	Salim Malik

GROUP B RESULTS TABLE

	P	*W*	*L*	*Points*
South Africa	5	5	–	10
Pakistan	5	4	1	8
New Zealand	5	3	2	6
England	5	2	3	4
UAE	5	1	4	2
Holland	5	–	5	–

Hundreds

Batsman	*Score*
N.J.Astle	101
G.Kirsten	188*
G.A.Hick	104*
Aamir Sohail	111
A.C.Hudson	161

Four or More Wickets

Bowler	*Analysis*
Waqar Younis	4-26
S.Dukanwala	5-29

SEMI-FINALS AND THE FINAL

Mar	*Venue*	*Country*	*Score*	*Country*	*Score*	*Winners*	*Match Award*
13	Calcutta	Sri Lanka	251-8	India	120-8	SL	P.A.de Silva
14	Mohali	Australia	207-8	West Indies	202	AUS	S.K.Warne
17	**Lahore**	**Australia**	**241-7**	**Sri Lanka**	**245-3**	**Sri Lanka**	**P.A.de Silva**

Hundreds

Batsman	*Score*
P.A.de Silva	107*

Four or More Wickets

Bowler	*Analysis*
S.K.Warne	4-36

Player of the Tournament: S.T.JAYASURIYA (Sri Lanka)

INDIA REGISTER

Test Match statistics to the start of the 1996 tour of England; Limited-Overs International statistics to the eve of the Wills World Cup (14 February 1996).

ANKOLA, Salil Ashok **(Bombay)**
Born Sholapur 1 Mar 1968. RHB, RMF. F-c debut 1988-89. **Tests:** 1 (1989-90). 6 runs (av 6.00); 2 wkts (av 64.00); 0 ct. HS 6 and BB 1-35 v P (Karachi) 1989-90. **LOI:** 14 (1989-90 to 1993-94). 14 runs (av 3.50); 11 wkts (av 35.09); 1 ct. HS 7*. BB 3-33 v SA (Mohali) 1993-94.

AZHARUDDIN, Mohammed (Hyderabad)
Born Hyderabad 8 Feb 1963. 5'11". Educated at Nizam C; Osmania U. RHB, RM/LB. F-c debut 1981-82. Derbyshire 1991 and 1994 (cap 1991). *Wisden* 1990. **Tests:** 68 (1984-85 to 1995-96, 34 as captain). 4320 runs (av 46.95), 14 hundreds; 0 wkts; 69 ct. HS 199 v SL (Kanpur) 1986-87. **LOI:** 199 (1984-85 to 1995-96, 101 as captain). 5400 runs (av 36.24), 3 hundreds; 12 wkts (av 39.00); 82 ct. HS 108* v NZ (Baroda) 1988-89. BB 3-19 v A (Delhi) 1987-88.

CHATTERJEE, Utpal (Bengal)
Born Calcutta 13 Jul 1964. LHB, SLA. F-c debut 1984-85. **Tests:** 0. **LOI:** 3 (1994-95 to 1995-96). 6 runs (av 6.00); 3 wkts (av 39.00); 1 ct. HS 3* and BB 2-35 v P (Sharjah) 1994-95.

CHAUHAN, Rajesh Kumar **(Madhya Pradesh)**
Born Ranchi 19 Dec 1966. RHB, OB. F-c debut 1988-89. **Tests:** 15 (1992-93 to 1995-96). 65 runs (av 8.12); 34 wkts (av 34.97); 8 ct. HS 15* v SL (PSS, Colombo) 1993-94. BB 3-8 v SL (Ahmedabad) 1993-94. **LOI:** 20 (1993-94 to 1994-95). 73 runs (av 14.60); 21 wkts (av 34.00); 5 ct. HS 26* v SL (Jalandhar) 1993-94. BB 3-29 v P (Sharjah) 1993-94.

HIRWANI, Narendra Deepchand **(Madhya Pradesh)**
Born Gorakhpur 18 Oct 1968. RHB, LBG. F-c debut 1984-85. **Tests:** 15 (1987-88 to 1995-96). 45 runs (av 5.62); 64 wkts (av 29.03), 5 wkts/inns (4), 10 wkts/match (1); 5 ct. HS 17 v NZ (Hyderabad) 1988-89. BB 8-61 (16-136 match) v WI (Madras) 1987-88 – on debut. **LOI:** 18 (1987-88 to 1991-92). 8 runs (av 2.00); 23 wkts (av 31.26); 2 ct. HS 4. BB 4-43 v NZ (Sharjah) 1987-88.

JADEJA, Ajaysinhji Daulatsinhji **(Haryana)**
Born Jamnagar 1 Feb 1971. RHB, RM. F-c debut 1988-89. **Tests:** 6 (1992-93 to 1995-96). 279 runs (av 34.87); 2 ct. HS 73 v NZ (Bangalore) 1995-96. **LOI:** 42 (1991-92 to 1995-96). 1166 runs (av 33.31), 1 hundred; 8 wkts (av 56.62); 12 ct. HS 104 v WI (Cuttack) 1994-95. BB 2-16 v SA (Mohali) 1993-94.

KAMBLI, Vinod Ganpat **(Bombay)**
Born Bombay 18 Jan 1972. LHB, OB. F-c debut 1989-90. **Tests:** 17 (1992-93 to 1995-96). 1084 runs (av 54.20), 4 hundreds; 7 ct. HS 227 v Z (Delhi) 1992-93. His first 8 innings in Test cricket were 16, 18*, 59, 224, 227, 125, 4 and 120. **LOI:** 61 (1991-92 to 1995-96). 1741 runs (av 40.48), 1 hundred; 1 wkt (av 7.00); 10 ct. HS 100* v E (Jaipur) 1992-93. BB 1-7.

KAPOOR, Aashish Rakesh **(Punjab)**
Born Madras 25 Mar 1971. RHB, OB. F-c debut 1989-90. **Tests:** 2 (1994-95 to 1995-96). 58 runs (av 19.33); 1 wkt (av 154.00); 1 ct. HS 42 v NZ (Cuttack) 1995-96. BB 1-90. **LOI:** 7 (1994-95 to 1995-96). 6 runs (av 6.00); 5 wkts (av 46.80); 0 ct. HS 6. BB 2-33 v NZ (Bombay) 1995-96.

KUMBLE, Anil (Karnataka)
Born Bangalore 17 Oct 1970. 6'1½". Educated at National HS; R.V. Engineering C, Bangalore. RHB, LBG. F-c debut 1989-90. Northamptonshire 1995 (cap 1995) – taking 105 f-c wickets. *Wisden* 1995. **Tests:** 23 (1990 to 1995-96). 257 runs (av 14.27); 109 wkts (av 24.42), 5 wkts/inns (6), 10 wkts/match (1); 11 ct. HS 52* v WI (Nagpur) 1994-95. BB 7-59 (11-128 match) v SL (Lucknow) 1993-94. **LOI:** 71 (1989-90 to 1995-96). 171 runs (av 9.00); 87 wkts (av 29.66); 21 ct. HS 24 v E (Bangalore) 1992-93. BB 6-12 v WI (Calcutta) 1993-94.

MANJREKAR, Sanjay Vijay **(Bombay)**
Born Mangalore 12 Jul 1965. RHB, OB. F-c debut 1984-85. **Tests:** 34 (1987-88 to 1995-96). 1899 runs (av 38.75), 4 hundreds; 0 wkts; 22 ct, 1 st. HS 218 v P (Lahore) 1989-90. **LOI:** 59 (1987-88 to 1995-96). 1604 runs (av 34.86), 1 hundred; 1 wkt (av 6.00); 19 ct. HS 105 v SA (Delhi) 1991-92. BB 1-2.

MONGIA, Nayan Ramlal **(Baroda)**
Born Baroda 19 Dec 1969. RHB, WK. F-c debut 1989-90. **Tests:** 10 (1993-94 to 1995-96). 388 runs (av 35.27); 20 ct, 2 st. HS 80 v WI (Bombay) 1994-95. **LOI:** 34 (1993-94 to 1995-96). 239 runs (av 23.90); 41 ct, 12 st. HS 40* v NZ (Christchurch) 1993-94.

PRABHAKAR, Manoj (Delhi)
Born Ghaziabad 15 Apr 1963. 5'8½". Educated at Ghaziabad SS; Delhi C. RHB, RM. F-c debut 1982-83. Durham 1995. **Tests:** 39 (1984-85 to 1995-96). 1600 runs (av 32.65), 1 hundred; 96 wkts (av 37.30), 5 wkts/inns (3); 20 ct. HS 120 v WI (Chandigarh) 1994-95. BB 6-132 v P (Faisalabad) 1989-90. **LOI:** 125 (1983-84 to 1995-96). 1844 runs (av 24.91), 2 hundreds; 154 wkts (av 28.40); 25 ct. HS 106 v P (Jamshedpur) 1986-87. BB 5-33 v NZ (Amritsar) 1995-96.

PRASAD, Bapu Krishnarao **Venkatesh (Karnataka)**
Born Bangalore 5 Aug 1969. RHB, RMF. F-c debut 1990-91. **Tests:** 0. **LOI:** 21 (1993-94 to 1995-96). 9 runs (av 2.25); 19 wkts (av 38.47); 8 ct. HS 5*. BB 3-36 v WI (Bombay) 1994-95.

RAJU, Sagi Lakshmi **Venkatapathy (Hyderabad)**
Born Hyderabad 9 Jul 1969. RHB, SLA. F-c debut 1985-86. **Tests:** 23 (1989-90 to 1995-96). 228 runs (av 12.00); 84 wkts (av 28.13), 5 wkts/inns (5), 10 wkts/match (1); 5 ct. HS 31 v A (Melbourne) 1991-92. BB 6-12 v SL (Chandigarh) 1990-91. **LOI:** 42 (1989-90 to 1994-95). 29 runs (av 4.14); 45 wkts (av 33.28); 7 ct. HS 8. BB 4-46 v WI (Jaipur) 1994-95.

SIDHU, Navjot Singh **(Punjab)**
Born Patiala 20 Oct 1963. RHB, RM. F-c debut 1981-82. **Tests:** 36 (1983-84 to 1995-96). 2087 runs (av 40.13), 6 hundreds; 0 wkts; 8 ct. HS 124 v SL (Lucknow) 1993-94. **LOI:** 92 (1987-88 to 1995-96). 3467 runs (av 42.80), 5 hundreds; 0 wkts; 15 ct. HS 134* v E (Gwalior) 1992-93.

SRINATH, Javagal (Karnataka)
Born Mysore 31 Aug 1969. 6'3". RHB, RFM. F-c debut 1989-90. **Tests:** 18 (1991-92 to 1995-96). 248 runs (av 22.54); 46 wkts (av 35.43); 8 ct. HS 60 v WI (Bombay) 1994-95. BB 4-33 v SA (Cape Town) 1992-93. **LOI:** 82 (1991-92 to 1995-96). 176 runs (av 8.80); 118 wkts (av 25.22); 12 ct. HS 37 v SA (Hamilton) 1994-95. BB 5-24 v SL (Kanpur) 1993-94.

TENDULKAR, Sachin Ramesh **(Bombay)**
Born Bombay 24 Apr 1973. RHB, RM. F-c debut 1988-89. Yorkshire 1992 (cap 1992). **Tests:** 38 (1989-90 to 1995-96). 2483 runs (av 51.72), 8 hundreds; 4 wkts (av 47.75); 31 ct. HS 179 v WI (Nagpur) 1994-95. BB 2-10 v A (Adelaide) 1991-92. **LOI:** 101 (1989-90 to 1995-96). 3201 runs (av 36.37), 4 hundreds; 34 wkts (av 51.52); 30 ct. HS 115 v NZ (Baroda) 1994-95. BB 4-34 v WI (Sharjah) 1991-92.

ENGLAND v INDIA

1932 to 1992-93

	Captains					
Season	*England*	*India*	*P*	*E*	*I*	*D*
1932	D.R.Jardine	C.K.Nayudu	1	1	0	0
1933-34	D.R.Jardine	C.K.Nayudu	3	2	0	1
1936	G.O.B.Allen	Maharaj of Vizianagram	3	2	0	1
1946	W.R.Hammond	Nawab of Pataudi, sn.	3	1	0	2
1951-52	N.D.Howard[1]	V.S.Hazare	5	1	1	3
1952	L.Hutton	V.S.Hazare	4	3	0	1
1959	P.B.H.May[2]	D.K.Gaekwad[3]	5	5	0	0
1961-62	E.R.Dexter	N.J.Contractor	5	0	2	3
1963-64	M.J.K.Smith	Nawab of Pataudi, jn	5	0	0	5
1967	D.B.Close	Nawab of Pataudi, jn	3	3	0	0
1971	R.Illingworth	A.L.Wadekar	3	0	1	2
1972-73	A.R.Lewis	A.L.Wadekar	5	1	2	2
1974	M.H.Denness	A.L.Wadekar	3	3	0	0
1976-77	A.W.Greig	B.S.Bedi	5	3	1	1
1979	J.M.Brearley	S.Venkataraghavan	4	1	0	3
1979-80	J.M.Brearley	G.R.Viswanath	1	1	0	0
1981-82	K.W.R.Fletcher	S.M.Gavaskar	6	0	1	5
1982	R.G.D.Willis	S.M.Gavaskar	3	1	0	2
1984-85	D.I.Gower	S.M.Gavaskar	5	2	1	2
1986	M.W.Gatting[4]	Kapil Dev	3	0	2	1
1990	G.A.Gooch	M.Azharuddin	3	1	0	2
1992-93	G.A.Gooch[5]	M.Azharuddin	3	0	3	0
	At Lord's		12	9	1	2
	At Manchester		8	3	0	5
	At The Oval		8	2	1	5
	At Leeds		5	3	1	1
	At Nottingham		1	1	0	0
	At Birmingham		4	3	0	1
	In England		38	21	3	14
	At Bombay		10	2	3	5
	At Calcutta		9	1	3	5
	At Madras		9	3	4	2
	At Delhi		7	3	0	4
	At Kanpur		6	1	0	5
	At Bangalore		2	0	1	1
	In India		43	10	11	22
	Totals		81	31	14	36

The Maharaja of Porbandar captained the 1932 Indian touring team but he did not play in the inaugural Test match.

The following deputised for the official touring captain or were appointed for only a minor portion of a home series:

[1]D.B.Carr (5th). [2]M.C.Cowdrey (4th and 5th). [3]Pankaj Roy (2nd). [4]D.I.Gower (1st). [5]A.J.Stewart (2nd).

HIGHEST INNINGS TOTALS

England	in England	653-4d	Lord's	1990
	in India	652-7d	Madras	1984-85
India	in England	606-9d	The Oval	1990
	in India	591	Bombay	1992-93

LOWEST INNINGS TOTALS

England	in England	101	The Oval	1971
	in India	102	Bombay	1981-82
India	in England	42	Lord's	1974
	in India	83	Madras	1976-77

HIGHEST MATCH AGGREGATE

1614 for 30 wickets	Lord's	1990

LOWEST MATCH AGGREGATE

482 for 31 wickets	Lord's	1936

HIGHEST INDIVIDUAL INNINGS

England	in England	333	G.A.Gooch	Lord's	1990
		246*	G.Boycott	Leeds	1967
		217	W.R.Hammond	The Oval	1936
		214*	D.Lloyd	Birmingham	1974
		208	I.T.Botham	The Oval	1982
		205*	J.Hardstaff, jr	Lord's	1946
		200*	D.I.Gower	Birmingham	1979
	in India	207	M.W.Gatting	Madras	1984-85
		201	G.Fowler	Madras	1984-85
India	in England	221	S.M.Gavaskar	The Oval	1979
	in India	224	V.G.Kambli	Bombay	1992-93
		222	G.R.Viswanath	Madras	1981-82
		203*	Nawab of Pataudi, jr	Delhi	1963-64

111 hundreds have been scored in this series: England 61, India 50.

HUNDRED IN EACH INNINGS

England	333	123	G.A.Gooch	Lord's	1990

HUNDRED ON DEBUT IN SERIES

England	136	B.H.Valentine	Bombay	1933-34
	137*	A.J.Watkins	Delhi	1951-52
	175	T.W.Graveney	Bombay	1951-52
	100	M.J.K.Smith	Manchester	1959
	246*	G.Boycott	Leeds	1967
	109	B.L.D'Oliveira	Leeds	1967
	200*	D.I.Gower	Birmingham	1979
	100*	R.A.Smith	Lord's	1990
India	118	L.Amarnath	Bombay	1933-34
	112	A.A.Baig	Manchester	1959
	105	Hanumant Singh	Delhi	1963-64
	110	M.Azharuddin	Calcutta	1984-85

HIGHEST AGGREGATE OF RUNS IN A SERIES

England	in England	752 (av 125.33)	G.A.Gooch	1990
	in India	594 (av 99.00)	K.F.Barrington	1961-62
India	in England	542 (av 77.42)	S.M.Gavaskar	1979
	in India	586 (av 83.71)	V.L.Manjrekar	1961-62

RECORD WICKET PARTNERSHIPS – ENGLAND

1st	225	G.A.Gooch (116), M.A.Atherton (131)	Manchester	1990
2nd	241	G.Fowler (201), M.W.Gatting (207)	Madras	1984-85
3rd	308	G.A.Gooch (333), A.J.Lamb (139)	Lord's	1990
4th	266	W.R.Hammond (217), T.S.Worthington (128)	The Oval	1936
5th	254	K.W.R.Fletcher (113), A.W.Greig (148)	Bombay	1972-73
6th	171	I.T.Botham (114), R.W.Taylor (43)	Bombay	1979-80
7th	125	D.W.Randall (126), P.H.Edmonds (64)	Lord's	1982
8th	168	R.Illingworth (107), P.Lever (88*)	Manchester	1971
9th	83	K.W.R.Fletcher (97*), N.Gifford (19)	Madras	1972-73
10th	70	P.J.W.Allott (41*), R.G.D.Willis (28)	Lord's	1982

RECORD WICKET PARTNERSHIPS – INDIA

1st	213	S.M.Gavaskar (221), C.P.S.Chauhan (80)	The Oval	1979
2nd	192	F.M.Engineer (121), A.L.Wadekar (87)	Bombay	1972-73
3rd	316†	G.R.Viswanath (222), Yashpal Sharma (140)	Madras	1981-82
4th	222	V.S.Hazare (89), V.L.Manjrekar (133)	Leeds	1952
5th	214	M.Azharuddin (110), R.J.Shastri (111)	Calcutta	1984-85
6th	130	S.M.H.Kirmani (43), Kapil Dev (97)	The Oval	1982
7th	235	R.J.Shastri (142), S.M.H.Kirmani (102)	Bombay	1984-85
8th	128	R.J.Shastri (93), S.M.H.Kirmani (67)	Delhi	1981-82
9th	104	R.J.Shastri (93), Madan Lal (44)	Delhi	1981-82
10th	51	R.G.Nadkarni (43*), B.S.Chandrasekhar (16)	Calcutta	1963-64
	51	S.M.H.Kirmani (75), C.Sharma (17*)	Madras	1984-85

† 415 runs were added for this wicket. D.B.Vengsarkar retired hurt and was replaced by Yashpal Sharma after 99 had been scored.

BEST INNINGS BOWLING ANALYSIS

England	in England	8- 31	F.S.Trueman	Manchester	1952
	in India	7- 46	J.K.Lever	Delhi	1976-77
India	in England	6- 35	L.Amar Singh	Lord's	1936
	in India	8- 55	M.H.Mankad	Madras	1951-52

BEST MATCH BOWLING ANALYSIS

England	in England	11- 93	A.V.Bedser	Manchester	1946
	in India	13-106	I.T.Botham	Bombay	1979-80
India	in England	10-188	C.Sharma	Birmingham	1986
	in India	12-108	M.H.Mankad	Madras	1951-52

HIGHEST AGGREGATE OF WICKETS IN A SERIES

England	in England	29 (av 13.31)	F.S.Trueman	1952
	in India	29 (av 17.55)	D.L.Underwood	1976-77
India	in England	17 (av 34.64)	S.P.Gupte	1959
	in India	35 (av 18.91)	B.S.Chandrasekhar	1972-73

PAKISTAN REGISTER

Test Match statistics to the start of the 1996 tour of England; Limited-Overs International statistics to the eve of the Wills World Cup (14 February 1996).

AAMIR SOHAIL (Lahore)
Born Lahore 14 Sep 1966. LHB, SLA. F-c debut 1983-84. **Tests:** 30 (1992 to 1995-96). 1960 runs (av 35.63), 2 hundreds; 17 wkts (av 38.35); 30 ct. HS 205 v E (Manchester) 1992. BB 4-54 v SL (Peshawar) 1995-96. **LOI:** 85 (1990-91 to 1995-96). 2682 runs (av 32.31), 3 hundreds; 59 wkts (av 35.23); 22 ct. HS 134 v NZ (Sharjah) 1993-94. BB 4-22 v SL (Sharjah) 1995-96.

AQIB JAVED (Islamabad)
Born Sheikhupura 5 Aug 1972. RHB, RFM. F-c debut 1984-85. Hampshire 1991 (uncapped). **Tests:** 21 (1988-89 to 1995-96). 100 runs (av 5.26); 54 wkts (av 33.07), 5 wkts/inns (1); 2 ct. HS 28* v SL (Peshawar) 1995-96. BB 5-84 v SL (Faisalabad) 1995-96. **LOI:** 121 (1988-89 to 1995-96). 144 runs (av 10.28); 134 wkts (av 31.05); 16 ct. HS 21 v SL (Faisalabad) 1995-96. BB 7-37 v I (Sharjah) 1991-92 – world record LOI analysis.

ATA-UR-REHMAN (Lahore)
Born Lahore 28 Mar 1975. RHB, RFM. F-c debut 1990-91. **Tests:** 11 (1992 to 1995-96). 66 runs (av 7.33); 26 wkts (av 34.53); 2 ct. HS 19 and BB 3-28 v WI (Port-of-Spain) 1992-93. **LOI:** 25 (1992-93 to 1995-96). 27 runs (av 6.75); 21 wkts (av 46.66); 0 ct. HS 11* v NZ (Auckland) 1993-94. BB 3-32 v UAE (Sharjah) 1993-94.

BASIT ALI (Karachi Whites; United Bank)
Born Karachi 13 Dec 1970. RHB, OB. F-c debut 1985-86. **Tests:** 19 (1992-93 to 1995-96). 858 runs (av 26.81), 1 hundred; 0 wkts; 6 ct. HS 103 v NZ (Christchurch) 1993-94. **LOI:** 47 (1992-93 to 1995-96). 1225 runs (av 35.00), 1 hundred; 1 wkt (av 21.00); 15 ct. HS 127* v WI (Sharjah) 1993-94. BB 1-17.

IJAZ AHMED (Habib Bank)
Born Sialkot 20 Sep 1968. RHB, LM. F-c debut 1983-84. **Tests:** 27 (1986-87 to 1995-96). 1379 runs (av 35.35), 4 hundreds; 1 wkt (av 18.00); 20 ct. HS 137 v A (Sydney) 1995-96. BB 1-9. **LOI:** 121 (1986-87 to 1995-96). 2391 runs (av 26.56), 4 hundreds; 3 wkts (av 90.66); 42 ct. HS 124* v Bangladesh (Chittagong) 1988-89. BB 2-31 v NZ (Sialkot) 1990-91. Unrelated to Ijaz Ahmed II.

IJAZ AHMED II (Faisalabad; Railways)
Born Lyallpur 2 Feb 1969. RHB, OB. F-c debut 1989-90. **Tests:** 2 (1995-96). 29 runs (av 9.66); 0 wkts; 3 ct. HS 16 v SL (Faisalabad) 1995-96. **LOI:** 0. Unrelated to his namesake.

INZAMAM-UL-HAQ (United Bank)
Born Multan 3 Mar 1970. RHB, SLA. F-c debut 1985-86. **Tests:** 30 (1992 to 1995-96). 2047 runs (av 45.48), 4 hundreds; 32 ct. HS 135* v NZ (Wellington) 1993-94. **LOI:** 96 (1991-92 to 1995-96). 3306 runs (av 41.32), 4 hundreds; 2 wkts (av 21.00); 25 ct. HS 137* v NZ (Sharjah) 1993-94. BB 1-4.

MOHAMMAD AKRAM (Rawalpindi)
Born Islamabad 10 Sep 1974. RHB, RFM. F-c debut 1992-93. **Tests:** 4 (1995-96). 8 runs (av 1.33); 9 wkts (av 43.55); 4 ct. HS 5 and BB 3-39 v SL (Sialkot) 1995-96. **LOI:** 5 (1995-96). 8 runs (av 8.00); 6 wkts (av 31.50); 0 ct. HS 7* and BB 2-36 v WI (Sharjah) 1995-96.

MOIN KHAN (Karachi Whites; PIA)
Born Rawalpindi 23 Sep 1971. RHB, WK. F-c debut 1986-87. **Tests:** 18 (1990-91 to 1995-96). 624 runs (av 26.00), 2 hundreds; 43 ct, 4 st. HS 117* v SL (Sialkot) 1995-96. **LOI:** 40 (1990-91 to 1995-96, 2 as captain). 277 runs (av 14.57); 45 ct, 12 st. HS 31 v SL (Faisalabad) 1995-96.

MUSHTAQ AHMED (United Bank)
Born Sahiwal 28 Jun 1970. 5'5". RHB, LBG. F-c debut 1986-87. Somerset debut/cap 1993. **Tests:** 21 (1989-90 to 1995-96). 202 runs (av 7.76); 72 wkts (av 30.00), 5 wkts/inns (3), 10 wkts/match (1); 6 ct. HS 27 v A (Lahore) 1994-95. BB 7-56 v NZ (Christchurch) 1995-96. **LOI:** 90 (1988-89 to 1995-96). 263 runs (av 9.06); 99 wkts (av 33.28); 19 ct. HS 26 v SL (Sharjah) 1995-96. BB 3-14 v SL (Sharjah) 1990-91.

RAMIZ RAJA (Islamabad; Lahore)
Born Lyallpur 14 Aug 1962. RHB, LB. F-c debut 1977-78. **Tests:** 55 (1983-84 to 1995-96, 3 as captain). 2747 runs (av 31.94), 2 hundreds; 32 ct. HS 122 v SL (PSS, Colombo) 1985-86. **LOI:** 170 (1984-85 to 1995-96, 8 as captain). 5257 runs (av 33.69), 9 hundreds; 0 wkts; 26 ct. HS 119* v NZ (Christchurch) 1991-92.

RASHID LATIF (Karachi Whites; United Bank)
Born Karachi 14 Oct 1968. RHB, WK. F-c debut 1986-87. **Tests:** 18 (1992 to 1995-96). 578 runs (av 24.08); 0 wkts; 55 ct, 8 st. HS 68* v Z (Karachi) 1993-94. **LOI:** 70 (1992-93 to 1995-96). 518 runs (av 15.23); 68 ct, 18 st. HS 39 v A (Hobart) 1992-93.

SAEED ANWAR (ADBP)
Born Karachi 6 Sep 1968. LHB, SLA. F-c debut 1986-87. **Tests:** 14 (1990-91 to 1995-96). 1038 runs (av 41.52), 2 hundreds; 0 wkts; 7 ct. HS 169 v NZ (Wellington) 1993-94. **LOI:** 82 (1988-89 to 1995-96, 1 as captain). 2541 runs (av 33.88), 8 hundreds; 3 wkts (av 43.33); 19 ct. HS 131 v WI (Sharjah) 1993-94. BB 1-9.

SALIM ELAHI (Lahore)
Born Sahiwal 21 Nov 1976. Brother of Manzoor Elahi. RHB, OB. F-c debut 1995-96. **Tests:** 2 (1995-96). 43 runs (av 10.75); 1 ct. HS 17 v A (Hobart) 1995-96. **LOI:** 8 (1995-96). 311 runs (av 44.42), 1 hundred; 2 ct. HS 102* v SL (Gujranwala) 1995-96 – on debut.

SALIM MALIK (Habib Bank)
Born Lahore 16 Apr 1963. RHB, LB. F-c debut 1978-79. **Tests:** 87 (1981-82 to 1995-96, 12 as captain). 4906 runs (av 44.60), 13 hundreds; 5 wkts (av 49.20); 57 ct. HS 237 v A (Rawalpindi) 1994-95. BB 1-3. **LOI:** 214 (1981-82 to 1995-96, 34 as captain). 5442 runs (av 32.78), 5 hundreds; 55 wkts (av 32.87); 64 ct. HS 102 v I (Sharjah) 1989-90 and 102 v SL (Rawalpindi) 1991-92. BB 5-35 v NZ (Lahore) 1990-91.

SAQLAIN MUSHTAQ (PIA; Islamabad)
Born Lahore 27 Nov 1976. RHB, OB. F-c debut 1994-95 taking 52 wickets in first season. **Tests:** 4 (1995-96). 53 runs (av 10.60); 13 wkts (av 37.84); 3 ct. HS 34 and BB 3-74 v SL (Faisalabad) 1995-96. **LOI:** 5 (1995-96). 30 runs (av 15.00); 8 wkts (av 21.62); 3 ct. HS 30 v SL (Sharjah) 1995-96. BB 4-47 v WI (Sharjah) 1995-96.

WAQAR YOUNIS (United Bank)
Born Vehari 16 Nov 1971. 6'0". Educated at Government C, Vehari. RHB, RF. F-c debut 1987-88. Surrey 1990 to 1993 (cap 1990). *Wisden* 1991. **Tests:** 38 (1989-90 to 1995-96, 1 as captain). 392 runs (av 9.80); 200 wkts (av 20.61), 5 wkts/inns (19), 10 wkts/match (4); 5 ct. HS 34 v NZ (Christchurch) 1995-96. BB 7-76 v NZ (Faisalabad) 1990-91. **LOI:** 112 (1989-90 to 1995-96, 1 as captain). 335 runs (av 9.57); 187 wkts (av 22.02); 10 ct. HS 37 v WI (Johannesburg) 1992-93. BB 6-26 v SL (Sharjah) 1989-90.

WASIM AKRAM (PIA)
Born Lahore 3 Jun 1966. 6'3". Educated at Islamia C. LHB, LF. F-c debut 1984-85. Lancashire debut 1988 (cap 1989). *Wisden* 1992. **Tests:** 67 (1984-85 to 1995-96, 9 as captain). 1554 runs (av 18.95), 1 hundred; 289 wkts (av 22.57), 5 wkts/inns (20), 10 wkts/match (3); 25 ct. HS 123 v A (Adelaide) 1989-90. BB 7-119 v NZ (Wellington) 1993-94. **LOI:** 193 (1984-85 to 1995-96, 30 as captain). 1746 runs (av 14.55); 282 wkts (av 22.27); 38 ct. HS 86 v A (Melbourne) 1989-90. BB 5-15 v Z (Karachi) 1993-94.

ENGLAND v PAKISTAN

1954 to 1992

	Captains					
Season	*England*	*Pakistan*	*P*	*E*	*P*	*D*
1954	L.Hutton[1]	A.H.Kardar	4	1	1	2
1961-62	E.R.Dexter	Imtiaz Ahmed	3	1	0	2
1962	E.R.Dexter[2]	Javed Burki	5	4	0	1
1967	D.B.Close	Hanif Mohammad	3	2	0	1
1968-69	M.C.Cowdrey	Saeed Ahmed	3	0	0	3
1971	R.Illingworth	Intikhab Alam	3	1	0	2
1972-73	A.R.Lewis	Majid Khan	3	0	0	3
1974	M.H.Denness	Intikhab Alam	3	0	0	3
1977-78	J.M.Brearley[3]	Wasim Bari	3	0	0	3
1978	J.M.Brearley	Wasim Bari	3	2	0	1
1982	R.G.D.Willis[4]	Imran Khan	3	2	1	0
1983-84	R.G.D.Willis[5]	Zaheer Abbas	3	0	1	2
1987	M.W.Gatting	Imran Khan	5	0	1	4
1987-88	M.W.Gatting	Javed Miandad	3	0	1	2
1992	G.A.Gooch	Javed Miandad	5	1	2	2
	At Lord's		9	2	2	5
	At Nottingham		3	2	0	1
	At Manchester		3	0	0	3
	At The Oval		6	2	2	2
	At Birmingham		6	3	0	3
	At Leeds		7	4	1	2
	In England		34	13	5	16
	At Lahore		6	1	1	4
	At Dacca		2	0	0	2
	At Karachi		6	0	1	5
	At Hyderabad		2	0	0	2
	At Faisalabad		2	0	0	2
	In Pakistan		18	1	2	15
	Totals		52	14	7	31

The following deputised for the official touring captain or were appointed for only a minor portion of a home series:
[1]D.S.Sheppard (2nd and 3rd). [2]M.C.Cowdrey (3rd). [3]G.Boycott (3rd). [4]D.I.Gower (2nd). [5]D.I.Gower (2nd and 3rd).

HIGHEST INNINGS TOTALS

England	in England	558-6d	Nottingham	1954
	in Pakistan	546-8d	Faisalabad	1983-84
Pakistan	in England	708	The Oval	1987
	in Pakistan	569-9d	Hyderabad	1972-73

LOWEST INNINGS TOTALS

England	in England	130	The Oval	1954
	in Pakistan	130	Lahore	1987-88
Pakistan	in England	87	Lord's	1954
	in Pakistan	191	Faisalabad	1987-88

HIGHEST MATCH AGGREGATE

1274 for 25 wickets	Hyderabad	1972-73
1274 for 37 wickets	Birmingham	1987

LOWEST MATCH AGGREGATE

509 for 28 wickets	Nottingham	1967

HIGHEST INDIVIDUAL INNINGS

England	in England	278	D.C.S.Compton	Nottingham	1954
		190	A.J.Stewart	Birmingham	1992
		183	D.L.Amiss	The Oval	1974
		182	M.C.Cowdrey	The Oval	1962
		172	E.R.Dexter	The Oval	1962
	in Pakistan	205	E.R.Dexter	Karachi	1961-62
		173*	D.I.Gower	Lahore	1983-84
Pakistan	in England	274	Zaheer Abbas	Birmingham	1971
		260	Javed Miandad	The Oval	1987
		240	Zaheer Abbas	The Oval	1974
		205	Aamir Sohail	Manchester	1992
		200	Mohsin Khan	Lord's	1982
		187*	Hanif Mohammad	Lord's	1967
	in Pakistan	157	Mushtaq Mohammad	Hyderabad	1972-73

77 hundreds have been scored in this series (England 44, Pakistan 33). At Karachi in 1972-73, three batsmen – Majid Khan, Mushtaq Mohammad and D.L.Amiss – each scored 99, a coincidence unique in Test cricket.

HUNDRED IN EACH INNINGS

Pakistan	111	104	Hanif Mohammad	Dacca	1961-62

HUNDRED ON DEBUT IN SERIES

England (8)	139	K.F.Barrington	Lahore	1961-62
	159	M.C.Cowdrey	Birmingham	1962
	108*	B.W.Luckhurst	Birmingham	1971
	106	C.T.Radley	Birmingham	1978
	100	I.T.Botham	Birmingham	1978
	166	R.T.Robinson	Manchester	1987
	190	A.J.Stewart	Birmingham	1992
	127	R.A.Smith	Birmingham	1992
Pakistan (4)	138	Javed Burki	Lahore	1961-62
	274	Zaheer Abbas	Birmingham	1971
	122	Haroon Rashid	Lahore	1977-78
	114	Mudassar Nazar	Lahore	1977-78

HIGHEST AGGREGATE OF RUNS IN A SERIES

England	in England	453 (av 90.60)	D.C.S.Compton	1954
	in Pakistan	449 (av 112.25)	D.I.Gower	1983-84
Pakistan	in England	488 (av 81.33)	Salim Malik	1992
	in Pakistan	407 (av 67.83)	Hanif Mohammad	1961-62

RECORD WICKET PARTNERSHIPS – ENGLAND

1st	198	G.Pullar (165), R.W.Barber (86)	Dacca	1961-62
2nd	248	M.C.Cowdrey (182), E.R.Dexter (172)	The Oval	1962
3rd	227	A.J.Stewart (190), R.A.Smith (127)	Birmingham	1992
4th	188	E.R.Dexter (205), P.H.Parfitt (111)	Karachi	1961-62
5th	192	D.C.S.Compton (278), T.E.Bailey (36*)	Nottingham	1954
6th	153*	P.H.Parfitt (101*), D.A.Allen (79*)	Birmingham	1962
7th	167	D.I.Gower (152), V.J.Marks (83)	Faisalabad	1983-84
8th	99	P.H.Parfitt (119), D.A.Allen (62)	Leeds	1962
9th	76	T.W.Graveney (153), F.S.Trueman (29)	Lord's	1962
10th	79	R.W.Taylor (54), R.G.D.Willis (28*)	Birmingham	1982

RECORD WICKET PARTNERSHIPS – PAKISTAN

1st	173	Mohsin Khan (104), Shoaib Mohammad (80)	Lahore	1983-84
2nd	291	Zaheer Abbas (274), Mushtaq Mohammad (100)	Birmingham	1971
3rd	180	Mudassar Nazar (114), Haroon Rashid (122)	Lahore	1977-78
4th	322	Javed Miandad (153*), Salim Malik (165)	Birmingham	1992
5th	197	Javed Burki (101), Nasim-ul-Ghani (101)	Lord's	1962
6th	145	Mushtaq Mohammad (157), Intikhab Alam (138)	Hyderabad	1972-73
7th	89	Ijaz Ahmed (69), Salim Yousuf (42)	The Oval	1987
8th	130	Hanif Mohammad (187*), Asif Iqbal (76)	Lord's	1967
9th	190	Asif Iqbal (146), Intikhab Alam (51)	The Oval	1967
10th	62	Sarfraz Nawaz (53), Asif Masood (4*)	Leeds	1974

BEST INNINGS BOWLING ANALYSIS

England	in England	8- 34	I.T.Botham	Lord's	1978
	in Pakistan	7- 66	P.H.Edmonds	Karachi	1977-78
Pakistan	in England	7- 40	Imran Khan	Leeds	1987
	in Pakistan	9- 56	Abdul Qadir	Lahore	1987-88

BEST MATCH BOWLING ANALYSIS

England	in England	13- 71	D.L.Underwood	Lord's	1974
	in Pakistan	11- 83	N.G.B.Cook	Karachi	1983-84
Pakistan	in England	12- 99	Fazal Mahmood	The Oval	1954
	in Pakistan	13-101	Abdul Qadir	Lahore	1987-88

HIGHEST AGGREGATE OF WICKETS IN A SERIES

England	in England	22 (av 19.95)	F.S.Trueman	1962
	in Pakistan	14 (av 31.71)	N.G.B.Cook	1983-84
Pakistan	in England	22 (av 25.31)	Waqar Younis	1992
	in Pakistan	30 (av 14.56)	Abdul Qadir	1987-88

THE FIRST-CLASS COUNTIES REGISTER, RECORDS AND 1995 AVERAGES

Career ststistics: Test and L-O Internationals to 13 February 1996; first-class to end of 1995 season

ABBREVIATIONS

General

*	not out/unbroken partnership	f-c	first-class
b	born	HS	Highest Score
BB	Best innings bowling analysis	LOI	Limited-Overs Internationals
Cap	Awarded 1st XI County Cap	Tests	Official Test Matches
Tours	Overseas tours involving first-class appearances		

Awards

BHC	Benson and Hedges Cup 'Gold' Award
NWT	NatWest Trophy/Gillette Cup 'Man of the Match' Award
Wisden 1995	One of *Wisden Cricketers' Almanack*'s Five Cricketers of 1995
YC 1995	Cricket Writers' Club Young Cricketer of 1995

Competitions

BHC	Benson and Hedges Cup
GC	Gillette Cup
NWT	NatWest Trophy
SL	Sunday (AXA Equity and Law) League

Playing Categories

LB	Bowls right-arm leg-breaks
LF	Bowls left-arm fast
LFM	Bowls left-arm fast-medium
LHB	Bats left-handed
LM	Bowls left-arm medium pace
LMF	Bowls left-arm medium-fast
OB	Bowls right-arm off-breaks
RF	Bowls right-arm fast
RFM	Bowls right-arm fast-medium
RHB	Bats right-handed
RM	Bowls right-arm medium pace
RMF	Bowls right-arm medium-fast
RSM	Bowls right-arm slow-medium
SLA	Bowls left-arm leg-breaks
SLC	Bowls left-arm 'Chinamen'
WK	Wicket-keeper

Education

BHS	Boys' High School
BS	Boys' School
C	College
CE	College of Education
CFE	College of Further Education
CHE	College of Higher Education
CS	Comprehensive School
GS	Grammar School
HS	High School
IHE	Institute of Higher Education
LSE	London School of Economics
RGS	Royal Grammar School
S	School
SFC	Sixth Form College
SM	Secondary Modern School
SS	Secondary School
TC	Technical College
T(H)S	Technical (High) School
U	University

Teams (see also p 129)

Cav	Cavaliers	NT	Northern Transvaal
CD	Central Districts	OFS	Orange Free State
DHR	D.H.Robins' XI	PIA	Pakistan International Airlines
Eng Co	English Counties XI	Q	Queensland
EP	Eastern Province	RW	Rest of the World XI
GW	Griqualand West	SAB	South African Breweries XI
Int XI	International XI	SAU	South African Universities
IW	International Wanderers	WA	Western Australia
ND	Northern Districts	WP	Western Province
NSW	New South Wales	Zim	Zimbabwe (Rhodesia)

DERBYSHIRE

Formation of Present Club: 4 November 1870
Colours: Chocolate, Amber and Pale Blue
Badge: Rose and Crown
Championships: (1) 1936
NatWest Trophy/Gillette Cup Winners: (1) 1981
Benson and Hedges Cup Winners: (1) 1993
Sunday League Champions: (1) 1990
Match Awards: NWT 35; BHC 60

Chief Executive: R.G.Taylor
County Cricket Ground, Nottingham Road, Derby DE2 6DA (Tel 01332 383211)
Captain: D.M.Jones
Scorer: S.W.Tacey
1996 Beneficiary: Derbyshire CCC

ADAMS, Christopher John (Repton S), b Whitwell 6 May 1970. 6'0". RHB, OB. Debut 1988. Cap 1992. 1000 runs (2); most – 1109 (1992). HS 216 v Kent (Maidstone) 1995. BB 4-29 v Lancs (Derby) 1991. Awards: NWT 1; BHC 2. **NWT:** HS 109* v Sussex (Hove) 1995. BB 1-15 v Berks (Derby) 1992. **BHC:** HS 94 v Northants (Derby) 1995. **SL:** HS 141* v Kent (Chesterfield) 1992. BB 2-15 v Essex (Chelmsford) 1993.

ALDRED, Paul (Lady Manner's S, Bakewell), b Chellaston 4 Feb 1969. RHB, RM. Debut 1995. Cheshire 1994. HS 33 v Warwks (Birmingham) 1995. BB 3-47 v Young A (Chesterfield) 1995. BAC BB 3-89 v Surrey (Derby) 1995. **SL:** HS 11* v Northants (Derby) 1995. BB 3-28 v Glos (Bristol) 1995. Hockey for Derbyshire.

BARNETT, Kim John (Leek HS), b Stoke-on-Trent, Staffs 17 Jul 1960. 6'1". RHB, LB. Debut 1979. Cap 1982. Captain 1983-95. Boland 1982-83/1987-88. Staffordshire 1976. *Wisden* 1988. Benefit 1992. **Tests:** 4 (1988 to 1989); HS 80 v A (Leeds) 1989. **LOI:** 1 (1988; HS 84). Tours: SA 1989-90 (Eng XI); NZ 1979-80 (DHR); SL 1985-86 (Eng B). 1000 runs (12); most – 1734 (1984). HS 239* v Leics (Leicester) 1988. BB 6-28 v Glam (Chesterfield) 1991. Awards: NWT 3; BHC 10. **NWT:** HS 113* v Glos (Bristol) 1994. BB 6-24 v Cumberland (Kendal) 1984. **BHC:** 115 v Glos (Derby) 1987. BB 1-10. **SL:** HS 131* v Essex (Derby) 1984. BB 3-39 v Yorks (Chesterfield) 1979.

BASE, Simon John (Fish Hoek HS, Cape Town), b Maidstone, Kent 2 Jan 1960. 6'2". RHB, RMF. W Province 1981-82/1983-84. Glamorgan 1986-87. Boland 1987-88/1988-89. Border 1989-90 to date. Derbyshire debut 1988. Cap 1990. HS 58 v Yorks (Chesterfield) 1990. 50 wkts (1): 60 (1989). BB 7-60 v Yorks (Chesterfield) 1989. **NWT:** HS 4. BB 2-49 Gm v Sussex (Hove) 1986. **BHC:** HS 15* v Somerset (Taunton) 1990. BB 3-33 v Minor C (Wellington) 1990. **SL:** HS 31 v Kent (Canterbury) 1993. BB 4-14 v Northants (Derby) 1991 and v Glos (Cheltenham) 1993.

CASSAR, Matthew Edward (Sir Joseph Banks HS, Sydney), b Sydney, Australia 16 Oct 1972. 6'0". RHB, RFM. Debut 1994. Qualified for England 1997. HS 66 v NZ (Derby) 1994. BB 4-54 v OU (Oxford) 1995.

CORK, Dominic Gerald (St Joseph's C, Stoke-on-Trent), b Newcastle-under-Lyme, Staffs 7 Aug 1971. 6'2". RHB, RFM. Debut 1990. Cap 1993. *Wisden* 1995. Staffordshire 1989-90. **Tests:** 10 (1995 to 1995-96); HS 56* v WI (Manchester) 1995; BB 7-43 v WI (Lord's) 1995 – on debut (record England analysis by Test match debutant); hat-trick v WI (Manchester) 1995 – the first in Test history to occur in the opening over of a day's play. **LOI:** 14 (1992 to 1995-96; HS 21; BB 3-27). Tours: A 1992-93 (Eng A); SA 1993-94 (Eng A), 1995-96; WI 1991-92 (Eng A); I 1994-95 (Eng A). HS 104 v Glos (Cheltenham) 1993. 50 wkts (2); most – 90 (1995). BB 9-43 (13-93 match) v Northants (Derby) 1995. Took 8-53 before lunch on his 20th birthday v Essex (Derby) 1991. 2 hat-tricks. Awards: NWT 2; BHC 2. **NWT:** HS 62 v Kent (Derby) 1994. BB 5-18 v Berks (Derby) 1992. **BHC:** HS 92* v Lancs (Lord's) 1993. BB 4-26 v Durham (Jesmond) 1992. **SL:** HS 66 v Sussex (Eastbourne) 1994. BB 4-44 v Warwks (Chesterfield) 1994.

DeFREITAS, Phillip Anthony Jason (Willesden HS, London), b Scotts Head, Dominica 18 Feb 1966. 6'0". RHB, RFM. UK resident since 1976. Leicestershire 1985-88 (cap 1986). Lancashire 1989-93 (cap 1989). Boland 1993-94 and 1995-96. Derbyshire debut/cap 1994. *Wisden* 1991. MCC YC. **Tests:** 44 (1986-87 to 1995-96); HS 88 v A (Adelaide) 1994-95. BB 7-70 v SL (Lord's) 1991. **LOI:** 97 (1986-87 to 1995-96; HS 49*; BB 4-35). Tours: A 1986-87, 1990-91, 1994-95; WI 1989-90; NZ 1987-88, 1991-92; P 1987-88; I 1992-93; Z 1988-89 (La). HS 113 Le v Notts (Worksop) 1988. De HS 108 v Leics (Derby) 1994. 50 wkts (8); most – 94 (1986). BB 7-21 La v Middx (Lord's) 1989. De BB 6-35 v Sussex (Derby) 1995. Hat-trick 1994. Awards: NWT 3; BHC 4. **NWT:** HS 69 Le v Lancs (Leicester) 1986. BB 5-13 La v Cumberland (Kendal) 1989. **BHC:** HS 75* La v Hants (Manchester) 1990. BB 5-16 La v Essex (Chelmsford) 1992. **SL:** HS 49* La v Hants (Manchester) 1992. BB 5-26 La v Hants (Southampton) 1993.

GRIFFITH, Frank Alexander (Beaconsfield HS; Wm Morris HS; Haringey Cricket C), b Whipps Cross, Essex 15 Aug 1968. 6'0". RHB, RM. Debut 1988. HS 81 v Glam (Chesterfield) 1992. BB 4-33 v Leics (Ilkeston) 1992. **NWT:** HS 8. BB 1-13. **BHC:** HS 13* and BB 2-48 v Glos (Bristol) 1993. **SL:** HS 31 v Lancs (Manchester) 1994. BB 4-48 v Glam (Derby) 1993.

GRIFFITHS, Steven Paul (Beechen Cliff S, Bath; Brunel C of Art & Technology, Bristol), b Hereford 31 May 1973. RHB, WK. 5'11". Debut 1995. HS 20 v Surrey (Derby) 1995.

HARRIS, Andrew James (Hadfield CS; Glossopdale Community C), b Ashton-under-Lyne, Lancs 26 Jun 1973. 6'1". RHB, RM. Debut 1994. HS 14* v Young A (Chesterfield) 1995. BAC HS 10 v Surrey (Oval) 1994. BB 4-84 v Glam (Derby) 1995. **BHC:** HS 5. BB 1-54. **SL:** HS 2. BB 3-15 v Durham (Chesterfield) 1995.

KRIKKEN, Karl Matthew (Rivington & Blackrod HS & SFC), b Bolton, Lancs 9 Apr 1969. Son of B.E. (Lancs and Worcs 1966-69). 5'9". RHB, WK. GW 1988-89. Derbyshire debut 1989. Cap 1992. HS 85* v Glam (Cardiff) 1994. **NWT:** HS 18 v Leics (Derby) 1992. **BHC:** HS 37* v Worcs (Worcester) 1992 and v Lancs (Lord's) 1993. **SL:** HS 44* v Essex (Chelmsford) 1991.

MALCOLM, Devon Eugene (St Elizabeth THS; Richmond C, Sheffield; Derby CHE), b Kingston, Jamaica 22 Feb 1963. Qualified for England 1987. 6'2". RHB, RF. Debut 1984. Cap 1989. Benefit 1997. *Wisden* 1994. **Tests:** 36 (1989 to 1995-96); HS 29 v A (Sydney) 1994-95; BB 9-57 v SA (Oval) 1994 – sixth best analysis in Test cricket. **LOI:** 10 (1990 to 1993-94; HS 4; BB 3-40). Tours: A 1990-91, 1994-95; SA 1995-96; WI 1989-90, 1991-92 (Eng A), 1993-94; I 1992-93; SL 1992-93. HS 51 v Surrey (Derby) 1989. 50 wkts (4); most – 69 (1994). BB 9-57 (*see Tests*). De BB 6-57 v Sussex (Derby) 1993. Award: BHC 1. **NWT:** HS 10* v Leics (Derby) 1992. BB 3-29 v Devon (Exmouth) 1993. **BHC:** HS 15 v Comb Us (Oxford) 1991. BB 5-27 v Middx (Derby) 1988. **SL:** HS 18 v Essex (Chelmsford) 1991. BB 4-21 v Surrey (Derby) 1989 and v Leics (Knypersley) 1990.

O'GORMAN, Timothy Joseph Gerard (St George's C, Weybridge; Durham U), b Woking, Surrey 15 May 1967. Grandson of J.G. (Surrey 1927). 6'2". RHB, OB. Debut 1987. Cap 1992. 1000 runs (2); most – 1116 (1991). HS 148 v Lancs (Manchester) 1991. BB 1-7. Award: NWT 1. **NWT:** HS 89 v Durham (Darlington) 1994. **BHC:** HS 49 v Northants (Derby) 1991 and v Lancs (Lord's) 1993. **SL:** HS 69 v Northants (Northampton) 1992.

OWEN, John Edward (Spondon S, Derby), b Derby 7 Aug 1971. 5'10". RHB, occ OB. Debut 1995. HS 65 v Young A (Chesterfield) 1995. BAC HS 50 v Leics (Leicester) 1995. **SL:** HS 45 v Surrey (Derby) 1995.

ROLLINS, Adrian Stewart (Little Ilford CS), b Barking, Essex 8 Feb 1972. Brother of R.J. (*see ESSEX*). 6'5". RHB, WK, occ RM. Debut 1993. Cap 1995. 1000 runs (1): 1095 (1995). HS 200* v Glos (Bristol) 1995. BB 1-19. **NWT:** HS 56 v Sussex (Hove) 1995. **BHC:** HS 70 v Lancs (Derby) 1994. **SL:** HS 126* v Surrey (Derby) 1995.

TWEATS, Timothy Andrew (Endon HS; Stoke-on-Trent SFC), b Stoke-on-Trent, Staffs 18 Apr 1974. 6'3". RHB, RM. Debut 1992. HS 78* v Worcs (Kidderminster) 1995. BB 1-23. **NWT:** HS 16 v Warwks (Derby) 1995. **SL:** HS 19 v Glam (Derby) 1995.

WARNER, Allan Esmond (Tabernacle S, St Kitts), b Birmingham 12 May 1957. 5'7". RHB, RFM. Worcestershire 1982-84. Derbyshire debut 1985. Cap 1987. Benefit 1995. HS 95* v Kent (Canterbury) 1993. BB 6-21 v Lancs (Derby) 1995. Award: NWT 1. **NWT:** HS 32 v Kent (Canterbury) 1987. BB 4-39 v Salop (Chesterfield) 1990. **BHC:** HS 35* v Comb Us (Oxford) 1991. BB 4-36 v Notts (Nottingham) 1987. **SL:** HS 68 v Hants (Heanor) 1986. BB 5-39 v Worcs (Knypersley) 1985.

WELLS, Colin Mark (Tideway CS, Newhaven), b Newhaven, Sussex 3 Mar 1960. Elder brother of A.P. (*see SUSSEX*). 5'11". RHB, RM. Sussex 1979-93 (cap 1982; benefit 1993). Derbyshire debut 1994. Cap 1995. Border 1980-81. W Province 1984-85. **LOI:** 2 (1984-85; HS 17). 1000 runs (6); most – 1456 (1987). HS 203 Sx v Hants (Hove) 1984. De HS 115 v OU (Oxford) 1995. 50 wkts (2); most – 59 (1984). BB 7-42 Sx v Derbys (Derby) 1991. De BB 4-52 v Middx (Derby) 1994. Awards: BHC 3. **NWT:** HS 76 Sx v Ire (Hove) 1985. BB 3-16 Sx v Scot (Edinburgh) 1991. **BHC:** HS 117 Sx v Glam (Swansea) 1989. BB 4-21 Sx v Middx (Lord's) 1980. **SL:** HS 104* Sx v Warwks (Hove) 1983. BB 4-15 Sx v Worcs (Worcester) 1983.

NEWCOMERS

DEAN, Kevin James, b Derby 16 Oct 1975. LHB, LFM.

JONES, Dean Mervyn, b Coburg, Victoria, Australia 24 Mar 1961. RHB, RM/OB. Victoria 1981-82 to date. Durham 1992 (cap 1992). Joins Derbyshire staff 1996 as captain. **Tests** (A): 52 (1983-84 to 1992-93); HS 216 v WI (Adelaide) 1988-89; BB 1-5. **LOI** (A): 164 (1983-84 to 1993-94; HS 145; BB 2-34). Tours (A): E 1987 (RW); 1989, 1991 (Vic); WI 1983-84, 1990-91; NZ 1989-90; I 1986-87; P 1988-89; SL 1992-93; Z 1985-86 (Young A). 1000 runs (2+5); most – 1510 (1989). HS 324* Victoria v S Australia (Melbourne) 1994-95. BAC HS 157 Du v Northants (Stockton) 1992. BB 1-0. **NWT:** HS 46 Du v Ireland (Dublin) 1992. **BHC:** HS 13 Du v Worcs (Worcester) 1992. BB 2-34 Du v Comb Us (Cambridge) 1992. **SL:** HS 114 Du v Lancs (Durham) 1992. BB 1-37.

LACEY, Simon James, b Nottingham 9 Mar 1975. RHB, OB.

MAY, Michael Robert, b Chesterfield 21 Jul 1971. RHB, OB.

SPENDLOVE, Benjamin Lee, b Belper 4 Nov 1978. RHB, OB.

DEPARTURES (who made first-class appearance in 1995)

BAIRSTOW, Andrew David, (Woodhouse Grove S, Leeds) b Dewsbury, Yorks 16 June 1975. 5'10". RHB, WK. Derbyshire 1995. HS 26 v Young A (Chesterfield) 1995. BAC HS 16 v Yorks (Chesterfield) 1995 – on debut. **SL:** HS 0.

COTTAM, Andrew Colin (Axminster SS), b Northampton 14 Jul 1973. Son of R.M.H. (Hants, Northants and England 1963-76). 6'1". RHB, SLA. Somerset 1992-93. Northamptonshire staff 1994 (no 1st XI appearances). Derbyshire 1995. Devon 1993. HS 36 and BB 2-5 v OU (Oxford) 1995. BAC HS 31 and BB 1-1 Sm v Glos (Gloucester) 1992. **NWT:** HS 2. BB 1-45. **SL:** HS –.

CULLINAN, Daryll John (Queens C, Queenstown; Stellenbosch U), b Kimberley, SA 4 Mar 1967. Brother of R.E. (Border and OFS 1984-85/1992-93). 5'10". RHB, OB. Border 1983-84/1984-85 and 1994-95 to date, making debut whilst at school. WP 1985-86/1990-91. Transvaal 1991-92/1993-94. At 16yr 304d remains youngest player to score f-c hundred in SA. Derbyshire 1995. **Tests** (SA): 19 (1992-93 to 1995-96); HS 102 v SL (Colombo) 1993-94. **LOI** (SA): 22 (HS 70*). Tours (SA): E 1994; A 1993-94; NZ 1994-95; SL 1993-94; Z 1995-96. 1000 runs (1): 1003 (1995). HS 337* Transvaal v N Transvaal (Jo'burg) 1993-94 (SA f-c record). De HS 161 v Somerset (Derby) 1995. BB 2-27 Border v Natal B (E London) 1983-84. Awards: NWT 1; BHC 1. **NWT:** HS 119* v Cambs (March) 1995. **BHC:** HS 101* v Scot (Glasgow) 1995. **SL:** HS 76* v Somerset (Derby) 1995.

DESSAUR, Wayne Anthony (Loughborough GS), b Nottingham 4 Feb 1971. 6'0". RHB, RM. Nottinghamshire 1992-94. Derbyshire 1995. HS 148 Nt v CU (Nottingham) 1992. BAC HS 104 Nt v Derbys (Nottingham) 1993. De HS 119* v OU (Oxford) 1995. BB 1-8. **NWT:** HS 85 v Cambs (March) 1995. **SL:** HS 18 v Middx (Derby) 1995.

continued on p 113

DERBYSHIRE 1995

RESULTS SUMMARY

	Place	Won	Lost	Tied	Drew	No Result
Britannic Assurance Championship	**14th**	4	10	–	3	–
All First-Class Matches		5	11	–	3	–
NatWest Trophy	Quarter-Finalist					
Benson and Hedges Cup	3rd in Group B					
Sunday League	**8th**	7	6	1	–	3

BRITANNIC ASSURANCE CHAMPIONSHIP AVERAGES

BATTING AND FIELDING

Cap		*M*	*I*	*NO*	*HS*	*Runs*	*Avge*	*100*	*50*	*Ct/St*
–	D.J.Cullinan	14	26	4	161	1003	45.59	5	1	8
1982	K.J.Barnett	16	31	3	169	1251	44.67	2	7	5
1992	C.J.Adams	13	25	–	216	1084	43.36	3	5	14
1995	A.S.Rollins	16	31	1	200*	1075	35.83	2	5	15
1995	C.M.Wells	15	29	3	106	861	33.11	1	6	16
–	W.A.Dessaur	6	12	1	84*	311	28.27	–	2	1
–	F.A.Griffith	8	13	4	53	240	26.66	–	1	10
1992	K.M.Krikken	10	14	3	61	271	24.63	–	1	34/1
1994	P.A.J.DeFreitas	15	24	3	94*	450	21.42	–	2	10
–	T.A.Tweats	7	14	1	78*	247	19.00	–	1	6
1987	A.E.Warner	14	22	8	43	265	18.92	–	–	2
1993	D.G.Cork	11	20	2	84*	311	17.27	–	1	5
1992	T.J.G.O'Gorman	4	7	–	39	108	15.42	–	–	3
–	J.E.Owen	3	6	–	50	90	15.00	–	1	–
–	A.C.Cottam	4	5	–	32	59	11.80	–	–	–
–	T.W.Harrison	5	10	1	61*	102	11.33	–	1	3
–	P.Aldred	5	9	–	33	77	8.55	–	–	3
–	S.P.Griffiths	5	9	–	20	75	8.33	–	–	14
1989	D.E.Malcolm	11	17	3	25*	106	7.57	–	–	1
–	A.D.Bairstow	2	4	–	16	25	6.25	–	–	5

Also batted: S.J.Base (1 match – cap 1990) 7*, 10; A.J.Harris (2 matches) 5*, 5, 2.

BOWLING

	O	*M*	*R*	*W*	*Avge*	*Best*	*5wI*	*10wM*
D.G.Cork	348	69	965	56	17.23	9-43	3	1
D.E.Malcolm	382.1	73	1333	56	23.80	6-61	3	1
A.E.Warner	375.1	90	1050	39	26.92	6-21	3	–
P.A.J.DeFreitas	564.1	124	1636	58	28.20	6-35	2	–
C.M.Wells	110	25	326	10	32.60	4-29	–	–
F.A.Griffith	190.4	42	614	17	36.11	4-89	–	–
K.J.Barnett	193.2	32	572	15	38.13	3-51	–	–

Also bowled: C.J.Adams 15-3-47-0; P.Aldred 67-10-241-9; S.J.Base 17-2-99-1; A.C.Cottam 56-8-257-1; W.A.Dessaur 4-1-16-0; A.J.Harris 31.4-3-152-6; T.W.Harrison 77-19-282-5; A.S.Rollins 3-1-19-1; T.A.Tweats 34.4-3-149-3.

The First-Class Averages (pp 129-143) give the records of Derbyshire players in all first-class county matches (their other opponents being Oxford University and Young Australia), with the exception of P.A.J.DeFreitas, whose full county figures are as above, and:

D.G.Cork 12-22-3-84*-383-20.15-0-2-6ct. 363.4-74-1020-57-17.89-9/43-3-1.
D.E.Malcolm 12-18-4-25*-110-7.85-0-0-1ct. 411.1-75-1472-60-24.53-6/61-3-1.

DERBYSHIRE RECORDS

FIRST-CLASS CRICKET

Highest Total	For 645		v	Hampshire	Derby	1898
	V 662		by	Yorkshire	Chesterfield	1898
Lowest Total	For 16		v	Notts	Nottingham	1879
	V 23		by	Hampshire	Burton upon T	1958
Highest Innings	For 274	G.A.Davidson	v	Lancashire	Manchester	1896
	V 343*	P.A.Perrin	for	Essex	Chesterfield	1904

Highest Partnership for each Wicket

1st	322	H.Storer/J.Bowden	v	Essex	Derby	1929
2nd	349	C.S.Elliott/J.D.Eggar	v	Notts	Nottingham	1947
3rd	291	P.N.Kirsten/D.S.Steele	v	Somerset	Taunton	1981
4th	328	P.Vaulkhard/D.Smith	v	Notts	Nottingham	1946
5th	302*†	J.E.Morris/D.G.Cork	v	Glos	Cheltenham	1993
6th	212	G.M.Lee/T.S.Worthington	v	Essex	Chesterfield	1932
7th	241*	G.H.Pope/A.E.G.Rhodes	v	Hampshire	Portsmouth	1948
8th	182	A.H.M.Jackson/W.Carter	v	Leics	Leicester	1922
9th	283	A.Warren/J.Chapman	v	Warwicks	Blackwell	1910
10th	132	A.Hill/M.Jean-Jacques	v	Yorkshire	Sheffield	1986

† *346 runs were added for this wicket in two separate partnerships.*

Best Bowling	For	10- 40	W.Bestwick	v	Glamorgan	Cardiff	1921
(Innings)	V	10- 45	R.L.Johnson	for	Middlesex	Derby	1994
Best Bowling	For	17-103	W.Mycroft	v	Hampshire	Southampton	1876
(Match)	V	16-101	G.Giffen	for	Australians	Derby	1886

Most Runs – Season	2165	D.B.Carr	(av 48.11)	1959
Most Runs – Career	20516†	D.Smith	(av 31.41)	1927-52
Most 100s – Season	8	P.N.Kirsten		1982
Most 100s – Career	46	K.J.Barnett		1979-95
Most Wkts – Season	168	T.B.Mitchell	(av 19.55)	1935
Most Wkts – Career	1670	H.L.Jackson	(av 17.11)	1947-63

† K.J.Barnett has scored 20114 runs.

LIMITED-OVERS CRICKET

Highest Total	NWT	365-3		v	Cornwall	Derby	1986
	BHC	366-4		v	Comb Univs	Oxford	1991
	SL	292-9		v	Worcs	Knypersley	1985
Lowest Total	NWT	79		v	Surrey	The Oval	1967
	BHC	98		v	Worcs	Derby	1994
	SL	61		v	Hampshire	Portsmouth	1990
Highest Innings	NWT	153	A.Hill	v	Cornwall	Derby	1986
	BHC	123	J.E.Morris	v	Somerset	Taunton	1990
	SL	141*	C.J.Adams	v	Kent	Chesterfield	1992
Best Bowling	NWT	8-21	M.A.Holding	v	Sussex	Hove	1988
	BHC	6-33	E.J.Barlow	v	Glos	Bristol	1978
	SL	6- 7	M.Hendrick	v	Notts	Nottingham	1972

DURHAM

Formation of Present Club: 10 May 1882
Colours: Navy blue, yellow and maroon
Badge: Coat of Arms of the County of Durham
Championships: (0) 16th 1994
NatWest Trophy/Gillette Cup Winners: (0) Quarter-Finalist 1992
Benson and Hedges Cup Winners: (0) Second Round 1994
Sunday League Champions: (0) Seventh 1993
Match Awards: NWT 18; BHC 7.

Chief Executive: G.A.Wright
County Ground, Riverside, Chester-le-Street, Co Durham DH3 3QR.
(Tel 0191 387 1717)
Captain: M.A.Roseberry
Scorer: B.Hunt
1996 Beneficiary: P.Bainbridge (Testimonial)

BAINBRIDGE, Philip (Hanley HS; Stoke-on-Trent SFC; Borough Road CE), b Sneyd Green, Stoke-on-Trent, Staffs 16 Apr 1958. 5'10". RHB, RM. Gloucestershire 1977-90 (cap 1981; benefit 1989). Durham debut/cap 1992. Captain 1994. Testimonial 1996. *Wisden* 1985. Tours: SL 1986-87 (Gs); Z 1984-85 (EC). 1000 runs (9); most – 1644 (1985). HS 169 Gs v Yorks (Cheltenham) 1988. Du HS 150* v Essex (Chelmsford) 1993. BB 8-53 Gs v Somerset (Bristol) 1986. Du BB 5-53 v Yorks (Leeds) 1993. Awards: NWT 1; BHC 3. **NWT:** HS 89 Gs v Leics (Leicester) 1988. BB 3-49 Gs v Scot (Bristol) 1983. **BHC:** HS 96 Gs v Hants (Southampton) 1988. BB 4-38 v Worcs (Worcester) 1992. **SL:** HS 106* Gs v Somerset (Bristol) 1986. BB 5-22 Gs v Middx (Lord's) 1987.

BETTS, Melvyn Morris (Fyndoune CS, Sacriston), b Sacriston 26 Mar 1975. 5'10". RHB, RMF. Debut 1993. Cap 1994. HS 14 v Yorks (Harrogate) 1995. BB 3-35 v Hants (Stockton) 1995. **NWT:** HS 9. BB 1-47. **SL:** HS 14* v Lancs (Manchester) and v Derbys (Chester-le-St) 1995. BB 3-39 v Notts (Chester-le-St) 1995.

BIRBECK, Shaun David (Hetton CS), b Easington Lane 26 Jul 1972. Brother of A. (Durham 1983-90). 5'11". LHB, RM. Debut/cap 1994. HS 75* v Derbys (Chester-le-St) 1995. BB 3-119 v Surrey (Oval) 1995. **NWT:** HS – . BB 2-27 v Herefords (Chester-le-St) 1995. **BHC:** HS 1. BB 3-64 v Minor C (Jesmond) 1995. **SL:** HS 23 v Surrey (Oval) 1995. BB 1-14.

BLENKIRON, Darren Andrew (Bishop Barrington CS, Bishop Auckland), b Solihull, Warwks 4 Feb 1974. Son of W. (Warwks 1964-74, Durham 1975-76). 5'10". LHB, RM. Durham staff/cap 1992. Debut 1994. HS 145 v Glam (Swansea) 1995. BB 1-10. **NWT:** HS 56 v Glam (Darlington) 1991. **SL:** HS 56 v Somerset (Chester-le-St) 1995. BB 1-25.

BOILING, James (Rutlish S, Merton; Durham U), b New Delhi, India 8 Apr 1968. 6'4". RHB, OB. Surrey 1988-94. Durham debut/cap 1995. Tour: A 1992-93 (Eng A). HS 69 v WI (Chester-le-St) 1995. BAC HS 34* Sy v Durham (Darlington) 1994. BB 6-84 (10-203 match) Sy v Glos (Bristol) 1992. Du BB 5-73 v Notts (Chester-le-St) 1995. Award: BHC 1. **NWT:** HS 24 Sy v Worcs (Oval) 1994. BB 4-22 v Herefords (Chester-le-St) 1995. **BHC:** HS 9* (twice). BB 3-9 Comb Us v Surrey (Cambridge) 1989. **SL:** HS 23* Sy v Worcs (Worcester) 1993. BB 5-24 Sy v Hants (Basingstoke) 1992.

BROWN, Simon John Emmerson (Boldon CS), b Cleadon 29 Jun 1969. 6'3". RHB, LFM. Northamptonshire 1987-90. Durham debut/cap 1992. HS 69 v Leics (Durham) 1994. 50 wkts (3); most – 75 (1994). BB 7-70 v A (Durham) 1993. BAC BB 7-105 v Kent (Canterbury) 1992. Award: NWT 1. **NWT:** HS 7*. BB 5-22 v Cheshire (Bowdon) 1994. **BHC:** HS 12 v Warwks (Birmingham) 1995. BB 3-39 v Notts (Stockton) 1995. **SL:** HS 7. BB 4-20 v Yorks (Leeds) 1995.

COX, David Mathew (Greenford HS), b Southall, Middx 2 Mar 1972. 5'10". LHB, SLA. Hertfordshire 1992. MCC YC. Durham staff/cap 1993. Debut 1994. HS 26* v SA (Chester-le-St) 1994. BAC HS 17 v Northants (Northampton) 1995. BB 4-141 v Glam (Swansea) 1995. **SL:** HS – . BB 1-25.

DALEY, James Arthur (Hetton CS), b Sunderland 24 Sep 1973. 5'10". RHB, RM. Debut/cap 1992. MCC YC. HS 159* v Hants (Portsmouth) 1994. **BHC:** HS 17 v Minor C (Jesmond) 1995. **SL:** HS 98* v Kent (Canterbury) 1994.

HUTTON, Stewart (De Brus S, Skelton; Cleveland TC), b Stockton-on-Tees 30 Nov 1969. 6'0". LHB, RSM. Debut/cap 1992. HS 101 v Northants (Hartlepool) 1994. Award: NWT 1. **NWT:** HS 125 v Herefords (Chester-le-St) 1995. **BHC:** HS 8. **SL:** HS 70 v Glam (Hartlepool) 1992.

KILLEEN, Neil (Greencroft CS; Derwentside C; Teesside U), b Shotley Bridge 17 Oct 1975. 6'2". RHB, RFM. Durham debut/cap 1995. HS 48 v Somerset (Chester-le-St) 1995. BB 5-118 v Sussex (Hartlepool) 1995. **BHC:** HS 8 and BB 2-43 Comb Us v H (Oxford) 1995. **SL:** HS 20 v Notts (Chester-le-St) 1995. BB 5-26 v Northants (Northampton) 1995. Soccer for Durham 1991. Athletics (javelin) for Durham 1990-92.

LIGERTWOOD, David George Coutts (St Peter's C, Adelaide; Adelaide U), b Oxford 16 May 1969. 5'8". RHB, WK. Surrey 1992. Hertfordshire 1990-91. Durham debut/cap 1995. HS 40 v Surrey (Oval) and v WI (Chester-le-St) 1995. **NWT:** HS 5. **SL:** HS 31 v Worcs (Darlington) 1995.

LONGLEY, Jonathan Ian (Tonbridge S; Durham U), b New Brunswick, New Jersey, USA 12 Apr 1969. 5'7". RHB. Kent 1989-93. Durham debut/cap 1994. Tour: Z 1992-93 (K). HS 110 K v CU (Cambridge) 1992. BAC/Du HS 100* v Derbys (Chesterfield) 1994 – on Du debut. **NWT:** HS 9. **BHC:** HS 57 K v Somerset (Canterbury) 1992. **SL:** HS 92 v Somerset (Chester-le-St) 1995.

LUGSDEN, Steven (St Edmund Campion S, Low Fell), b Gateshead 10 Jul 1976. 6'2". RHB, RFM. Debut 1993 aged 17yr 27d (youngest Durham f-c player). Cap 1994. HS 5* and BB 2-43 v Derbys (Durham) 1993. **SL:** HS – . BB 1-55.

MORRIS, John Edward (Shavington CS; Dane Bank CFE), b Crewe, Cheshire 1 Apr 1964. 5'10". RHB, RM. Derbyshire 1982-93 (cap 1986). GW 1988-89 and 1993-94. Durham debut/cap 1994. **Tests:** 3 (1990); HS 32 v I (Oval) 1990. **LOI:** 8 (1990-91; HS 63*). Tour: A 1990-91. 1000 runs (10); most – 1739 (1986). HS 229 De v Glos (Cheltenham) 1993. Du HS 204 v Warwks (Birmingham) 1994. BB 1-6. Du BB 1-37. Awards: NWT 1; BHC 2. **NWT:** HS 94* De v Salop (Chesterfield) 1990. **BHC:** HS 123 De v Somerset (Taunton) 1990. **SL:** HS 134 De v Somerset (Taunton) 1990.

ROSEBERRY, Michael Anthony (Durham S), b Sunderland 28 Nov 1966. Elder brother of A. (Leics and Glam 1992-94). 6'1". RHB, RM. Middlesex 1986-94 (cap 1990). Durham debut/cap 1995. Captain 1995-. Tour: A 1992-93 (Eng A). 1000 runs (4) inc 2000 (1): 2044 (1992). HS 185 M v Leics (Lord's) 1993. Du HS 90 v OU (Oxford) 1995. BB 1-1. Awards: NWT 1; BHC 1. **NWT:** HS 121 v Herefords (Chester-le-St) 1995. BB 1-22. **BHC:** HS 84 M v Minor C (Lord's) 1992. **SL:** HS 119* M v Surrey (Oval) 1994.

SCOTT, Christopher Wilmot (Robert Pattinson CS, N Hykeham), b Thorpe-on-the-Hill, Lincs 23 Jan 1964. 5'8". RHB, WK. Nottinghamshire 1981-91 (cap 1988). Durham debut/cap 1992. HS 108 v Surrey (Darlington) 1994. Held 10 catches for Notts in match v Derbys (Derby) 1988. **NWT:** HS 2. **BHC:** HS 18 Nt v Northants (Northampton) 1988. **SL:** HS 45 v Surrey (Darlington) 1994.

SEARLE, Jason Paul (John Bentley S, Calne; Swindon C), b Bath, Somerset 16 May 1976. 5'9". RHB, OB. Durham staff/cap 1993. Debut 1994. HS 5*. BB: 2-126 v Surrey (Oval) 1995. **BHC:** HS – . **SL:** HS – .

WALKER, Alan (Shelley HS), b Emley, Yorks 7 Jul 1962. 5'11". LHB, RFM. Northamptonshire 1983-93 (cap 1987). Durham debut/cap 1994. Tour: SA 1991-92 (Nh). HS 41* Nh v Warwks (Birmingham) 1987. Du HS 29 v WI (Chester-le-St) 1995. 50 wkts (1): 54 (1988).

WALKER – continued:
BB 8-118 (14-177 match) v Essex (Chelmsford) 1995. Award: NWT 1. **NWT:** HS 13 v Derbys (Darlington) 1994. BB 4-7 Nh v Ire (Northampton) 1987. **BHC:** HS 15* Nh v Notts (Nottingham) 1987. BB 4-42 v Minor C (Jesmond) 1995. **SL:** HS 30 Nh v Durham (Northampton) 1993. BB 4-21 Nh v Worcs (Worcester) 1985.

WESTON, Robin Michael Swann (Durham S; Loughborough U), b Durham 7 Jun 1975. Brother of W.P.C. (*see WORCESTERSHIRE*). 5'10". RHB, LB. Durham staff/cap 1994. Debut 1995. Minor C debut 1991 when aged 15yr 355d (Durham record). HS 9. BB 1-41.

WOOD, John (Crofton HS; Wakefield District C; Leeds Poly), b Wakefield, Yorks 22 Jul 1970. 6'3". RHB, RFM. GW in Nissan Shield 1990-91. Debut/cap 1992. HS 63* v Notts (Chester-le-St) 1993. BB 6-110 v Essex (Stockton) 1994. **NWT:** HS 1. BB 2-22 v Ireland (Dublin) 1992. **BHC:** HS 27 v Leics (Stockton) 1995. BB 3-50 v Warwicks (Birmingham) 1995. **SL:** HS 28 and BB 2-26 v Worcs (Worcester) 1994.

NEWCOMERS

CAMPBELL, Colin Lockey (Blaydon SFC), b Newcastle-upon-Tyne, Northumb 11 Aug 1977. RHB, RFM.

CAMPBELL, Sherwin Legay (Ellerslie SS), b Bridgetown, Barbados 1 Nov 1970. 5'4". RHB. Barbados 1990-91 to date. Durham staff/cap 1996. **Tests** (WI): 9 (1994-95 to 1995). HS 93 v E (Lord's) 1995. **LOI** (WI): 22 (1994-95 to 1995-96; HS 86). Tours (WI): E 1995; NZ 1994-95; I 1994-95. 1000 runs (1): 1225 (1995). HS 172 WI v Hants (Southampton) 1995.

COLLINGWOOD, Paul David (Blackfyne CS; Derwentside C), b Shotley Bridge 26 May 1976. 5'11". RHB, RM. Durham staff/cap 1996. **SL:** HS 33* v Notts (Chester-le-St) 1995.

PRATT, Andrew (Willington Parkside CS; Durham New C), Helmington Row, Crook 4 Mar 1975. LHB, WK. MCC YC. Durham staff/cap 1996.

DEPARTURES (who made first-class appearance in 1995)

LARKINS, Wayne (Bushmead SS, Eaton Socon), b Roxton, Beds 22 Nov 1953. 5'11". RHB, RM. Northamptonshire 1972-91 (cap 1976; benefit 1986). Durham 1992-95 (cap 1992). E Province 1982-83/1983-84. Bedfordshire 1996. **Tests:** 13 (1979-80 to 1990-91); HS 64 v A (Melbourne) 1990-91. **LOI:** 25 (1979 to 1990-91; HS 124). Tours: A 1979-80, 1990-91; SA 1981-82 (SAB); WI 1989-90; I 1979-80, 1980-81 (Overseas XI). 1000 runs (13); most – 1863 (1982). HS 252 Nh v Glam (Cardiff) 1983. Du HS 158* v Glos (Gateshead) 1994. BB 5-59 Nh v Worcs (Worcester) 1984. Awards: NWT 2; BHC 7. **NWT:** HS 121* Nh v Essex (Chelmsford) 1987. BB 2-38 Nh v Glos (Bristol) 1985. **BHC:** HS 132 Nh v Warwks (Birmingham) 1982. BB 4-37 Nh v Comb Us (Northampton) 1980. **SL:** HS 172* Nh v Warwks (Luton) 1983. BB 5-32 Nh v Essex (Ilford) 1978.

LAWRENCE, James Richard Geoffrey (Hurworth CS; Darlington QE SFC; Durham U), b Portsmouth, Hants 29 Nov 1976. 6'3". RHB, LMF. Durham 1995 (one match whilst attending SFC). HS 7* and BB 2-44 v Somerset (Chester-le-St) 1995.

PRABHAKAR, Manoj (Ghaziabad SS; Delhi U), b Ghaziabad, India 15 Apr 1963. 5'8½". RHB, RMF. Delhi 1982-83 to date. Durham 1995 (cap 1995). **Tests** (I): 39 (1984-85 to 1995-96); HS 120 v WI (Chandigarh) 1994-95. BB 6-132 v P (Faisalabad) 1989-90. **LOI** (I): 125 (1983-84 to 1995-96; HS 106; BB 5-33). Tours (I): E 1986, 1990; A 1991-92; SA 1992-93; NZ 1989-90, 1993-94; P 1989-90; SL 1993-94; Z 1983-84 (Young I), 1992-93. HS 229* Delhi v Himachal Pradesh (Delhi) 1988-89. Du HS 101 v Glam (Swansea) 1995. 50 wkts (1): 51 (1995). BB 7-65 v Leics (Leicester) 1995. **NWT:** HS 4. **BHC:** HS 69 v Notts (Stockton) 1995. BB 2-36 v Leics (Stockton) 1995. **SL:** HS 69 v Glam (Swansea) 1995. BB 3-30 v Essex (Chelmsford) 1995.

SAXELBY, Mark (Nottingham HS), b Worksop, Notts 4 Jan 1969. 6'3". LHB, RM. Younger brother of K. (Notts 1978-90). Nottinghamshire 1989-93. Durham debut/cap 1994. 1000 runs (1): 1102 (1994). HS 181 v Derbys (Chesterfield) 1994. BB 3-41 Nt v Derbys (Derby) 1991. Du BB 1-15. Award: BHC 1. **NWT:** HS 41 Nt v Bucks (Marlow) 1990. BB 2-42 Nt v Lincs (Nottingham) 1991. **BHC:** HS 80* v Leics (Stockton) 1995. BB 1-36. **SL:** HS 100* Nt v Durham (Chester-le-St) 1993. BB 4-29 Nt v Leics (Leicester) 1991.

DURHAM 1995

RESULTS SUMMARY

	Place	Won	Lost	Tied	Drew	No Result
Britannic Assurance Championship	**17th**	4	13	–	–	–
All First-Class Matches		4	13	–	2	–
NatWest Trophy	2nd Round					
Benson and Hedges Cup	4th in Group A					
Sunday League	**16th**	4	9	1	–	3

BRITANNIC ASSURANCE CHAMPIONSHIP AVERAGES

BATTING AND FIELDING

Cap		M	I	NO	HS	Runs	Avge	100	50	Ct/St
1992	J.A.Daley	6	10	1	55	362	40.22	–	3	5
1994	J.E.Morris	17	32	1	169	1123	36.22	3	4	8
1992	W.Larkins	13	23	–	121	737	32.04	2	1	11
1995	M.Prabhakar	17	31	3	101	896	32.00	1	5	9
1992	S.Hutton	10	19	1	98	551	30.61	–	4	6
1992	D.A.Blenkiron	8	15	1	145	413	29.50	1	2	3
1994	J.I.Longley	7	14	1	58	365	28.07	–	2	2
1994	S.D.Birbeck	4	6	2	75*	106	26.50	–	1	1
1992	C.W.Scott	6	11	–	56	270	24.54	–	2	14
1995	M.A.Roseberry	14	26	2	56	480	20.00	–	2	15
1994	M.Saxelby	5	10	–	68	194	19.40	–	1	4
1992	J.Wood	3	6	1	40*	67	13.40	–	–	–
1995	D.G.C.Ligertwood	11	19	2	40	225	13.23	–	–	33/3
1995	N.Killeen	6	11	3	48	100	12.50	–	–	3
1992	S.J.E.Brown	17	29	5	36	262	10.91	–	–	6
1995	J.Boiling	16	29	6	24	235	10.21	–	–	11
1994	A.Walker	9	13	2	19	72	6.54	–	–	3
1993	D.M.Cox	3	5	–	17	23	4.60	–	–	–
1994	M.M.Betts	8	14	4	14	44	4.40	–	–	2
1994	R.M.S.Weston	3	6	–	9	15	2.50	–	–	5

Also batted: P.Bainbridge (2 matches – cap 1992) 0, 4, 0 (1 ct); J.R.G.Lawrence (1 match) 0, 7*; J.P.Searle (1 match – cap 1993) 2*, 0.

BOWLING

	O	M	R	W	Avge	Best	5wI	10wM
J.Wood	74.4	16	255	12	21.25	4- 54	–	–
A.Walker	242.3	42	769	29	26.51	8-118	2	1
M.Prabhakar	579.1	163	1439	51	28.21	7- 65	1	–
S.J.E.Brown	557.3	107	1890	52	36.34	6- 69	4	1
D.M.Cox	129.5	28	422	11	38.36	4-141	–	–
N.Killeen	175.3	28	658	16	41.12	5-118	1	–
M.M.Betts	175.5	29	733	13	56.38	3- 35	–	–
J.Boiling	541	123	1575	25	63.00	5- 73	2	–

Also bowled: P.Bainbridge 15-2-55-1; S.D.Birbeck 64-8-271-4; D.A.Blenkiron 16-1-64-1; S.Hutton 2-0-13-0; J.R.G.Lawrence 40-8-123-3; J.I.Longley 4-0-47-0; M.A.Roseberry 2.4-0-14-0; M.Saxelby 13.4-0-60-1; C.W.Scott 3.2-0-30-0; J.P.Searle 36-3-126-2; R.M.S.Weston 22.1-2-70-1.

The First-Class Averages (pp 129-143) give the records of Durham players in all first-class county matches (their other opponents being the West Indians and Oxford University).

DURHAM RECORDS

FIRST-CLASS CRICKET

Highest Total	For	625-6d		v	Derbyshire	Chesterfield	1994
	V	810-4d		by	Warwicks	Birmingham	1994
Lowest Total	For	83		v	Lancs	Manchester	1993
	V	73		by	Oxford U	Oxford	1994
Highest Innings	For	204	J.E.Morris	v	Warwicks	Birmingham	1994
	V	501*	B.C.Lara	for	Warwicks	Birmingham	1994

Highest Partnership for each Wicket

1st	222	P.W.G.Parker/J.D.Glendenen	v	Oxford U	Oxford	1992
2nd	206	W.Larkins/D.M.Jones	v	Glamorgan	Cardiff	1992
3rd	205	G.Fowler/S.Hutton	v	Yorkshire	Leeds	1993
4th	201	W.Larkins/J.A.Daley	v	Somerset	Taunton	1992
5th	185	P.W.G.Parker/J.A.Daley	v	Warwicks	Darlington	1993
6th	152	I.T.Botham/A.C.Cummins	v	Worcs	Stockton	1993
7th	106	I.Smith/D.A.Graveney	v	Somerset	Taunton	1992
8th	134	A.C.Cummins/D.A.Graveney	v	Warwicks	Birmingham	1994
9th	88	C.W.Scott/D.A.Graveney	v	Surrey	Darlington	1994
10th	70	D.A.Graveney/S.J.E.Brown	v	Surrey	Durham	1992

Best Bowling	For	8-118	A.Walker	v	Essex	Chelmsford	1995
(Innings)	V	8- 69	A.R.Caddick	for	Somerset	Chester-le-St	1995
Best Bowling	For	14-177	A.Walker	v	Essex	Chelmsford	1995
(Match)	V	12- 68	J.N.B.Bovill	for	Hampshire	Stockton	1995

Most Runs – Season	1536	W.Larkins	(av 37.46)	1992
Most Runs – Career	4278	W.Larkins	(av 37.52)	1992-95
Most 100s – Season	4	D.M.Jones		1992
	4	W.Larkins		1992
	4	J.E.Morris		1994
Most 100s – Career	10	W.Larkins		1992-95
Most Wkts – Season	74	S.J.E.Brown	(av 27.62)	1994
Most Wkts – Career	236	S.J.E.Brown	(av 33.17)	1992-95

LIMITED-OVERS CRICKET

Highest Total	NWT	326-4		v	Herefords	Chester-le-St	1995
	BHC	271-6		v	Comb Univs	Cambridge	1992
	SL	281-2		v	Derbyshire	Durham	1993
Lowest Total	NWT	82		v	Worcs	Chester-le-St	1968
	BHC	165		v	Leics	Stockton	1995
	SL	105		v	Glamorgan	Colwyn Bay	1993
Highest Innings	NWT	125	S.Hutton	v	Herefords	Chester-le-St	1995
	BHC	123	W.Larkins	v	Minor C	Jesmond	1995
	SL	131*	W.Larkins	v	Hampshire	Portsmouth	1994
Best Bowling	NWT	7-32	S.P.Davis	v	Lancashire	Chester-le-St	1983
	BHC	4-38	P.Bainbridge	v	Worcs	Worcester	1992
	SL	5-26	N.Killeen	v	Northants	Northampton	1995

ESSEX

Formation of Present Club: 14 January 1876
Colours: Blue, Gold and Red
Badge: Three Seaxes above Scroll bearing 'Essex'
Championships: (6) 1979, 1983, 1984, 1986, 1991, 1992
NatWest Trophy/Gillette Cup Winners: (1) 1985
Benson and Hedges Cup Winners: (1) 1979
Sunday League Champions: (3) 1981, 1984, 1985
Match Awards: NWT 38; BHC 73

Secretary/General Manager: P.J.Edwards
County Ground, New Writtle Street, Chelmsford CM2 0PG (Tel 01245 252420)
Captain: P.J.Prichard
Scorer: C.F.Driver
1996 Beneficiary: P.J.Prichard

ANDREW, Stephen Jon Walter (Milton Abbey S; Portchester SS), b London 27 Jan 1966. 6'3". RHB, RMF. Hampshire 1984-89. Essex debut 1990. HS 35 v Northants (Chelmsford) 1990. BB 7-47 v Lancs (Manchester) 1993. Awards: BHC 2. **NWT:** HS 1*. BB 2-34 v Scot (Chelmsford) 1990. **BHC:** HS 4*. BB 5-24 H v Essex (Chelmsford) 1987. **SL:** HS 14 v Kent (Maidstone) 1993. BB 4-50 H v Middx (Southampton) 1988.

AYRES, Duncan Wallace (Falmouth CS; Millfield S), b Basildon 8 Oct 1976. 5'11". RHB, RMF. Essex staff 1993 – awaiting f-c debut.

CHILDS, John Henry (Audley Park SM, Torquay), b Plymouth, Devon 15 Aug 1951. 6'0". LHB, SLA. Gloucestershire 1975-84 (cap 1977). Essex debut 1985. Cap 1986. Benefit 1994. Devon 1973-74. Wisden 1986. **Tests:** 2 (1988); HS 2*; BB 1-13. HS 43 v Hants (Chelmsford) 1992. 50 wkts (9); most – 89 (1986). BB 9-56 Gs v Somerset (Bristol) 1981. Ex BB 8-58 v Glos (Colchester) 1986. Award: BHC 1. **NWT:** HS 14* Gs v Hants (Bristol) 1983. BB 2-15 Gs v Ire (Dublin) 1981. **BHC:** HS 10 Gs v Somerset (Bristol) 1979. BB 3-36 Gs v Glam (Bristol) 1982. **SL:** HS 16* Gs v Warwks (Bristol) 1981. BB 4-15 Gs v Northants (Northampton) 1976.

COUSINS, Darren Mark (Netherhall CS; Impington Village C), b Cambridge 24 Sep 1971. 6'2". RHB, RMF. Debut 1993. Cambridgeshire 1990. HS 18* v Durham (Chelmsford) 1995. BB 6-35 v CU (Cambridge) 1994. BAC BB 3-73 v Leics (Chelmsford) 1995. **NWT:** HS 1*. BB 1-33. **BHC:** HS 12* v Glam (Chelmsford) 1995. BB 1-46. **SL:** HS 6. BB 3-18 v Warwks (Birmingham) 1994.

COWAN, Ashley Preston (Framlingham C), b Hitchin, Herts 7 May 1975. 6'4". RHB, RM. Debut 1995. Cambridgeshire 1993. HS 22 v Yorks (Chelmsford) 1995. **SL:** HS 0*.

DERBYSHIRE, Nicholas Alexander (Ampleforth C; Goldsmith's C, London U), b Ramsbottom, Lancs 11 Sep 1970. 5'11½". RHB, RFM. Lancashire 1994. Essex debut 1995. HS 17 v Durham (Chelmsford) 1995. BB 1-18. BAC BB 1-20. **BHC:** HS –.

GOOCH, Graham Alan (Norlington Jr HS), b Leytonstone 23 Jul 1953. 6'0". RHB, RM. Debut 1973. Cap 1975. Captain 1986-87, 1989-94. Benefit 1985. Testimonial 1995. W Province 1982-83/1983-84. Wisden 1979. OBE 1991. **Tests:** 118 (1975 to 1994-95, 34 as captain); HS 333 and record match aggregate of 456 v I (Lord's) 1990; BB 3-39 v P (Manchester) 1992. **LOI:** 125 (1976 to 1994-95; HS 142; BB 3-19). Tours (C=captain): A 1978-79, 1979-80, 1990-91C, 1994-95; SA 1981-82 (SAB); WI 1980-81, 1985-86, 1989-90C; NZ 1991-92C; I 1979-80, 1981-82, 1992-93C; P 1987-88; SL 1981-82. 1000 runs (19+1) inc 2000 (5); most – 2746 (1990). HS 333 (*Tests*). Ex HS 275 v Kent (Chelmsford) 1988. BB 7-14 v Worcs (Ilford) 1982. Awards: NWT 9 (record); BHC 22 (record). **NWT:** HS 144 v Hants (Chelmsford) 1990. BB 5-8 v Cheshire (Chester) 1995. **BHC:** HS 198* v Sussex (Hove) 1982. BB 3-24 v Sussex (Hove) 1982. **SL:** HS 176 v Glam (Southend) 1983. BB 4-33 v Worcs (Chelmsford) 1984.

HIBBERT, Andrew James Edward (St Edward's CS and SFC, Romford), b Harold Wood 17 Dec 1974. 5'11½. RHB, RM. Debut 1995. Awaiting BAC debut. HS 24 v CU (Cambridge) 1995.

HUSSAIN, Nasser (Forest S, Snaresbrook; Durham U), b Madras, India 28 Mar 1968. Son of J. (Madras 1966-67); brother of M. (Worcs 1985). 5'11". RHB, LB. Debut 1987. Cap 1989. YC 1989. **Tests:** 7 (1989-90 to 1993); HS 71 v A (Nottingham) 1993. **LOI:** 4 (1989-90 to 1993-94; HS 16). Tours: WI 1989-90, 1991-92 (Eng A), 1993-94; P 1990-91 (Eng A), 1995-96 (Eng A – captain); SL 1990-91 (Eng A). 1000 runs (3); most – 1854 (1995). HS 197 v Surrey (Oval) 1990. BB 1-38. Awards: NWT 1; BHC 1. **NWT:** HS 108 v Cumberland (Chelmsford) 1992. **BHC:** HS 118 Comb Us v Somerset (Taunton) 1989. **SL:** HS 83 v Kent (Canterbury) 1995.

HYAM, Barry James (Havering SFC), b Romford 9 Sep 1975. RHB, WK. Debut 1993 (only match). HS 1.

ILOTT, Mark Christopher (Francis Combe S, Garston), b Watford, Herts 27 Aug 1970. 6'0½". LHB, LFM. Debut 1988. Cap 1993. Hertfordshire 1987-88 (at 16, the youngest to represent that county). **Tests:** 5 (1993 to 1995-96); HS 15 v A (Oval) 1993; BB 3-48 v SA (Durban) 1995-96. Tours: A 1992-93 (Eng A); SA 1993-94 (Eng A), 1995-96; I 1994-95 (Eng A – part); SL 1990-91 (Eng A). HS 60 Eng A v Warwks (Birmingham) 1995. Ex HS 51 v Sussex (Hove) 1993. 50 wkts (4); most – 78 (1995). BB 9-19 (14-105 match; inc hat-trick – all lbw) v Northants (Luton) 1995. Award: BHC 1. **NWT:** HS 54* v Cheshire (Chester) 1995. BB 2-23 v Cumberland (Chelmsford) 1992. **BHC:** HS 21 v Glam (Chelmsford) 1995. BB 5-21 v Scot (Forfar) 1993. **SL:** HS 56* v Sussex (Hove) 1995. BB 4-15 v Derbys (Derby) 1992.

IRANI, Ronald Charles (Smithills CS, Bolton), b Leigh, Lancs 26 Oct 1971. 6'3". RHB, RMF. Lancashire 1990-93. Essex debut/cap 1994. Tour (Eng A): P 1995-96. 1000 runs (1): 1165 (1995). HS 119 v Worcs (Worcester) 1994. BB 5-62 v Kent (Canterbury) 1995. Award: NWT 1. **NWT:** HS 30 v Glam (Cardiff) 1994. BB 4-49 v Sussex (Hove) 1994. **BHC:** HS 40 v Glos (Chelmsford) 1995. BB 3-40 v Comb Us (Cambridge) 1995. **SL:** HS 101* v Glos (Cheltenham) 1995. BB 3-22 v Worcs (Worcester) 1994.

LEWIS, Jonathan James Benjamin (King Edward VI S, Chelmsford; Roehampton IHE), b Isleworth, Middx 21 May 1970. 5'9½". RHB, RSM. Debut 1990 v Surrey (Oval), scoring 116*. Cap 1994. HS 136* v Notts (Nottingham) 1993. **NWT:** HS 24* v Sussex (Hove) 1994. **BHC:** HS 19 v Glos (Chelmsford) 1995. **SL:** HS 23 v Notts (Ilford) 1994.

PRICHARD, Paul John (Brentwood HS), b Billericay 7 Jan 1965. 5'10". RHB, RSM. Debut 1984. Cap 1986. Captain 1995-. Benefit 1996. Tour: A 1992-93 (Eng A). 1000 runs (7); most – 1485 (1992). HS 245 v Leics (Chelmsford) 1990. BB 1-28. Awards: NWT 1; BHC 2. **NWT:** HS 94 v Oxon (Chelmsford) 1985. **BHC:** HS 107 v Scot (Glasgow) 1990. **SL:** HS 107 v Notts (Nottingham) 1993.

ROBINSON, Darren David John (Tabor HS, Braintree; Chelmsford CFE), b Braintree 2 Mar 1973. 5'10½". RHB, RMF. Debut 1993. HS 123 v Glos (Cheltenham) 1995. **NWT:** HS 55 v Yorks (Chelmsford) 1995. **BHC:** HS 35* v Middx (Chelmsford) 1995. **SL:** HS 38 v Surrey (Oval) 1995.

ROLLINS, Robert John (Little Ilford CS), b Plaistow 30 Jan 1974. 5'9". RHB, RM, WK. Brother of A.S. (*see DERBYSHIRE*). Debut 1992. Cap 1995. HS 133* v Glam (Swansea) 1995. **NWT:** HS 21 v Yorks (Chelmsford) 1995. **BHC:** HS 0. **SL:** HS 28* v Warwks (Ilford) 1995.

SUCH, Peter Mark (Harry Carlton CS, Ex Leake, Notts), b Helensburgh, Dunbartonshire 12 Jun 1964. 5'11". RHB, OB. Nottinghamshire 1982-86. Leicestershire 1987-89. Essex debut 1990. Cap 1991. **Tests:** 8 (1993 to 1994); HS 14* and BB 6-67 v A (Manchester) 1993 – on debut. Tours (Eng A): A 1992-93; SA 1993-94. HS 54 v Worcs (Chelmsford) 1993. 50 wkts (3); most – 77 (1995). BB 8-93 (11-160 match) v Hants (Colchester) 1995. **NWT:** HS 8*. BB 2-29 v Devon (Exmouth) 1991. **BHC:** HS 5*. BB 4-43 v Northants (Northampton) 1992. **SL:** HS 19* v Notts (Ilford) 1994. BB 5-32 v Yorks (Chelmsford) 1993.

WILLIAMS, Neil FitzGerald (Acland Burghley CS), b Hope Well, St Vincent 2 Jul 1962. 5'11". RHB, RFM. Middlesex 1982-94 (cap 1984; benefit 1994). Essex debut 1995. Windward Is 1982-83 and 1989-90/1991-92. Tasmania 1983-84. MCC YC. **Tests:** 1 (1990); HS 38 and BB 2-148 v I (Oval) 1990. Tour: Z 1984-85 (EC). HS 77 M v Warwks (Birmingham) 1991. Ex HS 17 v Warwks (Ilford) 1995. 50 wkts (3); most – 63 (1983). BB 8-75 (12-139 match) M v Glos (Lord's) 1992. Ex BB 5-93 v Leics (Chelmsford) 1995. Award: BHC 1. **NWT:** HS 10 M v Northumb (Jesmond) 1984. BB 4-36 M v Derbys (Derby) 1983. **BHC:** HS 29* M v Surrey (Lord's) 1985. BB 3-16 M v Comb Us (Cambridge) 1982. **SL:** HS 43 M v Somerset (Lord's) 1988. BB 4-39 M v Surrey (Oval) 1988.

NEWCOMERS

GOODWIN, Giles Jeremy Anthony (Felsted S), b Isle of Sheppey 16 Sep 1976. RHB, SLA.

GRAYSON, Adrian Paul (Bedale CS), b Ripon, Yorks 31 Mar 1971. 6'1". RHB, SLA. Yorkshire 1990-95. Tour: SA 1991-92 (Y). 1000 runs (1): 1046 (1994). HS 100 Y v Worcs (Worcester) 1994. BB 2-5 Y v CU (Cambridge) 1995. BAC BB 2-43 Y v Hants (Leeds) 1994. **NWT:** HS 29 Y v Devon (Exmouth) 1994. BB 1-25. **BHC:** HS 22* Y v Hants (Southampton) 1994. BB 2-36 Y v Northants (Leeds) 1995. **SL:** HS 55 Y v Kent (Maidstone) 1994. BB 4-25 Y v Glam (Cardiff) 1994.

GROVE, Jamie Oliver, b Bury St Edmunds, Suffolk 3 Jul 1979. RHB, RF.

HODGSON, Timothy Paul, b Guildford, Surrey 27 Mar 1975. LHB.

LAW, Stuart Grant (Craigslea State HS), b Herston, Brisbane, Australia 18 Oct 1968. 6'2". RHB, RM/LB. Queensland 1988-89 to date. **Tests** (A): 1 (1995-96); HS 54* v SL (Perth) 1995-96. **LOI** (A): 14 (1994-95 to 1995-96; HS 110; BB 2-30). Tour (Young A): E 1995. 1000 runs (1): 1204 (1990-91). HS 179 Q v Tasmania (Brisbane) 1988-89. BB 3-25 Q v Victoria (Brisbane) 1992-93.

PETERS, Stephen David, b Harold Wood 10 Dec 1978. RHB.

POWELL, Jonathan Christopher, b Harold Wood 13 Jun 1979. RHB, OB.

DEPARTURES

GARNHAM, Michael Anthony (Camberwell GS, Melbourne; Scotch C, Perth; Barnstaple GS; N Devon SFC; East Anglia U), b Johannesburg, SA 20 Aug 1960. 5'10". RHB, WK. Gloucestershire 1979. Leicestershire 1980-85 and 1988. Essex 1989-95 (cap 1990). Cambridgeshire 1986-88. HS 123 Ex v Leics (Leicester) 1991. Awards: NWT 2; BHC 1. **NWT:** HS 110 Cambs v Warwks (Birmingham) 1988. **BHC:** HS 55 Le v Derbys (Leicester) 1982. **SL:** HS 79* Le v Lancs (Leicester) 1982.

PEARSON, R.M. – *see SURREY.*

WAUGH, Mark Edward (E Hills HS), b Canterbury, Sydney, Australia 2 Jun 1965. Younger twin of S.R. (NSW, Somerset and Australia). 6'1". RHB, RMF/OB. NSW 1985-86 to date. Essex 1988-90, 1992 and 1995 (cap 1989). *Wisden* 1990. **Tests** (A): 54 (1990-91 to 1995-96); HS 140 v E (Brisbane) 1994-95; BB 5-40 v E (Adelaide) 1994-95. **LOI** (A): 106 (1988-89 to 1995-96; HS 130; BB 5-24). Tours (A): E 1993, 1995 (NSW); SA 1993-94; WI 1990-91, 1994-95; NZ 1992-93; P 1994-95; SL 1992-93; Z 1985-86 (Young A), 1987-88 (NSW). 1000 runs (5+4) inc 2000 (1): 2072 (1990). HS 229* NSW v WA (Perth) 1990-91, sharing world record 5th wkt stand of 464* with S.R.Waugh. Ex HS 219* v Lancs (Ilford) 1992. BB 5-37 v Northants (Chelmsford) 1990. Awards: BHC 2. **NWT:** HS 47 v Hants (Chelmsford) 1990. BB 1-45. **BHC:** HS 100 v Northants (Northampton) 1992. BB 3-31 v Scot (Chelmsford) 1992. **SL:** HS 112* v Glam (Neath) 1989. BB 3-20 v Durham (Chelmsford) 1995.

ESSEX 1995

RESULTS SUMMARY

	Place	*Won*	*Lost*	*Tied*	*Drew*
Britannic Assurance Championship	**5th**	8	9	–	–
All First-Class Matches		8	9	–	2
NatWest Trophy	2nd Round				
Benson and Hedges Cup	4th in Group C				
Sunday League	**5th**	10	6	1	–

BRITANNIC ASSURANCE CHAMPIONSHIP AVERAGES

BATTING AND FIELDING

Cap		*M*	*I*	*NO*	*HS*	*Runs*	*Avge*	*100*	*50*	*Ct/St*
1989	N.Hussain	17	32	–	186	1688	52.75	6	8	33
1989	M.E.Waugh	15	28	2	173	1347	51.80	5	6	19
1975	G.A.Gooch	17	32	–	165	1510	47.18	6	5	12
1994	R.C.Irani	17	32	2	108	1135	37.83	1	9	7
1986	P.J.Prichard	17	31	–	109	1047	33.77	2	5	10
1995	R.J.Rollins	17	31	2	133*	727	25.06	1	4	48/9
–	D.D.J.Robinson	15	28	–	123	665	23.75	2	1	22
–	A.P.Cowan	2	4	1	22	47	15.66	–	–	1
1994	J.J.B.Lewis	5	10	–	75	141	14.10	–	1	5
1993	M.C.Ilott	15	27	3	37	288	12.00	–	–	3
1991	P.M.Such	17	30	8	32	214	9.72	–	–	11
–	D.M.Cousins	7	14	3	18*	99	9.00	–	–	2
–	N.F.Williams	8	12	2	17	90	9.00	–	–	1
1986	J.H.Childs	16	27	11	18	112	7.00	–	–	6

Also batted (1 match each): S.J.W.Andrew 0, 4; N.A.Derbyshire 9, 17.

BOWLING

	O	*M*	*R*	*W*	*Avge*	*Best*	*5wI*	*10wM*
M.C.Ilott	539.4	115	1684	76	22.15	9-19	6	2
P.M.Such	708.4	166	1940	75	25.86	8-93	6	2
J.H.Childs	648.3	171	1690	62	27.25	6-36	2	–
N.F.Williams	188.4	31	743	21	35.38	5-93	1	–
R.C.Irani	343.5	70	1134	25	45.36	5-62	1	–
M.E.Waugh	256	61	789	17	46.41	4-76	–	–

Also bowled: S.J.W.Andrew 19-2-70-0; D.M.Cousins 138-18-491-8; A.P.Cowan 24-2-113-1; N.A.Derbyshire 5-1-20-1; G.A.Gooch 20-4-68-4.

The First-Class Averages (pp 129-143) give the records of Essex players in all first-class county matches (their other opponents being the West Indians and Cambridge University), with the exception of M.E.Waugh, whose full county figures are as above, and:

M.C.Ilott 16-28-4-37-290-12.08-0-0-4ct. 551.4-117-1761-77-22.87-9/19-6-2.

ESSEX RECORDS

FIRST-CLASS CRICKET

Highest Total	For	761-6d		v	Leics	Chelmsford	1990
	V	803-4d		by	Kent	Brentwood	1934
Lowest Total	For	30		v	Yorkshire	Leyton	1901
	V	14		by	Surrey	Chelmsford	1983
Highest Innings	For	343*	P.A.Perrin	v	Derbyshire	Chesterfield	1904
	V	332	W.H.Ashdown	for	Kent	Brentwood	1934

Highest Partnership for each Wicket

1st	316	G.A.Gooch/P.J.Prichard	v	Kent	Chelmsford	1994
2nd	403	G.A.Gooch/P.J.Prichard	v	Leics	Chelmsford	1990
3rd	347*	M.E.Waugh/N.Hussain	v	Lancashire	Ilford	1992
4th	314	Salim Malik/N.Hussain	v	Surrey	The Oval	1991
5th	316	N.Hussain/M.A.Garnham	v	Leics	Leicester	1991
6th	206	J.W.H.T.Douglas/J.O'Connor	v	Glos	Cheltenham	1923
	206	B.R.Knight/R.A.G.Luckin	v	Middlesex	Brentwood	1962
7th	261	J.W.H.T.Douglas/J.Freeman	v	Lancashire	Leyton	1914
8th	263	D.R.Wilcox/R.M.Taylor	v	Warwicks	Southend	1946
9th	251	J.W.H.T.Douglas/S.N.Hare	v	Derbyshire	Leyton	1921
10th	218	F.H.Vigar/T.P.B.Smith	v	Derbyshire	Chesterfield	1947

Best Bowling (Innings)	For	10- 32	H.Pickett	v	Leics	Leyton	1895
	V	10- 40	E.G.Dennett	for	Glos	Bristol	1906
Best Bowling (Match)	For	17-119	W.Mead	v	Hampshire	Southampton	1895
	V	17- 56	C.W.L.Parker	for	Glos	Gloucester	1925

Most Runs – Season	2559	G.A.Gooch	(av 67.34)	1984
Most Runs – Career	29434†	K.W.R.Fletcher	(av 36.88)	1962-88
Most 100s – Season	9	J.O'Connor		1934
	9	D.J.Insole		1955
Most 100s – Career	86	G.A.Gooch		1973-95
Most Wkts – Season	172	T.P.B Smith	(av 27.13)	1947
Most Wkts – Career	1610	T.P.B.Smith	(av 26.68)	1929-51

† G.A.Gooch has scored 28388 runs.

LIMITED-OVERS CRICKET

Highest Total	NWT	386-5		v	Wiltshire	Chelmsford	1988
	BHC	388-7		v	Scotland	Chelmsford	1992
	SL	310-5		v	Glamorgan	Southend	1983
Lowest Total	NWT	100		v	Derbyshire	Brentwood	1965
	BHC	61		v	Lancashire	Chelmsford	1992
	SL	69		v	Derbyshire	Chesterfield	1974
Highest Innings	NWT	144	G.A.Gooch	v	Hampshire	Chelmsford	1990
	BHC	198*	G.A.Gooch	v	Sussex	Hove	1982
	SL	176	G.A.Gooch	v	Glamorgan	Southend	1983
Best Bowling	NWT	5- 8	J.K.Lever	v	Middlesex	Westcliff	1972
		5- 8	G.A.Gooch	v	Cheshire	Chester	1995
	BHC	5-13	J.K.Lever	v	Middlesex	Lord's	1985
	SL	8-26	K.D.Boyce	v	Lancashire	Manchester	1971

GLAMORGAN

Formation of Present Club: 6 July 1888
Colours: Blue and Gold
Badge: Gold Daffodil
Championships: (2) 1948, 1969
NatWest Trophy/Gillette Cup Winners: (0) Finalists 1977
Benson and Hedges Cup Winners: (0) Semi-Finalists 1988
Sunday League Champions: (1) 1993
Match Awards: NWT 36; BHC 45

Secretary: G.R.Stone. Cricket Secretary: M.J.Fatkin
Sophia Gardens, Cardiff, CF1 9XR (Tel 01222 343478)
Captain: M.P.Maynard
Scorer: B.T.Denning
1996 Beneficiary: M.P.Maynard

BARWICK, Stephen Royston (Cwrt Sart CS; Dwr-y-Felin CS), b Neath 6 Sep 1960. 6'2". RHB, RMF. Debut 1981. Cap 1987. Benefit 1995. Tour: Z 1994-95 (Gm). HS 30 v Hants (Bournemouth) 1988. 50 wkts (2); most – 64 (1989). BB 8-42 v Worcs (Worcester) 1983. Award: BHC 1. **NWT:** HS 6. BB 5-26 v Surrey (Swansea) 1992. **BHC:** HS 18 v Kent (Canterbury) 1984. BB 4-11 v Minor C (Swansea) 1985. **SL:** HS 48* v Worcs (Worcester) 1989. BB 6-28 v Derbys (Derby) 1993.

BUTCHER, Gary Paul (Trinity S; Riddlesdown S; Heath Clark C), b Clapham, London 11 Mar 1975. Son of A.R. (Surrey, Glam and England 1972-92); brother of M.A. (*see SURREY*). 5'9". RHB, RM. Debut 1994. Tour: Z 1994-95 (Gm). HS 41 v Leics (Cardiff) 1994. BB 2-36 v OU (Oxford) 1994. **BHC:** HS 0. **SL:** HS –. BB 2-8 v Somerset (Swansea) 1994.

COTTEY, Phillip Anthony (Bishopston CS, Swansea), b Swansea 2 Jun 1966. 5'4". RHB, OB. Debut 1986. Cap 1992. E Transvaal 1991-92. Tours (Gm): Z 1990-91, 1994-95. 1000 runs (5); most – 1465 (1995). HS 191 v Somerset (Swansea) 1994. BB 2-42 E Transvaal v W Transvaal (Potchefstroom) 1991-92. Gm BB 1-16. **NWT:** HS 61* v Leics (Leicester) 1995. BB 1-11. **BHC:** HS 68 v Hants (Southampton) 1989. **SL:** HS 92* v Hants (Ebbw Vale) 1991. BB 2-30 v Sussex (Hove) 1992.

CROFT, Robert Damien Bale (St John Lloyd Catholic CS; W Glam IHE), b Morriston 25 May 1970. 5'10½". RHB, OB. Debut 1989. Cap 1992. Tours: SA 1993-94 (Eng A): WI 1991-92 (Eng A); Z 1990-91 (Gm), 1994-95 (Gm). HS 143 v Somerset (Taunton) 1995. 50 wkts (3); most – 68 (1992, 1995). BB 8-66 (14-169 match) v Warwks (Swansea) 1992. **NWT:** HS 50 v Essex (Cardiff) 1994. BB 3-30 v Lincs (Swansea) 1994. **BHC:** HS 50 v Middx (Lord's) 1995. BB 3-28 v Comb Us (Cardiff) 1992. **SL:** HS 66* v Derbys (Derby) 1995. BB 6-20 v Worcs (Cardiff) 1994.

DALE, Adrian (Chepstow CS; Swansea U), b Germiston, SA 24 Oct 1968 (to UK at 6 mths). 5'11½". RHB, RM. Debut 1989. Cap 1992. Tours (Gm): SA 1993-94 (Eng A); Z 1990-91, 1994-95. 1000 runs (2); most – 1472 (1993). HS 214* v Middx (Cardiff) 1993. BB 6-18 v Warwks (Cardiff) 1993. Awards: NWT 1; BHC 1. **NWT:** HS 110 v Lincs (Swansea) 1994. BB 3-54 v Worcs (Swansea) 1993. **BHC:** HS 53 v Comb Us (Cardiff) 1992. BB 3-24 Comb Us v Surrey (Cambridge) 1989. **SL:** HS 67* v Derbys (Heanor) 1989. BB 6-22 v Durham (Colwyn Bay) 1993.

DALTON, Alistair John (Millfield S), b Bridgend 27 Apr 1973. 5'7". RHB, RM. Wales (MC) 1992-94. Debut 1994. HS 51* v SA (Pontypridd) 1994. BAC HS 46 v Derbys (Derby) 1995.

DAVIES, Andrew Philip (Christ C, Brecon; Trinity C, Carmarthen), b Neath 7 Nov 1976. RHB, RMF. Wales (MC). Debut 1995. HS – .

GIBSON, Ottis Delroy (Ellerslie SS), b Bridgetown, Barbados 16 Mar 1969. 6'2". RHB, RF. Barbados 1990-91 to date. Border 1992-93 to date. Glamorgan debut/cap 1994. **Tests** (WI): 1 (1995); HS 29 and BB 2-81 v E (Lord's) 1995. **LOI** (WI): 10 (1995 to 1995-96; HS 52; BB 5-40). Tour (WI): E 1995. HS 101* WI v Somerset (Taunton) 1995. Gm HS 85 v NZ (Swansea) 1994. BAC HS 81 v Somerset (Swansea) 1994. 50 wkts (1): 60 (1994). BB 7-55 Border v Natal (Durban) 1994-95. Gm BB 6-64 v Worcs (Cardiff) 1994. Award: NWT 1. **NWT:** HS 44 and BB 3-34 v Essex (Cardiff) 1994. **BHC:** HS 37 and BB 2-50 v Surrey (Oval) 1994. **SL:** HS 33 v Essex (Southend) 1994. BB 2-35 v Sussex (Hove) 1994.

HEMP, David Lloyd (Olchfa CS; Millfield S; W Glamorgan C), b Bermuda 15 Nov 1970. UK resident since 1976. 6'0". LHB, RM. Debut 1991. Cap 1994. Wales (MC) 1992-94. Tours: I 1994-95 (Eng A); Z 1994-95 (Gm). 1000 runs (1): 1452 (1994). HS 157 v Glos (Abergavenny) 1995. BB 1-9. Awards: NWT 1; BHC 1. **NWT:** HS 78 v Leics (Leicester) 1995. **BHC:** HS 121 v Comb Us (Cardiff) 1995. **SL:** HS 74 v Leics (Leicester) 1995.

JAMES, Stephen Peter (Monmouth S; Swansea U; Hughes Hall, Cambridge), b Lydney, Glos 7 Sep 1967. 6'0". RHB. Debut 1985. Cap 1992. Cambridge U 1989-90 (blue 1989-90). Mashonaland 1993-94 to date. Tour: Z 1990-91 (Gm). 1000 runs (3); most – 1376 (1992). HS 230* v Leics (Leicester) 1995. Awards: NWT 1; BHC 2. **NWT:** HS 123 v Lincs (Swansea) 1994. **BHC:** HS 135 v Comb Us (Cardiff) 1992. **SL:** HS 107 v Sussex (Llanelli) 1993.

JONES, Philip Steffan (Stradey CS; Neath TC), b Llanelli 9 Feb 1974. RHB, RFM. Wales (MC) 1992-94. Awaiting f-c debut. **BHC:** HS 26* Wales (MC) v Middx (Northop Hall) 1994.

KENDRICK, Neil Michael (Wilson's GS), b Bromley, Kent 11 Nov 1967. 5'11". RHB, SLA. Surrey 1988-94. Glamorgan debut 1994-95 (Z tour). Tour: Z 1994-95 (Gm). HS 59 v Surrey (Oval) 1995. 50 wkts (1): 51 (1992). BB 7-115 Sy v Notts (Oval) 1993. Gm BB 4-70 v Kent (Tunbridge Wells) 1995. **NWT:** HS – . BB 1-51. **BHC:** HS 24 and BB 2-47 Sy v Kent (Canterbury) 1992. **SL:** HS 13* and BB 2-48 Sy v Warwks (Guildford) 1994.

LEFEBVRE, Roland Philippe (Montessori Lyceum, Rotterdam; Hague Accademie of Physiotherapy), b Rotterdam, Holland 7 Feb 1963. 6'1". RHB, RMF. Somerset 1990-92 (cap 1991). Glamorgan debut/cap 1993. Holland 1983 to date; ICC Trophy 1986, 1989; World Cup 1995-96. Canterbury 1990-91. HS 100 Sm v Worcs (W-s-M) 1991. Gm HS 50 v Worcs (Worcester) 1993. BB 6-45 v OU (Oxford) 1995. BAC BB 5-30 Sm v Glos (Taunton) 1990. **NWT:** HS 21* Sm v Warwks (Birmingham) 1991. BB 7-15 Sm v Devon (Torquay) 1990. **BHC:** HS 37 Sm v Middx (Lord's) 1990. BB 3-42 v Middx (Lord's) 1995. **SL:** HS 36* v Northants (Pentrych) 1993. BB 4-23 v Durham (Hartlepool) 1994.

MAYNARD, Matthew Peter (David Hughes S, Anglesey), b Oldham, Lancs 21 Mar 1966. 5'10½". RHB, RM. Debut 1985 v Yorks (Swansea), scoring 102 out of 117 in 87 min, reaching 100 with 3 sixes off successive balls. Cap 1987. Captain 1996. Benefit 1996. N Districts 1990-91/1991-92. YC 1988. **Tests:** 4 (1988 to 1993-94); HS 35 v WI (Kingston) 1993-94. **LOI:** 5 (1993-94; HS 22*). Tours: SA 1989-90 (Eng XI); WI 1993-94; Z 1994-95 (Gm). 1000 runs (9); most – 1803 (1991). HS 243 v Hants (Southampton) 1991. BB 3-21 v OU (Oxford) 1987. BAC BB 1-3. Awards: NWT 4; BHC 5. **NWT:** HS 151* v Durham (Darlington) 1991. **BHC:** HS 115 v Comb Us (Cardiff) 1988. **SL:** HS 122* v Leics (Swansea) 1992.

METSON, Colin Peter (Enfield GS; Stanborough S, Welwyn Garden City; Durham U), b Goffs Oak, Herts 2 Jul 1963. 5'5½". RHB, WK. Middlesex 1981-86. Glamorgan debut/cap 1987. HS 96 M v Glos (Uxbridge) 1984. Gm HS 84 v Kent (Maidstone) 1991. Award: NWT 1. **NWT:** HS 21 v Notts (Nottingham) 1992. **BHC:** HS 23 v Kent (Swansea) 1990. **SL:** HS 30* v Hants (Bournemouth) 1990.

MORRIS, Hugh (Blundell's S), b Cardiff 5 Oct 1963. 5'8". LHB, RM. Debut 1981. Cap 1986. Captain 1986-89 and 1993-95. Benefit 1994. **Tests:** 3 (1991); HS 44 v WI (Oval) 1991. Tours (Eng A)(C=captain): SA 1993-94C; WI 1991-92C; SL 1990-91C; Z 1994-95C (Gm). 1000 runs (8) inc 2000 (1): 2276 – inc 10 hundreds – both Gm records (1990). HS 166* v Notts (Cardiff) 1995. BB 1-6. BAC BB 1-45. Awards: NWT 2; BHC 3. **NWT:** HS 154* v Staffs (Cardiff) 1989. **BHC:** HS 143* v Hants (Southampton) 1989. BB 1-14. **SL:** HS 127* v Surrey (Swansea) 1994.

PARKIN, Owen Thomas (Bournemouth GS, Bath U), b Coventry, Warwks 24 Sep 1972. 6'2". RHB, RFM. Dorset 1992. Debut 1994. HS 2* and BB 2-45 v Middx (Lord's) 1994.

SHAW, Adrian David (Neath Tertiary C), b Neath 17 Feb 1972. 5'11". RHB, WK. Wales (MC) 1990-92. Debut 1994. HS 14 v Middx (Lord's) 1994.

THOMAS, Stuart Darren (Graig CS, Llanelli; Neath Tertiary C), b Morriston 25 Jan 1975. 6'0". LHB, RFM. Debut v Derbys (Chesterfield) 1992, taking 5-80 when aged 17yr 217d. Tour: Z 1994-95 (Gm). HS 78* v Glos (Abergavenny) 1995. BB 5-76 v Worcs (Worcester) 1993. **NWT:** HS – . **BHC:** HS – . BB 6-20 v Comb Us (Cardiff) 1995. **SL:** HS 19 v Glos (Ebbw Vale) 1995. BB 3-44 v Ex (Pontypridd) 1995.

WATKIN, Steven Llewellyn (Cymer Afan CS; S Glamorgan CHE), b Maesteg 15 Sep 1964. 6'3". RHB, RMF. Debut 1986. Cap 1989. *Wisden* 1993. **Tests:** 3 (1991 to 1993); HS 13 and BB 4-65 v A (Oval) 1993. **LOI:** 4 (1993-94; HS 4; BB 4-49). Tours: WI 1991-92 (Eng A), 1993-94; P 1990-91 (Eng A); Z 1989-90 (Eng A), 1990-91 (Gm), 1994-95 (Gm). HS 41 v Worcs (Worcester) 1992. 50 wkts (7); most – 94 (1989). BB 8-59 v Warwks (Birmingham) 1988. Award: NWT 1. **NWT:** HS 9. BB 4-26 v Middx (Cardiff) 1995. **BHC:** HS 15 v Hants (Southampton) 1991. BB 3-28 v Minor C (Trowbridge) 1991. **SL:** 31* v Derbys (Checkley) 1991. BB 5-23 v Warwks (Birmingham) 1990.

WILLIAMS, James Robert Alexander (Clifton C), b Neath 20 Jul 1973. 5'11". RHB, OB. Debut 1993. HS 6.

NEWCOMERS

COSKER, Dean Andrew, b Weymouth, Dorset 7 Jan 1978. RHB, SLA.

EDWARDS, Gareth John Maldwyn, b St Asaph 13 Nov 1976. RHB, OB.

EVANS, Alun Wyn, b Fishguard 20 Aug 1975. RHB, RM.

DEPARTURE (who made first-class appearances in 1995)

ANTHONY, Hamish Aubrey Gervais (Urlings Village SS), b Urlings, Antigua 16 Jan 1971. Cousin of G.J.F.Ferris (Leeward Is and Leics 1982-83/1990). 6'1". RHB, RFM. Leeward Is 1989-90 to date. Glamorgan 1990, 1995. **LOI** (WI): 3 (1995-96; HS 21; BB 2-47). Tours (WI): E 1991; A 1991-92. HS 91 v Surrey (Oval) 1995. BB 6-22 Leeward Is v Windward Is (Castries) 1992-93. Gm BB 6-77 v Hants (Cardiff) 1995. **NWT:** HS 8. BB 4-25 v Middx (Cardiff) 1995. **BHC:** HS 2 and BB 3-40 v Middx (Cardiff) 1995. **SL:** HS 7. BB 3-40 v Northants (Cardiff) 1995.

GLAMORGAN 1995

RESULTS SUMMARY

	Place	Won	Lost	Drew	No Result
Britannic Assurance Championship	**16th**	3	8	6	–
All First-Class Matches		3	8	8	–
NatWest Trophy	Semi-Finalist				
Benson and Hedges Cup	3rd in Group C				
Sunday League	**6th**	8	6	–	3

BRITANNIC ASSURANCE CHAMPIONSHIP AVERAGES

BATTING AND FIELDING

Cap		M	I	NO	HS	Runs	Avge	100	50	Ct/St
1992	P.A.Cottey	16	27	2	130	1237	49.48	4	7	13
1986	H.Morris	16	30	2	166*	1373	49.03	5	8	5
1987	M.P.Maynard	17	31	1	164	1420	47.33	3	10	22
1992	S.P.James	13	24	3	230*	842	40.09	2	2	12
–	S.D.Thomas	10	14	3	78*	313	28.45	–	3	4
1994	D.L.Hemp	16	29	–	157	776	26.75	1	3	14
1992	A.Dale	10	19	2	133	420	24.70	1	2	4
1992	R.D.B.Croft	17	30	3	143	612	22.66	1	1	6
–	A.J.Dalton	4	8	1	46	129	18.42	–	–	2
–	N.M.Kendrick	13	20	4	59	291	18.18	–	1	6
1987	C.P.Metson	16	23	9	26*	253	18.07	–	–	45/6
–	H.A.G.Anthony	14	25	1	91	433	18.04	–	2	6
1989	S.L.Watkin	15	23	9	30	174	12.42	–	–	8
1987	S.R.Barwick	6	6	2	14	19	4.75	–	–	1

Also played: A.P.Davies (1 match) did not bat; R.P.Lefebvre (2 matches – cap 1993) 13, 18, 24; A.D.Shaw (1 match) 0, 2 (2 ct).

BOWLING

	O	M	R	W	Avge	Best	5wI	10wM
S.L.Watkin	561.4	135	1685	62	27.17	7- 49	2	1
H.A.G.Anthony	397.5	70	1402	44	31.86	6- 77	2	–
R.D.B.Croft	774.3	184	2180	56	38.92	6-104	3	1
N.M.Kendrick	334.1	85	1088	24	45.33	4- 70	–	–
S.D.Thomas	285.3	50	1257	26	48.34	5- 99	1	–
S.R.Barwick	213.4	52	619	12	51.58	4-116	–	–

Also bowled: P.A.Cottey 17.1-0-80-0; A.Dale 124.5-26-419-8; A.P.Davies 3-0-17-0; D.L.Hemp 22-2-110-3; R.P.Lefebvre 67-22-134-0.

The First-Class Averages (pp 129-143) give the records of Glamorgan players in all first-class county matches (their other opponents being Oxford University and Young Australia), with the exception of:

P.A.Cottey 18-31-3-130-1445-51.60-5-7-14ct. 32.1-2-109-1-109.00-1/29.
R.D.B.Croft 19-34-4-143-684-22.80-1-1-8ct. 829.1-207-2289-63-36.33-6/104-3-1.
D.L.Hemp 17-31-0-157-865-27.90-1-4-14ct. 22-2-110-3-36.66-1/9.
M.P.Maynard 19-34-1-164-1569-47.54-3-12-22ct. Did not bowl.
H.Morris 17-31-2-166*-1498-51.65-6-8-5ct. Did not bowl.

GLAMORGAN RECORDS

FIRST-CLASS CRICKET

Highest Total	For	587-8d		v	Derbyshire	Cardiff	1951
	V	657-7d		by	Warwicks	Birmingham	1994
Lowest Total	For	22		v	Lancashire	Liverpool	1924
	V	33		by	Leics	Ebbw Vale	1965
Highest Innings	For	287*	D.E.Davies	v	Glos	Newport	1939
	V	313*	S.J.Cook	for	Somerset	Cardiff	1990

Highest Partnership for each Wicket

1st	330	A.Jones/R.C.Fredericks	v	Northants	Swansea	1972
2nd	249	S.P.James/H.Morris	v	Oxford U	Oxford	1987
3rd	313	D.E.Davies/W.E.Jones	v	Essex	Brentwood	1948
4th	425*	A.Dale/I.V.A.Richards	v	Middlesex	Cardiff	1993
5th	264	M.Robinson/S.W.Montgomery	v	Hampshire	Bournemouth	1949
6th	230	W.E.Jones/B.L.Muncer	v	Worcs	Worcester	1953
7th	195*	W.Wooller/W.E.Jones	v	Lancashire	Liverpool	1947
8th	202	D.Davies/J.J.Hills	v	Sussex	Eastbourne	1928
9th	203*	J.J.Hills/J.C.Clay	v	Worcs	Swansea	1929
10th	143	T.Davies/S.A.B.Daniels	v	Glos	Swansea	1982

Best Bowling	For	10- 51	J.Mercer	v	Worcs	Worcester	1936
(Innings)	V	10- 18	G.Geary	for	Leics	Pontypridd	1929
Best Bowling	For	17-212	J.C.Clay	v	Worcs	Swansea	1937
(Match)	V	16- 96	G.Geary	for	Leics	Pontypridd	1929

Most Runs – Season	2276	H.Morris	(av 55.51)	1990
Most Runs – Career	34056	A.Jones	(av 33.03)	1957-83
Most 100s – Season	10	H.Morris		1990
Most 100s – Career	52	A.Jones		1957-83
Most Wkts – Season	176	J.C.Clay	(av 17.34)	1937
Most Wkts – Career	2174	D.J.Shepherd	(av 20.95)	1950-72

LIMITED-OVERS CRICKET

Highest Total	NWT	345-2		v	Durham	Darlington	1991
	BHC	302-6		v	Comb Univs	Cardiff	1988
	SL	287-8		v	Middlesex	Cardiff	1993
Lowest Total	NWT	76		v	Northants	Northampton	1968
	BHC	68		v	Lancashire	Manchester	1973
	SL	42		v	Derbyshire	Swansea	1979
Highest Innings	NWT	162*	I.V.A.Richards	v	Oxfordshire	Swansea	1993
	BHC	143*	H.Morris	v	Hampshire	Southampton	1989
	SL	130*	J.A.Hopkins	v	Somerset	Bath	1983
Best Bowling	NWT	5-13	R.J.Shastri	v	Scotland	Edinburgh	1988
	BHC	6-20	S.D.Thomas	v	Comb Univs	Cardiff	1995
	SL	6-20	R.D.B.Croft	v	Worcs	Cardiff	1994

GLOUCESTERSHIRE

Formation of Present Club: 1871
Colours: Blue, Gold, Brown, Silver, Green and Red
Badge: Coat of Arms of the City and County of Bristol
Championships (since 1890): (0) Second 1930, 1931, 1947, 1959, 1969, 1986
NatWest Trophy/Gillette Cup Winners: (1) 1973
Benson and Hedges Cup Winners: (1) 1977
Sunday League Champions: (0) Second 1988
Match Awards: NWT 40; BHC 47.

Chief Executive: P.G.M.August
County Ground, Nevil Road, Bristol BS7 9EJ (Tel 0117 924 5216)
Captain: C.A.Walsh
Scorer: B.H.Jenkins
1996 Beneficiary: A.J.Wright

ALLEYNE, Mark Wayne (Harrison C, Barbados; Cardinal Pole S, London E9; Haringey Cricket C), b Tottenham, London 23 May 1968. 5'10". RHB, RM. Debut 1986. Cap 1990. Tours (Gs): SL 1986-87, 1992-93. 1000 runs (4); most – 1121 (1991). HS 256 v Northants (Northampton) 1990. BB 5-78 v Kent (Cheltenham) 1994. Award: NWT 1. **NWT:** HS 73 v Herts (Bristol) 1993. BB 5-30 v Lincs (Gloucester) 1990. **BHC:** HS 42 v Middx (Bristol) 1995. BB 5-27 v Comb Us (Bristol) 1988. **SL:** HS 134* v Leics (Bristol) 1992. BB 5-28 v Glam (Ebbw Vale) 1995.

AVERIS, James Maxwell Michael (Bristol Cathedral S; Portsmouth U), b Bristol 28 May 1974. 5'11". RHB, RFM. Summer contract – awaiting f-c debut. **SL:** HS 2*. Rugby for Bristol.

BALL, Martyn Charles John (King Edmund SS; Bath CFE), b Bristol 26 Apr 1970. 5'8". RHB, OB. Debut 1988. Tour (Gs): SL 1992-93. HS 71 v Notts (Bristol) 1993. BB 8-46 (14-169 match) v Somerset (Taunton) 1993. **NWT:** HS 16* v Essex (Cheltenham) 1992. BB 3-42 v Lancs (Gloucester) 1989. **BHC:** HS 20* v Kent (Canterbury) 1994. BB 3-26 v Comb Us (Bristol) 1995. **SL:** HS 28* v Worcs (Worcester) 1994. BB 3-24 v Somerset (Taunton) 1993.

BODEN, David Jonathan Peter (Alleynes HS, Stone; Stafford CFE), b Eccleshall, Staffs 26 Nov 1970. 6'3". RHB, RMF. Middlesex 1989. Essex 1992-93. Gloucestershire debut 1995. HS 5. Gs HS 2. BB 4-11 M v OU (Oxford) 1989 – on debut. Gs BB 3-38 v OU (Bristol) 1995. BAC BB 2-73 v Hants (Bristol) 1995. **NWT:** HS – . BB 6-26 v Suffolk (Bristol) 1995. **SL:** HS 5. BB 3-34 v Hants (Bristol) 1995.

CAWDRON, Michael John (Cheltenham C), b Luton, Beds 7 Oct 1974. 6'2". LHB, RM. Joined staff 1994 – awaiting f-c debut. **SL:** HS 50 v Essex (Cheltenham) 1995. BB 1-23.

COOPER, Kevin Edwin (Hucknall National SS), b Hucknall, Notts 27 Dec 1957. 6'1". LHB, RFM. Nottinghamshire 1976-92 (cap 1980; benefit 1990). Gloucestershire debut 1992-93 (SL tour). Cap 1995. Tour: SL 1992-93 (Gs). HS 52 v Lancs (Cheltenham) 1993. 50 wkts (8) inc 100 (1): 101 (1988). BB 8-44 Nt v Middx (Lord's) 1984. Gs BB 5-83 v Yorks (Sheffield) 1993. Awards: NWT 1; BHC 2. **NWT:** HS 11 Nt v Glos (Nottingham) 1982. BB 4-49 Nt v Warwks (Nottingham) 1985. **BHC:** HS 25* Nt v Lancs (Manchester) 1983. BB 4-9 Nt v Yorks (Nottingham) 1989. **SL:** HS 31 Nt v Glos (Nottingham) 1984. BB 4-25 Nt v Hants (Nottingham) 1976.

CUNLIFFE, Robert John (Banbury S; Banbury TC), b Oxford 8 Nov 1973. 5'10". RHB, RM. Debut 1994. Oxfordshire 1991-94. HS 190* v OU (Bristol) 1995. BAC HS 92* v Lancs (Cheltenham) 1995. **NWT:** HS 40 v Durham (Chester-le-St) 1995. **SL:** HS 22 v Sussex (Hove) 1993.

DAWSON, Robert Ian (Millfield S; Newcastle Poly), b Exmouth, Devon 29 Mar 1970. 5'11". RHB, RM. Debut 1992. Devon 1988-91. 1000 runs (1): 1112 (1994). HS 127* v CU (Bristol) 1994. BAC HS 101 v Worcs (Gloucester) 1995. BB 2-38 v Derbys (Chesterfield) 1994. **NWT:** HS 60 v Devon (Bristol) 1994. BB 1-37. **BHC:** HS 38 v Middx (Bristol) and v Somerset (Bristol) 1995. **SL:** HS 45 v Middx (Lord's) 1994 and v Surrey (Oval) 1995. BB 1-19.

HANCOCK, Timothy Harold Coulter (St Edward's S, Oxford; Henley C), b Reading, Berks 20 Apr 1972. 5'10". RHB, RM. Debut 1991. Oxfordshire 1990. Tour: SL 1992-93 (Gs). HS 123 v Essex (Chelmsford) 1994. BB 3-10 v Glam (Abergavenny) 1993. **NWT:** HS 45 and BB 2-7 v Herts (Bristol) 1993. **BHC:** HS 36 v Essex (Chelmsford) 1995. **SL:** HS 46 v Sussex (Hove) 1993. BB 2-31 v Yorks (Cheltenham) 1994.

HEWSON, Dominic Robert (Cheltenham C), b Cheltenham 3 Oct 1974. 5'8". RHB, occ RM. Joined staff 1994 – awaiting f-c debut.

LEWIS, Jonathan (Churchfields S, Swindon; Swindon C), b Aylesbury, Bucks 26 Aug 1975. 6'2". RHB, RMF. Debut 1995. Wiltshire 1993. Northamptonshire staff 1994. HS 3. BB 4-34 (8-121 match) v Durham (Bristol) 1995. **SL:** HS 5. BB 3-27 v Warwks (Birmingham) 1995.

LYNCH, Monte Alan (Ryden's S, Walton-on-Thames), b Georgetown, British Guiana 21 May 1958. 5'8". RHB, OB. Surrey 1977-94 (cap 1982; benefit 1991). Gloucestershire debut/cap 1995. Guyana 1982-83. **LOI:** 3 (1988; HS 6). Tours: SA 1983-84 (WI XI); P 1981-82 (Int). 1000 (9); most – 1714 (1985). HS 172* Sy v Kent (Oval) 1989. Gs HS 114 v Kent (Canterbury) 1995. BB 3-6 Sy v Glam (Swansea) 1981. Awards: NWT 1; BHC 4. **NWT:** HS 129 Sy v Durham (Oval) 1982. BB 2-28 Sy v Glam (Swansea) 1992. **BHC:** HS 112* Sy v Kent (Oval) 1987. **SL:** HS 136 Sy v Yorks (Bradford) 1985. BB 2-2 Sy v Northants (Guildford) 1987 and Sy v Sussex (Hove) 1990.

RUSSELL, Robert Charles (***'Jack'***) (Archway CS), b Stroud 15 Aug 1963. 5'8½". LHB, WK, occ OB. Debut 1981 – youngest Glos wicket-keeper (17yr 307d), setting record for most match dismissals on f-c debut – 8 v SL (Bristol). Cap 1985. Benefit 1994. Captain 1995. *Wisden* 1989. **Tests:** 44 (1988 to 1995-96); HS 128* v A (Manchester) 1989. 11 ct v SA (Jo'burg) 1995-96 (Test record). 27 dis 1995-96 series v SA (Eng record). **LOI:** 31 (1987-88 to 1995-96; HS 50). Tours: A 1990-91, 1992-93 (Eng A); SA 1995-96; WI 1989-90, 1993-94; NZ 1991-92; P 1987-88; SL 1986-87 (Gs). HS 128* (*see Tests*). Gs HS 120 v Somerset (Bristol) 1990. BB 1-4. Awards: BHC 2. **NWT:** HS 59* v Suffolk (Bristol) 1995. **BHC:** HS 51 v Worcs (Worcester) 1991. **SL:** HS 108 v Worcs (Hereford) 1986.

SHEERAZ, Kamran Pasha (Licensed Victuallers' S, Ascot; E Berkshire C, Langley), b Wellington, Shropshire 28 Dec 1973. 6'0". RHB, RMF. Debut 1994. Bedfordshire 1992. HS 3. BB 6-67 v WI (Bristol) 1995. BAC BB 3-89 v Derbys (Bristol) 1995. **SL:** HS 14* v Surrey (Oval) 1995. BB 2-20 v Middx (Bristol) 1995.

SMITH, Andrew Michael (Queen Elizabeth GS, Wakefield; Exeter U), b Dewsbury, Yorks 1 Oct 1967. 5'9". RHB, LMF. Debut 1991. Cap 1995. Tour: P 1995-96 (Eng A – part). HS 51* v Warwks (Bristol) 1992. 50 wkts (1): 59 (1995). BB 7-70 v Essex (Cheltenham) 1995. Award: BHC 1. **NWT:** HS 8*. BB 3-45 v Somerset (Taunton) 1992. **BHC:** HS 15* Comb Us v Surrey (Oxford) 1990. BB 6-39 v Hants (Southampton) 1995. **SL:** HS 15* v Essex (Cheltenham) 1991. BB 4-38 v Leics (Bristol) 1992.

SYMONDS, Andrew (All Saints Anglican School, Mudgeeraba, Queensland), b Birmingham 9 Jun 1975. 6'1½". RHB, OB. Emigrated to Australia when 18 months old. Queensland 1994-95 to date. Australian CA. Gloucestershire debut/cap 1995. YC 1995. 1000 runs (1): 1438 (1995). HS 254* v Glam (Abergavenny) 1995 (including record 16 sixes); hit record 20 sixes in match. BB 3-77 Q v NSW (Sydney) 1994-95. Gs BB 1-13. Award: BHC 1. **NWT:** HS 48 v Northants (Bristol) 1995. **BHC:** HS 95 v Comb Us (Bristol) 1995. **SL:** HS 69 v Glam (Ebbw Vale) 1995. BB 3-38 v Northants (Northampton) 1995. Hockey for Queensland.

WALSH, Courtney Andrew (Excelsior HS), b Kingston, Jamaica 30 Oct 1962. 6'5½". RHB, RF. Jamaica 1981-82 to date (captain 1990-91 to date). Gloucestershire debut 1984. Cap 1985. Captain 1993-94, 1996. Benefit 1992. *Wisden* 1986. **Tests** (WI): 80 (1984-85 to 1995, 6 as captain); HS 30* v A (Melbourne) 1988-89; BB 7-37 (13-55 match) v NZ (Wellington) 1994-95. **LOI** (WI): 150 (1984-85 to 1995-96; HS 30; BB 5-1). Tours (WI)(C=captain): E 1984, 1988, 1991, 1995; A 1984-85, 1986-87, 1988-89, 1992-93; NZ

WALSH – continued:
1986-87, 1994-95C; I 1987-88, 1994-95C; P 1986-87, 1990-91; SL 1993-94; Z 1983-84 (Young WI). HS 66 v Kent (Cheltenham) 1994. 50 wkts (8+2) inc 100 (1): 118 (1986). BB 9-72 v Somerset (Bristol) 1986. Hat-trick 1988-89 (WI). Awards: NWT 2. **NWT:** HS 37 v Herts (Bristol) 1993. BB 6-21 v Kent (Bristol) 1990 and v Cheshire (Bristol) 1992. **BHC:** HS 28 v Comb Us (Bristol) 1989. BB 2-19 v Scot 1985. **SL:** HS 35 v Glam (Cardiff) 1986. BB 4-19 v Kent (Cheltenham) 1987.

WHITBY-COLES, James Graham (Clifton C), b Bath, Somerset 23 Aug 1974. RHB, OB. Awaiting f-c debut.

WILLIAMS, Richard Charles James (Millfield S), b Southmead, Bristol 8 Aug 1969. 5'8". LHB, WK. Debut 1990. Tour: SL 1992-93 (Gs). HS 90 v OU (Bristol) 1995. BAC HS 55* v Derbys (Gloucester) 1991. **SL:** HS 19 v Essex (Cheltenham) 1995.

WINDOWS, Matthew Guy Newman (Clifton C; Durham U), b Bristol 5 Apr 1973. Son of A.R. (Glos and CU 1960-68). 5'7". RHB, RSM. Debut 1992. Combined Us 1995. HS 106 v NZ (Bristol) 1994. BAC HS 85 v Lancs (Manchester) 1994. BB 1-6 (Comb Us). **NWT:** HS 33 v Devon (Bristol) 1994. **BHC:** HS 16* Comb Us v Lancs (Oxford) 1994. **SL:** HS 72 v Somerset (Bristol) 1994.

WRIGHT, Anthony John (Alleyn's GS) b Stevenage, Herts 27 Jun 1962. 6'0". RHB, RM. Gloucestershire debut 1982. Cap 1987. Captain 1990-93. Benefit 1996. Tours (Gs): SL 1986-87, 1992-93 (captain). 1000 runs (6); most – 1596 (1991). HS 193 v Notts (Bristol) 1995. BB 1-16. Awards: NWT 3; BHC 1. **NWT:** HS 142* v Suffolk (Bristol) 1995. **BHC:** HS 97 v Worcs (Bristol) 1990. **SL:** HS 93 v Durham (Stockton) 1992.

NEWCOMER

DAVIS, Richard Peter (King Ethelbert's S, Birchington; Thanet TC), b Westbrook, Margate, Kent 18 Mar 1966. 6'3". RHB, SLA. Kent 1986-93 (cap 1990). Warwickshire 1993-94/1995 (Cap 1994). Tours: SA 1994-95 (Wa); Z 1992-93 (K), 1993-94 (Wa). HS 67 K v Hants (Southampton) 1989. 50 wkts (2); most – 74 (1992). BB 7-64 K v Durham (Gateshead) 1992. Award: BHC 1. **NWT:** HS 22 K v Warwks (Birmingham) 1992. BB 3-19 K v Bucks (Canterbury) 1988. **BHC:** HS 18* K v Glam (Canterbury) 1993. BB 2-33 K v Sussex (Hove) 1988. **SL:** HS 40* K v Northants (Canterbury) 1991. BB 5-52 K v Somerset (Bath) 1989.

DEPARTURES (who made first-class appearances in 1995)

DAVIES, Mark (Cwrt Sart CS; Neath Tertiary C), b Neath, Glam 18 Apr 1969. 5'6". RHB, SLA. Glamorgan 1990. Gloucestershire debut 1992. MCC YC. Tour: SL 1992-93 (Gs). HS 54 v Notts (Nottingham) 1994. 50 wkts (1): 56 (1992). BB 5-57 (10-141 match) v Northants (Northampton) 1993. **SL:** HS 14 v Hants (Portsmouth) 1994. BB 2-23 v Middx (Lord's) 1994.

HODGSON, Geoffrey Dean (Nelson Thomlinson CS, Wigton; Loughborough U), b Carlisle, Cumberland 22 Oct 1966. 6'1". RHB. Debut 1989. Cap 1992. Cumberland 1984-88 (cap 1987 when aged 20 – county record). Warwickshire (SL only) 1987. 1000 runs (4); most – 1320 (1990). HS 166 v Hants (Bristol) 1993. Awards: BHC 2. **NWT:** HS 62 v Yorks (Bristol) 1993. **BHC:** HS 103* v Minor C (Cheltenham) 1992. **SL:** HS 104* v Durham (Bristol) 1993.

PIKE, Vyvian John (Taunton S; Portsmouth Poly), b Taunton, Somerset 13 Aug 1969. 6'2". RHB, LB. Debut 1994. Dorset 1993-94. HS 27 v Derbys (Chesterfield) 1994. BB 6-41 v CU (Bristol) 1994 – on debut. BAC BB 3-72 v Northants (Northampton) 1995.

SRINATH, Javagal, b Mysore, India 31 Aug 1969. 6'3". RHB, RFM. Karnataka 1989-90 to date. Gloucestershire 1995 (cap 1995). **Tests:** (I): 18 (1991-92 to 1995-96); HS 60 v WI (Bombay) 1994-95; BB 4-33 v SA (Cape Town) 1992-93. **LOI** (I): 82 (1991-92 to 1995-96; HS 37; BB 5-24). Tours (I): A 1991-92; SA 1992-93; NZ 1993-94; SL 1993-94; Z 1992-93. HS 60 (*see Tests*). Gs HS 44 v Kent (Canterbury) 1995. 50 wkts (1): 87 (1995). BB 9-76 (13-150 match) v Glam (Abergavenny) 1995. Awards: BHC 2. **NWT:** HS 11* v Durham (Chester-le-St) 1995. BB 4-38 v Northants (Bristol) 1995. **BHC:** HS 6. BB 4-33 v Comb Us (Bristol) 1995. **SL:** HS 11 v Notts (Bristol) 1995. BB 3-27 v Kent (Canterbury) 1995.

continued on p 113

GLOUCESTERSHIRE 1995

RESULTS SUMMARY

	Place	Won	Lost	Drew	No Result
Britannic Assurance Championship	6th	8	4	5	–
All First-Class Matches		9	5	5	–
NatWest Trophy	Quarter-Finalist				
Benson and Hedges Cup	Quarter-Finalist				
Sunday League	15th	5	10	–	2

BRITANNIC ASSURANCE CHAMPIONSHIP AVERAGES

BATTING AND FIELDING

Cap		*M*	*I*	*NO*	*HS*	*Runs*	*Avge*	*100*	*50*	*Ct/St*
–	A.Symonds	17	29	5	254*	1346	56.08	4	8	8
1987	A.J.Wright	17	32	4	193	1321	47.17	4	4	7
–	R.J.Cunliffe	6	7	2	92*	222	44.40	–	2	4
1985	R.C.Russell	14	21	3	87	778	43.22	–	7	41/1
1995	M.A.Lynch	17	29	2	114	1026	38.00	5	2	25
1990	M.W.Alleyne	17	29	2	141	988	36.59	1	7	6
1992	G.D.Hodgson	9	17	–	148	524	30.82	1	2	3
–	R.I.Dawson	7	13	1	101	312	26.00	1	3	2
–	T.H.C.Hancock	6	10	1	79*	214	23.77	–	1	3
–	M.C.J.Ball	16	25	8	48	395	23.23	–	–	14
–	M.G.N.Windows	6	12	1	56	230	20.90	–	2	8
–	M.Davies	5	6	3	22	62	20.66	–	–	–
–	R.C.J.Williams	3	6	–	52	107	17.83	–	1	13
1995	J.Srinath	15	24	4	44	314	15.70	–	–	5
–	R.C.Williams	2	4	–	22	41	10.25	–	–	–
1995	K.E.Cooper	3	5	1	32	36	9.00	–	–	1
–	V.J.Pike	5	8	3	22	42	8.40	–	–	3
1995	A.M.Smith	10	9	2	11	37	5.28	–	–	2
–	K.P.Sheeraz	8	9	3	3	7	1.16	–	–	4

Also batted: D.J.P.Boden (1 match) 2; J.Lewis (3 matches) 0, 0, 3.

BOWLING

	O	*M*	*R*	*W*	*Avge*	*Best*	*5wI*	*10wM*
J.Lewis	67.4	12	209	12	17.41	4-34	–	–
J.Srinath	568.4	147	1661	87	19.09	9-76	5	2
A.M.Smith	404.1	103	1218	56	21.75	7-70	4	1
M.C.J.Ball	521.5	129	1373	38	36.13	5-49	2	–
M.W.Alleyne	380.5	116	1093	25	43.72	3-59	–	–
V.J.Pike	195.3	39	592	11	53.81	3-72	–	–
K.P.Sheeraz	189	27	777	13	59.76	3-89	–	–

Also bowled: D.J.P.Boden 34-4-123-3; K.E.Cooper 77-20-188-6; M.Davies 88-20-252-6; R.I.Dawson 15-6-28-0; T.H.C.Hancock 5-1-20-0; M.A.Lynch 2-0-3-0; A.Symonds 35-9-87-0; R.C.Williams 61-9-223-1.

The First-Class Averages (pp 129-143) give the records of Gloucestershire players in all first-class county matches (their other opponents being the West Indians and Oxford University), with the exception of R.C.Russell, whose full county figures are as above, and:

M.G.N.Windows 8-15-1-56-256-18.28-0-2-10ct. Did not bowl.

GLOUCESTERSHIRE RECORDS

FIRST-CLASS CRICKET

Highest Total	For	653-6d		v	Glamorgan	Bristol	1928
	V	774-7d		by	Australians	Bristol	1948
Lowest Total	For	17		v	Australians	Cheltenham	1896
	V	12		by	Northants	Gloucester	1907
Highest Innings	For	318*	W.G.Grace	v	Yorkshire	Cheltenham	1876
	V	296	A.O.Jones	for	Notts	Nottingham	1903

Highest Partnership for each Wicket

1st	395	D.M.Young/R.B.Nicholls	v	Oxford U	Oxford	1962
2nd	256	C.T.M.Pugh/T.W.Graveney	v	Derbyshire	Chesterfield	1960
3rd	336	W.R.Hammond/B.H.Lyon	v	Leics	Leicester	1933
4th	321	W.R.Hammond/W.L.Neale	v	Leics	Gloucester	1937
5th	261	W.G.Grace/W.O.Moberley	v	Yorkshire	Cheltenham	1876
6th	320	G.L.Jessop/J.H.Board	v	Sussex	Hove	1903
7th	248	W.G.Grace/E.L.Thomas	v	Sussex	Hove	1896
8th	239	W.R.Hammond/A.E.Wilson	v	Lancashire	Bristol	1938
9th	193	W.G.Grace/S.A.P.Kitcat	v	Sussex	Bristol	1896
10th	131	W.R.Gouldsworthy/J.G.Bessant	v	Somerset	Bristol	1923

Best Bowling	For	10-40	E.G.Dennett	v	Essex	Bristol	1906
(Innings)	V	10-66	A.A.Mailey	for	Australians	Cheltenham	1921
		10-66	K.Smales	for	Notts	Stroud	1956
Best Bowling	For	17-56	C.W.L.Parker	v	Essex	Gloucester	1925
(Match)	V	15-87	A.J.Conway	for	Worcs	Moreton-in-M	1914

Most Runs – Season	2860	W.R.Hammond	(av 69.75)	1933
Most Runs – Career	33664	W.R.Hammond	(av 57.05)	1920-51
Most 100s – Season	13	W.R.Hammond		1938
Most 100s – Career	113	W.R.Hammond		1920-51
Most Wkts – Season	222	T.W.J.Goddard	(av 16.80)	1937
	222	T.W.J.Goddard	(av 16.37)	1947
Most Wkts – Career	3170	C.W.L.Parker	(av 19.43)	1903-35

LIMITED-OVERS CRICKET

Highest Total	NWT	327-7		v	Berkshire	Reading	1966
	BHC	300-4		v	Comb Univs	Oxford	1982
	SL	281-2		v	Hampshire	Swindon	1991
Lowest Total	NWT	82		v	Notts	Bristol	1987
	BHC	62		v	Hampshire	Bristol	1975
	SL	49		v	Middlesex	Bristol	1978
Highest Innings	NWT	158	Zaheer Abbas	v	Leics	Leicester	1983
	BHC	154*	M.J.Procter	v	Somerset	Taunton	1972
	SL	134*	M.W.Alleyne	v	Leics	Bristol	1992
Best Bowling	NWT	6-21	C.A.Walsh	v	Kent	Bristol	1990
		6-21	C.A.Walsh	v	Cheshire	Bristol	1992
	BHC	6-13	M.J.Procter	v	Hampshire	Southampton	1977
	SL	6-52	J.N.Shepherd	v	Kent	Bristol	1983

HAMPSHIRE

Formation of Present Club: 12 August 1863
Colours: Blue, Gold and White
Badge: Tudor Rose and Crown
Championships: (2) 1961, 1973
NatWest Trophy/Gillette Cup Winners: (1) 1991
Benson and Hedges Cup Winners: (2) 1988, 1992
Sunday League Champions: (3) 1975, 1978, 1986
Match Awards: NWT 51; BHC 60

Chief Executive: A.F.Baker
County Cricket Ground, Northlands Road, Southampton SO15 2UE (Tel 01703 333788)
Captain: J.P.Stephenson
Scorer: V.H Isaacs
1996 Beneficiary: R.A.Smith

AYMES, Adrian Nigel (Bellemoor SM, Southampton), b Southampton 4 Jun 1964. 6'0". RHB, WK. Debut 1987. Cap 1991. HS 107* v Sussex (Portsmouth) 1993. BB 1-75. **NWT:** HS 34 v Kent (Southampton) 1994. **BHC:** HS 29 v Comb Us (Oxford) 1995. **SL:** HS 54 v Durham (Portsmouth) 1994.

BENJAMIN, Winston Keithroy Matthew (All Saints S, Antigua), b St John's, Antigua 31 Dec 1964. 6'3". RHB, RFM. Debut (Rest of World XI) 1985. Leicestershire 1986-90 (cap 1989) and 1992. Leeward Is 1985-86 to date. Cheshire 1985. Hampshire 1994. **Tests** (WI): 21 (1987-88 to 1994-95); HS 85 v NZ (Christchurch) 1994-95; BB 4-46 v SL (Moratuwa) 1993-94. **LOI** (WI): 85 (1986-87 to 1995; HS 31; BB 5-22). Tours (WI): E 1985 (RW), 1988, 1995 (part); A 1986-87, 1988-89; NZ 1994-95; I 1987-88; P 1986-87; SL 1993-94. HS 101* Le v Derbys (Leicester) 1990. H HS 54 v Glos (Portsmouth) 1994. 50 wkts (1): 69 (1989). BB 7-54 (inc hat-trick) Le v A (Leicester) 1989. BAC BB 7-83 Le v Lancs (Leicester) 1993. H BB 6-46 v Worcs (Worcester) 1994. Awards: BHC 2. **NWT:** HS 24* Le v Durham (Leicester) 1992. BB 5-32 Le v Derbys (Derby) 1992. **BHC:** HS 45 Le v Middx (Leicester) 1992. BB 5-17 Le v Minor C (Leicester) 1986. **SL:** HS 55 v Glos (Leicester) 1993. BB 4-19 Le v Lancs (Leicester) 1986.

BOTHAM, Liam James (Rossall S), b Doncaster, Yorks 26 Aug 1977. Son of I.T. (Somerset, Worcs, Durham, Queensland and England 1974-93). 6'0". RHB, RMF. Staff 1996 – summer contract 1994-95. Awaiting f-c debut. Rugby for West Hartlepool.

BOVILL, James Noel Bruce (Charterhouse; Durham U), b High Wycombe, Bucks 2 Jun 1971. Son of M.E. (Dorset 1957-60). 6'1". RHB, RFM. Debut 1993. Combined Us 1994. Buckinghamshire 1990-92. HS 31 v Worcs (Southampton) 1995. BB 6-29 (12-68 match) v Durham (Stockton) 1995. **BHC:** HS 14* Comb Us v Glam (Cardiff) 1992. BB 2-21 Comb Us v Lancs (Oxford) 1994. **SL:** HS 7*. BB 3-40 v Surrey (Oval) 1993.

CONNOR, Cardigan Adolphus (The Valley SS, Anguilla; Langley C, Berkshire), b The Valley, Anguilla 24 Mar 1961. 5'9". RHB, RFM. Debut 1984. Cap 1988. Buckinghamshire 1979-83. HS 59 v Surrey (Oval) 1993. 50 wkts (5); most – 72 (1994). BB 7-31 v Glos (Portsmouth) 1989. Award: NWT 1. **NWT:** HS 13 v Yorks (Southampton) 1990. BB 4-11 v Cambs (March) 1994. **BHC:** HS 11 v Glos (Southampton) 1995. BB 4-19 v Sussex (Hove) 1989. **SL:** HS 25 v Middx (Lord's) 1993. BB 4-11 v Derbys (Portsmouth) 1990.

DIBDEN, Richard Rockley (Mountbatten S; Barton Peveril C; Loughborough U), b Southampton 29 Jan 1975. RHB, OB. Debut 1995. HS 0*. BB 2-36 v Yorks (Southampton) 1995.

GARAWAY, Mark (Sandown HS, IoW), b Swindon, Wilts 20 Jul 1973. 5'8". RHB, WK. MCC YC. Hampshire staff 1993 – awaiting f-c debut.

JAMES, Kevan David (Edmonton County HS), b Lambeth, London 18 Mar 1961. 6'0". LHB, LMF. Middlesex 1980-84. Wellington 1982-83. Hampshire debut 1985. Cap 1989. 1000 runs (2); most – 1274 (1991). HS 162 v Glam (Cardiff) 1989. BB 6-22 v A

JAMES – continued:
(Southampton) 1985. BAC BB 6-38 v Derbys (Derby) 1995. **NWT:** HS 42 v Glam (Cardiff) 1989. BB 3-22 v Dorset (Southampton) 1987. **BHC:** HS 45 v Essex (Chelmsford) 1989. BB 3-31 v Middx 1987 and v Glam 1988. **SL:** HS 66 v Glos (Trowbridge) 1989. BB 5-42 v Surrey (Southampton) 1994.

KEECH, Matthew (Northumberland Park S), b Hampstead 21 Oct 1970. 6'0". RHB, RM. Middlesex 1991-93. Hampshire debut 1994. MCC YC. HS 58* M v Notts (Lord's) 1991. H HS 57 v Middx (Southampton) 1994. BB 2-28 M v Glos (Bristol) 1993. H BB 1-43. Scored 251 (256 balls) v Glam II (Usk) – Hants II record. **NWT:** HS 3. **BHC:** HS 47 M v Warwks (Lord's) 1991. BB 1-37. **SL:** HS 98 v Worcs (Southampton) 1995. BB 2-22 M v Northants (Lord's) 1993.

KENDALL, William Salwey (Bradfield C; Keble C, Oxford), b Wimbledon, Surrey 18 Dec 1973. 5'10". RHB, RM. Oxford U 1994-95 (blue 1995). Awaiting Hampshire debut. HS 113* OU v Surrey (Oval) 1994. BB 3-37 OU v Derbys (Oxford) 1995. **BHC:** HS 23 v Hants (Oxford) 1995.

LANEY, Jason Scott (Pewsey Vale SS; St John's SFC, Marlborough; Leeds U), b Winchester 27 Apr 1973. 5'10". RHB, OB. Debut 1995. Matabeleland 1995-96. HS 73 v Somerset (Southampton) 1995. **SL:** HS 53 v Notts (Nottingham) 1995.

MARU, Rajesh Jamandass (Rook's Heath HS, Harrow; Pinner SFC), b Nairobi, Kenya 28 Oct 1962. 5'6". RHB, SLA. Middlesex 1980-82. Hampshire debut 1984. Cap 1986. Tour: Z 1980-81 (Mx). HS 74 v Glos (Gloucester) 1988. 50 wkts (4); most – 73 (1985). BB 8-41 v Kent (Southampton) 1989. **NWT:** HS 22 v Yorks (Southampton) 1990. BB 3-46 v Leics (Leicester) 1990. **BHC:** HS 9. BB 3-46 v Comb Us (Southampton) 1990. **SL:** HS 33* v Glam (Ebbw Vale) 1991. BB 3-30 v Leics (Leicester) 1988.

MORRIS, Robert **Sean** Millner (Stowe S; Durham U), b Great Horwood, Bucks 10 Sep 1968. RHB, OB. 6'0". Debut 1992. HS 174 v Notts (Basingstoke) 1994. **NWT:** HS 34* v Cambs (March) 1994. **SL:** HS 87 v Glos (Basingstoke) 1995.

SMITH, Robin Arnold (Northlands BHS), b Durban, SA 13 Sep 1963. Brother of C.L. (Natal, Glam, Hants and England 1977-78/1992) and grandson of Dr V.L.Shearer (Natal). 5'11". RHB, LB. Natal 1980-81/1984-85. Hampshire debut 1982. Cap 1985. Benefit 1996. *Wisden* 1989. **Tests:** 62 (1988 to 1995-96); HS 175 v WI (St John's) 1993-94. **LOI:** 69 (1988 to 1995-96; HS 167* – Eng record). Tours: A 1990-91; SA 1995-96; WI 1989-90, 1993-94; NZ 1991-92; I/SL 1992-93. 1000 runs (9); most – 1577 (1989). HS 209* v Essex (Southend) 1987. BB 2-11 v Surrey (Southampton) 1985. Awards: NWT 6; BHC 5. **NWT:** HS 125* v Surrey (Oval) 1989. BB 2-13 v Berks (Southampton) 1985. **BHC:** HS 155* v Glam (Southampton) 1989. **SL:** HS 131 v Notts (Nottingham) 1989. BB 1-0.

STEPHENSON, John Patrick (Felsted S; Durham U), b Stebbing 14 Mar 1965. 6'1". RHB, RM. Essex 1985-94 (cap 1989). Hampshire debut/cap 1995. Captain 1996. Boland 1988-89. **Tests:** 1 (1989); HS 25 v A (Oval) 1989. Tours: WI 1991-92 (Eng A); Z 1989-90 (Eng A). 1000 runs (5); most – 1887 (1990). HS 202* Ex v Somerset (Bath) 1990. H HS 127 v Lancs (Portsmouth) 1995. BB 7-51 v Middx (Lord's) 1995. Awards: BHC 4. **NWT:** HS 90 Ex v Northants (Chelmsford) 1993. BB 3-78 Ex v Lancs (Chelmsford) 1992. **BHC:** HS 142 Ex v Warwks (Birmingham) 1991. BB 3-22 Ex v Northants (Northampton) 1990. **SL:** HS 109 Ex v Lancs (Colchester) 1990. BB 5-58 Ex v Glos (Chelmsford) 1992.

TERRY, Vivian **Paul** (Millfield S), b Osnabruck, W Germany 14 Jan 1959. 6'0". RHB, RM. Debut 1978. Cap 1983. Benefit 1994. **Tests:** 2 (1984); HS 8. Tour: Z 1984-85 (EC). 1000 runs (11); most – 1469 (1993). HS 190 v SL (Southampton) 1988. BAC HS 180 v Derbys (Derby) 1990. Awards: NWT 4; BHC 4. **NWT:** HS 165* v Berks (Southampton) 1985. **BHC:** HS 134 v Comb Us (Southampton) 1990. **SL:** HS 142 v Leics (Southampton) 1986.

THURSFIELD, Martin John (Boldon CS), b South Shields, Co Durham 14 Dec 1971. 6'3". RHB, RM. Middlesex 1990. Hampshire debut 1992. MCC YC. HS 47 v Glam (Southampton) 1994. BB 6-130 v Middx (Southampton) 1994. **BHC:** HS 4*. BB 2-40 v Glos (Southampton) 1995. **SL:** HS 9. BB 3-31 v Leics (Leicester) 1994.

UDAL, Shaun David (Cove CS), b Cove, Farnborough 18 Mar 1969. Grandson of G.F.U. (Middx 1932 and Leics 1946); great-great-grandson of J.S. (MCC 1871-75). 6'2". RHB,

OB. Debut 1989. Cap 1992. **LOI:** 10 (1994 to 1995; HS 11*; BB 2-37). Tours: A 1994-95; P 1995-96 (Eng A). HS 94 v Glam (Southampton) 1994. 50 wkts (4); most – 74 (1993). BB 8-50 v Sussex (Southampton) 1992. Awards: NWT 1; BHC 1. **NWT:** HS 14* v Leics (Leicester) 1995. BB 3-39 v Kent (Southampton) 1992. **BHC:** HS 12 v Glos (Southampton) 1995. BB 4-40 v Middx (Southampton) 1992. **SL:** HS 44 v Lancs (Southampton) 1993. BB 4-51 v Northants (Bournemouth) 1992.

WHITAKER, Paul Robert (Whitcliffe Mount S), b Keighley, Yorks 28 Jun 1973. 5'9". LHB, OB. Debut 1994. Derbyshire staff 1992-93. HS 119 v Worcs (Southampton) 1995. BB 1-4. **NWT:** HS 13 v Leics (Leicester) 1995. **BHC:** HS 42 v Glos (Southampton) 1995. **SL:** HS 97 v Worcs (Southampton) 1995. BB 2-32 v Glos (Bristol) 1995.

WHITE, Giles William (Millfield S; Loughborough U), b Barnstaple, Devon 23 Mar 1972. 6'0". RHB, LB. Somerset 1991 (one match). Combined Us 1994. Hampshire debut 1994. Devon 1988-94. HS 104 Comb Us v NZ (Cambridge) 1994. H HS 73* v Durham (Portsmouth) 1994. BB 1-30. **NWT:** HS 11 and BB 1-45 Devon v Kent (Canterbury) 1992. **BHC:** HS 37* v Glam (Southampton) 1995. **SL:** HS 59 v Middx (Lord's) 1995.

NEWCOMERS

FRANCIS, Simon Richard George, b Bromley, Kent 15 Aug 1978. RHB, RF.

MILBURN, Stuart Mark (Upper Nidderdale HS), b Harrogate, Yorks 29 Sep 1972. 6'1". RHB, RMF. Yorkshire 1992-95. HS 7. BB 4-68 Y v Northants (Sheffield) 1995. **SL:** HS 13* Y v Surrey (Oval) 1995. BB 2-29 Y v Northants (Sheffield) 1995.

RENSHAW, Simon John (Birkenhead S; Leeds U), b Bebington, Cheshire 6 Mar 1974. 6'3". RHB, RMF. Combined Us 1995. Cheshire 1994-95. HS 0 and BB 2-135 Comb Us v WI (Oxford) 1995. **BHC:** HS 0*. BB 2-34 Comb Us v Hants (Oxford) 1995.

SAVIDENT, Lee, b Guernsey 22 Oct 1976. RHB, RM.

THOMAS, David Michael, b Frimley, Surrey 16 Nov 1976. RHB, RM.

TREAGUS, Glyn Robert, b Rustington, Sussex 10 Dec 1974. RHB, OB.

DEPARTURES (who made first-class appearances in 1995)

FLINT, Darren Peter John (Queen Mary's SFC), b Basingstoke 14 Jun 1970. 6'0". RHB, SLA. Debut 1993. HS 17* v Worcs (Southampton) 1995. BB 5-32 v Glos (Bristol) 1993 – on debut.

MIDDLETON, Tony Charles (Montgomery of Alamein S, and Peter Symonds SFC, Winchester), b Winchester 1 Feb 1964. 5'10½". RHB, SLA. Debut 1984. Cap 1990. Tour: A 1992-93 (Eng A). 1000 runs (2); most – 1780 (1992). HS 221 v Surrey (Southampton) 1992. BB 2-41 v Kent (Canterbury) 1991. Awards: BHC 2. **NWT:** HS 91* v Comb Us (Southampton) 1993. **BHC:** HS 65 v Middx (Southampton) 1992. **SL:** HS 98 v Northants (Bournemouth) 1992.

NICHOLAS, Mark Charles Jefford (Bradfield C), b London 29 Sep 1957. Grandson of F.W.H. (Essex 1912-29). 5'11". RHB, RM. Debut 1978. Cap 1982. Captain 1985-95. Benefit 1991. Tours (C=captain): SL 1985-86C (Eng B); Z 1984-85C (EC), 1989-90C (Eng A). 1000 runs (10); most – 1559 (1984). HS 206* v OU (Oxford) 1982. BAC HS 158 v Lancs (Portsmouth) 1984. BB 6-37 v Somerset (Southampton) 1989. Awards: NWT 1; BHC 1. **NWT:** HS 71 v Surrey (Oval) 1989. BB 2-39 v Berks (Southampton) 1985. **BHC:** HS 74 v Glam (Southampton) 1985. BB 4-34 v Minor C (Reading) 1985. **SL:** HS 108 v Glos (Bristol) 1984. BB 4-30 v Glos (Trowbridge) 1989.

STREAK, Heath Hilton (Falcon C), b Bulawayo, Rhodesia 16 Mar 1974. Son of D.H. (Rhodesia 1976-77/1978-79). 6'1". RHB, RFM. Debut for Zimbabwe B v Kent (Harare) 1992-93. Matabeleland 1993-94 to date. Hampshire 1995. **Tests** (Z): 12 (1993-94 to 1995-96); HS 53 v SA (Harare) 1995-96; BB 6-90 v P (1st) (Harare) 1994-95. **LOI** (Z): 21 (1993-94 to 1995-96; HS 36*; BB 4-25). Tours (Z): E 1993; A 1994-95; NZ 1995-96; P 1993-94. HS 98 Matabeleland v Glam (Bulawayo) 1994-95. H HS 69 v Young A (Southampton) 1995. BAC HS 38 v Worcs (Southampton) 1995. 50 wkts (1): 53 (1995). BB 6-90 (*see Tests*). H BB 4-40 v Leics (Basingstoke) 1995. **BHC:** HS 18 v Middx (Lord's) 1995. BB 3-28 v Glos (Southampton) 1995. **SL:** HS 32* v Yorks (Southampton) 1995. BB 4-56 v Worcs (Southampton) 1995.

HAMPSHIRE 1995

RESULTS SUMMARY

	Place	Won	Lost	Tied	Drew	No Result
Britannic Assurance Championship	**13th**	5	8	–	4	–
All First-Class Matches		5	9	–	6	–
NatWest Trophy	1st Round					
Benson and Hedges Cup	5th in Group C					
Sunday League	**18th**	3	12	1	–	1

BRITANNIC ASSURANCE CHAMPIONSHIP AVERAGES

BATTING AND FIELDING

Cap		M	I	NO	HS	Runs	Avge	100	50	Ct/St
1985	R.A.Smith	8	15	1	172	812	58.00	3	2	3
1982	M.C.J.Nicholas	17	30	3	147	1077	39.88	3	4	5
–	J.S.Laney	7	13	1	73	423	35.25	–	2	6
–	P.R.Whitaker	11	18	–	119	566	31.44	1	3	2
1995	J.P.Stephenson	15	26	4	127	689	31.31	1	5	8
1983	V.P.Terry	17	30	2	170	796	28.42	1	2	30
1991	A.N.Aymes	17	28	7	60*	547	26.04	–	3	51/3
–	G.W.White	14	23	2	62	497	23.66	–	2	14
1992	S.D.Udal	16	26	4	85	477	21.68	–	3	12
–	R.S.M.Morris	9	17	–	47	354	20.82	–	–	12
1989	K.D.James	10	17	2	53	274	18.26	–	1	4
–	J.N.B.Bovill	7	10	5	31	90	18.00	–	–	1
1988	C.A.Connor	15	24	5	33	275	14.47	–	–	5
–	H.H.Streak	16	25	2	38	301	13.08	–	–	6
–	R.R.Dibden	2	4	1	0*	0	0.00	–	–	–

Also batted: D.P.J.Flint (1 match) 17*; M.Keech (1 match) 35, 22; R.J.Maru (2 matches – cap 1986) 1, 0*, 7 (4 ct); T.C.Middleton (1 match – cap 1990) 7, 0 (1 ct); M.J.Thursfield (1 match) 16, 0.

BOWLING

	O	M	R	W	Avge	Best	5wI	10wM
J.N.B.Bovill	231.3	61	741	29	25.55	6-29	2	1
H.H.Streak	459.4	109	1448	52	27.84	4-40	–	–
C.A.Connor	513.2	112	1707	54	31.61	6-44	3	1
S.D.Udal	570.2	126	1692	53	31.92	6-65	5	1
J.P.Stephenson	326	61	1164	36	32.33	7-51	1	–
K.D.James	189.2	43	632	18	35.11	6-38	1	–

Also bowled: R.R.Dibden 63-10-255-4; D.P.J.Flint 32-11-64-2; M.Keech 10.3-0-43-1; R.J.Maru 105.5-47-199-9; M.C.J.Nicholas 7-0-26-0; M.J.Thursfield 25-5-82-1; P.R.Whitaker 4-0-15-1; G.W.White 4-1-22-0.

The First-Class Averages (pp 129-143) give the records of Hampshire players in all first-class county matches (their other opponents being the West Indians, Oxford University and Young Australia), with the exception of R.A.Smith whose full county figures are as above.

HAMPSHIRE RECORDS

FIRST-CLASS CRICKET

Highest Total	For	672-7d		v	Somerset	Taunton	1899
	V	742		by	Surrey	The Oval	1909
Lowest Total	For	15		v	Warwicks	Birmingham	1922
	V	23		by	Yorkshire	Middlesbrough	1965
Highest Innings	For	316	R.H.Moore	v	Warwicks	Bournemouth	1937
	V	302*	P.Holmes	for	Yorkshire	Portsmouth	1920

Highest Partnership for each Wicket

1st	347	V.P.Terry/C.L.Smith	v	Warwicks	Birmingham	1987
2nd	321	G.Brown/E.I.M.Barrett	v	Glos	Southampton	1920
3rd	344	C.P.Mead/G.Brown	v	Yorkshire	Portsmouth	1927
4th	263	R.E.Marshall/D.A.Livingstone	v	Middlesex	Lord's	1970
5th	235	G.Hill/D.F.Walker	v	Sussex	Portsmouth	1937
6th	411	R.M.Poore/E.G.Wynyard	v	Somerset	Taunton	1899
7th	325	G.Brown/C.H.Abercrombie	v	Essex	Leyton	1913
8th	227	K.D.James/T.M.Tremlett	v	Somerset	Taunton	1985
9th	230	D.A.Livingstone/A.T.Castell	v	Surrey	Southampton	1962
10th	192	H.A.W.Bowell/W.H.Livsey	v	Worcs	Bournemouth	1921

Best Bowling	For	9- 25	R.M.H.Cottam	v	Lancashire	Manchester	1965
(Innings)	V	10- 46	W.Hickton	for	Lancashire	Manchester	1870
Best Bowling	For	16- 88	J.A.Newman	v	Somerset	Weston-s-Mare	1927
(Match)	V	17-119	W.Mead	for	Essex	Southampton	1895

Most Runs – Season	2854	C.P.Mead	(av 79.27)	1928
Most Runs – Career	48892	C.P.Mead	(av 48.84)	1905-36
Most 100s – Season	12	C.P.Mead		1928
Most 100s – Career	138	C.P.Mead		1905-36
Most Wkts – Season	190	A.S.Kennedy	(av 15.61)	1922
Most Wkts – Career	2669	D.Shackleton	(av 18.23)	1948-69

LIMITED-OVERS CRICKET

Highest Total	NWT	371-4		v	Glamorgan	Southampton	1975
	BHC	321-1		v	Minor C (S)	Amersham	1973
	SL	313-2		v	Sussex	Portsmouth	1993
Lowest Total	NWT	98		v	Lancashire	Manchester	1975
	BHC	50		v	Yorkshire	Leeds	1991
	SL	43		v	Essex	Basingstoke	1972
Highest Innings	NWT	177	C.G.Greenidge	v	Glamorgan	Southampton	1975
	BHC	173*	C.G.Greenidge	v	Minor C (S)	Amersham	1973
	SL	172	C.G.Greenidge	v	Surrey	Southampton	1987
Best Bowling	NWT	7-30	P.J.Sainsbury	v	Norfolk	Southampton	1965
	BHC	5-13	S.T.Jefferies	v	Derbyshire	Lord's	1988
	SL	6-20	T.E.Jesty	v	Glamorgan	Cardiff	1975

KENT

Formation of Present Club: 1 March 1859
Substantial Reorganisation: 6 December 1870
Colours: Maroon and White
Badge: White Horse on a Red Ground
Championships: (6) 1906, 1909, 1910, 1913, 1970, 1978
Joint Championship: (1) 1977
NatWest Trophy/Gillette Cup Winners: (2) 1967, 1974
Benson and Hedges Cup Winners: (3) 1973, 1976, 1978
Sunday League Champions: (4) 1972, 1973, 1976, 1995
Match Awards: NWT 46; BHC 77

Secretary: S.T.W.Anderson OBE, MC
St Lawrence Ground, Canterbury, CT1 3NZ (Tel 01227 456886)
Captain: M.R.Benson
Scorer: J.C.Foley
1996 Beneficiary: C.Penn

BENSON, Mark Richard (Sutton Valence S), b Shoreham, Sussex 6 Jul 1958. 5'10". LHB, OB. Debut 1980. Cap 1981. Captain 1991-. Benefit 1991. **Tests:** 1 (1986); HS 30 v I (Birmingham) 1986. **LOI:** 1 (1986; HS 24). 1000 runs (11); most – 1725 (1987). HS 257 v Hants (Southampton) 1991. BB 2-55 v Surrey (Dartford) 1986. Awards: NWT 2; BHC 4. **NWT:** HS 113* v Warwks (Birmingham) 1984. **BHC:** HS 119 v Sussex (Hove) 1995. **SL:** HS 97 v Surrey (Oval) 1982.

COWDREY, Graham Robert (Tonbridge S; Durham U), b Farnborough 27 Jun 1964. Brother of C.S. (Kent, Glam and England 1977-92), son of M.C. (Kent and England 1950-76), grandson of E.A. (Europeans). 5'11". RHB, RM. Debut 1984. Cap 1988. Benefit 1997. 1000 runs (3); most – 1576 (1990). HS 147 v Glos (Bristol) 1992. BB 1-5. Award: BHC 1. **NWT:** HS 37 v Glos (Bristol) 1990. BB 2-4 v Devon (Canterbury) 1992. **BHC:** HS 70* v Leics (Canterbury) 1991. BB 1-6. **SL:** HS 105* v Hants (Southampton) 1995. BB 4-15 v Essex (Ilford) 1987.

EALHAM, Mark Alan (Stour Valley SS, Chartham), b Willesborough, Ashford 27 Aug 1969. Son of A.G.E. (Kent 1966-82). 5'9". RHB, RMF. Debut 1989. Cap 1992. Tour: Z 1992-93 (K). HS 121 v Notts (Nottingham) 1995. BB 7-53 v Hants (Canterbury) 1994. Awards: NWT 2; BHC 2. **NWT:** HS 58* v Warwks (Birmingham) 1993. BB 4-10 v Derbys (Derby) 1994. **BHC:** HS 52 v Somerset (Canterbury) 1995. BB 4-29 v Somerset (Canterbury) 1992. **SL:** HS 112 v Derbys (Maidstone) 1995 (off 44 balls – SL record). BB 6-53 v Hants (Basingstoke) 1993.

FLEMING, Matthew Valentine (St Aubyns S, Rottingdean; Eton C), b Macclesfield, Cheshire 12 Dec 1964. 5'11½". RHB, RM. Debut 1989. Cap 1990. Tour: Z 1992-93 (K). HS 116 v WI (Canterbury) 1991. BAC HS 113 v Surrey (Canterbury) 1991. BB 4-31 v Glos (Tunbridge W) 1993. Awards: NWT 1; BHC 4. **NWT:** HS 53 v Devon (Canterbury) 1992. BB 3-34 v Hants (Southampton) 1992. **BHC:** HS 69 v Somerset (Canterbury) 1992. BB 3-18 v Ire (Comber) 1995. **SL:** HS 79 v Glos (Cheltenham) 1994. BB 4-36 v Worcs (Canterbury) 1994.

FULTON, David Paul (The Judd S; Kent U), b Lewisham 15 Nov 1971. 6'2". RHB. Debut 1992. HS 116 v CU (Folkestone) 1995. BAC HS 75 v Northants (Canterbury) 1993. **NWT:** HS 19 v Staffs (Stone) 1995. **BHC:** HS 25 v Lancs (Lord's) 1995. **SL:** HS 29 v Lancs (Manchester) 1993.

HEADLEY, Dean Warren (Oldswinford Hospital S; Worcester RGS), b Norton, Stourbridge, Worcs 27 Jan 1970. Son of R.G.A. (Worcs, Jamaica and WI 1958-74); grandson of G.A. (Jamaica and WI 1927-28/1953-54). 6'4". RHB, RFM. Middlesex 1991-92; took 5-46 on BAC debut, including wicket of A.A.Metcalfe with his first ball. Kent debut 1992-93 (Z tour). Cap 1993. Tours: P 1995-96 (Eng A); Z 1992-93 (K). HS 91 M v Leics (Leicester) 1992. K HS 54 v Worcs (Worcester) 1995. BB 7-58 (9-127 match) v Sussex (Hove) 1995.

Award: BHC 1. **NWT:** HS 24* v Warwks (Birmingham) 1995. BB 5-20 M v Salop (Telford) 1992. **BHC:** HS 26 M v Surrey (Lord's) 1991. BB 4-19 M v Sussex (Hove) 1992. **SL:** HS 10* v Glam (Canterbury) 1993. BB 6-42 v Surrey (Canterbury) 1995.

HOOPER, Carl Llewellyn (Christchurch SS, Georgetown), b Georgetown, Guyana 15 Dec 1966. 6'1". RHB, OB. Demerara 1983-84. Guyana 1984-85 to date. Kent 1992-94 (cap 1992). **Tests** (WI): 52 (1987-88 to 1995); HS 178* v P (St John's) 1992-93; BB 5-40 v P (P-o-S) 1992-93. **LOI** (WI): 141 (1986-87 to 1995-96: HS 113*; BB 4-34). Tours (WI): E 1988, 1991, 1995; A 1988-89, 1991-92, 1992-93; NZ 1986-87; I 1987-88, 1994-95; P 1990-91; SL 1993-94; Z 1986-87 (Young WI), 1989-90 (Young WI). 1000 runs (5); most – 1579 (1994). HS 236* v Glam (Canterbury) 1993. BB 5-33 WI v Queensland (Brisbane) 1988-89. K BB 5-52 v Durham (Canterbury) 1994. Awards: NWT 1; BHC 1. **NWT:** HS 136* v Berks (Finchampstead) 1994. BB 2-12 v Middx (Canterbury) 1993. **BHC:** HS 50 v Surrey (Canterbury) 1992. BB 3-28 v Yorks (Leeds) 1992. **SL:** HS 122 v Northants (Northampton) 1994. BB 5-41 v Essex (Maidstone) 1993.

IGGLESDEN, Alan Paul (Churchill S, Westerham), b Farnborough 8 Oct 1964. 6'6". RHB, RFM. Debut 1986. Cap 1989. W Province 1987-88. Boland 1992-93. **Tests:** 3 (1989 to 1993-94); HS 3*; BB 2-91 v A (Oval) 1989. **LOI:** 4 (1993-94; HS 18; BB 2-12). Tours: WI 1993-94; Z 1989-90 (Eng A), 1992-93 (K). HS 41 v Surrey (Canterbury) 1988. 50 wkts (4); most – 56 (1989). BB 7-28 (12-66 match) Boland v GW (Kimberley) 1992-93. K BB 6-34 v Surrey (Canterbury) 1988. **NWT:** HS 12* v Oxon (Oxford) 1990. BB 4-29 v Cambs (Canterbury) 1991. **BHC:** HS 26* v Worcs (Worcester) 1991. BB 3-24 v Scot (Glasgow) 1991 and v Notts (Nottingham) 1992. **SL:** HS 13* (twice). BB 5-13 v Sussex (Hove) 1989.

LLONG, Nigel James (Ashford North S), b Ashford 11 Feb 1969. 6'0". LHB, OB. Debut 1990. Cap 1993. Tour: Z 1992-93 (K). HS 118 v Surrey (Canterbury) 1995. BB 5-63 v CU (Cambridge) 1994. BAC BB 3-70 v Worcs (Tunbridge W) 1992. **NWT:** HS 27* v Middx (Canterbury) 1993. BB 1-11. **BHC:** HS 5. BB 1-31. **SL:** HS 64* v Northants (Canterbury) 1993. BB 4-24 v Sussex (Hove) 1993.

McCAGUE, Martin John (Hedland Sr HS; Carine Tafe C), b Larne, N Ireland 24 May 1969. 6'5". RHB, RF. W Australia 1990-91/1991-92. Kent debut 1991. Cap 1992. **Tests:** 3 (1993 to 1994-95); HS 11 v A (Leeds) 1993; BB 4-121 v A (Nottingham) 1993. Tours: A 1994-95 (part); SA 1993-94 (Eng A). HS 59 v Notts (Nottingham) 1995. 50 wkts (3); most – 57 (1994). BB 9-86 (15-147 match) v Derbys (Derby) 1994. Award: NWT 1. **NWT:** HS 31* v Staffs (Stone) 1995. BB 5-26 v Middx (Canterbury) 1993. **BHC:** HS 30 v Derbys (Canterbury) 1992. BB 5-43 v Somerset (Canterbury) 1992. **SL:** HS 22* v Glam (Swansea) 1992. BB 5-40 v Essex (Canterbury) 1995.

MARSH, Steven Andrew (Walderslade SS; Mid-Kent CFE), b Westminster, London 27 Jan 1961. 5'10". RHB, WK. Debut 1982. Cap 1986. Benefit 1995. Tour: Z 1992-93 (K – captain). HS 125 v Yorks (Canterbury) 1992. BB 2-20 v Warwks (Birmingham) 1990. Set world f-c record by holding eight catches in an innings AND scoring a hundred (v Middx at Lord's) 1991. **NWT:** HS 55 v Warwks (Birmingham) 1995. **BHC:** HS 71 v Lancs (Manchester) 1991. **SL:** HS 59 v Leics (Canterbury) 1991.

PATEL, Minal Mahesh (Dartford GS; Erith TC), b Bombay, India 7 Jul 1970. 5'9". RHB, SLA. Debut 1989. Cap 1994. Tour: I 1994-95 (Eng A). HS 56 v Leics (Canterbury) 1995. 50 wkts (2); most – 90 (1994). BB 8-96 v Lancs (Canterbury) 1994. **NWT:** HS 4. BB 2-29 v Oxon (Oxford) 1990. **BHC:** HS 1. BB 2-29 v Somerset (Canterbury) 1995. **SL:** HS 5. BB 3-50 v Northants (Northampton) 1994.

PRESTON, Nicholas William (Meopham SS; Gravesend GS; Exeter U), b Dartford 22 Jan 1972. 6'1". RHB, RFM. Kent staff 1991 – awaiting f-c debut.

SPENCER, Duncan John (Gosnells HS, W Australia), b Nelson, Lancs 5 Apr 1972. 5'8". RHB, RF. Debut 1993. W Australia 1993-94. HS 75 v Z (Canterbury) 1993. BAC HS 13 v Notts (Canterbury) 1994. BB 4-31 v Leics (Leicester) 1994. **SL:** HS 17* v Northants (Canterbury) 1993. BB 2-16 v Essex (Chelmsford) 1994.

STANFORD, Edward John (The Downs SS, Dartford), b Dartford 21 Jan 1971. 5'10". LHB, SLA. Debut 1995. HS 4. BB 2-96 v Worcs (Worcester) 1995.

TAYLOR, Neil Royston (Cray Valley THS), b Orpington 21 Jul 1959. 6'1". RHB, OB. Debut 1979 v SL (Canterbury), scoring 110 and 11. Cap 1982. Benefit 1992. 1000 runs (10); most – 1979 (1990). HS 204 v Surrey (Canterbury) 1990. BB 2-20 v Somerset (Canterbury) 1985. Awards: BHC 8. **NWT:** HS 86 v Staffs (Stone) 1995. BB 3-29 v Dorset (Canterbury) 1989. **BHC:** HS 137 v Surrey (Oval) 1988. **SL:** HS 95 v Hants (Canterbury) 1990.

THOMPSON, Dr Julian Barton deCourcy (The Judd S, Tonbridge; Guy's Hospital Medical S, London U), b Cape Town, SA 28 Oct 1968. 6'4". RHB, RFM. Debut 1994. HS 40* and BB 2-10 v CU (Folkestone) 1995. BAC HS 17 v Somerset (Taunton) 1995. BAC BB 1-89. **SL:** HS 3*. BB 2-27 v Worcs (Worcester) 1995.

WALKER, Matthew Jonathan (King's S, Rochester), b Gravesend 2 Jan 1974. Grandson of Jack (Kent 1949). 5'8". LHB, RM. Debut 1992-93 (Z tour). UK debut 1994. Tour: Z 1992-93 (K). HS 107 v Surrey (Oval) 1994. Award: BHC 1. **BHC:** HS 69* v Sussex (Hove) 1995. **SL:** HS 69* v Derbys (Derby) 1994.

WARD, Trevor Robert (Hextable CS, nr Swanley), b Farningham 18 Jan 1968. 5'11". RHB, OB. Debut 1986. Cap 1989. Tour: Z 1992-93 (K). 1000 runs (4); most – 1648 (1992). HS 235* v Middx (Canterbury) 1991. BB 2-48 v Worcs (Canterbury) 1990. Awards: NWT 1; BHC 2. **NWT:** HS 120 v Berks (Finchampstead) 1994. BB 1-58. **BHC:** HS 125 v Surrey (Canterbury) 1995. **SL:** HS 131 v Notts (Nottingham) 1993. BB 3-20 v Glam (Canterbury) 1989.

WILLIS, Simon Charles (Wilmington GS), b Greenwich, London 19 Mar 1974. 5'8". RHB, OB, WK. Debut 1993. HS 82 v CU (Folkestone) 1995. BAC HS 53 v Notts (Nottingham) 1995. **NWT:** HS 19* v Staffs (Stone) 1995. **SL:** HS 13 v Notts (Nottingham) 1995.

WREN, Timothy Neil (Harvey GS, Folkestone), b Folkestone 26 Mar 1970. 6'3". RHB, LM. Debut 1990. Tour: Z 1992-93 (K). HS 23 v Sussex (Hove) 1995. BB 6-48 v Somerset (Canterbury) 1994. Award: BHC 1. **NWT:** HS 1*. BB 1-51. **BHC:** HS 7. BB 6-41 v Somerset (Canterbury) 1995. **SL:** HS 5*. BB 3-20 v Yorks (Leeds) 1995.

NEWCOMERS

FORD, James Antony, b Pembury 30 Mar 1976. RHB, SLA.

HOUSE, William John, b Sheffield, Yorks 16 Mar 1976. LHB, RMF.

PHILLIPS, Ben James, b Lewisham 30 Sep 1974. RHB, RFM.

SMITH, Edward Thomas, b Pembury 19 Jul 1977. RHB, RMF.

WALSH, Christopher David, b Pembury 6 Nov 1975. RHB, LB.

DEPARTURES (who made first-class appearance in 1995)

De SILVA, Pinnaduwage **Aravinda,** b Colombo, Sri Lanka 17 Oct 1965. 5'3½". RHB, OB. Debut (for SL) 1983-84. Nondescripts 1988-89 to date. Kent 1995 (cap 1995). *Wisden* 1995. **Tests** (SL): 53 (1984 to 1995-96, 5 as captain); HS 267 v NZ (Wellington) 1990-91; BB 3-39 v SA (Colombo) 1993-94. **LOI** (SL): 174 (1983-84 to 1995-96, 18 as captain; HS 107*; BB 3-36). Tours (SL)(C=captain): E 1984, 1988, 1990C, 1991C; A 1984-85, 1987-88, 1989-90, 1995-96; SA 1994-95; NZ 1990-91, 1994-95; I 1986-87, 1990-91, 1993-94; P 1985-86, 1991-92C, 1995-96; Z 1994-95. 1000 runs (1+1); most – 1781 (1995). HS 267 (*see Tests*). K HS 255 v Derbys (Maidstone) 1995. BB 7-24 Nondescripts v Panadura (Panadura) 1994-95. K BB 1-5. Award: BHC 1. **NWT:** HS 24 v Staffs (Stone) 1995. BB 2-45 v Warwks (Birmingham) 1995. **BHC:** HS 112 v Lancs (Lord's) 1995. BB 2-12 v Ire (Comber) 1995. **SL:** HS 124 v Surrey (Canterbury) 1995. BB 4-28 v M (Lord's) 1995.

HERZBERG, Steven, b Carshalton, Surrey 25 May 1967. Emigrated to Australia when aged 9. 6'4". RHB, OB. W Australia 1991-92 and 1992-93. Tasmania 1993-94. Kent 1995. Worcs 2nd XI 1990-91. HS 57* WA v NSW (Sydney) 1992-93. K HS 18 v Somerset (Taunton) 1995. BB 5-33 v Leics (Canterbury) 1995. **SL:** HS –.

1996 BENEFICIARY

PENN, Christopher (Dover GS), b Dover 19 Jun 1963. 6'1". LHB, RFM. Kent 1982-94 (cap 1987; benefit 1996). HS 115 v Lancs (Manchester) 1984. 50 wkts (2); most – 81 (1988). BB 7-70 v Middx (Lord's) 1988. **NWT:** HS 20* v Surrey (Oval) 1991. BB 3-30 v Warwks (Canterbury) 1988. **BHC:** HS 24* v Northants (Northampton) 1989. BB 4-34 v Surrey (Canterbury) 1982. **SL:** HS 40 v Sussex (Maidstone) 1982. BB 4-15 v Glos (Maidstone) 1989.

KENT 1995

RESULTS SUMMARY

	Place	Won	Lost	Drew	No Result
Britannic Assurance Championship	18th	3	10	4	–
All First-Class Matches		4	11	4	–
NatWest Trophy	2nd Round				
Benson and Hedges Cup	Finalist				
Sunday League	1st	12	4	–	1

BRITANNIC ASSURANCE CHAMPIONSHIP AVERAGES

BATTING AND FIELDING

Cap		M	I	NO	HS	Runs	Avge	100	50	Ct/St
1995	P.A.de Silva	15	28	–	255	1661	59.32	6	7	3
1988	G.R.Cowdrey	11	18	1	137	778	45.76	2	6	7
1982	N.R.Taylor	7	12	2	127	421	42.10	1	2	–
1993	N.J.Llong	8	14	–	118	516	36.85	2	1	10
1981	M.R.Benson	13	21	–	192	702	33.42	2	1	4
1989	T.R.Ward	17	30	1	114*	929	32.03	2	6	23
1992	M.A.Ealham	17	29	1	121	860	30.71	1	4	7
1986	S.A.Marsh	15	26	3	67*	673	29.26	–	4	27/2
1990	M.V.Fleming	8	13	1	61	335	27.91	–	2	2
–	D.P.Fulton	6	12	–	59	284	23.66	–	3	6
1992	M.J.McCague	13	23	5	59	327	18.16	–	1	9
1994	M.M.Patel	15	24	5	56	294	15.47	–	1	12
1993	D.W.Headley	14	24	6	54	253	14.05	–	1	7
–	M.J.Walker	8	12	–	53	160	13.33	–	1	5
1989	A.P.Igglesden	6	9	4	18	62	12.40	–	–	1
–	T.N.Wren	5	9	4	23	56	11.20	–	–	2
–	S.Herzberg	5	9	2	18	61	8.71	–	–	1

Also batted: E.J.Stanford (1 match) 0*, 4 (1 ct); J.B.D.Thompson (1 match) 17, 4; S.C.Willis (2 matches) 17, 1, 53 (6 ct).

BOWLING

	O	M	R	W	Avge	Best	5wI	10wM
D.W.Headley	430.5	101	1276	44	29.00	7- 58	3	–
M.J.McCague	401.4	71	1364	47	29.02	5- 47	2	–
A.P.Igglesden	142.2	26	501	17	29.47	5- 92	1	–
T.N.Wren	172.4	23	675	18	37.50	5-148	1	–
M.M.Patel	669.3	149	2095	51	41.07	6-206	2	–
M.A.Ealham	367.2	91	1114	27	41.25	3- 45	–	–

Also bowled: G.R.Cowdrey 3-0-46-0; P.A.de Silva 213-36-634-5; M.V.Fleming 112-19-395-5; S.Herzberg 115.4-21-401-9; N.J.Llong 62.4-11-232-3; S.A.Marsh 2-1-8-0; E.J.Stanford 51-12-145-2; J.B.D.Thompson 12-1-52-0; T.R.Ward 3.5-0-43-0.

The First-Class Averages (pp 129-143) give the records of Kent players in all first-class county matches (their other opponents being the West Indians and Cambridge University), with the exception of:

M.M.Patel 17-28-6-56-321-14.59-0-1-12ct. 753.2-182-2268-61-37.18-6/74-3-1.

KENT RECORDS

FIRST-CLASS CRICKET

Highest Total	For	803-4d		v	Essex	Brentwood	1934
	V	676		by	Australians	Canterbury	1921
Lowest Total	For	18		v	Sussex	Gravesend	1867
	V	16		by	Warwicks	Tonbridge	1913
Highest Innings	For	332	W.H.Ashdown	v	Essex	Brentwood	1934
	V	344	W.G.Grace	for	MCC	Canterbury	1876

Highest Partnership for each Wicket

1st	300	N.R.Taylor/M.R.Benson	v	Derbyshire	Canterbury	1991
2nd	366	S.G.Hinks/N.R.Taylor	v	Middlesex	Canterbury	1990
3rd	321*	A.Hearne/J.R.Mason	v	Notts	Nottingham	1899
4th	368	P.A.de Silva/G.R.Cowdrey	v	Derbyshire	Maidstone	1995
5th	277	F.E.Woolley/L.E.G.Ames	v	New Zealand	Canterbury	1931
6th	315	P.A.de Silva/M.A.Ealham	v	Notts	Nottingham	1995
7th	248	A.P.Day/E.Humphreys	v	Somerset	Taunton	1908
8th	157	A.L.Hilder/A.C.Wright	v	Essex	Gravesend	1924
9th	161	B.R.Edrich/F.Ridgway	v	Sussex	Tunbridge W	1949
10th	235	F.E.Woolley/A.Fielder	v	Worcs	Stourbridge	1909

Best Bowling	For	10- 30	C.Blythe	v	Northants	Northampton	1907
(Innings)	V	10- 48	C.H.G.Bland	for	Sussex	Tonbridge	1899
Best Bowling	For	17- 48	C.Blythe	v	Northants	Northampton	1907
(Match)	V	17-106	T.W.J.Goddard	for	Glos	Bristol	1939

Most Runs – Season	2894	F.E.Woolley	(av 59.06)	1928
Most Runs – Career	47868	F.E.Woolley	(av 41.77)	1906-38
Most 100s – Season	10	F.E.Woolley		1928
	10	F.E.Woolley		1934
Most 100s – Career	122	F.E.Woolley		1906-38
Most Wkts – Season	262	A.P.Freeman	(av 14.74)	1933
Most Wkts – Career	3340	A.P.Freeman	(av 17.64)	1914-36

LIMITED-OVERS CRICKET

Highest Total	NWT	384-6		v	Berkshire	Finchampstead	1994
	BHC	319-8		v	Scotland	Glasgow	1991
	SL	327-6		v	Leics	Canterbury	1993
Lowest Total	NWT	60		v	Somerset	Taunton	1979
	BHC	73		v	Middlesex	Canterbury	1979
	SL	83		v	Middlesex	Lord's	1984
Highest Innings	NWT	136*	C.L.Hooper	v	Berkshire	Finchampstead	1994
	BHC	143	C.J.Tavaré	v	Somerset	Taunton	1985
	SL	142	B.W.Luckhurst	v	Somerset	Weston-s-Mare	1970
Best Bowling	NWT	8-31	D.L.Underwood	v	Scotland	Edinburgh	1987
	BHC	6-41	T.N.Wren	v	Somerset	Canterbury	1995
	SL	6- 9	R.A.Woolmer	v	Derbyshire	Chesterfield	1979

LANCASHIRE

Formation of Present Club: 12 January 1864
Colours: Red, Green and Blue
Badge: Red Rose
Championships (since 1890): (7) 1897, 1904, 1926, 1927, 1928, 1930, 1934
Joint Championship: (1) 1950
NatWest Trophy/Gillette Cup Winners: (5) 1970, 1971, 1972, 1975, 1990
Benson and Hedges Cup Winners: (3) 1984, 1990, 1995
Sunday League Champions: (3) 1969, 1970, 1989
Match Awards: NWT 57; BHC 64

Chief Executive: J.M.Bower. **Cricket Secretary:** Miss R.B.FitzGibbon
Old Trafford, Manchester M16 0PX (Tel 0161 848 7021)
Captain: M.Watkinson
Scorer: W.Davies
1996 Beneficiary: M.Watkinson

ATHERTON, Michael Andrew (Manchester GS; Downing C, Cambridge), b Failsworth, Manchester 23 Mar 1968. 5'11". RHB, LB. Cambridge U 1987-89 (blue 1987-88-89; captain 1988-89). Lancashire debut 1987. Cap 1989. YC 1990. *Wisden* 1990. **Tests:** 56 (1989 to 1995-96, 29 as captain); HS 185* v SA (Jo'burg) 1995-96; BB 1-60. **LOI:** 31 (1990 to 1995-96, 21 as captain; HS 127). Tours (C=captain): A 1990-91, 1994-95C; SA 1995-96C: WI 1993-94C; I/SL 1992-93; Z 1989-90 (Eng A). 1000 runs (6); most – 1924 (1990). Scored 1193 in season of f-c debut. HS 199 v Durham (Gateshead) 1992. BB 6-78 v Notts (Nottingham) 1990. Awards: NWT 1; BHC 1. **NWT:** HS 109* v Oxon (Oxford) 1992. BB 2-15 v Glos (Manchester) 1990. **BHC:** HS 114 v Warwks (Birmingham) 1995. BB 4-42 Comb Us v Somerset (Taunton) 1989. **SL:** HS 111 v Essex (Colchester) 1990. BB 3-33 v Notts (Nottingham) 1990.

AUSTIN, Ian David (Haslingden HS), b Haslingden 30 May 1966. 5'10". LHB, RM. Debut 1987. Cap 1990. Tour: Z 1988-89 (La). HS 115* v Derbys (Blackpool) 1992. BB 5-23 (10-60 match) v Middx (Manchester) 1994. Award: BHC 1. **NWT:** HS 57 v Surrey (Oval) 1994. BB 3-32 v Yorks (Leeds) 1995. **BHC:** HS 80 v Worcs (Worcester) 1987. BB 4-8 v Minor C (Leek) 1995. **SL:** HS 48 v Middx (Lord's) 1991. BB 5-56 v Derbys (Derby) 1991.

BROWN, Christopher (Failsworth HS; Tameside TC), b Oldham 16 Aug 1974. 6'2". RHB, OB. Lancashire staff 1994 – awaiting f-c debut.

CHAPPLE, Glen (West Craven HS; Nelson & Colne C), b Skipton, Yorks 23 Jan 1974. 6'1". RHB, RFM. Debut 1992. Cap 1994. Tour: I 1994-95 (Eng A). HS 109* v Glam (Manchester) 1993 (100 off 27 balls in contrived circumstances). HS (authentic) 58 v Durham (Manchester) 1995. 50 wkts (1): 55 (1994). BB 6-48 v Durham (Stockton) 1994. **NWT:** HS –. BB 1-35. **BHC:** HS –. BB 2-30 v Derbys (Derby) 1994. **SL:** HS 9*. BB 3-29 v Hants (Manchester) 1994.

CRAWLEY, John Paul (Manchester GS; Trinity C, Cambridge), b Maldon, Essex 21 Sep 1971. Brother of M.A. (Oxford U, Lancs and Notts 1987-94) and P.M. (Cambridge U 1992). 6'1". RHB, RM. Debut 1990. Cap 1994. Cambridge U 1991-93 (blue 1991-92-93; captain 1992-93). YC 1994. **Tests:** 10 (1994 to 1995-96); HS 72 v A (Sydney) 1994-95. **LOI:** 3 (1994-95; HS 18). Tours: A 1994-95; SA 1993-94 (Eng A), 1995-96. 1000 runs (4); most – 1570 (1994). HS 286 England A v E Province (Port Elizabeth) 1993-94. La HS 281* v Somerset (Southport) 1994. BB 1-90. Award: BHC 1. **NWT:** HS 31 v Worcs (Manchester) 1995. **BHC:** HS 114 v Notts (Manchester) 1995. **SL:** HS 91 v Kent (Canterbury) 1994.

FAIRBROTHER, Neil Harvey (Lymm GS), b Warrington 9 Sep 1963. 5'8". LHB, LM. Debut 1982. Cap 1985. Captain 1992-93. Benefit 1995. Transvaal 1994-95. **Tests:** 10 (1987 to 1992-93); HS 83 v I (Madras) 1992-93. **LOI:** 51 (1986-87 to 1995-96; HS 113). Tours: NZ 1987-88, 1991-92; I/SL 1992-93; P 1987-88, 1990-91 (Eng A); SL 1990-91 (Eng A). 1000 runs (9); most – 1740 (1990). HS 366 v Surrey (Oval) 1990 (ground record), including 311 in a day and 100 or more in each session. BB 2-91 v Notts (Manchester) 1987. Awards: NWT 5; BHC 7. **NWT:** HS 93* v Leics (Leicester) 1986. **BHC:** HS 116* v Scot (Manchester) 1988. BB 1-17. **SL:** HS 116* v Notts (Nottingham) 1988. BB 1-33.

FLINTOFF, Andrew (Ribbleton Hall HS), b Preston 6 Dec 1976. 6'4". RHB, RM. Debut 1995. HS 7. **BHC:** HS –. BB 1-10. **SL:** HS 22 v Hants (Portsmouth) 1995.

GALLIAN, Jason Edward Riche (Pittwater House S, Sydney; Keble C, Oxford), b Manly, Sydney, Australia 25 Jun 1971. 6'0". RHB, RM. Debut 1990, taking wicket of D.A.Hagan (OU) with his first ball. Cap 1994. Qualified for England 1994. Oxford U 1992-93 (blue 1992-93; captain 1993). Captained Australia YC v England YC 1989-90, scoring 158* in 1st 'Test'. **Tests:** 3 (1995 to 1995-96); HS 28 v SA (Pt Elizabeth) 1995-96. Tours: SA 1995-96 (part); I 1994-95 (Eng A); P 1995-96 (Eng A). 1000 runs (1): 1122 (1995). HS 171 v Surrey (Manchester) 1994. BB 4-29 OU v Lancs (Oxford) 1992. La BB 3-14 v Derbys (Derby) 1995. Awards: NWT 1; BHC 1. **NWT:** HS 101* v Norfolk (Manchester) 1995. **BHC:** HS 134 v Notts (Manchester) 1995. BB 5-15 v Minor C (Leek) 1995. **SL:** HS 84 v Essex (Chelmsford) 1994. BB 2-10 v Somerset (Manchester) 1994.

GREEN, Richard James (Bridgewater HS, Cheshire; Mid-Cheshire C), b Warrington 13 Mar 1976. 6'1". RHB, RM. Debut 1995. HS 1. BB 2-40 v Surrey (Oval) 1995. **SL:** HS –. BB 3-38 v Durham (Manchester) 1995.

HARVEY, Mark Edward (Habergham HS; Loughborough U), b Burnley 26 Jun 1974. 5'9". RHB, RM/LB. Debut 1994. Combined Us 1995. HS 23 v Notts (Nottingham) 1994 and Comb Us v WI (Oxford) 1995. **BHC** (Comb Us): HS 3.

HEGG, Warren Kevin (Unsworth HS, Bury; Stand C, Whitefield), b Whitefield 23 Feb 1968. 5'8". RHB, WK. Debut 1986. Cap 1989. Tours: WI 1986-87 (La); SL 1990-91 (Eng A); Z 1988-89 (La). HS 130 v Northants (Northampton) 1987. Held 11 catches (equalling world f-c match record) v Derbys (Chesterfield) 1989. **NWT:** HS 32 v Surrey (Oval) 1994. **BHC:** HS 31* v Worcs (Lord's) 1990 and v Worcs (Worcester) 1995. **SL:** HS 52 v Glam (Colwyn Bay) 1994.

KEEDY, Gary (Garforth CS), b Wakefield, Yorks 27 Nov 1974. 6'0". LHB, SLA. Yorkshire 1994 (one match). Lancashire debut 1995. HS 15* v Durham and v Warwks (Manchester) 1995. BB 4-35 v Somerset (Taunton) 1995. **SL:** HS –. BB 1-40.

LLOYD, Graham David (Hollins County HS), b Accrington 1 Jul 1969. Son of D. (Lancs and England 1965-83). 5'9". RHB, RM. Debut 1988. Cap 1992. Tour: A 1992-93 (Eng A). 1000 runs (2); most – 1389 (1992). HS 132 v Kent (Manchester) 1992. BB 1-57. Award: BHC 1. **NWT:** HS 39 v Hants (Southampton) 1991. **BHC:** HS 81* v Leics (Manchester) 1995. **SL:** HS 100* v Kent (Maidstone) 1990.

MARTIN, Peter James (Danum S, Doncaster), b Accrington 15 Nov 1968. 6'4". RHB, RFM. Debut 1989. Cap 1994. **Tests:** 6 (1995 to 1995-96); HS 29 v WI (Lord's) 1995; BB 4-60 v SA (Durban) 1995-96. **LOI:** 7 (1995 to 1995-96; HS 6; BB 4-44). Tour: SA 1995-96. HS 133 v Durham (Gateshead) 1992. 50 wkts (1): 54 (1994). BB 5-35 v Yorks (Leeds) 1993 (not BAC). BAC BB 5-61 v Northants (Northampton) 1994. **NWT:** HS 16 and BB 3-63 v Surrey (Oval) 1994. **BHC:** HS 10* v Surrey (Oval) 1993. BB 2-35 v Warwks (Birmingham) 1995. **SL:** HS 18* v Sussex (Hove) 1992. BB 5-32 v Durham (Stockton) 1994.

SHADFORD, Darren James (Breeze Hill HS; Oldham TC), b Oldham 4 Mar 1975. 6'3". RHB, RMF. Debut 1995. HS 1. BB 2-40 v Surrey (Oval) 1995. **SL:** HS –.

SPEAK, Nicholas Jason (Parrs Wood HS, Manchester), b Manchester 21 Nov 1966. 6'0". RHB, RM/OB. Debut v Jamaica (Kingston) 1986-87. Cap 1992. Tour: WI 1986-87 (La). 1000 runs (3); most – 1892 (1992). HS 232 v Leics (Leicester) 1992. BB 1-0. **NWT:** HS 60 v Essex (Chelmsford) 1992. **BHC:** HS 82 v Hants (Manchester) 1992. **SL:** HS 102* v Yorks (Leeds) 1992.

THOMPSON, David James (Ernest Bevin S, Wandsworth; Westminster C), b Wandsworth, London 11 Mar 1976. 6'3". RHB, RFM. Surrey 1994 (one match). HS 22 and BB 2-37 Sy v OU (Oval) 1994. Awaiting Lancashire and BAC debuts.

TITCHARD, Stephen Paul (Lymm County HS; Priestley C), b Warrington 17 Dec 1967. 6'3". RHB, RM. Debut 1990. Cap 1995. HS 135 v Notts (Manchester) 1991. Award: NWT 1. **NWT:** HS 92 v Worcs (Manchester) 1995. **BHC:** HS 82 v Surrey (Oval) 1992. **SL:** HS 96 v Essex (Chelmsford) 1994.

WATKINSON, Michael (Rivington and Blackrod HS, Horwich), b Westhoughton 1 Aug 1961. 6'1". RHB, RMF/OB. Debut 1982. Cap 1987. Captain 1994-. Benefit 1996. Cheshire 1982. **Tests:** 4 (1995 to 1995-96); HS 82* v WI (Nottingham) 1995; BB 3-64 v WI (Manchester) 1995 – on debut. **LOI:** 1 (1995-96; HS –). Tour: SA 1995-96. 1000 runs (1): 1016 (1993). HS 161 v Essex (Manchester) 1995. 50 wkts (7); most – 66 (1992). BB 8-30 (11-87 match) v Hants (Manchester) 1994 – completing match 'double' with 128 runs. Hat-trick 1992. Awards: NWT 2; BHC 2. **NWT:** HS 90 and BB 3-14 v Glos (Manchester) 1990. **BHC:** HS 76 v Northants (Northampton) 1992. BB 5-49 v Yorks (Manchester) 1991. **SL:** HS 83 v Sussex (Manchester) 1991. BB 5-46 v Warwks (Manchester) 1990.

WOOD, Nathan Theo (Wm Hulme's GS), b Thornhill Edge, Yorks 4 Oct 1974. Son of B. (Yorks, Lancs, Derbys and England 1964-83). 5'8". LHB, OB. Lancashire staff 1993 – awaiting f-c debut.

YATES, Gary (Manchester GS), b Ashton-under-Lyne 20 Sep 1967. 6'0". RHB, OB. Debut 1990. Cap 1994. HS 134* v Northants (Manchester) 1993. BB 5-34 v Hants (Manchester) 1994. **NWT:** HS 9. BB 2-61 v Surrey (Oval) 1994. **BHC:** HS 19* v Worcs (Worcester) 1995. BB 3-42 v Warwks (Birmingham) 1995. **SL:** HS 24* v Sussex (Manchester) 1995. BB 4-34 v Warwks (Birmingham) 1994.

NEWCOMERS

CHILTON, Mark, b Sheffield, Yorks 2 Oct 1976. RHB, RM.

ELWORTHY, Steven (Chaplin HS, Gwelo; Sandown HS, Jo'burg; Witwatersrand U), b Bulawayo, Rhodesia 23 Feb 1965. RHB, RFM. Transvaal B 1987-88. N Transvaal 1988-89 to date. Tour: Z 1994-95 (SAA). HS 75 NT v EP (Pt Elizabeth) 1994-95. BB 7-65 NT v Natal (Durban) 1994-95.

HAYNES, Jamie Jonathan (St Edmunds C, Canberra; Canberra U), b Bristol 5 Jul 1974. 5'11". RHB, WK. Has represented Australian Capital Territory at Cricket and Australian Rules football.

McKEOWN, Patrick Christopher (Rossall S), b Liverpool 1 Jun 1976. 6'3". RHB, OB.

MARLAND, Lee John (Manchester GS; Northumbria U), b Withington 21 Sep 1975. 6'1". RHB, OB.

RIDGWAY, Paul Matthew, b Airedale, Yorks 13 Feb 1977. RHB, RFM.

DEPARTURE (who made first-class appearance in 1995)

WASIM AKRAM (Islamia C), b Lahore, Pakistan 3 Jun 1966. 6'3". LHB, LF. PACO 1984-85/1985-86. Lahore 1985-86/1986-87. PIA 1987-88 to date. Lancashire debut 1988. Cap 1989. *Wisden* 1992. **Tests** (P): 67 (1984-85 to 1995-96, 9 as captain); HS 123 v A (Adelaide) 1989-90; BB 7-119 v NZ (Wellington) 1993-94. **LOI** (P): 193 (1984-85 to 1995-96, 28 as captain; HS 86; BB 5-15). Tours (P)(C=captain): E 1987, 1992; A 1988-89, 1989-90, 1991-92, 1992-93, 1995-96C; SA 1994-95; WI 1987-88, 1992-93C; NZ 1984-85, 1992-93, 1993-94, 1995-96C; I 1986-87; SL 1984-85 (P U-23), 1985-86, 1994-95; Z 1994-95. HS 123 (*see Tests*). La HS 122 v Hants (Basingstoke) 1991. 50 wkts (5+1); most – 82 (1992). BB 8-30 (13-147 match) v Somerset (Southport) 1994. Hat-trick 1988. Awards: BHC 2. **NWT:** HS 50 v Surrey (Oval) 1994. BB 4-27 v Lincs (Manchester) 1988. **BHC:** HS 64 v Worcs (Worcester) 1995. BB 5-10 v Leics (Leicester) 1993. **SL:** HS 51* v Yorks (Manchester) 1993. BB 5-41 v Northants (Northampton) 1994. Expected to return in 1997.

LANCASHIRE 1995

RESULTS SUMMARY

	Place	Won	Lost	Drew	No Result
Britannic Assurance Championship	4th	10	4	3	–
All First-Class Matches		10	5	4	–
NatWest Trophy	Quarter-Finalist				
Benson and Hedges Cup	Winners				
Sunday League	4th	11	5	–	1

BRITANNIC ASSURANCE CHAMPIONSHIP AVERAGES

BATTING AND FIELDING

Cap		M	I	NO	HS	Runs	Avge	100	50	Ct/St
1994	J.P.Crawley	14	24	1	182	1203	52.30	3	8	17
1994	J.E.R.Gallian	14	26	3	158	1044	45.39	2	4	12
1989	M.A.Atherton	10	16	1	155*	659	43.93	2	4	9
1995	S.P.Titchard	12	22	2	130	689	34.45	1	5	6
1987	M.Watkinson	13	21	1	161	672	33.60	2	2	5
1992	N.J.Speak	15	27	2	83	795	31.80	–	7	11
1985	N.H.Fairbrother	13	22	2	132	578	28.90	2	1	16
1989	W.K.Hegg	16	25	4	101	556	26.47	1	1	53/7
1994	P.J.Martin	8	9	1	71	210	26.25	–	1	3
1992	G.D.Lloyd	12	19	2	97*	439	25.82	–	3	4
1990	I.D.Austin	11	19	4	80*	348	23.20	–	1	3
1989	Wasim Akram	14	22	3	61	423	22.26	–	4	1
1994	G.Chapple	14	20	6	58	275	19.64	–	1	6
–	G.Keedy	12	15	11	15*	73	18.25	–	–	2
1994	G.Yates	5	6	–	41	98	16.33	–	–	1

Also batted: A.Flintoff (1 match) 7, 0 (2 ct); R.J.Green (1 match) 1; D.J.Shadford (2 matches) 1, 0*.

BOWLING

	O	M	R	W	Avge	Best	5wI	10wM
Wasim Akram	518.1	108	1598	81	19.72	7- 52	7	3
P.J.Martin	211.5	65	547	27	20.25	4- 51	–	–
I.D.Austin	314.4	93	781	33	23.66	4- 50	–	–
M.Watkinson	466.4	119	1439	51	28.21	7-140	2	1
J.E.R.Gallian	98.5	11	374	13	28.76	3- 14	–	–
G.Chapple	361.1	75	1188	33	36.00	4- 44	–	–
G.Keedy	438.5	115	1275	33	38.63	4- 35	–	–

Also bowled: M.A.Atherton 1-0-1-0; N.H.Fairbrother 1.5-1-14-0; A.Flintoff 11-0-39-0; R.J.Green 20-2-87-3; D.J.Shadford 29.5-4-107-3; N.J.Speak 1-0-6-0; G.Yates 68-15-269-6.

The First-Class Averages (pp 129-143) give the records of Lancashire players in all first-class county matches (their other opponents being Yorkshire in a non-Championship match and Cambridge University), with the exception of G.Chapple, whose full county figures are as above, and:

M.A.Atherton 12-19-1-155*-835-46.38-3-4-11ct. 1-0-1-0.
J.P.Crawley 15-25-1-182-1277-53.20-3-9-17ct. Did not bowl.
J.E.R.Gallian 15-28-3-158-1088-43.52-2-4-13ct. 117.5-16-477-16-29.81-3/14.
P.J.Martin 10-11-2-71-248-27.55-0-1-3ct. 254.5-75-681-30-22.70-4/51.
M.Watkinson 15-25-2-161-731-31.78-2-2-6ct. 529.4-137-1621-57-28.43-7/140-2-1.

LANCASHIRE RECORDS

FIRST-CLASS CRICKET

Highest Total	For	863		v	Surrey	The Oval	1990
	V	707-9d		by	Surrey	The Oval	1990
Lowest Total	For	25		v	Derbyshire	Manchester	1871
	V	22		by	Glamorgan	Liverpool	1924
Highest Innings	For	424	A.C.MacLaren	v	Somerset	Taunton	1895
	V	315*	T.W.Hayward	for	Surrey	The Oval	1898

Highest Partnership for each Wicket

1st	368	A.C.MacLaren/R.H.Spooner	v	Glos	Liverpool	1903
2nd	371	F.B.Watson/G.E.Tyldesley	v	Surrey	Manchester	1928
3rd	364	M.A.Atherton/N.H.Fairbrother	v	Surrey	The Oval	1990
4th	324	A.C.MacLaren/J.T.Tyldesley	v	Notts	Nottingham	1904
5th	249	B.Wood/A.Kennedy	v	Warwicks	Birmingham	1975
6th	278	J.Iddon/H.R.W.Butterworth	v	Sussex	Manchester	1932
7th	245	A.H.Hornby/J.Sharp	v	Leics	Manchester	1912
8th	158	J.Lyon/R.M.Ratcliffe	v	Warwicks	Manchester	1979
9th	142	L.O.S.Poidevin/A.Kermode	v	Sussex	Eastbourne	1907
10th	173	J.Briggs/R.Pilling	v	Surrey	Liverpool	1885

Best Bowling	For	10-46	W.Hickton	v	Hampshire	Manchester	1870
(Innings)	V	10-40	G.O.B.Allen	for	Middlesex	Lord's	1929
Best Bowling	For	17-91	H.Dean	v	Yorkshire	Liverpool	1913
(Match)	V	16-65	G.Giffen	for	Australians	Manchester	1886

Most Runs – Season	2633	J.T.Tyldesley	(av 56.02)	1901
Most Runs – Career	34222	G.E.Tyldesley	(av 45.20)	1909-36
Most 100s – Season	11	C.Hallows		1928
Most 100s – Career	90	G.E.Tyldesley		1909-36
Most Wkts – Season	198	E.A.McDonald	(av 18.55)	1925
Most Wkts – Career	1816	J.B.Statham	(av 15.12)	1950-68

LIMITED-OVERS CRICKET

Highest Total	NWT	372-5		v	Glos	Manchester	1990
	BHC	353-7		v	Notts	Manchester	1995
	SL	300-7		v	Leics	Leicester	1993
Lowest Total	NWT	59		v	Worcs	Worcester	1963
	BHC	82		v	Yorkshire	Bradford	1972
	SL	71		v	Essex	Chelmsford	1987
Highest Innings	NWT	131	A.Kennedy	v	Middlesex	Manchester	1978
	BHC	136	G.Fowler	v	Sussex	Manchester	1991
	SL	134*	C.H.Lloyd	v	Somerset	Manchester	1970
Best Bowling	NWT	5-13	P.A.J.DeFreitas	v	Cumberland	Kendal	1989
	BHC	6-10	C.E.H.Croft	v	Scotland	Manchester	1982
	SL	6-29	D.P.Hughes	v	Somerset	Manchester	1977

LEICESTERSHIRE

Formation of Present Club: 25 March 1879
Colours: Dark Green and Scarlet
Badge: Gold Running Fox on Green Ground
Championships: (1) 1975
NatWest Trophy/Gillette Cup Winners: (0) Finalist 1992
Benson and Hedges Cup Winners: (3) 1972, 1975, 1985
Sunday League Champions: (2) 1974, 1977
Match Awards: NWT 36; BHC 60

Chief Executive: A.O.Norman. **Administrative Secretary:** K.P.Hill
County Ground, Grace Road, Leicester LE2 8AD (Tel 0116 283 2128/283 1880)
Captain: J.J.Whitaker
Scorer: G.A.York
1996 Beneficiary: none

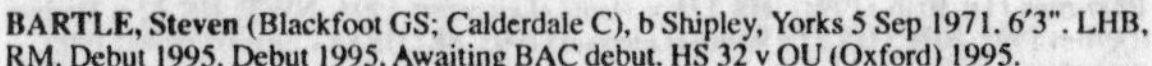

BARTLE, Steven (Blackfoot GS; Calderdale C), b Shipley, Yorks 5 Sep 1971. 6'3". LHB, RM. Debut 1995. Debut 1995. Awaiting BAC debut. HS 32 v OU (Oxford) 1995.

BRIERS, Nigel Edwin (Lutterworth GS; Borough Road CE), b Leicester 15 Jan 1955. 6'0". RHB, RM. Debut 1971 (aged 16yr 103d – youngest Leicestershire player). Cap 1981. Captain 1990-95. Benefit 1990. *Wisden* 1992. Tour: Z 1980-81 (Le). 1000 runs (11); most – 1996 (1990). HS 201* v Warwks (Birmingham) 1983. BB 4-29 v Derbys (Leicester) 1985. Awards: NWT 1; BHC 5. **NWT:** HS 88 v Essex (Leicester) 1992. BB 2-6 v Worcs (Leicester) 1979. **BHC:** HS 102 v Minor C (Stone) 1992. BB 1-26. **SL:** HS 119* v Hants (Bournemouth) 1981. BB 3-29 v Middx (Leicester) 1984.

BRIMSON, Matthew Thomas (Chislehurst & Sidcup GS; Durham U), b Plumstead, London 1 Dec 1970. 6'0". RHB, SLA. Kent staff 1991. Debut 1993. HS 25 v Surrey (Leicester) 1995. BB 2-11 v Glos (Leicester) 1995. **SL:** HS – . BB 1-28.

CLARKE, Vincent Paul (Sacred Heart C, Perth, Australia; Perth C), b Liverpool, Lancs 11 Nov 1971. 6'3". RHB, RM/LB. Somerset 1994. Leicestershire debut 1995. HS 38 Sm v Glos (Bristol) 1994 – on debut. BB 3-72 and Le HS 29 v Worcs (Worcester) 1995. **BHC:** HS 22 Sm v Surrey (Oval) 1994. **SL:** HS 26 Sm v Leics (Leicester) 1994. BB 1-15 (twice).

CROWE, Carl Daniel (Lutterworth GS), b Leicester 25 Nov 1975. 6'0". RHB, OB. Debut 1995. HS 9.

DAKIN, Jonathan Michael (King Edward VII S, Johannesburg) b Hitchin, Herts 28 Feb 1973. 6'4". LHB, RM. Debut 1993. HS 101* and BAC BB 2-20 v Notts (Leicester) 1995. BB 4-45 v CU (Cambridge) 1993 (on debut). **NWT:** HS 26 v Hants (Leicester) 1995. **BHC:** HS 8. **SL:** HS 45 v Notts (Leicester) 1995. BB 3-23 v Somerset (W-s-M) 1995.

HABIB, Aftab (Millfield S; Taunton S), b Reading, Berkshire 7 Feb 1972. 5'11". Cousin of Zahid Sadiq (Surrey and Derbys 1988-90). RHB, RMF. Middlesex 1992 (one match). Leicestershire debut 1995. HS 174* v OU (Oxford) 1995. BAC HS 12 M v Surrey (Oval) 1992. **SL:** HS 15 M v Northants (Lord's) 1993 and v Warwks (Leicester) 1995.

MACMILLAN, Gregor Innes (Guildford County S; Charterhouse; Southampton U; Keble C, Oxford), b Guildford, Surrey 7 Aug 1969. 6'5". RHB, OB. Oxford U 1993-94-95 (blue 1993-94-95; captain 1995). Leicestershire debut 1995 scoring 103 v Sussex (Hove). HS 122 v Surrey (Leicester) 1995. BB 3-13 OU v CU (Lord's) 1993. **NWT:** HS 9. BB 1-13. **BHC:** HS 77 Comb Us v Hants (Oxford) 1995. BB 1-18. **SL:** HS 48 v Glos (Moreton) 1994.

MADDY, Darren Lee (Wreake Valley C), b Leicester 23 May 1974. 5'9". RHB, RM/OB. Debut 1994. HS 131 v OU (Oxford) 1995. BAC HS 34 v Worcs (Leicester) 1994. **NWT:** HS 34 and BB 2-38 v Hants (Leicester) 1995. **BHC:** HS 50 v Notts (Nottingham) 1995. **SL:** HS 69 v Sussex (Hove) 1995. BB 3-29 v Surrey (Leicester) 1995.

MASON, Timothy James (Denstone C), b Leicester 12 Apr 1975. 5'8". RHB, OB. Debut 1994. HS 3. BB 1-22. **NWT:** HS 5. **BHC:** HS 5*. BB 1-34. **SL:** HS 17* v Somerset (W-s-M) 1995. BB 2-41 v Warwks (Leicester) 1995.

MILLNS, David James (Garibaldi CS), b Clipstone, Notts 27 Feb 1965. 6'3". LHB, RF. Nottinghamshire 1988-89. Leicestershire debut 1990. Cap 1991. Tour: A 1992-93 (Eng A). HS 70 v Essex (Chelmsford) 1995. 50 wkts (3); most – 76 (1994). BB 9-37 (12-91 match) v Derbys (Derby) 1991. Award: NWT 1. **NWT:** HS 29* v Derbys (Derby) 1992. BB 3-22 v Norfolk (Leicester) 1992. **BHC:** HS 11* v Sussex (Hove) 1991. BB 4-26 v Durham (Stockton) 1995. **SL:** HS 20* v Notts (Leicester) 1991. BB 2-11 v Somerset (Leicester) 1994.

MULLALLY, Alan David (Cannington HS, Perth, Australia; Wembley TC), b Southend-on-Sea, Essex 12 Jul 1969. 6'5". RHB, LFM. W Australia 1987-88/1989-90. Victoria 1990-91. Hampshire (1 match) 1988. Leicestershire debut 1990. Cap 1993. HS 34 WA v Tasmania (Perth) 1989-90. Le HS 29 v Hants (Leicester) 1990. 50 wkts (2); most – 62 (1993). BB 7-72 (10-170 match) v Glos (Leicester) 1993. **NWT:** HS 19* v Bucks (Marlow) 1993. BB 2-22 v Derbys (Derby) and v Northants (Lord's) 1992. **BHC:** HS 11 v Surrey (Leicester) 1992. BB 3-39 v Minor C (Leicester) 1995. **SL:** HS 38 v Kent (Leicester) 1994. BB 3-9 v Essex (Leicester) 1994.

NIXON, Paul Andrew (Ullswater HS, Penrith), b Carlisle, Cumberland 21 Oct 1970. 6'0". LHB, WK. Debut 1989. Cap 1994. Cumberland 1987. MCC YC. Tour: I 1994-95 (Eng A). 1000 runs (1): 1046 (1994). HS 131 v Hants (Leicester) 1994. **NWT:** HS 32 v Derbys (Derby) 1992. **BHC:** HS 27 v Worcs (Leicester) 1993. **SL:** HS 84 v Sussex (Hove) 1995.

ORMOND, James (St Thomas More S, Nuneaton), b Walsgrave-on-Sowe, Warwks 20 Aug 1977. 6'3". RHB, RMF. Debut 1995. Awaiting BAC debut. HS –. BB 2-65 v OU (Oxford) 1995. **SL:** HS –.

PARSONS, Gordon James (Woodside County SS, Slough), b Slough, Bucks 17 Oct 1959. Brother-in-law of W.J.Cronje (*see DEPARTURES*) 6'1". LHB, RMF. Leicestershire 1978-85 (cap 1984) and 1989-. Joint benefit 1994. Warwickshire 1986-88 (cap 1987). Boland 1983-84/1984-85. GW 1985-86/1986-87. OFS 1988-89 to date. Buckinghamshire 1977. Tours: NZ 1979-80 (DHR); Z 1980-81 (Le). HS 76 Boland v W Province B (Cape Town) 1984-85. Le HS 73 v Durham (Leicester) 1995. 50 wkts (3); most – 67 (1984). BB 9-72 Boland v Transvaal B (Johannesburg) 1984-85. Le BB 6-11 v OU (Oxford) 1985. BAC BB 6-70 v Surrey (Oval) 1992. Awards: BHC 2. **NWT:** HS 25* v Glam (Leicester) 1995. BB 2-11 v Wilts (Swindon) 1984. **BHC:** HS 63* and BB 4-12 v Scot (Leicester) 1989. **SL:** HS 38* v Lancs (Leicester) 1993. BB 4-19 v Essex (Harlow) 1982.

PIERSON, Adrian Roger Kirshaw (Kent C, Canterbury; Hatfield Poly), b Enfield, Middx 21 Jul 1963. 6'4". RHB, OB. Warwickshire 1985-91. Leicestershire debut 1993. Cap 1995. Cambridgeshire 1992. MCC YC. HS 58 v Lancs (Leicester) 1993. 50 wkts (1): 69 (1995). BB 8-42 v Warwks (Birmingham) 1994. Awards: NWT 1; BHC 1. **NWT:** HS 20* v Hants (Leicester) 1995. BB 3-20 Wa v Wilts (Birmingham) 1989. **BHC:** HS 11 Wa v Minor C (Walsall) 1986. BB 3-34 Wa v Lancs (Birmingham) 1988. **SL:** HS 29* v Kent (Leicester) 1994. BB 5-36 v Derbys (Leicester) 1995.

ROBINSON, Phillip Edward (Greenhead GS, Keighley), b Keighley, Yorks 3 Aug 1963. 5'9". RHB, LM. Yorkshire 1984-91 (cap 1988). Leicestershire debut 1992. Cumberland 1992. 1000 runs (3); most – 1402 (1990). HS 189 Y v Lancs (Scarborough) 1991. Le HS 86 v Glam (Cardiff) 1994. BB 1-10. Le BB 1-13. Awards: NWT 1; BHC 2. **NWT:** HS 73 v Norfolk (Leicester) 1992. **BHC:** HS 73* Y v Hants (Southampton) 1990. **SL:** HS 104 v Lancs (Manchester) 1992.

SIMMONS, Philip Verant (Holy Cross C, Arima), b Arima, Trinidad 18 Apr 1963. 6'3½". RHB, RM. Debut for N Trinidad 1982-83. Trinidad 1982-83 to date (captain 1988-89). Durham 1989-90 (NWT only). Leicestershire 1994 (cap 1994). **Tests** (WI): 22 (1987-88 to 1994-95); HS 110 and BB 2-34 v A (Melbourne) 1992-93. **LOI** (WI): 111 (1987-88 to 1995-96; HS 122; BB 4-3). Tours (WI): E 1988 (part), 1991, 1992 (RW), 1993 (RW), 1995; A 1992-93; I 1987-88, 1994-95; SL 1993-94; Z 1983-84 (Young WI), 1986-87 (Young WI). 1000 runs (1): 1031 (1991). HS 261 v Northants (Leicester) 1994 – on Le debut (county record). BB 5-24 Trinidad v Windward Is (Pointe-à-Pierre) 1990-91. Le BB 4-68 v Hants (Leicester) 1994. Award: BHC 1. **NWT:** HS 33 Du v Middx (Darlington) 1989. BB 3-31 v Cumb (Netherfield) 1994. **BHC:** HS 64 and BB 1-29 v Ire (Leicester) 1994. **SL:** HS 140 v Middx (Leicester) 1994. BB 4-19 v Essex (Leicester) 1994.

SMITH, Benjamin Francis (Kibworth HS), b Corby, Northants 3 Apr 1972. 5'9". RHB, RM. Debut 1990. Cap 1995. HS 112 v Northants (Northampton) 1995. BB 1-5. Award: NWT 1. **NWT:** HS 63* v Cumb (Netherfield) 1994. **BHC:** HS 43 v Warwks (Leicester) 1993. **SL:** HS 115 v Somerset (W-s-M) 1995.

SUTCLIFFE, Iain John (Leeds GS; Queen's C, Oxford U), b Leeds, Yorks 20 Dec 1974. 6'2". LHB, occ OB. Oxford U 1994-95 (blue 1995). Leicestershire debut 1995. HS 163* OU v Hants (Oxford) 1995. Le HS 34 v Sussex (Hove) 1995. BB (OU) 1-11. **NWT:** HS 68 v Glam (Leicester) 1995. **BHC:** HS 39 Comb Us v Essex (Cambridge) 1995. **SL:** HS 14 v Sussex (Hove) 1995. Boxing blue 1993-94.

WELLS, Vincent John (Sir William Nottidge S, Whitstable), b Dartford, Kent 6 Aug 1965. 6'0". RHB, RMF. Kent 1988-91. Leicestershire debut 1992. Cap 1994. HS 167 v Glam (Leicester) 1993. BB 5-43 K v Leics (Leicester) 1990. Le BB 5-50 (inc hat-trick) v Durham (Durham) 1994. Awards: NWT 1; BHC 1. **NWT:** 100* K v Oxon (Oxford) 1990. BB 3-38 v Durham (Leicester) 1992. **BHC:** HS 39 v Minor C (Leicester) 1995. BB 4-37 v Worcs (Leicester) 1993. **SL:** HS 101 v Middx (Leicester) 1994. BB 5-10 v Surrey (Oval) 1994.

WHITAKER, John James (Uppingham S), b Skipton, Yorks 5 May 1962. 5'10". RHB, OB. Debut 1983. Cap 1986. Benefit 1993. *Wisden* 1986. YC 1986. **Tests:** 1 (1986-87); HS 11 v A (Adelaide) 1986-87. **LOI:** 2 (1986-87; HS 44*). Tours: A 1986-87; Z 1989-90 (Eng A). 1000 runs (9); most – 1767 (1990). HS 200* v Notts (Leicester) 1986. BB 1-29. Awards: NWT 1; BHC 1. **NWT:** HS 155 v Wilts (Swindon) 1984. **BHC:** HS 100 v Kent (Canterbury) 1991. **SL:** HS 132 v Glam (Swansea) 1984.

WHITTICASE, Philip (Crestwood CS, Kingswinford), b Marston Green, Solihull 15 Mar 1965. 5'8". RHB, WK. Leicestershire 1984-92, 1995. Cap 1987. HS 114* v Hants (Bournemouth) 1991. **NWT:** HS 32 v Lancs (Leicester) 1986. **BHC:** HS 45 v Notts (Nottingham) 1990. **SL:** HS 38 v Northants (Leicester) 1990.

NEWCOMERS

REMY, Carlos Charles (St Aloyous C; Haringey Cricket C), b Castries, St Lucia 24 Jul 1968. 5'9". RHB, RM. Sussex 1989-95. HS 60 Sx v Northants (Northampton) 1994. BB 4-63 Sx v CU (Hove) 1990. BAC BB 3-27 Sx v Lancs (Hove) 1992. **NWT:** HS 1. **BHC:** HS 7. **SL:** HS 19 Sx v Essex (Hove) 1993. BB 4-31 Sx v Lancs (Hove) 1992.

STEVENS, Darren Ian (Charles Keene C), b Leicester 3 Apr 1976. RHB.

WILLIAMSON, Dominic (St Leonard's CS, Durham), b Durham 15 Nov 1975. MCC YC. RHB, RM.

DEPARTURES (who made first-class appearance in 1995)

BOON, Timothy James (Edlington CS, Doncaster), b Doncaster, Yorks 1 Nov 1961. 6'0". RHB, RM. Leicestershire 1980-95, (cap 1986; benefit 1995). Tour: Z 1980-81 (Le). 1000 runs (7); most – 1539 (1990). HS 144 v Glos (Leicester) 1984. BB 3-40 v Yorks (Leicester) 1986. Awards: NWT 2; BHC 1. **NWT:** HS 117 v Bucks (Marlow) 1993. **BHC:** HS 103 v Scot (Leicester) 1991. **SL:** HS 135* v Kent (Canterbury) 1993. BB 1-23.

CRONJE, Wessel Johannes (**'Hansie'**) (Grey C, Bloemfontein; OFS U), b Bloemfontein, SA 25 Sep 1969. Son of N.E. (OFS 1960-61/1971-72); brother of F.J.C. (Border 1985-86 to date); brother-in-law of G.J.Parsons *(see above)*. 6'4". RHB, RM. Orange Free State 1987-88 to date (captain 1990-91 to date). Leicestershire 1995 (cap 1995). **Tests** (SA): 27 (1991-92 to 1995-96, 12 as captain); HS 135 v I (Pt Eliz) 1992-93; BB 2-17 v I (Cape Town) 1992-93. **LOI** (SA): 77 (1991-92 to 1995-96, 27 as captain; HS 112; BB 5-32). Tours (SA)(C=captain): E 1994; A 1993-94; WI 1991-92; NZ 1994-95C; SL 1993-94; Z 1995-96C. 1000 runs (1+1); most – 1567 (1993-94). HS 251 OFS v A (Bloemfontein) 1993-94. Le HS 213 and Le BB 3-42 v Somerset (W-s-M) 1995. BB 4-47 SA v Kent (Canterbury) 1994. Award: BHC 1. **BHC:** HS 158 v Lancs (Manchester) 1995. BB 2-26 v Durham (Stockton) 1995. **SL:** HS 93* v Lancs (Leicester) 1995. BB 3-37 v Hants (Basingstoke) 1995.

SHERIYAR, A. – *see WORCESTERSHIRE.*

LEICESTERSHIRE 1995

RESULTS SUMMARY

	Place	Won	Lost	Drew	No Result
Britannic Assurance Championship	7th	7	8	2	–
All First-Class Matches		9	9	2	–
NatWest Trophy	2nd Round				
Benson and Hedges Cup	6th in Group A				
Sunday League	7th	8	7	–	2

BRITANNIC ASSURANCE CHAMPIONSHIP AVERAGES

BATTING AND FIELDING

Cap		M	I	NO	HS	Runs	Avge	100	50	Ct/St
1995	W.J.Cronje	15	26	1	213	1301	52.04	4	6	13
–	G.I.Macmillan	6	10	1	122	389	43.22	2	1	9
1981	N.E.Briers	15	27	2	175*	1046	41.84	3	3	1
1986	J.J.Whitaker	13	21	–	127	869	41.38	2	4	1
–	J.M.Dakin	6	10	2	101*	306	38.25	1	2	5
1987	P.Whitticase	3	5	1	62*	150	37.50	–	2	7/1
1995	B.F.Smith	15	25	4	112	698	33.23	1	6	8
1994	V.J.Wells	13	22	1	124	645	30.71	1	5	8
1991	D.J.Millns	7	12	2	70	259	25.90	–	2	4
–	M.T.Brimson	5	4	2	25	40	20.00	–	–	–
–	P.E.Robinson	3	6	1	60*	99	19.80	–	1	5
1994	P.A.Nixon	13	22	4	79	356	19.77	–	1	34
1984	G.J.Parsons	17	26	2	73	472	19.66	–	1	14
1995	A.R.K.Pierson	17	26	6	50	316	15.80	–	1	10
1986	T.J.Boon	6	12	–	38	177	14.75	–	–	5
–	D.L.Maddy	7	13	–	24	121	9.30	–	–	12
–	V.P.Clarke	2	4	–	29	35	8.75	–	–	1
1993	A.D.Mullally	17	26	6	22	150	7.50	–	–	–
–	A.Sheriyar	4	7	1	18	38	6.33	–	–	2

Also batted: C.D.Crowe (1 match) 1, 9 (1 ct); I.J.Sutcliffe (2 matches) 21, 34, 8.

BOWLING

	O	M	R	W	Avge	Best	5wI	10wM
V.J.Wells	131.3	35	393	19	20.68	3-28	–	–
A.R.K.Pierson	583.1	124	1872	65	28.80	5-48	2	–
A.D.Mullally	540	165	1534	52	29.50	6-50	2	–
G.J.Parsons	549.2	167	1527	50	30.54	4-46	–	–
A.Sheriyar	106.4	15	424	11	38.54	3-46	–	–
D.J.Millns	187.2	25	725	18	40.27	3-47	–	–
W.J.Cronje	248.2	80	676	14	48.28	3-42	–	–

Also bowled: M.T.Brimson 89-20-243-9; V.P.Clarke 44.2-6-155-4; C.D.Crowe 3-2-4-0; J.M.Dakin 54-9-194-2; D.L.Maddy 6-0-41-0; B.F.Smith 11.3-2-69-1.

The First-Class Averages (pp 129-143) give the records of Leicestershire players in all first-class county matches (their other opponents being the West Indians, Oxford University and Young Australia), with the exception of G.I.Macmillan, whose full county figures are as above, and :

A.D.Mullally 18-28-6-22-150-6.81-0-0-0ct. 567-169-1646-58-28.37-6/50-2-0.
P.A.Nixon 16-27-4-79-376-16.34-0-1-44ct-1st. Did not bowl.
A.R.K.Pierson 19-30-9-50-382-18.19-0-1-12ct. 622.1-130-2040-67-30.44-5/48-2-0.
A.G.Sheriyar 7-10-1-19-59-6.56-0-0-3ct. 182-27-757-29-26.10-6/30-2-1.
I.J.Sutcliffe 3-4-0-34-63-15.75-0-0-1ct. Did not bowl.

LEICESTERSHIRE RECORDS

FIRST-CLASS CRICKET

Highest Total	For	701-4d		v	Worcs	Worcester	1906
	V	761-6d		by	Essex	Chelmsford	1990
Lowest Total	For	25		v	Kent	Leicester	1912
	V	24		by	Glamorgan	Leicester	1971
		24		by	Oxford U	Oxford	1985
Highest Innings	For	261	P.V.Simmons	v	Northants	Leicester	1994
	V	341	G.H.Hirst	for	Yorkshire	Leicester	1905

Highest Partnership for each Wicket

1st	390	B.Dudleston/J.F.Steele	v	Derbyshire	Leicester	1979
2nd	289*	J.C.Balderstone/D.I.Gower	v	Essex	Leicester	1981
3rd	316*	W.Watson/A.Wharton	v	Somerset	Taunton	1961
4th	290*	P.Willey/T.J.Boon	v	Warwicks	Leicester	1984
5th	233	N.E.Briers/R.W.Tolchard	v	Somerset	Leicester	1979
6th	262	A.T.Sharpe/G.H.S.Fowke	v	Derbyshire	Chesterfield	1911
7th	219*	J.D.R.Benson/P.Whitticase	v	Hampshire	Bournemouth	1991
8th	164	M.R.Hallam/C.T.Spencer	v	Essex	Leicester	1964
9th	160	W.W.Odell/R.T.Crawford	v	Worcs	Leicester	1902
10th	228	R.Illingworth/K.Higgs	v	Northants	Leicester	1977

Best Bowling	For	10- 18	G.Geary	v	Glamorgan	Pontypridd	1929
(Innings)	V	10- 32	H.Pickett	for	Essex	Leyton	1895
Best Bowling	For	16- 96	G.Geary	v	Glamorgan	Pontypridd	1929
(Match)	V	16-102	C.Blythe	for	Kent	Leicester	1909

Most Runs – Season	2446	L.G.Berry	(av 52.04)	1937
Most Runs – Career	30143	L.G.Berry	(av 30.32)	1924-51
Most 100s – Season	7	L.G.Berry		1937
	7	W.Watson		1959
	7	B.F.Davison		1982
Most 100s – Career	45	L.G.Berry		1924-51
Most Wkts – Season	170	J.E.Walsh	(av 18.96)	1948
Most Wkts – Career	2130	W.E.Astill	(av 23.19)	1906-39

LIMITED-OVERS CRICKET

Highest Total	NWT	354-7		v	Wiltshire	Swindon	1984
	BHC	327-4		v	Warwicks	Coventry	1972
	SL	301-7		v	Middlesex	Leicester	1994
Lowest Total	NWT	56		v	Northants	Leicester	1964
	BHC	56		v	Minor C	Wellington	1982
	SL	36		v	Sussex	Leicester	1973
Highest Innings	NWT	156	D.I.Gower	v	Derbyshire	Leicester	1984
	BHC	158*	B.F.Davison	v	Warwicks	Coventry	1972
	SL	152	B.Dudleston	v	Lancashire	Manchester	1975
Best Bowling	NWT	6-20	K.Higgs	v	Staffs	Longton	1975
	BHC	6-35	L.B.Taylor	v	Worcs	Worcester	1982
	SL	6-17	K.Higgs	v	Glamorgan	Leicester	1973

MIDDLESEX

Formation of Present Club: 2 February 1864
Colours: Blue
Badge: Three Seaxes
Championships (since 1890): (10) 1903, 1920, 1921, 1947, 1976, 1980, 1982, 1985, 1990, 1993
Joint Championships: (2) 1949, 1977
NatWest Trophy/Gillette Cup Winners: (4) 1977, 1980, 1984, 1988
Benson and Hedges Cup Winners: (2) 1983, 1986
Sunday League Champions: (1) 1992
Match Awards: NWT 50; BHC 56

Secretary: J.Hardstaff MBE
Lord's Cricket Ground, London NW8 8QN (Tel 0171 289 1300/286 1310)
Captain: M.W.Gatting
Scorer: M.J.Smith
1996 Beneficiary: M.W.Gatting

BROWN, Keith Robert (Chace S, Enfield), b Edmonton 18 Mar 1963. Brother of G.K. (Middx 1986 and Durham 1992). 5'11". RHB, WK, RSM. Debut 1984. Cap 1990. MCC YC. 1000 runs (2); most – 1505 (1990). HS 200* v Notts (Lord's) 1990. BB 2-7 v Glos (Bristol) 1987. Awards: NWT 2; BHC 1. **NWT:** HS 103* v Surrey (Uxbridge) 1990. **BHC:** HS 75 v Comb Us (Lord's) 1995. **SL:** HS 102 v Somerset (Lord's) 1988.

CARR, John Donald (Repton S; Worcester C, Oxford), b St John's Wood 15 Jun 1963. Son of D.B. (Derbys, OU and England 1945-63). 5'11". RHB, RM. Oxford U 1983-85 (blue 1983-84-85). Middlesex 1983-89 (cap 1987) and 1992-. Hertfordshire 1982-84 and 1991. 1000 runs (5); most – 1543 (1994). HS 261* v Glos (Lord's) 1994. BB 6-61 v Glos (Lord's) 1985. **NWT:** HS 83 v Hants (Southampton) 1989. BB 2-19 v Surrey (Oval) 1988. **BHC:** HS 70 v Leics (Leicester) 1992. BB 3-22 Comb Us v Glos (Bristol) 1984. **SL:** HS 104* v Warwks (Lord's) 1992. BB 4-21 v Surrey (Lord's) 1989.

DUTCH, Keith Philip (Nower Hill HS; Weald C), b Harrow 21 Mar 1973. 5'10". RHB, OB. Debut 1993. MCC YC. HS – . **SL:** HS 21* v Sussex (Lord's) 1995.

FAY, Richard Anthony (Brondesbury & Kilburn HS; Queens Park Community S; City of Westminster C), b Kilburn, London 14 May 1974. Great-nephew of M.W.Tate (Sussex and England 1912-37). 6'4". RHB, RMF. MCC YC. Debut 1995. HS 1*. **SL:** HS 12* v Sussex (Lord's) 1995. BB 2-32 v Durham (Chester-le-St) 1995.

FELTHAM, Mark Andrew (Tiffin S), b St John's Wood 26 June 1963. 6'2½". RHB, RMF. Surrey 1983-92 (cap 1990). Middlesex debut 1993. Cap 1995. MCC YC. HS 101 Sy v Middx (Oval) 1990. M HS 73 v Notts (Lord's) 1993. 50 wkts (1): 56 (1988). BB 6-41 v WI (Lord's) 1995. BAC BB 6-53 Sy v Leics (Oval) 1990. Awards: BHC 2. **NWT:** HS 37* v Glam (Cardiff) 1995. BB 2-23 v Wales MC (Northop Hall) 1994. **BHC:** HS 35 Sy v Kent (Canterbury) 1992. BB 5-28 Sy v Comb Us (Cambridge) 1989. **SL:** HS 75 v Leics (Leicester) 1994. BB 5-51 v Hants (Lord's) 1995.

FOLLETT, David (Moorland Road HS, Burslem; Stoke-on-Trent TC), b Newcastle-under-Lyme, Staffs 14 Oct 1968. 6'2". RHB, RFM. Debut 1995. Staffordshire 1994. HS 4*. BB 1-61. **BHC:** HS 4. BB 2-44 v Hants (Lord's) 1995.

FRASER, Angus Robert Charles (Gayton HS, Harrow; Orange Sr HS, Edgware), b Billinge, Lancs 8 Aug 1965. Brother of A.G.J. (Middx and Essex 1986-92). 6'5". RHB, RMF. Debut 1984. Cap 1988. *Wisden* 1995. **Tests:** 32 (1989 to 1995-96); HS 29 v A (Nottingham) 1989; BB 8-75 v WI (Bridgetown) 1993-94 – record England analysis v WI. **LOI**: 33 (1989-90 to 1995; HS 38*; BB 4-22). Tours: A 1990-91, 1994-95 (part); SA 1995-96; WI 1989-90, 1993-94. HS 92 v Surrey (Oval) 1990. 50 wkts (6); most – 92 (1989). BB 8-75 (*see Tests*). M BB 7-40 v Leics (Lord's) 1993. **NWT:** HS 19 v Durham (Darlington) 1989. BB 4-34 v Yorks (Leeds) 1988. **BHC:** HS 13* v Essex (Lord's) 1988. BB 4-49 v Kent (Canterbury) 1995. **SL:** HS 30* v Kent (Canterbury) 1988. BB 5-32 v Derbys (Lord's) 1995.

GATTING, Michael William (John Kelly HS), b Kingsbury 6 Jun 1957. 5'10". RHB, RM. Debut 1975. Cap 1977. Captain 1983-. Benefits 1988, 1996. YC 1981. *Wisden* 1983. OBE 1987. **Tests:** 79 (1977-78 to 1994-95, 23 as captain); HS 207 v I (Madras) 1984-85; BB 1-14. **LOI**: 92 (1977-78 to 1992-93, 37 as captain; HS 115*; BB 3-32). Tours (C=captain): A 1986-87C, 1987-88C, 1994-95; SA 1989-90C (Eng XI); WI 1980-81, 1985-86; NZ 1977-78, 1983-84, 1987-88C; I/SL 1981-82, 1984-85, 1992-93; P 1977-78, 1983-84, 1987-88C; Z 1980-81 (Mx). 1000 runs (17+1) inc 2000 (3); most – 2257 (1984). HS 258 v Somerset (Bath) 1984. BB 5-34 v Glam (Swansea) 1982. Awards: NWT 6; BHC 11. **NWT:** HS 132* v Sussex (Lord's) 1989. BB 2-14 (twice). **BHC:** HS 143* v Sussex (Hove) 1985. BB 4-49 v Sussex (Lord's) 1984. **SL:** HS 124* v Leics (Leicester) 1990. BB 4-30 v Glos (Bristol) 1989.

HARRISON, Jason Christian (Great Marlow SM; Bucks CHE), b Amersham, Bucks 15 Jan 1972. 6'3". RHB, OB. Debut 1994. Awaiting BAC debut. Buckinghamshire 1991-93. HS 46* v CU (Cambridge) 1995. **SL:** HS 13* v Warwks (Birmingham) 1995. BB 1-3.

JOHNSON, Richard Leonard (Sunbury Manor S; S Pelthorne C), b Chertsey, Surrey 29 Dec 1974. 6'2". RHB, RMF. Debut 1992. Cap 1995. Tour: I 1994-95 (Eng A – part). HS 50* v CU (Cambridge) 1994. BAC HS 47 v Hants (Southampton) 1994. BB 10-45 v Derbys (Derby) 1994 (second youngest to take all ten wickets in any f-c match). **NWT:** HS 33 and BB 3-33 v Glam (Cardiff) 1995. **BHC:** HS 1. BB 1-17. **SL:** HS 18* v Lancs (Lord's) 1995. BB 4-66 v Worcs (Worcester) 1993.

KHAN, Amer Ali (Muslim Modle HS, Lahore; MAO C, Lahore), b Lahore, Pakistan 5 Nov 1969. 5'9½". RHB, LB. Rawalpindi 1987-88 (one match as AAMER ALI). Middlesex debut 1995. HS – . BB 4-51 v CU (Cambridge) 1995.

NASH, David Charles (Sunbury Manor S; Malvern C), b Chertsey, Surrey 19 Jan 1978. 5'8". RHB, WK. Awaiting f-c debut. **SL:** HS – .

NASH, Dion Joseph (Dargaville HS; Auckland GS, Otago U), b Auckland, NZ 20 Nov 1971. 6'1". RHB, RFM. N Districts 1990-91/1991-92. Otago 1992-93 to date. Middlesex debut/cap 1995. **Tests** (NZ): 14 (1992-93 to 1995-96); HS 56 and BB 6-76 (11-169 match) v E (Lord's) 1994. **LOI** (NZ): 22 (1992-93 to 1995-96; HS 40*; BB 3-30). Tours (NZ): E 1994; SA 1994-95; I 1995-96; SL 1992-93; Z 1992-93. HS 67 v Essex (Chelmsford) 1995. 50 wkts (1): 52 (1995). BB 6-30 NZ Academy XI v ND (Rotorua) 1993-94. M BB 5-35 v Hants (Lord's) 1995. **NWT:** HS 4. BB 1-36. **BHC:** HS 54 v Comb Us (Lord's) 1995. BB 2-31 v Glos (Bristol) 1995. **SL:** HS 35 v Notts (Lord's) 1995. BB 3-34 v Glos (Bristol) 1995.

POOLEY, Jason Calvin (Acton HS), b Hammersmith 8 Aug 1969. 6'0". LHB, occ OB. Debut 1989. Cap 1995. Tour: I 1995-96 (Eng A). 1000 runs (1): 1335 (1995). HS 136 v Glos (Bristol) 1995. **NWT:** HS 33 v Northants (Uxbridge) 1994. **BHC:** HS 47 v Glos (Bristol) and v Kent (Canterbury) 1995. **SL:** HS 109 v Derbys (Lord's) 1991.

RAMPRAKASH, Mark Ravin (Gayton HS; Harrow Weald SFC), b Bushey, Herts 5 Sep 1969. 5'9". RHB, RM. Debut 1987. Cap 1990. YC 1991. **Tests:** 19 (1991 to 1995-96); HS 72 v A (Perth) 1994-95. **LOI**: 10 (1991 to 1995-96; HS 32). Tours: A 1994-95 (part); SA 1995-96; WI 1991-92 (Eng A), 1993-94; NZ 1991-92; I 1994-95 (Eng A); P 1990-91 (Eng A); SL 1990-91 (Eng A). 1000 runs (6) inc 2000 (1): 2258 (1995). HS 235 v Yorks (Leeds) 1995. BB 3-91 v Somerset (Taunton) 1995. Awards: NWT 1; BHC 3. **NWT:** HS 104 v Surrey (Uxbridge) 1990. BB 2-15 v Ire (Dublin) 1991. **BHC:** HS 119* v Northants (Lord's) 1994. **SL:** HS 147* v Worcs (Lord's) 1990. BB 5-38 v Leics (Lord's) 1993.

RASHID, Umer Bin Abdul (Ealing Green HS; Ealing Tertiary C; Southbank U), b Southampton, Hants 6 Feb 1976. 6'3". LHB, SLA. Awaiting f-c debut. **BHC** (Comb Us): HS 9. BB 1-52. **SL:** HS 8. BB 2-34 v Yorks (Leeds) 1995.

SHAH, Owais Alam (Isleworth & Syon S), b Karachi, Pakistan 22 Oct 1978. 6'0". RHB. Awaiting f-c debut. **SL:** HS 64 v Yorks (Leeds) 1995.

TUFNELL, Philip Clive Roderick (Highgate S), b Barnet, Herts 29 Apr 1966. 6'0". RHB, SLA. Debut 1986. Cap 1990. MCC YC. **Tests:** 22 (1990-91 to 1994-95); HS 22* v I (Madras) 1992-93; BB 7-47 (11-147 match) v NZ (Christchurch) 1991-92. **LOI:** 19 (1991 to 1994-95; HS 5*; BB 3-40). Tours: A 1990-91, 1994-95; WI 1993-94; NZ 1991-92; I/SL 1992-93. HS 37 v Leics (Leicester) and v Yorks (Leeds) 1990. 50 wkts (5); most – 88 (1991). BB 8-29 v Glam (Cardiff) 1993. Award: NWT 1. **NWT:** HS 8. BB 3-29 v Herts (Lord's) 1988. **BHC:** HS 18 v Warwks (Lord's) 1991. BB 3-32 v Northants (Lord's) 1994. **SL:** HS 13* v Glam (Merthyr Tydfil) 1989. BB 5-28 v Leics (Lord's) 1993.

WEEKES, Paul Nicholas (Homerton House SS, Hackney), b Hackney, London 8 Jul 1969. 5'10". LHB, OB. Debut 1990. Cap 1993. Tour: I 1994-95 (Eng A). MCC YC. HS 143 v OU (Oxford) 1995. BAC HS 127* v Northants (Uxbridge) 1995. BB 5-12 v CU (Cambridge) 1994. BAC BB 4-79 v Glam (Lord's) 1994. Awards: NWT 1; BHC 2. **NWT:** HS 143* v Cornwall (St Austell) 1995. BB 2-36 v Kent (Canterbury) 1993. **BHC:** HS 67* v Essex (Chelmsford) 1995. BB 3-32 v Warwks (Lord's) 1994. **SL:** HS 66* v Surrey (Lord's) 1993. BB 4-37 v Somerset (Lord's) 1992.

NEWCOMERS

BLANCHETT, Ian Neale, b Melbourne, Australia 2 Oct 1975. RHB, RFM.

EVANS, Matthew Robert, b Gravesend, Kent 27 Nov 1974. RHB, RFM.

GOODCHILD, David John (Weald C), b Harrow 17 Sep 1976. RHB, RM.

HEWITT, James Peter (Teddington S; Richmond C; City of Westminster C), b Southwark, London 26 Feb 1976. 6'2½". LHB, RMF. **SL:** HS 3 and BB 2-31 v Yorks (Leeds) 1995.

MOFFAT, Scott Park, b Germiston, SA 1 Feb 1973. RHB, OB.

WELLINGS, Peter Edward, b Wolverhampton, Staffs 5 Feb 1970. RHB, RM.

DEPARTURES (who made first-class appearances in 1995)

EMBUREY, J.E. – *see NORTHAMPTONSHIRE.*

FARBRACE, Paul (Geoffrey Chaucer S, Canterbury), b Ash, Kent 7 Jul 1967. 5'10". RHB, WK. Kent 1987-89. Middlesex 1990-95. HS 79 v CU (Cambridge) 1990. BAC HS 75* K v Yorks (Canterbury) 1987. BB 1-64. **NWT:** HS 17 v Berks (Lord's) 1990. **SL:** HS 26* v Lancs (Lord's) 1991.

MARC, Kervin (The London Oratory S; Central St Martin C of Art & Design), b Mon Repos, St Lucia 9 Jan 1975. 6'5". RHB, RFM. Debut 1994. MCC YC. HS 9 and BB 2-52 v Lancs (Manchester) 1994.

RADFORD, Toby Alexander (St Bartholomew's S, Newbury; Loughborough U), b Caerphilly, Glam 3 Dec 1971. 5'10". RHB, OB. Middlesex 1994-95. HS 69 v Essex (Chelmsford) 1995 – on BAC debut. BB 1-0. **NWT:** HS 82 v Surrey (Oval) 1995. **SL:** HS 38 v Worcs (Worcester) 1993.

SHINE, K.J. – *see SOMERSET.*

TAYLOR, Charles William (Spendlove S, Charlbury), b Banbury, Oxon 12 Aug 1966. 6'5½". LHB, LMF. Middlesex 1990-95. Oxfordshire 1986 and 1990. HS 28* v OU (Oxford) 1993. BAC HS 21 v Kent (Lord's) 1991. BB 5-33 v Yorks (Leeds) 1990. **NWT:** HS –. BB 1-54. **SL:** HS 3*. BB 2-33 v Northants (Lord's) 1993.

MIDDLESEX 1995

RESULTS SUMMARY

	Place	Won	Lost	Drew	No Result
Britannic Assurance Championship	**2nd**	12	2	3	–
All First-Class Matches		12	2	6	–
NatWest Trophy	Quarter-Finalist				
Benson and Hedges Cup	Quarter-Finalist				
Sunday League	**17th**	4	11	–	2

BRITANNIC ASSURANCE CHAMPIONSHIP AVERAGES

BATTING AND FIELDING

Cap		*M*	*I*	*NO*	*HS*	*Runs*	*Avge*	*100*	*50*	*Ct/St*
1990	M.R.Ramprakash	16	26	3	235	2147	93.34	10	6	10
1977	M.W.Gatting	16	22	1	148	1139	54.23	5	3	13
1995	J.C.Pooley	16	27	3	136	1181	49.20	4	6	25
1990	K.R.Brown	17	25	4	147*	894	42.57	1	6	43/5
1987	J.D.Carr	17	26	5	129	830	39.52	2	3	32
–	T.A.Radford	3	5	1	69	122	30.50	–	1	4
1993	P.N.Weekes	17	27	1	127*	771	29.65	1	5	15
1977	J.E.Emburey	16	19	1	87	379	21.05	–	1	17
1995	D.J.Nash	17	22	3	67	351	18.47	–	2	9
1995	M.A.Feltham	12	13	4	25	97	10.77	–	–	7
1995	R.L.Johnson	9	10	–	25	92	9.20	–	–	8
1990	P.C.R.Tufnell	16	14	6	23*	65	8.12	–	–	5
1988	A.R.C.Fraser	12	13	4	20	73	8.11	–	–	1

Also played (1 match each): R.A.Fay 1*; D.Follett 1, 4* (1 ct); A.A.Khan did not bat.

BOWLING

	O	*M*	*R*	*W*	*Avge*	*Best*	*5wI*	*10wM*
R.L.Johnson	222.5	58	596	36	16.55	5-48	2	1
J.E.Emburey	678.4	191	1619	74	21.87	7-82	5	2
P.C.R.Tufnell	638.1	199	1523	68	22.39	5-74	4	1
A.R.C.Fraser	404.2	104	1069	40	26.72	5-56	1	–
D.J.Nash	424.2	85	1388	51	27.21	5-35	2	–
M.A.Feltham	229.3	58	675	21	32.14	4-55	–	–
P.N.Weekes	172.4	36	449	10	44.90	3-26	–	–

Also bowled: K.R.Brown 15-0-114-1; R.A.Fay 3-0-25-0; D.Follett 30-6-95-1; M.W.Gatting 5-0-31-0; A.A.Khan 2-2-0-0; J.C.Pooley 4-0-15-0; M.R.Ramprakash 20-3-91-3.

The First-Class Averages (pp 129-143) give the records of Middlesex players in all first-class county matches (their other opponents being the West Indians, Cambridge University and Oxford University), with the exception of J.E.Emburey and A.R.C.Fraser, whose full county figures are as above, and:

M.R.Ramprakash 17-27-3-235-2157-89.87-10-6-10ct. 22.2-3-108-4-27.00-3/91.

MIDDLESEX RECORDS

FIRST-CLASS CRICKET

Highest Total	For	642-3d		v	Hampshire	Southampton	1923
	V	665		by	W Indians	Lord's	1939
Lowest Total	For	20		v	MCC	Lord's	1864
	V	31		by	Glos	Bristol	1924
Highest Innings	For	331*	J.D.B.Robertson	v	Worcs	Worcester	1949
	V	316*	J.B.Hobbs	for	Surrey	Lord's	1926

Highest Partnership for each Wicket

1st	367*	G.D.Barlow/W.N.Slack	v	Kent	Lord's	1981
2nd	380	F.A.Tarrant/J.W.Hearne	v	Lancashire	Lord's	1914
3rd	424*	W.J.Edrich/D.C.S.Compton	v	Somerset	Lord's	1948
4th	325	J.W.Hearne/E.H.Hendren	v	Hampshire	Lord's	1919
5th	338	R.S.Lucas/T.C.O'Brien	v	Sussex	Hove	1895
6th	270	J.D.Carr/P.N.Weekes	v	Glos	Lord's	1994
7th	271*	E.H.Hendren/F.T.Mann	v	Notts	Nottingham	1925
8th	182*	M.H.C.Doll/H.R.Murrell	v	Notts	Lord's	1913
9th	160*	E.H.Hendren/T.J.Durston	v	Essex	Leyton	1927
10th	230	R.W.Nicholls/W.Roche	v	Kent	Lord's	1899

Best Bowling	For	10- 40	G.O.B.Allen	v	Lancashire	Lord's	1929
(Innings)	V	9- 38	R.C.Glasgow†	for	Somerset	Lord's	1924
Best Bowling	For	16-114	G.Burton	v	Yorkshire	Sheffield	1888
(Match)		16-114	J.T.Hearne	v	Lancashire	Manchester	1898
	V	16-109	C.W.L.Parker	for	Glos	Cheltenham	1930

Most Runs – Season	2669	E.H.Hendren	(av 83.41)	1923
Most Runs – Career	40302	E.H.Hendren	(av 48.81)	1907-37
Most 100s – Season	13	D.C.S.Compton		1947
Most 100s – Career	119	E.H.Hendren		1907-37
Most Wkts – Season	158	F.J.Titmus	(av 14.63)	1955
Most Wkts – Career	2361	F.J.Titmus	(av 21.27)	1949-82

LIMITED-OVERS CRICKET

Highest Total	NWT	304-7		v	Surrey	The Oval	1995
	BHC	304-8		v	Cornwall	St Austell	1995
	SL	290-6		v	Worcs	Lord's	1990
Lowest Total	NWT	41		v	Essex	Westcliff	1972
	BHC	73		v	Essex	Lord's	1985
	SL	23		v	Yorkshire	Leeds	1974
Highest Innings	NWT	158	G.D.Barlow	v	Lancashire	Lord's	1984
	BHC	143*	M.W.Gatting	v	Sussex	Hove	1985
	SL	147*	M.R.Ramprakash	v	Worcs	Lord's	1990
Best Bowling	NWT	6-15	W.W.Daniel	v	Sussex	Hove	1980
	BHC	7-12	W.W.Daniel	v	Minor C (E)	Ipswich	1978
	SL	6- 6	R.W.Hooker	v	Surrey	Lord's	1969

† R.C.Robertson-Glasgow

NORTHAMPTONSHIRE

Formation of Present Club: 31 July 1878
Colours: Maroon
Badge: Tudor Rose
Championships: (0) Second 1912, 1957, 1965, 1976
NatWest Trophy/Gillette Cup Winners: (2) 1976, 1992
Benson and Hedges Cup Winners: (1) 1980
Sunday League Champions: (0) Third 1991
Match Awards: NWT 49; BHC 44

Chief Executive: S.P.Coverdale
County Cricket Ground, Wantage Road, Northampton, NN1 4TJ (Tel 01604 32917)
Captain: R.J.Bailey
Scorer: A.C.Kingston
1996 Beneficiary: A.J.Lamb (Testimonial)

AMBROSE, Curtly Elconn Lynwall (All Saints Village SS), b Swetes Village, Antigua 21 Sep 1963. Cousin of R.M.Otto (Leeward Is 1979-80/1990-91). 6'7". LHB, RF. Leeward Is 1985-86 to date. Northamptonshire 1989-94 (cap 1990). *Wisden* 1991. **Tests** (WI): 59 (1987-88 to 1995); HS 53 v A (P-of-S) 1990-91; BB 8-45 v E (Bridgetown) 1989-90. **LOI** (WI): 122 (1987-88 to 1995-96; HS 26*; BB 5-17). Tours (WI): E 1988, 1991, 1995; A 1988-89, 1992-93; NZ 1994-95; P 1990-91; SL 1993-94. HS 78 v Somerset (Taunton) 1994. 50 wkts (5+1); most – 77 (1994). BB 8-45 (*see Tests*). Nh BB 7-44 v Hants (Southampton) 1994. Award: NWT 1. **NWT:** HS 48 v Lancs (Lord's) 1990. BB 4-7 v Yorks (Northampton) 1992. **BHC:** HS 17* v Kent (Northampton) 1989. BB 4-31 v Essex (Northampton) 1992. **SL:** HS 37 v Notts (Nottingham) 1994. BB 4-20 v Lancs (Northampton) and v Kent (Northampton) 1994.

BAILEY, Robert John (Biddulph HS), b Biddulph, Staffs 28 Oct 1963. 6'3". RHB, OB. Debut 1982. Cap 1985. Benefit 1993. Captain 1996. Staffordshire 1980. YC 1984. **Tests:** 4 (1988 to 1989-90); HS 43 v WI (Oval) 1988. **LOI**: 4 (1984-85 to 1989-90; HS 43*). Tours: SA 1991-92 (Nh); WI 1989-90; Z 1994-95 (Nh). 1000 runs (12); most – 1987 (1990). HS 224* v Glam (Swansea) 1986. BB 5-54 v Notts (Northampton) 1993. Awards: NWT 7; BHC 6. **NWT:** HS 145 v Staffs (Stone) 1991. BB 3-47 v Notts (Northampton) 1990. **BHC:** HS 134 v Glos (Northampton) 1987. BB 1-22. **SL:** HS 125* v Derbys (Derby) 1987. BB 3-23 v Leics (Leicester) 1987.

BOSWELL, Scott Antony John (Pocklington S; Wolverhampton U), b Fulford, Yorks 11 Sep 1974. 6'5". RHB, RFM. Northamptonshire staff 1995 – awaiting f-c debut. **BHC:** HS –. BB 1-6. **SL:** HS 2. BB 1-20.

BROWN, Jason Fred (St Margaret Ward HS & SFC), b Newcastle-under-Lyme, Staffs 10 Oct 1974. 6'0". RHB, OB. Staffordshire 1994. Northamptonshire staff 1995 – awaiting f-c debut.

CAPEL, David John (Roade CS), b Northampton 6 Feb 1963. 5'11". RHB, RMF. Debut 1981. Cap 1986. Benefit 1994. E Province 1985-86/1986-87. **Tests:** 15 (1987 to 1989-90); HS 98 v P (Karachi) 1987-88; BB 3-88 v WI (Bridgetown) 1989-90. **LOI**: 23 (1986-87 to 1989-90; HS 50*; BB 3-38). Tours: A 1987-88, 1992-93 (Eng A); WI 1989-90; NZ 1987-88; P 1987-88. 1000 runs (3); most – 1311 (1989). HS 175 v Leics (Northampton) 1995. 50 wkts (4); most – 63 (1986). BB 7-44 v Warwks (Birmingham) 1995. Awards: NWT 3. **NWT:** HS 101 v Notts (Northampton) 1990. BB 3-21 v Glam (Swansea) 1992. **BHC:** HS 97 v Yorks (Lord's) 1987. BB 4-29 v Warwks (Birmingham) 1986. **SL:** HS 121 v Glam (Northampton) 1990. BB 4-30 v Yorks (Middlesbrough) 1982.

CURRAN, Kevin Malcolm (Marandellas HS), b Rusape, S Rhodesia 7 Sep 1959. Son of K.P. (Rhodesia 1947-48/1953-54). 6'1". RHB, RMF. Zimbabwe 1980-81/1987-88. Qualified for England 1994. Natal 1988-89. Gloucestershire 1985-90 (cap 1985).

CURRAN – continued:
Northamptonshire debut 1991. Cap 1992. Boland 1994-95. **LOI** (Z): 11 (1983 to 1987-88; HS 73; BB 3-65). Tours (Z): E 1982; SL 1983-84. 1000 runs (5); most – 1353 (1986). HS 144* Gs v Sussex (Bristol) 1990. Nh HS 117 v Surrey (Northampton) 1995. 50 wkts (5); most – 67 (1993). BB 7-47 Natal v Transvaal (Johannesburg) 1988-89 and v Yorks (Harrogate) 1993. Awards: NWT 2; BHC 2. **NWT:** HS 78* v Cambs (Northampton) 1992. BB 4-34 Gs v Northants (Bristol) 1985. **BHC:** HS 57 Gs v Derbys (Derby) 1987. BB 4-38 v Worcs (Northampton) 1995. **SL:** HS 119* v Kent (Canterbury) 1990. BB 5-15 Gs v Leics (Gloucester) 1988.

FORDHAM, Alan (Bedford Modern S; Durham U), b Bedford 9 Nov 1964. 6'1". RHB, RM. Debut 1986. Cap 1990. Bedfordshire 1982-85. Tours (Nh): SA 1991-92; Z 1994-95. 1000 runs (5); most – 1840 (1991). HS 206* v Yorks (Leeds) 1990. BB 1-0. Awards: NWT 4; BHC 3. **NWT:** HS 132* v Leics (Northampton) 1991. BB 1-3. **BHC:** HS 108 v Scot (Northampton) 1995. **SL:** HS 111 v Durham (Hartlepool) 1994.

HUGHES, John Gareth (Sir Christopher Hatton SS, Wellingborough; Sheffield City Poly), b Wellingborough 3 May 1971. 6'1". RHB, RM. Debut 1990. Tours (Nh): SA 1991-92; Z 1994-95. HS 17 and BB 5-69 v Hants (Southampton) 1994. **BHC:** HS 9. BB 2-47 v Derbys (Derby) 1995. **SL:** HS 21 v Kent (Canterbury) 1993. BB 2-39 v Derbys (Northampton) 1995.

INNES, Kevin John (Weston Favell Upper S), b Wellingborough 24 Sep 1975. 5'10". RHB, RM. 2nd XI debut 1990 (aged 14yr 8m – Northamptonshire record). Debut 1994. HS 0. **BHC:** HS 1. BB 1-25. **SL:** HS 5. BB 1-35.

LAMB, Allan Joseph (Wynberg HS; Abbotts C) b Langebaanweg, Cape Province, SA 20 Jun 1954. 5'8". RHB, RM. W Province 1972-73/1981-82 and 1992-93. OFS 1987-88. Northamptonshire debut/cap 1978. Captain 1989-95. Benefit 1988. Testimonial 1996. *Wisden* 1980. **Tests:** 79 (1982 to 1992, 3 as captain); HS 142 v NZ (Wellington) 1991-92; BB 1-6. **LOI**: 122 (1982 to 1992; HS 118). Tours: A 1982-83, 1986-87, 1990-91; WI 1985-86, 1989-90; NZ 1983-84, 1991-92; I/SL 1984-85; P 1983-84; Z 1994-95 (Nh – captain). 1000 runs (13) inc 2000 (1): 2049 (1981). HS 294 OFS v E Province (Bloemfontein) 1987-88 – sharing record SA 5th wkt stand of 355 with J.J.Strydom. Nh HS 235 v Yorks (Leeds) 1990. BB 2-29 v Lancs (Lytham) 1991. Awards: NWT 4; BHC 9. **NWT:** HS 129* v Middx (Uxbridge) 1994. BB 1-4. **BHC:** HS 126* v Kent (Canterbury) 1987. BB 1-11. **SL:** HS 132* v Surrey (Guildford) 1985.

LOYE, Malachy Bernhard (Moulton S), b Northampton 27 Sep 1972. 6'2". RHB, OB. Debut 1991. Cap 1994. Tours: SA 1993-94 (Eng A); Z 1994-95 (Nh). HS 153* v Kent (Canterbury) 1993. **NWT:** HS 65 v Essex (Chelmsford) 1993. **BHC:** HS 68* v Middx (Lord's) 1994. **SL:** HS 122 v Somerset (Luton) 1993.

MALLENDER, Neil Alan (Beverley GS), b Kirk Sandall, Yorks 13 Aug 1961. 6'0". RHB, RFM. Northamptonshire 1980-86 (cap 1984). Somerset 1987-94 (Cap 1987; benefit 1994). Otago 1983-84/1992-93 (captain 1990-91/1992-93). **Tests:** 2 (1992); HS 4; BB 5-50 v P (Leeds) 1992 – on debut. Tour: Z 1994-95 (Nh). HS 100* Otago v CD (Palmerston N) 1991-92. BAC HS 87* Sm v Sussex (Hove) 1990. Nh HS 71* v OU (Oxford) 1983. 50 wkts (6); most – 56 (1983). BB 7-27 Otago v Auckland (Auckland) 1984-85. BB 7-41 v Derbys (Northampton) 1982. Award: NWT 1. **NWT:** HS 11* (twice). BB 7-37 v Worcs (Northampton) 1984. **BHC:** HS 16* Sm v Hants (Taunton) 1988. BB 5-53 v Leics (Northampton) 1986. **SL:** HS 31* Sm v Durham (Hartlepool) 1993. BB 5-34 v Middx (Tring) 1981.

MONTGOMERIE, Richard Robert (Rugby S; Worcester C, Oxford), b Rugby, Warwks 3 Jul 1971. 5'10½". RHB, OB. Oxford U 1991-94 (blue 1991-92-93-94; captain 1994). Northamptonshire debut 1991. Cap 1995. Tour: Z 1994-95 (Nh). 1000 runs (1): 1062 (1994). HS 192 v Kent (Canterbury) 1995. **NWT:** HS 109 v Notts (Nottingham) 1995. **BHC:** HS 75 Comb Us v Worcs (Oxford) 1992. **SL:** HS 74 v Somerset (Taunton) 1994. Half blues for rackets and real tennis.

PENBERTHY, Anthony Leonard (Camborne CS), b Troon, Cornwall 1 Sep 1969. 6'1". LHB, RM. Debut 1989. Cap 1994. Cornwall 1987-89. Tours (Nh): SA 1991-92; Z 1994-95 (Nh). HS 101* v CU (Cambridge) 1990. BAC HS 88* v Somerset (Taunton) 1994. BB 5-37 v Glam (Swansea) 1993. Dismissed M.A.Taylor with his first ball in f-c cricket. **NWT:** HS 41* v Essex (Chelmsford) 1993. BB 2-29 v Glam (Swansea) 1992. **BHC:** HS 26 and BB 3-39 v Yorks (Leeds) 1995. **SL:** HS 69* v Glam (Northampton) 1994. BB 5-36 v Glos (Northampton) 1993.

RIPLEY, David (Royds SS, Leeds), b Leeds, Yorks 13 Sep 1966. 5'9". RHB, WK. Debut 1984. Cap 1987. Benefit 1997. Tours (Nh): SA 1991-92; Z 1994-95. HS 134* v Yorks (Scarborough) 1986. BB 2-89 v Essex (Ilford) 1987. Award: BHC 1. **NWT:** HS 27* v Durham (Darlington) 1984. **BHC:** HS 36* v Glos (Bristol) 1991. **SL:** HS 52* v Surrey (Northampton) 1993.

ROBERTS, Andrew Richard (Bishop Stopford CS, Kettering), b Kettering 16 Apr 1971. 5'6". RHB, LB. Debut 1989. Tour: SA 1991-92 (Nh). HS 62 v Notts (Nottingham) 1992. BB 6-72 v Lancs (Lytham) 1991. **NWT:** HS –. BB 1-23. **SL:** HS 20 v Essex (Chelmsford) 1994. BB 3-26 v Hants (Northampton) 1991.

ROBERTS, David James (Mullion CS), b Truro, Cornwall 29 Dec 1976. Cousin of C.K.Bullen (Surrey 1982-91). 5'11". RHB, RSM. Northamptonshire staff 1994 – awaiting f-c debut.

SALES, David John Grimwood (Caterham S), b Carshalton, Surrey 3 Dec 1977. 6'0". RHB, RM. Northamptonshire staff 1995 – awaiting f-c debut. **SL:** HS 70* (off 56 balls) v Essex (Chelmsford) 1994, when 16yr 289d (youngest to score SL fifty). Soccer for Wimbledon and Crystal Palace.

SNAPE, Jeremy Nicholas (Denstone C; Durham U), b Stoke-on-Trent, Staffs 27 Apr 1973. 5'8½". RHB, OB. Debut 1992. Combined Us 1994. Tour: Z 1994-95 (Nh). HS 87 v Mashonaland Select XI (Harare) 1994-95. UK HS 55 v Glam (Cardiff) 1995. BB 5-65 v Durham (Northampton) 1995. Award: BHC 1. **NWT:** HS 21 v Warwks (Lord's) 1995. BB 2-44 v Glos (Bristol) 1995. **BHC:** HS 52 Comb Us v Hants (Southampton) 1993. BB 3-35 Comb Us v Worcs (Oxford) 1992. **SL:** HS 31* v Leics (Leicester) 1994. BB 3-25 v Essex (Northampton) 1993.

STEELE, Mark Vincent (Wellingborough S), b Kettering 13 Nov 1976. Son of D.S. (Northants, Derbys and England 1963-81); nephew of J.F. (Leics, Natal and Glamorgan 1970-86). 6'0". LHB, RMF. Northamptonshire staff 1995 – awaiting f-c debut.

SWANN, Alec James (Sponne S, Towcester), b Northampton 26 Oct 1976. 6'1". RHB, OB. Bedfordshire 1994. Northamptonshire staff 1995 – awaiting f-c debut.

TAYLOR, Jonathan Paul (Pingle S, Swadlincote), b Ashby-de-la-Zouch, Leics 8 Aug 1964. 6'2". LHB, LFM. Derbyshire 1984-86. Northamptonshire debut 1991. Cap 1992. Staffordshire 1989-90 (cap 1989). **Tests:** 2 (1992-93 to 1994); HS 17* v I (Calcutta) 1992-93. BB 1-18. **LOI:** 1 (1992-93; HS 1). Tours: SA 1993-94 (Eng A – part); I 1992-93; Z 1994-95 (Nh). HS 86 v Durham (Northampton) 1995. 50 wkts (3); most – 69 (1993). BB 7-23 v Hants (Bournemouth) 1992. **NWT:** HS 9. BB 4-34 v Glos (Bristol) 1995. **BHC:** HS 7*. BB 3-38 v Lancs (Northampton) 1992. **SL:** HS 24 v Worcs (Northampton) 1993. BB 3-14 De v Glos (Gloucester) 1986.

WALTON, Timothy Charles (Leeds GS; Newcastle upon Tyne Poly), b Low Head, Yorks 8 Nov 1972. 6'0½". RHB, RM. Debut 1994. HS 71 v Somerset (Northampton) 1995. BB 1-46. **BHC:** HS 29 and BB 1-27 v Scot (Northampton) 1995. **SL:** HS 72 v Glos (Bristol) 1994. BB 2-27 v Leics (Leicester) 1992.

WARREN, Russell John (Kingsthorpe Upper S), b Northampton 10 Sep 1971. 6'1". RHB, OB. Debut 1992. Cap 1995. HS 154 v Notts (Northampton) 1995. Award: NWT 1. **NWT:** HS 100* v Ire (Northampton) 1994. **BHC:** HS 23 v Derbys (Derby) 1995. **SL:** HS 71* v Leics (Northampton) 1993.

NEWCOMERS and DEPARTURES – see p 113

NORTHAMPTONSHIRE 1995

RESULTS SUMMARY

	Place	Won	Lost	Tied	Drew	No Result
Britannic Assurance Championship	3rd	12	2	–	3	–
All First-Class Matches		12	2	–	4	–
NatWest Trophy	Finalist					
Benson and Hedges Cup	4th in Group B					
Sunday League	13th	6	8	1	–	2

BRITANNIC ASSURANCE CHAMPIONSHIP AVERAGES

BATTING AND FIELDING

Cap		M	I	NO	HS	Runs	Avge	100	50	Ct/St
1978	A.J.Lamb	16	26	4	166	1237	56.22	3	6	15
1995	R.J.Warren	15	26	5	154	877	41.76	1	5	27/1
1985	R.J.Bailey	17	29	3	157	1008	38.76	4	2	20
1986	D.J.Capel	17	26	3	175	885	38.47	3	3	11
1990	A.Fordham	15	28	1	130	1025	37.96	4	4	14
1992	K.M.Curran	17	27	3	117	863	35.95	1	4	22
1987	D.Ripley	5	4	1	40	87	29.00	–	–	7/2
–	J.N.Snape	12	15	3	55	344	28.66	–	2	16
1995	R.R.Montgomerie	13	23	1	192	605	27.50	1	2	27
1992	J.P.Taylor	17	20	8	86	277	23.08	–	2	6
–	T.C.Walton	3	6	1	71	104	20.80	–	1	–
1995	A.Kumble	17	21	5	40*	321	20.06	–	–	11
1994	M.B.Loye	7	10	1	51*	134	14.88	–	1	2
1994	A.L.Penberthy	3	5	1	35	42	10.50	–	–	1
1984	N.A.Mallender	6	9	2	18	72	10.28	–	–	1
–	J.G.Hughes	5	6	1	16	32	6.40	–	–	–

Also batted (1 match each): C.S.Atkins 5, 8*; A.R.Roberts 11, 10.

BOWLING

	O	M	R	W	Avge	Best	5wI	10wM
A.Kumble	899.4	265	2143	105	20.40	7-82	8	2
N.A.Mallender	130.2	29	382	17	22.47	4-49	–	–
D.J.Capel	338.2	68	1129	47	24.02	7-44	2	–
J.P.Taylor	558.4	118	1685	57	29.56	7-50	2	–
K.M.Curran	357.1	84	1202	37	32.48	4-78	–	–
J.N.Snape	212	47	681	19	35.84	5-65	1	–

Also bowled: C.S.Atkins 11-4-46-1; R.J.Bailey 106.3-20-376-7; A.Fordham 6-0-51-0; J.G.Hughes 90-15-320-7; A.L.Penberthy 41-6-141-4; A.R.Roberts 11-2-45-0.

The First-Class Averages (pp 129-143) give the records of Northamptonshire players in all first-class county matches (their other opponents being the West Indians), with the exception of:

D.J.Capel 18-27-3-175-897-37.37-3-3-11ct. 349.2-69-1166-48-24.29-7/44-2-0.

NORTHAMPTONSHIRE RECORDS

FIRST-CLASS CRICKET

Highest Total	For	781-7d		v	Notts	Northampton	1995
	V	670-9d		by	Sussex	Hove	1921
Lowest Total	For	12		v	Glos	Gloucester	1907
	V	33		by	Lancashire	Northampton	1977
Highest Innings	For	300	R.Subba Row	v	Surrey	The Oval	1958
	V	333	K.S.Duleepsinhji	for	Sussex	Hove	1930

Highest Partnership for each Wicket

1st	361	N.Oldfield/V.Broderick	v	Scotland	Peterborough	1953
2nd	344	G.Cook/R.J.Boyd-Moss	v	Lancashire	Northampton	1986
3rd	393	A.Fordham/A.J.Lamb	v	Yorkshire	Leeds	1990
4th	370	R.T.Virgin/P.Willey	v	Somerset	Northampton	1976
5th	347	D.Brookes/D.W.Barrick	v	Essex	Northampton	1952
6th	376	R.Subba Row/A.Lightfoot	v	Surrey	The Oval	1958
7th	229	W.W.Timms/F.A.Walden	v	Warwicks	Northampton	1926
8th	164	D.Ripley/N.G.B.Cook	v	Lancashire	Manchester	1987
9th	156	R.Subba Row/S.Starkie	v	Lancashire	Northampton	1955
10th	148	B.W.Bellamy/J.V.Murdin	v	Glamorgan	Northampton	1925

Best Bowling	For	10-127	V.W.C.Jupp	v	Kent	Tunbridge W	1932
(Innings)	V	10- 30	C.Blythe	for	Kent	Northampton	1907
Best Bowling	For	15- 31	G.E.Tribe	v	Yorkshire	Northampton	1958
(Match)	V	17- 48	C.Blythe	for	Kent	Northampton	1907

Most Runs – Season	2198	D.Brookes	(av 51.11)	1952
Most Runs – Career	28980	D.Brookes	(av 36.13)	1934-59
Most 100s – Season	8	R.A.Haywood		1921
Most 100s – Career	67	D.Brookes		1934-59
Most Wkts – Season	175	G.E.Tribe	(av 18.70)	1955
Most Wkts – Career	1097	E.W.Clark	(av 21.31)	1922-47

LIMITED-OVERS CRICKET

Highest Total	**NWT**	360-2		v	Staffs	Northampton	1990
	BHC	304-6		v	Scotland	Northampton	1995
	SL	306-2		v	Surrey	Guildford	1985
Lowest Total	**NWT**	62		v	Leics	Leicester	1974
	BHC	85		v	Sussex	Northampton	1978
	SL	41		v	Middlesex	Northampton	1972
Highest Innings	**NWT**	145	R.J.Bailey	v	Staffs	Stone	1991
	BHC	134	R.J.Bailey	v	Glos	Northampton	1987
	SL	172*	W.Larkins	v	Warwicks	Luton	1983
Best Bowling	**NWT**	7-37	N.A.Mallender	v	Worcs	Northampton	1984
	BHC	5-21	Sarfraz Nawaz	v	Middlesex	Lord's	1980
	SL	7-39	A.Hodgson	v	Somerset	Northampton	1976

NOTTINGHAMSHIRE

Formation of Present Club: March/April 1841
Substantial Reorganisation: 11 December 1866
Colours: Green and Gold
Badge: Badge of City of Nottingham
Championships (since 1890): (4) 1907, 1929, 1981, 1987
NatWest Trophy/Gillette Cup Winners: (1) 1987
Benson and Hedges Cup Winners: (1) 1989
Sunday League Champions: (1) 1991
Match Awards: NWT 37; BHC 61

Secretary/General Manager: B.Robson
Trent Bridge, Nottingham NG2 6AG (Tel 0115 982 1525)
Captain: P.Johnson
Scorer: G.Stringfellow
1996 Beneficiary: R.A.Pick

AFFORD, John Andrew (Spalding GS; Stamford CFE), b Crowland, Lincs 12 May 1964. 6'1½". RHB, SLA. Debut 1984. Cap 1990. Tour: Z 1989-90 (Eng A). HS 22* v Leics (Nottingham) 1989. 50 wkts (4); most – 57 (1991, 1993). BB 6-68 (10-185 match) v Sussex (Nottingham) 1992. Award: BHC 1. **NWT:** HS 2*. BB 3-32 v Herts (Hitchin) 1989. **BHC:** HS 1*. BB 4-38 v Kent (Nottingham) 1989. **SL:** HS 1. BB 3-33 v Northants (Northampton) 1993.

AFZAAL, Usman (Manvers Pierrepont CS; S Notts C), b Rawalpindi, Pakistan 9 Jun 1977. 6'0". LHB, SLA. Debut 1995. HS 37 and BB 2-41 v Yorks (Nottingham) 1995. **NWT:** HS 26* v Northants (Nottingham) 1995. **SL:** HS 2. BB 2-25 v Yorks (Cleethorpes) 1995.

ARCHER, Graeme Francis (Heron Brook Middle S; King Edward VI HS, Stafford), b Carlisle, Cumberland 26 Sep 1970. 6'1". RHB, OB. Debut 1992. Cap 1995. Staffordshire 1990. 1000 runs (1): 1171 (1995). HS 168 v Glam (Worksop) 1994. BB 3-50 v Durham (Chester-le-St) 1995. **NWT:** HS 39 v Cheshire (Warrington) 1993. **BHC:** HS 74 v Lancs (Manchester) 1995. **SL:** HS 53 v Hants (Nottingham) 1995. BB 2-16 v Surrey (Guildford) 1995.

BATES, Richard Terry (Bourne GS; Stamford CFE), b Stamford, Lincs 17 Jun 1972. 6'1". RHB, OB. Lincolnshire 1990-91. Debut 1993. HS 33* v OU (Oxford) 1993. BAC HS 18* v Glos (Bristol) 1993. BB 5-88 v Durham (Chester-le-St) 1995. **SL:** HS 16 v Worcs (Worcester) 1994. BB 3-43 v Derbys (Nottingham) 1993.

BROADHURST, Mark (Kingstone S, Barnsley) , b Worsborough Common, Barnsley, Yorks 20 Jun 1974. 6'0". RHB, RFM. Yorkshire 1991-94. Tour: SA 1992-93 (Y). Awaiting BAC debut. HS 6. BB 3-61 Y v OU (Oxford) 1991. **SL:** HS – .

CAIRNS, Christopher Lance (Christchurch BHS), b Picton, NZ 13 Jun 1970. Son of B.L. (CD, Otago, ND and NZ 1971-86). 6'2". RHB, RFM. Nottinghamshire 1988-89, 1992-93 and 1995 (cap 1993). N Districts 1988-89. Canterbury 1990-91 to date. **Tests** (NZ): 16 (1989-90 to 1995-96); HS 120 v Z (Auckland) 1995-96; BB 6-52 v E (Auckland) 1991-92. **LOI** (NZ): 38 (1990-91 to 1995-96; HS 103; BB 4-55). Tours (NZ): A 1989-90, 1993-94; I 1995-96. 1000 runs (1): 1171 (1995). HS 115 v Middx (Lord's) 1995. 50 wkts (3); most – 56 (1992). BB 8-47 (15-83 match) v Sussex (Arundel) 1995. Awards: NWT 2; BHC 1. **NWT:** HS 77 v Glam (Nottingham) 1992. BB 4-18 v Cheshire (Warrington) 1993. **BHC:** HS 46 and BB 4-47 v Durham (Stockton) 1995. **SL:** HS 126* v Surrey (Oval) 1993. BB 6-52 v Kent (Nottingham) 1993.

CHAPMAN, Robert James (Farnborough CS; S Notts CFE), b Nottingham 28 Jul 1972. Son of footballer R.O. ('Sammy') (Nottingham Forest, Notts County and Shrewsbury Town). 6'1". RHB, RFM. Debut 1992. HS 25 v Lancs (Nottingham) 1994. BB 3-119 v Surrey (Guildford) 1995. **NWT:** HS – . **SL:** HS 4*. BB 2-36 v Kent (Nottingham) 1995.

DOWMAN, Mathew Peter (St Hugh's CS; Grantham C), b Grantham, Lincs 10 May 1974. 5'10". LHB, RMF. Debut 1994. Scored 267 for England YC v WI YC (Hove) 1993 – record score in youth 'Tests'. HS 107 v OU (Oxford) 1995. BAC HS 73 v Essex (Nottingham) 1995. **BHC:** HS 6. **SL:** HS 52* v Glam (Nottingham) 1994. BB 1-33.

EVANS, Kevin Paul (Colonel Frank Seely S) b Calverton 10 Sep 1963. Elder brother of R.J. (Notts 1987-90). 6'2". RHB, RMF. Debut 1984. Cap 1990. HS 104 v Surrey (Nottingham) 1992 and v Sussex (Nottingham) 1994. BB 6-67 v Yorks (Nottingham) 1993. Awards: BHC 2. **NWT:** HS 21 v Worcs (Worcester) 1994. BB 6-10 v Northumb (Jesmond) 1994. **BHC:** HS 47 v Lancs (Manchester) 1995. BB 4-19 v Minor C (Leek) 1995. **SL:** HS 30 v Kent (Canterbury) 1990 and v Hants (Southampton) 1992. BB 4-26 v Kent (Canterbury) 1994.

GIE, Noel Addison (Trent C), b Pretoria, SA 12 Apr 1977. UK resident since 1984. Son of C.A. (WP and SAU 1970-71 to 1980-81). 6'0". RHB, RM. Debut 1995. HS 34 v Glam (Cardiff) 1995.

HART, Jamie Paul (Millfield S), b Blackpool, Lancs 31 Dec 1975. Son of P. (Nottingham Forest footballer). 6'3". RHB, RM. Awaiting f-c debut. **SL:** HS –. BB 1-48.

HINDSON, James Edward (Toot Hill CS, Bingham), b Huddersfield, Yorks 13 Sep 1973. 6'1". RHB, SLA. Debut 1992. HS 53* v OU (Oxford) 1995. BAC HS 47 v Kent (Nottingham) 1995. 50 wkts (1): 65 (1995). BB 5-42 v CU (Nottingham) 1992. BAC BB 5-53 v Glam (Worksop) 1994. **NWT:** HS 16* and BB 2-57 v Northants (Nottingham) 1995. **BHC:** HS 41* and BB 1-69 v Lancs (Manchester) 1995. **SL:** HS 21 v Middx (Nottingham) 1994. BB 4-19 v Worcs (Worcester) 1994.

JOHNSON, Paul (Grove CS, Balderton), b Newark 24 Apr 1965. 5'7". RHB, RM. Debut 1982. Cap 1986. Benefit 1995. Captain 1996. Tour: WI 1991-92 (Eng A). 1000 runs (8); most – 1518 (1990). HS 187 v Lancs (Manchester) 1993. BB 1-9. BAC BB 1-14. Awards: NWT 2; BHC 3. **NWT:** HS 146 v Northumb (Jesmond) 1994. **BHC:** HS 104* v Essex (Chelmsford) 1990. **SL:** HS 167* v Kent (Nottingham) 1993.

MIKE, Gregory Wentworth (Claremont CS; Basford Hall C), b Nottingham 14 Jul 1966. 6'0". RHB, RMF. Debut 1989. HS 66* v OU (Oxford) 1995. BAC HS 61* v Warwks (Birmingham) 1992. BB 5-44 v Yorks (Middlesbrough) 1994. **NWT:** HS 5*. BB 1-71. **BHC:** HS 29 v Kent (Nottingham) 1989. BB 4-44 v Somerset (Nottingham) 1993. **SL:** HS 51* v Middx (Lord's) 1993. BB 4-41 v Northants (Nottingham) 1994.

NEWELL, Michael (West Bridgford CS), b Blackburn, Lancs 25 Feb 1965. 5'8". RHB, LB. Debut 1984. Cap 1987. 1000 runs (1): 1054 (1987). HS 203* v Derbys (Derby) 1987. BB 2-38 v SL (Nottingham) 1988. BAC BB 1-0. **NWT:** HS 60 v Derbys (Derby) 1987. **BHC:** HS 39 v Somerset (Taunton) 1989. **SL:** HS 109* v Essex (Southend) 1990.

NOON, Wayne Michael (Caistor S), b Grimsby, Lincs 5 Feb 1971. 5'9". RHB, WK. Northamptonshire 1989-93. Nottinghamshire debut 1994. Cap 1995. Canterbury 1994-95. Worcs 2nd XI debut when aged 15yr 199d. Tour: SA 1991-92 (Nh). HS 75 v Northants (Nottingham) 1994. **NWT:** HS 34 v Worcs (Worcester) 1994. **BHC:** HS 23 v Warwks (Nottingham) 1995. **SL:** HS 38 v Durham (Chester-le-St) 1995.

PENNETT, David Barrington (Benton Park GS, Rawdon), b Leeds, Yorks 26 Oct 1969. 6'0". RHB, RMF. Debut 1992. HS 50 v Durham (Chester-le-St) 1995. BB 5-36 v Durham (Chester-le-St) 1993. **NWT:** HS –. BB 1-22. **SL:** HS 12* v Durham (Nottingham) 1992. BB 3-27 v Worcs (Nottingham) 1995.

PICK, Robert **Andrew** (Alderman Derbyshire CS; High Pavement SFC), b Nottingham 19 Nov 1963. 5'10". LHB, RFM. Debut 1983. Cap 1987. Benefit 1996. Wellington 1989-90. Tours: WI 1991-92 (Eng A); SL 1990-91 (Eng A). HS 65* v Northants (Nottingham) 1994. 50 wkts (5); most – 67 (1991). BB 7-128 v Leics (Leicester) 1990. Awards: NWT 2; BHC 1. **NWT:** HS 34* v Sussex (Hove) 1983. BB 5-22 v Glos (Bristol) 1987. **BHC:** HS 25* v Hants (Southampton) 1991. BB 4-42 v Northants (Nottingham) 1987. **SL:** HS 58* v Essex (Nottingham) 1995. BB 4-32 v Glos (Moreton) 1987.

POLLARD, Paul Raymond (Gedling CS), b Carlton, Nottingham 24 Sep 1968. 5'11". LHB, RM. Debut 1987. Cap 1992. 1000 runs (3); most – 1463 (1993). HS 180 v Derbys (Nottingham) 1993. BB 2-79 v Glos (Bristol) 1993. **NWT:** HS 96 v Northants (Nottingham) 1995. **BHC:** HS 104 v Surrey (Nottingham) 1994. **SL:** HS 132* v Somerset (Nottingham) 1995.

RICHES, Ian (Ancaster HS, Lincoln; Luton U), b Lincoln 12 Sep 1975. 6'2". RHB, LFM. Summer contract – awaiting f-c debut. **SL:** HS –.

ROBINSON, Robert Timothy (Dunstable GS; High Pavement SFC; Sheffield U), b Sutton in Ashfield 21 Nov 1958. 6'0". RHB, RM. Debut 1978. Cap 1983. Captain 1988-95. Benefit 1992. *Wisden* 1985. **Tests:** 29 (1984-85 to 1988); HS 175 v A (Leeds) 1985. **LOI:** 26 (1984-85 to 1988; HS 83). Tours: A 1987-88; SA 1989-90 (Eng XI); NZ 1987-88; WI 1985-86; I/SL 1984-85; P 1987-88. 1000 runs (13) inc 2000 (1): 2032 (1984). HS 220* v Yorks (Nottingham) 1990. BB 1-22. Awards: NWT 4; BHC 7. **NWT:** HS 139 v Worcs (Worcester) 1985. **BHC:** HS 120 v Scot (Glasgow) 1985. **SL:** HS 119* v Lancs (Nottingham) 1994.

WALKER, Lyndsay Nicholas Paton (Cardiff HS, NSW), b Armidale, NSW, Australia 22 Jun 1974. 6'0". RHB, WK. Debut 1994. HS 24 v OU (Oxford) 1995. Awaiting BAC debut.

WILEMAN, Jonathan Ritchie (Stancliffe Hall S, Darley Dale; Malvern C; Salford), b Sheffield, Yorks 19 Aug 1970. 6'1". RHB, RSM. Nottinghamshire debut 1992, scored 109 v CU (Nottingham) in his first f-c innings for the County. Subsequently appeared for Comb U v A (Oxford) 1993 and Minor C v SA (Torquay) 1994. Lincolnshire 1993-94. HS 109 (*see above*). BAC HS 37 v Lancs (Liverpool) 1995. BB 2-33 v Hants (Nottingham) 1995. **NWT:** HS 12 v Northants (Nottingham) 1995. BB 1-9. **BHC:** HS 0. **SL:** HS 51* v Sussex (Arundel) 1995. BB 4-21 v Glos (Bristol) 1995.

NEWCOMERS

BOWEN, Mark Nicholas (Sacred Heart, Redcar; St Mary's C; Tees Side Poly), b Redcar, Yorks 6 Dec 1967. 6'2". RHB, RM. Northamptonshire 1991-92/1994. Tour: SA 1991-92 (Nh). HS 23* Nh v Durham (Northampton) 1993. BB 4-124 Nh v Kent (Canterbury) 1993. **BHC:** HS 0. BB 1-39. **SL:** HS 27* Nh v Kent (Northampton) 1994. BB 3-35 Nh v Derbys (Derby) 1993.

METCALFE, Ashley Anthony (Bradford GS; University C, London), b Horsforth, Yorks 25 Dec 1963. 5'8". RHB, OB. Yorkshire 1983-95 (scoring 122 v Notts (Bradford) on debut; cap 1986; benefit 1995). YC 1986. OFS 1988-89. Tours (Y): SA 1991-92, 1992-93; WI 1986-87. 1000 runs (6) inc 2000 (1): 2047 (1990). HS 216* Y v Middx (Leeds) 1988. BB 2-18 Y v Warwks (Scarborough) 1987. Awards: NWT 2; BHC 5. **NWT:** HS 127* Y v Warwks (Leeds) 1990. BB 2-44 Y v Wilts (Trowbridge) 1987. **BHC:** HS 114 Y v Lancs (Manchester) 1991. **SL:** HS 116 Y v Middx (Lord's) 1991.

TOLLEY, Christopher Mark (King Edward VI C, Stourbridge; Loughborough U), b Kidderminster, Worcs 30 Dec 1967. 5'9". RHB, LMF. Worcestershire 1989-95 (cap 1993). Tours (Wo): Z 1990-91, 1993-94. HS 84 Wo v Derbys (Derby) 1994. BB 5-55 Wo v Kent (Worcester) 1993. Award: BHC 1. **NWT:** HS 12* Wo v Glam (Swansea) 1993. BB 3-25 Wo v Derbys (Worcester) 1993. **BHC:** HS 77 Comb Us v Lancs (Cambridge) 1990. BB 1-12. **SL:** HS 30 Wo v Hants (Southampton) 1995. BB 4-50 Wo v Hants (Portsmouth) 1993.

WELTON, Guy Edward (Healing CS), b Grimsby, Lincs 4 May 1978. RHB, OB.

DEPARTURES (who made first-class appearances in 1995)

BANTON, Colin (Fish Hoek HS), b Fish Hoek, SA 15 Sep 1969. 6'0". RHB, RM. Nottinghamshire 1995. HS 80* v CU (Cambridge) 1995 – on debut. BAC HS 37 v Yorks (Nottingham) 1995. **BHC:** HS 40 v Lancs (Manchester) 1995. **SL:** HS 1.

FIELD-BUSS, Michael Gwyn (Wanstead HS), b Mtarfa, Malta 23 Sep 1964. 5'10". RHB, OB. Essex 1987. Nottinghamshire 1989-95. HS 34* Ex v Middx (Lord's) 1987. Nt HS 25 v Middx (Lord's) 1991. BB 6-42 v Kent (Nottingham) 1993. **NWT:** HS 5*. BB 4-62 v Worcs (Nottingham) 1992. **BHC:** HS –. **SL:** HS 10* v Hants (Southampton) 1992. BB 3-25 v Worcs (Nottingham) 1993.

FRENCH, Bruce Nicholas (The Meden CS), b Warsop 13 Aug 1959. 5'6". RHB, WK. Nottinghamshire 1976-95 (debut when aged 16yr 287d) (cap 1980; benefit 1991). **Tests:** 16 (1986 to 1987-88); HS 59 v P (Manchester) 1987. **LOI:** 13 (1984-85 to 1987-88; HS 9*). Tours: A 1986-87, 1987-88; SA 1989-90 (Eng XI); WI 1985-86; NZ 1987-88; I/SL 1984-85; P 1987-88. HS 123 v Durham (Chester-le-St) 1993. BB 1-37. Award: BHC 1. **NWT:** HS 49 v Staffs (Nottingham) 1985. **BHC:** HS 48* v Worcs (Nottingham) 1984. **SL:** HS 37 v Glos (Bristol) 1985.

NOTTINGHAMSHIRE 1995

RESULTS SUMMARY

	Place	Won	Lost	Drew	No Result
Britannic Assurance Championship	**11th**	5	9	3	–
All First-Class Matches		5	9	5	–
NatWest Trophy	2nd Round				
Benson and Hedges Cup	Quarter-Finalist				
Sunday League	**11th**	7	9	–	1

BRITANNIC ASSURANCE CHAMPIONSHIP AVERAGES

BATTING AND FIELDING

Cap		*M*	*I*	*NO*	*HS*	*Runs*	*Avge*	*100*	*50*	*Ct/St*
1983	R.T.Robinson	17	31	–	209	1627	52.48	6	5	6
1995	G.F.Archer	17	32	3	158	1171	40.37	3	4	16
1993	C.L.Cairns	16	29	1	115	1061	37.89	1	7	6
1986	P.Johnson	16	29	1	120*	923	32.96	1	7	9
1992	P.R.Pollard	11	19	2	120	506	29.76	1	2	13
1995	W.M.Noon	16	29	6	64*	672	29.21	–	4	32/5
–	D.B.Pennett	7	12	8	50	89	22.25	–	1	3
–	M.P.Dowman	7	14	1	73	278	21.38	–	2	7
1990	K.P.Evans	6	12	2	78*	207	20.70	–	1	9
1987	R.A.Pick	16	26	4	50*	395	17.95	–	1	9
–	N.A.Gie	3	6	–	34	98	16.33	–	–	–
–	J.R.Wileman	7	14	3	37	160	14.54	–	–	3
–	C.Banton	5	10	2	37	114	14.25	–	–	2
–	U.Afzaal	7	12	2	37	134	13.40	–	–	3
–	J.E.Hindson	15	26	4	47	251	11.40	–	–	9
–	R.J.Chapman	7	11	3	22	78	9.75	–	–	–
1990	J.A.Afford	6	9	3	15*	57	9.50	–	–	3
–	R.T.Bates	3	6	–	11	41	6.83	–	–	1
–	G.W.Mike	3	6	1	9*	23	4.60	–	–	1

Also batted (1 match each): M.G.Field-Buss 2, 2; B.N.French (cap 1980) 2, 16 (1 ct).

BOWLING

	O	*M*	*R*	*W*	*Avge*	*Best*	*5wI*	*10wM*
C.L.Cairns	363.5	84	1022	49	20.85	8- 47	3	1
R.A.Pick	462.4	95	1554	45	34.53	5- 82	2	–
J.E.Hindson	628	147	2059	59	34.89	5- 67	5	2
R.T.Bates	112.1	30	367	10	36.70	5- 88	1	–
K.P.Evans	213.1	55	514	14	36.71	3- 66	–	–
J.A.Afford	276.5	50	921	18	51.16	4- 58	–	–
R.J.Chapman	164.2	22	719	10	71.90	3-119	–	–

Also bowled: U.Afzaal 182-42-582-5; G.F.Archer 79-11-261-6; C.Banton 3-1-12-0; M.P.Dowman 5-0-30-0; M.G.Field-Buss 32-7-95-0; G.W.Mike 67.5-15-242-4; D.B.Pennett 191.1-33-730-9; J.R.Wileman 89-33-214-4.

The First-Class Averages (pp 129-143) give the records of Nottinghamshire players in all first-class county matches (their other opponents being Cambridge University and Oxford University).

NOTTINGHAMSHIRE RECORDS

FIRST-CLASS CRICKET

Highest Total	For	739-7d		v	Leics	Nottingham	1903
	V	781-7d		by	Northants	Northampton	1995
Lowest Total	For	13		v	Yorkshire	Nottingham	1901
	V	16		by	Derbyshire	Nottingham	1879
		16		by	Surrey	The Oval	1880
Highest Innings	For	312*	W.W.Keeton	v	Middlesex	The Oval	1939
	V	345	C.G.Macartney	for	Australians	Nottingham	1921

Highest Partnership for each Wicket

1st	391	A.O.Jones/A.Shrewsbury	v	Glos	Bristol	1899
2nd	398	A.Shrewsbury/W.Gunn	v	Sussex	Nottingham	1890
3rd	369	W.Gunn/J.R.Gunn	v	Leics	Nottingham	1903
4th	361	A.O.Jones/J.R.Gunn	v	Essex	Leyton	1905
5th	266	A.Shrewsbury/W.Gunn	v	Sussex	Hove	1884
6th	303*	F.H.Winrow/P.F.Harvey	v	Derbyshire	Nottingham	1947
7th	301	C.C.Lewis/B.N.French	v	Durham	Chester-le-St	1993
8th	220	G.F.H.Heane/R.Winrow	v	Somerset	Nottingham	1935
9th	170	J.C.Adams/K.P.Evans	v	Somerset	Taunton	1994
10th	152	E.B.Alletson/W.Riley	v	Sussex	Hove	1911

Best Bowling	For	10-66	K.Smales	v	Glos	Stroud	1956
(Innings)	V	10-10	H.Verity	for	Yorkshire	Leeds	1932
Best Bowling	For	17-89	F.C.Matthews	v	Northants	Nottingham	1923
(Match)	V	17-89	W.G.Grace	for	Glos	Cheltenham	1877

Most Runs – Season	2620	W.W.Whysall	(av 53.46)	1929
Most Runs – Career	31592	G.Gunn	(av 35.69)	1902-32
Most 100s – Season	9	W.W.Whysall		1928
	9	M.J.Harris		1971
	9	B.C.Broad		1990
Most 100s – Career	65	J.Hardstaff, jr		1930-55
Most Wkts – Season	181	B.Dooland	(av 14.96)	1954
Most Wkts – Career	1653	T.G.Wass	(av 20.34)	1896-1920

LIMITED-OVERS CRICKET

Highest Total	NWT	344-6		v	Northumb	Jesmond	1994
	BHC	296-6		v	Kent	Nottingham	1989
	SL	329-6		v	Derbyshire	Nottingham	1993
Lowest Total	NWT	123		v	Yorkshire	Scarborough	1969
	BHC	74		v	Leics	Leicester	1987
	SL	66		v	Yorkshire	Bradford	1969
Highest Innings	NWT	149*	D.W.Randall	v	Devon	Torquay	1988
	BHC	130*	C.E.B.Rice	v	Scotland	Glasgow	1982
	SL	167*	P.Johnson	v	Kent	Nottingham	1993
Best Bowling	NWT	6-10	K.P.Evans	v	Northumb	Jesmond	1994
	BHC	6-22	M.K.Bore	v	Leics	Leicester	1980
		6-22	C.E.B.Rice	v	Northants	Northampton	1981
	SL	6-12	R.J.Hadlee	v	Lancashire	Nottingham	1980

SOMERSET

Formation of Present Club: 18 August 1875
Colours: Black, White and Maroon
Badge: Somerset Dragon
Championships: (0) Third 1892, 1958, 1963, 1966, 1981
NatWest Trophy/Gillette Cup Winners: (2) 1979, 1983
Benson and Hedges Cup Winners: (2) 1981, 1982
Sunday League Champions: (1) 1979
Match Awards: NWT 46; BHC 58

Chief Executive: P.W.Anderson
The County Ground, Taunton TA1 1JT (Tel 01823 272946)
Captain: A.N.Hayhurst
Scorer: D.A.Oldam
1996 Beneficiary: R.J.Harden

BATTY, Jeremy David (Bingley GS; Horsforth C), b Bradford, Yorks 15 May 1971. Brother of G.J. (*see YORKSHIRE*) 6'1". RHB, OB. Yorkshire 1989-94. Somerset debut 1995. Tours (Y): SA 1991-92, 1992-93. HS 51 Y v SL (Leeds) 1991. BAC HS 50 Y v Notts (Nottingham) 1993. Sm HS 45* v WI (Taunton) 1995. BB 6-48 Y v Notts (Worksop) 1991. Sm BB 4-70 v Middx (Taunton) 1995. Award: BHC 1. **NWT:** HS 4. BB 1-17. **BHC:** HS 19* v Surrey (Taunton) 1995. BB 2-13 v Glos (Bristol) 1995. **SL:** HS 13* and BB 4-33 Y v Kent (Scarborough) 1991.

BOWLER, Peter Duncan (Educated at Canberra, Australia), b Plymouth, Devon 30 Jul 1963. 6'1". RHB, OB, occ WK. Leicestershire 1986 – first to score hundred on f-c debut for Leics (100* and 62 v Hants). Tasmania 1986-87. Derbyshire 1988-94 (cap 1989); scored 155* v CU (Cambridge) on debut – only instance of hundreds on debut for two counties. Somerset debut/cap 1995. 1000 runs (7) inc 2000 (1): 2044 (1992). HS 241* De v Hants (Portsmouth) 1992. Sm HS 196 v Essex (Southend) 1995. BB 3-41 De v Leics (Leicester) 1991 and De v Yorks (Chesterfield) 1991. Sm BB 1-13. Awards: BHC 3. **NWT:** HS 111 De v Berks (Derby) 1992. **BHC:** HS 109 De v Somerset (Taunton) 1990. BB 1-15. **SL:** HS 138* De v Somerset (Derby) 1993. BB 3-31 De v Glos (Cheltenham) 1991.

CADDICK, Andrew Richard (Papanui HS), b Christchurch, NZ 21 Nov 1968. Son of English emigrants – qualified for England 1992. 6'5". RHB, RFM. Debut 1991. Cap 1992. Represented NZ in 1987-88 Youth World Cup. **Tests:** 8 (1993 to 1993-94); HS 29* v WI (Kingston) 1993-94; BB 6-65 v WI (P-o-S) 1993-94. **LOI:** 5 (1993 to 1993-94; HS 21*; BB 3-39). Tours: A 1992-93 (Eng A); WI 1993-94. HS 92 v Worcs (Worcester) 1995. 50 wkts (3); most – 71 (1992). BB 9-32 (12-120 match) v Lancs (Taunton) 1993. Award: NWT 1. **NWT:** HS 8. BB 6-30 v Glos (Taunton) 1992. **BHC:** HS 28 v Kent (Canterbury) 1995. BB 2-20 v Yorks (Taunton) 1992. **SL:** HS 36* v Durham (Hartlepool) 1993. BB 4-18 v Lancs (Manchester) 1992.

DIMOND, Matthew (Castle S; Richard Huish C), b Taunton 24 Sep 1975. 6'1". RHB, RMF. Debut 1994. HS 26 v Derbys (Derby) 1995. BB 4-73 v Yorks (Bradford) 1994. **SL:** HS –.

ECCLESTONE, Simon Charles (Bryanston S; Durham U; Keble C, Oxford), b Great Dunmow, Essex 16 Jul 1971. 6'3". LHB, RM. Oxford U 1994 (blue 1994). Somerset debut 1994. Cambridgeshire 1990-94. HS 81 v Northants (Northampton) 1995. BB 4-66 OU v Surrey (Oval) 1994. **NWT:** HS 0. **BHC:** HS 30 v Surrey (Taunton) 1995. BB 2-44 v Kent (Canterbury) 1995. **SL:** HS 66 v Durham (Taunton) 1994. BB 4-31 v Essex (W-s-M) 1994.

HALLETT, Jeremy Charles (Millfield S; Durham U), b Yeovil 18 Oct 1970. 6'2". RHB, RMF. Debut 1990. Combined Us 1994. HS 111* v Middx (Taunton) 1995. BB 4-59 v Kent (Canterbury) 1994. **BHC:** HS 5*. BB 3-36 Comb Us v Worcs (Cambridge) 1991. **SL:** HS 26 v Sussex (Taunton) 1993. BB 3-33 v Worcs (Worcester) 1995.

HARDEN, Richard John (King's C, Taunton), b Bridgwater 16 Aug 1965. 5'11". RHB, SLA. Debut 1985. Cap 1989. Benefit 1996. C Districts 1987-88. 1000 runs (7); most – 1460 (1990). HS 187 v Notts (Taunton) 1992. BB 2-7 CD v Canterbury (Blenheim) 1987-88. Sm BB 2-24 v Hants (Taunton) 1986. Award: NWT 1. **NWT:** HS 108* v Scot (Taunton) 1992. **BHC:** HS 76 v Kent (Canterbury) 1992. **SL:** HS 100* v Durham (Chester-le-St) 1995.

HAYHURST, Andrew Neil (Worsley Wardley HS; Eccles SFC; Leeds Poly), b Davyhulme, Manchester 23 Nov 1962. 5'11". RHB, RM. Lancashire 1985-89. Somerset debut/cap 1990. Captain 1994-. Tours: WI 1986-87 (La); Z 1988-89 (La). 1000 runs (3); most – 1559 (1990). HS 172* v Glos (Bath) 1991. BB 4-27 La v Middx (Manchester) 1987. Sm BB 3-27 v Yorks (Middlesbrough) 1992. Awards: NWT 2; BHC 2. **NWT:** HS 91* and BB 5-60 v Warwks (Birmingham) 1991. **BHC:** HS 95 v Notts (Nottingham) 1992. BB 4-50 La v Worcs (Worcester) 1987. **SL:** HS 84 La v Leics (Manchester) 1988. BB 4-37 La v Glam (Pontypridd) 1988 and Sm v Sussex (Hove) 1990.

HOLLOWAY, Piran Christopher Laity (Millfield S; Taunton S; Loughborough U), b Helston, Cornwall 1 Oct 1970. 5'8". LHB, WK. Warwickshire 1988-93. Somerset debut 1994. HS 129* v Sussex (Bath) 1995. **NWT:** HS 50 v Warwks (Birmingham) 1995. **BHC:** HS 27 Comb Us v Derbys (Oxford) 1991. **SL:** HS 66 v Leics (W-s-M) 1995.

KERR, Jason Ian Douglas (Withins HS; Bolton C), b Bolton, Lancs 7 Apr 1974. 6'2". RHB, RMF. Debut 1993. HS 80 and BB 5-82 v WI (Taunton) 1995. BAC HS 42 v Worcs (Worcester) 1995. BAC BB 4-68 v Sussex (Bath) 1995. **NWT:** HS 3. BB 2-74 v Warwks (Birmingham) 1995. **BHC:** HS – . BB 2-35 v Sussex (Taunton) 1995. **SL:** HS 17 v Northants (Luton) 1993. BB 3-34 v Essex (Chelmsford) 1993.

LATHWELL, Mark Nicholas (Braunton S, Devon), b Bletchley, Bucks 26 Dec 1971. 5'8". RHB, RM. Debut 1991. Cap 1992. YC 1993. MCC YC. **Tests:** 2 (1993); HS 33 v A (Nottingham) 1993. Tours (Eng A): A 1992-93; SA 1993-94. 1000 runs (4); most – 1230 (1994). HS 206 v Surrey (Bath) 1994. BB 2-21 v Sussex (Hove) 1994. Awards: NWT 1; BHC 1. **NWT:** HS 103 and BB 1-23 v Salop (Telford) 1993. **BHC:** HS 120 v Surrey (Oval) 1994. **SL:** HS 117 v Notts (Taunton) 1994.

PARSONS, Keith Alan (The Castle S, Taunton; Richard Huish SFC), b Taunton 2 May 1973. Identical twin brother of K.J. (Somerset staff 1992-94). 6'1". RHB, RM. Debut 1992. HS 105 v Young A (Taunton) 1995. BAC HS 78 v Leics (W-s-M) 1995. BB 2-11 v Derbys (Derby) 1995. **NWT:** HS 48 v Warwks (Birmingham) 1995. BB 2-47 v Salop (Telford) 1993. **BHC:** HS – . **SL:** HS 52* v Derbys (Derby) 1995. BB 2-16 v Leics (W-s-M) 1995.

ROSE, Graham David (Northumberland Park S, Tottenham), b Tottenham, London 12 Apr 1964. 6'4". RHB, RM. Middlesex 1985-86. Somerset debut 1987. Cap 1988. Benefit 1997. 1000 runs (1): 1000 (1990). HS 138 v Sussex (Taunton) 1993. 50 wkts (2); most – 57 (1988). BB 6-41 M v Worcs (Worcester) 1985 – on debut. Sm BB 6-47 v Warwks (Bath) 1988. Awards: BHC 3. **NWT:** HS 110 v Devon (Torquay) 1990. BB 3-11 v Salop (Telford) 1993. **BHC:** HS 79 v Surrey (Taunton) 1995. BB 4-21 v Ire (Erlington) 1995. **SL:** HS 148 v Glam (Neath) 1990. BB 4-26 v Kent (Taunton) 1993.

TRESCOTHICK, Marcus Edward (Sir Bernard Lovell S), b Keynsham 25 Dec 1975. 6'2". LHB, RM. Debut 1993. HS 151 v Northants (Taunton) 1995. BB 4-36 (inc hat-trick) v Young A (Taunton) 1995. Award: NWT 1. **NWT:** HS 116 v Oxon (Aston Rowant) 1994. **BHC:** HS 122 v Ire (Erlington) 1995. **SL:** HS 74 v Yorks (Leeds) 1994.

TRUMP, Harvey Russell John (Millfield S), b Taunton 11 Oct 1968. 6'0". RHB, OB. Debut 1988. Cap 1994. HS 48 v Notts (Taunton) 1988 – on debut. 50 wkts (1): 51 (1991). BB 7-52 (inc hat-trick; 14-104 match) v Glos (Gloucester) 1992. **NWT:** HS 10* v Warwks (Birmingham) 1995. BB 2-44 v Essex (Taunton) 1989. **BHC:** HS 11 v Kent (Canterbury). BB 3-17 v Ire (Erlington) 1995. **SL:** HS 19 v Kent (Taunton) 1991. BB 3-19 v Essex (W-s-M) 1994.

TURNER, Robert Julian (Millfield S; Magdalene C, Cambridge), b Malvern, Worcs 25 Nov 1967. 6'1½". RHB, WK. Brother of S.J. (Somerset 1984-85). Cambridge U 1988-91 (blue 1988-89-90-91; captain 1991). Somerset debut 1991. Cap 1994. HS 106 v Derbys (Derby) 1995. **NWT:** HS 15 v Warwks (Taunton) 1994. **BHC:** HS 37* v Kent (Canterbury) 1995. **SL:** HS 37* v Sussex (Hove) 1994.

Van TROOST, Adrianus Pelrus (**Andre**) (Spieringshoek C, Schiedam), b Schiedam, Holland Oct 1972. 6'7". RHB, RF. Debut 1991. Qualified for England 1998. Holland 1990 (opened bowling in ICC Trophy final v Zimbabwe). HS 35 v Lancs (Taunton) 1993. BB 6-48 v Essex (Taunton) 1992. **NWT:** HS 17* v Surrey (Taunton) 1993. BB 5-22 v Oxon (Aston Rowant) 1994. **BHC:** HS 9* and BB 2-38 v Notts (Nottingham) 1993. **SL:** HS 9*. BB 4-23 v Notts (Taunton) 1994.

NEWCOMERS

BISHOP, Ian Emlyn, b Taunton 26 Aug 1977. RHB, RF.

LEE, Shane, b Wollongong, NSW, Australia 8 Aug 1973. RHB, RFM. NSW 1992-93 to date. Australian CA. **LOI** (A): 6 (1995-96; HS 39; BB 1-20). Tour (NSW): E 1995. HS 104* NSW v Q (Sydney) 1993-94. BB 3-53 NSW v Victoria (Melbourne) 1994-95.

SHINE, Kevin James (Maiden Erlegh CS), b Bracknell, Berks 22 Feb 1969. 6'2½". RHB, RFM. Hampshire 1989-93. Middlesex 1994-95. Berkshire 1986. HS 26* H v Middx (Lord's) 1989. BB 8-47 (8 wkts in 38 balls inc hat-trick and 4 in 5; 13-105 match) H v Lancs (Manchester) 1992. **NWT:** HS – . BB 3-31 M v Wales MC (Northop Hall) 1994. **BHC:** HS 0. BB 4-68 H v Surrey (Oval) 1990. **SL:** HS 2*. BB 2-15 H v Northants (Northampton) 1993.

DEPARTURES (who made first-class appearances in 1995)

MUSHTAQ AHMED, b Sahiwal, Pakistan 28 Jun 1970. 5'5". RHB, LB. Multan 1986-87/1990-91. United Bank 1986-87 to date. Somerset 1993-95 (cap 1993). **Tests** (P): 21 (1989-90 to 1995-96); HS 27 v A (Lahore) 1994-95; BB 7-56 (10-171 match) v NZ (Christchurch) 1995-96. **LOI** (P): 90 (1988-89 to 1995-96; HS 26; BB 3-14). Tours (P): E 1992; A 1989-90, 1991-92, 1992-93, 1995-96; WI 1992-93; NZ 1992-93, 1993-94, 1995-96; SL 1994-95. HS 90 and Sm BB 7-91 (12-175 match) v Sussex (Taunton) 1993. 50 wkts (3+1); most – 95 (1995). BB 9-93 Multan v Peshawar (Sahiwal) 1990-91. Awards: NWT 1; BHC 1. **NWT:** HS 35 v Surrey (Taunton) 1993. BB 3-26 v Oxon (Aston Rowant) 1994. **BHC:** HS 21 v Surrey (Taunton) 1995. BB 4-29 v Sussex (Taunton) 1995. **SL:** HS 32 v Middx (Bath) 1993. BB 3-17 v Glos (Taunton) 1993.

SOMERSET 1995

RESULTS SUMMARY

	Place	Won	Lost	Drew	No Result
Britannic Assurance Championship	**9th**	7	5	5	–
All First-Class Matches		7	7	6	–
NatWest Trophy	1st Round				
Benson and Hedges Cup	Semi-Finalist				
Sunday League	**14th**	5	9	–	3

BRITANNIC ASSURANCE CHAMPIONSHIP AVERAGES

BATTING AND FIELDING

Cap		*M*	*I*	*NO*	*HS*	*Runs*	*Avge*	*100*	*50*	*Ct/St*
–	J.C.Hallett	2	4	1	111*	229	76.33	1	–	1
–	S.C.Ecclestone	5	9	2	81	417	59.57	–	3	–
1995	P.D.Bowler	16	28	3	196	1483	59.32	6	4	8
–	P.C.L.Holloway	10	18	4	129*	758	54.14	2	5	2
1989	R.J.Harden	17	32	6	129*	1319	50.73	5	5	12
1990	A.N.Hayhurst	15	26	5	107	803	38.23	1	5	3
1992	A.R.Caddick	6	7	–	92	237	33.85	–	2	1
1994	R.J.Turner	16	24	5	106*	594	31.26	1	3	42/7
1988	G.D.Rose	14	22	–	84	658	29.90	–	5	5
–	K.A.Parsons	13	22	1	78	617	29.38	–	5	11
1992	M.N.Lathwell	14	27	–	111	737	27.29	2	2	7
–	M.E.Trescothick	10	18	–	151	373	20.72	1	1	12
1994	H.R.J.Trump	13	18	8	47	197	19.70	–	–	10
–	J.I.D.Kerr	11	15	2	42	252	19.38	–	–	4
1993	Mushtaq Ahmed	16	22	2	62*	299	14.95	–	1	3
–	A.P.van Troost	6	9	3	34	73	12.16	–	–	–

Also batted: J.D.Batty (2 matches) 35, 11 (1 ct); M.Dimond (1 match) 7, 26.

BOWLING

	O	*M*	*R*	*W*	*Avge*	*Best*	*5wI*	*10wM*
A.R.Caddick	183.1	34	613	24	25.54	8-69	1	1
Mushtaq Ahmed	928	281	2716	92	29.52	6-38	7	2
G.D.Rose	376	82	1217	34	35.79	5-78	1	–
J.I.D.Kerr	241.1	50	898	22	40.81	4-68	–	–
H.R.J.Trump	470	141	1316	32	41.12	5-85	1	–

Also bowled: J.D.Batty 63.4-10-282-5; P.D.Bowler 16.2-3-68-1; M.Dimond 14-2-70-1; S.C.Ecclestone 66-14-222-7; J.C.Hallett 14-1-86-2; R.J.Harden 1-0-17-0; A.N.Hayhurst 120.2-20-405-8; P.C.L.Holloway 2-1-12-0; M.N.Lathwell 24-5-76-2; K.A.Parsons 66-10-270-5; M.E.Trescothick 15-1-63-0; A.P.van Troost 107.3-17-451-9.

The First-Class Averages (pp 129-143) give the records of Somerset players in all first-class county matches (their other opponents being the West Indians – twice – and Young Australia).

SOMERSET RECORDS

FIRST-CLASS CRICKET

Highest Total	For	675-9d		v	Hampshire	Bath	1924
	V	811		by	Surrey	The Oval	1899
Lowest Total	For	25		v	Glos	Bristol	1947
	V	22		by	Glos	Bristol	1920
Highest Innings	For	322	I.V.A.Richards	v	Warwicks	Taunton	1985
	V	424	A.C.MacLaren	for	Lancashire	Taunton	1895

Highest Partnership for each Wicket

1st	346	H.T.Hewett/L.C.H.Palairet	v	Yorkshire	Taunton	1892
2nd	290	J.C.W.MacBryan/M.D.Lyon	v	Derbyshire	Buxton	1924
3rd	319	P.M.Roebuck/M.D.Crowe	v	Leics	Taunton	1984
4th	310	P.W.Denning/I.T.Botham	v	Glos	Taunton	1980
5th	235	J.C.White/C.C.C.Case	v	Glos	Taunton	1927
6th	265	W.E.Alley/K.E.Palmer	v	Northants	Northampton	1961
7th	240	S.M.J.Woods/V.T.Hill	v	Kent	Taunton	1898
8th	172	I.V.A.Richards/I.T.Botham	v	Leics	Leicester	1983
9th	183	C.H.M.Greetham/H.W.Stephenson	v	Leics	Weston-s-Mare	1963
	183	C.J.Tavaré/N.A.Mallender	v	Sussex	Hove	1990
10th	143	J.J.Bridges/A.H.D.Gibbs	v	Essex	Weston-s-Mare	1919

Best Bowling	For	10- 49	E.J.Tyler	v	Surrey	Taunton	1895
(Innings)	V	10- 35	A.Drake	for	Yorkshire	Weston-s-Mare	1914
Best Bowling	For	16- 83	J.C.White	v	Worcs	Bath	1919
(Match)	V	17-137	W.Brearley	for	Lancashire	Manchester	1905

Most Runs – Season	2761	W.E.Alley	(av 58.74)	1961
Most Runs – Career	21142	H.Gimblett	(av 36.96)	1935-54
Most 100s – Season	11	S.J.Cook		1991
Most 100s – Career	49	H.Gimblett		1935-54
Most Wkts – Season	169	A.W.Wellard	(av 19.24)	1938
Most Wkts – Career	2166	J.C.White	(av 18.02)	1909-37

LIMITED-OVERS CRICKET

Highest Total	NWT	413-4		v	Devon	Torquay	1990
	BHC	321-5		v	Sussex	Hove	1990
	SL	360-3		v	Glamorgan	Neath	1990
Lowest Total	NWT	59		v	Middlesex	Lord's	1977
	BHC	98		v	Middlesex	Lord's	1982
	SL	58		v	Essex	Chelmsford	1977
Highest Innings	NWT	162*	C.J.Tavaré	v	Devon	Torquay	1990
	BHC	177	S.J.Cook	v	Sussex	Hove	1990
	SL	175*	I.T.Botham	v	Northants	Wellingborough	1986
Best Bowling	NWT	7-15	R.P.Lefebvre	v	Devon	Torquay	1990
	BHC	5-14	J.Garner	v	Surrey	Lord's	1981
	SL	6-24	I.V.A.Richards	v	Lancashire	Manchester	1983

SURREY

Formation of Present Club: 22 August 1845
Colours: Chocolate
Badge: Prince of Wales' Feathers
Championships (since 1890): (15) 1890, 1891, 1892, 1894, 1895, 1899, 1914, 1952, 1953, 1954, 1955, 1956, 1957, 1958, 1971. Joint: (1) 1950
NatWest Trophy/Gillette Cup Winners: (1) 1982
Benson and Hedges Cup Winners: (1) 1974
Sunday League Champions: (0) Third 1993
Match Awards: NWT 41; BHC 56

Chief Executive: P.C.J.Sheldon
Kennington Oval, London, SE11 5SS (Tel 0171 582 6660)
Captain: A.J.Stewart
Scorer: K.R.Booth
1996 Beneficiary: D.M.Ward

BENJAMIN, Joseph Emmanuel (Cayon HS, St Kitts; Mount Pleasant S, Highgate, Birmingham), b Christ Church, St Kitts 2 Feb 1961. 6'2". RHB, RMF. Warwickshire 1988-91. Surrey debut 1992. Cap 1993. Staffordshire 1986-88. **Tests:** 1 (1994); HS 0 and BB 4-42 v SA (Oval) 1994. **LOI:** 2 (1994-95; HS 0; BB 1-22). Tour: A 1994-95. HS 49 v Essex (Oval) 1995. 50 wkts (3); most – 80 (1994). BB 6-19 v Notts (Oval) 1993. Awards: NWT 2; BHC 1. **NWT:** HS 25 v Worcs (Oval) 1994. BB 4-20 v Berks (Oval) 1995. **BHC:** HS 20 Wa v Worcs (Birmingham) 1990. BB 4-27 v Somerset (Taunton) 1995. **SL:** HS 24 Wa v Lancs (Manchester) 1990. BB 4-44 v Middx (Oval) 1992.

BICKNELL, Darren John (Robert Haining SS; Guildford TC), b Guildford 24 Jun 1967. Elder brother of M.P. 6'4". LHB, SLA. Debut 1987. Cap 1990. Tours (Eng A): WI 1991-92; P 1990-91; SL 1990-91; Z 1989-90. 1000 runs (6); most – 1888 (1991). HS 235* v Notts (Nottingham) 1994. BB 3-88 v Kent (Canterbury) 1995. Awards: NWT 1; BHC 3. **NWT:** HS 135* v Yorks (Oval) 1989. **BHC:** HS 119 v Hants (Oval) 1990. **SL:** HS 125 v Durham (Durham) 1992. BB 1-11.

BICKNELL, Martin Paul (Robert Haining SS), b Guildford 14 Jan 1969. Younger brother of D.J. 6'3". RHB, RFM. Debut 1986. Cap 1989. **Tests:** 2 (1993); HS 14 and BB 3-99 v A (Birmingham) 1993. **LOI:** 7 (1990-91; HS 31*; BB 3-55). Tours: A 1990-91; SA 1993-94 (Eng A); Z 1989-90 (Eng A). HS 88 v Hants (Southampton) 1992. 50 wkts (5); most – 71 (1992). BB 9-45 v CU (Oval) 1988. BAC BB 7-52 v Sussex (Oval) 1991. Award: BHC 1. **NWT:** HS 66* v Northants (Oval) 1991. BB 4-35 v Somerset (Taunton) 1993. **BHC:** HS 43 v Kent (Canterbury) 1995. BB 4-49 v Somerset (Oval) 1994. **SL:** HS 25 v Glam (Oval) 1995. BB 5-12 v Northants (Oval) 1994.

BROWN, Alistair Duncan (Caterham S), b Beckenham, Kent 11 Feb 1970. 5'10". RHB, occ LB. Debut 1992. Cap 1994. 1000 runs (3); most – 1382 (1993). HS 187 v Glos (Oval) 1995. **NWT:** HS 52 v Worcs (Oval) 1994. **BHC:** HS 82 v Sussex (Oval) 1995. **SL:** HS 142* v Middx (Oval) 1994.

BUTCHER, Mark Alan (Trinity S; Archbishop Tenison's S, Croydon), b Croydon 23 Aug 1972. Son of A.R. (Surrey, Glamorgan and England 1972-92); brother of G.P. (*see GLAMORGAN*). 5'11". LHB, RM. Debut 1992. 1000 runs (1): 1210 (1995). HS 167 v Durham (Oval) 1995. BB 4-31 v Worcs (Oval) 1994. **NWT:** HS 79* v Berks (Oval) 1995. BB 2-57 v Somerset (Taunton) 1993. **BHC:** HS 5. BB 3-37 v Somerset (Oval) 1994. **SL:** HS 48* v Glam (Oval) 1991 (on 1st XI debut and against team captained by his father). BB 3-23 v Sussex (Oval) 1992.

De la PENA, Jason Michael (Stowe S; Bournside S), b London 16 Sep 1972. 6'4". RHB, RFM. Gloucestershire 1991-93. Surrey debut 1995. HS 7*. Sy/BAC HS 2*. BB 4-77 Gs v A (Bristol) 1993. Sy/BAC BB 3-53 v Yorks (Oval) 1995. **SL:** HS 2*.

HOLLIOAKE, Adam John (St George's C, Weybridge), b Melbourne, Australia 5 Sep 1971. Brother of B.C. (*see below*). 5'11". RHB, RMF. Debut 1993, scoring 13 and 123 v Derbys (Ilkeston). Cap 1995. Qualified for England 1992. 1000 runs (1): 1099 (1995). HS 138 v Leics (Oval) 1994. BB 4-22 v Yorks (Oval) 1995. **NWT:** HS 60 v Worcs (Oval) 1994. BB 4-53 v Middx (Oval) 1995. **BHC:** HS 23 v Kent (Canterbury) 1995. BB 3-48 v Notts (Nottingham) 1994. **SL:** HS 93 v Kent (Canterbury) 1995. BB 4-22 v Warwks (Birmingham) 1995.

KENLOCK, Stratford Garfield (*'Mark'*) (Stockwell Manor S), b Portland, Jamaica 16 Apr 1965. 6'0". LHB, LFM. Debut 1994. HS 12 v Northants (Northampton) 1995. BB 3-104 v Kent (Oval) 1994. Award: BHC 1. **BHC:** HS – . BB 5-15 v Ire (Oval) 1995. **SL:** HS 9. BB 4-30 v Yorks (Scarborough) 1994.

KENNIS, Gregor John (Tiffin S), b Yokohama, Japan 9 Mar 1974. 6'1". RHB, OB. MCC YC. Debut 1994. HS 23 v OU (Oval) 1994. Scored 258 (395 balls, 41 fours) v Leics II (Kibworth) 1995 – Surrey II record. HS 29 v Kent (Canterbury) 1995. **SL:** HS 5.

KERSEY, Graham James (Bexley & Erith Technical HS), b Plumstead, London 19 May 1971. 5'7". RHB, WK. Kent 1991-92. Surrey debut 1993. HS 83 v Yorks (Oval) 1995. **NWT:** HS 21 v Middx (Oval) 1995. **SL:** HS 50 v Durham (Oval) 1993.

KNOTT, James Alan (City of Westminster C), b Canterbury, Kent 14 Jun 1975. Son of A.P.E. (Kent, Tasmania and England 1964-85). 5'6". RHB, WK. Debut 1995. MCC YC. HS – .

NOWELL, Richard William (Trinity S, Croydon), b Croydon 29 Dec 1975. 6'1". LHB, SLA. Debut 1995. HS 27 v Warwks (Birmingham) 1995. BB 4-43 v Notts (Guildford) 1995. **NWT:** HS 2*. **BHC:** HS 15* and BB 1-35 v Sussex (Oval) 1995. **SL:** HS 0.

PIGOTT, Anthony Charles Shackleton (Harrow S), b Fulham, London 4 Jun 1958. 6'1". RHB, RFM. Sussex 1978-93 (cap 1982; benefit 1991). Surrey debut 1994. Cap 1995. Wellington 1982-83/1983-84. **Tests:** 1 (1983-84); HS 8* and BB 2-75 v NZ (Christchurch) 1983-84. Tours: NZ 1979-80 (DHR), 1983-84 (part). HS 104* Sx v Warwks (Birmingham) 1986. Sy HS 40 v Warwks (Guildford) 1994. 50 wkts (5); most – 74 (1988). BB 7-74 Sx v Northants (Eastbourne) 1982. Sy BB 6-46 v Notts (Nottingham) 1994. Hat-trick 1978 (Sx – his first f-c wkts). **NWT:** HS 53 Sx v Derbys (Hove) 1988. BB 3-4 Sx v Ire (Hove) 1985. **BHC:** HS 49* Sx v Essex (Hove) 1989. BB 3-29 Sx v Leics (Hove) 1991. **SL:** HS 51* Sx v Northants (Hove) 1989. BB 5-24 Sx v Lancs (Manchester) 1986.

RATCLIFFE, Jason David (Sharman's Cross SS; Solihull SFC), b Solihull, Warwks 19 Jun 1969. Son of D.P. (Warwks 1957-68). 6'4". RHB, RM. Warwickshire 1988-94. Surrey debut 1995. Tours (Wa): SA 1991-92, 1992-93; Z 1993-94. HS 127* Wa v CU (Cambridge) 1989. BAC HS 101 Wa v Sussex (Birmingham) 1993. Sy HS 75 v Glam (Oval) 1995. BB 1-4. BAC BB 1-6. Awards: NWT 2. **NWT:** HS 105 Wa v Yorks (Leeds) 1993. **BHC:** HS 29 Wa v Surrey (Oval) 1991. **SL:** HS 37 Wa v Somerset (Birmingham) 1989. BB 2-11 Wa v Glam (Neath) 1993.

SARGEANT, Neil Fredrick (Whitmore HS), b Hammersmith 8 Nov 1965. 5'8". RHB, WK. Debut 1989. HS 49 v Lancs (Manchester) 1991. BB 1-88. **SL:** HS 22 v Glos (Cheltenham) 1990.

SHAHID, Nadeem (Ipswich S), b Karachi, Pakistan 23 Apr 1969. 6'0". RHB, LB. Essex 1989-94. Surrey debut 1995. Suffolk 1988. 1000 runs (1): 1003 (1990). HS 139 v Yorks (Oval) 1995. BB Ex 3-91 v Surrey (Oval) 1990. Sy BB 2-29 v Derbys (Derby) 1995. **NWT:** HS 85* Ex v Glam (Cardiff) 1994. BB 1-0. **BHC:** HS 65* and BB 1-59 v Kent (Canterbury) 1995. **SL:** HS 101 v Derbys (Derby) 1995.

SMITH, Andrew William (Sutton Manor HS), b Sutton 30 May 1969. Son of W.A. (Surrey 1961-70). 5'8". RHB, OB. Debut 1993. HS 202* v OU (Oval) 1994. BAC HS 88 v Somerset (Oval) 1995. BB 5-103 v Somerset (Bath) 1994. Award: NWT 1. **NWT:** HS – . BB 3-25 v Leics (Leicester) 1993. **BHC:** HS 15* and BB 2-38 v Glam (Oval) 1994. **SL:** HS 58 v Derbys (Ilkeston) 1993. BB 3-36 v Glos (Oval) 1995.

STEWART, Alec James (Tiffin S), b Merton 8 Apr 1963. Son of M.J. (Surrey and England 1954-72). 5'11". RHB, WK. Debut 1981. Cap 1985. Captain 1992-. Benefit 1994. *Wisden* 1992. **Tests:** 53 (1989-90 to 1995-96, 2 as captain); HS 190 v P (Birmingham) 1992. **LOI:** 68 (1989-90 to 1995-96, 7 as captain; HS 103). Tours: A 1990-91, 1994-95; SA 1995-96; WI 1989-90, 1993-94; NZ 1991-92; I 1992-93; SL 1992-93 (captain). 1000 runs (8); most –

STEWART – continued:
1665 (1986). HS 206* v Essex (Oval) 1989. BB 1-7. Held 11 catches (equalling world f-c match record) v Leics (Leicester) 1989. Awards: NWT 2; BHC 4. **NWT:** HS 107* v Middx (Oval) 1988. **BHC:** HS 167* v Somerset (Oval) 1994. **SL:** HS 125 v Lancs (Oval) 1990.

THORPE, Graham Paul (Weydon CS; Farnham SFC), b Farnham 1 Aug 1969. 5'11". LHB, RM. Debut 1988. Cap 1991. **Tests:** 26 (1993 to 1995-96); HS 123 v A (Perth) 1994-95; scored 114* v A (Nottingham) 1993 on debut. **LOI:** 19 (1993 to 1995-96; HS 89 – twice). Tours: A 1992-93 (Eng A), 1994-95; SA 1995-96; WI 1991-92 (Eng A), 1993-94; P 1990-91 (Eng A); SL 1990-91 (Eng A); Z 1989-90 (Eng A). 1000 runs (6); most – 1895 (1992). HS 216 v Somerset (Oval) 1992. BB 4-40 v A (Oval) 1993. BAC BB 2-31 v Essex (Oval) 1989. Award: NWT 1. **NWT:** HS 145* v Lancs (Oval) 1994. **BHC:** HS 103 v Lancs (Oval) 1993. BB 3-35 v Middx (Lord's) 1989. **SL:** HS 115* v Lancs (Manchester) 1991. BB 3-21 v Somerset (Oval) 1991.

TUDOR, Alex Jeremy (St Mark's S, Hammersmith; City of Westminster C), b London 23 Oct 1977. RHB, RFM. Debut 1995. HS 56 v Leics (Leicester) 1995. BB 5-32 v Derbys (Derby) 1995. **NWT:** HS –. BB 1-27. **SL:** HS 29* v Essex (Oval) 1995. BB 1-19.

WARD, David Mark (Haling Manor HS), b Croydon 10 Feb 1961. 6'1". RHB, OB, occ WK. Debut 1985. Cap 1990. Benefit 1996. 1000 runs (2) inc 2000 (1): 2072 (1990). **HS** 294* v Derbys (Oval) 1994. BB 2-66 v Glos (Guildford) 1991. Awards: NWT 1; BHC 1. **NWT:** HS 101* v Glam (Swansea) 1992. **BHC:** HS 73 v Notts (Nottingham) 1994. **SL:** HS 102* v Hants (Southampton) 1990.

NEWCOMERS

HOLLIOAKE, Benjamin Caine, b Melbourne, Australia 11 Nov 1977. Brother of A.J. (*see above*). RHB, RM.

LEWIS, Clairmonte **Christopher** (Willesden HS, London), b Georgetown, Guyana 14 Feb 1968. 6'2½". RHB, RFM. Leicestershire 1987-91 (cap 1990). Nottinghamshire 1992-94 (cap 1994). **Tests:** 27 (1990 to 1994-95); HS 117 v I (Madras) 1992-93; BB 6-111 v WI (Birmingham) 1991. **LOI:** 48 (1989-90 to 1994; HS 33; BB 4-30). Tours: A 1990-91 (part), 1994-95 (part); WI 1989-90 (part), 1993-94; NZ 1991-92; I/SL 1992-93. HS 247 Nt v Durham (Chester-le-St) 1993. 50 wkts (2); most – 56 (1990). BB 6-22 Le v OU (Oxford) 1988. BAC BB 6-55 Le v Glam (Cardiff) 1990. Award: NWT 1. **NWT:** HS 89 Nt v Northumb (Jesmond) 1994. BB 3-24 Nt v Somerset (Nottingham) 1993. **BHC:** HS 48* Nt v Minor C (Nottingham) 1994. BB 5-46 Nt v Kent (Nottingham) 1992. **SL:** HS 93* Le v Essex (Leicester) 1990. BB 4-13 Le v Essex (Leicester) 1988.

McMILLAN, Brian Mervin (Carleton Jones HS; Witwatersrand U), b Welkom, OFS, SA 22 Dec 1963. 6'4". RHB, RFM. Transvaal 1984-85/1988-89. Warwickshire 1986. W Province 1989-90 to date. **Tests** (SA): 23 (1992-93 to 1995-96); HS 113 v P (Johannesburg) 1994-95. BB 4-65 v NZ (Cape Town) 1994-95. **LOI** (SA): 48 (1991-92 to 1995-96; HS 127; BB 4-32). Tours (SA): E 1994; A 1993-94; SL 1993-94; Z 1995-96. HS 140 WP v Boland (Cape Town) 1994-95. BB 5-35 WP v Natal (Cape Town) 1993-94.

PEARSON, Richard Michael (Batley GS; St John's, Cambridge), b Batley, Yorks 27 Jan 1972. 6'3". RHB, OB. Cambridge U 1991-92 (blue 1991-92). Northamptonshire 1992. Essex 1994-95. HS 33* CU v Surrey (Cambridge) 1992. BAC HS 11 Ex v Glos (Chelmsford) 1994. BB 5-108 CU v Warwks (Cambridge) 1992. BAC BB 2-90 Nh v Warwks (Northampton) 1992. **NWT:** HS –. BB 1-47. **BHC:** HS 8. BB 3-46 Ex v Glos (Chelmsford) 1995. **SL:** HS 7. BB 3-33 Ex v Leics (Leicester) 1994.

DEPARTURES (who made first-class appearances in 1995)

RACKEMANN, Carl Grey, b Wondai, Brisbane, Australia 3 Jun 1960. RHB, RFM. Queensland 1979-80 to date. Surrey 1995. **Tests** (A): 12 (1982-83 to 1990-91); HS 15* v NZ (Perth) 1989-90; BB 6-86 v P (Perth) 1983-84. **LOI** (A): 52 (1982-83 to 1990-91; HS 9*; BB 5-16). Tours (A): E 1989; SA 1985-86 (Aus XI), 1986-87 (Aus XI); WI 1983-84, 1994-95 (part); NZ 1989-90. HS 33 Q v Tasmania (Hobart) 1993-94. Sy HS 20* v Leics (Leicester) 1995. 50 wkts (0+2); most – 52 (1994-95). BB 8-84 Australian XI v SA XI (Jo'burg) 1985-86. Sy BB 6-60 v Sussex (Horsham) 1995. **NWT:** HS 6. BB 3-40 v Berks (Oval) 1995. **SL:** HS 15* v Essex (Oval) 1995. BB 3-36 v Sussex (Horsham) 1995.

SURREY 1995

RESULTS SUMMARY

	Place	Won	Lost	Drew	No Result
Britannic Assurance Championship	**12th**	5	8	4	–
All First-Class Matches		5	8	5	–
NatWest Trophy	2nd Round				
Benson and Hedges Cup	3rd in Group D				
Sunday League	**9th**	7	8	–	2

BRITANNIC ASSURANCE CHAMPIONSHIP AVERAGES

BATTING AND FIELDING

Cap		*M*	*I*	*NO*	*HS*	*Runs*	*Avge*	*100*	*50*	*Ct/St*
1985	A.J.Stewart	7	13	1	151	534	44.50	2	2	14
1994	A.D.Brown	15	29	4	187	1054	42.16	3	3	19
1991	G.P.Thorpe	10	18	–	152	717	39.83	2	4	11
1990	D.J.Bicknell	14	27	2	228*	981	39.24	2	4	5
–	N.Shahid	13	25	2	139	900	39.13	2	5	14
1995	A.J.Hollioake	17	30	2	117*	1094	39.07	1	8	12
–	M.A.Butcher	16	31	–	167	1175	37.90	2	10	13
–	J.D.Ratcliffe	8	16	–	75	536	33.50	–	5	2
–	G.J.Kersey	15	28	4	83	708	29.50	–	6	60/5
1989	M.P.Bicknell	8	12	3	61	213	23.66	–	1	1
–	A.W.Smith	8	13	–	88	272	20.92	–	2	2
1990	D.M.Ward	2	4	–	51	66	16.50	–	1	2
–	C.G.Rackemann	12	20	12	20*	120	15.00	–	–	3
–	A.J.Tudor	5	9	–	56	123	13.66	–	1	1
1993	J.E.Benjamin	11	18	4	49	174	12.42	–	–	1
–	S.G.Kenlock	4	8	2	12	50	8.33	–	–	3
1995	A.C.S.Pigott	6	11	1	19	76	7.60	–	–	1
–	R.W.Nowell	11	20	2	27	134	7.44	–	–	5

Also batted: J.M.de la Pena (2 matches) 0*, 0*, 2*; G.J.Kennis (1 match) 29, 18; N.F.Sargeant (2 matches) 6, 2 (11 ct).

BOWLING

	O	*M*	*R*	*W*	*Avge*	*Best*	*5wI*	*10wM*
M.P.Bicknell	272	64	899	41	21.92	5-61	3	–
A.J.Tudor	83.3	7	320	14	22.85	5-32	1	–
J.E.Benjamin	401.4	84	1244	51	24.39	5-37	3	–
C.G.Rackemann	445	111	1394	47	29.65	6-60	1	–
A.C.S.Pigott	209.3	50	667	22	30.31	6-91	2	1
A.J.Hollioake	230.3	46	721	21	34.33	4-22	–	–
R.W.Nowell	424.5	117	1264	32	39.50	4-43	–	–
M.A.Butcher	226.5	37	865	21	41.19	4-72	–	–

Also bowled: D.J.Bicknell 24.3-5-96-3; J.M.de la Pena 44-8-208-6; S.G.Kenlock 119-20-440-8; G.J.Kennis 3-3-0-0; N.Shahid 114-14-524-7; A.W.Smith 144-25-543-8; A.J.Stewart 3-0-18-0; G.P.Thorpe 23-4-59-2.

The First-Class Averages (pp 129-143) give the records of Surrey players in all first-class county matches (their other opponents being New South Wales), with the exception of A.J.Hollioake, A.J.Stewart and G.P.Thorpe, whose full county figures are as above, and:
M.A.Butcher 17-32-1-167-1185-38.22-2-10-14ct. 234.5-37-935-22-42.50-4/72.

SURREY RECORDS

FIRST-CLASS CRICKET

Highest Total	For	811		v	Somerset	The Oval	1899
	V	863		by	Lancashire	The Oval	1990
Lowest Total	For	14		v	Essex	Chelmsford	1983
	V	16		by	MCC	Lord's	1872
Highest Innings	For	357*	R.Abel	v	Somerset	The Oval	1899
	V	366	N.H.Fairbrother	for	Lancashire	The Oval	1990

Highest Partnership for each Wicket

1st	428	J.B.Hobbs/A.Sandham	v	Oxford U	The Oval	1926
2nd	371	J.B.Hobbs/E.G.Hayes	v	Hampshire	The Oval	1909
3rd	413	D.J.Bicknell/D.M.Ward	v	Kent	Canterbury	1990
4th	448	R.Abel/T.W.Hayward	v	Yorkshire	The Oval	1899
5th	308	J.N.Crawford/F.C.Holland	v	Somerset	The Oval	1908
6th	298	A.Sandham/H.S.Harrison	v	Sussex	The Oval	1913
7th	262	C.J.Richards/K.T.Medlycott	v	Kent	The Oval	1987
8th	205	I.A.Greig/M.P.Bicknell	v	Lancashire	The Oval	1990
9th	168	E.R.T.Holmes/E.W.J.Brooks	v	Hampshire	The Oval	1936
10th	173	A.Ducat/A.Sandham	v	Essex	Leyton	1921

Best Bowling	For	10-43	T.Rushby	v	Somerset	Taunton	1921
(Innings)	V	10-28	W.P.Howell	for	Australians	The Oval	1899
Best Bowling	For	16-83	G.A.R.Lock	v	Kent	Blackheath	1956
(Match)	V	15-57	W.P.Howell	for	Australians	The Oval	1899

Most Runs – Season	3246	T.W.Hayward	(av 72.13)	1906
Most Runs – Career	43554	J.B.Hobbs	(av 49.72)	1905-34
Most 100s – Season	13	T.W.Hayward		1906
	13	J.B.Hobbs		1925
Most 100s – Career	144	J.B.Hobbs		1905-34
Most Wkts – Season	252	T.Richardson	(av 13.94)	1895
Most Wkts – Career	1775	T.Richardson	(av 17.87)	1892-1904

LIMITED-OVERS CRICKET

Highest Total	NWT	350		v	Worcs	The Oval	1994
	BHC	331-5		v	Hampshire	The Oval	1990
	SL	375-4		v	Yorkshire	Scarborough	1994
Lowest Total	NWT	74		v	Kent	The Oval	1967
	BHC	89		v	Notts	Nottingham	1984
	SL	64		v	Worcs	Worcester	1978
Highest Innings	NWT	146	G.S.Clinton	v	Kent	Canterbury	1985
	BHC	167*	A.J.Stewart	v	Somerset	The Oval	1994
	SL	142*	A.D.Brown	v	Middlesex	The Oval	1994
Best Bowling	NWT	7-33	R.D.Jackman	v	Yorkshire	Harrogate	1970
	BHC	5-15	S.G.Kenlock	v	Ireland	The Oval	1995
	SL	6-25	Intikhab Alam	v	Derbyshire	The Oval	1974

SUSSEX

Formation of Present Club: 1 March 1839
Substantial Reorganisation: August 1857
Colours: Dark Blue, Light Blue and Gold
Badge: County Arms of Six Martlets
Championships: (0) Second 1902, 1903, 1932, 1933, 1934, 1953, 1981
NatWest Trophy/Gillette Cup Winners: (4) 1963, 1964, 1978, 1986
Benson and Hedges Cup Winners: (0) Semi-Finalists 1982
Sunday League Champions: (1) 1982
Match Awards: NWT 50; BHC 50

Secretary: N.Bett
County Ground, Eaton Road, Hove BN3 3AN (Tel 01273 732161)
Captain: A.P.Wells
Scorer: L.V.Chandler
1996 Beneficiary: A.P.Wells

ATHEY, Charles William Jeffrey (Stainsby SS; Acklam Hall HS), b Middlesbrough, Yorks 27 Sep 1957. 5'9½". RHB, RM. Yorkshire 1976-83 (cap 1980). Gloucestershire 1984-92 (cap 1985; captain 1989; benefit 1990). Sussex debut/cap 1993. **Tests:** 23 (1980 to 1988); HS 123 v P (Lord's) 1987. **LOI:** 31 (1980 to 1987-88; HS 142*). Tours: A 1986-87, 1987-88; SA 1989-90 (Eng A); WI 1980-81; NZ 1979-80 (DHR), 1987-88; P 1987-88; SL 1985-86 (Eng B). 1000 runs (12); most – 1812 (1984). HS 184 Eng B v Sri Lanka (Galle) 1985-86. BAC HS 181 Gs v Sussex (Cheltenham) 1992. Sx HS 169* v Kent (Tunbridge W) 1994. BB 3-3 Gs v Hants (Bristol) 1985. Sx BB 2-40 v Notts (Eastbourne) 1993. Awards: NWT 4; BHC 6. **NWT:** HS 115 Y v Kent (Leeds) 1980. BB 1-18. **BHC:** HS 118 v Kent (Hove) 1995. BB 4-48 Gs v Comb Us (Bristol) 1984. **SL:** HS 121* Gs v Worcs (Moreton) 1985. BB 5-35 Y v Derbys (Chesterfield) 1981.

BATES, Justin Jonathan (Hurstpierpoint C), b Farnborough, Hants 9 Apr 1976. 5'11". RHB, OB. Sussex staff 1995 – awaiting f-c debut.

EDWARDS Alexander David (Imberhorne CS, E Grinstead; Loughborough U), b Cuckfield 2 Aug 1975. 6'0". RHB, RFM. Combined Us 1995. Sussex debut 1995. Awaiting BAC debut. HS 22 and BB 3-83 v Young A (Hove) 1995. **BHC:** HS 7*. BB 2-51 Comb Us v Middx (Lord's) 1995. **SL:** HS –.

GIDDINS, Edward Simon Hunter (Eastbourne C), b Eastbourne 20 Jul 1971. 6'4½". RHB, RMF. Debut 1991. Cap 1994. MCC YC. Tour: P 1995-96 (Eng A). HS 34 v Essex (Hove) 1995. 50 wkts (2); most – 68 (1995). BB 6-73 v Somerset (Bath) 1995. **NWT:** HS 13 v Essex (Hove) 1994. BB 2-21 v Northants (Northampton) 1993. **BHC:** HS 0*. BB 3-28 v Surrey (Oval) 1995. **SL:** HS 9*. BB 4-23 v Kent (Tunbridge W) 1994.

GREENFIELD, Keith (Falmer HS), b Brighton 6 Dec 1968. 6'0". RHB, RM. Debut 1987. HS 127* v CU (Hove) 1991. BAC HS 121 v Essex (Hove) 1995. BB 2-40 v Essex (Hove) 1993. Award: NWT 1. **NWT:** HS 96* v Wales (Hove) 1993. BB 2-35 v Glam (Hove) 1993. **BHC:** HS 62 v Leics (Leicester) 1992. BB 1-35. **SL:** HS 102 v Notts (Arundel) 1995. BB 3-34 v Northants (Hove) 1995.

HALL, James William (Chichester HS), b Chichester 30 Mar 1968. 6'3". RHB, OB. Debut 1990. Cap 1992. 1000 runs (2); most – 1140 (1990 – debut season). HS 140* v Lancs (Hove) 1992. Award: BHC 1. **NWT:** HS 70 v Derbys (Hove) 1995. **BHC:** HS 81 v Surrey (Hove) 1992. **SL:** HS 77 v Notts (Nottingham) 1992.

HUMPHRIES, Shaun (The Weald, Billingshurst; Kingston C, London), b Horsham 11 Jan 1973. 5'9". RHB, WK. Debut 1993. HS – . Awaiting BAC debut.

JARVIS, Paul William (Bydales CS, Marske), b Redcar, Yorks 29 Jun 1965. 5'10". RHB, RFM. Yorkshire 1981-93 (cap 1986); youngest Yorkshire debutant at 16yr 75d. Sussex debut 1994. **Tests:** 9 (1987-88 to 1992-93); HS 29* and BB 4-107 v WI (Lord's) 1988. **LOI:** 16 (1987-88 to 1993; HS 16*; BB 5-35). Tours: SA 1989-90 (Eng XI); WI 1986-87 (Y); NZ 1987-88; I/SL 1992-93; P 1987-88. HS 80 Y v Northants (Scarborough) 1992. Sx HS 70* v SA (Hove) 1994. 50 wkts (4); most – 81 (1987). BB 7-55 Y v Surrey (Leeds) 1986. Sx BB 7-58 v Somerset (Hove) 1994. Hat-trick 1985 (Y). **NWT:** HS 16 Y v Somerset (Leeds) 1985. BB 4-41 Y v Leics (Leeds) 1987. **BHC:** HS 42 Y v Lancs (Leeds) 1990. BB 4-34 Y v Warwks (Birmingham) 1992. **SL:** HS 38* Y v Glam (Middlesbrough) 1993. BB 6-27 Y v Somerset (Taunton) 1989.

KIRTLEY, Robert James (Clifton C), b Eastbourne 10 Jan 1975. 6'0". RHB, RFM. Debut 1995. HS 2*. BB 1-28. **SL:** HS 2. BB 1-49.

LAW, Danny Richard (Steyning GS), b Lambeth, London 15 Jul 1975. 6'5". RHB, RFM. Debut 1993. HS 115 v Young A (Hove) 1995. BAC HS 19 v Middx (Lord's) 1995. BB 2-38 v Worcs (Hove) 1993. **SL:** HS 41* v Derbys (Derby) 1995.

LENHAM, Neil John (Brighton C), b Worthing 17 Dec 1965. Son of L.J. (Sussex 1956-70). 5'11". RHB, RM. Debut 1984. Cap 1990. 1000 runs (3); most – 1663 (1990). HS 222* v Kent (Hove) 1992. BB 4-13 v Durham (Durham) 1993. Awards: NWT 2; BHC 1. **NWT:** HS 129* v Devon (Hove) 1995. BB 2-12 v Ire (Downpatrick) 1990. **BHC:** HS 82 v Somerset (Hove) 1986. BB 1-3. **SL:** HS 86 v Kent (Hove) 1991. BB 5-28 v Durham (Durham) 1993.

LEWRY, Jason David (Durrington HS, Worthing), b Worthing 2 Apr 1971. 6'2". LHB, LMF. Debut 1994. HS 34 v Kent (Hove) 1995. BB 6-43 v Worcs (Eastbourne) 1995. **NWT:** HS 2*. BB 3-63 v Devon (Hove) 1995. **BHC:** HS 14* v Ire (Hove) 1995. **SL:** HS 7*. BB 4-29 v Somerset (Bath) 1995.

MARTIN-JENKINS, Robin Simon Christopher (Radley C; Durham U), b Guildford, Surrey 28 Oct 1975. Son of C.M.J. (*Daily Telegraph* Cricket Correspondent). 6'5". RHB, RFM. Debut 1995. HS 50 v Northants (Hove) 1995. **SL:** HS 10 v Northants (Hove) 1995. BB 2-41 v Middx (Lord's) 1995.

MOORES, Peter (King Edward VI S, Macclesfield), b Macclesfield, Cheshire 18 Dec 1962. 6'0". RHB, WK. Worcestershire 1983-84. Sussex debut 1985. Cap 1989. OFS 1988-89. HS 116 v Somerset (Hove) 1989. **NWT:** HS 26 v Scot (Edinburgh) 1991. **BHC:** HS 76 v Middx (Hove) 1990. **SL:** HS 89* v Leics (Hove) 1995.

NEWELL, Keith (Ifield Community C), b Crawley 25 Mar 1972. Brother of M. 6'0". RHB, RM. Debut 1995. Matabeleland 1995-96. HS 135 v WI (Hove) 1995. BAC HS 63 v Glam (Swansea) 1995 – on debut. **NWT:** HS 52 v Derbys (Hove) 1995. **BHC:** HS 35 v Kent (Hove) 1995. **SL:** HS 76* v Kent (Hove) 1995.

NEWELL, Mark (Hazelwick SS; City of Westminster C), b Crawley 19 Dec 1973. Brother of K. 6'1½". RHB, OB. Sussex staff 1995 – awaiting f-c debut.

PHILLIPS, Nicholas Charles (Wm Parker S, Hastings), b Pembury, Kent 10 May 1974. 5'10½". RHB, OB. Debut 1993. HS 53 v Young A (Hove) 1995. BB 3-39 v CU (Hove) 1993. BAC HS 52 and BB 3-78 v Lancs (Lytham) 1995. **SL:** HS 11* v Worcs (Worcester) 1994. BB 2-19 v Somerset (Hove) 1994.

SALISBURY, Ian David Kenneth (Moulton CS), b Northampton 21 Jan 1970. 5'11". RHB, LB. Debut 1989. Cap 1991. MCC YC. YC 1992. *Wisden* 1992. **Tests:** 7 (1992 to 1994); HS 50 v P (Manchester) 1992; BB 4-163 v WI (Georgetown) 1993-94. **LOI:** 4 (1992-93 to 1993-94; HS 5; BB 3-41). Tours (Eng A): WI 1991-92, 1993-94 (Eng); I 1992-93 (Eng), 1994-95; P 1990-91, 1995-96; SL 1990-91. HS 74 v Glos (Hove) 1995. 50 wkts (3); most – 87 (1992). BB 7-54 (12-138 match) v Yorks (Hove) 1992. Award: BHC 1. **NWT:** HS 14* v Essex (Hove) 1991. BB 3-28 v Bucks (Beaconsfield) 1992. **BHC:** HS 17* and BB 3-40 v Kent (Canterbury) 1991. **SL:** HS 48* v Glam (Swansea) 1995. BB 5-30 v Leics (Leicester) 1992.

SPEIGHT, Martin Peter (Hurstpierpoint C; Durham U), b Walsall, Staffs 24 Oct 1967. 5'9". RHB, WK. Debut 1986. Cap 1991. Wellington 1989-90/1992-93. 1000 runs (3); most – 1375 (1990). HS 184 v Notts (Eastbourne) 1993. BB 1-2. Award: BHC 1. **NWT:** HS 50 v Warwks (Lord's) 1993. **BHC:** HS 83 Comb Us v Glos (Bristol) 1988. **SL:** HS 126 v Somerset (Taunton) 1993. Missed entire 1995 season through severe viral infection.

WELLS, Alan Peter (Tideway CS, Newhaven), b Newhaven 2 Oct 1961. Younger brother of C.M. (*see DERBYSHIRE*). 6'0". RHB, RM. Debut 1981. Cap 1986. Captain 1992-. Benefit 1996. Border 1981-82. **Tests:** 1 (1995); HS 3*. **LOI:** 1 (1995; HS 15). Tours (Eng A): SA 1989-90 (Eng XI), 1993-94; I 1994-95 (captain). 1000 runs (9); most – 1784 (1991). HS 253* v Yorks (Middlesbrough) 1991. BB 3-67 v Worcs (Worcester) 1987. Awards: NWT 2. **NWT:** HS 119 v Bucks (Beaconsfield) 1992. **BHC:** HS 74 v Middx (Hove) 1990. BB 1-17. **SL:** HS 127 v Hants (Portsmouth) 1993. BB 1-0.

NEWCOMER

DRAKES, Vasbert Conneil (St Lucy SS), b St James, Barbados 5 Aug 1969. 6'2". RHB, RFM. Barbados 1991-92 to date. **LOI** (WI): 5 (1994-95; HS 16; BB 1-36). Tour (WI): E 1995. HS 180* Barbados v Leeward Is (Anguilla) 1994-95. UK HS 48* WI v Yorks (Scarborough) 1995. BB 7-47 Barbados v Guyana (Bridgetown) 1994-95. UK BB 5-20 WI v Kent (Canterbury) 1995.

DEPARTURES (who made first-class appearances in 1995)

HEMMINGS, Edward Ernest (Campion S), b Leamington Spa, Warwks 20 Feb 1949. 5'10". RHB, OB. Warwickshire 1966-78 (cap 1974). Nottinghamshire 1979-92 (cap 1980; benefit 1987). Sussex 1993-95 (cap 1993). **Tests:** 16 (1982 to 1990-91); HS 95 v A (Sydney) 1982-83; BB 6-58 v NZ (Birmingham) 1990. **LOI:** 33 (1982 to 1990-91; HS 8*; BB 4-52). Tours: A 1982-83, 1987-88, 1990-91; SA 1974-75 (DHR); WI 1982-83 (Int), 1989-90; NZ 1987-88; P 1981-82 (Int), 1987-88. HS 127* Nt v Yorks (Worksop) 1982. Sx HS 18 v Somerset (Bath) 1995. 50 wkts (15); most – 94 (1984). BB 10-175 Int XI v WI XI (Kingston) 1982-83. BAC BB 7-23 Nt v Lancs (Nottingham) 1983. Sx BB 7-31 (12-58 match) v Leics (Horsham) 1993. 2 hat-tricks: 1977 (Wa), 1984 (Nt). Awards: NWT 1; BHC 1. **NWT:** HS 31* Nt v Staffs (Nottingham) 1985. BB 3-27 Nt v Warwks (Nottingham) 1985. **BHC:** HS 61* Wa v Leics (Birmingham) 1974. BB 4-47 Nt v Glos (Bristol) 1989. **SL:** HS 44* Wa v Kent (Birmingham) 1971. BB 5-22 Wa v Notts (Birmingham) 1974.

PEIRCE, Michael Toby Edward (Ardingly C; Durham U), b Maidenhead, Berks 14 Jun 1973. 5'10". LHB, SLA. Combined Us 1994. Sussex 1995. HS 24 Comb Us v NZ (Cambridge) 1994. HS 60 v Worcs (Eastbourne) 1995. **BHC:** HS 44 Comb Us v Middx (Lord's) 1995. **SL:** HS 7.

REMY, C.C. – *see LEICESTERSHIRE.*

STEPHENSON, Franklyn Dacosta (Samuel Jackson Prescod Poly), b St James, Barbados 8 Apr 1959. 6'3½". RHB, RFM. Barbados 1981-82 and 1989-90. Tasmania 1981-82. Gloucestershire 1982-83. Nottinghamshire 1988-91 (cap 1988). OFS 1991-92 to date. Sussex 1992-95 (cap 1992). Staffordshire 1980. *Wisden* 1988. Tours (WI XI): SA 1982-83, 1983-84. 1000 runs (1): 1018 (1988). HS 165 Barbados v Leeward Is (Basseterre) 1981-82. Sx HS 133 v Somerset (Hove) 1992. 50 wkts (5) inc 100 (1): 125 (1988). BB 8-47 (15-106 match) Nt v Essex (Nottingham) 1989. Sx BB 7-29 (11-107 match) v Worcs (Worcester) 1992. Scored 111 and 117 and took 11-222 Nt v Yorks (Nottingham) 1988. Double 1988. Awards: NWT 1; BHC 3. **NWT:** HS 40 v Warwks (Birmingham) 1992. BB 3-8 v Bucks (Beaconsfield) 1992. **BHC:** HS 98* Nt v Worcs (Nottingham) 1990. BB 5-30 Nt v Yorks (Nottingham) 1991. **SL:** HS 103 v Surrey (Hove) 1993. BB 5-23 v Essex (Hove) 1993.

SUSSEX 1995

RESULTS SUMMARY

	Place	Won	Lost	Drew	No Result
Britannic Assurance Championship	**15th**	4	7	6	–
All First-Class Matches		5	8	6	–
NatWest Trophy	2nd Round				
Benson and Hedges Cup	4th in Group D				
Sunday League	**10th**	7	8	–	2

BRITANNIC ASSURANCE CHAMPIONSHIP AVERAGES

BATTING AND FIELDING

Cap		*M*	*I*	*NO*	*HS*	*Runs*	*Avge*	*100*	*50*	*Ct/St*
1986	A.P.Wells	15	26	1	142	1322	52.88	6	4	8
1993	C.W.J.Athey	14	25	1	163*	869	36.20	2	5	6
1990	N.J.Lenham	13	22	3	104	624	32.84	1	3	9
1992	F.D.Stephenson	12	22	–	106	658	29.90	1	3	2
–	K.Greenfield	17	29	1	121	794	28.35	1	5	11
1992	J.W.Hall	11	20	–	100	504	25.20	1	2	5
1991	I.D.K.Salisbury	17	29	3	74	599	23.03	–	2	16
–	K.Newell	9	18	2	63	365	22.81	–	2	3
–	M.T.E.Peirce	5	8	–	60	174	21.75	–	1	4
1989	P.Moores	17	29	2	94	570	21.11	–	5	38/2
–	N.C.Phillips	5	8	1	52	130	18.57	–	2	2
–	P.W.Jarvis	8	12	2	38	177	17.70	–	–	8
1993	E.E.Hemmings	6	12	7	18	70	14.00	–	–	1
–	J.D.Lewry	10	16	3	34	139	10.69	–	–	1
1994	E.S.H.Giddins	17	25	10	34	127	8.46	–	–	3
–	D.R.Law	6	10	–	19	82	8.20	–	–	4

Also batted: R.J.Kirtley (2 matches) 2*, 1* (2 ct); R.S.C.Martin-Jenkins (2 matches) 0*, 50; C.C.Remy (1 match) 4, 1.

BOWLING

	O	*M*	*R*	*W*	*Avge*	*Best*	*5wI*	*10wM*
J.D.Lewry	287.4	50	1008	38	26.52	6-43	3	–
P.W.Jarvis	202.4	39	629	23	27.34	5-55	1	–
E.S.H.Giddins	583.4	104	1929	67	28.79	6-73	4	1
I.D.K.Salisbury	550.2	128	1649	52	31.71	7-72	5	1
F.D.Stephenson	346.2	71	1069	31	34.48	5-64	1	–
E.E.Hemmings	159.5	46	402	11	36.54	4-57	–	–

Also bowled: C.W.J.Athey 7-1-35-0; K.Greenfield 17.1-1-71-0; R.J.Kirtley 38-11-103-2; D.R.Law 45-6-215-4; N.J.Lenham 2-0-10-1; R.S.C.Martin-Jenkins 3-1-11-0; K.Newell 40-8-127-0; M.T.E.Peirce 6-1-14-0; N.C.Phillips 114.5-23-364-7; C.C.Remy 22.3-2-114-0.

The First-Class Averages (pp 129-143) give the records of Sussex players in all first-class county matches (their other opponents being the West Indians and Young Australia), with the exception of:

A.D.Edwards 1-2-0-22-23-11.50-0-0-0ct. 23-4-87-3-29.00-3/83.

A.P.Wells 16-27-1-142-1343-51.65-6-4-9ct. Did not bowl.

SUSSEX RECORDS

FIRST-CLASS CRICKET

Highest Total	For	705-8d		v	Surrey	Hastings	1902
	V	726		by	Notts	Nottingham	1895
Lowest Total	For	19		v	Surrey	Godalming	1830
		19		v	Notts	Hove	1873
	V	18		by	Kent	Gravesend	1867
Highest Innings	For	333	K.S.Duleepsinhji	v	Northants	Hove	1930
	V	322	E.Paynter	for	Lancashire	Hove	1937

Highest Partnership for each Wicket

1st	490	E.H.Bowley/J.G.Langridge	v	Middlesex	Hove	1933
2nd	385	E.H.Bowley/M.W.Tate	v	Northants	Hove	1921
3rd	298	K.S.Ranjitsinhji/E.H.Killick	v	Lancashire	Hove	1901
4th	326*	J.Langridge/G.Cox	v	Yorkshire	Leeds	1949
5th	297	J.H.Parks/H.W.Parks	v	Hampshire	Portsmouth	1937
6th	255	K.S.Duleepsinhji/M.W.Tate	v	Northants	Hove	1930
7th	344	K.S.Ranjitsinhji/W.Newham	v	Essex	Leyton	1902
8th	229*	C.L.A.Smith/G.Brann	v	Kent	Hove	1902
9th	178	H.W.Parks/A.F.Wensley	v	Derbyshire	Horsham	1930
10th	156	G.R.Cox/H.R.Butt	v	Cambridge U	Cambridge	1908

Best Bowling	For	10- 48	C.H.G.Bland	v	Kent	Tonbridge	1899
(Innings)	V	9- 11	A.P.Freeman	for	Kent	Hove	1922
Best Bowling	For	17-106	G.R.Cox	v	Warwicks	Horsham	1926
(Match)	V	17- 67	A.P.Freeman	for	Kent	Hove	1922

Most Runs – Season	2850	J.G.Langridge	(av 64.77)	1949
Most Runs – Career	34152	J.G.Langridge	(av 37.69)	1928-55
Most 100s – Season	12	J.G.Langridge		1949
Most 100s – Career	76	J.G.Langridge		1928-55
Most Wkts – Season	198	M.W.Tate	(av 13.47)	1925
Most Wkts – Career	2211	M.W.Tate	(av 17.41)	1912-37

LIMITED-OVERS CRICKET

Highest Total	NWT	327-6		v	Bucks	Beaconsfield	1992
	BHC	305-6		v	Kent	Hove	1982
	SL	312-8		v	Hampshire	Portsmouth	1993
Lowest Total	NWT	49		v	Derbyshire	Chesterfield	1969
	BHC	61		v	Middlesex	Hove	1978
	SL	61		v	Derbyshire	Derby	1978
Highest Innings	NWT	141*	G.D.Mendis	v	Warwicks	Hove	1980
	BHC	118	C.W.J.Athey	v	Kent	Hove	1995
	SL	129	A.W.Greig	v	Yorkshire	Scarborough	1976
Best Bowling	NWT	6- 9	A.I.C.Dodemaide	v	Ireland	Downpatrick	1990
	BHC	5- 8	Imran Khan	v	Northants	Northampton	1978
	SL	7-41	A.N.Jones	v	Notts	Nottingham	1986

WARWICKSHIRE

Formation of Present Club: 8 April 1882
Substantial Reorganisation: 19 January 1884
Colours: Dark Blue, Gold and Silver
Badge: Bear and Ragged Staff
Championships: (5) 1911, 1951, 1972, 1994, 1995
NatWest Trophy/Gillette Cup Winners: (5) 1966, 1968, 1989, 1993, 1995
Benson and Hedges Cup Winners: (1) 1994
Sunday League Champions: (2) 1980, 1994
Match Awards: NWT 58; BHC 49

Chief Executive: D.L.Amiss MBE
County Ground, Edgbaston, Birmingham, B5 7QU (Tel 0121 446 4422)
Captain: D.A.Reeve OBE
Scorer: A.E.Davis
1996 Beneficiary: D.A.Reeve OBE

ALTREE, Darren Anthony (Ashlawn S, Rugby), b Rugby 30 Sep 1974. 5'10". RHB, LM. Warwickshire staff 1994 – awaiting f-c debut.

BELL, Michael Anthony Vincent (Bishop Milner CS; Dudley TC), b Birmingham 19 Dec 1966. 6'2". RHB, LMF. Debut 1992. MCC YC. Tour (Wa): Z 1993-94. HS 22* and BB 7-48 v Glos (Birmingham) 1993. **NWT:** HS – . BB 2-41 v Northants (Lord's) 1995. **BHC:** HS – . BB 2-34 v Middx (Lord's) 1994. **SL:** HS 8*. BB 5-19 v Leics (Birmingham) 1994.

BROWN, Douglas Robert (Alloa Academy; W London IHE), b Stirling, Scotland 29 Oct 1969. 6'2". RHB, RFM. Scotland 1989. Warwickshire debut 1991-92 (SA tour). Cap 1995. Wellington 1995-96. Tours (Wa): SA 1991-92, 1994-95. HS 85 v Essex (Ilford) 1995. BB 4-24 v Yorks (Birmingham) 1995. **NWT:** HS 58 v Derbys (Derby) 1995. BB 2-35 v Northants (Lord's) 1995. **BHC:** HS 24 Scot v Notts (Glasgow) 1990. BB 3-43 v Leics (Leicester) 1995. **SL:** HS 78* v Notts (Nottingham) 1995. BB 3-21 v Hants (Birmingham) 1992.

BURNS, Michael (Walney CS), b Barrow-in-Furness, Lancs 6 Jun 1969. 6'0". RHB, WK, occ RM. Cumberland 1988-90. Debut 1992. HS 78 v CU (Cambridge) 1992. BAC HS 35 v Middx (Birmingham) 1995. **BHC:** HS 22 v Leics (Leicester) 1993. **SL:** HS 37 v Derbys (Birmingham) 1994.

FROST, Tony (James Brinkley HS; Stoke-on-Trent C), b Stoke-on-Trent, Staffs 17 Nov 1975. 5'11". RHB, WK. Warwickshire staff 1994 – awaiting f-c debut.

GILES, Ashley Fraser (George Abbot S, Guildford), b Chertsey, Surrey 19 Mar 1973. 6'3". RHB, SLA. Debut 1993. HS 32 v Hants (Southampton) 1995. BB 5-23 v Worcs (Birmingham) 1995. **NWT:** HS 21* v Derbys (Derby) 1995. BB 3-14 v Glam (Cardiff) 1995. **SL:** HS – .

KHAN, Wasim Gulzar (Small Heath CS; Josiah Mason SFC, Erdington), b Birmingham 26 Feb 1971. 6'1". LHB, LB. Debut 1995. HS 181 v Hants (Southampton) 1995. **SL:** HS 7.

KNIGHT, Nicholas Verity (Felsted S; Loughborough U), b Watford, Herts 28 Nov 1969. 6'0". LHB, occ RM. Essex 1991-94 (cap 1994). Warwickshire debut 1994-95 (SA tour). Cap 1995. **Tests:** 2 (1995): HS 57 v WI (Nottingham) 1995. Tours (Eng A): SA 1994-95 (Wa); I 1994-95; P 1995-96. HS 174 v Kent (Canterbury) 1995. BB 1-61. Awards: NWT 1; BHC 1. **NWT:** HS 151 v Somerset (Birmingham) 1995. **BHC:** HS 91 v Durham (Birmingham) 1995. **SL:** HS 80 v Glam (Cardiff) 1995. BB 1-14.

MOLES, Andrew James (Finham Park CS; Butts CHE), b Solihull 12 Feb 1961. 5'10". RHB, RM. Debut 1986. Cap 1987. Benefit 1997. GW 1986-87/1988-89. Tours (Wa): SA 1991-92, 1992-93, 1994-95. 1000 runs (6); most – 1854 (1990). HS 230* GW v N Transvaal B (Verwoerdburg) 1988-89. Wa HS 224* v Glam (Swansea) 1990. BB 3-21 v OU (Oxford) 1987. BAC BB 3-50 v Essex (Chelmsford) 1987. Awards: NWT 2; BHC 2. **NWT:** HS 127 v Bucks (Birmingham) 1987. **BHC:** HS 89 v Lancs (Birmingham) 1995. BB 1-11. **SL:** HS 96* v Glam (Birmingham) 1992. BB 2-24 v Worcs (Worcester) 1987.

MUNTON, Timothy Alan (Sarson HS; King Edward VII Upper S), b Melton Mowbray, Leics 30 Jul 1965. 6'5". RHB, RMF. Debut 1985. Cap 1989. *Wisden* 1994. **Tests:** 2 (1992); HS 25* v P (Manchester) 1992; BB 2-22 v P (Leeds) 1992. Tours: SA 1992-93 (Wa); WI 1991-92 (Eng A); P 1990-91 (Eng A), 1995-96 (Eng A – part); SL 1990-91 (Eng A); Z 1993-94 (Wa). HS 47 v Kent (Birmingham) 1992. 50 wkts (5); most – 81 (1994). BB 8-89 (11-128 match) v Middx (Birmingham) 1991. Awards: NWT 2; BHC 1. **NWT:** HS 5. BB 3-36 v Kent (Canterbury) 1989. **BHC:** HS 13 v Leics (Leicester) 1989. BB 4-35 v Surrey (Oval) 1991. **SL:** HS 15* v Yorks (Scarborough) 1994. BB 5-23 v Glos (Moreton) 1990.

OSTLER, Dominic Piers (Princethorpe C; Solihull TC), b Solihull 15 Jul 1970. 6'3". RHB, occ RM. Debut 1990. Cap 1991. Tours: SA 1992-93 (Wa); P 1995-96 (Eng A). 1000 runs (4); most – 1284 (1991). HS 208 v Surrey (Birmingham) 1995. Awards: NWT 2. **NWT:** HS 104 and BB 1-4 v Norfolk (Lakenham) 1993. **BHC:** HS 87 v Notts (Birmingham) 1995. **SL:** HS 84* v Sussex (Hove) 1994.

PENNEY, Trevor Lionel (Prince Edward S, Salisbury), b Salisbury, Rhodesia 12 Jun 1968. 6'0". RHB, RM. Qualified for England 1992. Debut for Boland 1991-92. Warwickshire debut 1991-92 (SA tour). UK debut v CU (Cambridge) 1992, scoring 102*. Cap 1994. Mashonaland 1993-94. Tours (Wa): SA 1991-92, 1992-93, 1994-95; Z 1993-94. 1000 runs (1): 1198 (1995). HS 151 v Middx (Lord's) 1992. BB 3-18 Mashonaland v Mashonaland U-24 (Harare) 1993-94. Award: NWT 1. **NWT:** HS 65* v Leics (Leicester) 1994. BB 1-8. **BHC:** HS 39 v Middx (Lord's) 1994. **SL:** HS 83* v Kent (Canterbury) 1993.

PIPER, Keith John (Haringey Cricket C), b Leicester 18 Dec 1969. 5'6". RHB, WK. Debut 1989. Cap 1992. Tours (Wa): SA 1991-92, 1992-93, 1994-95; I 1994-95 (Eng A); P 1995-96 (Eng A); Z 1993-94. HS 116* v Durham (Birmingham) 1994. BB 1-57. **NWT:** HS 16* v Worcs (Lord's) 1994. **BHC:** HS 11* v Surrey (Oval) 1991. **SL:** HS 30 v Lancs (Manchester) 1990.

POWELL, Michael James (Lawrence Sheriff S, Rugby), b Bolton, Lancs 5 Apr 1975. 5'11". RHB, RM. Warwickshire staff 1994 – awaiting f-c debut.

REEVE, Dermot Alexander (King George V S, Kowloon), b Kowloon, Hong Kong 2 Apr 1963. 6'0". RHB, RMF. Sussex 1983-87 (cap 1986). Warwickshire debut 1988. Cap 1989. Captain 1993-. Benefit 1996. *Wisden* 1995. OBE 1996. Hong Kong 1982 (ICC Trophy). MCC YC. **Tests:** 3 (1991-92); HS 59 v NZ (Christchurch) 1991-92 (on debut); BB 1-4. **LOI:** 27 (1991 to 1995-96; HS 33*; BB 3-20). Tours (C=captain): SA 1992-93C (Wa), 1994-95C (Wa); NZ 1991-92; I 1992-93; Z 1993-94C (Wa). 1000 runs (2); most – 1412 (1990). HS 202* v Northants (Northampton) 1990. 50 wkts (2); most – 55 (1984). BB 7-37 Sx v Lancs (Lytham) 1987. Wa BB 6-73 v Kent (Tunbridge W) 1991. Awards: NWT 5; BHC 2. **NWT:** HS 81* v Sussex (Lord's) 1993. BB 4-20 Sx v Lancs (Lord's) 1986. **BHC:** HS 80 v Essex (Birmingham) 1991. BB 4-37 v Durham (Birmingham) 1995. **SL:** HS 100 v Lancs (Birmingham) 1991. BB 5-23 v Essex (Birmingham) 1988.

SINGH, Anurag (King Edward's, Birmingham; Gonville & Caius C, Cambridge), b Kanpur, India 9 Sep 1975. 5'10". RHB, OB. Debut 1995. HS 7.

SMALL, Gladstone Cleophas (Moseley S; Hall Green TC), b St George, Barbados 18 Oct 1961. 5'11". RHB, RFM. Debut 1979-80 (DHR XI in NZ). Warwickshire debut 1980. Cap 1982. Benefit 1992. S Australia 1985-86. **Tests:** 17 (1986 to 1990); HS 59 v A (Oval) 1989; BB 5-48 v A (Melbourne) 1986-87. **LOI:** 53 (1986-87 to 1992; HS 18*; BB 4-31). Tours: A 1986-87, 1990-91; SA 1992-93 (Wa), 1994-95 (Wa); WI 1989-90; NZ 1979-80 (DHR); P 1981-82 (Int); Z 1993-94 (Wa). HS 70 v Lancs (Manchester) 1988. 50 wkts (6); most – 80 (1988). BB 7-15 v Notts (Birmingham) 1988. Award: NWT 1. **NWT:** HS 33 v Surrey (Lord's) 1982. BB 3-22 v Glam (Cardiff) 1982. **BHC:** HS 22 v Kent (Canterbury) 1990. BB 4-22 v Glam (Birmingham) 1990. **SL:** HS 40* v Essex (Ilford) 1984. BB 5-29 v Surrey (Birmingham) 1980.

SMITH, Neil Michael Knight (Warwick S), b Birmingham 27 Jul 1967. Son of M.J.K. (Leics, Warwks and England 1951-75). 6'0". RHB, OB. Debut 1987. Cap 1993. MCC YC.

SMITH, N.M.K. – continued:
LOI: 2 (1995-96; HS 3; BB 2-46). Tours (Wa): SA 1991-92, 1994-95; Z 1993-94. HS 161 v Yorks (Leeds) 1989. BB 7-42 v Lancs (Birmingham) 1994. Awards: NWT 1; BHC 1. **NWT:** HS 65 v Kent (Birmingham) 1995. BB 5-17 v Norfolk (Lakenham) 1993. **BHC:** HS 32 v Somerset (Taunton) 1992. BB 3-29 v Middx (Lord's) 1994. **SL:** HS 71 v Somerset (Birmingham) 1995. BB 6-33 v Sussex (Birmingham) 1995.

SMITH, Paul Andrew (Heaton GS), b Jesmond, Northumb 15 Apr 1964. Son of K.D. sr (Leics 1950-51) and brother of K.D. jr (Warwks 1973-85). 6'2". RHB, RFM. Debut 1982. Cap 1986. Benefit 1995. MCC YC. Tours (Wa): SA 1991-92, 1994-95. 1000 runs (2); most – 1508 (1986). HS 140 v Worcs (Worcester) 1989. BB 6-91 v Derbys (Birmingham) 1992. 2 hat-tricks: 1989, 1990. Awards: BHC 3. **NWT:** HS 79 v Durham (Birmingham) 1986. BB 4-37 v Yorks (Leeds) 1993. **BHC:** HS 74 v Northants (Birmingham) 1989. BB 3-28 v Middx (Lord's) 1991. **SL:** HS 93* v Middx (Birmingham) 1989. BB 5-36 v Worcs (Birmingham) 1993.

WELCH, Graeme (Hetton CS), b Durham 21 Mar 1972. 5'11½". RHB, RM. Debut 1994. Tour: SA 1994-95 (Wa). HS 84* v Notts (Birmingham) 1994. BB 4-74 v Yorks (Scarborough) 1994. **NWT:** HS 0*. **BHC:** HS 27* v Lancs (Birmingham) 1995. BB 1-24. **SL:** HS 26 v Surrey (Guildford) and v Yorks (Scarborough) 1994. BB 2-30 v Sussex (Hove) 1994.

NEWCOMERS

EDMOND, Michael b Barrow-in-Furness, Lancs 30 Jul 1969. RHB, RFM.

McDONALD, Stephen (Bristnall Hall HS; Rowley Regis C), b Birmingham 2 Oct 1974. 5'10". RHB, OB.

POLLOCK, Shaun Maclean (Northwood HS; Durban U), b Port Elizabeth, SA 16 Jul 1973. Son of P.M. (EP and SA 1958-59/1971-72); nephew of R.G. (EP, Transvaal and SA 1960-61/1986-87). RHB, RFM. Natal 1991-92 to date. **Tests** (SA): 5 (1995-96); HS 36* v E (Durban) 1995-96; BB 5-32 v E (Cape Town) 1995-96. **LOI** (SA): 7 (1995-96; HS 66* and BB 4-34 v E (Cape Town) 1995-96 – on debut). HS 56 Natal v Border (East London) 1993-94. BB (*see Tests*).

VESTERGAARD, Soren (Fredericksberg C), b Copenhagen, Denmark 1 Mar 1972. 6'2". RHB, RFM. Represented Denmark in 1994 ICC Trophy.

WAGH, Mark Anant (King Edward's S, Birmingham; Keble C, Oxford), b Birmingham 20 Feb 1976. 6'2". RHB, OB.

DEPARTURES (who made first-class appearances in 1995)

DAVIS, R.P. *see GLOUCESTERSHIRE.*

DONALD, Allan Anthony (Grey College HS), b Bloemfontein, SA 20 Oct 1966. 6'2". RHB, RF. OFS 1985-86 to date. Warwickshire 1987-93, 1995 (cap 1989). *Wisden* 1991. **Tests** (SA): 25 (1991-92 to 1995-96); HS 33 and BB 8-71 (11-113 match) v Z (Harare) 1995-96. **LOI** (SA): 57 (1991-92 to 1995-96; HS 7*; BB 5-29). Tours (SA): E 1994; A 1993-94; WI 1991-92; NZ 1994-95; SL 1993-94; Z 1995-96. HS 46* OFS v W Province (Cape Town) 1990-91. Wa HS 44 v Essex (Ilford) 1995. 50 wkts (4+1); most – 89 (1995). BB 8-37 OFS v Transvaal (Johannesburg) 1986-87. Wa BB 7-37 v Durham (Birmingham) 1992. Awards: NWT 3. **NWT:** HS 14* v Northants (Birmingham) 1992. BB 5-12 v Wilts (Birmingham) 1989. **BHC:** HS 23* v Leics (Leicester) 1989. BB 4-28 v Scot (Perth) 1987. **SL:** HS 18* v Middx (Lord's) 1988. BB 6-15 v Yorks (Birmingham) 1995.

TWOSE, Roger Graham (King's C, Taunton), b Torquay, Devon 17 Apr 1968. Nephew of R.W.Tolchard (Leics and England 1965-83). 6'0". LHB, RM. Warwickshire 1989-95 (cap 1992). N Districts 1989-90. C Districts 1991-92/1993-94 (captain 1993-94). Wellington 1994-95 to date. Devon 1988-89. MCC YC. **Tests** (NZ): 5 (1995-96); HS 94 v Z (Auckland) 1995-96; BB 2-36 v Z (Hamilton) 1995-96. **LOI** (NZ): 12 (1995-96; HS 60; BB 2-31). Tours (Wa): SA 1991-92, 1992-93; I 1995-96 (NZ); Z 1993-94. 1000 runs (3); most – 1412 (1992). HS 277* v Glam (Birmingham) 1994. BB 6-28 v Surrey (Guildford) 1994. Awards: NWT 3. **NWT:** HS 110 v Beds (Birmingham) 1994. BB 3-39 v Sussex (Birmingham) 1992. **BHC:** HS 90 v Durham (Birmingham) 1995. BB 1-23. **SL:** HS 100 v Leics (Birmingham) 1992. BB 3-31 v Durham (Darlington) 1993.

WARWICKSHIRE 1995

RESULTS SUMMARY

	Place	Won	Lost	Drew	No Result
Britannic Assurance Championship	**1st**	14	2	1	–
All First-Class Matches		14	3	2	–
NatWest Trophy	**Winners**				
Benson and Hedges Cup	3rd in Group A				
Sunday League	**2nd**	12	4	–	1

BRITANNIC ASSURANCE CHAMPIONSHIP AVERAGES

BATTING AND FIELDING

Cap		*M*	*I*	*NO*	*HS*	*Runs*	*Avge*	*100*	*50*	*Ct/St*
1995	N.V.Knight	11	19	5	174	798	57.00	1	6	21
1994	T.L.Penney	17	24	2	144	1133	51.50	4	4	7
–	W.G.Khan	12	21	5	181	740	46.25	1	5	16
1992	R.G.Twose	17	27	4	191	1036	45.04	4	2	6
1991	D.P.Ostler	16	23	2	208	909	43.28	2	6	25
1987	A.J.Moles	7	13	–	131	532	40.92	1	4	4
1989	D.A.Reeve	15	20	3	77*	575	33.82	–	4	16
1995	D.R.Brown	13	17	2	85	441	29.40	–	3	6
1992	K.J.Piper	14	16	2	99	388	27.71	–	2	55/1
1993	N.M.K.Smith	16	20	1	75	413	21.73	–	3	6
–	A.F.Giles	6	5	–	32	84	16.80	–	–	–
1986	P.A.Smith	2	4	–	44	67	16.75	–	–	1
1982	G.C.Small	5	7	4	15	50	16.66	–	–	–
1989	T.A.Munton	10	10	6	19*	66	16.50	–	–	2
1989	A.A.Donald	14	14	5	44	145	16.11	–	–	7
–	M.Burns	3	5	–	35	78	15.60	–	–	9/1
1994	R.P.Davis	5	7	1	30	79	13.16	–	–	5

Also batted: M.A.V.Bell (3 matches) 0* (2 ct); A.Singh (1 match) 5, 7 (1 ct).

BOWLING

	O	*M*	*R*	*W*	*Avge*	*Best*	*5wI*	*10wM*
A.A.Donald	511.3	128	1363	88	15.48	6-56	6	1
D.A.Reeve	293.4	112	620	36	17.22	5-30	1	–
T.A.Munton	353.5	104	900	46	19.56	5-37	3	1
A.F.Giles	146.5	46	354	16	22.12	5-23	1	–
D.R.Brown	268.4	62	842	34	24.76	4-24	–	–
G.C.Small	159.5	41	444	17	26.11	5-71	1	–
N.M.K.Smith	400	88	1190	36	33.05	6-72	3	–

Also bowled: M.A.V.Bell 80-25-265-7; R.P.Davis 187.2-48-495-12; W.G.Khan 7-1-22-0; A.J.Moles 7-0-22-0; P.A.Smith 35-8-107-4; R.G.Twose 96-28-261-8.

The First-Class Averages (pp 129-143) give the records of Warwickshire players in all first-class county matches (their other opponents being England A and Cambridge University), with the exception of N.V.Knight whose full county figures are as above.

WARWICKSHIRE RECORDS

FIRST-CLASS CRICKET

Highest Total	For	810-4d		v	Durham	Birmingham	1994
	V	887		by	Yorkshire	Birmingham	1896
Lowest Total	For	16		v	Kent	Tonbridge	1913
	V	15		by	Hampshire	Birmingham	1922
Highest Innings	For	501*	B.C.Lara	v	Durham	Birmingham	1994
	V	322	I.V.A.Richards	for	Somerset	Taunton	1985

Highest Partnership for each Wicket

1st	377*	N.F.Horner/K.Ibadulla	v	Surrey	The Oval	1960
2nd	465*	J.A.Jameson/R.B.Kanhai	v	Glos	Birmingham	1974
3rd	327	S.P.Kinneir/W.G.Quaife	v	Lancashire	Birmingham	1901
4th	470	A.I.Kallicharran/G.W.Humpage	v	Lancashire	Southport	1982
5th	322*	B.C.Lara/K.J.Piper	v	Durham	Birmingham	1994
6th	220	H.E.Dollery/J.Buckingham	v	Derbyshire	Derby	1938
7th	250	H.E.Dollery/J.S.Ord	v	Kent	Maidstone	1953
8th	228	A.J.W.Croom/R.E.S.Wyatt	v	Worcs	Dudley	1925
9th	154	G.W.Stephens/A.J.W.Croom	v	Derbyshire	Birmingham	1925
10th	128	F.R.Santall/W.Sanders	v	Yorkshire	Birmingham	1930

Best Bowling	For	10-41	J.D.Bannister	v	Comb Servs	Birmingham	1959
(Innings)	V	10-36	H.Verity	for	Yorkshire	Leeds	1931
Best Bowling	For	15-76	S.Hargreave	v	Surrey	The Oval	1903
(Match)	V	17-92	A.P.Freeman	for	Kent	Folkestone	1932

Most Runs – Season	2417	M.J.K.Smith	(av 60.42)	1959
Most Runs – Career	35146	D.L.Amiss	(av 41.64)	1960-87
Most 100s – Season	9	A.I.Kallicharran		1984
	9	B.C.Lara		1994
Most 100s – Career	78	D.L.Amiss		1960-87
Most Wkts – Season	180	W.E.Hollies	(av 15.13)	1946
Most Wkts – Career	2201	W.E.Hollies	(av 20.45)	1932-57

LIMITED-OVERS CRICKET

Highest Total	**NWT**	392-5		v	Oxfordshire	Birmingham	1984
	BHC	308-4		v	Scotland	Birmingham	1988
	SL	301-6		v	Essex	Colchester	1982
Lowest Total	**NWT**	109		v	Kent	Canterbury	1971
	BHC	96		v	Leics	Leicester	1972
	SL	65		v	Kent	Maidstone	1979
Highest Innings	**NWT**	206	A.I.Kallicharran	v	Oxfordshire	Birmingham	1984
	BHC	137*	T.A.Lloyd	v	Lancashire	Birmingham	1985
	SL	132*	Asif Din	v	Hampshire	Southampton	1993
Best Bowling	**NWT**	6-32	K.Ibadulla	v	Hampshire	Birmingham	1965
		6-32	A.I.Kallicharran	v	Oxfordshire	Birmingham	1984
	BHC	7-32	R.G.D.Willis	v	Yorkshire	Birmingham	1981
	SL	6-15	A.A.Donald	v	Yorkshire	Birmingham	1995

WORCESTERSHIRE

Formation of Present Club: 11 March 1865
Colours: Dark Green and Black
Badge: Shield Argent a Fess between three Pears Sable
Championships: (5) 1964, 1965, 1974, 1988, 1989
NatWest Trophy/Gillette Cup Winners: (1) 1994
Benson and Hedges Cup Winners: (1) 1991
Sunday League Champions: (3) 1971, 1987, 1988
Match Awards: NWT 43; BHC 62

Secretary: Revd M.D.Vockins
County Ground, New Road, Worcester, WR2 4QQ (Tel 01905 748474)
Captain: T.M.Moody
Scorer: J.W.Sewter
1996 Beneficiary: S.J.Rhodes

BRINKLEY, James Edward (Marist C, Canberra; Trinity C, Perth), b Helensburgh, Scotland 13 Mar 1974. 6'3". RHB, RFM. Debut 1993-94 (Z tour). Matabeleland 1994-95 to date. Tour: Z 1993-94 (Wo). HS 29 Matabeleland v Mashonaland U-24 (Harare) 1994-95. BAC HS 5. BB 6-35 Matabeleland v Mashonaland CD (Harare South) 1994-95. BAC BB 6-98 v Surrey (Oval) 1994 on UK debut. **SL:** HS –.

CHURCH, Matthew John (St George's C, Weybridge), b Guildford, Surrey 26 Jul 1972. 6'2". RHB, RM. Debut 1994. MCC YC. HS 38 v Yorks (Worcester) 1994. **BHC:** HS –. **SL:** HS 18 v Notts (Worcester) 1994.

CURTIS, Timothy Stephen (Worcester RGS; Durham U; Magdalene C, Cambridge), b Chislehurst, Kent 15 Jan 1960. 5'11". RHB, LB. Debut 1979. Cap 1984. Captain 1992-95. Benefit 1994. Cambridge U 1983 (blue). **Tests:** 5 (1988 to 1989), HS 41 v A (Birmingham) 1989. Tours (Wo): Z 1990-91, 1993-94 (captain). 1000 runs (11); most – 1829 (1992). HS 248 v Somerset (Worcester) 1991. BB 2-17 v OU (Oxford) 1991. BAC BB 2-72 v Warwks (Worcester) 1987 and v Derbys (Worcester) 1992. Awards: NWT 6; BHC 2. **NWT:** HS 136* v Surrey (Oval) 1994. BB 1-6. **BHC:** HS 97 v Warwks (Birmingham) 1990. **SL:** HS 124 v Somerset (Taunton) 1990.

ELLIS, Scott William Kenneth (Shrewsbury S; Warwick U), b Newcastle-under-Lyme, Staffs 3 Oct 1975. 6'3". RHB, RMF. Combined Us 1995. Awaiting Worcestershire debut. HS 0 and BB 5-59 Comb Us v WI (Oxford) 1995.

HAYNES, Gavin Richard (High Park S; King Edward VI S, Stourbridge), b Stourbridge 29 Sep 1969. 5'10". RHB, RM. Debut 1991. Cap 1994. Tour: Z 1993-94 (Wo). 1000 runs (1): 1021 (1994). HS 158 v Kent (Worcester) 1993. BB 4-33 v Kent (Worcester) 1995. Awards: NWT 2; BHC 1. **NWT:** HS 116* v Cumberland (Worcester) 1995. BB 1-9. **BHC:** HS 65 v Hants (Worcester) 1994. BB 3-17 v Derbys (Worcester) 1995. **SL:** HS 83 v Hants (Worcester) 1994. BB 4-21 v Surrey (Worcester) 1995.

HICK, Graeme Ashley (Prince Edward HS, Salisbury), b Salisbury, Rhodesia 23 May 1966. 6'3". RHB, OB. Zimbabwe 1983-84/1985-86. Worcestershire debut 1984. Cap 1986. N Districts 1987-88/1988-89. Queensland 1990-91. *Wisden* 1986. **Tests:** 42 (1991 to 1995-96); HS 178 v I (Bombay) 1992-93; BB 4-126 v NZ (Wellington) 1991-92. **LOI:** 54 (1991 to 1995-96; HS 105*; BB 3-41). Tours: E 1985 (Z); A 1994-95; SA 1995-96; WI 1993-94; NZ 1991-92; I 1992-93; SL 1983-84 (Z), 1992-93; Z 1990-91 (Wo). 1000 runs (11+1) inc 2000 (3); most – 2713 (1988); youngest to score 2000 (1986). Scored 1019 runs before June 1988, including a record 410 runs in April. Fewest innings for 10,000 runs in county cricket (179). Youngest (24) to score 50 first-class hundreds. Scored 645 runs without being dismissed (UK record) in 1990. HS 405* (Worcs record and then second highest in UK f-c matches) v Somerset (Taunton) 1988. BB 5-15 v Leics (Worcester) 1995. Awards: NWT 4; BHC 10. **NWT:** HS 172* v Devon (Worcester) 1987. BB 4-54 v Hants (Worcester) 1988 and v Surrey (Oval) 1994. **BHC:** HS 127* v Derbys (Worcester) 1995. BB 3-36 v Warwks (Birmingham) 1990. **SL:** HS 130 v Durham (Darlington) 1995. BB 4-21 v Somerset (Worcester) 1995.

ILLINGWORTH, Richard Keith (Salts GS), b Bradford, Yorks 23 Aug 1963. 5'11". RHB, SLA. Debut 1982. Cap 1986. Natal 1988-89. **Tests:** 9 (1991 to 1995-96); HS 28 v SA (Pt Elizabeth) 1995-96. BB 4-96 v WI (Nottingham) 1995. Took wicket of P.V.Simmons with his first ball in Tests – v WI (Nottingham) 1991. **LOI:** 21 (1991 to 1995-96; HS 14; BB 3-33). Tours: SA 1995-96; NZ 1991-92; P 1990-91 (Eng A); SL 1990-91 (Eng A); Z 1989-90 (Eng A), 1990-91 (Wo), 1993-94 (Wo). HS 120* v Warwks (Worcester) 1987 – as night-watchman. Scored 106 for England A v Z (Harare) 1989-90 – also as night-watchman. 50 wkts (4); most – 75 (1990). BB 7-50 v OU (Oxford) 1985. BAC BB 6-28 v Glos (Gloucester) 1993. **NWT:** HS 22 v Northants (Northampton) 1984. BB 4-20 v Devon (Worcester) 1987. **BHC:** HS 36* v Kent (Worcester) 1990. BB 4-36 v Yorks (Bradford) 1985. **SL:** HS 31 v Yorks (Worcester) 1994. BB 5-24 v Somerset (Worcester) 1983.

LAMPITT, Stuart Richard (Kingswinford S; Dudley TC), b Wolverhampton, Staffs 29 Jul 1966. 5'11". RHB, RMF. Debut 1985. Cap 1989. Tours (Wo): Z 1990-91, 1993-94. HS 122 v Middx (Lord's) 1994. 50 wkts (4); most – 64 (1994). BB 5-32 v Kent (Worcester) 1989. Awards: NWT 1; BHC 4. **NWT:** HS 29 v Lancs (Manchester) 1995. BB 5-22 v Suffolk (Bury St E) 1990. **BHC:** HS 41 v Glam (Worcester) 1990. BB 6-26 v Derbys (Derby) 1994. **SL:** HS 41* v Leics (Worcester) 1993. BB 5-67 v Middx (Lord's) 1990.

LEATHERDALE, David Anthony (Pudsey Grangefield S), b Bradford, Yorks 26 Nov 1967. 5'10½". RHB, RM. Debut 1988. Cap 1994. Tour: Z 1993-94 (Wo). HS 157 v Somerset (Worcester) 1991. BB 2-11 v CU (Cambridge) 1994. BAC BB 2-36 v Essex (Chelmsford) 1995. **NWT:** HS 43 v Hants (Worcester) 1988. BB 3-14 v Norfolk (Lakenham) 1994. **BHC:** HS 30 v Hants (Worcester) 1994. **SL:** HS 62* v Kent (Folkestone) 1988. BB 2-15 v Warwks (Birmingham) 1994.

MOODY, Thomas Masson (Guildford GS, WA), b Adelaide, Australia 2 Oct 1965. 6'6½". RHB, RM. W Australia 1985-86 to date; captain 1995-96. Warwickshire 1990 (cap 1990). Worcestershire 1991-92 (cap 1991) and 1994. Captain 1995-. **Tests** (A): 8 (1989-90 to 1992-93); HS 106 v SL (Brisbane) 1989-90; BB 1-17. **LOI** (A): 34 (1987-88 to 1992-93; HS 89; BB 3-56). Tours (A): E 1989; I 1989-90 (WA); SL 1992-93. 1000 runs (4+1); most – 1887 (1991). HS 272 WA v Tasmania (Hobart) 1994-95. Wo/BAC HS 210 v Warwks (Worcester) 1991. BB 7-43 (10-109 match) WA v Victoria (Perth) 1990-91. Wo/BAC BB 4-24 v Derbys (Derby) 1994. Awards: NWT 2; BHC 5. **NWT:** HS 180* v Surrey (Oval) 1994. BB 2-33 v Norfolk (Lakenham) 1994. **BHC:** HS 110* v Derbys (Worcester) 1991. BB 4-59 v Somerset (Worcester) 1992. **SL:** HS 160 v Kent (Worcester) 1991 (on Wo 1st XI debut). BB 3-18 v Somerset (Taunton) 1994.

NEWPORT, Philip John (High Wycombe RGS; Portsmouth Poly), b High Wycombe, Bucks 11 Oct 1962. 6'3". RHB, RFM. Debut 1982. Cap 1986. Boland 1987-88. N Transvaal 1992-93. Buckinghamshire 1981-82. **Tests:** 3 (1988 to 1990-91); HS 40* v A (Perth) 1990-91; BB 4-87 v SL (Lord's) 1988 (on debut). Tours: A 1990-91 (part); P 1990-91 (Eng A); SL 1990-91 (Eng A); Z 1993-94 (Wo). HS 98 v NZ (Worcester) 1990. BAC HS 96 v Essex (Worcester) 1990. 50 wkts (8); most – 93 (1988). BB 8-52 v Middx (Lord's) 1988. Award: BHC 1. **NWT:** HS 25 v Northants (Northampton) 1984. BB 4-30 v Northants (Worcester) 1994. **BHC:** HS 28 v Kent (Worcester) 1990. BB 5-22 v Warwks (Birmingham) 1987. **SL:** HS 26* v Leics (Leicester) 1987 and v Surrey (Worcester) 1993. BB 5-32 v Essex (Chelmsford) 1995.

RHODES, Steven John (Lapage Middle S; Carlton-Bolling S, Bradford), b Bradford, Yorks 17 Jun 1964. Son of W.E. (Notts 1961-64). 5'7". RHB, WK. Yorkshire 1981-84. Worcestershire debut 1985. Cap 1986. Benefit 1996. *Wisden* 1994. **Tests:** 11 (1994 to 1994-95); HS 65* v SA (Leeds) 1994. **LOI:** 9 (1989 to 1994-95; HS 56). Tours: A 1994-95; SA 1993-94 (Eng A); WI 1991-92 (Eng A); SL 1985-86 (Eng B), 1990-91 (Eng A); Z 1989-90 (Eng A), 1990-91 (Wo), 1993-94 (Wo). 1000 runs (1): 1018 (1995). HS 122* v Young A (Worcester) 1995. BAC HS 116* v Warwks (Worcester) 1992. Awards: NWT 1; BHC 1. **NWT:** HS 61 v Derbys (Worcester) 1989. **BHC:** HS 51* v Warwks (Birmingham) 1987. **SL:** HS 48* v Kent (Worcester) 1989.

SOLANKI, Vikram Singh (Regis S, Wolverhampton), b Udaipur, India 1 Apr 1976. 6'0". RHB, OB. Debut 1995. HS 36 and BB 1-10 v Northants (Northampton) 1995. **NWT:** HS 29 and BB 1-48 v Cumberland (Worcester) 1995. **SL:** HS 22 v Middx (Worcester) 1993.

SPIRING, Karl Ruben (Monmouth S; Durham U), b Southport, Lancs 13 Nov 1974. 5'11". RHB, OB. Debut 1994. HS 56 v OU (Worcester) 1994 – on debut (also scored 52). Awaiting BAC debut. **BHC:** HS 35 Comb Us v Essex (Cambridge) 1995. **SL:** HS 7.

THOMAS, Paul Anthony (Brodway S; Sutton C; Sandwell C), b Perry Barr, Birmingham 3 Jun 1971. 5'11". RHB, RFM. Debut 1995. Shropshire 1992-94. HS 25 v Warwks (Birmingham) 1995. BB 5-70 v WI (Worcester) 1995 – on debut. BAC BB 4-78 v Sussex (Eastbourne) 1995. **NWT:** HS –. BB 2-30 v Cumberland (Worcester) 1995.

WESTON, William **Philip** Christopher (Durham S), b Durham 16 Jun 1973. Son of M.P. (Durham; England RFU); brother of R.M.S. (*see DURHAM*). 6'3". LHB, LM. Debut 1991. Cap 1995. Tour: Z 1993-94 (Wo). 1000 runs (1): 1207 (1995). HS 113 v OU (Worcester) 1993. BAC HS 111 v Sussex (Eastbourne) 1995. BB 2-39 v P (Worcester) 1992. BAC BB –. **NWT:** HS 31 v Scot (Edinburgh) 1993. **BHC:** HS 32* v Essex (Worcester) 1993. **SL:** HS 26 v Lancs (Worcester) 1993.

NEWCOMERS

DAWOOD, Ismail (Batley GS), b Dewsbury, Yorks 23 Jul 1976. 5'8". RHB, WK. Northamptonshire 1994. HS 2*. **SL:** HS 2.

DIWAN, Muneeb (Sir George Monoux S, Walthamstow), b St Stephen, Canada 20 Mar 1972. 5'9". RHB, RM. Essex 1994. HS 0. **SL:** HS 14 Ex v Notts (Ilford) 1994.

HARRISON, Christopher Paul, b Bury, Lancs 23 Oct 1976. RHB, OB.

PREECE, Benjamin Edward Ashley, b Birmingham 8 Nov 1976. RHB, RFM.

RALPH, James Trevor (Harry Cheshire HS, Kidderminster), b Kidderminster 9 Oct 1975. RHB, LB.

RAWNSLEY, Matthew, b Birmingham 8 Jun 1976. RHB, SLA.

SHERIYAR, Alamgir (George Dixon S; Joseph Chamberlain SFC; Oxford Poly), b Birmingham 15 Nov 1973. 6'1". RHB, LF. Leicestershire 1994-95. HS 19 Le v WI (Leicester) 1995. BAC HS 18 Le v Northants (Northampton) 1995. BB 6-30 Le v Young A (Leicester) 1995. BAC BB 4-44 (inc hat-trick) Le v Durham (Durham) 1994 – his second match. **SL:** HS 0*.

DEPARTURES (who made first-class appearances in 1995)

D'OLIVEIRA, Damian Basil (Blessed Edward Oldcorne SS), b Cape Town, SA 19 Oct 1960. Son of B.L. (Worcs and England 1964-80). 5'9". RHB, OB. Worcestershire 1982-95 (cap 1985; joint benefit 1993). MCC YC. Tours: Z 1984-85 (EC), 1990-91 (Wo), 1993-94. 1000 runs (4); most – 1263 (1990). HS 237 v OU (Oxford) 1991. BAC HS 155 v Lancs (Manchester) 1990. BB 4-68 v OU (Worcester) 1994. BAC BB 3-36 v Essex (Chelmsford) 1993. Awards: NWT 2; BHC 2. **NWT:** HS 99 v Oxon (Worcester) 1986. BB 2-17 v Suffolk (Bury St E) 1990. **BHC:** HS 66 v Yorks (Leeds) 1986. BB 3-12 v Scot (Glasgow) 1986. **SL:** HS 103 v Surrey (Worcester) 1985. BB 3-23 v Derbys (Derby) 1983. Appointed 2nd XI captain and assistant coach 1995.

MIRZA, Parvaz (Small Heath S), b Birmingham 17 Dec 1970; d Birmingham 24 Sep 1995. 5'11". RHB, RM. Worcestershire 1994-95. Herefordshire 1992. HS 40 v Kent (Canterbury) 1994. BB 5-110 v Derbys (Kidderminster) 1995. **NWT:** HS –. BB 1-61. **SL:** HS 2*. BB 4-27 v Derbys (Worcester) 1995.

RADFORD, Neal Victor (Athlone BHS, Johannesburg), b Luanshya, N Rhodesia 7 Jun 1957. Brother of W.R. (OFS). 5'11". RHB, RFM. Transvaal 1978-79/1988-89. Lancashire 1980-84. Worcestershire 1985-95. Cap 1985. Benefit 1995. *Wisden* 1985. **Tests:** 3 (1986 to 1987-88); HS 12* v NZ (Lord's) 1986; BB 2-131 v I (Birmingham) 1986. **LOI:** 6 (1987-88 to 1988; HS 0*; BB 1-32). Tours: NZ 1987-88; Z 1990-91 (Wo), 1993-94 (Wo). HS 76* La v Derbys (Blackpool) 1981. Wo HS 73* v Notts (Nottingham) 1992. 50 wkts (6) inc 100 (2); most – 109 (1987). BB 9-70 v Somerset (Worcester) 1986. Awards: NWT 1; BHC 1. **NWT:** HS 37 v Essex (Chelmsford) 1987. BB 7-19 v Beds (Bedford) 1991. **BHC:** HS 40 v Glam (Worcester) 1990. BB 4-25 v Northants (Northampton) 1988. **SL:** HS 70 v Durham (Stockton) 1993. BB 5-32 v Warwks (Worcester) 1987.

TOLLEY, C.M. – *see NOTTINGHAMSHIRE.*

WYLIE, Alex (Bromsgrove S; Warwick C of Ag), b Tamworth, Staffs 20 Feb 1973. 6'2½". LHB, RF. Worcestershire 1993-95. HS 7. BB 1-50.

WORCESTERSHIRE 1995

RESULTS SUMMARY

	Place	*Won*	*Lost*	*Tied*	*Drew*	*No Result*
Britannic Assurance Championship	10th	6	7	–	4	–
All First-Class Matches		6	7	–	7	–
NatWest Trophy	2nd Round					
Benson and Hedges Cup	Semi-Finalist					
Sunday League	3rd	11	3	1	–	2

BRITANNIC ASSURANCE CHAMPIONSHIP AVERAGES

BATTING AND FIELDING

Cap		*M*	*I*	*NO*	*HS*	*Runs*	*Avge*	*100*	*50*	*Ct/St*
1991	T.M.Moody	17	29	1	168	1518	54.21	5	7	30
1986	G.A.Hick	10	16	1	152	768	51.20	3	2	16
1984	T.S.Curtis	17	31	4	169*	1064	39.40	2	4	8
1986	S.J.Rhodes	17	29	6	81*	867	37.69	–	7	43/4
1994	D.A.Leatherdale	16	27	3	93	866	36.08	–	7	14
1995	W.P.C.Weston	17	31	1	111	1020	34.00	2	6	12
1986	P.J.Newport	16	22	7	50	401	26.73	–	1	2
1989	S.R.Lampitt	14	21	4	97	454	26.70	–	1	10
1994	G.R.Haynes	15	25	–	78	586	23.44	–	3	8
–	V.S.Solanki	6	9	1	36	150	18.75	–	–	8
1985	D.B.D'Oliveira	2	4	–	25	59	14.75	–	–	2
1986	R.K.Illingworth	8	11	4	23*	91	13.00	–	–	3
1993	C.M.Tolley	3	5	–	24	62	12.40	–	–	1
1985	N.V.Radford	8	10	2	22	80	10.00	–	–	–
–	M.J.Church	2	4	–	25	26	6.50	–	–	–
–	P.Mirza	5	9	2	18*	37	5.28	–	–	5
–	P.A.Thomas	12	14	4	25	49	4.90	–	–	1
–	A.Wylie	2	4	1	7	14	4.66	–	–	–

BOWLING

	O	*M*	*R*	*W*	*Avge*	*Best*	*5wI*	*10wM*
P.J.Newport	508	134	1445	63	22.93	5- 45	4	–
R.K.Illingworth	371.5	115	899	33	27.24	4- 30	–	–
S.R.Lampitt	430.1	113	1302	46	28.30	4- 34	–	–
N.V.Radford	181.2	40	626	18	34.77	5- 45	1	–
G.R.Haynes	244	68	761	20	38.05	4- 33	–	–
P.Mirza	149.1	35	557	13	42.84	5-110	1	–
P.A.Thomas	343.4	60	1352	25	54.08	4- 78	–	–

Also bowled: T.S.Curtis 1-0-5-0; D.B.D'Oliveira 113.5-15-369-5; G.A.Hick 156-35-462-8; D.A.Leatherdale 28-3-123-4; T.M.Moody 71.1-19-209-5; V.S.Solanki 88-15-359-3; C.M.Tolley 4-0-23-0; W.P.C.Weston 13.4-0-58-0; A.Wylie 35-7-143-1.

The First-Class Averages (pp 129-143) give the records of Worcestershire players in all first-class county matches (their other opponents being the West Indians, Oxford University and Young Australia), with the exception of:

G.A.Hick 11-17-1-152-790-49.37-3-2-17ct. 156-35-462-8-57.75-5/18-1-0.
R.K.Illingworth 10-11-4-23*-91-13.00-0-0-3ct. 424-132-997-39-25.56-4/30.

WORCESTERSHIRE RECORDS

FIRST-CLASS CRICKET

Highest Total	For	670-7d		v	Somerset	Worcester	1995
	V	701-4d		by	Leics	Worcester	1906
Lowest Total	For	24		v	Yorkshire	Huddersfield	1903
	V	30		by	Hampshire	Worcester	1903
Highest Innings	For	405*	G.A.Hick	v	Somerset	Taunton	1988
	V	331*	J.D.B.Robertson	for	Middlesex	Worcester	1949

Highest Partnership for each Wicket

1st	309	F.L.Bowley/H.K.Foster	v	Derbyshire	Derby	1901
2nd	287*	T.S.Curtis/G.A.Hick	v	Glamorgan	Neath	1986
3rd	314	M.J.Horton/T.W.Graveney	v	Somerset	Worcester	1962
4th	281	J.A.Ormrod/Younis Ahmed	v	Notts	Nottingham	1979
5th	393	E.G.Arnold/W.B.Burns	v	Warwicks	Birmingham	1909
6th	265	G.A.Hick/S.J.Rhodes	v	Somerset	Taunton	1988
7th	205	G.A.Hick/P.J.Newport	v	Yorkshire	Worcester	1988
8th	184	S.J.Rhodes/S.R.Lampitt	v	Derbyshire	Kidderminster	1991
9th	181	J.A.Cuffe/R.D.Burrows	v	Glos	Worcester	1907
10th	119	W.B.Burns/G.A.Wilson	v	Somerset	Worcester	1906

Best Bowling (Innings)	For	9- 23	C.F.Root	v	Lancashire	Worcester	1931
	V	10- 51	J.Mercer	for	Glamorgan	Worcester	1936
Best Bowling (Match)	For	15- 87	A.J.Conway	v	Glos	Moreton-in-M	1914
	V	17-212	J.C.Clay	for	Glamorgan	Swansea	1937

Most Runs – Season	2654	H.H.I.Gibbons	(av 52.03)	1934
Most Runs – Career	33490	D.Kenyon	(av 33.19)	1946-67
Most 100s – Season	10	G.M.Turner		1970
	10	G.A.Hick		1988
Most 100s – Career	72†	G.M.Turner		1967-82
Most Wkts – Season	207	C.F.Root	(av 17.52)	1925
Most Wkts – Career	2143	R.T.D.Perks	(av 23.73)	1930-55

† G.A.Hick has scored 58 hundreds.

LIMITED-OVERS CRICKET

Highest Total	NWT	404-3		v	Devon	Worcester	1987
	BHC	314-5		v	Lancashire	Manchester	1980
	SL	307-4		v	Derbyshire	Worcester	1975
Lowest Total	NWT	98		v	Durham	Chester-le-St	1968
	BHC	81		v	Leics	Worcester	1983
	SL	86		v	Yorkshire	Leeds	1969
Highest Innings	NWT	180*	T.M.Moody	v	Surrey	The Oval	1994
	BHC	143*	G.M.Turner	v	Warwicks	Birmingham	1976
	SL	160	T.M.Moody	v	Kent	Worcester	1991
Best Bowling	NWT	7-19	N.V.Radford	v	Beds	Bedford	1991
	BHC	6- 8	N.Gifford	v	Minor C (S)	High Wycombe	1979
	SL	6-26	A.P.Pridgeon	v	Surrey	Worcester	1978

YORKSHIRE

Formation of Present Club: 8 January 1863
Substantial Reorganisation: 10 December 1891
Colours: Dark Blue, Light Blue and Gold
Badge: White Rose
Championships (since 1890): (29) 1893, 1896, 1898, 1900, 1901, 1902, 1905, 1908, 1912, 1919, 1922, 1923, 1924, 1925, 1931, 1932, 1933, 1935, 1937, 1938, 1939, 1946, 1959, 1960, 1962, 1963, 1966, 1967, 1968. Joint: (1) 1949
NatWest Trophy/Gillette Cup Winners: (2) 1965, 1969
Benson and Hedges Cup Winners: (1) 1987
Sunday League Champions: (1) 1983
Match Awards: NWT 29; BHC 58

Chief Executive: C.D.Hassell. **Secretary:** D.M.Ryder
Headingley Cricket Ground, Leeds, LS6 3BU (Tel 0113 278 7394)
Captain: D.Byas
Scorer: J.T.Potter
1996 Beneficiary: P.J.Hartley

BEVAN, Michael Gwyl, b Belconnen, ACT, Australia 8 May 1970. LHB, SLC. S Australia 1989-90. NSW 1990-91 to date. Yorkshire debut/cap 1995. **Tests** (A): 6 (1994-95); HS 91 and BB 1-21 v P (Lahore) 1994-95. **LOI** (A): 25 (1993-94 to 1995-96; HS 78*; BB 2-31). Tours (A): P 1994-95; Z 1991-92 (Aus B). 1000 runs (1+1); most – 1598 (1995). HS 203* NSW v WA (Sydney) 1993-94. Y HS 153* v Surrey (Oval) 1995. BB 3-6 NSW v Wellington (Sydney) 1990-91. Y BB 3-55 v Sussex (Scarborough) 1995. Awards: NWT 2; BHC 2. **NWT:** HS 91* v Essex (Chelmsford) 1995. BB 1-14. **BHC:** HS 83* v Worcs (Leeds) 1995. **SL:** HS 103* and BB 3-21 v Glos (Middlesbrough) 1995.

BLAKEY, Richard John (Rastrick GS), b Huddersfield 15 Jan 1967. 5'9". RHB, WK. Debut 1985. Cap 1987. YC 1987. **Tests:** 2 (1992-93); HS 6. **LOI:** 3 (1992-93; HS 25). Tours: SA 1991-92 (Y); WI 1986-87 (Y); I 1992-93; P 1990-91 (Eng A); SL 1990-91 (Eng A); Z 1989-90 (Eng A). 1000 runs (5); most – 1361 (1987). HS 221 Eng A v Z (Bulawayo) 1989-90. Y HS 204* v Glos (Leeds) 1987. BB 1-68. Awards: BHC 2. **NWT:** HS 75 v Warwks (Leeds) 1993. **BHC:** HS 79 v Surrey (Oval) 1990. **SL:** HS 130* v Kent (Scarborough) 1991.

BYAS, David (Scarborough C), b Kilham 26 Aug 1963. 6'4". LHB, RM. Debut 1986. Cap 1991. Captain 1996. Tours (Y): SA 1991-92, 1992-93. 1000 runs (4); most – 1913 (1995). HS 213 v Worcs (Scarborough) 1995. BB 3-55 v Derbys (Chesterfield) 1990. **NWT:** HS 71 v Somerset (Leeds) 1994. BB 1-23. **BHC:** HS 92 v Hants (Leeds) 1991. BB 2-38 v Somerset (Leeds) 1989. **SL:** HS 106* v Derbys (Chesterfield) 1993. BB 3-19 v Notts (Leeds) 1989.

CHAPMAN, Colin Anthony (Beckfoot GS, Bingley; Bradford & Ilkley Art C), b Bradford 8 Jun 1971. 5'8½". RHB, WK. Debut 1990. Tour: SA 1992-93 (Y). HS 20 v Middx (Uxbridge) 1990. **NWT:** HS –. **BHC:** HS –. **SL:** HS 36* v Middx (Scarborough) 1990.

GOUGH, Darren (Priory CS, Lundwood), b Barnsley 18 Sep 1970. 5'11". RHB, RFM. Debut 1989. Cap 1993. **Tests:** 12 (1994 to 1995-96); HS 65 v NZ (Manchester) 1994 – on debut; BB 6-49 v A (Sydney) 1994-95. **LOI:** 16 (HS 45; BB 5-44). Took wickets with his sixth balls in both Tests and LOIs. Tours: A 1994-95; SA 1991-92 (Y), 1992-93 (Y), 1993-94 (Eng A), 1995-96. HS 72 v Northants (Northampton) 1991. 50 wkts (3); most – 62 (1994).

BB 7-28 (10-80 match) v Lancs (Leeds) 1995 (friendly). BAC BB 7-42 (10-96 match) v Somerset (Taunton) 1993. Hat-trick (and four wickets in 5 balls) v Kent (Leeds) 1995. **NWT:** HS 33 v Ire (Leeds) 1995. BB 3-31 v Warwks (Leeds) 1993. **BHC:** HS 14 v Northants (Leeds) 1995. BB 2-21 v Scot (Glasgow) 1995. **SL:** HS 72* v Leics (Leicester) 1991. BB 5-13 v Sussex (Hove) 1994.

HAMILTON, Gavin Mark (Hurstmere SS, Kent), b Broxburn, Scotland 16 Sep 1974. 6'1". RHB, RFM. Scotland 1993-94. Yorkshire debut 1994. HS 48 v Kent (Maidstone) 1994. BB 5-65 Scot v Ire (Eglinton) 1993. Y BB 3-41 v CU (Cambridge) 1995. BAC BB 2-76 v Kent (Maidstone) 1994. **SL:** HS 16* v Kent (Maidstone) 1994. BB 4-27 v Warwks (Birmingham) 1995.

HARTLEY, Peter John (Greenhead GS; Bradford C), b Keighley 18 Apr 1960. 6'0". RHB, RMF. Warwickshire 1982. Yorkshire debut 1985. Cap 1987. Benefit 1996. Tours (Y): SA 1991-92; WI 1986-87. HS 127* v Lancs (Manchester) 1988. 50 wkts (5); most – 81 (1995). BB 9-41 (inc hat-trick, 4 wkts in 5 balls and 5 in 9; 11-68 match) v Derbys (Chesterfield) 1995. Awards: NWT 1; BHC 2. **NWT:** HS 52 and BB 5-46 v Hants (Southampton) 1990. **BHC:** HS 29* v Notts (Nottingham) 1986. BB 5-43 v Scot (Leeds) 1986. **SL:** HS 51 v Northants (Tring) 1990. BB 5-36 v Sussex (Scarborough) 1993.

KETTLEBOROUGH, Richard Allan (Worksop C), b Sheffield 15 Mar 1973. 6'0". LHB, RM. Debut 1994. HS 55 v Essex (Chelmsford) 1995. **SL:** HS 28 v Somerset (Leeds) 1994. BB 2-43 v Surrey (Oval) 1995.

McGRATH, Anthony (Yorkshire Martyrs Collegiate S), b Bradford 6 Oct 1975. 6'2". RHB, OB. Debut 1995. Tour: P 1995-96 (Eng A). HS 84 v Somerset (Taunton) 1995. **BHC:** HS 2. **SL:** HS 72 v Sussex (Scarborough) 1995.

MORRIS, Alexander Corfield (Holgate S; Barnsley C), b Barnsley 4 Oct 1976. 6'3". LHB, RMF. Debut 1995. Yorks 2nd XI debut when 16yr 332d. HS 1. **NWT:** HS 1*. BB 1-43. **SL:** HS 7. BB 1-8.

MOXON, Martyn Douglas (Holgate GS, Barnsley), b Barnsley 4 May 1960. 6'0". RHB, RM. Debut 1981 v Essex (Leeds), scoring 5 and 116. Cap 1984. Captain 1990-95. Benefit 1993. GW 1982-83/1983-84. *Wisden* 1992. **Tests:** 10 (1986 to 1989); HS 99 v NZ (Auckland) 1987-88. **LOI:** 8 (1984-85 to 1987-88; HS 70). Tours (C=captain): A 1987-88, 1992-93C (Eng A); SA 1992-93C (Y); WI 1986-87 (Y); NZ 1987-88; I 1984-85; SL 1984-85, 1985-86 (Eng B). 1000 runs (11); most – 1669 (1991). HS 274* v Worcs (Worcester) 1994. BB 3-24 v Hants (Southampton) 1989. Awards: NWT 4; BHC 7. **NWT:** HS 107* v Warwks (Leeds) 1990. BB 2-19 v Norfolk (Leeds) 1990. **BHC:** HS 141* v Glam (Cardiff) 1991. BB 5-31 v Warwks (Leeds) 1991. **SL:** HS 129* v Surrey (Oval) 1991. BB 3-29 v Sussex (Hove) 1990.

PARKER, Bradley (Bingley GS), b Mirfield 23 Jun 1970. 5'11". RHB, RM. Debut 1992. HS 127 v Surrey (Scarborough) 1994. **NWT:** HS – . **SL:** HS 36 v Sussex (Hove) 1994.

ROBINSON, Mark Andrew (Hull GS), b Hull 23 Nov 1966. 6'3". RHB, RFM. Northamptonshire 1987-90 (cap 1990). Canterbury 1988-89. Yorkshire debut 1991. Cap 1992. Tours (Y): SA 1991-92, 1992-93. Failed to score in 12 successive f-c innings 1990 – world record. HS 23 v Glos (Middlesbrough) 1995. 50 wkts (1): 50 (1992). BB 9-37 (12-124 match) v Northants (Harrogate) 1993. Award: BHC 1. **NWT:** HS 3*. BB 4-32 Nh v Somerset (Taunton) 1989. **BHC:** HS 3*. BB 3-20 Nh v Scot (Glasgow) 1989. **SL:** HS 7. BB 4-23 v Northants (Leeds) 1993.

SCHOFIELD, Christopher John (Kingstone S, Barnsley), b Barnsley 21 Mar 1976. 5'7". RHB. Awaiting f-c debut.

SILVERWOOD, Christopher Eric Wilfred (Garforth CS), b Pontefract 5 Mar 1975. 6'1". RHB, RFM. Debut 1993. HS 50 v Lancs (Manchester) 1995. BB 5-62 v Surrey (Oval) 1995. **NWT:** HS 8*. BB 1-38. **BHC:** HS 2. BB 1-19. **SL:** HS 9. BB 3-29 v Worcs (Worcester) 1994.

STEMP, Richard David (Britannia HS, Rowley Regis), b Erdington, Birmingham 11 Dec 1967. 6'0". RHB, SLA. Worcestershire 1990-92. Yorkshire debut 1993. Tours (Eng A): SA 1992-93 (Y); I 1994-95; P 1995-96. HS 37 v Essex (Chelmsford) 1993. BB 6-37 v Durham (Durham) 1994. **NWT:** HS 1*. BB 1-31. **BHC:** HS 0*. BB 2-28 v Scot (Glasgow) 1995. **SL:** HS 23* v Warwks (Birmingham) 1993. BB 3-18 Wo v Derbys (Worcester) 1991.

VAUGHAN, Michael Paul (Silverdale CS, Sheffield), b Manchester, Lancs 29 Oct 1974. 6'2". RHB, OB. Debut 1993. Cap 1995. Tour: I 1994-95 (Eng A). 1000 runs (2); most – 1244 (1995). HS 117 v Northants (Luton) 1994. BB 4-39 v OU (Oxford) 1994. BAC BB 3-32 v Leics (Leicester) 1995. **NWT:** HS 34 v Northants (Leeds) 1995. **BHC:** HS 50* v Scot (Glasgow) 1995. **SL:** HS 46 v Notts (Cleethorpes) 1995.

WHARF, Alexander George (Buttershaw Upper S), b Bradford 4 Jun 1975. 6'5". RHB, RMF. Debut 1994. HS 46 and BB 1-78 v Warwks (Scarborough) 1994 – on debut. **SL:** HS – and BB 3-39 v Warwks (Scarborough) 1994.

WHITE, Craig (Flora Hill HS, Bendigo, Australia; Bendigo HS), b Morley 16 Dec 1969. 6'0". RHB, RFM. Debut 1990. Cap 1993. Victoria 1990-91 (2 matches). **Tests:** 6 (1994 to 1995); HS 51 v NZ (Lord's) 1994; BB 3-18 v NZ (Manchester) 1994. **LOI:** 8 (1994-95 to 1995-96; HS 34; BB 2-18). Tours: A 1994-95; SA 1991-92 (Y), 1992-93 (Y); P 1995-96 (Eng A). HS 146 v Durham (Leeds) 1993. BB 5-40 v Essex (Leeds) 1994. **NWT:** HS 113 and BB 3-38 v Ire (Leeds) 1995. **BHC:** HS 43 v Worcs (Leeds) 1995. BB 2-30 v Northants (Leeds) 1993. **SL:** HS 63 v Surrey (Scarborough) 1992. BB 3-25 v Hants (Leeds) 1994.

NEWCOMERS

BATTY, Gareth Jon, b Bradford 13 Oct 1977. Brother of J.D. (*see SOMERSET*). RHB, OB.

FISHER, Ian Douglas (Beckfoot GS, Bingley), b Bradford 31 Mar 1976. LHB, SLA.

HOGGARD, Matthew James (Grangefield S, Pudsey), b Leeds 31 Dec 1976. 6'2". RHB, RFM.

HUTCHISON, Paul Michael (Crawshaw HS, Pudsey), b Leeds 9 Jun 1977. 6'3". LHB, LFM

SIDEBOTTOM, Ryan Jay (King James's GS, Almondbury), b Huddersfield 15 Jan 1978. Son of A. (Yorks, OFS and England 1973-91). 6'3". LHB, LFM.

WOOD, Matthew James (Shelley HS & SFC), b Huddersfield 6 Apr 1977. 5'9". RHB, OB.

DEPARTURES (who made first-class appearances in 1995)

GRAYSON, A.P. – *see ESSEX.*

KELLETT, Simon Andrew (Whitcliffe Mount S), b Mirfield 16 Oct 1967. 6'2". RHB. Yorkshire 1989-95 (cap 1992). Wellington 1991-92. Tours (Y): SA 1991-92, 1992-93. 1000 runs (2); most – 1326 (1992). HS 125* v Derbys (Chesterfield) 1991. Award: NWT 1. **NWT:** HS 107 v Ire (Leeds) 1995. **BHC:** HS 45 v Surrey (Oval) 1990. **SL:** HS 118* v Derbys (Leeds) 1992.

METCALFE, A.A. – *see NOTTINGHAMSHIRE.*

MILBURN, S.M. – *see HAMPSHIRE.*

YORKSHIRE 1995

RESULTS SUMMARY

	Place	Won	Lost	Drew	No Result
Britannic Assurance Championship	**8th**	7	8	2	–
All First-Class Matches		8	8	4	–
NatWest Trophy	Semi-Finalist				
Benson and Hedges Cup	Quarter-Finalist				
Sunday League	**12th**	7	9	–	1

BRITANNIC ASSURANCE CHAMPIONSHIP AVERAGES

BATTING AND FIELDING

Cap		*M*	*I*	*NO*	*HS*	*Runs*	*Avge*	*100*	*50*	*Ct/St*
1984	M.D.Moxon	10	18	7	203*	839	76.27	2	6	6
1991	D.Byas	17	32	3	213	1476	50.89	2	10	39
1995	M.G.Bevan	17	29	4	153*	1249	49.96	3	7	15
1995	M.P.Vaughan	17	32	–	88	1151	35.96	–	9	11
1993	C.White	14	23	3	110	627	31.35	3	–	6
–	A.McGrath	5	10	–	84	280	28.00	–	1	3
1993	D.Gough	9	11	1	60	235	23.50	–	1	3
–	B.Parker	4	8	1	40	161	23.00	–	–	3
1992	S.A.Kellett	6	11	1	86	228	22.80	–	1	5
–	A.P.Grayson	7	11	1	73	160	16.00	–	1	2
–	C.E.W.Silverwood	7	9	2	50	106	15.14	–	1	1
1987	P.J.Hartley	15	20	2	38	235	13.05	–	–	4
1987	R.J.Blakey	17	25	3	45	284	12.90	–	–	51/3
–	R.D.Stemp	17	23	3	22*	178	8.90	–	–	7
1992	M.A.Robinson	15	19	8	23	70	6.36	–	–	3
–	S.M.Milburn	3	6	1	7	15	3.00	–	–	–

Also batted: G.M.Hamilton (2 matches) 9, 12*, 29 (2 ct); R.A.Kettleborough (1 match) 55, 4; A.A.Metcalfe (3 matches – cap 1986) 79, 1, 20* (4 ct); A.C.Morris (1 match) 1, 0* (1 ct).

BOWLING

	O	*M*	*R*	*W*	*Avge*	*Best*	*5wI*	*10wM*
S.M.Milburn	69	15	204	10	20.40	4-68	–	–
P.J.Hartley	470.2	107	1556	71	21.91	9-41	4	1
D.Gough	283.5	68	895	32	27.96	4-34	–	–
M.A.Robinson	413.1	117	1158	38	30.47	4-46	–	–
C.White	216.1	39	687	20	34.35	4-40	–	–
C.E.W.Silverwood	147.1	23	630	18	35.00	5-62	1	–
R.D.Stemp	610.1	193	1628	36	45.22	4-68	–	–
M.P.Vaughan	238.4	57	744	19	39.15	3-32	–	–

Also bowled: M.G.Bevan 85-20-292-6; A.P.Grayson 24-7-75-0; G.M.Hamilton 47-11-169-4; A.C.Morris 17-5-62-0.

The First-Class Averages (pp 129-143) give the records of Yorkshire players in all first-class county matches (their other opponents being Lancashire in a non-Championship match, the West Indians and Cambridge University), with the exception of:

D.Gough 11-13-1-60-259-21.58-0-1-4ct. 344.5-83-1110-45-24.66-7/28-1-1.
R.D.Stemp 20-24-3-22*-179-8.52-0-0-8ct. 690.1-214-1860-38-48.94-4/68.
M.P.Vaughan 20-38-1-88-1235-33.37-0-10-13ct. 272.4-64-876-22-39.81-3/32.
C.White 17-29-5-110-848-35.33-3-3-8ct. 257.4-49-858-25-34.32-4/40.

YORKSHIRE RECORDS

FIRST-CLASS CRICKET

Highest Total	For	887		v	Warwicks	Birmingham	1896
	V	630		by	Somerset	Leeds	1901
Lowest Total	For	23		v	Hampshire	Middlesbrough	1965
	V	13		by	Notts	Nottingham	1901
Highest Innings	For	341	G.H.Hirst	v	Leics	Leicester	1905
	V	318*	W.G.Grace	for	Glos	Cheltenham	1876

Highest Partnerships for each Wicket

1st	555	P.Holmes/H.Sutcliffe	v	Essex	Leyton	1932
2nd	346	W.Barber/M.Leyland	v	Middlesex	Sheffield	1932
3rd	323*	H.Sutcliffe/M.Leyland	v	Glamorgan	Huddersfield	1928
4th	312	D.Denton/G.H.Hirst	v	Hampshire	Southampton	1914
5th	340	E.Wainwright/G.H.Hirst	v	Surrey	The Oval	1899
6th	276	M.Leyland/E.Robinson	v	Glamorgan	Swansea	1926
7th	254	W.Rhodes/D.C.F.Burton	v	Hampshire	Dewsbury	1919
8th	292	R.Peel/Lord Hawke	v	Warwicks	Birmingham	1896
9th	192	G.H.Hirst/S.Haigh	v	Surrey	Bradford	1898
10th	149	G.Boycott/G.B.Stevenson	v	Warwicks	Birmingham	1982

Best Bowling	For	10-10	H.Verity	v	Notts	Leeds	1932
(Innings)	V	10-37	C.V.Grimmett	for	Australians	Sheffield	1930
Best Bowling	For	17-91	H.Verity	v	Essex	Leyton	1933
(Match)	V	17-91	H.Dean	for	Lancashire	Liverpool	1913

Most Runs – Season	2883	H.Sutcliffe	(av 80.08)	1932
Most Runs – Career	38561	H.Sutcliffe	(av 50.20)	1919-45
Most 100s – Season	12	H.Sutcliffe		1932
Most 100s – Career	112	H.Sutcliffe		1919-45
Most Wkts – Season	240	W.Rhodes	(av 12.72)	1900
Most Wkts – Career	3608	W.Rhodes	(av 16.00)	1898-1930

LIMITED-OVERS CRICKET

Highest Total	**NWT**	317-4		v	Surrey	Lord's	1965
	BHC	317-5		v	Scotland	Leeds	1986
	SL	318-7		v	Leics	Leicester	1993
Lowest Total	**NWT**	76		v	Surrey	Harrogate	1970
	BHC	88		v	Worcs	Leeds	1995
	SL	56		v	Warwicks	Birmingham	1995
Highest Innings	**NWT**	146	G.Boycott	v	Surrey	Lord's	1965
	BHC	142	G.Boycott	v	Worcs	Worcester	1980
	SL	130*	R.J.Blakey	v	Kent	Scarborough	1991
Best Bowling	**NWT**	6-15	F.S.Trueman	v	Somerset	Taunton	1965
	BHC	6-27	A.G.Nicholson	v	Minor C (N)	Middlesbrough	1972
	SL	7-15	R.A.Hutton	v	Worcs	Leeds	1969

DERBYSHIRE – DEPARTURES (continued from p 25)

HARRISON, Tom William (Oundle S; Manchester U), b Peterborough, Hunts 11 Dec 1971. 6'2". LHB, SLA. Derbyshire 1995. Northamptonshire staff 1994. HS 61* v Surrey (Derby) 1995. BB 4-153 v Essex (Chelmsford) 1995. **BHC:** HS 25 v Worcs (Worcester) 1995. **SL:** HS 15 v Worcs (Worcester) 1995. Maroon for Rugby at Manchester U.

RICHARDSON, Alan (Alleyne's HS; Stafford CFE), b Newcastle-under-Lyme, Staffs 6 May 1975. 6'2". RHB, RM. Derbyshire 1995 (one match). HS 4 and BB 3-27 v OU (Oxford) 1995. **SL:** HS –.

GLOUCESTERSHIRE – DEPARTURES (continued from p 45)

WILLIAMS, Ricardo Cecil (Ellerslie SS, Barbados; Haringey Cricket C), b Camberwell, London 3 Feb 1968. 5'9". RHB, RM. Debut 1991. HS 44 v Notts (Worksop) 1992. BB 4-28 v CU (Bristol) 1994. BAC BB 3-13 v Kent (Cheltenham) 1994. **SL:** HS 40 v Yorks (Middlesbrough) 1995. BB 4-51 v Middx (Bristol) 1994.

NORTHAMPTONSHIRE – NEWCOMERS (continued from p 75)

BAILEY, Tobin Michael Barnaby (Bedford S), b Kettering 28 Aug 1976. RHB, WK. Bedfordshire 1994.

EMBUREY, John Ernest (Peckham Manor SS), b Peckham, London 20 Aug 1952. 6'2". RHB, OB. Middlesex 1973-95 (cap 1977; benefit 1986; testimonial 1995). *Wisden* 1983. W Province 1982-83/1983-84. **Tests:** 64 (1978 to 1995, 2 as captain); HS 75 v NZ (Nottingham) 1986; BB 7-78 v A (Sydney) 1986-87. **LOI**: 61 (HS 34; BB 4-37). Tours: A 1978-79, 1979-80, 1986-87, 1987-88; SA 1981-82 (SAB), 1989-90 (Eng XI); WI 1980-81, 1985-86; NZ 1987-88; I 1979-80, 1981-82, 1992-93; P 1987-88; SL 1977-78 (DHR), 1981-82, 1991-92; Z 1980-81 (Mx). HS 133 v Essex (Chelmsford) 1983. 50 wkts (17) inc 100 (1): 103 (1983). BB 8-40 (12-115 match) v Hants (Lord's) 1993. Awards: NWT 2; BHC 6. **NWT:** HS 36* v Lancs (Manchester) 1978. BB 3-11 v Sussex (Lord's) 1989. **BHC:** HS 50 v Kent (Lord's) 1984. BB 5-37 v Somerset (Taunton) 1991. **SL:** HS 50 v Lancs (Blackpool) 1988. BB 5-23 v Somerset (Taunton) 1991. Appointed Northamptonshire coach 1996. Playing registration subject to TCCB approval.

DEPARTURES (who made first-class appearances in 1995)

ATKINS, Craig Stuart (Swan Hill TS, Victoria), b Melbourne, Australia 29 May 1966. 6'2". LHB, SLA. Northamptonshire 1995 (one match). HS 8*. BB 1-46. **SL:** HS 1.

KUMBLE, Anil (National HS; R.V. Engineering C, Bangalore), b Bangalore, India 17 Oct 1970. 6'1½". RHB, LB. Karnataka 1989-90 to date. Northamptonshire 1995 (cap 1995). *Wisden* 1995. **Tests** (I): 23 (1990 to 1995-96); HS 52* v WI (Nagpur) 1994-95; BB 7-59 (11-128 match) v SL (Lucknow) 1993-94. **LOI** (I): 71 (1989-90 to 1995-96; HS 24; BB 6-12). Tours (I): E 1990; SA 1992-93; NZ 1993-94; SL 1993-94; Z 1992-93. HS 154* Karnataka v Kerala (Bijapur) 1991-92. Nh HS 40* v Glos (Northampton) 1995. 50 wkts (1) inc 100 (1): 105 (1995). BB 8-41 Karnataka v Kerala (Tellicherry) 1994-95. Nh BB 7-82 v Warwks (Birmingham) 1995. **NWT:** HS 6*. BB 4-50 v Holland (Northampton) 1995. **BHC:** HS 3. BB 2-30 v Yorks (Leeds) 1995. **SL:** HS 8. BB 3-25 v Derbys (Derby) 1995.

CAMBRIDGE v OXFORD 1995
150th UNIVERSITY MATCH

At Lord's, London, on 5, 6, 7 July.
Toss: Cambridge University. Result: OXFORD UNIVERSITY won by 9 wickets.

CAMBRIDGE UNIVERSITY

R.T.Ragnauth c Ricketts b MacRobert	35		c Ridley b Kendall	14
†D.R.H.Churton c Sutcliffe b Ricketts	31		c Townsend b Kendall	1
J.Ratledge c Ridley b Mather	67		c MacRobert b Yeabsley	8
R.Q.Cake c Ricketts b Sutcliffe	101		b MacRobert	43
J.P.Carroll c Townsend b Ricketts	17	(6)	lbw b Yeabsley	13
R.A.Battye c Townsend b Ricketts	6	(7)	c Macmillan b MacRobert	1
*A.R.Whittall lbw b MacRobert	2	(8)	c and b Yeabsley	17
N.J.Haste c Townsend b Yeabsley	6	(5)	c Malik b Yeabsley	0
A.N.Janisch not out	4		not out	18
J.W.O.Freeth c Malik b MacRobert	13		c Mather b Ricketts	1
E.J.How lbw b MacRobert	0		b Mather	0
Extras (B5, LB7, W1)	13		(B4, LB6)	10
Total	**295**			**126**

OXFORD UNIVERSITY

C.M.Gupte c Ragnauth b Whittall	5	(3)	not out	13
I.J.Sutcliffe c Ragnauth b Janisch	71		c Churton b How	52
A.C.Ridley c Churton b Haste	2			
*G.I.Macmillan lbw b Haste	2	(1)	not out	113
W.S.Kendall c Whittall b Haste	41			
H.S.Malik c Whittall b Haste	64			
R.S.Yeabsley c Ragnauth b Haste	3			
J.D.Ricketts c Cake b Janisch	10			
A.D.MacRobert c Ratledge b Janisch	7			
†C.J.Townsend not out	9			
D.P.Mather				
Extras (B4, LB11, W1, NB2)	19		(B6, LB2, W2, NB2)	12
Total (9 wickets declared)	**233**		(1 wicket)	**190**

OXFORD	*O*	*M*	*R*	*W*		*O*	*M*	*R*	*W*
MacRobert	23	8	41	4		23	5	55	2
Mather	17	3	70	1	(5)	0.1	0	0	1
Yeabsley	18	6	45	1		19	7	34	4
Ricketts	29	8	59	3		12	5	14	1
Kendall	5	2	7	0	(2)	8	2	13	2
Malik	5	1	24	0					
Macmillan	13	3	26	0					
Sutcliffe	4	1	11	1					
CAMBRIDGE									
Whittall	19	7	47	1		13	3	19	0
Haste	19	4	73	5		9	0	51	0
How	8	2	32	0	(5)	4	0	24	1
Janisch	12	2	38	3		6	0	22	0
Freeth	12	1	28	0	(3)	14	1	52	0
Battye						0.4	0	14	0

FALL OF WICKETS

Wkt	*CU 1st*	*OU 1st*	*CU 2nd*	*OU 2nd*
1st	57	10	14	143
2nd	83	13	19	–
3rd	185	15	30	–
4th	215	89	33	–
5th	267	174	55	–
6th	267	183	60	–
7th	276	196	81	–
8th	276	215	103	–
9th	295	233	106	–
10th	295	–	126	–

Umpires: B.Dudleston and K.E.Palmer.

UNIVERSITY MATCH RESULTS

Played: 150. Wins: Cambridge 55; Oxford 48. Drawn: 47. Abandoned: 1.
This, the oldest surviving first-class fixture, dates from 1827 and, wartime interruptions apart, has been played annually since 1838. With the exception of five matches played in the area of Oxford (1829, 1843, 1846, 1848 and 1850), all the fixtures have been played at Lord's.

1827	Drawn	1873	Oxford	1911	Oxford	1959	Oxford
1829	Oxford	1874	Oxford	1912	Cambridge	1960	Drawn
1836	Oxford	1875	Oxford	1913	Cambridge	1961	Drawn
1838	Oxford	1876	Cambridge	1914	Oxford	1962	Drawn
1839	Cambridge	1877	Oxford	1919	Oxford	1963	Drawn
1840	Cambridge	1878	Cambridge	1920	Drawn	1964	Drawn
1841	Cambridge	1879	Cambridge	1921	Cambridge	1965	Drawn
1842	Cambridge	1880	Cambridge	1922	Cambridge	1966	Oxford
1843	Cambridge	1881	Oxford	1923	Oxford	1967	Drawn
1844	Drawn	1882	Cambridge	1924	Cambridge	1968	Drawn
1845	Cambridge	1883	Cambridge	1925	Drawn	1969	Drawn
1846	Oxford	1884	Oxford	1926	Cambridge	1970	Drawn
1847	Cambridge	1885	Cambridge	1927	Cambridge	1971	Drawn
1848	Oxford	1886	Oxford	1928	Drawn	1972	Cambridge
1849	Cambridge	1887	Oxford	1929	Drawn	1973	Drawn
1850	Oxford	1888	Drawn	1930	Cambridge	1974	Drawn
1851	Cambridge	1889	Cambridge	1931	Oxford	1975	Drawn
1852	Oxford	1890	Cambridge	1932	Drawn	1976	Oxford
1853	Oxford	1891	Cambridge	1933	Drawn	1977	Drawn
1854	Oxford	1892	Oxford	1934	Drawn	1978	Drawn
1855	Oxford	1893	Cambridge	1935	Cambridge	1979	Cambridge
1856	Cambridge	1894	Oxford	1936	Cambridge	1980	Drawn
1857	Oxford	1895	Cambridge	1937	Oxford	1981	Drawn
1858	Oxford	1896	Oxford	1938	Drawn	1982	Cambridge
1859	Cambridge	1897	Cambridge	1939	Oxford	1983	Drawn
1860	Cambridge	1898	Oxford	1946	Oxford	1984	Oxford
1861	Cambridge	1899	Drawn	1947	Drawn	1985	Drawn
1862	Cambridge	1900	Drawn	1948	Oxford	1986	Cambridge
1863	Oxford	1901	Drawn	1949	Cambridge	1987	Drawn
1864	Oxford	1902	Cambridge	1950	Drawn	1988	Abandoned
1865	Oxford	1903	Oxford	1951	Oxford	1989	Drawn
1866	Oxford	1904	Drawn	1952	Drawn	1990	Drawn
1867	Cambridge	1905	Cambridge	1953	Cambridge	1991	Drawn
1868	Cambridge	1906	Cambridge	1954	Drawn	1992	Cambridge
1869	Cambridge	1907	Cambridge	1955	Drawn	1993	Oxford
1870	Cambridge	1908	Oxford	1956	Drawn	1994	Drawn
1871	Oxford	1909	Drawn	1957	Cambridge	1995	Oxford
1872	Cambridge	1910	Oxford	1958	Cambridge		

CAMBRIDGE UNIVERSITY

BATTYE, Richard Antony (Salendine Nook HS; Huddersfield New C; Trinity C), b Huddersfield, Yorks 19 Oct 1969. 6'2". RHB. Debut/blue 1995. HS 70* v Middx (Cambridge) 1995.

BIRKS, Malcolm James (S Craven CS; Jesus C), b Keighley, Yorks 29 Jul 1975. 6'3½". RHB, WK. Debut 1995. HS 23* v Notts (Cambridge) 1995. Made 2 stumpings as a substitute v Yorks 1995.

CAKE, Russell Quentin (KCS, Wimbledon; St John's C), b Chertsey, Surrey 16 May 1973. 5'7". RHB. Debut 1993; blue 1993-94-95; captain 1996. HS 108 Comb Us v A (Oxford) 1993. CU HS 107 v Glam (Cambridge) 1994. Hockey blue.

CARROLL, John Paul (Rendcomb C, Cirencester; Homerton C), b Bebington, Cheshire 14 Jul 1972. 6'2". RHB, RM. Debut 1992; blue 1992-93-94-95. HS 92 v Kent (Cambridge) 1992.

CHURTON, David Richard Harding (Wellington C; St Catharine's C); b Salisbury, Wilts 29 Mar 1975. 5'9". RHB, WK. Debut/blue 1995. HS 39 v Warwks (Cambridge) 1995. Hockey blue.

CLARKE, Lionel Paul (Silverdale S, Sheffield; Bristol U; St Catharine's C), b Sheffield, Yorks 11 Oct 1972. 6'0". RHB. Debut 1995. HS 14 and BB 1-55 v Yorks (Cambridge) 1995.

FREETH, James William Owen (Sherborne S; Pembroke C), b Bournemouth, Hants 9 Apr 1974. 5'9½". RHB, OB. Debut/blue 1995. HS 18 v Kent (Folkestone) 1995. BB 2-62 v Lancs (Cambridge) 1995.

HASTE, Nicholas John (Wellingborough S; Pembroke C), b Northampton 13 Nov 1972. 6'0". RHB, RM. Debut 1993; blue 1993-94-95. HS 36 v OU (Lord's) 1993. BB 5-73 v OU (Lord's) 1995.

HOW, Edward Joseph (Dr Challoner's GS, Amersham; Gonville & Caius C), b Amersham, Bucks 16 May 1974. 5'10". RHB, LMF. Debut/blue 1995. HS 0* (*his only innings were 0*, 0*, 0 and 0*). BB 1-24 (*his only wicket*) v OU (Lord's) 1995.

HUGHES, Edward Robert (Hadleigh HS; Ipswich S; Downing C), b Ipswich, Suffolk 12 Dec 1973. 5'9½". RHB, RM. Debut 1995. HS 0. BB 1-62.

JANISCH, Adam Nicholas (Abingdon S; Trinity C), b Hammersmith Hospital, London 21 Oct 1975. 6'0". RHB, RM. Debut/blue 1995. HS 18* and BB 3-38 v OU (Lord's) 1995.

RAGNAUTH, Reimell Tagenath (The Perse S; Trinity Hall), b Cambridge 29 Mar 1975. 5'9". RHB. Debut/blue 1995. HS 82 v Kent (Folkestone) 1995. Hockey blue.

RATLEDGE, John (Bolton S; St John's C), b Preston, Lancs 8 Aug 1974. 5'8". RHB, RM. Debut 1994; blue 1994-95. HS 79 v Lancs (Cambridge) 1994. BB 1-16.

STANLEY, Donald Eric (Abingdon S; Gonville & Caius C), b Bromley, Kent 8 Mar 1972. 6'2". RHB. Debut/blue 1994. HS 48 v Glam (Cambridge) 1994.

WHITTALL, Andrew Richard (Falcon C, Zimbabwe; Trinity C), b Mutare, Zimbabwe 28 Mar 1973. Cousin of G.J. (Zimbabwe). 6'3", RHB, OB. Debut 1993; blue 1993-94-95; captain 1994-95. HS 91* v OU (Lord's) 1994. BB 6-46 (11-113 match) v Essex (Cambridge) 1995. **BHC** (Comb Us): HS 21 and BB 2-49 v Glos (Bristol) 1995.

YEABSLEY, Michael Ian (Haberdashers' Aske's S, Elstree; Durham U; Queens' C), b St Albans, Herts 8 Aug 1972. Son of D.I. (Devon 1959-89; Minor Counties 1974-79), brother of R.S. (*see OXFORD U*). 6'0". RHB, OB. Debut 1995. HS 2. BB 1-28. Represented Durham in UAU Rugby final 1991.

RESULTS SUMMARY

	Played	Won	Lost	Drew
All first-class matches	8	0	2	6

1995 FIRST-CLASS AVERAGES

BATTING AND FIELDING

	M	I	NO	HS	Runs	Avge	100	50	Ct/St
† R.Q.Cake	7	14	3	101	511	46.45	1	2	4
† R.A.Battye	8	14	2	70*	391	32.58	–	5	3
† J.P.Carroll	8	15	2	42	292	22.46	–	–	4
† J.Ratledge	8	16	–	67	358	22.37	–	3	4
† R.T.Ragnauth	8	16	1	82	335	22.33	–	3	10
† A.R.Whittall	8	13	2	81*	185	16.81	–	1	6
† N.J.Haste	7	10	4	16	83	13.83	–	–	1
† D.R.H.Churton	6	10	–	39	118	11.80	–	–	7/3
† A.N.Janisch	7	8	4	18*	38	9.50	–	–	2
† J.W.O.Freeth	7	6	1	18	35	7.00	–	–	2
D.E.Stanley	2	4	–	6	10	2.50	–	–	–
M.I.Yeabsley	2	4	–	2	2	0.50	–	–	–
† E.J.How	4	4	2	0*	0	0.00	–	–	1

Also batted (2 matches each): M.J.Birks 18*, 2, 23* (2 ct); L.P.Clarke 14, 3, 0 (1 ct); E.R.Hughes 0.

BOWLING

	O	*M*	*R*	*W*	*Avge*	*Best*	*5wI*	*10wM*
N.J.Haste	197	41	655	18	36.38	5-73	1	–
A.R.Whittall	328.4	85	1064	29	36.68	6-46	2	1
A.N.Janisch	185	21	723	10	72.30	3-38	–	–
J.W.O.Freeth	210.3	33	721	8	90.12	2-62	–	–

Also bowled: R.A.Battye 0.4-0-14-0; J.P.Carroll 26-3-98-0; L.P.Clarke 7-0-55-1; E.J.How 75-9-299-1; E.R.Hughes 54-5-234-2; J.Ratledge 4.4-0-42-1; M.I.Yeabsley 18-3-84-2.

† Blue 1995.

CAMBRIDGE UNIVERSITY RECORDS

ALL FIRST-CLASS MATCHES

Highest Total	For	703-9d		v	Sussex	Hove	1890
	V	730-3		by	W Indians	Cambridge	1950
Lowest Total	For	30		v	Yorkshire	Cambridge	1928
	V	32		by	Oxford U	Lord's	1878
Highest Innings	For	254*	K.S.Duleepsinhji	v	Middlesex	Cambridge	1927
	V	304	E.de C.Weekes	for	W Indians	Cambridge	1950

Highest Partnership for each Wicket

1st	349	J.G.Dewes/D.S.Sheppard	v	Sussex	Hove	1950
2nd	429*	J.G.Dewes/G.H.G.Doggart	v	Essex	Cambridge	1949
3rd	284	E.T.Killick/G.C.Grant	v	Essex	Cambridge	1929
4th	275	R.de W.K.Winlaw/J.H.Human	v	Essex	Cambridge	1934
5th	220	R.Subba Row/F.C.M.Alexander	v	Notts	Nottingham	1953
6th	245	J.L.Bryan/C.T.Ashton	v	Surrey	The Oval	1921
7th	289	G.Goonesena/G.W.Cook	v	Oxford U	Lord's	1957
8th	145	H.Ashton/A.E.R.Gilligan	v	F Foresters	Cambridge	1920
9th	200	G.W.Cook/C.S.Smith	v	Lancashire	Liverpool	1957
10th	177	A.E.R.Gilligan/J.H.Naumann	v	Sussex	Hove	1919

Best Bowling	For	10-69	S.M.J.Woods	v	Thornton's XI	Cambridge	1890
(Innings)	V	10-38	S.E.Butler	for	Oxford U	Lord's	1871
Best Bowling	For	15-88	S.M.J.Woods	v	Thornton's XI	Cambridge	1890
(Match)	V	15-95	S.E.Butler	for	Oxford U	Lord's	1871

Most Runs – Season	1581	D.S.Sheppard	(av 79.05)	1952
Most Runs – Career	4310	J.M.Brearley	(av 38.48)	1961-68
Most 100s – Season	7	D.S.Sheppard		1952
Most 100s – Career	14	D.S.Sheppard		1950-52
Most Wkts – Season	80	O.S.Wheatley	(av 17.63)	1958
Most Wkts – Career	208	G.Goonesena	(av 21.82)	1954-57

UNIVERSITY MATCH RECORDS

Highest Total	432-9d		1936
Lowest Total	39		1858
Highest Innings	211	G.Goonesena	1957
Best Bowling (Innings)	8-44	G.E.Jeffery	1873
Best Bowling (Match)	13-73	A.G.Steel	1878

Hat-Tricks F.C.Cobden (1870), A.G.Steel (1879), P.H.Morton (1880), J.F.Ireland (1911), R.G.Lowe (1926)

Match Double No instance

OXFORD UNIVERSITY

ATTFIELD, Jeremy Mark (Wellingborough S; Kingston U; Keble C), b Kettering, Northants 5 Mar 1972. 5'10". RHB, OB. Debut 1995. HS 23* and BB 2-76 v Notts (Oxford) 1995.

GUPTE, Chinmay Madhukar (John Lyon S, Harrow; Pembroke C), b Poona, India 5 Jul 1972. Son of M.S. (Maharashtra). 5'7". RHB, SLA. Debut 1991; blue 1991-93-94-95; captain 1996. HS 122 v CU (Lord's) 1994. BB 2-41 v Notts (Oxford) 1991. **BHC** (Comb Us): HS 19 v Middx (Lord's) 1995.

JARRETT, Michael Eugene Dominic (Harrow S; Girton C, Cambridge; St John's C, Oxford), b St Thomas' Hospital, London 18 Sep 1972. 5'9". RHB, RM. Cambridge U 1992-93; blue 1992-93. Oxford U debut 1995. HS 51 CU v Leics (Cambridge) 1993. OU HS 40 v Derbys (Oxford) 1995.

KENDALL, William Salwey – *see HAMPSHIRE.*

MACROBERT, Angus David (Grey HS, Pt Elizabeth; Cape Town U; Keble C), b Pretoria, SA 15 Oct 1968. 6'1". LHB, RMF. Debut/blue 1995. HS 29 v Derbys (Oxford) 1995. BB 4-41 v CU (Lord's) 1995. **BHC** (Comb Us): HS 6. BB 3-51 v Glos (Bristol) 1995.

MACMILLAN, Gregor Innes (captain 1995) – *see LEICESTERSHIRE.*

MALIK, Hasnain Siddiq (KCS, Wimbledon; Keble C), b Sargodha, Pakistan 21 Apr 1973. 5'11". LHB, OB. Debut 1992; blue 1994-95. HS 64* v Hants (Oxford) 1993. BB 3-10 v Hants (Oxford) 1994.

MARTIN, Neil Frederick Clay (King Edward's S, Birmingham; Durham U; Birmingham U; Keble C), b Birmingham 19 Oct 1969. 6'3". RHB, RM. Debut/blue 1994. HS 26 v Hants (Oxford) 1994. BB 2-84 v Surrey (Oval) 1994. Rugby blue.

MATHER, David Peter (Wirral G; St Hugh's C), b Bebington, Cheshire 20 Nov 1975. 5'11". LHB, LM. Debut/blue 1995. HS 8*. BB 4-65 v Durham (Oxford) 1995.

RICKETTS, Justin Donald (Sherborne S; Balliol C), b Salisbury, Wilts 8 Nov 1973. 6'2". RHB, LBG. Debut/blue 1995. HS 63 v Middx (Oxford) 1995. BB 3-30 v Glam (Oxford) 1995.

RIDLEY, Andrew Claude (St Aloysius C, Sydney; Sydney U; Exeter C), b Sydney, Australia 2 Aug 1968. 5'11". LHB, RM. Debut 1994; blue 1995. HS 71 v Notts (Oxford) 1995.

SUTCLIFFE, Iain John – *see LEICESTERSHIRE.*

TOWNSEND, Christopher James (Dean Close S; Brasenose C), b Wokingham, Berks 1 Dec 1972. 6'0". RHB, WK. Grandson of W.D.Wickson (Surrey President 1992). Debut 1992; blue 1992-94-95. HS 27 v Glos (Bristol) 1995.

WINDSOR, Jason Michael (Repton S; Worcester C), b Chesterfield, Derbys 7 Aug 1972. 6'1". RHB, RFM. Debut 1995. HS 14 v Derbys (Oxford) 1995. BB 3-51 v Middx (Oxford) 1995.

YEABSLEY, Richard Stuart (Haberdashers' Aske's S, Elstree; Keble C), b St Albans, Herts 2 Nov 1973. Son of D.I. (Devon 1959-89; Minor Counties 1974-79), brother of M.I. (*see CAMBRIDGE U*). 6'4½". RHB, RMF. Debut 1993; blue 1993-94-95. L-O appearances for Middlesex 1994-95. Devon 1990. HS 52* OU v Yorks (Oxford) 1994. BB 6-54 (10-104 match) OU v CU (Lord's) 1994. **NWT:** HS 2. **SL:** HS –. BB 5-32 M v Essex (Uxbridge) 1994. Rugby blue.

OXFORD UNIVERSITY

RESULTS SUMMARY

	Played	Won	Lost	Drew
All first-class matches	10	1	3	6

1995 FIRST-CLASS AVERAGES

BATTING AND FIELDING

	M	I	NO	HS	Runs	Avge	100	50	Ct/St
† I.J.Sutcliffe	10	18	3	163*	673	44.86	1	4	8
† W.S.Kendall	10	15	2	94	442	34.00	–	3	5
† C.M.Gupte	9	16	2	119	472	33.71	1	2	1
† G.I.Macmillan	10	15	2	113*	357	27.46	1	1	11
† A.C.Ridley	10	16	1	71	375	25.00	–	2	4
† C.J.Townsend	6	7	4	27	72	24.00	–	–	11/1
M.E.D.Jarrett	7	11	4	40	137	19.57	–	–	8/1
† H.S.Malik	8	10	1	64	160	17.77	–	1	8
† J.D.Ricketts	10	11	1	63	148	14.80	–	1	3
J.M.Attfield	6	8	2	23*	76	12.66	–	–	2
† A.D.MacRobert	9	9	2	29	80	11.42	–	–	3
† D.P.Mather	8	6	3	8*	19	6.33	–	–	2
† R.S.Yeabsley	3	4	–	4	13	3.25	–	–	1

Also batted (2 matches each): N.F.C.Martin 3, 7; J.M.Windsor 6*, 14, 8.

BOWLING

	O	M	R	W	Avge	Best	5wI	10wM
W.S.Kendall	76	13	233	8	29.12	3-37	–	–
R.S.Yeabsley	85	16	277	8	34.62	4-34	–	–
D.P.Mather	227.1	49	710	18	39.44	4-65	–	–
J.D.Ricketts	224.5	34	732	17	43.05	3-30	–	–
A.D.MacRobert	264	37	843	18	46.83	4-41	–	–
H.S.Malik	152	22	539	6	89.83	2-55	–	–
G.I.Macmillan	129.3	12	460	5	92.00	1-53	–	–

Also bowled: J.M.Attfield 87.3-12-310-3; N.F.C.Martin 23-2-123-1; I.J.Sutcliffe 9-1-31-1; J.M.Windsor 41.4-12-93-3.

† Blue 1995.

The following appeared in other first-class matches in 1995: C.M.Gupte, W.S. Kendall, G.I.Macmillan and I.J.Sutcliffe for Combined Universities v West Indians, the latter two players also appearing for Leicestershire. Their records in all first-class matches appear on pp 129-143.

OXFORD UNIVERSITY RECORDS

ALL FIRST-CLASS MATCHES

Highest Total	For	651	v	Sussex	Hove	1895
	V	679-7d	by	Australians	Oxford	1938
Lowest Total	For	12	v	MCC	Oxford	1877
	V	24	by	MCC	Oxford	1846
Highest Innings	For	281 K.J.Key	v	Middlesex	Chiswick Park	1887
	V	338 W.W.Read	for	Surrey	The Oval	1888

Highest Partnership for each Wicket

1st	338	T.Bowring/H.Teesdale	v	Gentlemen	Oxford	1908
2nd	226	W.G.Keighley/H.A.Pawson	v	Cambridge U	Lord's	1947
3rd	273	F.C.de Saram/N.S.Mitchell-Innes	v	Glos	Oxford	1934
4th	276	P.G.T.Kingsley/N.M.Ford	v	Surrey	The Oval	1930
5th	256*	A.A.Baig/C.A.Fry	v	F Foresters	Oxford	1959
6th	270	D.R.Walsh/S.A.Westley	v	Warwks	Oxford	1969
7th	340	K.J.Key/H.Philipson	v	Middlesex	Chiswick Park	1887
8th	160	H.Philipson/A.C.M.Croome	v	MCC	Lord's	1889
9th	157	H.M.G.-Wells†/C.K.H.Hill-Wood	v	Kent	Oxford	1928
10th	149	F.H.Hollins/B.A.Collins	v	MCC	Oxford	1901

Best Bowling	For	10-38	S.E.Butler	v Cambridge U	Lord's	1871
(Innings)	V	10-49	W.G.Grace	for MCC	Oxford	1886
Best Bowling	For	15-65	B.J.T.Bosanquet	v Sussex	Oxford	1900
(Match)	V	16-225	J.E.Walsh	for Leics	Oxford	1953

Most Runs – Season	1307	Nawab of Pataudi sr	(av 93.35)	1931
Most Runs – Career	3319	N.S.Mitchell-Innes	(av 47.41)	1934-37
Most 100s – Season	6	Nawab of Pataudi sr		1931
Most 100s – Career	9	A.M.Crawley		1927-30
	9	Nawab of Pataudi sr		1928-31
	9	N.S.Mitchell-Innes		1934-37
	9	M.P.Donnelly		1946-47
Most Wkts – Season	70	I.A.R.Peebles	(av 18.15)	1930
Most Wkts – Career	182	R.H.B.Bettington	(av 19.38)	1920-23

UNIVERSITY MATCH RECORDS

Highest Total	503		1900
Lowest Total	32		1878
Highest Innings	238*	Nawab of Pataudi sr	1931
Best Bowling (Innings)	10-38	S.E.Butler	1871
Best Bowling (Match)	15-95	S.E.Butler	1871
Hat-Tricks	No instance		
Match Double	160 and 11-66	P.R.le Couter	1910
	149 and 10-93	G.J.Toogood	1985

† H.M.Garland-Wells

FIRST-CLASS UMPIRES 1996

BALDERSTONE, John Christopher (Paddock Council S, Huddersfield), b Longwood, Huddersfield, Yorks 16 Nov 1940. RHB, SLA. Yorkshire 1961-69. Leicestershire 1971-86 (cap 1973; testimonial 1984). **Tests:** 2 (1976); HS 35 v WI (Leeds) 1976; BB 1-80. Tour: Z 1980-81 (Le). 1000 runs (11); most – 1482 (1982). HS 181* Le v Glos (Leicester) 1984. BB 6-25 Le v Hants (Southampton) 1978. Hat-trick 1976 (Le). F-c career: 390 matches; 19034 runs @ 34.11, 32 hundreds; 310 wickets @ 26.32; 210 ct. Soccer for Huddersfield Town, Carlisle United, Doncaster Rovers and Queen of the South. Appointed 1988. Umpired 1 LOI (1994).

BIRD, Harold Dennis (***'Dickie'***) (Raley SM, Barnsley), b Barnsley, Yorks 19 Apr 1933. RHB, RM. Yorkshire 1956-59. Leicestershire 1960-64 (cap 1960). MBE 1986. 1000 runs (1): 1028 (1960). HS 181* Y v Glam (Bradford) 1959. F-c career: 93 matches; 3314 runs @ 20.71, 2 hundreds. Appointed 1970. Umpired world record 65 Tests (1973 to 1995-96), with a final appearance scheduled at Lord's in June 1996. Umpired in 71 LOI (1973 to 1995), including 1975, 1979 and 1983 World Cup finals, 1985-86 Asia Cup and 7 Sharjah tournaments. International Panel 1994 to 1995-96.

BOND, John David (Bolton S), b Kearsley, Lancs 6 May 1932. RHB, LB. Lancashire 1955-72 (cap 1955; captain 1968-72; coach 1973; manager 1980-86; benefit 1970). Nottinghamshire 1974 (captain/coach 1974). 1000 runs (2); most – 2125 (1963). HS 157 La v Hants (Manchester) 1962. Test selector 1974. F-c career: 362 matches; 12125 runs @ 25.90, 14 hundreds; 222 ct. Appointed 1988.

BURGESS, Graham Iefvion (Millfield S), b Glastonbury, Somerset 5 May 1943. RHB, RM. Somerset 1966-79 (cap 1968; testimonial 1977). HS 129 v Glos (Taunton) 1973. BB 7-43 (13-75 match) v OU (Oxford) 1975. F-c career: 252 matches; 7129 runs @ 18.90, 2 hundreds; 474 wickets @ 28.57. Appointed 1991.

CLARKSON, Anthony (Harrogate GS), b Killinghall, Harrogate, Yorks 5 Sep 1939. RHB, OB. Yorkshire 1963. Somerset 1966-71 (cap 1968). Devon. 1000 runs (2); most – 1246 (1970). HS 131 Sm v Northants (Northampton) 1969. BB 3-51 Sm v Essex (Yeovil) 1967. F-c career: 110 matches; 4458 runs @ 25.18, 2 hundreds; 13 wickets @ 28.23. Appointed 1996.

CONSTANT, David John, b Bradford-on-Avon, Wilts 9 Nov 1941. LHB, SLA. Kent 1961-63. Leicestershire 1965-68. HS 80 Le v Glos (Bristol) 1966. F-c career: 61 matches; 1517 runs @ 19.20; 1 wicket @ 36.00. Appointed 1969. Umpired 36 Tests (1971 to 1988) and 29 LOI (1972 to 1990). Represented Gloucestershire at bowls 1984-86.

DUDLESTON, Barry (Stockport S), b Bebington, Cheshire 16 Jul 1945. RHB, SLA. Leicestershire 1966-80 (cap 1969; benefit 1980). Gloucestershire 1981-83. Rhodesia 1976-80. 1000 runs (8); most – 1374 (1970). HS 202 Le v Derbys (Leicester) 1979. BB 4-6 Le v Surrey (Leicester) 1972. F-c career: 295 matches; 14747 runs @ 32.48, 32 hundreds; 47 wickets @ 29.04. Appointed 1984. Umpired 2 Tests (1991 to 1992) and 1 LOI (1992).

HAMPSHIRE, John Harry (Oakwood THS, Rotherham), b Thurnscoe, Yorks 10 Feb 1941. RHB, LB. Son of J. (Yorks 1937); brother of A.W. (Yorks 1975). Yorkshire 1961-81 (cap 1963; benefit 1976; captain 1979-80). Derbyshire 1982-84 (cap 1982). Tasmania 1967-69, 1977-79. **Tests:** 8 (1969 to 1975); 403 runs @ 26.86, HS 107 v WI (Lord's) 1969 on debut (only England player to score hundred at Lord's on Test debut). Tours: A 1970-71; SA 1972-73 (DHR), 1974-75 (DHR); WI 1964-65 (Cav); NZ 1970-71; P 1967-68 (Cwlth XI); SL 1969-70; Z 1980-81 (Le XI). 1000 runs (15); most – 1596 (1978). HS 183* Y v Sussex (Hove) 1971. BB 7-52 Y v Glam (Cardiff) 1963. F-c career: 577 matches; 28059 runs @ 34.55, 43 hundreds; 30 wickets @ 54.56; 445 ct. Appointed 1985. Umpired 11 Tests (1989 to 1993) and 5 LOI (1989 to 1992).

HARRIS, John Henry, b Taunton, Somerset 13 Feb 1936. LHB, RFM. Somerset 1952-59. Suffolk 1960-62. Devon 1975. HS 41 v Worcs (Taunton) 1957. BB 3-29 v Worcs (Bristol) 1959. F-c career: 15 matches; 154 runs @ 11.00; 19 wickets @ 32.57. Appointed 1983.

HOLDER, John Wakefield (Combermere S, Barbados), b St George, Barbados 19 Mar 1945. RHB, RFM. Hampshire 1968-72. Hat-trick 1972. HS 33 v Sussex (Hove) 1971. BB 7-79 v Glos (Gloucester) 1972. F-c career: 47 matches; 374 runs @ 10.68; 139 wickets @ 24.56. Appointed 1983. Umpired 10 Tests (1988 to 1991) and 13 LOI (1988 to 1993-94) including 1989-90 Nehru Cup and one Sharjah tournament.

HOLDER, Vanburn Alonza (Richmond SM, Barbados), b Bridgetown, Barbados 8 Oct 1945. RHB, RFM. Barbados 1966-78. Worcestershire 1968-80 (cap 1970; benefit 1979). Shropshire 1981. **Tests** (WI): 40 (1969 to 1978-79); 682 runs @ 14.20, HS 42 v NZ (P-o-S) 1971-72; 109 wkts @ 33.27, BB 6-28 v A (P-o-S) 1977-78. **LOI** (WI): 12. Tours (WI): E 1969, 1973, 1976; A 1975-76; I 1974-75, 1978-79; P 1973-74 (RW), 1974-75; SL 1974-75, 1978-79. HS 122 Barbados v Trinidad (Bridgetown) 1973-74. BB 7-40 Wo v Glam (Cardiff) 1974. F-c career: 311 matches; 3559 runs @ 13.03, 1 hundred; 947 wickets @ 24.48. Appointed 1992.

JESTY, Trevor Edward (Privet County SS, Gosport), b Gosport, Hants 2 Jun 1948. RHB, RM. Hampshire 1966-84 (cap 1971; benefit 1982). Surrey 1985-87 (cap 1985; captain 1985). Lancashire 1988-91 (cap 1989). Border 1973-74. GW 1974-76, 1980-81. Canterbury 1979-80. *Wisden* 1982. **LOI**: 10. Tours: WI 1982-83 (Int); Z 1988-89 (La). 1000 runs (10); most – 1645 (1982). HS 248 H v CU (Cambridge) 1984. Scored 122* La v OU (Oxford) 1991 in his final f-c innings. 50 wkts (2); most – 52 (1981). BB 7-75 H v Worcs (Southampton) 1976. F-c career: 490 matches; 21916 runs @ 32.71, 35 hundreds; 585 wickets @ 27.47. Appointed 1994.

JONES, Allan Arthur (St John's C, Horsham), b Horley, Surrey 9 Dec 1947. RHB, RFM. Sussex 1966-69. Somerset 1970-75 (cap 1972). Northern Transvaal 1972-73. Middlesex 1976-79 (cap 1976). Orange Free State 1976-77. Glamorgan 1980-81. HS 33 M v Kent (Canterbury) 1978. BB 9-51 Sm v Sussex (Hove) 1972. F-c career: 214 matches; 799 runs @ 5.39; 549 wickets @ 28.07. Appointed 1985.

JULIAN, Raymond (Wigston SM), b Cosby, Leics 23 Aug 1936. RHB, WK. Leicestershire 1953-71 (cap 1961). HS 51 v Worcs (Worcester) 1962. F-c career: 192 matches; 2581 runs @ 9.73; 421 dismissals (382 ct, 39 st). Appointed 1972.

KITCHEN, Mervyn John (Backwell SM, Nailsea), b Nailsea, Somerset 1 Aug 1940. LHB, RM. Somerset 1960-79 (cap 1966; testimonial 1973). Tour: Rhodesia 1972-73 (Int W). 1000 runs (7); most – 1730 (1968). HS 189 v Pakistanis (Taunton) 1967. BB 1-4. F-c career: 354 matches; 15230 runs @ 26.25, 17 hundreds; 2 wickets @ 54.50. Appointed 1982. Umpired 11 Tests (1990 to 1995-96) and 12 LOI (1983 to 1995). **Appointed to International Panel 1995.**

LEADBEATER, Barrie (Harehills SS), b Harehills, Leeds, Yorks 14 Aug 1943. RHB, RM. Yorkshire 1966-79 (cap 1969; joint benefit with G.A.Cope 1980). Tour: WI 1969-70 (DN). HS 140* v Hants (Portsmouth) 1976. F-c career: 147 matches; 5373 runs @ 25.34, 1 hundred; 1 wicket @ 5.00. Appointed 1981. Umpired 4 LOI (1983).

LYONS, Kevin James (Lady Mary's HS), b Cardiff, Glam 18 Dec 1946. RHB, RM. Glamorgan 1967-77. Tour: WI 1969-70 (Glam). HS 92 v CU (Cambridge) 1972. F-c career: 62 matches; 1673 runs @ 19.68; 2 wickets @ 126.00. F-c umpire 1985 to 1991. Worcestershire coach 1992-93. Re-appointed 1994.

MEYER, Barrie John (Boscombe SS), b Bournemouth, Hants 21 Aug 1932. RHB, WK. Gloucestershire 1957-71 (cap 1958; benefit 1971). HS 63 v Indians (Cheltenham) 1959, v OU (Bristol) 1962, and v Sussex (Bristol) 1964. F-c career: 406 matches; 5367 runs @ 14.16; 826 dismissals (707 ct, 119 st). Soccer for Bristol Rovers, Plymouth Argyle, Newport County and Bristol City. Appointed 1973. Umpired 26 Tests (1978 to 1993) and 23 LOI (1977 to 1993), including 1979 and 1983 World Cup finals.

PALMER, Kenneth Ernest (Southbroom SM, Devizes), b Winchester, Hants 22 Apr 1937. RHB, RFM. Brother of R. (*below*) and father of G.V. (Somerset 1982-88). Somerset 1955-69 (cap 1958; testimonial 1968). Tours: WI 1963-64 (Cav); P 1963-64 (Cwlth XI). **Tests:** 1 (1964-65; while coaching in South Africa); 10 runs; 1 wicket. 1000 runs (1): 1036 (1961). 100 wickets (4); most – 139 (1963). HS 125* v Northants (Northampton) 1961. BB 9-57 v Notts (Nottingham) 1963. F-c career: 314 matches; 7761 runs @ 20.64, 2 hundreds; 866 wickets @ 21.34. Appointed 1972. Umpired 22 Tests (1978 to 1994) and 19 LOI (1977 to 1994). International Panel 1994.

PALMER, Roy (Southbroom SM, Devizes), b Devizes, Wilts 12 Jul 1942. RHB, RFM. Brother of K.E. (*above*). Somerset 1965-70. HS 84 v Leics (Taunton) 1967. BB 6-45 v Middx (Lord's) 1967. F-c career: 74 matches; 1037 runs @ 13.29; 172 wickets @ 31.62. Appointed 1980. Umpired 2 Tests (1992 to 1993) and 8 LOI (1983 to 1995).

PLEWS, Nigel Trevor (Mundella GS, Nottingham), b Nottingham 5 Sep 1934. Former policeman (Fraud Squad). No first-class appearances. Appointed 1982. Umpired 11 Tests (1988 to 1995-96) and 15 LOI (1986 to 1995-96), including 2 Sharjah tournaments. International Panel 1994 to 1995-96.

SHARP, George (Elwick Road SS, Hartlepool), b West Hartlepool, Co Durham 12 Mar 1950. RHB, WK, occ LM. Northamptonshire 1968-85 (cap 1973; benefit 1982). HS 98 v Yorks (Northampton) 1983. BB 1-47. F-c career: 306 matches; 6254 runs @ 19.85; 1 wicket @ 70.00; 655 dismissals (565 ct, 90 st). Appointed 1992. **Appointed to International Panel 1996.**

SHEPHERD, David Robert (Barnstaple GS; St Luke's C, Exeter), b Bideford, Devon 27 Dec 1940. RHB, RM. Gloucestershire 1965-79 (cap 1969; joint benefit with J.Davey 1978). Scored 108 on debut (v OU). Devon 1959-64. 1000 runs (2); most – 1079 (1970). HS 153 v Middx (Bristol) 1968. F-c career: 282 matches; 10672 runs @ 24.47, 12 hundreds; 2 wickets @ 53.00. Appointed 1981. Umpired 28 Tests (1985 to 1995-96) and 62 LOI (1983 to 1995-96), including 1987-88, 1991-92 and 1995-96 World Cups, 1985-86 Asia Cup and 5 Sharjah tournaments. **Appointed to International Panel 1994.**

WHITE, Robert Arthur (Chiswick GS), b Fulham, London 6 Oct 1936. LHB, OB. Middlesex 1958-65 (cap 1963). Nottinghamshire 1966-80 (cap 1966; benefit 1974). 1000 runs (1): 1355 (1963). HS 116* Nt v Surrey (Oval) 1967. BB 7-41 Nt v Derbys (Ilkeston) 1971. F-c career: 413 matches; 12452 runs @ 23.18, 5 hundreds; 693 wickets @ 30.50. Appointed 1983.

WHITEHEAD, Alan Geoffrey Thomas, b Butleigh, Somerset 28 Oct 1940. LHB, SLA. Somerset 1957-61. HS 15 v Hants (Southampton) 1959 and v Leics (Leicester) 1960. BB 6-74 v Sussex (Eastbourne) 1959. F-c career: 38 matches; 137 runs @ 5.70; 67 wickets @ 34.41. Appointed 1970. Umpired 5 Tests (1982 to 1987) and 12 LOI (1979 to 1987).

WILLEY, Peter (Seaham SS), b Sedgefield, Co Durham 6 Dec 1949. RHB, OB. Northamptonshire 1966-83 (cap 1971; benefit 1981). Leicestershire 1984-91 (cap 1984; captain 1987). E Province 1982-85. Northumberland 1992. **Tests:** 26 (1976 to 1986); 1184 runs @ 26.90, HS 102* v WI (St John's) 1980-81; 7 wkts @ 65.14, BB 2-73 v WI (Lord's) 1980. **LOI:** 26. Tours: A 1979-80; SA 1972-73 (DHR), 1981-82 (SAB); WI 1980-81, 1985-86; I 1979-80; SL 1977-78 (DHR). 1000 runs (10); most – 1783 (1982). HS 227 Nh v Somerset (Northampton) 1976. 50 wkts (3); most – 52 (1979). BB 7-37 Nh v OU (Oxford) 1975. F-c career: 559 matches; 24361 runs @ 30.56, 44 hundreds; 756 wickets @ 30.95. Appointed 1993. **Appointed to International Panel 1996.**

RESERVE FIRST-CLASS LIST: P.Adams, N.G.Cowley, M.J.Harris, J.W.Lloyds, M.K.Reed, J.F.Steele.

INTERNATIONAL PANEL: M.J.Kitchen, G.Sharp, D.R.Shepherd, P.Willey (England); D.B.Hair, S.G.Randell (Australia); V.K.Ramaswamy, S.Venkataraghavan (India); R.S.Dunne, A.N.Other (New Zealand); Khizer Hayat, Mahboob Shah (Pakistan); K.E.Liebenberg, C.J.Mitchley (South Africa); B.C.Cooray, K.T.Francis (Sri Lanka); S.A.Bucknor, L.H.Barker (West Indies); I.D.Robinson, R.B.Tiffin (Zimbabwe).

TEXACO TROPHY PANEL: H.D.Bird, D.J.Constant, J.W.Holder, A.A.Jones, R.Julian, M.J.Kitchen, N.T.Plews, G.Sharp, D.R.Shepherd, A.G.T.Whitehead, P.Willey.

Test Match and LOI statistics to 18 March 1996. See page 22 for key to abbreviations.

THE 1995 FIRST-CLASS SEASON STATISTICAL HIGHLIGHTS

HIGHEST INNINGS TOTALS (*† County record*)

781-7d†	Northamptonshire v Nottinghamshire	Northampton
696-6d	West Indians v Hampshire	Southampton
692-8d	West Indies v England (6th Test)	The Oval
670-7d†	Worcestershire v Somerset	Worcester
662-7d	Essex v Hampshire	Colchester
652-9d	Surrey v Durham	The Oval
637-5d	West Indians v Combined Universities	Oxford
603-6d	Derbyshire v Sussex	Derby
602-7d	Middlesex v Sussex	Lord's
600-4d	Yorkshire v Worcestershire	Scarborough
587	Middlesex v Nottinghamshire	Lord's
580-8d	Young Australia v Sussex	Hove
575	Kent v Leicestershire	Canterbury
564	Northamptonshire v Leicestershire	Northampton
561-8d	Northamptonshire v Kent	Canterbury
560	Hampshire v Northamptonshire	Northampton
559	Surrey v Kent	Canterbury
546-9d	Derbyshire v Kent	Maidstone
535-8d	Warwickshire v Hampshire	Southampton
534	Hampshire v Sussex	Portsmouth
534	Kent v Derbyshire	Maidstone
533	Kent v Nottinghamshire	Nottingham
530	Middlesex v Glamorgan	Colwyn Bay
528-9d	Surrey v Nottinghamshire	Guildford
527-7d	Young Australia v Hampshire	Southampton
527	Nottinghamshire v Northamptonshire	Northampton
516-9d	Middlesex v Yorkshire	Leeds
513	Warwickshire v Essex	Ilford
505	Yorkshire v Lancashire	Manchester
503	England A v Warwickshire	Birmingham
503	Leicestershire v Surrey	Leicester
501-8d	Surrey v Sussex	Horsham

HIGHEST FOURTH INNINGS TOTALS

467-9	Worcestershire (set 517) v Derbyshire	Kidderminster
430	Somerset (set 461) v Young Australia	Taunton
413	Worcestershire (set 484) v Hampshire	Southampton
404-5	Leicestershire (set 404) v Oxford University	Oxford

LOWEST INNINGS TOTALS (*† One man absent hurt*)

46	Northamptonshire v Essex	Luton
59	Northamptonshire v Surrey	Northampton
67†	Leicestershire v Warwickshire	Leicester
83†	Leicestershire v Worcestershire	Worcester
85	Durham v Kent	Chester-le-Street
87	Somerset v West Indians	Taunton
88	Middlesex v Lancashire	Lord's
89†	England v West Indies (3rd Test)	Birmingham
91	Cambridge University v Nottinghamshire	Cambridge
95	Kent v West Indians	Canterbury
96	Yorkshire v Warwickshire	Birmingham
97	Oxford University v Derbyshire	Oxford

MATCH AGGREGATES OF 1500 RUNS

Runs-Wkts		
1642-29	Nottinghamshire v Kent	Nottingham
1601-35	Kent v Surrey	Canterbury
1587-32	Kent v Derbyshire	Maidstone
1559-39	Glamorgan v Gloucestershire	Abergavenny
1502-32	Somerset v Young Australia	Taunton

BATSMEN'S MATCH (Qualification: 1200 runs, average 70 per wicket)

86	Yorkshire (600-4d, 231-3d) v Worcs (453-5d, 189-5)	Scarborough

VICTORY AFTER FOLLOWING ON

Surrey (217 & 475) beat Gloucestershire (392 & 207)	The Oval
Somerset (189 & 434) beat Derbyshire (376 & 168)	Derby

FOUR HUNDREDS IN AN INNINGS

West Indians (637-5d) v Combined Universities — Oxford
C.L.Hooper 118, S.C.Williams 114, J.C.Adams 114*, K.L.T.Arthurton 102*

Northamptonshire (781-7d) v Nottinghamshire — Northampton
A.Fordham 130, A.J.Lamb 115, R.J.Warren 154, D.J.Capel 114*

FIRST TO INDIVIDUAL TARGETS

1000 RUNS	D.Byas	Yorkshire	June 29
2000 RUNS	M.R.Ramprakash	Middlesex	September 11
100 WICKETS	A.Kumble	Northamptonshire	September 9

DOUBLE HUNDREDS (15)

C.J.Adams		216	Derbyshire v Kent	Maidstone
D.J.Bicknell		228*	Surrey v Nottinghamshire	Guildford
D.Byas		213	Yorkshire v Worcestershire	Scarborough
W.J.Cronje		213	Leicestershire v Somerset	Weston-s-Mare
P.A.de Silva	(2)	225	Kent v Nottinghamshire	Nottingham
		255	Kent v Derbyshire	Maidstone
S.P.James		230*	Glamorgan v Leicestershire	Leicester
M.D.Moxon		203*	Yorkshire v Kent	Leeds
D.P.Ostler		208	Warwickshire v Surrey	Birmingham
M.R.Ramprakash	(3)	214	Middlesex v Surrey	Lord's
		205	Middlesex v Sussex	Lord's
		235	Middlesex v Yorkshire	Leeds
R.T.Robinson		209	Nottinghamshire v Northamptonshire	Northampton
A.S.Rollins		200*	Derbyshire v Gloucestershire	Bristol
A.Symonds		254*	Gloucestershire v Glamorgan	Abergavenny

HUNDREDS IN THREE CONSECUTIVE INNINGS

M.W.Gatting (Middx)	108 v Glos (Bristol), 101 v Sussex (Lord's), 148 v Notts (Lord's)
T.M.Moody (Worcs)	157 and 106 v Notts (Nottingham), 110 v Lancs (Worcester)
M.R.Ramprakash (Middx)	158 and 111* v Leics (Uxbridge), 115 v Somerset (Taunton)

HUNDRED IN EACH INNINGS OF A MATCH (10)

R.J.Bailey	157	119	Northamptonshire v Middlesex	Uxbridge
J.P.Crawley	182	108	Lancashire v Glamorgan	Manchester
P.A.de Silva	255	116	Kent v Derbyshire	Maidstone
M.A.Lynch	108	114	Gloucestershire v Kent	Canterbury
T.M.Moody	157	106	Worcestershire v Nottinghamshire	Nottingham
H.Morris	166*	104*	Glamorgan v Nottinghamshire	Cardiff
M.R.Ramprakash	158	111*	Middlesex v Leicestershire	Uxbridge
P.V.Simmons	112	139*	West Indians v Essex	Chelmsford
M.E.Waugh	121*	121	Essex v Derbyshire	Chelmsford
A.P.Wells	107	136	Sussex v Kent	Hove

FASTEST HUNDRED (TEAM CENTURY AWARD)

C.L.Cairns	65 balls	Nottinghamshire v Cambridge University	Cambridge

In 76 minutes, including 7 sixes and 7 fours

HUNDRED BEFORE LUNCH

		Day		
G.A.Hick	27-144	2	Worcestershire v Lancashire	Worcester
C.L.Hooper	105*	1	West Indians v Combined Universities	Oxford
J.C.Pooley	100*	1	Middlesex v Nottinghamshire	Lord's
M.R.Ramprakash	111*	4	Middlesex v Leicestershire	Uxbridge
N.R.Taylor	101*	1	Kent v Leicestershire	Canterbury

HUNDRED ON FIRST-CLASS DEBUT IN BRITAIN

M.G.Bevan	113*	Yorkshire v Cambridge University	Cambridge
A.C.Gilchrist	122	Young Australia v Somerset	Taunton
M.L.Love	181	Young Australia v Somerset	Taunton
A.Symonds	161*	Gloucestershire v Surrey	The Oval
S.Young	110	Young Australia v Somerset	Taunton

CARRYING BAT THROUGH COMPLETED INNINGS (*† One man absent*)

N.E.Briers	175*	Leicestershire (359) v Worcestershire	Worcester
T.S.Curtis	75*	Worcestershire (177) v Warwickshire	Birmingham
J.C.Pooley	85*	Middlesex (174) v Derbyshire	Lord's
A.S.Rollins	200*†	Derbyshire (463) v Gloucestershire	Bristol
T.R.Ward	114*	Kent (215) v Northamptonshire	Canterbury

MOST SIXES IN AN INNINGS (World Record)

16	A.Symonds	Gloucestershire v Glamorgan	Abergavenny

MOST SIXES IN A MATCH (World Record)

20	A.Symonds	Gloucestershire v Glamorgan	Abergavenny

FIRST-WICKET PARTNERSHIP OF 100 IN EACH INNINGS

107	103	M.P.Dowman/R.T.Robinson	Nottinghamshire v Essex	Nottingham
123	106*	J.E.R.Gallian/N.J.Speak	Lancashire v Essex	Manchester

OTHER NOTABLE PARTNERSHIPS (*† County record*)

First Wicket

362	A.J.Wright/G.D.Hodgson	Gloucestershire v Nottinghamshire	Bristol
283	C.M.Gupte/I.J.Sutcliffe	Oxford University v Hampshire	Oxford
263	N.J.Lenham/K.Newell	Sussex v West Indians	Hove
260*	S.Chanderpaul/P.V.Simmons	West Indians v Essex	Chelmsford

Second Wicket

294	R.T.Robinson/G.F.Archer	Nottinghamshire v Northamptonshire	Northampton
260	D.J.Bicknell/G.P.Thorpe	Surrey v Kent	Canterbury

Third Wicket

306	D.L.Hemp/M.P.Maynard	Glamorgan v Gloucestershire	Abergavenny
259	V.P.Terry/R.A.Smith	Hampshire v Sussex	Portsmouth
253	M.R.Ramprakash/J.D.Carr	Middlesex v Hampshire	Lord's
250	G.A.Hick/T.M.Moody	Worcestershire v Lancashire	Worcester

Fourth Wicket

368†	P.A.de Silva/G.R.Cowdrey	Kent v Derbyshire	Maidstone
261	M.L.Hayden/J.L.Langer	Young Australia v Sussex	Hove

Fifth Wicket

282	A.J.Lamb/K.M.Curran	Northamptonshire v Surrey	Northampton
237	J.P.Crawley/W.K.Hegg	Lancashire v Northamptonshire	Manchester
225	S.P.Titchard/M.Watkinson	Lancashire v Essex	Manchester

Sixth Wicket

337	R.R.Montgomerie/D.J.Capel	Northamptonshire v Kent	Canterbury
315†	P.A.de Silva/M.A.Ealham	Kent v Nottinghamshire	Nottingham

Tenth Wicket

122	N.E.Briers/A.R.K.Pierson	Leicestershire v Worcestershire	Worcester
100	A.J.Hollioake/J.E.Benjamin	Surrey v Warwickshire	Birmingham

EIGHT OR MORE WICKETS IN AN INNINGS (8)

A.R.Caddick	8- 69	Somerset v Durham	Chester-le-Street
C.L.Cairns	8- 47	Nottinghamshire v Sussex	Arundel
D.G.Cork	9- 43	Derbyshire v Northamptonshire	Derby
P.J.Hartley	9- 41	Yorkshire v Derbyshire	Chesterfield
M.C.Ilott	9- 19	Essex v Northamptonshire	Luton
J.Srinath	9- 76	Gloucestershire v Glamorgan	Abergavenny
P.M.Such	8- 93	Essex v Hampshire	Colchester
A.Walker	8-118	Durham v Essex	Chelmsford

TEN OR MORE WICKETS IN A MATCH (44)

K.C.G.Benjamin		10-174	West Indies v England (5th Test)	Nottingham
J.N.B.Bovill		12- 68	Hampshire v Durham	Stockton
S.J.E.Brown		11-192	Durham v Warwickshire	Chester-le-Street
A.R.Caddick		10-131	Somerset v Durham	Chester-le-Street
C.L.Cairns		15- 83	Nottinghamshire v Sussex	Arundel
C.A.Connor		10-127	Hampshire v Leicestershire	Basingstoke
D.G.Cork		13- 93	Derbyshire v Northamptonshire	Derby
R.D.B.Croft		10-191	Glamorgan v Essex	Swansea
A.A.Donald		10-136	Warwickshire v Northamptonshire	Birmingham
J.E.Emburey	(2)	10- 98	Middlesex v Surrey	Lord's
		12-157	Middlesex v Yorkshire	Leeds
E.S.H.Giddins		10-144	Sussex v Durham	Hartlepool
D.Gough		10- 80	Yorkshire v Lancashire	Leeds
P.J.Hartley		11- 68	Yorkshire v Derbyshire	Chesterfield
J.E.Hindson	(2)	10-197	Nottinghamshire v Essex	Nottingham
		10-145	Nottinghamshire v Somerset	Nottingham
M.C.Ilott	(2)	10-157	Essex v Sussex	Hove
		14-105	Essex v Northamptonshire	Luton
R.L.Johnson		10- 98	Middlesex v Durham	Chester-le-Street
A.Kumble	(2)	13-192	Northamptonshire v Hampshire	Northampton
		10-151	Northamptonshire v Warwickshire	Birmingham
D.E.Malcolm		10-179	Derbyshire v Worcestershire	Kidderminster
T.A.Munton		10-116	Warwickshire v Nottinghamshire	Nottingham
Mushtaq Ahmed	(2)	10-116	Somerset v Sussex	Bath
		11-144	Somerset v Kent	Taunton
M.M.Patel		10-117	Kent v Cambridge University	Folkestone
A.C.S.Pigott		11-111	Surrey v Northamptonshire	Northampton
I.D.K.Salisbury		11-171	Sussex v Leicestershire	Hove
K.P.Sheeraz		11-111	Gloucestershire v West Indians	Bristol
A.G.Sheriyar		10- 85	Leicestershire v Young Australia	Leicester
A.M.Smith		10-125	Gloucestershire v Worcestershire	Gloucester
J.Srinath	(2)	10- 97	Gloucestershire v Yorkshire	Middlesbrough

		13-150	Gloucestershire v Glamorgan	Abergavenny
P.M.Such	(2)	12-178	Essex v Worcestershire	Chelmsford
		11-160	Essex v Hampshire	Colchester
P.C.R.Tufnell		10-202	Middlesex v Leicestershire	Uxbridge
S.D.Udal		11-170	Hampshire v Nottinghamshire	Nottingham
A.Walker		14-177	Durham v Essex	Chelmsford
Wasim Akram	(3)	10-172	Lancashire v Northamptonshire	Manchester
		12-165	Lancashire v Leicestershire	Leicester
		10-156	Lancashire v Hampshire	Portsmouth
S.L.Watkin		10-104	Glamorgan v Somerset	Taunton
M.Watkinson		10-222	Lancashire v Sussex	Lytham
A.R.Whittall		11-113	Cambridge University v Essex	Cambridge

FOUR WICKETS IN FIVE BALLS (*† Also five wickets in nine balls*)

D.Gough	Yorkshire v Kent	Leeds
P.J.Hartley†	Yorkshire v Derbyshire	Chesterfield

HAT-TRICKS (5) (*† All lbw*)

D.G.Cork	England v West Indies (4th Test)	Manchester
D.Gough	Yorkshire v Kent	Leeds
P.J.Hartley	Yorkshire v Derbyshire	Chesterfield
M.C.Ilott†	Essex v Northamptonshire	Luton
M.E.Trescothick	Somerset v Young Australia	Taunton

200 RUNS CONCEDED IN AN INNINGS

J.A.Afford	41-4-223-3	Nottinghamshire v Northamptonshire	Northampton
M.M.Patel	59.5-10-206-6	Kent v Surrey	Canterbury

60 OVERS IN AN INNINGS

Mushtaq Ahmed	60-17-192-2	Somerset v Worcestershire	Worcester

SIX OR MORE WICKET-KEEPING DISMISSALS IN AN INNINGS (5)

A.C.Gilchrist	4ct, 2st	Young Australia v TCCB XI	Birmingham
W.K.Hegg	6ct	Lancashire v Derbyshire	Derby
K.M.Krikken	6ct	Derbyshire v Oxford University	Oxford
K.J.Piper	6ct	Warwickshire v Gloucestershire	Birmingham
R.J.Turner	6ct	Somerset v West Indians	Taunton

NINE OR MORE WICKET-KEEPING DISMISSALS IN A MATCH (4)

C.O.Browne	9ct	West Indies v England (5th Test)	Nottingham
A.C.Gilchrist	7ct, 3st	Young Australia v TCCB XI	Birmingham
C.P.Metson	9ct	Glamorgan v Surrey	The Oval
K.J.Piper	8ct, 1st	Warwickshire v Hampshire	Southampton

NO BYES CONCEDED IN TOTAL OF 500 OR MORE

W.M.Noon	Nottinghamshire v Middlesex (587)	Lord's
P.Whitticase	Leicestershire v Kent (575)	Canterbury
S.A.Marsh	Kent v Surrey (559)	Canterbury
W.M.Noon	Nottinghamshire v Kent (533)	Nottingham
G.J.Kersey	Surrey v Leicestershire (503)	Leicester

FIVE OR MORE CATCHES IN AN INNINGS IN THE FIELD

J.D.Carr	6	Middlesex v Warwickshire	Birmingham

SEVEN OR MORE CATCHES IN A MATCH IN THE FIELD

J.D.Carr	8	Middlesex v Warwickshire	Birmingham
W.Larkins	7	Durham v Somerset	Chester-le-Street

UNUSUAL DISMISSALS – STUMPED BY A SUBSTITUTE

A.P.Grayson	by M.J.Birks	Cambridge University v Yorkshire	Cambridge
R.J.Blakey	by M.J.Birks	Cambridge University v Yorkshire	Cambridge

1995 FIRST-CLASS AVERAGES

These averages involve the 448 cricketers who played in the 201 first-class matches staged in the British Isles during the 1995 season.

'Cap' denotes the season in which the player was awarded a 1st XI cap by the county he represented in 1995. Durham do not award caps on merit; each player receives his cap on joining the staff.

Team abbreviations: CU – Cambridge University; De – Derbyshire; Du – Durham; E – England; EA – England A; Ex – Essex; Gm – Glamorgan; Gs – Gloucestershire; H – Hampshire; K – Kent; La – Lancashire; Le – Leicestershire; M – Middlesex; NSW – New South Wales; Nh – Northamptonshire; Nt – Nottinghamshire; OU – Oxford University; Sm – Somerset; Sy – Surrey; Sx – Sussex; TCCB – TCCB XI; Us – Combined Universities; Wa – Warwickshire; WI – West Indies/Indians; Wo – Worcestershire; Y – Yorkshire; YA – Young Australia.

† Left-handed batsman.

BATTING AND FIELDING

	Cap	*M*	*I*	*NO*	*HS*	*Runs*	*Avge*	*100*	*50*	*Ct/St*
Adams, C.J.(De)	1992	15	27	–	216	1096	40.59	3	5	17
†Adams, J.C.(WI)	—	13	22	5	114*	741	43.58	1	5	5
Afford, J.A.(Nt)	1990	7	9	3	15*	57	9.50	–	–	3
†Afzaal, U.(Nt)	—	7	12	2	37	134	13.40	–	–	3
Aldred, P.(De)	—	7	12	–	33	97	8.08	–	–	4
Alleyne, M.W.(Gs)	1990	19	32	2	141	1007	33.56	1	7	9
†Ambrose, C.E.L.(WI)	—	10	13	7	27*	147	24.50	–	–	8
Andrew, S.J.W.(Ex)	—	2	4	–	4	7	1.75	–	–	–
†Angel, J.(YA)	—	6	7	4	29*	103	34.33	–	–	6
Anthony, H.A.G.(Gm)	—	14	25	1	91	433	18.04	–	2	6
Archer, G.F.(Nt)	1995	17	32	3	158	1171	40.37	3	4	16
†Arthurton, K.L.T.(WI)	—	15	23	4	146	1077	56.68	3	6	8
Atherton, M.A.(La/E)	1989	18	31	1	155*	1323	44.10	4	6	14
Athey, C.W.J.(Sx)	1993	15	27	1	163*	929	35.73	2	5	6
†Atkins, C.S.(Nh)	—	1	2	1	8*	13	13.00	–	–	–
Attfield, J.M.(OU)	—	6	8	2	23*	76	12.66	–	–	2
†Austin, I.D.(La)	1990	13	22	4	80*	412	22.88	–	1	3
Aymes, A.N.(H)	1991	20	33	9	62*	720	30.00	–	5	53/3
Bailey, R.J.(Nh)	1985	18	30	3	157	1038	38.44	4	2	21
Bainbridge, P.(Du)	1992	2	3	–	4	4	1.33	–	–	1
Bairstow, A.D.(De)	—	3	6	–	26	73	12.16	–	–	7/1
Ball, M.C.J.(Gs)	—	18	28	9	48	417	21.94	–	–	16
Banton, C.(Nt)	—	7	14	4	80*	292	29.20	–	2	4
Barnett, K.J.(De)	1982	17	31	3	169	1251	44.67	2	7	5
†Bartle, S.(Le)	—	1	1	–	32	32	32.00	–	–	1
Barwick, S.R.(Gm)	1987	7	6	2	14	19	4.75	–	–	1
Base, S.J.(De)	1990	1	2	1	10	17	17.00	–	–	–
Bates, R.T.(Nt)	—	4	7	–	11	50	7.14	–	–	1
Batty, J.D.(Y)	—	4	6	1	45*	125	25.00	–	–	3
Batty, J.N.(Us)	—	1	1	1	31*	31	–	–	–	1
Battye, R.A.(CU)	—	8	14	2	70*	391	32.58	–	5	3
Bell, M.A.V.(Wa)	—	3	1	1	0*	0	–	–	–	2
Benjamin, J.E.(Sy)	1993	12	18	4	49	174	12.42	–	–	1
Benjamin, K.C.G.(WI)	—	11	12	4	44	154	19.25	–	–	–
Benjamin, W.K.M.(WI)	—	3	2	–	7	11	5.50	–	–	1
†Benson, M.R.(K)	1981	13	21	–	192	702	33.42	2	1	4
Betts, M.M.(Du)	1994	9	15	5	14	55	5.50	–	–	2

	Cap	M	I	NO	HS	Runs	Avge	100	50	Ct/St
†Bevan, M.G.(Y)	1995	20	34	5	153*	1598	55.10	6	7	18
†Bicknell, D.J.(Sy)	1990	15	28	3	228*	997	39.88	2	4	5
Bicknell, M.P.(Sy)	1989	9	12	3	61	213	23.66	–	1	1
†Birbeck, S.D.(Du)	1994	4	6	2	75*	106	26.50	–	1	1
Birks, M.J.(CU)	—	2	3	2	23*	43	43.00	–	–	2
Bishop, I.R.(WI)	—	10	11	1	25	102	10.20	–	–	5
Blakey, R.J.(Y)	1987	20	29	6	77*	398	17.30	–	1	59/4
†Blenkiron, D.A.(Du)	1992	9	17	1	145	446	27.87	1	2	3
Boden, D.J.P.(Gs)	—	2	1	–	2	2	2.00	–	–	2
Boiling, J.(Du)	1995	18	32	7	69	312	12.48	–	1	11
Boon, T.J.(Le)	1986	6	12	–	38	177	14.75	–	–	5
Bovill, J.N.B.(H)	—	8	10	5	31	90	18.00	–	–	1
Bowler, P.D.(Sm)	1995	19	33	3	196	1619	53.96	6	5	9
Briers, N.E.(Le)	1981	15	27	2	175*	1046	41.84	3	3	1
Brimson, M.T.(Le)	—	7	5	3	25	40	20.00	–	–	1
Brinkley, J.E.(Wo)	—	1	1	1	5*	5	–	–	–	–
Brown, A.D.(Sy)	1994	16	29	4	187	1054	42.16	3	3	20
Brown, D.R.(Wa)	1995	15	20	2	85	506	28.11	–	4	7
Brown, K.R.(M)	1990	19	27	4	147*	970	42.17	1	7	45/6
Brown, S.J.E.(Du)	1992	18	30	6	36	278	11.58	–	–	6
Browne, C.O.(WI)	—	12	16	5	102*	498	45.27	2	1	47/7
Burns, M.(Wa)	—	3	5	–	35	78	15.60	–	–	9/1
Butcher, G.P.(Gm)	—	1	2	2	4*	7	–	–	–	–
†Butcher, M.A.(Sy/TCCB)	—	18	34	1	167	1210	36.66	2	10	15
†Byas, D.(Y)	1991	20	37	3	213	1913	56.26	4	10	42
Caddick, A.R.(Sm)	1992	6	7	–	92	237	33.85	–	2	1
Cairns, C.L.(Nt)	1993	17	30	1	115	1171	40.37	2	7	7
Cake, R.Q.(CU)	—	7	14	3	101	511	46.45	1	2	4
Campbell, S.L.(WI)	—	16	26	–	172	1225	47.11	3	6	15
Capel, D.J.(Nh/TCCB)	1986	19	29	3	175	926	35.61	3	3	13
Carr, J.D.(M)	1987	20	29	6	129	1098	47.73	4	3	39
Carroll, J.P.(CU)	—	8	15	2	42	292	22.46	–	–	4
Cassar, M.E.(De)	—	2	3	–	32	68	22.66	–	–	2
†Chanderpaul, S.(WI)	—	15	25	8	140*	1003	59.00	4	5	11
Chapman, R.J.(Nt)	—	8	11	3	22	78	9.75	–	–	1
Chapple, G.(La/EA)	1994	15	21	6	58	292	19.46	–	1	6
†Childs, J.H.(Ex)	1986	17	28	11	18	113	6.64	–	–	6
Church, M.J.(Wo)	—	5	9	1	35	126	15.75	–	–	3
Churton, D.R.H.(CU)	—	6	10	–	39	118	11.80	–	–	7/3
Clarke, L.P.(CU)	—	2	3	–	14	17	5.66	–	–	1
Clarke, V.P.(Sm)	—	4	7	1	29	55	9.16	–	–	1
Connor, C.A.(H)	1988	17	27	6	33	336	16.00	–	–	7
†Cooper, K.E.(Gs)	1995	4	5	1	32	36	9.00	–	–	1
Cork, D.G.(De/E/EA)	1993	18	31	4	84*	589	21.81	–	3	8
Cottam, A.C.(De)	—	5	6	–	36	95	15.83	–	–	–
Cottey, P.A.(Gm/TCCB)	1992	19	33	3	130	1465	48.83	5	7	14
Cousins, D.M.(Ex)	—	9	16	4	18*	121	10.08	–	–	3
Cowan, A.P.(Ex)	—	2	4	1	22	47	15.66	–	–	1
Cowdrey, G.R.(K)	1988	13	22	1	137	930	44.28	2	6	8
†Cox, D.M.(Du)	1993	3	5	–	17	23	4.60	–	–	–
Crawley, J.P.(La/E)	1994	18	31	2	182	1377	47.48	3	10	21
Croft, R.D.B.(Gm/TCCB)	1992	20	36	4	143	716	22.37	1	1	8
Cronje, W.J.(Le)	1995	16	28	1	213	1362	50.44	4	7	13
Crowe, C.D.(Le)	—	1	2	–	9	10	5.00	–	–	1
Cullinan, D.J.(De)	—	14	26	4	161	1003	45.59	5	1	8
Cummins, A.C.(WI)	—	2	1	–	16	16	16.00	–	–	–

	Cap	M	I	NO	HS	Runs	Avge	100	50	Ct/St
Cunliffe, R.J.(Gs)	—	7	8	3	190*	412	82.40	1	2	5
Curran, K.M.(Nh)	1992	17	27	3	117	863	35.95	1	4	22
Curtis, T.S.(Wo)	1984	20	35	5	169*	1221	40.70	2	5	8
†Dakin, J.M.(Le)	—	8	13	2	101*	326	29.63	1	2	6
Dale, A.(Gm)	1992	12	23	2	133	622	29.61	2	2	7
Daley, J.A.(Du)	1992	7	12	2	55	435	43.50	–	4	5
Dalton, A.J.(Gm)	—	5	10	1	46	201	22.33	–	–	4
Davies, A.P.(Gm)	—	1	–	–	–	–	–	–	–	–
Davies, M.(Gs)	—	6	7	4	22	77	25.66	–	–	–
Davis, R.P.(Wa)	1994	6	8	2	30	79	13.16	–	–	5
Dawson, R.I.(Gs)	—	9	16	1	101	355	23.66	1	3	3
DeFreitas, P.A.J.(De/E)	1994	16	26	3	94*	474	20.60	–	2	10
De la Pena, J.M.(Sy)	—	2	3	3	2*	2	–	–	–	–
Derbyshire, N.A.(Ex)	—	2	4	1	17	47	15.66	–	–	–
De Silva, P.A.(K)	1995	16	30	–	255	1781	59.36	7	7	3
Dessaur, W.A.(De)	—	8	16	2	119*	478	34.14	1	2	1
Dhanraj, R.(WI)	—	15	13	3	22	81	8.10	–	–	5
Dibden, R.R.(H)	—	4	7	2	0*	0	0.00	–	–	–
Dimond, M.(Sm)	—	1	2	–	26	33	16.50	–	–	–
D'Oliveira, D.B.(Wo)	1985	2	4	–	25	59	14.75	–	–	2
Donald, A.A.(Wa)	1989	15	16	5	44	194	17.63	–	–	7
†Dowman, M.P.(Nt)	—	9	18	2	107	548	34.25	2	2	7
Drakes, V.C.(WI)	—	6	9	1	48*	118	14.75	–	–	2
Dutch, K.P.(M)	—	1	–	–	–	–	–	–	–	2
Ealham, M.A.(K)	1992	18	31	1	121	891	29.70	1	4	7
†Ecclestone, S.C.(Sm)	—	7	12	2	81	472	47.20	–	3	1
Edwards, A.D.(Sx/Us)	—	2	3	–	22	38	12.66	–	–	2
†Elliott, M.T.G.(YA)	—	6	12	3	89*	357	39.66	–	3	5
†Ellis, S.W.K.(Us)	—	1	1	–	0	0	0.00	–	–	1
Emburey, J.E.(M/E)	1977	17	20	1	87	387	20.36	–	1	18
†Emery, P.A.(NSW)	—	1	1	1	10*	10	–	–	–	–
Evans, K.P.(Nt)	1990	7	13	2	78*	260	23.63	–	2	9
†Fairbrother, N.H.(La)	1985	14	23	3	132	602	30.10	2	1	17
Farbrace, P.(M)	—	2	2	–	16	17	8.50	–	–	3
Fay, R.A.(M)	—	1	1	1	1*	1	–	–	–	–
Feltham, M.A.(M)	1995	14	15	4	25	115	10.45	–	–	8
Field-Buss, M.G.(Nt)	—	2	2	–	2	4	2.00	–	–	1
Fleming, M.V.(K)	1990	10	16	1	100	447	29.80	1	2	2
Flint, D.P.J.(H)	—	2	1	1	17*	17	–	–	–	–
Flintoff, A.(La)	—	1	2	–	7	7	3.50	–	–	2
Follett, D.(M)	—	1	2	1	4*	5	5.00	–	–	1
Fordham, A.(Nh)	1990	16	29	1	130	1025	36.60	4	4	14
Fraser, A.R.C.(M/E)	1988	17	21	8	20	95	7.30	–	–	2
Freedman, D.A.(NSW)	—	1	–	–	–	–	–	–	–	–
Freeth, J.W.O.(CU)	—	7	6	1	18	35	7.00	–	–	2
French, B.N.(Nt)	1980	2	3	1	16	19	9.50	–	–	3
Fulton, D.P.(K)	—	8	16	1	116	502	33.46	1	4	12
Gallian, J.E.R.(La/E/EA)	1994	18	33	3	158	1122	37.40	2	4	18
Garnham, M.A.(Ex)	1990	1	2	–	41	48	24.00	–	–	1
Gatting, M.W.(M)	1977	16	22	1	148	1139	54.23	5	3	13
George, S.P.(YA)	—	3	3	–	29	46	15.33	–	–	1
Gibson, O.D.(WI)	—	11	13	2	101*	303	27.54	1	–	5
Giddins, E.S.H.(Sx)	1994	18	27	12	34	137	9.13	–	–	3
Gie, N.A.(Nt)	—	3	6	–	34	98	16.33	–	–	–
†Gilchrist, A.C.(YA)	—	8	11	3	122	495	61.87	2	2	33/5
Giles, A.F.(Wa)	—	6	5	–	32	84	16.80	–	–	–

	Cap	M	I	NO	HS	Runs	Avge	100	50	Ct St
Gooch, G.A.(Ex)	1975	18	34	1	165	1669	50.57	7	6	12
Gough, D.(Y/E)	1993	14	19	1	60	332	18.44	–	1	6
Grayson, A.P.(Y)	—	9	14	1	73	235	18.07	–	2	4
Green, R.J.(La)	—	1	1	–	1	1	1.00	–	–	–
Greenfield, K.(Sx)	—	19	32	1	121	853	27.51	1	5	11
Griffith, F.A.(De)	—	8	13	4	53	240	26.66	–	1	10
Griffiths, S.P.(De)	—	5	9	–	20	75	8.33	–	–	14
Gupte, C.M.(OU/Us)	—	10	18	2	119	554	34.62	1	3	1
Habib, A.(Le)	—	3	5	2	174*	230	76.66	1	–	–
Hall, J.W.(Sx)	1992	12	22	–	100	537	24.40	1	2	5
Hallett, J.C.(Sm)	—	2	4	1	111*	229	76.33	1	–	1
Hamilton, G.M.(Y)	—	3	4	2	29	59	29.50	–	–	2
Hancock, T.H.C.(Gs)	—	8	13	1	79*	275	22.91	–	1	6
Harden, R.J.(Sm)	1989	19	35	6	129*	1429	49.27	5	6	13
Harris, A.J.(De)	—	4	6	3	14*	47	15.66	–	–	–
Harrison, J.C.(M)	—	2	3	1	46*	95	47.50	–	–	–
†Harrison, T.W.(De)	—	5	10	1	61*	102	11.33	–	1	3
Harrity, M.A.(YA)	—	5	3	–	18	18	6.00	–	–	2
Hartley, P.J.(Y)	1987	18	23	4	38	256	13.47	–	–	4
Harvey, M.E.(Us)	—	1	1	–	23	23	23.00	–	–	–
Haste, N.J.(CU)	—	7	10	4	16	83	13.83	–	–	1
†Hayden, M.L.(YA)	—	7	14	2	178	551	45.91	2	1	3
Hayhurst, A.N.(Sm)	1990	17	29	5	107	825	34.37	1	5	3
Haynes, G.R.(Wo)	1994	18	30	–	78	737	24.56	–	4	10
Headley, D.W.(K)	1993	14	24	6	54	253	14.05	–	1	7
Hegg, W.K.(La)	1989	18	28	4	101	669	27.87	1	2	53/9
Hemmings, E.E.(Sx)	1993	7	12	7	18	70	14.00	–	–	1
†Hemp, D.L.(Gm/EA)	1994	18	32	–	157	872	27.25	1	4	14
Herzberg, S.(K)	—	5	9	2	18	61	8.71	–	–	1
Hibbert, A.J.E.(Ex)	—	1	2	–	24	31	15.50	–	–	–
Hick, G.A.(Wo/E)	1986	16	27	3	152	1193	49.70	4	5	22
Hindson, J.E.(Nt)	—	17	28	5	53*	309	13.43	–	1	10
Hodgson, G.D.(Gs)	1992	9	17	–	148	524	30.82	1	2	3
Hollioake, A.J.(Sy/TCCB)	1995	18	32	2	117*	1099	36.63	1	8	12
†Holloway, P.C.L.(Sm)	—	12	22	6	129*	863	53.93	2	6	3
Hooper, C.L.(WI)	—	15	25	2	195	1063	46.21	5	2	10
How, E.J.(CU)	—	4	4	2	0*	0	0.00	–	–	1
Hughes, E.R.(CU)	—	2	1	–	0	0	0.00	–	–	–
Hughes, J.G.(Nh)	—	5	6	1	16	32	6.40	–	–	–
Hussain, N.(Ex)	1989	19	35	1	186	1854	54.52	6	10	34
†Hutton, S.(Du)	1992	12	23	1	98	634	28.81	–	4	6
Igglesden, A.P.(K)	1989	7	9	4	18	62	12.40	–	–	1
Illingworth, R.K.(Wo/E)	1986	14	19	9	23*	160	16.00	–	–	5
†Ilott, M.C.(Ex/EA)	1993	17	29	4	60	350	14.00	–	1	4
Irani, R.C.(Ex)	1994	18	34	2	108	1165	36.40	1	9	7
†James, K.D.(H)	1989	12	21	3	53	341	18.94	–	1	5
James, S.P.(Gm)	1992	15	28	3	230*	1011	40.44	3	2	12
Janisch, A.N.(CU)	—	7	8	4	18*	38	9.50	–	–	2
Jarrett, M.E.D.(OU)	—	7	11	4	40	137	19.57	–	–	8/1
Jarvis, P.W.(Sx)	—	9	13	2	38	177	16.09	–	–	8
Johnson, P.(Nt)	1986	17	30	1	120*	996	34.34	1	8	9
Johnson, R.L.(M)	1995	12	13	2	29*	164	14.90	–	–	8
Kasprowicz, M.S.(YA)	—	5	6	2	43*	65	16.25	–	–	–
Keech, M.(H)	—	2	4	–	41	100	25.00	–	–	2
†Keedy. G.(La)	—	14	17	12	15*	73	14.60	–	–	2
Kellett, S.A.(Y)	1992	6	11	1	86	228	22.80	–	1	5

	Cap	M	I	NO	HS	Runs	Avge	100	50	Ct/St
Kendall, W.S.(OU/Us)	—	11	16	2	94	457	32.64	–	3	5
Kendrick, N.M.(Gm)	—	15	21	4	59	291	17.11	–	1	6
†Kenlock, S.G.(Sy)	—	4	8	2	12	50	8.33	–	–	3
Kennis, G.J.(Sy)	—	1	2	–	29	47	23.50	–	–	–
Kerr, J.I.D.(Sm)	—	13	19	2	80	349	20.52	–	1	5
Kersey, G.J.(Sy)	—	15	28	4	83	708	29.50	–	6	60/5
†Kettleborough, R.A.(Y)	—	1	2	–	55	59	29.50	–	1	–
Khan, A.A.(M)	—	3	–	–	–	–	–	–	–	1
†Khan, W.G.(Wa)	—	13	23	6	181	847	49.82	1	6	17
Killeen, N.(Du)	1995	7	13	3	48	137	13.70	–	–	4
Kirtley, R.J.(Sx)	—	2	2	2	2*	3	–	–	–	2
†Knight, N.V.(Wa/E)	1995	13	23	5	174	887	49.27	1	7	26
Knott, J.A.(Sy)	—	1	–	–	–	–	–	–	–	1
Krikken, K.M.(De)	1992	11	16	5	61	288	26.18	–	1	42/1
Kumble, A.(Nh)	1995	17	21	5	40*	321	20.06	–	–	11
Lamb, A.J.(Nh)	1978	16	26	4	166	1237	56.22	3	6	15
Lampitt, S.R.(Wo)	1989	17	25	6	97	488	25.68	–	1	11
Laney, J.S.(H)	—	9	17	1	73	470	29.37	–	2	7
†Langer, J.L.(YA)	—	7	12	3	149	516	57.33	2	2	5
†Lara, B.C.(WI)	—	13	20	1	179	1126	59.26	3	7	14
Larkins, W.(Du)	1992	13	23	–	121	737	32.04	2	1	11
Lathwell, M.N.(Sm)	1992	17	33	–	111	1033	31.30	2	5	9
Law, D.R.(Sx)	—	8	13	–	115	248	19.07	1	–	6
Law, S.G.(YA)	—	7	11	2	134	397	44.11	1	1	13
Lawrence, J.R.G.(Du)	—	1	2	1	7*	7	7.00	–	–	–
Leatherdale, D.A.(Wo)	1994	18	30	3	93	993	36.77	–	8	15
Lee, S.(NSW)	—	1	1	–	30	30	30.00	–	–	–
Lefebvre, R.P.(Gm)	1993	3	3	–	24	55	18.33	–	–	–
Lenham, N.J.(Sx)	1990	15	25	3	128	867	39.40	2	4	10
Lewis, J.(Gs)	—	3	3	–	3	3	1.00	–	–	–
Lewis, J.J.B.(Ex)	1994	7	14	–	75	299	21.35	–	2	9
†Lewry, J.D.(Sx)	—	12	19	4	34	150	10.00	–	–	2
Ligertwood, D.G.C.(Du)	1995	12	21	2	40	303	15.94	–	–	33/3
†Llong, N.J.(K)	1993	9	16	–	118	538	33.62	2	1	11
Lloyd, G.D.(La)	1992	14	23	2	117	584	27.80	1	3	4
Longley, J.I.(Du)	1994	9	18	1	58	420	24.70	–	2	3
Love, M.L.(YA)	—	7	13	2	181	510	46.36	2	1	10
Loye, M.B.(Nh)	1994	7	10	1	51*	134	14.88	–	1	2
Lynch, M.A.(Gs)	1995	17	29	2	114	1026	38.00	5	2	25
McCague, M.J.(K)	1992	14	25	6	59	344	18.10	–	1	9
McGrath, A.(Y)	—	5	10	–	84	280	28.00	–	1	3
McGrath, G.D.(NSW)	—	1	–	–	–	–	–	–	–	–
McIntyre, P.E.(YA)	—	8	8	1	13	26	3.71	–	–	4
Macmillan, G.I.(Le/OU/Us)	—	17	26	3	122	817	35.52	3	3	23
†MacRobert, A.D.(OU)	—	9	9	2	29	80	11.42	–	–	3
Maddy, D.L.(Le)	—	9	17	1	131	264	16.50	1	–	14
Malcolm, D.E.(De/E)	1989	14	21	4	25*	125	7.35	–	–	1
†Malik, H.S.(OU)	—	8	10	1	64	160	17.77	–	1	8
Mallender, N.A.(Nh)	1984	7	10	3	49*	121	17.28	–	–	3
Marc, K.(M)	—	1	–	–	–	–	–	–	–	–
Marsh, S.A.(K)	1986	16	28	3	67*	688	27.52	–	4	32/2
Martin, N.F.C.(OU)	—	2	2	–	7	10	5.00	–	–	–
Martin, P.J.(La/E)	1994	13	17	2	71	300	20.00	–	1	7
Martin-Jenkins, R.S.C.(Sx)	—	2	2	1	50	50	50.00	–	1	–
Maru, R.J.(H)	1986	2	3	1	7	8	4.00	–	–	4
Mason, T.J.(Le)	—	1	–	–	–	–	–	–	–	1

	Cap	M	I	NO	HS	Runs	Avge	100	50	Ct/St
†Mather, D.P.(OU)	—	8	6	3	8*	19	6.33	–	–	2
†Matthews, G.R.J.(NSW)	—	1	1	–	40	40	40.00	–	–	–
Maynard, M.P.(Gm/TCCB)	1987	20	36	1	164	1590	45.42	3	12	23
Metcalfe, A.A.(Y)	1986	4	4	1	100	200	66.66	1	1	5
Metson, C.P.(Gm)	1987	17	23	9	26*	253	18.07	–	–	47/7
Middleton, T.C.(H)	1990	2	4	–	31	48	12.00	–	–	1
Mike, G.W.(Nt)	—	5	9	3	66*	143	23.83	–	2	1
Milburn, S.M.(Y)	—	3	6	1	7	15	3.00	–	–	–
†Millns, D.J.(Le)	1991	8	14	2	70	307	25.58	–	2	4
Mirza, P.(Wo)	—	6	10	2	18*	39	4.87	–	–	5
Moles, A.J.(Wa)	1987	9	16	–	131	710	44.37	1	6	5
Montgomerie, R.R.(Nh)	1995	14	24	1	192	632	27.47	1	2	27
Moody, T.M.(Wo)	1991	18	31	2	168	1600	55.17	5	7	31
Moores, P.(Sx)	1989	19	32	2	94	660	22.00	–	5	44/2
†Morris, A.C.(Y)	—	1	2	1	1	1	1.00	–	–	1
†Morris, H.(Gm/TCCB)	1986	18	33	3	166*	1574	52.46	6	8	5
Morris, J.E.(Du)	1994	19	35	1	169	1297	38.14	3	6	9
Morris, R.S.M.(H)	—	10	18	–	47	368	20.44	–	–	13
Moxon, M.D.(Y)	1984	13	23	8	203*	1145	76.33	3	8	6
Mullally, A.D.(Le/TCCB)	1993	19	30	6	22	150	6.25	–	–	–
Munton, T.A.(Wa)	1989	11	10	6	19*	66	16.50	–	–	3
Murray, J.R.(WI)	—	12	19	3	100	440	27.50	1	1	27/3
Mushtaq Ahmed (Sm)	1993	17	23	2	62*	311	14.80	–	1	4
Nash, D.J.(M)	1995	19	25	4	67	433	20.61	–	3	10
Newell, K.(Sx)	—	10	19	2	135	500	29.41	1	2	3
Newport, P.J.(Wo)	1986	18	23	8	50	404	26.93	–	1	2
Nicholas, M.C.J.(H)	1982	19	33	3	147	1210	40.33	4	4	5
†Nixon, P.A.(Le/EA/TCCB)	1994	18	30	5	79	461	18.44	–	2	46/2
Noon, W.M.(Nt)	1995	17	31	6	66	745	29.80	–	5	32/5
†Nowell, R.W.(Sy)	—	11	20	2	27	134	7.44	–	–	5
O'Gorman, T.J.G.(De)	1992	5	8	–	39	125	15.62	–	–	3
Ormond, J.(Le)	—	1	–	–	–	–	–	–	–	1
Ostler, D.P.(Wa)	1991	18	26	2	208	983	40.95	2	6	25
Owen, J.E.(De)	—	4	8	–	65	200	25.00	–	2	–
Parker, B.(Y)	—	4	8	1	40	161	23.00	–	–	3
†Parsons, G.J.(Le)	1984	18	28	2	73	501	19.26	–	1	15
Parsons, K.A.(Sm)	—	16	28	2	105	821	31.57	1	6	13
Patel, M.M.(K/EA)	1994	18	29	6	56	376	16.34	–	2	13
Patterson, M.W.(NSW)	—	1	1	–	46	46	46.00	–	–	–
Pearson, R.M.(Ex)	—	2	2	–	27	27	13.50	–	–	–
†Peirce, M.T.E.(Sx)	—	6	10	–	60	219	21.90	–	1	4
†Penberthy, A.L.(Nh)	1994	4	6	1	73	115	23.00	–	1	1
Pennett, D.B.(Nt)	—	8	12	8	50	89	22.25	–	1	3
Penney, T.L.(Wa)	1994	19	27	3	144	1198	49.91	4	4	9
Phillips, N.C.(Sx)	—	6	10	1	53	183	20.33	–	3	3
†Pick, R.A.(Nt)	1987	17	26	4	50*	395	17.95	–	1	9
Pierson, A.R.K.(Le/TCCB)	1995	20	32	10	50	392	17.81	–	1	13
Pigott, A.C.S.(Sy)	1995	6	11	1	19	76	7.60	–	–	1
Pike, V.J.(Gs)	—	5	8	3	22	42	8.40	–	–	3
Piper, K.J.(Wa)	1992	16	19	2	99	398	23.41	–	2	59/2
†Pollard, P.R.(Nt)	1992	11	19	2	120	506	29.76	1	2	13
Ponting, K.R.(YA)	—	7	12	2	103*	460	46.00	1	4	7
†Pooley, J.C.(M)	1995	18	30	4	136	1335	51.34	5	6	25
Prabhakar, M.(Du)	1995	17	31	3	101	896	32.00	1	5	9
Prichard, P.J.(Ex)	1986	18	33	1	109	1080	33.75	2	5	10
Rackemann, C.G.(Sy)	—	13	20	12	20*	120	15.00	–	–	3

	Cap	M	I	NO	HS	Runs	Avge	100	50	Ct/St
Radford, N.V.(Wo)	1985	10	11	2	50	130	14.44	–	1	–
Radford, T.A.(M)	—	6	11	4	69	244	34.85	–	2	7
Ragnauth, R.T.(CU)	—	8	16	1	82	335	22.33	–	3	10
Ramprakash, M.R.(M/E/EA)	1990	20	32	3	235	2258	77.86	10	7	14
Ratcliffe, J.D.(Sy)	—	9	17	–	75	550	32.35	–	5	3
Ratledge, J.(CU)	—	8	16	–	67	358	22.37	–	3	4
Reeve, D.A.(Wa)	1989	16	22	4	77*	652	36.22	–	5	17
Remy, C.C.(Sx)	—	1	2	–	4	5	2.50	–	–	–
Renshaw, S.J.(Us)	—	1	1	–	0	0	0.00	–	–	–
Rhodes, S.J.(Wo)	1986	20	33	8	122*	1018	40.72	1	7	51/7
Richardson, A.(De)	—	1	1	–	4	4	4.00	–	–	–
Richardson, R.B.(WI)	—	15	23	3	101*	804	40.20	1	5	12
Ricketts, J.D.(OU)	—	10	11	1	63	148	14.80	–	1	3
†Ridley, A.C.(OU)	—	10	16	1	71	375	25.00	–	2	4
Ripley, D.(Nh)	1987	6	5	1	40	90	22.50	–	–	7/2
Roberts, A.R.(Nh)	—	1	2	–	11	21	10.50	–	–	–
Roberts, K.J.(NSW)	—	1	1	–	53	53	53.00	–	1	–
Robinson, D.D.J.(Ex)	—	17	32	–	123	712	22.25	2	1	25
Robinson, M.A.(Y)	1992	18	20	8	23	75	6.25	–	–	4
Robinson, P.E.(Le)	—	3	6	1	60*	99	19.80	–	1	5
Robinson, R.T.(Nt)	1983	18	32	–	209	1728	54.00	7	5	7
Rollins, A.S.(De)	1995	17	33	1	200*	1095	34.21	2	5	16
Rollins, R.J.(Ex)	1995	19	35	3	133*	809	25.28	1	4	53/9
Rose, G.D.(Sm)	1988	16	25	–	84	771	30.84	–	6	9
Roseberry, M.A.(Du)	1995	16	29	2	90	669	24.77	–	4	17
†Russell, R.C.(Gs/E)	1985	17	26	4	91	977	44.40	–	8	50/2
Salisbury, I.D.K.(Sx)	1991	18	30	3	74	599	22.18	–	2	17
Sargeant, N.F.(Sy)	—	2	2	–	6	8	4.00	–	–	11
†Saxelby, M.(Du)	1994	7	14	–	68	251	17.92	–	1	5
Scott, C.W.(Du)	1992	7	13	1	56	311	25.91	–	2	18
Searle, J.P.(Du)	1993	1	2	1	2*	2	2.00	–	–	–
Shadford, D.J.(La)	—	2	2	1	1	1	1.00	–	–	–
Shahid, N.(Ex)	—	14	25	2	139	900	39.13	2	5	15
Shaw, A.D.(Gm)	—	2	4	1	14	20	6.66	–	–	3/2
Sheeraz, K.P.(Gs)	—	9	11	4	3	8	1.14	–	–	4
Sheriyar, A.(Le/TCCB)	—	8	12	1	19	59	5.36	–	–	3
Shine, K.J.(M)	—	2	1	–	6	6	6.00	–	–	–
Silverwood, C.E.W.(Y)	—	7	9	2.	50	106	15.14	–	1	1
Simmons, P.V.(WI)	—	2	3	1	139*	261	130.50	2	–	–
Singh, A.(Wa)	—	1	2	–	7	12	6.00	–	–	1
Slater, M.J.(NSW)	—	1	1	–	69	69	69.00	–	1	–
Small, G.C.(Wa)	1982	6	9	4	15	72	14.40	–	–	–
Smith, A.M.(Gs)	1995	11	11	2	11	37	4.11	–	–	2
Smith, A.W.(Sy)	—	9	13	–	88	272	20.92	–	2	2
Smith, B.F.(Le)	1995	18	31	5	112	802	30.84	1	6	8
Smith, N.M.K.(Wa)	1993	18	23	2	75	486	23.14	–	4	6
Smith, P.A.(Wa)	1986	3	5	–	57	124	24.80	–	1	1
Smith, R.A.(H/E)	1985	12	23	2	172	1117	53.19	3	4	3
Snape, J.N.(Nh)	—	13	16	3	55	361	27.76	–	2	16
Solanki, V.S.(Wo)	—	6	9	1	36	150	18.75	–	–	8
Speak, N.J.(La)	1992	17	30	2	116	919	32.82	1	7	11
Spiring, K.R.(Wo)	—	1	2	–	3	4	2.00	–	–	1
Srinath, J.(Gs)	1995	15	24	4	44	314	15.70	–	–	5
†Stanford, E.J.(K)	—	2	2	1	4	4	4.00	–	–	1
Stanley, D.E.(CU)	—	2	4	–	6	10	2.50	–	–	–
Stemp, R.D.(Y/EA)	—	21	25	4	22*	179	8.52	–	–	9

	Cap	M	I	NO	HS	Runs	Avge	100	50	Ct/St
Stephenson, F.D.(Sx)	1992	13	23	–	106	690	30.00	1	3	4
Stephenson, J.P.(H)	1995	17	30	4	127	892	34.30	1	6	9
Stewart, A.J.(Sy/E)	1985	10	18	1	151	647	38.05	2	2	23
Streak, H.H.(H)	—	19	28	3	69	378	15.12	–	1	6
Stuart, A.M.(NSW)	—	1	–	–	–	–	–	–	–	–
Such, P.M.(Ex)	1991	18	30	8	32	214	9.72	–	–	11
†Sutcliffe, I.J.(Le/OU/Us)	—	14	24	4	163*	847	42.35	1	5	9
Symonds, A.(Gs)	—	18	31	5	254*	1438	55.30	4	9	8
†Taylor, C.W.(M)	—	1	–	–	–	–	–	–	–	–
†Taylor, J.P.(Nh)	1992	18	21	8	86	284	21.84	–	2	6
†Taylor, M.A.(NSW)	—	1	1	–	61	61	61.00	–	1	–
Taylor, N.R.(K)	1982	7	12	2	127	421	42.10	1	2	–
Terry, V.P.(H)	1983	20	35	2	170	1012	30.66	2	3	30
Thomas, P.A.(Wo)	—	14	15	4	25	57	5.18	–	–	1
†Thomas, S.D.(Gm)	—	11	15	4	78*	331	30.09	–	3	4
Thompson, J.B.D.(K)	—	3	6	2	40*	83	20.75	–	–	1
†Thorpe, G.P.(Sy/E)	1991	16	30	–	152	1223	40.76	2	9	13
Thursfield, M.J.(H)	—	3	3	–	30	46	15.33	–	–	–
Titchard, S.P.(La)	1995	13	24	2	130	697	31.68	1	5	6
Tolley, C.M.(Wo)	1993	3	5	–	24	62	12.40	–	–	1
Townsend, C.J.(OU)	—	6	7	4	27	72	24.00	–	–	11/1
†Trescothick, M.E.(Sm)	—	12	22	–	151	417	18.95	1	1	14
†Trimby, P.W.(Us)	—	1	1	–	5	5	5.00	–	–	2
Trump, H.R.J.(Sm)	1994	16	22	10	47	207	17.25	–	–	12
Tudor, A.J.(Sy)	—	5	9	–	56	123	13.66	–	1	1
Tufnell, P.C.R.(M)	1990	17	15	7	23*	65	8.12	–	–	5
Turner, R.J.(Sm)	1994	19	30	7	106*	717	31.17	1	4	54/10
Tweats, T.A.(De)	—	8	16	1	78*	308	20.53	–	2	7
†Twose, R.G.(Wa)	1992	19	30	4	191	1186	45.61	4	3	6
Udal, S.D.(H)	1992	18	29	4	85	512	20.48	–	3	12
Van Troost, A.P.(Sm)	—	7	11	3	34	82	10.25	–	–	–
Vaughan, M.P.(Y/EA)	1995	21	39	1	88	1244	32.73	–	10	13
†Walker, A.(Du)	1994	11	16	3	29	102	7.84	–	–	4
Walker, L.N.P.(Nt)	—	1	2	–	24	42	21.00	–	–	2/1
†Walker, M.J.(K)	—	9	14	1	53	162	12.46	–	1	7
Walsh, C.A.(WI)	—	11	11	1	40	111	11.10	–	–	3
Walton, T.C.(Nh)	—	4	7	1	71	104	17.33	–	1	–
Ward, D.M.(Sy)	1990	3	4	–	51	66	16.50	–	1	2
Ward, T.R.(K)	1989	18	32	1	114*	932	30.06	2	6	23
Warner, A.E.(De)	1987	14	22	8	43	265	18.92	–	–	2
Warren, R.J.(Nh)	1995	16	27	5	154	914	41.54	1	5	27/1
†Wasim Akram (La)	1989	14	22	3	61	423	22.26	–	4	1
Watkin, S.L.(Gm)	1989	16	23	9	30	174	12.42	–	–	8
Watkinson, M.(La/E)	1987	18	29	3	161	887	34.11	2	3	7
Waugh, M.E.(Ex/NSW)	1989	16	29	2	173	1392	51.55	5	6	19
Weekes, P.N.(M)	1993	20	31	2	143	995	34.31	2	6	20
Welch, G.(Wa)	—	1	2	–	2	2	1.00	–	–	–
Wells, A.P.(Sx/E/EA)	1986	18	30	2	178	1524	54.42	7	4	10
Wells, C.M.(De)	1995	16	30	3	115	976	36.14	2	6	16
Wells, V.J.(Le)	1994	14	24	1	124	654	28.43	1	5	8
Weston, R.M.S.(Du)	1994	3	6	–	9	15	2.50	–	–	5
†Weston, W.P.C.(Wo)	1995	20	35	1	111	1207	35.50	3	7	14
Whitaker, J.J.(Le)	1986	15	25	–	127	1055	42.20	3	5	4
†Whitaker, P.R.(H)	—	13	21	–	119	624	29.71	1	3	3
White, C.(Y/E)	1993	19	33	5	110	874	31.21	3	3	8
White, G.W.(H)	—	15	24	2	62	554	25.18	–	3	14

	Cap	M	I	NO	HS	Runs	Avge	100	50	Ct/St
Whittall, A.R.(CU)	—	8	13	2	81*	185	16.81	–	1	6
Whitticase, P.(Le)	1987	3	5	1	62*	150	37.50	–	2	7/1
Wileman, J.R.(Nt)	—	8	16	4	43	230	19.16	–	–	3
Williams, B.A.(YA)	—	5	6	1	28	72	14.40	–	–	–
Williams, N.F.(Ex)	—	8	12	2	17	90	9.00	–	–	1
Williams, R.C.(Gs)	—	4	7	–	22	60	8.57	–	–	1
†Williams, R.C.J.(Gs)	—	5	9	–	90	223	24.77	–	2	24
Williams, S.C.(WI)	—	13	20	–	137	770	38.50	3	3	13
Willis, S.C.(K)	—	3	4	–	82	153	38.25	–	2	10
Windows, M.G.N.(Gs/Us)	—	9	17	2	56	313	20.86	–	2	11
Windsor, J.M.(OU)	—	2	3	1	14	28	14.00	–	–	–
Wood, J.(Du)	1992	4	7	2	40*	86	17.20	–	–	–
Wren, T.N.(K)	—	7	11	4	23	60	8.57	–	–	2
Wright, A.J.(Gs)	1987	18	34	4	193	1401	46.70	4	5	8
†Wylie, A.(Wo)	—	2	4	1	7	14	4.66	–	–	–
Yates, G.(La)	1994	7	9	2	42*	162	23.14	–	–	1
Yeabsley, M.I.(CU)	—	2	4	–	2	2	0.50	–	–	–
Yeabsley, R.S.(OU)	—	3	4	–	4	13	3.25	–	–	1
†Young, S.(YA)	—	7	10	–	110	228	22.80	1	1	4

BOWLING

See BATTING and FIELDING section for details of caps and teams.

	Cat	O	M	R	W	Avge	Best	5wI	10wM
Adams, C.J.	OB	15	3	47	0				
Adams, J.C	SLA	42.1	9	114	5	22.80	3- 41	–	–
Afford, J.A.	SLA	314.5	69	991	21	47.19	4- 58	–	–
Afzaal, U.	SLA	182	42	582	5	116.40	2- 41	–	–
Aldred, P.	RM	108.2	22	375	15	25.00	3- 47	–	–
Alleyne, M.W.	RM	421.5	125	1228	29	42.34	3- 59	–	–
Ambrose, C.E.L.	RF	262.1	70	744	25	29.76	5- 96	1	–
Andrew, S.J.W.	RMF	38	9	107	1	107.00	1- 24	–	–
Angel, J.	RFM	179.5	39	709	27	26.25	4- 31	–	–
Anthony, H.A.G.	RFM	397.5	70	1402	44	31.86	6- 77	2	–
Archer, G.F.	OB	79	11	261	6	43.50	3- 50	–	–
Arthurton, K.L.T.	SLA	88.5	17	264	6	44.00	2- 19	–	–
Atherton, M.A.	LB	1	0	1	0				
Athey, C.W.J.	RM	7	1	35	0				
Atkins, C.S.	SLA	11	4	46	1	46.00	1- 46	–	–
Attfield, J.M.	OB	87.3	12	310	3	103.33	2- 76	–	–
Austin, I.D.	RM	363.4	111	889	35	25.40	4- 50	–	–
Bailey, R.J.	OB	114.3	21	403	8	50.37	4- 66	–	–
Bainbridge, P.	RM	15	2	55	1	55.00	1- 5	–	–
Ball, M.C.J.	OB	577.2	144	1481	42	35.26	5- 49	2	–
Banton, C.	RM	8	1	37	0				
Barnett, K.J.	LB	218.2	42	635	16	39.68	3- 51	–	–
Bartle, S.	RM	2	0	42	0				
Barwick, S.R.	RMF	233.4	58	681	14	48.64	4-116	–	–
Base, S.J.	RMF	17	2	99	1	99.00	1- 99	–	–
Bates, R.T.	OB	115.1	32	369	10	36.90	5- 88	1	–
Batty, J.D.	OB	111.4	13	583	7	83.28	4- 70	–	–
Battye, R.A.	RSM	0.4	0	14	0				
Bell, M.A.V.	LMF	80	25	265	7	37.85	2- 59	–	–
Benjamin, J.E.	RMF	420.4	85	1326	53	25.01	5- 37	3	–
Benjamin, K.C.G.	RFM	284.1	71	923	43	21.46	5- 52	3	1
Benjamin, W.K.M.	RFM	33	10	73	1	73.00	1- 10	–	–

	Cat	O	M	R	W	Avge	Best	5wI	10wM
Betts, M.M.	RMF	194.5	31	853	17	50.17	3- 35	–	–
Bevan, M.G.	SLC	99	24	351	6	58.50	3- 55	–	–
Bicknell, D.J.	SLA	24.3	5	96	3	32.00	3- 88	–	–
Bicknell, M.P.	RFM	285	65	978	41	23.85	5- 61	3	–
Birbeck, S.D.	RM	64	8	271	4	67.75	3-119	–	–
Bishop, I.R.	RF	334	69	983	38	25.86	5- 32	1	–
Blenkiron, D.A.	RM	16	1	64	1	64.00	1- 10	–	–
Boden, D.J.P.	RMF	59.4	10	187	7	26.71	3- 38	–	–
Boiling, J.	OB	599	149	1702	27	63.03	5- 73	2	–
Bovill, J.N.B.	RFM	251.3	62	814	30	27.13	6- 29	2	1
Bowler, P.D.	OB	16.2	3	68	1	68.00	1- 13	–	–
Brimson, M.T.	SLA	110	24	310	12	25.83	2- 11	–	–
Brinkley, J.E.	RFM	26	5	99	1	99.00	1- 50	–	–
Brown, D.R.	RFM	311.4	71	1011	37	27.32	4- 24	–	–
Brown, K.R.	(WK)	15	0	114	1	114.00	1-114	–	–
Brown, S.J.E.	LFM	589.3	117	1951	57	34.22	6- 69	4	1
Browne, C.O.	(WK)	2	0	16	0				
Butcher, G.P.	RM	16	5	45	0				
Butcher, M.A.	RM	234.5	37	935	22	42.50	4- 72	–	–
Byas, D.	RM	6	1	37	0				
Caddick, A.R.	RFM	183.1	34	613	24	25.54	8- 69	1	1
Cairns, C.L.	RFM	375.5	89	1035	52	19.90	8- 47	3	1
Capel, D.J.	RMF	358.2	70	1206	51	23.64	7- 44	2	–
Carroll, J.P.	RM	26	3	98	0				
Cassar, M.E.	RFM	30.2	9	91	5	18.20	4- 54	–	–
Chanderpaul, S.	LB	42	5	154	2	77.00	2- 41	–	–
Chapman, R.J.	RFM	179.2	23	777	11	70.63	3-119	–	–
Chapple, G.	RMF	380.1	81	1229	36	34.13	4- 44	–	–
Childs, J.H.	SLA	678.2	184	1757	68	25.83	6- 36	2	–
Clarke, L.P.	RM	7	0	55	1	55.00	1- 55	–	–
Clarke, V.P.	RM/LB	73.3	10	284	5	56.80	3- 72	–	–
Connor, C.A.	RFM	554.2	115	1944	57	34.10	6- 44	3	1
Cooper, K.E.	RFM	103	32	228	13	17.53	4- 34	–	–
Cork, D.G.	RFM	587	111	1800	90	20.00	9- 43	4	1
Cottam, A.C.	SLA	79.3	16	291	4	72.75	2- 5	–	–
Cottey, P.A.	OB	32.1	2	109	1	109.00	1- 29	–	–
Cousins, D.M.	RMF	176	23	640	12	53.33	3- 73	–	–
Cowan, A.P.	RM	24	2	113	1	113.00	1- 53	–	–
Cowdrey, G.R.	RM	3	0	46	0				
Cox, D.M.	SLA	129.5	28	422	11	38.36	4-141	–	–
Croft, R.D.B.	OB	847	210	2353	68	34.60	6-104	4	1
Cronje, W.J.	RM	256.2	82	688	15	45.86	3- 42	–	–
Crowe, C.D.	OB	3	2	4	0				
Cummins, A.C.	RFM	42	4	180	7	25.71	5- 60	1	–
Curran, K.M.	RMF	357.1	84	1202	37	32.48	4- 78	–	–
Curtis, T.S.	LB	3	1	8	0				
Dakin, J.M.	RM	99	15	370	6	61.66	2- 20	–	–
Dale, A.	RM	144.5	28	472	9	52.44	2- 38	–	–
Davies, A.P.	RMF	3	0	17	0				
Davies, M.	SLA	107.2	28	288	6	48.00	4- 86	–	–
Davis, R.P.	SLA	216.4	58	576	15	38.40	5-118	1	–
Dawson, R.I.	RM	15	6	28	0				
DeFreitas, P.A.J.	RFM	591.1	127	1751	60	29.18	6- 35	2	–
De la Pena, J.M.	RFM	44	8	208	6	34.66	3- 53	–	–
Derbyshire, N.A.	RFM	21	5	48	2	24.00	1- 18	–	–
De Silva, P.A.	OB	215	36	641	5	128.20	1- 5	–	–

	Cat	O	M	R	W	Avge	Best	5wI	10wM
Dessaur, W.A.	RM	7	1	24	1	24.00	1- 8	–	–
Dhanraj, R.	LBG	475.3	79	1596	61	26.16	6- 50	4	–
Dibden, R.R.	OB	103.1	20	428	6	71.33	2- 36	–	–
Dimond, M.	RMF	14	2	70	1	70.00	1- 16	–	–
D'Oliveira, D.B.	OB	113.5	15	369	5	73.80	3- 88	–	–
Donald, A.A.	RF	535.3	134	1431	89	16.07	6- 56	6	1
Dowman, M.P.	RM	5	0	30	0				
Drakes, V.C.	RF	106	17	400	16	25.00	5- 20	1	–
Dutch, K.P.	OB	14	7	24	0				
Ealham, M.A.	RMF	384.2	95	1151	30	38.36	3- 37	–	–
Ecclestone, S.C.	RMF	105	20	383	11	34.81	2- 31	–	–
Edwards, A.D.	RFM	47	4	246	3	82.00	3- 83	–	–
Elliott, M.T.G.	LM/SLC	7	2	23	1	23.00	1- 23	–	–
Ellis, S.W.K.	RFM	35	3	146	5	29.20	5- 59	1	–
Emburey, J.E.	OB	708.4	198	1701	74	22.98	7- 82	5	2
Evans, K.P.	RMF	238.1	60	590	14	42.14	3- 66	–	–
Fairbrother, N.H.	LM	1.5	1	14	0				
Farbrace, P.	(WK)	1	1	0	0				
Fay, R.A.	RMF	3	0	25	0				
Feltham, M.A.	RMF	273.1	72	783	29	27.00	6- 41	1	–
Field-Buss, M.G.	OB	57	14	172	1	172.00	1- 28	–	–
Fleming, M.V.	RM	127	19	436	6	72.66	3- 93	–	–
Flint, D.P.J.	SLA	50	16	123	2	61.50	2- 52	–	–
Flintoff, A.	RM	11	0	39	0				
Follett, D.	RMF	30	6	95	1	95.00	1- 61	–	–
Fordham, A.	RM	7	1	51	1	51.00	1- –	–	–
Fraser, A.R.C.	RMF	592.1	156	1632	56	29.14	5- 56	2	–
Freeth, J.W.O.	OB	210.3	33	721	8	90.12	2- 62	–	–
Gallian, J.E.R.	RM	129.5	17	533	16	33.31	3- 14	–	–
Gatting, M.W.	RM	5	0	31	0				
George, S.P.	RFM	72	6	422	7	60.28	3- 91	–	–
Gibson, O.D.	RF	242.4	36	966	31	31.16	4- 32	–	–
Giddins, E.S.H.	RMF	605.4	110	2004	68	29.47	6- 73	4	1
Giles, A.F.	SLA	146.5	46	354	16	22.12	5- 23	1	–
Gooch, G.A.	RM	29.4	4	112	6	18.66	2- 15	–	–
Gough, D.	RFM	414.5	89	1365	51	26.76	7- 28	1	1
Grayson, A.P.	SLA	32	13	80	2	40.00	2- 5	–	–
Green, R.J.	RM	20	2	87	3	29.00	2- 40	–	–
Greenfield, K.	RM	21.1	1	82	0				
Griffith, F.A.	RM	190.4	42	614	17	36.11	4- 89	–	–
Hallett, J.C.	RMF	14	1	86	2	43.00	2- 22	–	–
Hamilton, G.M.	RMF	75.2	24	224	7	32.00	3- 41	–	–
Hancock, T.H.C.	RM	5	1	20	0				
Harden, R.J.	SLA	1	0	17	0				
Harris, A.J.	RM	85.5	16	354	14	25.28	4- 84	–	–
Harrison, T.W.	SLA	77	19	282	5	56.40	4-153	–	–
Harrity, M.A.	LF	135.2	33	497	13	38.23	4- 37	–	–
Hartley, P.J.	RMF	549	120	1861	81	22.97	9- 41	4	1
Haste, N.J.	RM	197	41	655	18	36.38	5- 73	1	–
Hayhurst, A.N.	RM	139.2	21	519	10	51.90	2- 39	–	–
Haynes, G.R.	RM	272	76	840	21	40.00	4- 33	–	–
Headley, D.W.	RFM	430.5	101	1276	44	29.00	7- 58	3	–
Hemmings, E.E.	OB	177.5	51	442	15	29.46	4- 33	–	–
Hemp, D.L.	RM	22	2	110	3	36.66	1- 9	–	–
Herzberg, S.	OB	115.4	21	401	9	44.55	5- 33	1	–
Hick, G.A.	OB	174	39	526	9	58.44	5- 18	1	–

	Cat	O	M	R	W	Avge	Best	5wI	10wM
Hindson, J.E	SLA	692	165	2219	65	34.13	5- 67	5	2
Hollioake, A.J.	RMF	230.3	46	721	21	34.33	4- 22	–	–
Holloway, P.C.L.	(WK)	2	1	12	0				
Hooper, C.L.	OB	267.4	54	821	17	48.29	3- 22	–	–
How, E.J.	LMF	75	9	299	1	299.00	1- 24	–	–
Hughes, E.R.	RM	54	5	234	2	117.00	1- 62	–	–
Hughes, J.G.	RM	90	15	320	7	45.71	3- 69	–	–
Hutton, S.	RSM	2	0	13	0				
Igglesden, A.P.	RFM	171.2	37	563	21	26.80	5- 92	1	–
Illingworth, R.K.	SLA	524	172	1212	45	26.93	4- 30	–	–
Ilott, M.C.	LFM	582.4	126	1897	78	24.32	9- 19	6	2
Irani, R.C.	RM	361.5	71	1222	27	45.25	5- 62	1	–
James, K.D.	LMF	235.2	47	867	19	45.63	6- 38	1	–
Janisch, A.N.	RM	185	21	723	10	72.30	3- 38	–	–
Jarvis, P.W.	RFM	228.4	45	719	26	27.65	5- 55	1	–
Johnson, R.L.	RMF	301.4	79	812	40	20.30	5- 48	2	1
Kasprowicz, M.S.	RFM	175.1	42	599	27	22.18	5- 19	1	–
Keech, M.	RM	20.3	0	98	2	49.00	1- 43	–	–
Keedy, G.	SLA	505	128	1498	37	40.48	4- 35	–	–
Kendall, W.S.	RM	81	13	255	8	31.87	3- 37	–	–
Kendrick, N.M.	SLA	389.5	102	1255	27	46.48	4- 70	–	–
Kenlock, S.G.	LMF	119	20	440	8	55.00	2- 71	–	–
Kennis, G.J.	OB	3	3	0	0				
Kerr, J.I.D.	RMF	280.1	53	1134	28	40.50	5- 82	1	–
Khan, A.A.	LB	76	24	142	8	17.75	4- 51	–	–
Khan, W.G.	LB	7	1	22	0				
Killeen, N.	RFM	195.3	30	767	17	45.11	5-118	1	–
Kirtley, R.J.	RFM	38	11	103	2	51.50	1- 28	–	–
Kumble, A.	LBG	899.4	265	2143	105	20.40	7- 82	8	2
Lampitt, S.R.	RMF	494.1	124	1524	55	27.70	4- 34	–	–
Lara, B.C.	LB	9	1	45	0				
Lathwell, M.N.	RM	25	5	82	2	41.00	1- 15	–	–
Law, D.R.	RFM	69.3	11	303	6	50.50	2-115	–	–
Lawrence, J.R.G.	LMF	40	8	123	3	41.00	2- 44	–	–
Leatherdale, D.A.	RM	28	3	123	4	30.75	2- 36	–	–
Lefebvre, R.P.	RMF	85.3	28	179	6	29.83	6- 45	1	–
Lenham, N.J.	RM	6	0	27	1	27.00	1- 10	–	–
Lewis, J.	RMF	67.4	12	209	12	17.41	4- 34	–	–
Lewry, J.D.	LMF	350.1	62	1247	47	26.53	6- 43	3	–
Llong, N.J.	OB	71.4	11	273	3	91.00	2- 47	–	–
Longley, J.I.	RSM	4	0	47	0				
Lynch, M.A.	OB	2	0	3	0				
McCague, M.J.	RF	424.2	79	1457	50	29.14	5- 47	2	–
McGrath, G.D.	RF	7	1	21	0				
McIntyre, P.E.	LBG	297	70	1018	34	29.94	5- 38	1	–
Macmillan, G.I.	OB	158.3	13	568	7	81.14	2-108	–	–
MacRobert, A.D.	RMF	264	37	843	18	46.83	4- 41	–	–
Maddy, D.L.	RM/OB	6	0	41	0				
Malcolm, D.E.	RF	461.4	82	1692	65	26.03	6- 61	3	1
Malik, H.S.	OB	152	22	539	6	89.83	2- 55	–	–
Mallender, N.A.	RFM	142.2	32	427	17	25.11	4- 49	–	–
Marc, K.	RF	9	0	37	0				
Marsh, S H.	(WK)	2	1	8	0				
Martin, N.F.C.	RM	23	2	123	1	123.00	1- 61	–	–
Martin, P.J.	RFM	338.5	96	922	35	26.34	4- 51	–	–
Martin-Jenkins, R.S.C.	RFM	3	1	11	0				

	Cat	O	M	R	W	Avge	Best	5wI	10wM
Maru, R.J.	SLA	105.5	47	199	9	22.11	3- 38	–	–
Mason, T.J.	OB	25	4	79	0				
Mather, D.P.	LM	227.1	49	710	18	39.44	4- 65	–	–
Matthews, G.R.J.	OB	2	2	0	0				
Metcalfe, A.A.	OB	6	0	46	0				
Mike, G.W.	RMF	88.5	18	294	7	42.00	4- 87	–	–
Milburn, S.M.	RMF	69	15	204	10	20.40	4- 68	–	–
Millns, D.J.	RF	205.2	27	792	19	41.68	3- 47	–	–
Mirza, P.	RM	175.1	40	661	14	47.21	5-110	1	–
Moles, A.J.	RM	7	0	22	0				
Moody, T.M.	RM	72.1	20	209	5	41.80	2- 23	–	–
Morris, A.C.	RMF	17	5	62	0				
Mullally, A.D.	LFM	583.4	172	1700	59	28.81	6- 50	2	–
Munton, T.A.	RMF	373.5	111	952	48	19.83	5- 37	3	1
Mushtaq Ahmed	LBG	952	286	2821	95	29.69	6- 38	7	2
Nash, D.J.	RFM	460.1	90	1512	52	29.07	5- 35	2	–
Newell, K.	RM	40	8	127	0				
Newport, P.J.	RFM	548	148	1551	69	22.47	5- 45	4	–
Nicholas, M.C.J.	RM	7	0	26	0				
Nowell, R.W.	SLA	424.5	117	1264	32	39.50	4- 43	–	–
Ormond, J.	RMF	17	6	65	2	32.50	2- 65	–	–
Parsons, G.J.	RMF	579.2	179	1570	53	29.62	4- 46	–	–
Parsons, K.A.	RM	105	16	458	6	76.33	2- 11	–	–
Patel, M.M.	SLA	788	194	2336	66	35.39	6- 74	3	1
Pearson, R.M.	OB	81	13	302	7	43.14	3- 58	–	–
Peirce, M.T.E.	SLA	9	1	30	0				
Penberthy, A.L.	RM	52	7	177	4	44.25	2- 6	–	–
Pennett, D.B.	RMF	208.1	35	811	10	81.10	3-136	–	–
Phillips, N.C.	OB	154.5	34	521	8	65.12	3- 78	–	–
Pick, R.A.	RFM	490.2	105	1602	51	31.41	5- 82	2	–
Pierson, A.R.K.	OB	637.1	131	2115	69	30.65	5- 48	2	–
Pigott, A.C.S.	RFM	209.3	50	667	22	30.31	6- 91	2	1
Pike, V.J.	LB	195.3	39	592	11	53.81	3- 72	–	–
Ponting, K.R.	OB	10	1	36	0				
Pooley, J.C.	OB	4	0	15	0				
Prabhakar, M.	RMF	579.1	163	1439	51	28.21	7- 65	1	–
Rackemann, C.G.	RFM	457	114	1430	48	29.79	6- 60	1	–
Radford, N.V.	RFM	220.1	46	780	22	35.45	5- 45	1	–
Radford, T.A.	OB	1	1	0	1	0.00	1- 0	–	–
Ramprakash, M.R.	RM	22.2	3	108	4	27.00	3- 91	–	–
Ratledge, J.	RM	4.4	0	42	1	42.00	1- 16	–	–
Reeve, D.A.	RMF	312	117	661	38	17.39	5- 30	1	–
Remy, C.C.	RM	22.3	2	114	0				
Renshaw, S.J.	RMF	40	5	191	2	95.50	2-135	–	–
Richardson, A.	RM	19	3	60	3	20.00	3- 27	–	–
Ricketts, J.D.	LBG	224.5	35	732	17	43.05	3- 30	–	–
Roberts, A.R.	LB	11	2	45	0				
Robinson, D.D.J.	RMF	1	0	7	0				
Robinson, M.A.	RFM	483.1	134	1375	46	29.89	4- 46	–	–
Rollins, A.S.	RM	3	1	19	1	19.00	1- 19	–	–
Rose, G.D.	RM	426	93	1402	39	35.94	5- 78	1	–
Roseberry, M.A.	RM	3.4	0	19	0				
Salisbury, I.D.K.	LB	558.2	130	1674	54	31.00	7- 72	5	1
Saxelby, M.	RM	37.4	5	138	2	69.00	1- 15	–	–
Scott, C.W.	(WK)	3.2	0	30	0				
Searle, J.P.	OB	36	3	126	2	63.00	2-126	–	–

	Cat	O	M	R	W	Avge	Best	5wI	10wM
Shadford, D.J.	RMF	29.5	4	107	3	35.66	2- 40	–	–
Shahid, N.	LB	120	16	547	8	68.37	2- 29	–	–
Sheeraz, K.P.	RMF	225.1	35	888	24	37.00	6- 67	2	1
Sheriyar, A.	LF	189	27	799	29	27.55	6- 30	2	1
Shine, K.J.	RFM	43	6	173	7	24.71	4- 23	–	–
Silverwood, C.E.W.	RFM	147.1	23	630	18	35.00	5- 62	1	–
Simmons, P.V.	RM	39	9	121	1	121.00	1- 30	–	–
Small, G.C.	RFM	182.5	48	507	17	29.82	5- 71	1	–
Smith, A.M.	LM	415.3	104	1275	59	21.61	7- 70	4	1
Smith, A.W.	OB	165.3	27	647	10	64.70	3-112	–	–
Smith, B.F.	RM	11.3	2	69	1	69.00	1- 69	–	–
Smith, N.M.K.	OB	460	105	1375	39	35.25	6- 72	3	–
Smith, P.A.	RFM	43	10	136	4	34.00	2- 22	–	–
Snape, J.N.	OB	231	53	747	19	39.31	5- 65	1	–
Solanki, V.S.	OB	88	15	359	3	119.66	1- 10	–	–
Speak, N.J.	RM/OB	4	0	26	0				
Srinath, J.	RFM	568.4	147	1661	87	19.09	9- 76	5	2
Stanford, E.J.	SLA	77.5	19	220	3	73.33	2- 96	–	–
Stemp, R.D.	SLA	721.1	226	1929	42	45.92	4- 68	–	–
Stephenson, F.D.	RFM	361.2	73	1113	35	31.80	5- 64	1	–
Stephenson, J.P.	RM	358	62	1316	36	36.55	7- 51	1	–
Stewart, A.J.	RM	3	0	18	0				
Streak, H.H.	RFM	516.2	115	1629	53	30.73	4- 40	–	–
Stuart, A.M.	RFM	5	0	29	0				
Such, P.M.	OB	748.4	174	2064	77	26.80	8- 93	6	2
Sutcliffe, I.J.	OB	12	1	51	1	51.00	1- 11	–	–
Symonds, A.	OB	38	9	100	1	100.00	1- 13	–	–
Taylor, C.W.	LMF	11	4	26	4	6.50	4- 15	–	–
Taylor, J.P.	LFM	573.4	122	1713	59	29.03	7- 50	2	–
Thomas, P.A.	RF	386.4	67	1554	33	47.09	5- 70	1	–
Thomas, S.D.	RFM	303.3	51	1356	28	48.42	5- 99	1	–
Thompson, J.B.D.	RMF	38	8	157	6	26.16	2- 10	–	–
Thorpe, G.P.	RM	23	4	59	2	29.50	2- 42	–	–
Thursfield, M.J.	RM	72	13	238	4	59.50	3-108	–	–
Tolley, C.M.	LMF	4	0	23	0				
Trescothick, M.E.	RM	33	6	143	5	28.60	4- 36	–	–
Trimby, P.W.	LB	25	0	156	0				
Trump, H.R.J.	OB	596.2	173	1745	40	43.62	5- 85	1	–
Tudor, A.J.	RFM	83.3	7	320	14	22.85	5- 32	1	–
Tufnell, P.C.R.	SLA	678.1	207	1634	74	22.08	6-111	5	1
Tweats, T.A.	RM	43.4	3	194	4	48.50	1- 23	–	–
Twose, R.G.	RM	108	29	301	11	27.36	3- 50	–	–
Udal, S.D.	OB	628.2	137	1864	55	33.89	6- 65	5	1
Van Troost, A.P.	RF	145.3	23	624	16	39.00	5-120	1	–
Vaughan, M.P.	OB	272.4	64	876	22	39.81	3- 32	–	–
Walker, A.	RFM	285.3	53	958	31	30.90	8-118	2	1
Walsh, C.A.	RF	384.2	76	1124	39	28.82	5- 45	1	–
Walton, T.C.	RM	8	2	26	0				
Ward, T.R.	OB	3.5	0	43	0				
Warner, A.E.	RFM	375.1	90	1050	39	26.92	6- 21	3	–
Wasim Akram	LF	518.1	108	1598	81	19.72	7- 52	7	3
Watkin, S.L.	RMF	590.4	144	1755	65	27.00	7- 49	2	1
Watkinson, M.	RMF	622.4	158	1910	65	29.38	7-140	2	1
Waugh, M.E.	RMF	256	61	789	17	46.41	4- 76	–	–
Weekes, P.N.	OB	258.4	55	679	13	52.23	3- 26	–	–
Welch, G.	RM	17	1	80	2	40.00	2- 80	–	–

	Cat	O	M	R	W	Avge	Best	5wI	10wM
Wells, C.M.	RM	110	25	326	10	32.60	4- 29	–	–
Wells, V.J.	RMF	139.3	33	438	19	23.05	3- 28	–	–
Weston, R.M.S.	LB	22.1	2	70	1	70.00	1- 41	–	–
Weston, W.P.C.	LM	21.4	2	91	0				
Whitaker, P.R.	OB	10	2	30	1	30.00	1- 4	–	–
White, C.	RFM	273.4	49	934	25	37.36	4- 40	–	–
White, G.W.	LB	4	1	22	0				
Whittall, A.R.	OB	328.4	85	1064	29	36.68	6- 46	2	1
Wileman, J.R.	RSM	95	36	217	4	54.25	2- 33	–	–
Williams, B.A.	RF	134.3	26	443	14	31.64	4- 79	–	–
Williams, N.F.	RFM	188.4	31	743	21	35.38	5- 93	1	–
Williams, R.C.	RM	103.3	20	361	6	60.16	3- 44	–	–
Williams, S.C.	RSM	1	0	2	0				
Windows, M.G.N.	RSM	7.3	1	36	2	18.00	1- 6	–	–
Windsor, J.M.	RFM	41.4	12	93	3	31.00	3- 51	–	–
Wood, J.	RFM	97.4	25	303	14	21.64	4- 54	–	–
Wren, T.N.	LM	205.4	31	785	23	34.13	5-148	1	–
Wylie, A.	RF	35	7	143	1	143.00	1- 65	–	–
Yates, G.	OB	136	33	494	11	44.90	4- 67	–	–
Yeabsley, M.I.	OB	18	3	84	2	42.00	1- 28	–	–
Yeabsley, R.S.	RMF	85	16	277	8	34.62	4- 34	–	–
Young, S.	RFM	128	36	359	16	22.43	3- 23	–	–

YOUNG CRICKETER OF THE YEAR

This annual award, made by The Cricket Writers' Club (founded in 1946), is currently restricted to players qualified for England and under the age of 23 on 1 April. In 1986 their ballot resulted in a dead heat. Only six of their selections (marked †) have failed to win an England cap.

1950	R.Tattersall	1974	P.H.Edmonds
1951	P.B.H.May	1975	A.Kennedy†
1952	F.S.Trueman	1976	G.Miller
1953	M.C.Cowdrey	1977	I.T.Botham
1954	P.J.Loader	1978	D.I.Gower
1955	K.F.Barrington	1979	P.W.G.Parker
1956	B.Taylor†	1980	G.R.Dilley
1957	M.J.Stewart	1981	M.W.Gatting
1958	A.C.D.Ingleby-Mackenzie†	1982	N.G.Cowans
1959	G.Pullar	1983	N.A.Foster
1960	D.A.Allen	1984	R.J.Bailey
1961	P.H.Parfitt	1985	D.V.Lawrence
1962	P.J.Sharpe	1986	A.A.Metcalfe†
1963	G.Boycott	1986	J.J.Whitaker
1964	J.M.Brearley	1987	R.J.Blakey
1965	A.P.E.Knott	1988	M.P.Maynard
1966	D.L.Underwood	1989	N.Hussain
1967	A.W.Greig	1990	M.A.Atherton
1968	R.M.H.Cottam	1991	M.R.Ramprakash
1969	A.Ward	1992	I.D.K.Salisbury
1970	C.M.Old	1993	M.N.Lathwell
1971	J.Whitehouse†	1994	J.P.Crawley
1972	D.R.Owen-Thomas†	1995	A.Symonds
1973	M.Hendrick		

BRITANNIC ASSURANCE COUNTY CHAMPIONSHIP 1995 FINAL TABLE

		P	*W*	*L*	*D*	*Bonus Bat*	*Points Bowl*	*Total Points*
1	WARWICKSHIRE (1)	17	14	2	1	49	64	337
2	Middlesex (4)	17	12	2	3	51	62	305
3	Northamptonshire (5)	17	12	2	3	41	57	290
4	Lancashire (10)	17	10	4	3	48	61	269
5	Essex (6)	17	8	9	–	42	58	228
6	Gloucestershire (12)	17	8	4	5	45	50	223
7	Leicestershire (2)	17	7	8	2	41	61	214
8	Yorkshire (13)	17	7	8	2	39	55	206
9	Somerset (11)	17	7	5	5	40	49	201
10	Worcestershire (15)	17	6	7	4	29	57	182
11	Nottinghamshire (3)	17	5	9	3	41	54	175
12	Surrey (7)	17	5	8	4	34	55	169
13	Hampshire (13)	17	5	8	4	32	56	168
14	Derbyshire (17)	17	4	10	3	39	64	167
15	Sussex (8)	17	4	7	6	37	51	152
16	Glamorgan (18)	17	3	8	6	40	57	145
17	Durham (16)	17	4	13	–	20	53	137
18	Kent (9)	17	3	10	4	40	44	132

1994 final positions are shown in brackets.

SCORING OF POINTS 1995

(a) For a win, 16 points, plus any points scored in the first innings.

(b) In a tie, each side to score eight points, plus any points scored in the first innings.

(c) If the scores are equal in a drawn match, the side batting in the fourth innings to score eight points, plus any points scored in the first innings.

(d) **First Innings Points** (awarded only for performances **in the first 120 overs** of each first innings and retained whatever the result of the match).

(i) A maximum of four batting points to be available as under—

200 to 249 runs — 1 point
250 to 299 runs — 2 points
300 to 349 runs — 3 points
350 runs or over — 4 points

(ii) A maximum of four bowling points to be available as under—

3 to 4 wickets taken — 1 point
5 to 6 wickets taken — 2 points
7 to 8 wickets taken — 3 points
9 to 10 wickets taken — 4 points

(c) If play starts when less than eight hours playing time remains (in which event a one innings match shall be played as provided for in First-Class Playing Condition 20), no first innings points shall be scored. The side winning on the one innings to score 12 points. In a tie, each side to score six points. If the scores are equal in a drawn match, the side batting in the second innings to score six points.

(f) A County which is adjudged to have prepared a pitch which is 'unsuitable for First-Class Cricket' shall be liable to have 25 points deducted from its aggregate of points under the procedure agreed by the Board in December 1988 and revised in December 1993. In addition, a penalty of 10 or 15 points may in certain circumstances be imposed on a County in respect of a 'Poor' pitch under the procedure agreed by the Board in March 1995. There shall be no right of appeal against any points penalty provided for in this Clause.

(g) The side which has the highest aggregate of points gained at the end of the season shall be the Champion County. Should any sides in the Championship table be equal on points, the side with most wins will have priority.

COUNTY CHAMPIONS

The English County Championship was not officially constituted until December 1889. Prior to that date there was no generally accepted method of awarding the title; although the 'least matches lost' method existed, it was not consistently applied. Rules governing playing qualifications were not agreed until 1873, and the first unofficial points system was not introduced until 1888.

Research has produced a list of champions dating back to 1826, but at least seven different versions exist for the period from 1864 to 1889 (see *The Wisden Book of Cricket Records*). Only from 1890 can any authorised list of county champions commence.

That first official Championship was contested between eight counties: Gloucestershire, Kent, Lancashire, Middlesex, Nottinghamshire, Surrey, Sussex and Yorkshire. The remaining counties were admitted in the following seasons: 1891 – Somerset, 1895 – Derbyshire, Essex, Hampshire, Leicestershire and Warwickshire, 1899 – Worcestershire, 1905 – Northamptonshire, 1921 – Glamorgan, and 1992 – Durham.

The Championship pennant was introduced by the 1951 champions, Warwickshire, and the Lord's Taverners' Trophy was first presented in 1973. The first sponsors, Schweppes (1977 to 1983), were succeeded by BRITANNIC ASSURANCE in 1984.

1890	Surrey	1927	Lancashire	1964	Worcestershire
1891	Surrey	1928	Lancashire	1965	Worcestershire
1892	Surrey	1929	Nottinghamshire	1966	Yorkshire
1893	Yorkshire	1930	Lancashire	1967	Yorkshire
1894	Surrey	1931	Yorkshire	1968	Yorkshire
1895	Surrey	1932	Yorkshire	1969	Glamorgan
1896	Yorkshire	1933	Yorkshire	1970	Kent
1897	Lancashire	1934	Lancashire	1971	Surrey
1898	Yorkshire	1935	Yorkshire	1972	Warwickshire
1899	Surrey	1936	Derbyshire	1973	Hampshire
1900	Yorkshire	1937	Yorkshire	1974	Worcestershire
1901	Yorkshire	1938	Yorkshire	1975	Leicestershire
1902	Yorkshire	1939	Yorkshire	1976	Middlesex
1903	Middlesex	1946	Yorkshire	1977	Kent / Middlesex
1904	Lancashire	1947	Middlesex		
1905	Yorkshire	1948	Glamorgan	1978	Kent
1906	Kent	1949	Middlesex / Yorkshire	1979	Essex
1907	Nottinghamshire			1980	Middlesex
1908	Yorkshire	1950	Lancashire / Surrey	1981	Nottinghamshire
1909	Kent			1982	Middlesex
1910	Kent	1951	Warwickshire	1983	Essex
1911	Warwickshire	1952	Surrey	1984	Essex
1912	Yorkshire	1953	Surrey	1985	Middlesex
1913	Kent	1954	Surrey	1986	Essex
1914	Surrey	1955	Surrey	1987	Nottinghamshire
1919	Yorkshire	1956	Surrey	1988	Worcestershire
1920	Middlesex	1957	Surrey	1989	Worcestershire
1921	Middlesex	1958	Surrey	1990	Middlesex
1922	Yorkshire	1959	Yorkshire	1991	Essex
1923	Yorkshire	1960	Yorkshire	1992	Essex
1924	Yorkshire	1961	Hampshire	1993	Middlesex
1925	Yorkshire	1962	Yorkshire	1994	Warwickshire
1926	Lancashire	1963	Yorkshire	1995	Warwickshire

INVENTIVE REEVE TRIUMPHS

Led with great panache by the hyper-inventive Dermot Reeve, Warwickshire won a closely contested final at 3.43 on the second afternoon, the final margin being four wickets with seven balls to spare. Without Reeve's maverick captaincy, nagging 12-over spell for 31 runs in mid-innings and decisive undefeated 37 off 47 balls at the death, Allan Lamb would most certainly have celebrated the end of his seven-year reign as Northamptonshire's captain by holding aloft the distinctive NatWest Trophy.

Limited-overs matches are at the mercy of the climate and there must be a strong case for moving the longest variation of this form of cricket away from the shortest day of the season and its most unstable weather. The side batting first has enjoyed scant success in recent September finals and Lamb astonished every pundit when he chose to bat after rain had delayed the start until 3pm. He must have entertained doubts himself when he edged his third ball to slip and departed with the scoreboard showing 39-2 in the 12th over. Visions of the match still ending on its appointed day were dashed when the middle order rallied the total to 197-8, the light failing at 7.05pm with just nine balls remaining.

Before a much diminished audience, Northamptonshire added only three runs on Sunday morning but their meagre total assumed more regal proportions when inspired opening spells by Paul Taylor (7-4-6-2) and Kevin Curran (7-3-9-0) reduced the 'Bears' to 17-2 after 14 overs. Roger Twose, a key player in the outstanding team of the nineties, marked his final major appearance prior to becoming a New Zealand Test cricketer by contributing the only fifty of the contest. For nearly three hours he played the vital anchor role, sharing partnerships of 46, 48 and 54 with Dominic Ostler, Trevor Penney and his captain respectively. When he ran himself out calling for an imaginative bye to the keeper, Warwickshire still required 25 off 20 balls and the game, to quote John Arlott, 'was still in the hazard'. Reeve, reprieved by umpire Bird in the closest of lbw decisions, soon ended the matter by conjuring four boundaries off his next nine balls. Richie Benaud needed to look no further for his player of the match nor Raymond Illingworth for his World Cup all-rounder.

GILLETTE CUP WINNERS

1963 Sussex
1964 Sussex
1965 Yorkshire
1966 Warwickshire
1967 Kent
1968 Warwickshire
1969 Yorkshire
1970 Lancashire
1971 Lancashire
1972 Lancashire
1973 Gloucestershire
1974 Kent
1975 Lancashire
1976 Northamptonshire
1977 Middlesex
1978 Sussex
1979 Somerset
1980 Middlesex

NATWEST TROPHY WINNERS

1981 Derbyshire
1982 Surrey
1983 Somerset
1984 Middlesex
1985 Essex
1986 Sussex
1987 Nottinghamshire
1988 Middlesex
1989 Warwickshire
1990 Lancashire
1991 Hampshire
1992 Northamptonshire
1993 Warwickshire
1994 Worcestershire
1995 Warwickshire

1995 NATWEST TROPHY FINAL

NORTHAMPTONSHIRE v WARWICKSHIRE

At Lord's, London, on 2, 3 September.
Toss: Northamptonshire. Result: WARWICKSHIRE won by 4 wickets.
Match Award: D.A.Reeve.

NORTHAMPTONSHIRE		Runs	Min	Balls	6s	4s	Fall
R.R.Montgomerie	b Donald	1	19	17	–	–	1- 4
A.Fordham	b Brown	20	49	30	–	2	2- 39
R.J.Bailey	b N.M.K.Smith	44	95	90	–	4	4- 89
*A.J.Lamb	c Ostler b Brown	0	3	3	–	–	3- 39
K.M.Curran	b Donald	30	108	80	–	2	6-128
D.J.Capel	c Piper b Reeve	12	20	28	1	–	5-110
†R.J.Warren	b Bell	41	93	66	1	3	10-200
A.L.Penberthy	run out (Penney)	5	28	12	–	–	7-158
J.N.Snape	c Piper b Donald	21	30	28	–	2	8-197
A.Kumble	c Twose b Bell	2	6	5	–	–	9-200
J.P.Taylor	not out	0	1	0	–	–	
Extras (B4, LB9, W11)		24					
Total (59.5 overs; 232 minutes)		200					

WARWICKSHIRE		Runs	Min	Balls	6s	4s	Fall
N.V.Knight	c Bailey b Taylor	2	42	34	–	–	2- 14
N.M.K.Smith	c Warren b Taylor	2	19	13	–	–	1- 5
D.P.Ostler	b Kumble	45	109	77	–	5	4- 74
D.R.Brown	c Warren b Penberthy	8	28	18	–	1	3- 28
R.G.Twose	run out (Warren)	68	170	127	–	2	6-176
T.L.Penney	c Montgomerie b Penberthy	20	53	35	–	1	5-122
*D.A.Reeve	not out	37	72	47	–	5	
P.A.Smith	not out	4	13	2	–	–	
†K.J.Piper							
A.A.Donald							
M.A.V.Bell							
Extras (B2, LB14, W1)		17					
Total (6 wickets; 58.5 overs; 256 mins)		203					

WARWICKSHIRE	*O*	*M*	*R*	*W*	NORTHAMPTONSHIRE	*O*	*M*	*R*	*W*
Donald	12	1	33	3	Taylor	11.5	4	37	2
Brown	10	2	35	2	Curran	11	3	31	0
Bell	8.5	1	41	2	Penberthy	11	1	44	2
N.M.K.Smith	12	1	23	1	Kumble	12	0	29	1
Reeve	12	1	31	1	Capel	12	0	40	0
P.A.Smith	5	0	24	0	Snape	1	0	6	0

Umpires: H.D.Bird and M.J.Kitchen.

THE NATWEST TROPHY 1995 RESULTS CHART

First Round *27 June*	Second Round *12 July*	Quarter-finals *1 August*	Semi-finals *15 August*	Final *2, 3 September*
WARWICKSHIRE†	WARWICKSHIRE†	WARWICKSHIRE	WARWICKSHIRE	WARWICKSHIRE (£35,000)
Somerset				
KENT	Kent			
Staffordshire†				
DERBYSHIRE	DERBYSHIRE	Derbyshire† (£4,375)		
Cambridgeshire†				
SUSSEX†	Sussex†			
Devon				
GLAMORGAN†	GLAMORGAN	GLAMORGAN†	Glamorgan† (£8,750)	
Dorset				
LEICESTERSHIRE†	Leicestershire†			
Hampshire				
MIDDLESEX	MIDDLESEX	Middlesex (£4,375)		
Cornwall†				
SURREY†	Surrey†			
Berkshire				
LANCASHIRE†	LANCASHIRE†	Lancashire (£4,375)	Yorkshire† (£8,750)	Northamptonshire (£17,500)
Norfolk				
WORCESTERSHIRE†	Worcestershire			
Cumberland				
YORKSHIRE†	YORKSHIRE	YORKSHIRE†		
Ireland				
ESSEX	Essex†			
Cheshire†				
DURHAM†	Durham†	Gloucestershire† (£4,375)	NORTHAMPTONSHIRE	
Herefordshire				
GLOUCESTERSHIRE†	GLOUCESTERSHIRE			
Suffolk				
NOTTINGHAMSHIRE†	Nottinghamshire†	NORTHAMPTONSHIRE		
Scotland				
NORTHAMPTONSHIRE†	NORTHAMPTONSHIRE			
Holland				

NATWEST TROPHY PRINCIPAL RECORDS 1963-95

(Including The Gillette Cup)

Highest Total	413-4	Somerset v Devon	Torquay	1990
Highest Total in a Final	322-5	Warwicks v Sussex	Lord's	1993
Highest Total by a Minor County	305-9	Durham v Glam	Darlington	1991
Highest Total Batting Second	350	Surrey v Worcs	The Oval	1994
Highest Total to Win Batting 2nd	322-5	Warwicks v Sussex	Lord's	1993
Lowest Total	39	Ireland v Sussex	Lord's	1985
Lowest Total in a Final	118	Lancashire v Kent	Lord's	1974
Lowest Total to Win Batting First	98	Worcs v Durham	Chester-le-St	1968

Highest Score	206 A.I.Kallicharran	Warwicks v Oxon	Birmingham	1984
HS (Minor County)	132 G.Robinson	Lincs v Northumb	Jesmond	1971
Hundreds	266 (Gillette Cup 93; NatWest Trophy 173)			1963-95
Fastest Hundred	36 balls – G.D.Rose	Somerset v Devon	Torquay	1990
Most Hundreds	7 C.L.Smith	Hampshire		1980-91
Most Runs	2417 (av 51.42)	G.A.Gooch	Essex	1973-95

Highest Partnership for each Wicket

1st	255	M.A.Roseberry/S.Hutton	Durham v Herefords	Chester-le-St	1995
2nd	286	I.S.Anderson/A.Hill	Derbys v Cornwall	Derby	1986
3rd	309*	T.S.Curtis/T.M.Moody	Worcs v Surrey	The Oval	1994
4th	234*	D.Lloyd/C.H.Lloyd	Lancashire v Glos	Manchester	1978
5th	166	M.A.Lynch/G.R.J.Roope	Surrey v Durham	The Oval	1982
6th	123	D.A.Reeve/T.L.Penney	Warwicks v Leics	Leicester	1994
7th	160*	C.J.Richards/I.R.Payne	Surrey v Lincs	Sleaford	1983
8th	83	J.Hartley/D.A.Hale	Oxon v Glos	Oxford	1989
9th	87	M.A.Nash/A.E.Cordle	Glamorgan v Lincs	Swansea	1974
10th	81	S.Turner/R.E.East	Essex v Yorkshire	Leeds	1982

Best Bowling	8-21	M.A.Holding	Derbys v Sussex	Hove	1988
	8-31	D.L.Underwood	Kent v Scotland	Edinburgh	1987
Most Wickets	81	(av 14.85)	G.G.Arnold	Surrey	1963-80
Hat-Tricks		J.D.F.Larter	Northants v Sussex	Northampton	1963
		D.A.D.Sydenham	Surrey v Cheshire	Hoylake	1964
		R.N.S.Hobbs	Essex v Middlesex	Lord's	1968
		N.M.McVicker	Warwicks v Lincs	Birmingham	1971
		G.S.Le Roux	Sussex v Ireland	Hove	1985
		M.Jean-Jacques	Derbyshire v Notts	Derby	1987
		J.F.M.O'Brien	Cheshire v Derbys	Chester	1988
		R.A.Pick	Notts v Scotland	Nottingham	1995

Most Wicket-Keeping Dismissals in an Innings

7 (7ct) A.J.Stewart Surrey v Glamorgan Swansea 1994

Most Catches in an Innings

4 – A.S.Brown (Glos 1963), G.Cook (Northants 1972), C.G.Greenidge (Hants 1981), D.C.Jackson (Durham 1984), T.S.Smith (Herts 1984), H.Morris (Glam 1988), C.C.Lewis (Notts 1992).

Most Appearances	61	D.P.Hughes	Lancashire	1969-91
Most Match Awards	9	G.A.Gooch	Essex	1973-93
Most Match Wins	66 Warwickshire.	**Most Cup/Trophy Wins**	5 – Lancs, Warwicks.	

1995 BENSON AND HEDGES CUP FINAL

KENT v LANCASHIRE

At Lord's, London, on 15 July.
Toss: Kent. Result: LANCASHIRE won by 35 runs.
Match Award: P.A.de Silva.

LANCASHIRE		Runs	Min	Balls	6s	4s	Fall
M.A.Atherton	c Fulton b Headley	93	163	141	–	9	2-201
J.E.R.Gallian	b Ealham	36	76	64	–	2	1- 80
J.P.Crawley	c Taylor b McCague	83	116	89	1	5	4-258
N.H.Fairbrother	c McCague b Headley	16	16	13	–	1	3-236
G.D.Lloyd	run out (McCague)	12	14	12	–	–	5-259
Wasim Akram	run out (Ward/McCague)	10	12	7	–	1	7-274
*M.Watkinson	c McCague b Fleming	0	3	1	–	–	6-266
I.D.Austin	not out	5	5	6	–	–	
†W.K.Hegg							
G.Chapple							
G.Yates							
Extras (LB2, W10, NB7)		19					
Total (7 wickets; 55 overs; 206 minutes)		274					

KENT		Runs	Min	Balls	6s	4s	Fall
D.P.Fulton	lbw b Chapple	25	42	49	–	4	2- 37
T.R.Ward	c Hegg b Chapple	7	25	11	–	1	1- 28
N.R.Taylor	b Yates	14	49	38	–	2	3- 81
P.A.de Silva	c Lloyd b Austin	112	140	95	3	11	7-214
G.R.Cowdrey	lbw b Yates	25	50	48	–	1	4-142
M.V.Fleming	b Yates	11	24	24	–	1	5-162
M.A.Ealham	lbw b Watkinson	3	12	11	–	–	6-180
*†S.A.Marsh	c Crawley b Austin	4	19	16	–	–	8-214
M.J.McCague	not out	11	20	10	–	1	
D.W.Headley	c Chapple b Watkinson	5	5	6	–	1	9-219
T.N.Wren	c Austin b Watkinson	7	13	8	–	1	10-239
Extras (LB7, W2, NB6)		15					
Total (52.1 overs; 205 minutes)		239					

KENT	O	M	R	W
Wren	5	0	21	0
Headley	11	0	57	2
McCague	11	0	65	1
Ealham	11	0	33	1
De Silva	8	0	36	0
Fleming	9	0	60	1

LANCASHIRE	O	M	R	W
Wasim	10	0	57	0
Chapple	10	1	55	2
Austin	11	4	36	2
Watkinson	10.1	0	42	3
Yates	11	0	42	3

Umpires: N.T.Plews and D.R.Shepherd.

1995 BENSON AND HEDGES CUP

FINAL GROUP TABLES

GROUP A	*P*	*W*	*L*	*NR*	*Pts*	*Net Run Rate*
LANCASHIRE	5	4	–	1	9	22.56
NOTTINGHAMSHIRE	5	3	1	1	7	0.70
Warwickshire	5	2	2	1	5	4.69
Durham	5	2	2	1	5	–3.18
Minor Counties	5	1	3	1	3	–11.76
Leicestershire	5	–	4	1	1	–7.58
GROUP B						
YORKSHIRE	4	3	–	1	7	17.34
WORCESTERSHIRE	4	3	1	–	6	26.02
Derbyshire	4	2	1	1	5	–3.11
Northamptonshire	4	1	3	–	2	–1.49
Scotland	4	–	4	–	–	–37.35
GROUP C						
GLOUCESTERSHIRE	5	5	–	–	10	9.99
MIDDLESEX	5	4	1	–	8	7.70
Glamorgan	5	3	2	–	6	16.45
Essex	5	1	3	1	3	–2.48
Hampshire	5	1	3	1	3	–6.10
Combined Universities	5	–	5	–	–	–28.04
GROUP D						
KENT	4	4	–	–	8	27.14
SOMERSET	4	2	2	–	4	12.17
Surrey	4	2	2	–	4	4.67
Sussex	4	2	2	–	4	0.46
Ireland	4	–	4	–	–	–46.00

FINAL ROUNDS

QUARTER-FINALS *30, 31 May*	SEMI-FINALS *13, 14 June*	FINAL *15 July*
KENT† Middlesex (£4,375)	KENT†	Kent (£17,500)
SOMERSET Gloucestershire† (£4,375)	Somerset (£8,750)	
WORCESTERSHIRE Yorkshire† (£4,375)	Worcestershire† (£8,750)	LANCASHIRE (£35,000)
Nottinghamshire (£4,375) LANCASHIRE†	LANCASHIRE	

† Home team. Winning teams are in capitals. Prize-money in brackets.

BENSON AND HEDGES CUP PRINCIPAL RECORDS 1972-95

Highest Total		388-7	Essex v Scotland	Chelmsford	1992
Highest Total Batting Second		318-5	Lancashire v Leics	Manchester	1995
Highest Total to Lose Batting 2nd		303-7	Derbys v Somerset	Taunton	1990
Lowest Total		50	Hampshire v Yorks	Leeds	1991
Highest Score	198* G.A.Gooch		Essex v Sussex	Hove	1982
Hundreds	257				1972-95
Fastest Hundred	62 min – M.A.Nash		Glamorgan v Hants	Swansea	1976

Highest Partnership for each Wicket

1st	252	V.P.Terry/C.L.Smith	Hants v Comb Us	Southampton	1990
2nd	285*	C.G.Greenidge/D.R.Turner	Hants v Minor C (S)	Amersham	1973
3rd	269*	P.M.Roebuck/M.D.Crowe	Somerset v Hants	Southampton	1987
4th	184*	D.Lloyd/B.W.Reidy	Lancashire v Derbys	Chesterfield	1980
5th	160	A.J.Lamb/D.J.Capel	Northants v Leics	Northampton	1986
6th	121	P.A.Neale/S.J.Rhodes	Worcs v Yorkshire	Worcester	1988
7th	149*	J.D.Love/C.M.Old	Yorks v Scotland	Bradford	1981
8th	109	R.E.East/N.Smith	Essex v Northants	Chelmsford	1977
9th	83	P.G.Newman/M.A.Holding	Derbyshire v Notts	Nottingham	1985
10th	80*	D.L.Bairstow/M.Johnson	Yorkshire v Derbys	Derby	1981

Best Bowling	7-12	W.W.Daniel	Middx v Minor C (E)	Ipswich	1978
	7-22	J.R.Thomson	Middx v Hampshire	Lord's	1981
	7-32	R.G.D.Willis	Warwicks v Yorks	Birmingham	1981
Hat-Tricks		G.D.McKenzie	Leics v Worcs	Worcester	1972
		K.Higgs	Leics v Surrey	Lord's	1974
		A.A.Jones	Middlesex v Essex	Lord's	1977
		M.J.Procter	Glos v Hampshire	Southampton	1977
		W.Larkins	Northants v Comb Us	Northampton	1980
		E.A.Moseley	Glamorgan v Kent	Cardiff	1981
		G.C.Small	Warwickshire v Leics	Leicester	1984
		N.A.Mallender	Somerset v Comb Us	Taunton	1987
		W.K.M.Benjamin	Leics v Notts	Leicester	1987
		A.R.C.Fraser	Middlesex v Sussex	Lord's	1988

Most Wicket-Keeping Dismissals in an Innings

8 (8ct)	D.J.S.Taylor	Somerset v Comb Us	Taunton	1982

Most Catches in an Innings

5	V.J.Marks	Comb Us v Kent	Oxford	1976

Most Match Awards	22	G.A.Gooch	Essex	1973-95

BENSON AND HEDGES CUP WINNERS

1972	Leicestershire	1980	Northamptonshire	1988	Hampshire
1973	Kent	1981	Somerset	1989	Nottinghamshire
1974	Surrey	1982	Somerset	1990	Lancashire
1975	Leicestershire	1983	Middlesex	1991	Worcestershire
1976	Kent	1984	Lancashire	1992	Hampshire
1977	Gloucestershire	1985	Leicestershire	1993	Derbyshire
1978	Kent	1986	Middlesex	1994	Warwickshire
1979	Essex	1987	Yorkshire	1995	Lancashire

SUNDAY LEAGUE FINAL TABLE 1995

		P	W	L	T	NR	Pts
1	KENT (3)	17	12	4	–	1	50
2	Warwickshire (1)	17	12	4	–	1	50
3	Worcestershire (2)	17	11	3	1	2	50
4	Lancashire (4)	17	11	5	–	1	46
5	Essex (17)	17	10	6	1	–	42
6	Glamorgan (7)	17	8	6	–	3	38
7	Leicestershire (10)	17	8	7	–	2	36
8	Derbyshire (8)	17	7	6	1	3	36
9	Surrey (6)	17	7	8	–	2	32
10	Sussex (15)	17	7	8	–	2	32
11	Nottinghamshire (11)	17	7	9	–	1	30
12	Yorkshire (5)	17	7	9	–	1	30
13	Northamptonshire (13)	17	6	8	1	2	30
14	Somerset (16)	17	5	9	–	3	26
15	Gloucestershire (18)	17	5	10	–	2	24
16	Durham (9)	17	4	9	1	3	24
17	Middlesex (14)	17	4	11	–	2	20
18	Hampshire (12)	17	3	12	1	1	16

Win = 4 points. Tie/No Result = 2 points. When counties finish with an equal number of points, their places are decided by most wins or, if equal, by higher run-rate. Kent won the title by virtue of a run-rate superior to that of Warwickshsire, Worcestershire taking third place by having won fewer matches.

1994 final positions are shown in brackets.

The Sunday League's sponsors have been John Player & Sons (1969-1986), Refuge Assurance (1987-1991), TCCB (1992) and AXA Equity & Law Insurance (1993 to date). The competition has been limited to 40 overs per innings, apart from 1993 when it was experimentally extended to 50.

WINNERS

1969 Lancashire
1970 Lancashire
1971 Worcestershire
1972 Kent
1973 Kent
1974 Leicestershire
1975 Hampshire
1976 Kent
1977 Leicestershire
1978 Hampshire
1979 Somerset
1980 Warwickshire
1981 Essex
1982 Sussex
1983 Yorkshire
1984 Essex
1985 Essex
1986 Hampshire
1987 Worcestershire
1988 Worcestershire
1989 Lancashire
1990 Derbyshire
1991 Nottinghamshire
1992 Middlesex
1993 Glamorgan
1994 Warwickshire
1995 Kent

SUNDAY LEAGUE PRINCIPAL RECORDS 1969-95

Highest Total		375-4	Surrey v Yorkshire	Scarborough	1994
Highest Total Batting Second		317-6	Surrey v Notts	The Oval	1993
Lowest Total		23	Middlesex v Yorks	Leeds	1974
Highest Score	176	G.A.Gooch	Essex v Glamorgan	Southend	1983
Hundreds	516				1969-95
Fastest Hundred	44 balls	M.A.Ealham	Kent v Derbyshire	Maidstone	1995

Highest Partnership for each Wicket

1st	239	G.A.Gooch/B.R.Hardie	Essex v Notts	Nottingham	1985
2nd	273	G.A.Gooch/K.S.McEwan	Essex v Notts	Nottingham	1983
3rd	223	S.J.Cook/G.D.Rose	Somerset v Glam	Neath	1990
4th	219	C.G.Greenidge/C.L.Smith	Hampshire v Surrey	Southampton	1987
5th	190	R.J.Blakey/M.J.Foster	Yorkshire v Leics	Leicester	1993
6th	124*	J.J.Whitaker/P.A.Nixon	Leics v Surrey	The Oval	1992
7th	132	K.R.Brown/N.F.Williams	Middx v Somerset	Lord's	1988
8th	110*	C.L.Cairns/B.N.French	Notts v Surrey	The Oval	1993
9th	105	D.G.Moir/R.W.Taylor	Derbyshire v Kent	Derby	1984
10th	57	D.A.Graveney/J.B.Mortimore	Glos v Lancashire	Tewkesbury	1973

Best Bowling	8-26	K.D.Boyce	Essex v Lancashire	Manchester	1971
	7-15	R.A.Hutton	Yorkshire v Worcs	Leeds	1969
	7-39	A.Hodgson	Northants v Somerset	Northampton	1976
	7-41	A.N.Jones	Sussex v Notts	Nottingham	1986

Four Wkts in Four Balls	A.Ward	Derbyshire v Sussex	Derby	1970

Hat-Tricks (24): Derbyshire – A.Ward (1970), C.J.Tunnicliffe (1979); Essex – K.D.Boyce (1971); Glamorgan – M.A.Nash (1975), A.E.Cordle (1979), G.C.Holmes (1987), A.Dale (1993); Gloucestershire – K.M.Curran (1989); Hampshire – J.M.Rice (1975), M.D.Marshall (1981); Kent – R.M.Ellison (1983), M.J.McCague (1992); Leicestershire – G.D.McKenzie (1972); Northamptonshire – A.Hodgson (1976); Nottinghamshire – K.Saxelby (1987), K.P.Evans (1994); Somerset – R.Palmer (1970), I.V.A.Richards (1982); Surrey – M.P.Bicknell (1992); Sussex – A.Buss (1974); Warwickshire – R.G.D.Willis (1973), W.Blenkiron (1974); Worcestershire – R.K.Illingworth (1993); Yorkshire – P.W.Jarvis (1982).

Most Wicket-Keeping Dismissals in an Innings

7 (6ct, 1st)	R.W.Taylor	Derbyshire v Lancs	Manchester	1975

Most Catches in an Innings

5	J.M.Rice	Hampshire v Warwicks	Southampton	1978

COUNTY CAPS AWARDED IN 1995

Derbyshire	A.S.Rollins, C.M.Wells
Durham	J.Boiling, N.Killeen, D.G.C.Ligertwood, M.Prabhakar, M.A.Roseberry.
Essex	R.J.Rollins
Glamorgan	–
Gloucestershire	K.E.Cooper, M.A.Lynch, A.M.Smith, J.Srinath
Hampshire	J.P.Stephenson
Kent	P.A.de Silva
Lancashire	S.P.Titchard
Leicestershire	W.J.Cronje, A.R.K.Pierson, B.F.Smith.
Middlesex	M.A.Feltham, R.L.Johnson, D.J.Nash, J.C.Pooley
Northamptonshire	A.Kumble, R.R.Montgomerie, R.J.Warren
Nottinghamshire	G.F.Archer, W.M.Noon
Somerset	P.D.Bowler
Surrey	A.J.Hollioake, A.C.S.Pigott
Sussex	–
Warwickshire	D.R.Brown, N.V.Knight
Worcestershire	W.P.C.Weston
Yorkshire	M.G.Bevan, M.P.Vaughan

MINOR COUNTIES CHAMPIONSHIP

FINAL TABLE 1995

								Bonus Points		*Total*
		P	*W*	*L*	*T*	*D*	*NR*	*Bat*	*Bowl*	*Points*
EASTERN DIVISION										
Lincolnshire	NW	9	4	0	0	4	1	23	17	109
Norfolk	NW	9	3	1	0	5	0	25	26	107
Suffolk	NW	9	3	1	0	5	0	23	24	95
Cumberland	NW	9	3	4	0	2	0	11	28	87
Cambridgeshire	NW	9	3	2	0	4	0	13	24	85
Staffordshire	NW	9	2	2	0	5	0	23	29	84
Buckinghamshire		9	2	3	0	4	0	24	22	78
Hertfordshire		9	2	3	0	4	0	25	20	77
Northumberland		9	2	3	0	3	1	15	18	70
Bedfordshire		9	1	6	0	2	0	15	22	53
WESTERN DIVISION										
Devon	NW	9	5	0	0	4	0	29	26	135
Cheshire	NW	9	4	3	0	2	0	26	28	118
Berkshire	NW	9	3	2	0	4	0	18	25	91
Cornwall	NW	9	3	3	0	3	0	19	20	87
Oxfordshire	NW	9	3	2	0	4	0	15	23	86
Herefordshire		9	2	1	0	6	0	25	23	80
Shropshire		9	2	3	0	4	0	22	19	73
Dorset		9	2	3	0	4	0	18	18	68
Wiltshire		9	1	4	0	4	0	14	12	42
Wales		9	0	4	0	5	0	24	18	42

Norfolk's record includes eight points for a drawn match in which the scores finished level.

NW signifies qualification for 1996 NatWest Trophy.

1995 CHAMPIONSHIP FINAL
DEVON v LINCOLNSHIRE

At Worcester on 10, 11 September.
Toss: Lincolnshire. Result: DEVON won by 57 runs (match reduced to 50 overs).

DEVON		
N.R.Gaywood	not out	138
J.G.Wyatt	c Fell b Bradford	50
*P.M.Roebuck	lbw b Towse	33
G.T.J.Townsend	not out	35
A.J.Pugh		
A.M.Small		
A.O.F.le Fleming		
K.Donohue		
†D.K.Boase		
M.C.Woodman		
A.W.Allin		
Extras (B3, LB2, NB2)		7
Total (2 wickets; 50 overs)		263

LINCOLNSHIRE		
D.B.Storer	lbw b Le Fleming	25
G.M.Evison	c Boase b Allin	7
D.E.Gillett	b Le Fleming	31
R.J.Evans	b Le Fleming	42
*M.A.Fell	b Allin	32
D.A.Christmas	b Roebuck	12
A.D.Towse	c Woodman b Roebuck	10
N.French	run out	2
S.N.Warman	not out	21
S.A.Bradford	not out	10
†G.B.Wilson		
Extras (B1, LB13)		14
Total (8 wickets; 50 overs)		206

LINCOLNSHIRE	O	M	R	W
French	7	2	35	0
Towse	16	2	75	1
Bradford	17	2	101	1
Christmas	4	0	26	0
Fell	6	0	21	0
DEVON				
Donohue	6	2	19	0
Woodman	10	1	42	0
Allin	9	1	45	2
Le Fleming	10	0	33	3
Roebuck	14	3	42	2
Gaywood	1	0	11	0

FALL OF WICKETS

Wkt	D	L
1st	133	15
2nd	177	58
3rd	–	79
4th	–	149
5th	–	162
6th	–	162
7th	–	164
8th	–	179
9th	–	–
10th	–	–

Umpires: P.Adams and T.G.Wilson.

MINOR COUNTIES CHAMPIONS

1895	Norfolk Durham Worcestershire	1928	Berkshire	1966	Lincolnshire
		1929	Oxfordshire	1967	Cheshire
		1930	Durham	1968	Yorkshire II
1896	Worcestershire	1931	Leicestershire II	1969	Buckinghamshire
1897	Worcestershire	1932	Buckinghamshire	1970	Bedfordshire
1898	Worcestershire	1933	*Undecided*	1971	Yorkshire II
1899	Northamptonshire Buckinghamshire	1934	Lancashire II	1972	Bedfordshire
		1935	Middlesex II	1973	Shropshire
1900	Glamorgan Durham Northamptonshire	1936	Hertfordshire	1974	Oxfordshire
		1937	Lancashire II	1975	Hertfordshire
		1938	Buckinghamshire	1976	Durham
1901	Durham	1939	Surrey II	1977	Suffolk
1902	Wiltshire	1946	Suffolk	1978	Devon
1903	Northamptonshire	1947	Yorkshire II	1979	Suffolk
1904	Northamptonshire	1948	Lancashire II	1980	Durham
1905	Norfolk	1949	Lancashire II	1981	Durham
1906	Staffordshire	1950	Surrey II	1982	Oxfordshire
1907	Lancashire II	1951	Kent II	1983	Hertfordshire
1908	Staffordshire	1952	Buckinghamshire	1984	Durham
1909	Wiltshire	1953	Berkshire	1985	Cheshire
1910	Norfolk	1954	Surrey II	1986	Cumberland
1911	Staffordshire	1955	Surrey II	1987	Buckinghamshire
1912	*In abeyance*	1956	Kent II	1988	Cheshire
1913	Norfolk	1957	Yorkshire II	1989	Oxfordshire
1920	Staffordshire	1958	Yorkshire II	1990	Hertfordshire
1921	Staffordshire	1959	Warwickshire II	1991	Staffordshire
1922	Buckinghamshire	1960	Lancashire II	1992	Staffordshire
1923	Buckinghamshire	1961	Somerset II	1993	Staffordshire
1924	Berkshire	1962	Warwickshire II	1994	Devon
1925	Buckinghamshire	1963	Cambridgeshire	1995	Devon
1926	Durham	1964	Lancashire II		
1927	Staffordshire	1965	Somerset II		

MINOR COUNTIES CHAMPIONSHIP RECORDS

Highest Total	621		Surrey II v Devon	The Oval	1928
Lowest Total	14		Cheshire v Staffs	Stoke	1909
Highest Score	282	E.Garnett	Berkshire v Wiltshire	Reading	1908
Most Runs – Season	1212	A.F.Brazier	Surrey II		1949
Record Partnership					
2nd 388*		T.H.Clark and A.F.Brazier	Surrey II v Sussex II	The Oval	1949
Best Bowling – Innings	10- 11	S.Turner	Cambs v Cumberland	Penrith	1987
– Match	18-100	N.W.Harding	Kent II v Wiltshire	Swindon	1937
Most Wickets – Season	119	S.F.Barnes	Staffordshire		1906

1995 MINOR COUNTIES CHAMPIONSHIP

LEADING BATTING AVERAGES

(Qualification: 8 completed innings (or 500 runs), average 45.00)

		I	*NO*	*HS*	*Runs*	*Avge*
N.A.Folland	Devon	16	6	151*	963	96.30
H.V.Patel	Herefordshire	16	1	135	1094	72.93
R.J.Evans	Lincolnshire	10	2	114*	534	66.75
K.Sharp	Shropshire	17	3	146*	925	66.07
D.B.Storer	Lincolnshire	14	2	150*	716	59.66
S.M.Brogan	Herefordshire	12	3	105	535	59.44
S.C.Goldsmith	Norfolk	17	3	156*	816	58.28
J.G.Wyatt	Devon	13	2	112*	641	58.27
A.Habib	Berkshire	16	2	146*	805	57.50
N.R.Gaywood	Devon	16	2	138*	801	57.21
J.P.J.Sylvester	Wales	16	2	138	793	56.64
D.W.Randall	Suffolk	13	0	118	727	55.92
S.V.Laudat	Oxfordshire	10	1	104*	492	54.66
A.C.H.Seymour	Cornwall	17	2	111	798	53.20
S.G.Plumb	Norfolk	18	5	109*	684	52.61
J.R.Wood	Berkshire	11	1	220*	507	50.70
J.J.E.Hardy	Dorset	12	2	86	493	49.30
G.T.J.Townsend	Devon	14	3	123	515	46.81
P.J.Caley	Suffolk	15	5	114*	465	46.50
M.P.Briers	Cornwall	13	3	111*	462	46.20
R.S.Jerome	Hertfordshire	14	5	73*	413	45.88
K.J.Parsons	Wiltshire	11	2	87	412	45.77
G.D.Reynolds	Dorset	16	1	106*	682	45.46

LEADING BOWLING AVERAGES

(Qualification: 20 wickets, average 28.00)

		O	*M*	*R*	*W*	*Avge*
C.C.Lovell	Cornwall	88.1	20	262	20	13.10
J.H.Shackleton	Dorset	155.2	53	401	26	15.42
L.Potter	Staffordshire	319	112	657	42	15.64
A.K.Golding	Suffolk	379	86	1150	66	17.42
P.J.Humphries	Staffordshire	103	17	355	20	17.75
P.M.Roebuck	Devon	339.1	111	724	38	19.05
P.G.Newman	Staffordshire	272.3	72	706	36	19.61
N.D.Peel	Cheshire	200.2	43	697	34	20.50
A.D.Greasley	Cheshire	137.4	38	434	21	20.66
R.A.Bunting	Norfolk	180.1	54	500	24	20.83
M.G.Scothern	Cumberland	140.1	30	459	22	20.86
R.A.Evans	Oxfordshire	257	60	732	34	21.52
I.J.Curtis	Oxfordshire	190.1	41	583	27	21.59
N.A.Foster	Norfolk	203	48	637	29	21.96
M.A.Sharp	Cumberland	157.1	47	490	22	22.27
A.J.Murphy	Cheshire	264.5	49	970	42	23.09
S.F.Stanway	Buckinghamshire	208.2	32	678	27	25.11
Z.A.Sher	Bedfordshire	172.5	27	705	28	25.17
A.Griffiths	Wales	145.2	23	563	22	25.59
R.G.Pitcher	Berkshire	269.3	55	843	32	26.34
M.G.Powell	Norfolk	211.5	49	668	25	26.72
K.Donohue	Devon	190	37	540	20	27.00
T.J.A.Scriven	Buckinghamshire	259.3	63	871	32	27.21
M.J.Bailey	Herefordshire	217.2	50	631	23	27.43
D.J.Angove	Cornwall	153.2	30	551	20	27.55

SECOND XI CHAMPIONSHIP 1995
FINAL TABLE

	P	W	L	D	Bonus Points Bat	Bonus Points Bowl	Total Points
1 HAMPSHIRE (13)	17	10	2	5	56	62	278
2 Northamptonshire (5)	17	9	3	5	66	62	272
3 Durham (7)	17	8	3	6	58	57	243
4 Kent (3)	17	8	4	5	52	59	239
5 Yorkshire (2)	17	7	1	9	55	53	220
6 Warwickshire (14)	17	7	2	8	54	50	216
7 Surrey (11)	17	5	5	7	56	52	188
8 Worcestershire (8)	17	5	7	5	46	56	182
9 Sussex (9)	17	5	5	7	46	46	172
10 Middlesex (10)	17	4	8	5	48	53	165
11 Nottinghamshire (18)	17	4	8	5	37	54	163
12 Leicestershire (4)	17	4	5	8	48	47	159
13 Lancashire (15)	17	4	10	3	37	53	154
14 Gloucestershire (6)	17	4	6	7	35	47	146
15 Somerset (1)	17	3	7	7	40	51	139
16 Derbyshire (16)	17	3	7	7	43	47	138
17 Essex (12)	17	3	6	8	38	51	137
18 Glamorgan (17)	17	3	7	7	38	49	135

Win = 16 points. 1994 final positions are shown in brackets.
Nottinghamshire's total includes 8 points from a match drawn with the scores level.

TCCB SECOND XI PLAYER OF THE SEASON:

A.R.Roberts (Northamptonshire) – 791 runs (av 43.94), 73 wickets (av 24.53).

SECOND XI CHAMPIONS

1959 Gloucestershire
1960 Northamptonshire
1961 Kent
1962 Worcestershire
1963 Worcestershire
1964 Lancashire
1965 Glamorgan
1966 Surrey
1967 Hampshire
1968 Surrey
1969 Kent
1970 Kent
1971 Hampshire
1972 Nottinghamshire
1973 Essex
1974 Middlesex
1975 Surrey
1976 Kent
1977 Yorkshire
1978 Sussex
1979 Warwickshire
1980 Glamorgan
1981 Hampshire
1982 Worcestershire
1983 Leicestershire
1984 Yorkshire
1985 Nottinghamshire
1986 Lancashire
1987 Kent/Yorkshire
1988 Surrey
1989 Middlesex
1990 Sussex
1991 Yorkshire
1992 Surrey
1993 Middlesex
1994 Somerset
1995 Hampshire

FIRST-CLASS CAREER RECORDS

Compiled by Philip Bailey

The following career records are for all players who appeared in first-class cricket during the 1995 season, and are complete to the end of that season. Some players who did not appear in 1995 but may do so in 1996 are also included.

BATTING AND FIELDING

'1000' denotes instances of scoring 1000 runs in a season. Where these have been achieved outside the UK, they are shown after a plus sign.

	M	*I*	*NO*	*HS*	*Runs*	*Avge*	*100*	*1000*	*Ct/St*
Adams, C.J.	120	192	16	216	5922	33.64	13	2	120
Adams, J.C.	106	175	32	174*	6200	43.35	14	–	101
Afford, J.A.	151	142	58	22*	351	4.17	–	–	50
Afzaal, U.	7	12	2	37	134	13.40	–	–	3
Aldred, P.	7	12	–	33	97	8.08	–	–	4
Alleyne, M.W.	182	299	30	256	8293	30.82	11	4	139/2
Ambrose, C.E.L.	173	129	53	78	2506	15.09	–	–	60
Andrew, S.J.W.	119	95	36	35	411	6.96	–	–	24
Angel, J.	45	59	19	84*	622	15.55	–	–	13
Anthony, H.A.G.	60	86	7	91	1373	17.37	–	–	22
Archer, G.F.	46	80	8	168	2732	37.94	6	1	44
Arthurton, K.L.T.	104	163	23	157*	6401	45.72	18	1	55
Asif Din	210	341	45	217	9058	30.60	9	2	114
Atherton, M.A.	198	343	32	199	13722	44.12	38	6	167
Athey, C.W.J.	437	730	69	184	23680	35.82	51	12	405/2
Atkins, C.S.	1	2	1	8*	13	13.00	–	–	–
Attfield, J.M.	6	8	2	23*	76	12.66	–	–	2
Austin, I.D.	77	107	22	115*	2078	24.44	2	–	15
Aymes, A.N.	108	157	40	107*	3528	30.15	1	–	244/21
Bailey, R.J.	288	485	73	224*	17299	41.98	38	12	214
Bainbridge, P.	313	520	72	169	15090	33.68	24	9	139
Bairstow, A.D.	3	6	–	26	73	12.16	–	–	7/1
Ball, M.C.J.	72	110	21	71	1408	15.82	–	–	83
Banton, C.	7	14	4	80*	292	29.20	–	–	4
Barnett, K.J.	381	612	57	239*	21816	39.30	46	12	234
Bartle, S.	1	1	–	32	32	32.00	–	–	1
Barwick, S.R.	205	196	73	30	839	6.82	–	–	44
Base, S.J.	132	169	35	58	1525	11.38	–	–	60
Bates, R.T.	11	16	4	33*	135	11.25	–	–	4
Batty, J.D.	68	73	21	51	828	15.92	–	–	28
Batty, J.N.	2	3	1	31*	40	20.00	–	–	2
Battye, R.A.	8	14	2	70*	391	32.58	–	–	3
Bell, M.A.V.	17	21	10	22*	79	7.18	–	–	7
Benjamin, J.E.	92	105	28	49	802	10.41	–	–	22
Benjamin, K.C.G.	74	86	25	52*	773	12.67	–	–	11
Benjamin, W.K.M.	169	209	36	101*	3845	22.22	1	–	92
Benson, M.R.	292	491	34	257	18387	40.23	48	11	140
Betts, M.M.	10	17	6	14	59	5.36	–	–	2
Bevan, M.G.	88	150	23	203*	6486	51.07	22	1+1	52
Bicknell, D.J.	174	306	31	235*	11133	40.48	26	6	65
Bicknell, M.P.	150	177	48	88	2341	18.14	–	–	53
Birbeck, S.D.	5	7	2	75*	112	22.40	–	–	2

	M	I	NO	HS	Runs	Avge	100	1000	Ct/St
Bird, P.J.	2	3	1	7	12	6.00	–	–	–
Birks, M.J.	2	3	2	23*	43	43.00	–	–	2
Bishop, I.R.	111	145	35	103*	1644	14.94	1	–	31
Blakey, R.J.	219	356	53	221	9805	32.35	9	5	420/38
Blenkiron, D.A.	10	17	1	145	446	27.87	1	–	3
Boden, D.J.P.	6	4	–	5	12	3.00	–	–	4
Boiling, J.	63	88	30	69	747	12.87	–	–	49
Boon, T.J.	248	419	42	144	11821	31.35	14	7	124
Bovill, J.N.B.	15	21	12	31	128	14.22	–	–	2
Bowen, M.N.	13	14	4	23*	116	11.60	–	–	3
Bowler, P.D.	177	308	28	241*	11544	41.22	26	7	115/1
Briers, N.E.	381	628	61	201*	18726	33.02	31	11	152
Brimson, M.T.	14	15	6	25	85	9.44	–	–	1
Brinkley, J.E.	14	16	4	29	89	7.41	–	–	5
Broadhurst, M.	5	3	–	6	7	2.33	–	–	–
Brown, A.D.	63	103	10	187	4225	45.43	11	3	60
Brown, D.R.	22	31	6	85	711	28.44	–	–	9
Brown, K.R.	193	288	55	200*	8393	36.02	12	12	318/24
Brown, S.J.E.	88	117	40	69	965	12.53	–	–	29
Browne, C.O.	43	65	15	102*	1540	30.80	2	–	141/16
Burns, M.	12	19	1	78	295	16.38	–	–	25/3
Butcher, G.P.	5	7	2	41	64	12.80	–	–	2
Butcher, M.A.	38	66	7	167	2093	35.47	3	1	40
Byas, D.	159	269	25	213	8799	36.06	15	4	188
Caddick, A.R.	64	81	13	92	1156	17.00	–	–	22
Cairns, C.L.	107	158	17	115	4813	34.13	5	1	47
Cake, R.Q.	28	51	10	108	1630	39.75	3	–	13
Campbell, S.L.	37	61	3	172	2417	41.67	8	1	40
Capel, D.J.	291	440	64	175	11248	29.91	15	3	142
Carr, J.D.	195	303	50	261*	10112	39.96	24	5	232
Carroll, J.P.	30	51	5	92	782	17.00	–	–	8
Cassar, M.E.	3	4	–	66	134	33.50	–	–	2
Chanderpaul, S.	42	67	17	140*	2540	50.80	6	1	32
Chapman, C.A.	4	7	1	20	72	12.00	–	–	5/2
Chapman, R.J.	12	15	3	25	114	9.50	–	–	2
Chapple, G.	44	63	26	109*	777	21.00	1	–	18
Childs, J.H.	375	354	170	43	1689	9.17	–	–	115
Church, M.J.	8	14	1	38	191	14.69	–	–	4
Churton, D.R.H.	6	10	–	39	118	11.80	–	–	7/3
Clarke, L.P.	2	3	–	14	17	5.66	–	–	1
Clarke, V.P.	6	11	1	38	101	10.10	–	–	1
Connor, C.A.	202	189	48	59	1640	11.63	–	–	61
Cooper, K.E.	304	329	83	52	2479	10.07	–	–	93
Cork, D.G.	101	149	19	104	2938	22.60	1	–	64
Cottam, A.C.	11	14	1	36	138	10.61	–	–	1
Cottey, P.A.	146	238	36	191	7524	37.24	15	5	90
Cousins, D.M.	14	23	5	18*	145	8.05	–	–	5
Cowan, A.P.	2	4	1	22	47	15.66	–	–	1
Cowans, N.G.	239	248	68	66	1605	8.91	–	–	63
Cowdrey, G.R.	159	252	29	147	7887	35.36	15	3	85
Cox, D.M.	6	9	1	26*	55	6.87	–	–	1
Crawley, J.P.	107	179	17	286	7890	48.70	14	4	90
Croft, R.D.B.	138	201	41	143	4090	25.56	2	–	59
Cronje, W.J.	101	180	16	251	6931	42.26	20	1+1	70
Crowe, M.D.	1	2	–	9	10	5.00	–	–	1
Cullinan, D.J.	120	214	32	337*	7404	40.68	17	1	106

	M	I	NO	HS	Runs	Avge	100	1000	Ct/St
Cummins, A.C.	62	87	10	107	1593	20.68	1	–	14
Cunliffe, R.J.	14	21	4	190*	766	45.05	2	–	10
Curran, K.M.	267	413	67	144*	12448	35.97	21	5	157
Curtis, T.S.	308	525	64	248	19131	41.49	37	11	170
Dakin, J.M.	11	17	2	101*	360	24.00	1	–	6
Dale, A.	111	186	18	214*	5551	33.04	11	2	46
Daley, J.A.	32	56	5	159*	1701	33.35	1	–	17
Dalton, A.J.	11	20	3	51*	389	22.88	–	–	9
Davies, A.P.	1	–	–	–	–	–	–	–	–
Davies, M.	45	64	22	54	632	15.04	–	–	19
Davis, R.P.	145	174	44	67	2009	15.45	–	–	128
Dawood, I.	1	1	1	2*	2	–	–	–	–
Dawson, R.I.	40	71	6	127*	1905	29.30	2	1	24
DeFreitas, P.A.J.	235	330	34	113	6490	21.92	6	–	78
De la Pena, J.M.	6	7	5	7*	10	5.00	–	–	–
Derbyshire, N.A.	4	5	1	17	52	13.00	–	–	–
De Silva, P.A.	148	227	21	267	10007	48.57	27	1+1	79
Dessaur, W.A.	22	38	3	148	1121	32.02	3	–	6
Dhanraj, R.	58	73	28	47	354	7.86	–	–	18
Dibden, R.R.	4	7	2	0*	0	0.00	–	–	–
Dimond, M.	4	4	1	26	67	22.33	–	–	4
D'Oliveira, D.B.	234	366	22	237	9504	27.62	10	4	205
Donald, A.A.	212	242	95	46*	1744	11.86	–	–	84
Dowman, M.P.	12	23	2	107	659	31.38	2	–	7
Drakes, V.C.	26	38	8	180*	880	29.33	2	–	6
Dutch, K.P.	2	–	–	–	–	–	–	–	4
Ealham, M.A.	71	114	14	121	2879	28.79	1	–	25
Ecclestone, S.C.	20	31	6	81	806	32.24	–	–	4
Edwards, A.D.	2	3	–	22	38	12.66	–	–	2
Elliott, M.T.G.	28	55	4	175*	2205	43.23	5	0+1	29
Ellis, S.W.K.	1	1	–	0	0	0.00	–	–	1
Elworthy, S.	51	84	16	75	1379	20.27	–	–	18
Emburey, J.E.	499	628	126	133	11782	23.47	7	–	452
Emery, P.A.	79	112	33	92	2039	25.81	–	–	237/23
Evans, K.P.	122	171	40	104	3379	25.79	3	–	99
Fairbrother, N.H.	275	439	66	366	15227	40.82	33	9	191
Farbrace, P.	40	50	11	79	711	18.23	–	–	89/12
Fay, R.A.	1	1	1	1*	1	–	–	–	–
Feltham, M.A.	157	192	47	101	3185	21.96	1	–	67
Field-Buss, M.G.	38	43	14	34*	311	10.72	–	–	13
Fleming, M.V.	113	183	21	116	5044	31.13	6	–	46
Flint, D.P.J.	15	16	7	17*	72	8.00	–	–	8
Flintoff, A.	1	2	–	7	7	3.50	–	–	2
Follett, D.	1	2	1	4*	5	5.00	–	–	1
Fordham, A.	148	262	19	206*	9764	40.18	24	5	99
Foster, M.J.	5	7	1	63*	165	27.50	–	–	6
Fraser, A.R.C.	178	200	49	92	1657	10.97	–	–	34
Freedman, D.A.	26	29	8	50	259	12.33	–	–	10
Freeth, J.W.D.	7	6	1	18	35	7.00	–	–	2
French, B.N.	360	471	92	123	7160	18.89	2	–	817/100
Fulton, D.P.	26	47	2	116	1300	28.88	2	–	42
Gallian, J.E.R.	56	98	7	171	3510	38.57	7	1	35
Garnham, M.A.	207	282	55	123	6240	27.48	5	–	429/41
Gatting, M.W.	499	778	118	258	33456	50.69	89	17+1	441
George, S.P.	43	50	10	62	374	9.35	–	–	14
Gibson, O.D.	68	98	14	101*	1811	21.55	1	–	23

	M	I	NO	HS	Runs	Avge	100	1000	Ct/St
Giddins, E.S.H.	63	77	31	34	261	5.67	–	–	12
Gie, N.A.	3	6	–	34	98	16.33	–	–	–
Gilchrist, A.C.	29	44	7	126	1210	32.70	3	–	99/5
Giles, A.F.	8	9	1	32	137	17.12	–	–	–
Gooch, G.A.	553	941	73	333	42528	48.99	120	19+1	525
Gough, D.	95	125	26	72	1674	16.90	–	–	24
Grayson, A.P.	52	80	10	100	1958	27.97	1	1	36
Green, R.J.	1	1	–	1	1	1.00	–	–	–
Greenfield, K.	53	88	11	127*	2262	29.37	5	–	43
Griffith, F.A.	42	63	9	81	1087	20.12	–	–	28
Griffiths, S.P.	5	9	–	20	75	8.33	–	–	14
Gupte, C.M.	42	66	9	122	1728	30.31	3	–	14
Habib, A.	4	7	3	174*	249	62.25	1	–	–
Hall, J.W.	90	162	10	140*	4667	30.70	6	2	41
Hallett, J.C.	18	19	4	111*	349	23.26	1	–	7
Hamilton, G.M.	8	9	2	48	129	18.42	–	–	4
Hancock, T.H.C.	60	107	7	123	2452	24.52	2	–	37
Harden, R.J.	210	343	55	187	11525	40.01	25	7	158
Harris, A.J.	6	9	3	14*	58	9.66	–	–	–
Harrison, J.C.	3	5	1	46*	99	24.75	–	–	2
Harrison, T.W.	5	10	1	61*	102	11.33	–	–	3
Harrity, M.A.	14	13	6	18	25	3.57	–	–	7
Hartley, P.J.	172	207	49	127*	3278	20.74	2	–	53
Harvey, M.E.	3	4	–	23	67	16.75	–	–	1
Haste, N.J.	26	31	7	36	271	11.29	–	–	8
Hayden, M.L.	67	123	14	201*	6219	57.05	19	1+3	59
Hayhurst, A.N.	155	250	33	172*	7595	35.00	14	3	51
Haynes, G.R.	62	95	6	158	2630	29.55	3	1	31
Headley, D.W.	67	86	22	91	1140	17.81	–	–	31
Hegg, W.K.	185	271	51	130	5451	24.77	3	–	432/56
Hemmings, E.E.	518	683	169	127*	9533	18.54	1	–	212
Hemp, D.L.	67	118	10	157	3458	32.01	5	1	45
Herzberg, S.	14	18	5	57*	187	14.38	–	–	4
Hibbert, A.J.E.	1	2	–	24	31	15.50	–	–	–
Hick, G.A.	300	492	50	405*	25194	57.00	84	11+1	369
Hindson, J.E.	24	32	5	53*	330	12.22	–	–	12
Hodgson, G.D.	103	179	10	166	5675	33.57	9	4	45
Hollioake, A.J.	40	64	5	138	2173	36.83	5	1	28
Holloway, P.C.L.	30	49	13	129*	1481	41.13	3	–	35/1
Hooper, C.L.	190	297	30	236*	11921	44.64	30	5	204
How, E.J.	4	4	2	0*	0	0.00	–	–	1
Hughes, E.R.	2	1	–	0	0	0.00	–	–	–
Hughes, J.G.	16	22	1	17	101	4.80	–	–	4
Humphries, S.	1	–	–	–	–	–	–	–	2
Hussain, N.	160	248	32	197	9687	44.84	26	3	208
Hutton, S.	44	79	3	101	2171	28.56	1	–	27
Igglesden, A.P.	145	158	59	41	862	8.70	–	–	37
Illingworth, R.K.	297	333	93	120*	5101	21.25	3	–	127
Ilott, M.C.	100	119	29	60	1235	13.72	–	–	27
Innes, K.J.	1	2	–	0	0	0.00	–	–	–
Irani, R.C.	45	74	9	119	2273	34.96	3	1	18
James, K.D.	182	269	45	162	6831	30.49	8	2	59
James, S.P.	129	226	20	230*	6924	33.61	17	3	101
Janisch, A.N.	7	8	4	18*	38	9.50	–	–	2
Jarrett, M.E.D.	24	37	7	51	520	17.33	–	–	13/1
Jarvis, P.W.	182	223	60	80	2651	16.26	–	–	51

	M	I	NO	HS	Runs	Avge	100	1000	Ct/St
Johnson, P.	265	439	41	187	14732	37.01	32	8	166/1
Johnson, R.L.	27	33	6	50*	442	16.37	–	–	16
Jones, D.M.	190	316	35	324*	14837	52.80	43	2+5	145
Kasprowicz, M.S.	56	76	11	49	934	14.36	–	–	20
Keech, M.	27	47	4	58*	825	19.18	–	–	17
Keedy, G.	15	18	12	15*	74	12.33	–	–	2
Kellett, S.A.	87	149	10	125*	4234	30.46	2	2	77
Kendall, W.S.	20	26	5	113*	710	33.80	1	–	13
Kendrick, N.M.	71	95	24	59	1171	16.49	–	–	53
Kenlock, S.G.	6	8	2	12	50	8.33	–	–	4
Kennis, G.J.	2	4	–	29	88	22.00	–	–	2
Kerr, J.I.D.	21	32	5	80	421	15.59	–	–	9
Kersey, G.J.	38	62	10	83	1176	22.61	–	–	124/11
Kettleborough, R.A.	2	4	1	55	108	36.00	–	–	–
Khan, A.A.	4	–	–	–	–	–	–	–	1
Khan, W.G.	13	23	6	181	847	49.82	1	–	17
Killeen, N.	7	13	3	48	137	13.70	–	–	4
Kirtley, R.J.	2	2	2	2*	3	–	–	–	2
Knight, N.V.	65	109	13	174	3669	38.21	8	–	96
Knott, J.A.	1	–	–	–	–	–	–	–	1
Krikken, K.M.	113	165	35	85*	2617	20.13	–	–	265/20
Kumble, A.	77	96	21	154*	1964	26.18	3	–	41
Lamb, A.J.	467	772	108	294	32502	48.94	89	13	371
Lampitt, S.R.	141	178	36	122	3249	22.88	1	–	85
Laney, J.S.	9	17	1	73	470	29.37	–	–	7
Langer, J.L.	49	83	7	241*	3821	50.27	9	0+1	39
Lara, B.C.	105	169	6	501*	9171	56.26	26	2+1	129
Larkins, W.	482	842	54	252	27142	34.44	59	13	306
Lathwell, M.N.	84	152	4	206	5058	34.17	9	4	61
Law, D.R.	11	15	–	115	259	17.26	1	–	6
Law, S.G.	82	140	14	179	5313	42.16	14	0+1	69
Lawrence, J.R.G.	1	2	1	7*	7	7.00	–	–	–
Leatherdale, D.A.	96	148	14	157	4290	32.01	5	–	88
Lee, S.	16	26	4	104*	667	30.31	2	–	12
Lefebvre, R.P.	77	89	16	100	1494	20.46	1	–	36
Lenham, N.J.	169	292	26	222*	8942	33.61	18	3	68
Lewis, C.C.	134	200	25	247	5411	30.92	7	–	106
Lewis, J.	3	3	–	3	3	1.00	–	–	–
Lewis, J.J.B.	52	90	12	136*	2721	34.88	4	–	38
Lewry, J.D.	16	25	8	34	164	9.64	–	–	2
Ligertwood, D.C.G.	16	28	2	40	366	14.07	–	–	40/4
Llong, N.J.	44	58	8	118	1973	32.88	4	–	36
Lloyd, G.D.	113	186	21	132	5981	36.24	11	2	71
Longley, J.I.	33	60	3	110	1375	24.12	2	–	18
Love, M.L.	30	55	3	187	2229	42.05	7	0+1	30
Loye, M.B.	60	93	10	153*	2647	31.89	5	–	41
Lugsden, S.	6	6	3	5*	7	2.33	–	–	–
Lynch, M.A.	336	547	62	172*	17307	35.68	39	9	348
McCague, M.J.	77	103	23	59	1144	14.30	–	–	45
McGrath, A.	5	10	–	84	280	28.00	–	–	3
McGrath, G.D.	32	31	10	9	50	2.38	–	–	2
McIntyre, P.E.	50	56	15	32	323	7.87	–	–	20
McMillan, B.M.	102	161	25	140	5279	38.81	9	–	103
Macmillan, G.I.	36	57	7	122	1548	30.96	3	–	48
MacRobert, A.D.	9	9	2	29	80	11.42	–	–	3
Maddy, D.L.	12	23	1	131	344	15.63	1	–	17

	M	I	NO	HS	Runs	Avge	100	1000	Ct/St
Malcolm, D.E.	190	224	66	51	1251	7.91	–	–	30
Malik, H.S.	23	31	5	64*	508	19.53	–	–	17
Mallender, N.A.	342	393	122	100*	4678	17.26	1	–	110
Marc, K.	2	2	–	9	17	8.50	–	–	–
Marsh, S.A.	227	328	56	125	7697	28.29	7	–	529/42
Martin, N.F.C.	12	12	1	26	84	7.63	–	–	5
Martin, P.J.	97	111	29	133	1723	21.01	1	–	28
Martin-Jenkins, R.S.C.	2	2	1	50	50	50.00	–	–	–
Maru, R.J.	212	208	51	74	2568	16.35	–	–	229
Mason, T.J.	2	1	–	3	3	3.00	–	–	3
Mather, D.P.	8	6	3	8*	19	6.33	–	–	2
Matthews, G.R.J.	165	243	44	184	7921	39.80	12	–	130
Maynard, M.P.	248	410	40	243	15521	41.94	34	9	230/5
Metcalfe, A.A.	194	333	20	216*	10892	34.79	25	6	74
Metson, C.P.	221	288	67	96	3990	18.05	–	–	538/48
Middleton, T.C.	109	187	16	221	5753	33.64	13	2	79
Mike, G.W.	40	61	11	66*	994	19.88	–	–	11
Milburn, S.M.	6	8	2	7	22	3.66	–	–	–
Millns, D.J.	106	126	47	70	1389	17.58	–	–	56
Mirza, P.	9	15	3	40	86	7.16	–	–	6
Moles, A.J.	205	369	37	230*	13767	41.46	26	6	129
Montgomerie, R.R.	60	102	10	192	2993	32.53	5	1	56
Moody, T.M.	204	339	26	272	14647	46.79	43	4+1	200
Moores, P.	192	279	33	116	5942	24.15	4	–	414/42
Morris, A.C.	1	2	1	1	1	1.00	–	–	1
Morris, H.	278	482	46	166*	16780	38.48	43	8	169
Morris, J.E.	279	466	29	229	17301	39.59	42	10	118
Morris, R.S.M.	32	58	4	174	1635	30.27	2	–	38
Moxon, M.D.	289	495	44	274*	19446	43.11	41	11	209
Mullally, A.D.	107	124	31	34	710	7.63	–	–	23
Munton, T.A.	191	191	76	47	1162	10.10	–	–	66
Murray, J.R.	76	119	17	141*	2808	27.52	4	–	179/12
Mushtaq Ahmed	118	148	19	90	1809	14.02	–	–	63
Nash, D.J.	56	81	17	67	1163	18.17	–	–	28
Newell, K.	10	19	2	135	500	29.41	1	–	3
Newell, M.	102	178	26	203*	4636	30.50	6	1	93/1
Newport, P.J.	251	293	87	98	5202	25.25	–	–	71
Nicholas, M.C.J.	377	620	89	206*	18262	34.39	36	10	215
Nixon, P.A.	104	152	34	131	3149	26.68	5	1	268/21
Noon, W.M.	49	81	14	75	1549	23.11	–	–	99/13
North, J.A.	23	31	6	114	513	20.52	1	–	4
Nowell, R.W.	11	20	2	27	134	7.44	–	–	5
O'Gorman, T.J.G.	106	177	21	148	4736	30.35	9	2	69
Ormond, J.	1	–	–	–	–	–	–	–	1
Ostler, D.P.	111	186	16	208	6271	36.88	9	4	110
Owen, J.E.H.	4	8	–	65	200	25.00	–	–	–
Parker, B.	15	28	3	127	776	31.04	1	–	10
Parkin, O.T.	2	2	2	2*	2	–	–	–	–
Parsons, G.J.	313	418	93	76	6330	19.47	–	–	123
Parsons, K.A.	25	44	4	105	994	24.85	1	–	18
Patel, M.M.	61	89	20	56	915	13.26	–	–	33
Patterson, M.W.	3	5	–	46	125	25.00	–	–	2
Pearson, R.M.	36	41	7	33*	332	9.76	–	–	11
Peirce, M.T.E.	7	12	–	60	243	20.25	–	–	5
Penberthy, A.L.	70	103	15	101*	1876	21.31	1	–	41
Pennett, D.B.	28	27	11	50	169	10.56	–	–	6

	M	I	NO	HS	Runs	Avge	100	1000	Ct/St
Penney, T.L.	79	122	25	151	4189	43.18	10	1	42
Phillips, N.C.	8	12	2	53	220	22.00	–	–	4
Pick, R.A.	184	195	54	65*	2161	15.32	–	–	49
Pierson, A.R.K.	110	139	50	58	1391	15.62	–	–	48
Pigott, A.C.S.	260	317	66	104*	4841	19.28	1	–	121
Pike, V.J.	14	20	7	27	156	12.00	–	–	5
Piper, K.J.	112	151	23	116*	2553	19.94	2	–	307/17
Pollard, P.R.	129	225	13	180	6930	32.68	12	3	125
Ponting, R.T.	38	65	5	211	2998	49.96	10	0+1	31
Pooley, J.C.	40	67	6	136	2129	34.90	5	1	37
Prabhakar, M.	142	198	33	229*	6876	41.67	18	–	61
Prichard, P.J.	244	396	44	245	12626	35.86	25	7	156
Rackemann, C.G.	163	184	72	33	860	7.67	–	–	40
Radford, N.V.	296	298	73	76*	3537	15.72	–	–	130
Radford, T.A.	7	12	4	69	248	31.00	–	–	8
Ragnauth, R.T.	8	16	1	82	335	22.33	–	–	10
Ramprakash, M.R.	183	295	41	235	11519	45.35	29	6	103
Ratcliffe, J.D.	87	161	8	127*	4413	28.84	3	–	50
Ratledge, J.	17	32	–	79	585	18.28	–	–	5
Reeve, D.A.	236	314	76	202*	8190	34.41	6	2	193
Remy, C.C.	21	29	3	60	480	18.46	–	–	7
Renshaw, S.J.	1	1	–	0	0	0.00	–	–	–
Rhodes, S.J.	290	396	115	122*	9246	32.90	8	1	733/96
Richardson, A.	1	1	–	4	4	4.00	–	–	–
Richardson, R.B.	215	356	29	194	13857	42.37	37	1+2	198
Ricketts, J.D.	10	11	1	63	148	14.80	–	–	3
Ridley, A.C.	13	20	2	71	440	24.44	–	–	4
Ripley, D.	219	283	74	134*	5029	24.06	6	–	473/67
Roberts, A.R.	55	75	18	62	1032	18.10	–	–	22
Roberts, K.J.	6	11	–	53	244	22.18	–	–	1
Robinson, D.D.J.	20	37	–	123	862	23.29	2	–	28
Robinson, M.A.	155	161	68	23	312	3.35	–	–	31
Robinson, P.E.	159	261	35	189	7617	33.70	7	3	130
Robinson, R.T.	367	637	76	220*	24365	43.43	58	13	226
Rollins, A.S.	40	75	7	200*	2195	32.27	2	1	39/1
Rollins, R.J.	24	42	4	133*	851	22.39	1	–	59/12
Rose, G.D.	171	237	40	138	5910	30.00	6	1	92
Roseberry, M.A.	175	294	34	185	9362	36.00	18	4	135
Russell, R.C.	318	462	102	128*	10446	29.01	4	–	751/96
Salisbury, I.D.K.	142	181	45	74	2462	18.10	–	–	111
Sargeant, N.F.	52	67	11	49	786	14.03	–	–	120/16
Saxelby, M.	60	104	7	181	2893	29.82	2	1	18
Scott, C.W.	122	166	30	108	3020	22.20	2	–	263/17
Searle, J.P.	2	4	3	5*	7	7.00	–	–	–
Shadford, D.J.	2	2	1	1	1	1.00	–	–	–
Shahid, N.	80	124	18	139	3462	32.66	4	1	79
Shaw, A.D.	5	7	2	14	38	7.60	–	–	9/2
Sheeraz, K.P.	10	13	6	3	9	1.28	–	–	4
Sheriyar, A.	12	15	3	19	87	7.25	–	–	3
Shine, K.J.	69	56	26	26*	303	10.10	–	–	11
Silverwood, C.E.W.	17	25	5	50	233	11.65	–	–	4
Simmons, P.V.	134	235	9	261	7876	34.84	15	1	141
Singh, A.	1	2	–	7	12	6.00	–	–	1
Slater, M.J.	67	116	8	176	5283	48.91	14	1+3	33
Small, G.C.	305	391	91	70	4341	14.47	–	–	92
Smith, A.M.	56	63	12	51*	515	10.09	–	–	9

	M	I	NO	HS	Runs	Avge	100	1000	Ct/St
Smith, A.W.	37	57	7	202*	1356	27.12	1	–	12
Smith, B.F.	75	117	17	112	2827	28.27	2	–	33
Smith, N.M.K.	96	133	18	161	2816	24.48	1	–	26
Smith, P.A.	219	349	42	140	8150	26.54	4	2	59
Smith, R.A.	291	498	75	209*	18930	44.75	48	9	177
Snape, J.N.	18	24	5	87	556	29.26	–	–	22
Solanki, V.S.	6	9	1	36	150	18.75	–	–	8
Speak, N.J.	110	191	17	232	6788	39.01	11	3	72
Speight, M.P.	112	185	13	184	6300	36.62	12	3	91
Spencer, D.J.	14	16	2	75	200	14.28	–	–	9
Spiring, K.R.	2	4	–	56	112	28.00	–	–	3
Srinath, J.	63	84	18	60	1110	16.32	–	–	27
Stanford, E.J.	2	2	1	4	4	4.00	–	–	1
Stanley, D.E.	7	12	2	48	101	10.10	–	–	2
Stemp, R.D.	84	99	28	37	863	12.15	–	–	36
Stephenson, F.D.	207	324	34	165	8073	27.83	10	1	91
Stephenson, J.P.	205	354	36	202*	11122	34.97	19	5	122
Stewart, A.J.	284	471	55	206*	16462	39.57	33	8	367/13
Streak, H.H.	43	61	10	98	921	18.05	–	–	18
Stuart, A.M.	3	3	2	14*	29	29.00	–	–	–
Such, P.M.	199	196	59	54	967	7.05	–	–	81
Sutcliffe, I.J.	19	28	5	163*	865	37.60	1	–	11
Symonds, A.	23	39	6	254*	1762	53.39	6	1	10
Taylor, C.W.	33	25	9	28*	175	10.93	–	–	6
Taylor, J.P.	99	101	43	86	739	12.74	–	–	35
Taylor, M.A.	181	311	14	219	13020	43.83	32	1+5	249
Taylor, N.R.	303	515	68	204	17771	39.75	42	10	151
Terry, V.P.	285	481	43	190	16048	36.63	38	11	320
Thomas, P.A.	14	15	4	25	57	5.18	–	–	1
Thomas, S.D.	23	32	12	78*	417	20.85	–	–	7
Thompson, D.J.	1	2	–	22	39	19.50	–	–	–
Thompson, J.B.D.	4	8	3	40*	86	17.20	–	–	1
Thorpe, G.P.	167	282	36	216	10393	42.24	18	6	121
Thursfield, M.J.	17	19	3	47	188	11.75	–	–	1
Titchard, S.P.	56	99	6	135	2826	30.38	2	–	39
Tolley, C.M.	63	74	21	84	1105	20.84	–	–	27
Townsend, C.J.	22	21	9	27	141	11.75	–	–	34/5
Trescothick, M.E.	26	48	1	151	1355	28.82	3	–	31
Trimby, P.W.	13	9	4	11	31	6.20	–	–	7
Trump, H.R.J.	104	119	40	48	991	12.54	–	–	73
Tudor, A.J.	5	9	–	56	123	13.66	–	–	1
Tufnell, P.C.R.	178	178	74	37	985	9.47	–	–	76
Turner, R.J.	84	131	27	106*	2694	25.90	3	–	157/31
Tweats, T.A.	9	17	1	78*	332	20.75	–	–	8
Twose, R.G.	129	216	28	277*	7450	39.62	15	3	67
Udal, S.D.	88	126	22	94	2214	21.28	–	–	43
Van Troost, A.P.	54	62	21	35	353	8.60	–	–	9
Vaughan, M.P.	42	79	2	117	2478	32.18	3	2	21
Walker, A.	112	114	50	41*	800	12.50	–	–	43
Walker, L.N.P.	2	4	–	24	43	10.75	–	–	2/1
Walker, M.J.	15	23	2	107	440	20.95	1	–	10
Walsh, C.A.	320	400	90	66	3837	12.37	–	–	82
Walton, T.C.	6	9	1	71	120	15.00	–	–	2
Ward, D.M.	153	240	33	294*	7997	38.63	16	2	118/3
Ward, T.R.	150	257	16	235*	8971	37.22	20	4	138
Warner, A.E.	199	272	52	95*	3763	17.10	–	–	46

	M	I	NO	HS	Runs	Avge	100	1000	Ct/St
Warren, R.J.	35	57	9	154	1563	32.56	1	–	44/1
Wasim Akram	179	244	29	123	4679	21.76	4	–	56
Watkin, S.L.	174	194	63	41	1235	9.42	–	–	42
Watkinson, M.	255	379	45	161	8984	26.89	9	1	125
Waugh, M.E.	224	356	46	229*	17260	55.67	57	5+4	262
Weekes, P.N.	69	98	13	143	2768	32.56	3	–	55
Welch, G.	14	19	3	84*	456	28.50	–	–	6
Wells, A.P.	302	502	75	253*	17302	40.51	41	9	191
Wells, C.M.	306	491	75	203	13680	32.88	23	6	107
Wells, V.J.	76	123	14	167	3135	28.76	2	–	45
Weston, R.M.S.	3	6	–	9	15	2.50	–	–	5
Weston, W.P.C.	68	114	10	113	3443	33.10	5	1	31
Wharf, A.G.	1	2	–	46	46	23.00	–	–	–
Whitaker, J.J.	276	442	46	200*	14941	37.72	30	9	163
Whitaker, P.R.	15	24	–	119	758	31.58	1	–	3
White, C.	87	133	23	146	3616	32.87	5	–	52
White, G.W.	27	45	3	104	1063	25.30	1	–	27
Whittall, A.R.	27	33	6	91*	458	16.96	–	–	11
Whitticase, P.	132	174	40	114*	3113	23.23	1	–	309/14
Wileman, J.R.	11	21	6	109	447	29.80	1	–	9
Williams, B.A.	8	12	4	32*	130	16.25	–	–	1
Williams, J.R.A.	1	2	–	6	6	3.00	–	–	–
Williams, N.F.	230	265	53	77	3999	18.86	–	–	60
Williams, R.C.	26	41	6	44	453	12.94	–	–	6
Williams, R.C.J.	30	36	8	90	507	18.10	–	–	82/13
Williams, S.C.	55	93	5	157	2898	32.93	7	–	37
Willis, S.C.	4	5	1	82	153	38.25	–	–	12
Windows, M.G.N.	23	43	2	106	1252	30.53	1	–	24
Windsor, J.M.	2	3	1	14	28	14.00	–	–	–
Wood, J.	36	52	9	63*	610	14.18	–	–	6
Wren, T.N.	22	28	10	23	115	6.38	–	–	9
Wright, A.J.	254	445	35	193	12264	29.91	17	6	191
Wylie, A.	3	5	1	7	14	3.50	–	–	–
Yates, G.	52	69	30	134*	1281	32.84	3	–	17
Yeabsley, M.I.	2	4	–	2	2	0.50	–	–	–
Yeabsley, R.S.	19	20	5	52*	204	13.60	–	–	11
Young, S.	48	78	12	152*	2620	39.69	4	–	34

BOWLING

'50wS' denotes instances of taking 50 or more wickets in a season. Where these have been achieved outside the UK, they are shown after a plus sign.

	Runs	Wkts	Avge	Best	5wI	10wM	50wS
Adams, C.J.	1028	18	57.11	4- 29	–	–	–
Adams, J.C.	1902	50	38.04	4- 43	–	–	–
Afford, J.A.	13926	414	33.63	6- 68	14	2	4
Afzaal, U.	582	5	116.40	2- 41	–	–	–
Aldred, P.	375	15	25.00	3- 47	–	–	–
Alleyne, M.W.	5543	158	35.08	5- 78	1	–	–
Ambrose, C.E.L.	14393	694	20.73	8- 45	34	7	5+1
Andrew, S.J.W.	9815	298	32.93	7- 47	7	–	–
Angel, J.	4934	191	25.83	6- 71	8	1	0+1
Anthony, H.A.G.	5211	181	28.79	6- 22	5	–	–
Archer, G.F.	333	6	55.50	3- 50	–	–	–
Arthurton, K.L.T.	777	22	35.31	3- 14	–	–	–

	Runs	Wkts	Avge	Best	5wI	10wM	50wS
Asif Din	4393	79	55.60	5- 61	2	–	–
Atherton, M.A.	4691	107	43.84	6- 78	3	–	–
Athey, C.W.J.	2652	48	55.25	3- 3	–	–	–
Atkins, C.S.	46	1	46.00	1- 46	–	–	–
Attfield, J.M.	310	3	103.33	2- 76	–	–	–
Austin, I.D.	4603	147	31.31	5- 23	4	1	–
Aymes, A.N.	75	1	75.00	1- 75	–	–	–
Bailey, R.J.	4033	93	43.36	5- 54	2	–	–
Bainbridge, P.	12712	342	37.16	8- 53	10	–	–
Ball, M.C.J.	5427	153	35.47	8- 46	7	1	–
Banton, C.	37	0	–	–	–	–	–
Barnett, K.J.	6210	168	36.96	6- 28	3	–	–
Bartle, S.	42	0	–	–	–	–	–
Barwick, S.R.	15795	451	35.02	8- 42	10	1	2
Base, S.J.	11258	387	29.09	7- 60	16	1	1
Bates, R.T.	794	18	44.11	5- 88	1	–	–
Batty, J.D.	5869	147	39.92	6- 48	3	–	–
Battye, R.A.	14	0	–	–	–	–	–
Bell, M.A.V.	1333	46	28.97	7- 48	3	–	–
Benjamin, J.E.	8908	312	28.55	6- 19	16	1	3
Benjamin, K.C.G.	6368	253	25.16	7- 51	11	1	–
Benjamin, W.K.M.	12157	470	25.86	7- 54	23	2	1
Benson, M.R.	493	5	98.60	2- 55	–	–	–
Betts, M.M.	872	18	48.44	3- 35	–	–	–
Bevan, M.G.	1198	16	74.87	3- 6	–	–	–
Bicknell, D.J.	383	6	63.83	3- 88	–	–	–
Bicknell, M.P.	13598	520	26.15	9- 45	23	2	5
Birbeck, S.D.	284	6	47.33	3-119	–	–	–
Bird, P.J.	166	0	–	–	–	–	–
Bishop, I.R.	8732	413	21.14	7- 34	21	1	2
Blakey, R.J.	68	1	68.00	1- 68	–	–	–
Blenkiron, D.A.	64	1	64.00	1- 10	–	–	–
Boden, D.J.P.	471	14	33.64	4- 11	–	–	–
Boiling, J.	5126	110	46.60	6- 84	4	1	–
Boon, T.J.	563	11	51.18	3- 40	–	–	–
Bovill, J.N.B.	1283	47	27.29	6- 29	3	1	–
Bowen, M.N.	1196	30	39.86	4-124	–	–	–
Bowler, P.D.	1579	21	75.19	3- 41	–	–	–
Briers, N.E.	988	32	30.87	4- 29	–	–	–
Brimson, M.T.	723	19	38.05	2- 11	–	–	–
Brinkley, J.E.	1115	34	32.79	6- 35	2	–	–
Broadhurst, M.	231	7	33.00	3- 61	–	–	–
Brown, A.D.	131	0	–	–	–	–	–
Brown, D.R.	1394	52	26.80	4- 24	–	–	–
Brown, K.R.	276	6	46.00	2- 7	–	–	–
Brown, S.J.E.	8707	262	33.23	7- 70	16	1	3
Browne, C.O.	16	0	–	–	–	–	–
Burns, M.	8	0	–	–	–	–	–
Butcher, G.P.	239	2	119.50	2- 36	–	–	–
Butcher, M.A.	2156	54	39.92	4- 31	–	–	–
Byas, D.	719	12	59.91	3- 55	–	–	–
Caddick, A.R.	6535	244	26.78	9- 32	14	5	3
Cairns, C.L.	9228	326	28.30	8- 47	13	3	3
Campbell, S.L.	3	0	–	–	–	–	–
Capel, D.J.	16146	508	31.78	7- 44	14	–	4
Carr, J.D.	2939	68	43.22	6- 61	3	–	–

	Runs	Wkts	Avge	Best	5wI	10wM	50wS
Carroll, J.P.	120	0	–	–	–	–	–
Cassar, M.E.	185	8	23.12	4- 54	–	–	–
Chanderpaul, S.	1295	32	40.46	4- 48	–	–	–
Chapman, R.J.	1041	17	61.23	3-119	–	–	–
Chapple, G.	3675	127	28.93	6- 48	6	–	1
Childs, J.H.	29835	1009	29.56	9- 56	52	8	9
Church, M.J.	4	0	–	–	–	–	–
Clarke, L.P.	55	1	55.00	1- 55	–	–	–
Clarke, V.P.	389	6	64.83	3- 72	–	–	–
Connor, C.A.	17837	550	32.43	7- 31	15	4	5
Cooper, K.E.	21928	812	27.00	8- 44	26	1	8
Cork, D.G.	8052	318	25.32	9- 43	9	2	2
Cottam, A.C.	571	10	57.10	2- 5	–	–	–
Cottey, P.A.	641	9	71.22	2- 42	–	–	–
Cousins, D.M.	1086	26	41.76	6- 35	1	–	–
Cowan, A.P.	113	1	113.00	1- 53	–	–	–
Cowans, N.G.	16461	662	24.86	6- 31	23	1	6
Cowdrey, G.R.	799	11	72.63	1- 5	–	–	–
Cox, D.M.	767	12	63.91	4-141	–	–	–
Crawley, J.P.	108	1	108.00	1- 90	–	–	–
Croft, R.D.B.	13250	330	40.15	8- 66	14	2	3
Cronje, W.J.	2146	51	42.07	4- 47	–	–	–
Crowe, C.D.	4	0	–	–	–	–	–
Cullinan, D.J.	70	3	23.33	2- 27	–	–	–
Cummins, A.C.	5804	188	30.87	6- 64	8	1	2
Curran, K.M.	14878	551	27.00	7- 47	15	4	5
Curtis, T.S.	730	11	66.36	2- 17	–	–	–
Dakin, J.M.	490	11	44.45	4- 45	–	–	–
Dale, A.	4616	120	38.46	6- 18	1	–	–
Daley, J.A.	9	0	–	–	–	–	–
Davies, A.P.	17	0	–	–	–	–	–
Davies, M.	3878	110	35.25	5- 57	3	1	1
Davis, R.P.	12883	374	34.44	7- 64	16	2	2
Dawson, R.I.	103	2	51.50	2- 38	–	–	–
DeFreitas, P.A.J.	21765	771	28.22	7- 21	38	3	8
De la Pena, J.M.	502	13	38.61	4- 77	–	–	–
Derbyshire, N.A.	216	4	54.00	1- 18	–	–	–
De Silva, P.A.	2254	66	34.15	7- 24	4	–	–
Dessaur, W.A.	118	1	118.00	1- 8	–	–	–
Dhanraj, R.	6137	209	29.36	8- 51	10	1	1
Dibden, R.R.	428	6	71.33	2- 36	–	–	–
Dimond, M.	286	6	47.66	4- 73	–	–	–
D'Oliveira, D.B.	2480	55	45.09	4- 68	–	–	–
Donald, A.A.	18433	792	23.27	8- 37	43	6	4+1
Dowman, M.P.	75	0	–	–	–	–	–
Drakes, V.C.	2250	85	26.47	7- 47	3	–	–
Dutch, K.P.	42	0	–	–	–	–	–
Ealham, M.A.	4701	147	31.97	7- 53	5	–	–
Ecclestone, S.C.	1208	33	36.60	4- 66	–	–	–
Edwards, A.D.	246	3	82.00	3- 83	–	–	–
Elliott, M.T.G.	59	1	59.00	1- 23	–	–	–
Ellis, S.W.K.	146	5	29.20	5- 59	1	–	–
Elworthy, S.	5238	183	28.62	7- 65	8	1	–
Emburey, J.E.	40657	1577	25.78	8- 40	72	12	17
Emery, P.A.	14	0	–	–	–	–	–
Evans, K.P.	8798	259	33.96	6- 67	4	–	–

	Runs	Wkts	Avge	Best	5wI	10wM	50wS
Fairbrother, N.H.	440	5	88.00	2- 91	–	–	–
Farbrace, P.	64	1	64.00	1- 64	–	–	–
Fay, R.A.	25	0	–	–	–	–	–
Feltham, M.A.	12094	384	31.49	6- 41	8	–	1
Field-Buss, M.G.	2464	63	39.11	6- 42	1	–	–
Fleming, M.V.	5097	118	43.19	4- 31	–	–	–
Flint, D.P.J.	1318	34	38.76	5- 32	1	–	–
Flintoff, A.	39	0	–	–	–	–	–
Follett, D.	95	1	95.00	1- 61	–	–	–
Fordham, A.	289	4	72.25	1- 0	–	–	–
Foster, M.J.	150	6	25.00	3- 39	–	–	–
Fraser, A.R.C.	14782	556	26.58	8- 75	22	2	6
Freedman, D.A.	2000	59	33.89	6- 89	1	1	–
Freeth, J.W.D.	721	8	90.12	2- 62	–	–	–
French, B.N.	70	1	70.00	1- 37	–	–	–
Fulton, D.P.	0	0	–	–	–	–	–
Gallian, J.E.R.	2240	56	40.00	4- 29	–	–	–
Garnham, M.A.	39	0	–	–	–	–	–
Gatting, M.W.	4623	156	29.63	5- 34	2	–	–
George, S.P.	4859	130	37.37	6- 51	2	–	–
Gibson, O.D.	6891	241	28.59	7- 55	11	3	1
Giddins, E.S.H.	6000	190	31.57	6- 73	9	1	2
Giles, A.F.	482	19	25.36	5- 23	1	–	–
Gooch, G.A.	8397	244	34.41	7- 14	3	–	–
Gough, D.	8856	300	29.52	7- 28	11	2	3
Grayson, A.P.	846	13	65.07	2- 5	–	–	–
Green, R.J.	87	3	29.00	2- 40	–	–	–
Greenfield, K.	427	5	85.40	2- 40	–	–	–
Griffith, F.A.	2434	72	33.80	4- 33	–	–	–
Gupte, C.M.	276	4	69.00	2- 41	–	–	–
Hall, J.W.	14	0	–	–	–	–	–
Hallett, J.C.	1342	31	43.29	4- 59	–	–	–
Hamilton, G.M.	688	17	40.47	5- 65	1	–	–
Hancock, T.H.C.	499	13	38.38	3- 10	–	–	–
Harden, R.J.	969	19	51.00	2- 7	–	–	–
Harris, A.J.	519	19	27.31	4- 84	–	–	–
Harrison, T.W.	282	5	56.40	4-153	–	–	–
Harrity, M.A.	1476	37	39.89	5- 92	1	–	–
Hartley, P.J.	15452	497	31.09	9- 41	18	1	5
Haste, N.J.	2280	41	55.60	5- 73	1	–	–
Hayden, M.L.	116	1	116.00	1- 24	–	–	–
Hayhurst, A.N.	4870	108	45.09	4- 27	–	–	–
Haynes, G.R.	1643	35	46.94	4- 33	–	–	–
Headley, D.W.	5999	182	32.96	7- 58	9	–	–
Hegg, W.K.	7	0	–	–	–	–	–
Hemmings, E.E.	44403	1515	29.30	10-175	70	15	15
Hemp, D.L.	151	3	50.33	1- 9	–	–	–
Herzberg, S.	1532	37	41.40	5- 33	1	–	–
Hick, G.A.	8015	187	42.86	5- 18	5	1	–
Hindson, J.E.	2751	82	33.54	5- 42	7	2	1
Hodgson, G.D.	65	0	–	–	–	–	–
Hollioake, A.J.	1984	52	36.74	4- 22	–	–	–
Holloway, P.C.L.	12	0	–	–	–	–	–
Hooper, C.L.	11175	314	35.58	5- 33	10	–	–
How, E.J.	299	1	299.00	1- 24	–	–	–
Hughes, E.R.	234	2	117.00	1- 62	–	–	–

	Runs	Wkts	Avge	Best	5wI	10wM	50wS
Hughes, J.G.	1260	30	42.00	5- 69	1	–	–
Hussain, N.	307	2	153.50	1- 38	–	–	–
Hutton, S.	18	0	–	–	–	–	–
Igglesden, A.P.	12748	483	26.39	7- 28	23	4	4
Illingworth, R.K.	21045	686	30.67	7- 50	22	5	4
Ilott, M.C.	9969	353	28.24	9- 19	18	3	4
Innes, K.J.	33	0	–	–	–	–	–
Irani, R.C.	2354	60	39.23	5- 62	1	–	–
James, K.D.	9937	300	33.12	6- 22	8	–	–
James, S.P.	3	0	–	–	–	–	–
Janisch, A.N.	723	10	72.30	3- 38	–	–	–
Jarvis, P.W.	16103	572	28.15	7- 55	20	3	4
Johnson, P.	510	5	102.00	1- 9	–	–	–
Johnson, R.L.	2110	83	25.42	10- 45	3	2	–
Jones, D.M.	1100	17	64.70	1- 0	–	–	–
Kasprowicz, M.S.	5913	193	30.63	7- 83	10	–	1+1
Keech, M.	286	7	40.85	2- 28	–	–	–
Keedy, G.	1498	37	40.48	4- 35	–	–	–
Kellett, S.A.	19	0	–	–	–	–	–
Kendall, W.S.	255	8	31.87	3- 37	–	–	–
Kendrick, N.M.	6185	162	38.17	7-115	6	1	1
Kenlock, S.G.	626	11	56.90	3-104	–	–	–
Kennis, G.J.	0	0	–	–	–	–	–
Kerr, J.I.D.	1630	43	37.90	5- 82	1	–	–
Kettleborough, R.A.	18	0	–	–	–	–	–
Khan, A.A.	160	8	20.00	4- 51	–	–	–
Khan, W.G.	22	0	–	–	–	–	–
Killeen, N.	767	17	45.11	5-118	1	–	–
Kirtley, R.J.	103	2	51.50	1- 28	–	–	–
Knight, N.V.	105	1	105.00	1- 61	–	–	–
Krikken, K.M.	40	0	–	–	–	–	–
Kumble, A.	8489	371	22.88	8- 41	24	6	1
Lamb, A.J.	199	8	24.87	2- 29	–	–	–
Lampitt, S.R.	9879	341	28.97	5- 32	10	–	4
Langer, J.L.	20	0	–	–	–	–	–
Lara, B.C.	268	1	268.00	1- 22	–	–	–
Larkins, W.	1915	42	45.59	5- 59	1	–	–
Lathwell, M.N.	597	11	54.27	2- 21	–	–	–
Law, D.R.	519	11	47.18	2- 38	–	–	–
Law, S.G.	1262	30	42.06	3- 25	–	–	–
Lawrence, J.R.G.	123	3	41.00	2- 44	–	–	–
Leatherdale, D.A.	521	10	52.10	2- 11	–	–	–
Lee, S.	977	16	61.06	3- 53	–	–	–
Lefebvre, R.P.	5399	149	36.23	6- 45	3	–	–
Lenham, N.J.	1701	39	43.61	4- 13	–	–	–
Lewis, C.C.	11799	403	29.27	6- 22	15	3	2
Lewis, J.	209	12	17.41	4- 34	–	–	–
Lewis, J.J.B.	32	0	–	–	–	–	–
Lewry, J.D.	1562	54	28.92	6- 43	3	–	–
Llong, N.J.	810	20	40.50	5- 63	1	–	–
Lloyd, G.D.	186	1	186.00	1- 57	–	–	–
Longley, J.I.	47	0	–	–	–	–	–
Loye, M.B.	1	0	–	–	–	–	–
Lugsden, S.	497	5	99.40	2- 43	–	–	–
Lynch, M.A.	1398	26	53.76	3- 6	–	–	–
McCague, M.J.	7347	268	27.41	9- 86	17	2	3

	Runs	Wkts	Avge	Best	5wI	10wM	50wS
McGrath, G.D.	3111	126	24.69	6- 47	7	1	–
McIntyre, P.E.	6333	155	40.85	6- 43	5	–	–
McMillan, B.M.	6873	254	27.05	5- 35	4	–	–
Macmillan, G.I.	1103	21	52.52	3- 13	–	–	–
MacRobert, A.D.	843	18	46.83	4- 41	–	–	–
Maddy, D.L.	41	0	–	–	–	–	–
Malcolm, D.E.	19438	627	31.00	9- 57	20	3	4
Malik, H.S.	1282	20	64.10	3- 10	–	–	–
Mallender, N.A.	24517	936	26.19	7- 27	36	5	6
Marc, K.	170	3	56.66	2- 52	–	–	–
Marsh, S.A.	235	2	117.50	2- 20	–	–	–
Martin, N.F.C.	603	8	75.37	2- 84	–	–	–
Martin, P.J.	7504	223	33.65	5- 35	3	–	1
Martin-Jenkins, R.S.C.	11	0	–	–	–	–	–
Maru, R.J.	16477	504	32.69	8- 41	15	1	4
Mason, T.J.	101	1	101.00	1- 22	–	–	–
Mather, D.P.	710	18	39.44	4- 65	–	–	–
Matthews, G.R.J.	14217	450	31.59	8- 52	19	5	0+2
Maynard, M.P.	686	6	114.33	3- 21	–	–	–
Metcalfe, A.A.	362	4	90.50	2- 18	–	–	–
Metson, C.P.	0	0	–	–	–	–	–
Middleton, T.C.	241	5	48.20	2- 41	–	–	–
Mike, G.W.	3108	83	37.44	5- 44	2	–	–
Milburn, S.M.	431	14	30.78	4- 68	–	–	–
Millns, D.J.	9574	334	28.66	9- 37	17	2	3
Mirza, P.	854	23	37.13	5-110	1	–	–
Moles, A.J.	1882	40	47.05	3- 21	–	–	–
Montgomerie, R.R.	65	0	–	–	–	–	–
Moody, T.M.	4833	150	32.22	7- 43	1	1	–
Moores, P.	16	0	–	–	–	–	–
Morris, A.C.	62	0	–	–	–	–	–
Morris, H.	380	2	190.00	1- 6	–	–	–
Morris, J.E.	902	7	128.85	1- 6	–	–	–
Morris, R.S.M.	1	0	–	–	–	–	–
Moxon, M.D.	1481	28	52.89	3- 24	–	–	–
Mullally, A.D.	9162	273	33.56	7- 72	6	1	2
Munton, T.A.	14369	550	26.12	8- 89	25	6	5
Mushtaq Ahmed	12960	495	26.18	9- 93	32	8	3+1
Nash, D.J.	4100	146	28.08	6- 30	7	1	1
Newell, K.	127	0	–	–	–	–	–
Newell, M.	282	7	40.28	2- 38	–	–	–
Newport, P.J.	20928	772	27.10	8- 52	33	3	8
Nicholas, M.C.J.	3245	72	45.06	6- 37	2	–	–
North, J.A.	1577	44	35.84	4- 47	–	–	–
Nowell, R.W.	1264	32	39.50	4- 43	–	–	–
O'Gorman, T.J.G.	215	3	71.66	1- 7	–	–	–
Ormond, J.	65	2	32.50	2- 65	–	–	–
Ostler, D.P.	122	0	–	–	–	–	–
Parkin, O.T.	170	4	42.50	2- 45	–	–	–
Parsons, G.J.	22416	749	29.92	9- 72	19	1	3
Parsons, K.A.	493	6	82.16	2- 11	–	–	–
Patel, M.M.	6552	217	30.19	8- 96	13	6	2
Pearson, R.M.	3917	67	58.46	5-108	1	–	–
Peirce, M.T.E.	30	0	–	–	–	–	–
Penberthy, A.L.	4049	111	36.47	5- 37	2	–	–
Pennett, D.B.	2321	53	43.79	5- 36	1	–	–

	Runs	Wkts	Avge	Best	5wI	10wM	50wS
Penney, T.L.	183	6	30.50	3- 18	–	–	–
Phillips, N.C.	751	13	57.76	3- 39	–	–	–
Pick, R.A.	15606	482	32.37	7-128	16	3	5
Pierson, A.R.K.	8506	235	36.19	8- 42	10	–	1
Pigott, A.C.S.	20831	672	30.99	7- 74	26	2	5
Pike, V.J.	1170	31	37.74	6- 41	1	–	–
Piper, K.J.	57	1	57.00	1- 57	–	–	–
Pollard, P.R.	268	4	67.00	2- 79	–	–	–
Ponting, R.T.	190	2	95.00	1- 7	–	–	–
Pooley, J.C.	26	0	–	–	–	–	–
Prabhakar, M.	10612	360	29.47	7- 65	10	1	1
Prichard, P.J.	497	2	248.50	1- 28	–	–	–
Rackemann, C.G.	16206	608	26.65	8- 84	22	3	0+2
Radford, N.V.	26707	994	26.86	9- 70	48	7	6
Radford, T.A.	0	1	0.00	1- 0	–	–	–
Ramprakash, M.R.	860	12	71.66	3- 91	–	–	–
Ratcliffe, J.D.	235	4	58.75	1- 4	–	–	–
Ratledge, J.	108	1	108.00	1- 16	–	–	–
Reeve, D.A.	12037	447	26.92	7- 37	7	–	2
Remy, C.C.	1051	19	55.31	4- 63	–	–	–
Renshaw, S.J.	191	2	95.50	2-135	–	–	–
Rhodes, S.J.	30	0	–	–	–	–	–
Richardson, A.	60	3	20.00	3- 27	–	–	–
Richardson, R.B.	238	6	39.66	5- 40	1	–	–
Ricketts, J.D.	732	17	43.05	3- 30	–	–	–
Ripley, D.	103	2	51.50	2- 89	–	–	–
Roberts, A.R.	4302	97	44.35	6- 72	1	–	–
Robinson, D.D.J.	7	0	–	–	–	–	–
Robinson, M.A.	12059	369	32.68	9- 37	7	2	1
Robinson, P.E.	329	3	109.66	1- 10	–	–	–
Robinson, R.T.	285	4	71.25	1- 22	–	–	–
Rollins, A.S.	51	1	51.00	1- 19	–	–	–
Rose, G.D.	11968	390	30.68	6- 41	8	–	2
Roseberry, M.A.	406	4	101.50	1- 1	–	–	–
Russell, R.C.	53	1	53.00	1- 4	–	–	–
Salisbury, I.D.K.	14430	407	35.45	7- 54	20	3	3
Sargeant, N.F.	88	1	88.00	1- 88	–	–	–
Saxelby, M.	903	11	82.09	3- 41	–	–	–
Scott, C.W.	40	0	–	–	–	–	–
Searle, J.P.	133	2	66.50	2-126	–	–	–
Shadford, D.J.	107	3	35.66	2- 40	–	–	–
Shahid, N.	1628	35	46.51	3- 91	–	–	–
Sheeraz, K.P.	922	26	35.46	6- 67	2	1	–
Sheriyar, A.	1199	40	29.97	6- 30	2	1	–
Shine, K.J.	5885	155	37.96	8- 47	7	1	–
Silverwood, C.E.W.	1588	46	34.52	5- 62	1	–	–
Simmons, P.V.	3178	90	35.31	5- 24	1	–	–
Slater, M.J.	24	1	24.00	1- 4	–	–	–
Small, G.C.	23698	830	28.55	7- 15	29	2	6
Smith, A.M.	4769	156	30.57	7- 70	5	1	1
Smith, A.W.	2374	43	55.20	5-103	1	–	–
Smith, B.F.	190	2	95.00	1- 5	–	–	–
Smith, N.M.K.	7617	199	38.27	7- 42	12	–	–
Smith, P.A.	10021	281	35.66	6- 91	7	–	–
Smith, R.A.	693	12	57.75	2- 11	–	–	–
Snape, J.N.	1194	27	44.22	5- 65	1	–	–

	Runs	Wkts	Avge	Best	5wI	10wM	50wS
Solanki, V.S.	359	3	119.66	1- 10	–	–	–
Speak, N.J.	130	2	65.00	1- 0	–	–	–
Speight, M.P.	32	2	16.00	1- 2	–	–	–
Spencer, D.J.	1257	34	36.97	4- 31	–	–	–
Srinath, J.	6033	231	26.11	9- 76	9	2	1
Stanford, E.J.	220	3	73.33	2- 96	–	–	–
Stemp, R.D.	6721	197	34.11	6- 37	8	1	–
Stephenson, F.D.	18278	758	24.11	8- 47	43	10	5
Stephenson, J.P.	6193	181	34.21	7- 51	5	–	–
Stewart, A.J.	393	3	131.00	1- 7	–	–	–
Streak, H.H.	3461	125	27.68	6- 90	3	–	1
Stuart, A.M.	248	4	62.00	2- 57	–	–	–
Such, P.M.	15897	536	29.65	8- 93	27	5	3
Sutcliffe, I.J.	51	1	51.00	1- 11	–	–	–
Symonds, A.	298	5	59.60	3- 77	–	–	–
Taylor, C.W.	2421	72	33.62	5- 33	1	–	–
Taylor, J.P.	8671	286	30.31	7- 23	10	1	3
Taylor, M.A.	68	2	34.00	1- 4	–	–	–
Taylor, N.R.	891	16	55.68	2- 20	–	–	–
Terry, V.P.	58	0	–	–	–	–	–
Thomas, P.A.	1554	33	47.09	5- 70	1	–	–
Thomas, S.D.	2533	71	35.67	5- 76	4	–	–
Thompson, D.J.	123	3	41.00	2- 37	–	–	–
Thompson, J.B.D.	277	7	39.57	2- 10	–	–	–
Thorpe, G.P.	1108	22	50.36	4- 40	–	–	–
Thursfield, M.J.	1070	30	35.66	6-130	1	–	–
Tolley, C.M.	3463	96	36.07	5- 55	1	–	–
Trescothick, M.E.	143	5	28.60	4- 36	–	–	–
Trimby, P.W.	1343	38	35.34	5- 84	1	–	–
Trump, H.R.J.	9245	239	38.68	7- 52	9	2	1
Tudor, A.J.	320	14	22.85	5- 32	1	–	–
Tufnell, P.C.R.	18563	605	30.68	8- 29	29	3	5
Turner, R.J.	26	0	–	–	–	–	–
Tweats, T.A.	194	4	48.50	1- 23	–	–	–
Twose, R.G.	3782	117	32.32	6- 28	2	–	–
Udal, S.D.	9363	285	32.85	8- 50	19	4	4
Van Troost, A.P.	4218	115	36.67	6- 48	4	–	–
Vaughan, M.P.	1623	38	42.71	4- 39	–	–	–
Walker, A.	8276	263	31.46	8-118	4	1	1
Walsh, C.A.	29200	1305	22.37	9- 72	75	15	8+2
Walton, T.C.	124	2	62.00	1- 46	–	–	–
Ward, D.M.	113	2	56.50	2- 66	–	–	–
Ward, T.R.	580	6	96.66	2- 48	–	–	–
Warner, A.E.	13358	425	31.43	6- 21	8	1	–
Wasim Akram	16075	747	21.51	8- 30	59	14	5+1
Watkin, S.L.	17458	595	29.34	8- 59	22	4	7
Watkinson, M.	21169	639	33.12	8- 30	25	3	7
Waugh, M.E.	6319	163	38.76	5- 37	2	–	–
Weekes, P.N.	3391	82	41.35	5- 12	1	–	–
Welch, G.	1089	26	41.88	4- 74	–	–	–
Wells, A.P.	765	10	76.50	3- 67	–	–	–
Wells, C.M.	14308	419	34.14	7- 42	7	–	2
Wells, V.J.	3361	130	25.85	5- 43	2	–	–
Weston, R.M.S.	70	1	70.00	1- 41	–	–	–
Weston, W.P.C.	480	4	120.00	2- 39	–	–	–
Wharf, A.G.	78	1	78.00	1- 78	–	–	–

	Runs	Wkts	Avge	Best	5wI	10wM	50wS
Whitaker, J.J.	268	2	134.00	1- 29	–	–	–
Whitaker, P.R.	34	1	34.00	1- 4	–	–	–
White, C.	2900	95	30.52	5- 40	3	–	–
White, G.W.	65	1	65.00	1- 30	–	–	–
Whittall, A.R.	3093	59	52.42	6- 46	2	1	–
Whitticase, P.	7	0	–	–	–	–	–
Wileman, J.R.	217	4	54.25	2- 33	–	–	–
Williams, B.A.	805	25	32.20	5- 88	1	–	–
Williams, N.F.	18103	601	30.12	8- 75	19	2	3
Williams, R.C.	1960	44	44.54	4- 28	–	–	–
Williams, S.C.	2	0	–	–	–	–	–
Windows, M.G.N.	39	2	19.50	1- 6	–	–	–
Windsor, J.M.	93	3	31.00	3- 51	–	–	–
Wood, J.	3073	92	33.40	6-110	4	–	–
Wren, T.N.	1985	55	36.09	6- 48	2	–	–
Wright, A.J.	68	1	68.00	1- 16	–	–	–
Wylie, A.	216	2	108.00	1- 50	–	–	–
Yates, G.	4533	103	44.00	5- 34	2	–	–
Yeabsley, M.I.	84	2	42.00	1- 28	–	–	–
Yeabsley, R.S.	1606	49	32.77	6- 54	1	1	–
Young, S.	4181	125	33.44	5- 36	5	1	–

ICC TOURS PROGRAMME

(Full Member Countries)

Current at 14 February 1996. *Unconfirmed

1996-97

Aug	Australia to Sri Lanka*
Sep/Oct	Australia to India
Oct/Dec	South Africa to India
Nov/Dec	England to Sri Lanka*
Nov/Dec	New Zealand to Pakistan
Nov/Feb	West Indies to Australia
Dec	England to Zimbabwe
Dec/Jan	Pakistan to Australia
Dec/Feb	India to South Africa
Jan/Mar	England to New Zealand
Jan	Zimbabwe to South Africa
Feb/Apr	Australia to South Africa
Feb/Apr	India to West Indies
Mar	Australia to Zimbabwe*

1997

May/Aug	Australia to England

1997-98

Aug/Sep	New Zealand to Sri Lanka*
Oct	South Africa to Pakistan
Oct/Dec	West Indies to Pakistan
Nov/Jan	New Zealand to Australia
Dec/Jan	South Africa to Australia
Jan/Apr	England to West Indies
Jan/Feb	Zimbabwe to Sri Lanka
Feb/Mar	India to New Zealand*
Feb/Mar	Pakistan to South Africa
Mar/Apr	Australia to India
Mar/Apr	Pakistan to Zimbabwe

1998

May/Aug	South Africa to England

1998-99

Sep/Nov	Australia to Pakistan
Oct	West Indies to Zimbabwe
Nov/Feb	England to Australia
Nov	Zimbabwe to India
Nov/Jan	West Indies to South Africa
Dec	Zimbabwe to Pakistan
Dec/Jan	Sri Lanka to Australia and NZ

1999	New Zealand to England
	World Cup in England
1999-2000	England to Pakistan*
2000	West Indies to England

LEADING CURRENT PLAYERS

The leading career records of players currently registered for first-class county cricket. All figures are to the end of the 1995 English season.

BATTING

(Qualification: 100 innings)

	Runs	Avge
G.A.Hick	25194	57.00
M.E.Waugh	17260	55.67
D.M.Jones	14837	52.80
M.G.Bevan	6486	51.07
M.W.Gatting	33456	50.69
G.A.Gooch	42528	48.99
A.J.Lamb	32502	48.94
J.P.Crawley	7890	48.70
T.M.Moody	14647	46.79
A.D.Brown	4225	45.43
M.R.Ramprakash	11519	45.35
N.Hussain	9687	44.84
R.A.Smith	18930	44.75
C.L.Hooper	11921	44.64
M.A.Atherton	13722	44.12
R.T.Robinson	24365	43.43
T.L.Penney	4189	43.18
M.D.Moxon	19446	43.11
G.P.Thorpe	10393	42.24
R.J.Bailey	17229	41.98
M.P.Maynard	15521	41.94
T.S.Curtis	19131	41.49
A.J.Moles	13767	41.46
P.D.Bowler	11544	41.22
N.H.Fairbrother	15227	40.82
A.P.Wells	17302	40.51
D.J.Bicknell	11133	40.48
M.R.Benson	18387	40.23
A.Fordham	9764	40.18
R.J.Harden	11525	40.01
J.D.Carr	10112	39.96
N.R.Taylor	17771	39.75
J.E.Morris	17301	39.59
A.J.Stewart	16462	39.57
K.J.Barnett	21816	39.30
N.J.Speak	6788	39.01

BOWLING

(Qualification: 100 wickets)

	Wkts	Avge
C.E.L.Ambrose	694	20.73
C.A.Walsh	1305	22.37
D.G.Cork	318	25.32
J.E.Emburey	1577	25.78
V.J.Wells	130	25.85
W.K.M.Benjamin	470	25.86
T.A.Munton	550	26.12
M.P.Bicknell	520	26.15
N.A.Mallender	936	26.19
A.P.Igglesden	483	26.39
A.R.C.Fraser	556	26.58
A.R.Caddick	244	26.78
D.A.Reeve	447	26.92
K.M.Curran	551	27.001
K.E.Cooper	812	27.004
P.J.Newport	772	27.10
M.J.McCague	268	27.41
D.J.Nash	146	28.08
P.W.Jarvis	572	28.15
P.A.J.DeFreitas	771	28.22
M.C.Ilott	353	28.24
C.L.Cairns	326	28.30
J.E.Benjamin	312	28.5512
G.C.Small	830	28.5518
O.D.Gibson	241	28.59
D.J.Millns	334	28.66
G.Chapple	127	28.93
S.R.Lampitt	341	28.97
S.J.Base	387	29.09
C.C.Lewis	403	29.27
S.L.Watkin	595	29.34
D.Gough	300	29.52
J.H.Childs	1009	29.56
M.W.Gatting	156	29.63
P.M.Such	536	29.65
G.J.Parsons	749	29.92

WICKET-KEEPING

	Total	Ct	St
R.C.Russell	847	751	96
S.J.Rhodes	829	733	96
C.P.Metson	586	538	48
S.A.Marsh	571	529	42
D.Ripley	540	473	67
W.K.Hegg	488	432	56
R.J.Blakey	458	420	38
P.Moores	456	414	42

FIELDING

	Ct
G.A.Gooch	525
J.E.Emburey	452
M.W.Gatting	441
C.W.J.Athey	405
A.J.Lamb	371
G.A.Hick	369
M.A.Lynch	348
V.P.Terry	320

TEST CAREER RECORDS

These records, complete to the end of the 1995-96 season (excluding West Indies v New Zealand), include all players registered for county cricket in 1996, plus those who have appeared in international cricket since 31 August 1994 or gained selection for the World Cup. Full career records for all Tests prior to that date are published in *The Wisden Book of Test Cricket* (Fourth Edition).

ENGLAND

BATTING AND FIELDING

	M	*I*	*NO*	*HS*	*Runs*	*Avge*	*100*	*50*	*Ct/St*
M.A.Atherton	56	104	2	185*	4202	41.19	9	27	39
C.W.J.Athey	23	41	1	123	919	22.97	1	4	13
R.J.Bailey	4	8	–	43	119	14.87	–	–	–
K.J.Barnett	4	7	–	80	207	29.57	–	2	1
J.E.Benjamin	1	1	–	0	0	0.00	–	–	–
M.R.Benson	1	2	–	30	51	25.50	–	–	–
M.P.Bicknell	2	4	–	14	26	6.50	–	–	–
R.J.Blakey	2	4	–	6	7	1.75	–	–	2
A.R.Caddick	8	14	2	29*	170	14.16	–	–	4
D.J.Capel	15	25	1	98	374	15.58	–	2	6
J.H.Childs	2	4	4	2*	2	–	–	–	1
D.G.Cork	10	14	2	56*	266	22.16	–	1	2
J.P.Crawley	10	16	1	72	330	22.00	–	3	10
T.S.Curtis	5	9	–	41	140	15.55	–	–	3
P.A.J.DeFreitas	44	68	5	88	934	14.82	–	4	14
J.E.Emburey	64	96	20	75	1713	22.53	–	10	34
N.H.Fairbrother	10	15	1	83	219	15.64	–	1	4
A.R.C.Fraser	32	46	10	29	265	7.36	–	–	7
J.E.R.Gallian	3	6	–	28	74	12.33	–	–	1
M.W.Gatting	79	138	14	207	4409	35.55	10	21	59
G.A.Gooch	118	215	6	333	8900	42.58	20	46	103
D.Gough	12	18	3	65	319	21.26	–	2	7
G.A.Hick	42	74	6	178	2629	38.66	4	15	59
N.Hussain	7	13	2	71	284	25.81	–	1	3
A.P.Igglesden	3	5	3	3*	6	3.00	–	–	1
R.K.Illingworth	9	14	7	28	128	18.28	–	–	5
M.C.Ilott	5	6	2	15	28	7.00	–	–	–
P.W.Jarvis	9	15	2	29*	132	10.15	–	–	2
N.V.Knight	2	4	–	57	89	22.25	–	1	5
A.J.Lamb	79	139	10	142	4656	36.09	14	18	75
M.N.Lathwell	2	4	–	33	78	19.50	–	–	–
C.C.Lewis	27	44	2	117	1009	24.02	1	4	23
M.J.McCague	3	5	–	11	21	4.20	–	–	1
D.E.Malcolm	36	53	18	29	224	6.40	–	–	5
N.A.Mallender	2	3	–	4	8	2.66	–	–	–
P.J.Martin	6	9	–	29	65	7.22	–	–	5
M.P.Maynard	4	8	–	35	87	10.87	–	–	3
H.Morris	3	6	–	44	115	19.16	–	–	3
J.E.Morris	3	5	2	32	71	23.66	–	–	3
M.D.Moxon	10	17	1	99	455	28.43	–	3	10
T.A.Munton	2	2	1	25*	25	25.00	–	–	–
P.J.Newport	3	5	1	40*	110	27.50	–	–	1

ENGLAND – BATTING AND FIELDING (continued)

	M	I	NO	HS	Runs	Avge	100	50	Ct/St
A.C.S.Pigott	1	2	1	8*	12	12.00	–	–	–
M.R.Ramprakash	19	33	1	72	533	16.65	–	2	13
D.A.Reeve	3	5	–	59	124	24.80	–	1	1
S.J.Rhodes	11	17	5	65*	294	24.50	–	1	46/3
R.T.Robinson	29	49	5	175	1601	36.38	4	6	8
R.C.Russell	44	70	14	128*	1594	28.46	1	6	124/11
I.D.K.Salisbury	7	13	1	50	205	17.08	–	1	3
G.C.Small	17	24	7	59	263	15.47	–	1	9
R.A.Smith	62	112	15	175	4236	43.67	9	28	39
J.P.Stephenson	1	2	–	25	36	18.00	–	–	–
A.J.Stewart	53	95	6	190	3403	38.23	7	16	65/4
P.M.Such	8	11	4	14*	65	9.28	–	–	2
J.P.Taylor	2	4	2	17*	34	17.00	–	–	–
V.P.Terry	2	3	–	8	16	5.33	–	–	2
G.P.Thorpe	26	49	4	123	1842	40.93	2	15	22
P.C.R.Tufnell	22	32	17	22*	62	4.13	–	–	10
S.L.Watkin	3	5	–	13	25	5.00	–	–	1
M.Watkinson	4	6	1	82*	167	33.40	–	1	1
A.P.Wells	1	2	1	3*	3	3.00	–	–	–
J.J.Whitaker	1	1	–	11	11	11.00	–	–	1
C.White	6	10	–	51	157	15.70	–	1	3
N.F.Williams	1	1	–	38	38	38.00	–	–	–

ENGLAND

BOWLING

	Overs	Runs	Wkts	Avge	Best	5wI	10wM
M.A.Atherton	61	282	1	282.00	1- 60	–	–
K.J.Barnett	6	32	0	–	–	–	–
J.E.Benjamin	28	80	4	20.00	4- 42	–	–
M.P.Bicknell	87	263	4	65.75	3- 99	–	–
A.R.Caddick	323.2	1033	23	44.91	6- 65	2	–
D.J.Capel	333.2	1064	21	50.66	3- 88	–	–
J.H.Childs	86	183	3	61.00	1- 13	–	–
D.G.Cork	373.4	1146	45	25.46	7- 43	2	–
T.S.Curtis	3	7	0	–	–	–	–
P.A.J.DeFreitas	1639.4	4700	140	33.57	7- 70	4	–
J.E.Emburey	2565.1	5646	147	38.40	7- 78	6	–
N.H.Fairbrother	2	9	0	–	–	–	–
A.R.C.Fraser	1327.5	3509	119	29.48	8- 75	8	–
J.E.R.Gallian	14	62	0	–	–	–	–
M.W.Gatting	125.2	317	4	79.25	1- 14	–	–
G.A.Gooch	442.3	1069	23	46.47	3- 39	–	–
D.Gough	420.1	1358	43	31.58	6- 49	1	–
G.A.Hick	463.3	1154	21	54.95	4-126	–	–
A.P.Igglesden	92.3	329	6	54.83	2- 91	–	–
R.K.Illingworth	247.3	615	19	32.36	4- 96	–	–

ENGLAND – BOWLING (continued)

	Overs	*Runs*	*Wkts*	*Avge*	*Best*	*5wI*	*10wM*
M.C.Ilott	173.4	542	12	45.16	3- 48	–	–
P.W.Jarvis	318.4	965	21	45.95	4-107	–	–
A.J.Lamb	5	23	1	23.00	1- 6	–	–
C.C.Lewis	939.2	2870	77	37.27	6-111	2	–
M.J.McCague	98.5	390	6	65.00	4-121	–	–
D.E.Malcolm	1320.2	4441	122	36.40	9- 57	5	2
N.A.Mallender	74.5	215	10	21.50	5- 50	1	–
P.J.Martin	189	459	16	28.68	4- 60	–	–
M.D.Moxon	8	30	0	–	–	–	–
T.A.Munton	67.3	200	4	50.00	2- 22	–	–
P.J.Newport	111.3	417	10	41.70	4- 87	–	–
A.C.S.Pigott	17	75	2	37.50	2- 75	–	–
M.R.Ramprakash	44.1	149	0	–	–	–	–
D.A.Reeve	24.5	60	2	30.00	1- 4	–	–
R.T.Robinson	1	0	0	–	–	–	–
I.D.K.Salisbury	234.1	933	16	58.31	4-163	–	–
G.C.Small	654.3	1871	55	34.01	5- 48	2	–
R.A.Smith	4	6	0	–	–	–	–
A.J.Stewart	3.2	13	0	–	–	–	–
P.M.Such	362.5	805	22	36.59	6- 67	1	–
J.P.Taylor	48	156	3	52.00	1- 18	–	–
G.P.Thorpe	8	15	0	–	–	–	–
P.C.R.Tufnell	1063	2671	68	39.27	7- 47	4	1
S.L.Watkin	89	305	11	27.72	4- 65	–	–
M.Watkinson	112	348	10	34.80	3- 64	–	–
C.White	94.1	334	8	41.75	3- 18	–	–
N.F.Williams	41	148	2	74.00	2-148	–	–

AUSTRALIA

BATTING AND FIELDING

	M	I	NO	HS	Runs	Avge	100	50	Ct/St
J.Angel	4	7	1	11	35	5.83	–	–	1
M.G.Bevan	6	10	–	91	324	32.40	–	3	5
G.S.Blewett	9	15	1	115	468	33.42	2	2	11
D.C.Boon	107	190	20	200	7422	43.65	21	32	99
P.A.Emery	1	1	1	8*	8	–	–	–	5/1
D.W.Fleming	4	4	–	24	40	10.00	–	–	2
I.A.Healy	79	117	14	113*	2803	27.21	2	17	255/20
B.P.Julian	7	9	1	56*	128	16.00	–	1	4
J.L.Langer	6	9	–	69	241	26.77	–	3	2
S.G.Law	1	1	1	54*	54	–	–	1	1
C.J.McDermott	71	90	13	42*	940	12.20	–	–	19
G.D.McGrath	19	20	5	9	32	2.13	–	–	2
P.E.McIntyre	1	2	–	0	0	0.00	–	–	–
T.B.A.May	24	28	12	42*	225	14.06	–	–	6
R.T.Ponting	3	4	–	96	193	48.25	–	2	4
P.R.Reiffel	21	27	9	56	412	22.88	–	2	11
M.J.Slater	33	57	3	219	2611	48.35	7	10	11
M.A.Taylor	72	129	9	219	5502	45.85	14	33	105
S.K.Warne	44	58	9	74*	669	13.65	–	1	30
M.E.Waugh	54	86	4	140	3627	44.23	10	22	68
S.R.Waugh	81	125	26	200	5002	50.52	11	28	61

AUSTRALIA

BOWLING

	Overs	Runs	Wkts	Avge	Best	5wI	10wM
J.Angel	124.4	463	10	46.30	3-54	–	–
M.G.Bevan	15	67	1	67.00	1-21	–	–
G.S.Blewett	40	122	2	61.00	2-25	–	–
D.C.Boon	6	14	0	–	–	–	–
D.W.Fleming	150.2	435	17	25.58	4-75	–	–
B.P.Julian	183	599	15	39.93	4-36	–	–
S.G.Law	3	9	0	–	–	–	–
C.J.McDermott	2764.2	8332	291	28.63	8-97	14	2
G.D.McGrath	757.1	2107	78	27.01	6-47	4	–
P.E.McIntyre	27.3	87	2	43.50	2-51	–	–
T.B.A.May	1096.1	2606	75	34.74	5- 9	3	–
R.T.Ponting	4	8	1	8.00	1- 8	–	–
P.R.Reiffel	644.5	1744	63	27.68	6-71	3	–
M.J.Slater	1.1	4	1	4.00	1- 4	–	–
M.A.Taylor	7	26	1	26.00	1-11	–	–
S.K.Warne	2186.2	4870	207	23.52	8-71	10	3
M.E.Waugh	488	1342	38	35.31	5-40	1	–
S.R.Waugh	1019.1	2710	77	35.19	5-28	3	–

SOUTH AFRICA

BATTING AND FIELDING

	M	I	NO	HS	Runs	Avge	100	50	Ct/St
P.R.Adams	2	3	1	29	29	14.50	–	–	2
J.B.Commins	3	6	1	45	125	25.00	–	–	2
W.J.Cronje	27	46	5	135	1516	36.97	5	4	10
D.J.Cullinan	19	31	2	102	1095	37.75	1	9	13
P.S.de Villiers	14	19	5	66*	230	16.42	–	1	7
A.A.Donald	25	32	17	33	233	15.53	–	–	7
C.E.Eksteen	6	10	2	22	87	10.87	–	–	5
A.C.Hudson	25	44	2	163	1444	34.38	3	10	24
S.D.Jack	2	2	–	7	7	3.50	–	–	1
J.H.Kallis	2	2	–	7	8	4.00	–	–	1
G.Kirsten	20	35	2	110	1265	38.33	1	9	18
B.M.McMillan	23	35	6	113	1226	42.27	2	7	28
C.R.Matthews	18	25	6	62*	348	18.31	–	1	4
S.M.Pollock	5	6	1	36*	133	26.60	–	–	2
M.W.Pringle	4	6	2	33	67	16.75	–	–	–
J.N.Rhodes	27	43	5	101*	1223	32.18	1	7	14
D.J.Richardson	28	41	4	109	1006	27.18	1	7	107
B.N.Schultz	7	6	2	6	6	1.50	–	–	–
R.P.Snell	5	8	1	48	95	13.57	–	–	1
P.J.R.Steyn	3	6	–	46	127	21.16	–	–	–
P.L.Symcox	6	7	–	50	164	23.42	–	1	–

SOUTH AFRICA

BOWLING

	Overs	Runs	Wkts	Avge	Best	5wI	10wM
P.R.Adams	107.1	231	8	28.87	3-75	–	–
W.J.Cronje	273.1	512	8	64.00	2-17	–	–
P.S.de Villiers	668.1	1733	70	24.75	6-43	4	2
A.A.Donald	963.3	2836	114	24.87	8-71	6	2
C.E.Eksteen	243	447	8	55.87	3-12	–	–
S.D.Jack	77	196	8	24.50	4-68	–	–
J.H.Kallis	4	2	0	–	–	–	–
G.Kirsten	54.1	135	2	67.50	1- 0	–	–
B.M.McMillan	706.5	1789	60	29.81	4-65	–	–
C.R.Matthews	663.2	1502	52	28.88	5-42	2	–
S.M.Pollock	149.5	377	16	23.56	5-32	1	–
M.W.Pringle	108.4	270	5	54.00	2-62	–	–
J.N.Rhodes	2	5	0	–	–	–	–
B.N.Schultz	236.5	600	30	20.00	5-48	2	–
R.P.Snell	170.5	538	19	28.31	4-74	–	–
P.L.Symcox	164.5	426	9	47.33	3-75	–	–

WEST INDIES

BATTING AND FIELDING

	M	I	NO	HS	Runs	Avge	100	50	Ct/St
J.C.Adams	22	34	8	174*	1616	62.15	4	8	24
C.E.L.Ambrose	59	84	18	53	815	12.34	–	1	13
K.L.T.Arthurton	33	50	5	157*	1382	30.71	2	8	22
K.C.G.Benjamin	21	27	7	43*	184	9.20	–	–	1
W.K.M.Benjamin	21	26	1	85	470	18.80	–	2	12
I.R.Bishop	24	36	9	30*	302	11.18	–	–	3
C.O.Browne	3	5	3	34	94	47.00	–	–	14
S.L.Campbell	9	14	–	93	599	42.78	–	6	11
S.Chanderpaul	9	13	4	80	536	59.55	–	7	4
C.E.Cuffy	2	3	1	1	1	0.50	–	–	1
A.C.Cummins	5	6	1	50	98	19.60	–	1	1
R.Dhanraj	3	3	–	4	8	2.66	–	–	–
O.D.Gibson	1	2	–	29	43	21.50	–	–	–
R.A.Harper	25	32	3	74	535	18.44	–	3	36
C.L.Hooper	52	87	7	178*	2548	31.85	5	12	57
B.C.Lara	31	52	2	375	3048	60.96	7	16	42
J.R.Murray	24	31	3	101*	712	25.42	1	2	86/2
R.B.Richardson	86	146	12	194	5949	44.39	16	27	90
P.V.Simmons	22	41	2	110	919	23.56	1	3	21
C.A.Walsh	80	106	30	30*	683	8.98	–	–	12
S.C.Williams	12	19	2	62	386	22.70	–	1	14

WEST INDIES

BOWLING

	Overs	Runs	Wkts	Avge	Best	5wI	10wM
J.C.Adams	150.4	481	9	53.44	4-43	–	–
C.E.L.Ambrose	2311.4	5493	258	21.29	8-45	13	3
K.L.T.Arthurton	78.5	183	1	183.00	1-17	–	–
K.C.G.Benjamin	674.3	2257	80	28.21	6-66	4	1
W.K.M.Benjamin	615.4	1648	61	27.01	4-46	–	–
I.R.Bishop	895.3	2347	110	21.33	6-40	6	–
S.Chanderpaul	96	304	2	152.00	1-63	–	–
C.E.Cuffy	52.2	190	5	38.00	3-80	–	–
A.C.Cummins	103	342	8	42.75	4-54	–	–
R.Dhanraj	125	430	6	71.66	2-49	–	–
O.D.Gibson	34	132	2	66.00	2-81	–	–
R.A.Harper	602.3	1291	46	28.06	6-57	1	–
C.L.Hooper	1010	2672	51	52.39	5-40	2	–
B.C.Lara	7	12	0	–	–	–	–
R.B.Richardson	11	18	0	–	–	–	–
P.V.Simmons	66	158	2	79.00	2-34	–	–
C.A.Walsh	2848.5	7534	301	25.02	7-37	11	2

NEW ZEALAND

BATTING AND FIELDING

	M	I	NO	HS	Runs	Avge	100	50	Ct/St
G.I.Allott	2	2	1	0*	0	0.00	–	–	–
N.J.Astle	2	4	–	32	77	19.25	–	–	4
C.L.Cairns	16	26	–	120	675	25.96	1	4	7
M.D.Crowe	77	131	11	299	5444	45.36	17	18	71
R.P.de Groen	5	10	4	26	45	7.50	–	–	–
S.B.Doull	11	18	2	31*	210	13.12	–	–	8
S.P.Fleming	18	30	–	92	1025	34.16	–	7	16
L.K.Germon	6	9	2	48	196	28.00	–	–	16/1
M.J.Greatbatch	39	67	5	146*	1981	31.95	3	10	27
C.Z.Harris	5	10	1	56	116	12.88	–	1	2
M.N.Hart	14	24	4	45	353	17.65	–	–	9
M.J.Haslam	4	2	1	3	4	4.00	–	–	2
A.H.Jones	39	74	8	186	2922	44.27	7	11	25
R.J.Kennedy	2	2	1	2*	2	2.00	–	–	2
G.R.Larsen	6	10	3	26*	92	13.14	–	–	5
G.B.Loveridge	1	1	1	4*	4	–	–	–	–
D.K.Morrison	45	66	22	42	329	7.47	–	–	14
D.J.Murray	8	16	1	52	303	20.20	–	1	6
D.J.Nash	14	21	6	56	236	15.73	–	1	7
A.C.Parore	26	44	6	100*	1012	26.63	1	5	59/2
D.N.Patel	30	54	7	99	983	20.91	–	4	11
C.Pringle	14	21	4	30	175	10.29	–	–	3
K.R.Rutherford	56	99	8	107*	2465	27.08	3	18	32
C.J.Spearman	3	6	–	112	254	42.33	1	–	3
M.L.Su'a	13	18	5	44	165	12.69	–	–	9
S.A.Thomson	19	35	4	120*	958	30.90	1	5	7
R.G.Twose	5	7	1	94	308	51.33	–	3	1
K.P.Walmsley	2	3	–	4	8	2.66	–	–	–
B.A.Young	18	36	1	120	1052	30.05	1	8	29

BOWLING

	Overs	Runs	Wkts	Avge	Best	5wI	10wM
G.I.Allott	66	209	4	52.25	3-56	–	–
N.J.Astle	4	7	0	–	–	–	–
C.L.Cairns	538.1	1782	51	34.94	6-52	2	–
M.D.Crowe	229.3	676	14	48.28	2-25	–	–
R.P.de Groen	176.4	505	11	45.90	3-40	–	–
S.B.Doull	335.2	1077	33	32.63	5-66	2	–
M.J.Greatbatch	1	0	0	–	–	–	–
C.Z.Harris	22	103	0	–	–	–	–
M.N.Hart	494.2	1438	29	49.58	5-77	1	–
M.J.Haslam	82.1	245	2	122.50	1-33	–	–
A.H.Jones	54.4	194	1	194.00	1-40	–	–
R.J.Kennedy	59	181	5	36.20	3-28	–	–
G.R.Larsen	251.5	517	19	27.21	3-57	–	–
D.K.Morrison	1575.1	5132	150	34.21	7-89	9	–
D.J.Nash	462	1308	44	29.72	6-76	2	1
D.N.Patel	903.5	2617	63	41.53	6-50	3	–
C.Pringle	497.3	1389	30	46.30	7-52	1	1
K.R.Rutherford	42.4	161	1	161.00	1-38	–	–
M.L.Su'a	473.5	1377	36	38.25	5-73	2	–
S.A.Thomson	331.4	953	19	50.15	3-63	–	–
R.G.Twose	22	60	3	20.00	2-36	–	–
K.P.Walmsley	111	344	7	49.14	3-70	–	–

INDIA

BATTING AND FIELDING

	M	I	NO	HS	Runs	Avge	100	50	Ct/St
M.Azharuddin	68	96	4	199	4320	46.95	14	15	69
R.K.Chauhan	15	11	3	15*	65	8.12	–	–	8
N.D.Hirwani	15	18	10	17	45	5.62	–	–	5
A.D.Jadeja	6	9	1	73	279	34.87	–	2	2
V.G.Kambli	17	21	1	227	1084	54.20	4	3	7
A.R.Kapoor	2	3	–	42	58	19.33	–	–	1
A.Kumble	23	23	5	52*	257	14.27	–	1	11
S.V.Manjrekar	34	55	6	218	1899	38.75	4	8	22/1
N.R.Mongia	10	13	2	80	388	35.27	–	1	20/2
M.Prabhakar	39	58	9	120	1600	32.65	1	9	20
S.L.V.Raju	23	28	9	31	228	12.00	–	–	5
N.S.Sidhu	36	54	2	124	2087	40.13	6	10	8
J.Srinath	18	23	12	60	248	22.54	–	2	8
S.R.Tendulkar	38	55	7	179	2483	51.72	8	13	31

INDIA

BOWLING

	Overs	Runs	Wkts	Avge	Best	5wI	10wM
M.Azharuddin	1.1	12	0	–	–	–	–
R.K.Chauhan	542.5	1189	34	34.97	3- 8	–	–
N.D.Hirwani	676.2	1858	64	29.03	8- 61	4	1
A.R.Kapoor	54	154	1	154.00	1- 90	–	–
A.Kumble	1166.5	2662	109	24.42	7- 59	6	1
S.V.Manjrekar	2.5	15	0	–	–	–	–
M.Prabhakar	1245.5	3581	96	37.30	6-132	3	–
S.L.V.Raju	1057	2363	84	28.13	6- 12	5	1
N.S.Sidhu	1	9	0	–	–	–	–
J.Srinath	624	1630	46	35.43	4- 33	–	–
S.R.Tendulkar	72	191	4	47.75	2- 10	–	–

PAKISTAN

BATTING AND FIELDING

	M	I	NO	HS	Runs	Avge	100	50	Ct/St
Aamer Malik	14	19	3	117	565	35.31	2	3	15/1
Aamir Nazir	6	11	6	11	31	6.20	–	–	2
Aamir Sohail	30	56	1	205	1960	35.63	2	13	30
Akram Raza	9	12	2	32	153	15.30	–	–	8
Aqib Javed	21	25	6	28*	100	5.26	–	–	2
Asif Mujtaba	21	35	3	65*	762	23.81	–	7	17
Ata-ur-Rehman	11	13	4	19	66	7.33	–	–	2
Basit Ali	19	33	1	103	858	26.81	1	5	6
Ijaz Ahmed	27	40	1	137	1379	35.35	4	6	20
Ijaz Ahmed II	2	3	–	16	29	9.66	–	–	3
Inzamam-ul-Haq	30	52	7	135*	2047	45.48	4	14	32
Javed Miandad	124	189	21	280*	8832	52.57	23	43	93/1
Kabir Khan	4	5	2	10	24	8.00	–	–	1
Manzoor Elahi	6	10	2	52	123	15.37	–	1	7
Mohammad Akram	4	8	2	5	8	1.33	–	–	4
Mohsin Kamal	9	11	7	13*	37	9.25	–	–	4
Moin Khan	18	28	4	117*	624	26.00	2	2	43/4
Mushtaq Ahmed	21	32	6	27	202	7.76	–	–	6
Ramiz Raja	55	91	5	122	2747	31.94	2	21	32
Rashid Latif	18	28	4	68*	578	24.08	–	3	55/8
Saeed Anwar	14	25	–	169	1038	41.52	2	8	7
Salim Elahi	2	4	–	17	43	10.75	–	–	1
Salim Malik	87	129	19	237	4906	44.60	13	24	57
Saqlain Mushtaq	4	7	2	34	53	10.60	–	–	3
Shakil Ahmed	3	5	–	33	74	14.80	–	–	4
Shoaib Mohammad	45	68	7	203*	2705	44.34	7	13	22
Waqar Younis	38	50	10	34	392	9.80	–	–	5
Wasim Akram	67	93	11	123	1554	18.95	1	4	25
Zahid Fazal	9	16	–	78	288	18.00	–	1	5

BOWLING

	Overs	Runs	Wkts	Avge	Best	5wI	10wM
Aamer Malik	26	89	1	89.00	1- 0	–	–
Aamir Nazir	176.1	597	20	29.85	5- 46	1	–
Aamir Sohail	240.5	652	17	38.35	4- 54	–	–
Akram Raza	254.2	732	13	56.30	3- 46	–	–
Aqib Javed	625.4	1786	54	33.07	5- 84	1	–
Asif Mujtaba	44	152	2	76.00	1- 0	–	–
Ata-ur-Rehman	280.1	898	26	34.53	3- 28	–	–
Basit Ali	1	6	0	–	–	–	–
Ijaz Ahmed	9	18	1	18.00	1- 9	–	–
Ijaz Ahmed II	4	6	0	–	–	–	–
Javed Miandad	245	682	17	40.11	3- 74	–	–
Kabir Khan	109.1	370	9	41.11	3- 26	–	–
Manzoor Elahi	74	194	7	27.71	2- 38	–	–
Mohammad Akram	131.1	392	9	43.55	3- 39	–	–
Mohsin Kamal	224.4	822	24	34.25	4-116	–	–
Mushtaq Ahmed	756	2160	72	30.00	7- 56	3	1
Rashid Latif	2	10	0	–	–	–	–
Saeed Anwar	3	4	0	–	–	–	–
Salim Malik	70.2	246	5	49.20	1- 3	–	–
Saqlain Mushtaq	179	492	13	37.84	3- 74	–	–
Shoaib Mohammad	66	170	5	34.00	2- 8	–	–
Waqar Younis	1288.5	4122	200	20.61	7- 76	19	4
Wasim Akram	2544.2	6524	289	22.57	7-119	20	3

SRI LANKA

BATTING AND FIELDING

	M	I	NO	HS	Runs	Avge	100	50	Ct/St
P.B.Dassanayake	11	17	2	36	196	13.06	–	–	19/5
P.A.de Silva	53	93	4	267	3176	35.68	8	13	23
H.D.P.K.Dharmasena	10	18	1	62*	307	18.05	–	2	4
C.I.Dunusinghe	5	10	–	91	160	16.00	–	1	13/2
A.P.Gurusinha	39	68	7	143	2312	37.90	7	6	30
U.C.Hathurusinghe	24	42	1	83	1260	30.73	–	8	6
S.T.Jayasuriya	17	27	5	112	771	35.04	1	4	17
R.S.Kalpage	8	14	1	63	265	20.38	–	2	6
R.S.Kaluwitharana	6	10	1	132*	350	38.88	1	2	12
R.S.Mahanama	37	63	–	153	1838	29.17	3	9	26
M.Muralitharan	23	32	17	20*	205	13.66	–	–	13
K.R.Pushpakumara	7	12	6	17*	45	7.50	–	–	4
A.Ranatunga	61	104	6	135*	3471	35.41	4	23	25
S.Ranatunga	8	15	1	118	522	37.28	2	2	2
D.P.Samaraweera	7	14	–	42	211	15.07	–	–	5
K.J.Silva	1	2	1	6*	6	6.00	–	–	–
H.P.Tillekeratne	36	61	8	119	2166	40.86	4	12	69
W.P.U.C.J.Vaas	12	21	2	51	320	16.84	–	1	1
G.P.Wickremasinghe	23	37	4	28	280	8.48	–	–	8

SRI LANKA

BOWLING

	Overs	Runs	Wkts	Avge	Best	5wI	10wM
P.A.de Silva	191.3	605	17	35.58	3- 39	–	–
H.D.P.K.Dharmasena	432.3	1046	23	45.47	6- 99	1	–
A.P.Gurusinha	227.4	674	20	33.70	2- 7	–	–
U.C.Hathurusinghe	284	668	16	41.75	4- 66	–	–
S.T.Jayasuriya	108	386	4	96.50	2- 46	–	–
R.S.Kalpage	152.5	405	6	67.50	2- 27	–	–
R.S.Mahanama	6	30	0	–	–	–	–
M.Muralitharan	1016.3	2745	81	33.88	5- 64	5	–
K.R.Pushpakumara	179.4	691	18	38.38	7-116	1	–
A.Ranatunga	360.2	942	14	67.28	2- 17	–	–
K.J.Silva	35	120	1	120.00	1-120	–	–
H.P.Tillekeratne	3.4	11	0	–	–	–	–
W.P.U.C.J.Vaas	466.5	1117	48	23.27	6- 87	4	1
G.P.Wickremasinghe	725.5	2220	46	48.26	5- 73	1	–

ZIMBABWE

BATTING AND FIELDING

	M	*I*	*NO*	*HS*	*Runs*	*Avge*	*100*	*50*	*Ct/St*
D.H.Brain	9	13	2	28	115	10.45	–	–	1
E.A.Brandes	8	12	2	39	102	10.20	–	–	4
I.P.Butchart	1	2	–	15	23	11.50	–	–	1
A.D.R.Campbell	16	27	1	99	819	31.50	–	7	10
S.V.Carlisle	5	8	1	58	171	24.42	–	1	8
M.H.Dekker	9	13	1	68*	233	19.41	–	2	10
A.Flower	16	26	5	156	1049	49.95	2	8	39/2
G.W.Flower	16	27	1	201*	796	30.61	1	4	8
D.L.Houghton	16	25	2	266	1113	48.39	4	2	11
W.R.James	4	4	–	33	61	15.25	–	–	16
M.P.Jarvis	5	3	1	2*	4	2.00	–	–	2
A.C.I.Lock	1	2	1	8*	8	8.00	–	–	–
H.K.Olonga	2	1	–	0	0	0.00	–	–	3
S.G.Peall	4	6	2	30	60	15.00	–	–	1
J.A.Rennie	3	4	1	19*	24	8.00	–	–	–
B.C.Strang	5	8	3	25*	49	9.80	–	–	4
P.A.Strang	7	10	1	49	204	22.66	–	–	4
H.H.Streak	12	17	2	53	188	12.53	–	1	4
G.J.Whittall	12	19	2	113*	482	28.35	1	2	6
C.B.Wishart	2	4	1	24	56	18.66	–	–	1

ZIMBABWE

BOWLING

	Overs	*Runs*	*Wkts*	*Avge*	*Best*	*5wI*	*10wM*
D.H.Brain	301.4	915	30	30.50	5- 42	1	–
E.A.Brandes	274.4	806	22	36.63	3- 45	–	–
I.P.Butchart	3	11	0	–	–	–	–
A.D.R.Campbell	5	7	0	–	–	–	–
M.H.Dekker	10	15	0	–	–	–	–
A.Flower	0.1	0	0	–	–	–	–
G.W.Flower	72	214	2	107.00	1- 8	–	–
D.L.Houghton	0.5	0	0	–	–	–	–
M.P.Jarvis	212.1	393	11	35.72	3- 30	–	–
A.C.I.Lock	30	105	5	21.00	3- 68	–	–
H.K.Olonga	27	112	2	56.00	1- 27	–	–
S.G.Peall	148	303	4	75.75	2- 89	–	–
J.A.Rennie	109.4	256	3	85.33	2- 22	–	–
B.C.Strang	216.1	437	18	24.27	5-101	1	–
P.A.Strang	195	548	7	78.28	3- 65	–	–
H.H.Streak	497.4	1257	58	21.67	6- 90	3	–
G.J.Whittall	266	675	19	35.52	4- 70	–	–

LIMITED-OVERS INTERNATIONALS CAREER RECORDS

These records, complete to 13 February 1996 (prior to the World Cup), include all players registered for county cricket in 1996, plus those who have appeared in internationals since 31 August 1994 or gained selection for the World Cup.

ENGLAND

BATTING AND FIELDING

	M	I	NO	HS	Runs	Avge	100	50	Ct/St
M.A.Atherton	31	31	2	127	1214	41.86	1	9	10
C.W.J.Athey	31	30	3	142*	848	31.40	2	4	1
R.J.Bailey	4	4	2	43*	137	68.50	–	–	1
K.J.Barnett	1	1	–	84	84	84.00	–	1	–
J.E.Benjamin	2	1	–	0	0	0.00	–	–	–
M.R.Benson	1	1	–	24	24	24.00	–	–	–
M.P.Bicknell	7	6	2	31*	96	24.00	–	–	2
R.J.Blakey	3	2	–	25	25	12.50	–	–	2/1
A.R.Caddick	5	3	3	21*	24	–	–	–	1
D.J.Capel	23	19	2	50*	327	19.23	–	1	6
D.G.Cork	14	8	–	21	56	7.00	–	–	1
J.P.Crawley	3	3	–	18	34	11.33	–	–	–
P.A.J.DeFreitas	97	64	23	49*	601	14.65	–	–	26
N.H.Fairbrother	51	49	11	113	1451	38.18	1	11	22
A.R.C.Fraser	33	14	6	38*	80	10.00	–	–	1
M.W.Gatting	92	88	17	115*	2095	29.50	1	9	22
G.A.Gooch	125	122	6	142	4290	36.98	8	23	45
D.Gough	16	12	3	45	93	10.33	–	–	3
G.A.Hick	54	53	6	105*	1770	37.65	1	14	29
N.Hussain	4	4	1	16	43	14.33	–	–	2
A.P.Igglesden	4	3	1	18	20	10.00	–	–	1
R.K.Illingworth	21	9	3	14	64	10.66	–	–	8
P.W.Jarvis	16	8	2	16*	31	5.16	–	–	1
A.J.Lamb	122	118	16	118	4010	39.31	4	26	31
C.C.Lewis	48	36	11	33	315	12.60	–	–	20
M.A.Lynch	3	3	–	6	8	2.66	–	–	1
D.E.Malcolm	10	5	2	4	9	3.00	–	–	1
P.J.Martin	7	5	4	6	21	21.00	–	–	–
M.P.Maynard	5	5	1	22*	59	14.75	–	–	1
J.E.Morris	8	8	1	63*	167	23.85	–	1	2
M.D.Moxon	8	8	–	70	174	21.75	–	1	5
M.R.Ramprakash	10	10	3	32	184	26.28	–	–	5
D.A.Reeve	27	19	9	33*	253	25.30	–	–	12
S.J.Rhodes	9	8	2	56	107	17.83	–	1	9/2
R.T.Robinson	26	26	–	83	597	22.96	–	3	6
R.C.Russell	31	24	7	50	354	20.82	–	1	32/5
I.D.K.Salisbury	4	2	1	5	7	7.00	–	–	1
G.C.Small	53	24	9	18*	98	6.53	–	–	7
N.M.K.Smith	2	1	–	3	3	3.00	–	–	–
R.A.Smith	69	68	8	167*	2319	38.65	4	14	25
A.J.Stewart	68	63	5	103	1796	30.96	1	12	55/4
J.P.Taylor	1	1	–	1	1	1.00	–	–	–

ENGLAND – BATTING AND FIELDING (continued)

	M	I	NO	HS	Runs	Avge	100	50	Ct/St
G.P.Thorpe	19	19	1	89	586	32.55	–	5	10
P.C.R.Tufnell	19	10	9	5*	15	15.00	–	–	3
S.D.Udal	10	6	4	11*	35	17.50	–	–	1
S.L.Watkin	4	2	–	4	4	2.00	–	–	–
M.Watkinson	1	–	–	–	–	–	–	–	–
A.P.Wells	1	1	–	15	15	15.00	–	–	–
C.M.Wells	2	2	–	17	22	11.00	–	–	–
J.J.Whitaker	2	2	1	44*	48	48.00	–	–	1
C.White	8	7	–	34	100	14.28	–	–	–

ENGLAND

BOWLING

	O	R	W	Avge	Best	4wI
C.W.J.Athey	1	10	0	–	–	–
R.J.Bailey	6	25	0	–	–	–
J.E.Benjamin	12	47	1	47.00	1-22	–
M.P.Bicknell	68.5	347	13	26.69	3-55	–
A.R.Caddick	53	258	6	43.00	3-39	–
D.J.Capel	173	805	17	47.35	3-38	–
D.G.Cork	142	608	21	28.95	3-27	–
P.A.J.DeFreitas	901.5	3553	109	32.59	4-35	1
N.H.Fairbrother	1	9	0	–	–	–
A.R.C.Fraser	312.4	1132	38	29.78	4-22	1
M.W.Gatting	65.2	336	10	33.60	3-32	–
G.A.Gooch	344.2	1516	36	42.11	3-19	–
D.Gough	151.4	551	28	19.67	5-44	2
G.A.Hick	120	577	15	38.46	3-41	–
A.P.Igglesden	28	122	2	61.00	2-12	–
R.K.Illingworth	210.1	885	26	34.03	3-33	–
P.W.Jarvis	146.3	672	24	28.00	5-35	2
A.J.Lamb	1	3	0	–	–	–
C.C.Lewis	391.4	1735	61	28.44	4-30	3
D.E.Malcolm	87.4	404	16	25.25	3-40	–
P.J.Martin	61.2	261	13	20.07	4-44	1
M.R.Ramprakash	2	14	0	–	–	–
D.A.Reeve	180.3	769	19	40.47	3-20	–
I.D.K.Salisbury	31	177	5	35.40	3-41	–
N.M.K.Smith	12	55	2	27.50	2-46	–
G.C.Small	465.3	1942	58	33.48	4-31	1
J.P.Taylor	3	20	0	–	–	–
P.C.R.Tufnell	160	676	15	45.06	3-40	–
S.D.Udal	95	372	8	46.50	2-37	–
S.L.Watkin	36.5	193	7	27.57	4-49	1
M.Watkinson	9	43	0	–	–	–
C.White	57.1	242	8	30.25	2-18	–

AUSTRALIA

BATTING AND FIELDING

	M	I	NO	HS	Runs	Avge	100	50	Ct/St
J.Angel	3	1	–	0	0	0.00	–	–	–
M.G.Bevan	25	23	13	78*	821	82.10	–	4	10
G.S.Blewett	8	8	–	46	111	13.87	–	–	1
D.C.Boon	181	177	16	122	5964	37.04	5	37	45
P.A.Emery	1	1	1	11*	11	–	–	–	3
D.W.Fleming	14	5	4	5*	14	14.00	–	–	3
I.A.Healy	139	96	32	56	1496	23.37	–	4	168/29
B.P.Julian	2	1	–	11	11	11.00	–	–	–
M.S.Kasprowicz	2	–	–	–	–	–	–	–	–
J.L.Langer	7	6	2	36	131	32.75	–	–	1/1
S.G.Law	14	14	1	110	385	29.61	1	2	4
S.Lee	6	5	1	39	52	13.00	–	–	4
C.J.McDermott	137	78	17	37	432	7.08	–	–	27
G.D.McGrath	44	14	7	10	26	3.71	–	–	4
T.B.A.May	47	12	8	15	39	9.75	–	–	3
R.T.Ponting	16	16	2	123	464	33.14	1	4	2
P.R.Reiffel	55	34	14	58	365	18.25	–	1	18
G.R.Robertson	4	3	2	5*	7	7.00	–	–	–
M.A.Slater	33	33	–	73	765	23.18	–	6	8
M.A.Taylor	89	86	1	97	2834	33.34	–	25	47
S.K.Warne	52	25	8	55	240	14.11	–	1	17
M.E.Waugh	106	102	8	130	3244	34.51	5	22	43
S.R.Waugh	189	169	40	102*	3980	30.85	1	19	64

AUSTRALIA

BOWLING

	O	R	W	Avge	Best	4wI
J.Angel	27	113	4	28.25	2-47	–
M.G.Bevan	31.3	155	5	31.00	2-31	–
G.S.Blewett	43.5	249	4	62.25	1-30	–
D.C.Boon	13.4	86	0	–	–	–
D.W.Fleming	127.2	517	20	25.85	4-39	2
B.P.Julian	21	116	3	38.66	3-50	–
M.S.Kasprowicz	16	83	2	41.50	1-32	–
S.G.Law	70	276	6	46.00	2-30	–
S.Lee	47	176	4	44.00	1-20	–
C.J.McDermott	1240.3	5006	202	24.78	5-44	5
G.D.McGrath	392.3	1512	62	24.38	5-52	4
T.B.A.May	417.2	1771	39	45.41	3-19	–
P.R.Reiffel	489.1	1814	74	24.51	4-13	4
G.R.Robertson	24	127	0	–	–	–
M.A.Slater	2	11	0	–	–	–
S.K.Warne	482.4	1870	87	21.49	4-19	5
M.E.Waugh	330.3	1581	58	27.25	5-24	2
S.R.Waugh	1226	5442	162	33.59	4-33	2

SOUTH AFRICA

BATTING AND FIELDING

	M	I	NO	HS	Runs	Avge	100	50	Ct/St
P.R.Adams	3	2	1	0*	0	0.00	–	–	1
N.Boje	2	1	1	2*	2	–	–	–	–
D.J.Callaghan	27	24	6	169*	478	26.55	1	–	6
W.J.Cronje	77	74	11	112	2263	35.92	2	12	29
D.N.Crookes	3	3	–	20	30	10.00	–	–	–
D.J.Cullinan	41	40	4	70*	927	25.75	–	5	15
P.S.de Villiers	62	27	12	20	123	8.20	–	–	12
A.A.Donald	57	18	10	7*	34	4.25	–	–	7
C.E.Eksteen	5	1	1	0*	0	–	–	–	1
A.C.Hudson	60	59	–	108	1714	29.05	1	13	7
S.D.Jack	2	2	–	6	7	3.50	–	–	3
J.H.Kallis	7	7	1	67	166	27.66	–	1	1
G.Kirsten	35	35	3	116	1143	35.71	2	6	9
L.Klusener	1	1	–	0	0	0.00	–	–	–
A.P.Kuiper	25	23	7	63*	539	33.68	–	3	3
G.F.J.Liebenberg	1	1	–	12	12	12.00	–	–	–
B.M.McMillan	48	33	11	127	598	27.18	1	–	28
C.R.Matthews	43	19	6	26	124	9.53	–	–	7
S.J.Palframan	1	1	–	10	10	10.00	–	–	1
S.M.Pollock	7	6	3	66*	96	32.00	–	1	2
M.W.Pringle	17	8	3	13*	48	9.60	–	–	2
J.N.Rhodes	76	72	10	66	1745	28.14	–	6	27
D.J.Richardson	77	54	21	53	670	20.30	–	1	101/12
M.J.R.Rindel	8	8	2	106*	215	35.83	1	–	4
T.G.Shaw	9	6	4	17*	26	13.00	–	–	2
E.O.Simons	23	18	4	24	217	15.50	–	–	6
R.P.Snell	42	28	8	63	322	16.10	–	2	7
P.J.R.Steyn	1	1	–	4	4	4.00	–	–	–
P.L.Symcox	19	15	2	35	113	8.69	–	–	6

SOUTH AFRICA

BOWLING

	O	R	W	Avge	Best	4wI
P.R.Adams	20	66	4	16.50	3-26	–
N.Boje	14	54	0	–	–	–
D.J.Callaghan	74	365	10	36.50	3-32	–
W.J.Cronje	431.3	1800	54	33.33	5-32	2
D.N.Crookes	10	48	0	–	–	–
P.S.de Villiers	554	1918	67	28.62	4-27	2
A.A.Donald	510.2	2069	81	25.54	5-29	3
C.E.Eksteen	35	163	2	81.50	1-26	–
S.D.Jack	18	86	3	28.66	2-41	–
J.H.Kallis	11	50	0	–	–	–
G.Kirsten	2	14	0	–	–	–
L.Klusener	4	19	0	–	–	–
A.P.Kuiper	98	518	18	28.77	3-33	–
B.M.McMillan	378.5	1652	44	37.54	4-32	1
C.R.Matthews	393.5	1558	66	23.60	4-10	3
S.M.Pollock	65.1	212	13	16.30	4-34	1
M.W.Pringle	145	604	22	27.45	4-11	1

SOUTH AFRICA – BOWLING (continued)

	O	R	W	Avge	Best	4wI
M.J.R.Rindel	19	89	3	29.66	2-15	–
T.G.Shaw	84	298	9	33.11	2-19	–
E.O.Simons	202	810	33	24.54	4-42	1
R.P.Snell	349.1	1574	44	35.77	5-40	3
P.L.Symcox	149	534	18	29.66	3-20	–

WEST INDIES

BATTING AND FIELDING

	M	I	NO	HS	Runs	Avge	100	50	Ct/St
J.C.Adams	50	37	12	81*	692	27.68	–	6	26/4
C.E.L.Ambrose	122	64	28	26*	403	11.19	–	–	33
H.A.G.Anthony	3	3	–	21	23	7.66	–	–	–
K.L.T.Arthurton	81	71	15	84	1650	29.46	–	9	20
K.C.G.Benjamin	23	11	7	17	54	13.50	–	–	4
W.K.M.Benjamin	85	52	12	31	298	7.45	–	–	16
I.R.Bishop	66	33	14	33*	270	14.21	–	–	11
B.St A.Browne	4	3	2	8*	8	8.00	–	–	–
C.O.Browne	13	11	3	22	82	10.25	–	–	22/3
S.L.Campbell	22	22	–	86	553	25.13	–	2	9
S.Chanderpaul	18	16	1	77	443	29.53	–	3	4
C.E.Cuffy	9	5	3	17*	20	10.00	–	–	2
A.C.Cummins	63	41	11	44*	459	15.30	–	–	11
R.Dhanraj	6	2	1	8	8	8.00	–	–	1
V.C.Drakes	5	2	–	16	25	12.50	–	–	1
O.D.Gibson	10	8	1	52	131	18.71	–	1	2
R.A.Harper	93	63	18	45*	744	16.53	–	–	44
R.I.C.Holder	18	15	3	50	330	27.50	–	1	6
C.L.Hooper	141	126	29	113*	3270	33.71	2	19	70
B.C.Lara	92	91	7	169	3702	44.07	6	27	48
J.R.Murray	38	19	6	86	213	16.38	–	1	35/5
R.B.Richardson	218	211	28	122	6012	32.85	5	43	73
P.V.Simmons	111	109	6	122	2963	28.76	4	17	45
C.A.Walsh	150	55	23	30	259	8.09	–	–	21
S.C.Williams	24	24	2	73*	646	29.36	–	4	5

WEST INDIES

BOWLING

	O	R	W	Avge	Best	4wI
J.C.Adams	13	59	2	29.50	1- 2	–
C.E.L.Ambrose	1083.5	3783	164	23.06	5-17	8
H.A.G.Anthony	26	143	3	47.66	2-47	–
K.L.T.Arthurton	112.5	558	21	26.57	3-31	–
K.C.G.Benjamin	192.1	800	31	25.80	3-34	–
W.K.M.Benjamin	740.2	3079	100	30.79	5-22	1
I.R.Bishop	584.1	2441	106	23.02	5-25	8
B.St A.Browne	30	156	2	78.00	2-50	–
S.Chanderpaul	34	206	1	206.00	1-18	–

WEST INDIES – BOWLING (continued)

	O	R	W	Avge	Best	4wI
C.E.Cuffy	74.1	288	6	48.00	2-19	–
A.C.Cummins	523.5	2246	78	28.79	5-31	3
R.Dhanraj	44	170	10	17.00	4-26	1
V.C.Drakes	39.5	204	3	68.00	1-36	–
O.D.Gibson	85.3	422	28	15.07	5-40	3
R.A.Harper	747	2972	81	36.69	4-40	2
C.L.Hooper	937.4	4107	129	31.83	4-34	1
B.C.Lara	4	22	2	11.00	2- 5	–
R.B.Richardson	9.4	46	1	46.00	1- 4	–
P.V.Simmons	451.4	1931	57	33.87	4- 3	2
C.A.Walsh	1319	5038	166	30.34	5- 1	6

NEW ZEALAND

BATTING AND FIELDING

	M	I	NO	HS	Runs	Avge	100	50	Ct/St
N.J.Astle	17	17	1	120	582	36.37	2	2	4
C.L.Cairns	38	34	4	103	820	27.33	1	3	14
M.D.Crowe	143	141	19	107*	4704	38.55	4	34	66
R.P.de Groen	12	8	3	7*	12	2.40	–	–	2
M.W.Douglas	6	6	–	30	55	9.16	–	–	2
S.B.Doull	9	8	4	19*	63	15.75	–	–	–
S.P.Fleming	37	36	3	90	984	29.81	–	8	12
L.K.Germon	13	8	–	40	96	12.00	–	–	4/1
M.J.Greatbatch	78	78	5	111	2086	28.57	2	12	32
C.Z.Harris	58	50	14	68*	844	23.44	–	3	14
M.N.Hart	10	6	–	16	49	8.16	–	–	7
B.A.Hartland	16	16	1	68*	311	20.73	–	2	5
R.L.Hayes	1	1	–	13	13	13.00	–	–	–
A.H.Jones	87	87	9	93	2784	35.69	–	25	23
R.J.Kennedy	2	1	1	8*	8	–	–	–	–
G.R.Larsen	76	45	20	37	444	17.76	–	–	12
D.K.Morrison	86	37	19	20*	154	8.55	–	–	17
D.J.Murray	1	1	–	3	3	3.00	–	–	–
D.J.Nash	22	15	4	40*	113	10.27	–	–	6
A.C.Parore	45	41	9	108	1165	36.40	1	6	31/8
D.N.Patel	56	44	5	40	454	11.64	–	–	19
M.W.Priest	12	10	2	24	95	11.87	–	–	2
C.Pringle	64	41	19	34*	193	8.77	–	–	7
K.R.Rutherford	121	115	9	108	3143	29.65	2	18	41
C.M.Spearman	7	7	–	48	145	20.71	–	–	3
M.L.Su'a	12	7	2	12*	24	4.80	–	–	1
S.A.Thomson	48	45	8	83	851	23.00	–	5	14
R.G.Twose	12	11	–	60	375	34.09	–	3	3
J.T.C.Vaughan	13	12	4	33	131	16.37	–	–	3
B.A.Young	47	46	4	74	997	23.73	–	3	19

NEW ZEALAND

BOWLING

	O	R	W	Avge	Best	4wI
N.J.Astle	84.4	409	7	58.42	3-42	–
C.L.Cairns	261	1211	39	31.05	4-55	1
M.D.Crowe	216	954	29	32.89	2- 9	–
R.P.de Groen	91.3	477	8	59.62	2-34	–
S.B.Doull	74.4	447	9	49.66	3-42	–
S.P.Fleming	0.5	5	0	–	–	–
M.J.Greatbatch	1	5	0	–	–	–
C.Z.Harris	407.2	1887	53	35.60	3-15	–
M.N.Hart	81.2	314	11	28.54	5-22	1
R.L.Hayes	7	31	0	–	–	–
A.H.Jones	51	216	4	54.00	2-42	–
R.J.Kennedy	19	124	0	–	–	–
G.R.Larsen	682	2552	61	41.83	4-24	1
D.K.Morrison	696.1	3133	112	27.97	5-46	2
D.J.Nash	167	796	19	41.89	3-30	–
D.N.Patel	390.5	1604	35	45.82	3-22	–
M.W.Priest	84.3	418	4	104.50	2-27	–
C.Pringle	552.2	2455	103	23.83	5-45	3
K.R.Rutherford	64.5	323	10	32.30	2-39	–
M.L.Su'a	77.1	367	9	40.77	4-59	1
S.A.Thomson	302	1345	37	36.35	3-14	–
R.G.Twose	29.2	139	4	34.75	2-31	–
J.T.C.Vaughan	72	314	10	31.40	4-33	1

INDIA

BATTING AND FIELDING

	M	I	NO	HS	Runs	Avge	100	50	Ct/St
S.A.Ankola	14	8	4	7*	14	3.50	–	–	1
M.Azharuddin	199	184	35	108*	5400	36.24	3	30	82
A.C.Bedade	12	10	3	51	158	22.57	–	1	4
U.Chatterjee	3	2	1	3*	6	6.00	–	–	1
R.K.Chauhan	20	8	3	26*	73	14.60	–	–	5
A.D.Jadeja	42	38	3	104	1166	33.31	1	7	12
V.G.Kambli	61	57	14	100*	1741	40.48	1	11	10
Kapil Dev	224	198	39	175*	3783	23.79	1	14	71
A.R.Kapoor	7	1	–	6	6	6.00	–	–	–
A.Kumble	71	30	11	24	171	9.00	–	–	21
S.V.Manjrekar	59	55	9	105	1604	34.86	1	12	19
N.R.Mongia	34	18	8	40*	239	23.90	–	–	41/12
M.Prabhakar	125	94	20	106	1844	24.91	2	11	25
B.K.V.Prasad	21	6	2	5*	9	2.25	–	–	8
S.L.V.Raju	42	12	5	8	29	4.14	–	–	7
C.Sharma	65	35	16	101*	456	24.00	1	–	6
N.S.Sidhu	92	89	8	134*	3467	42.80	5	28	15
J.Srinath	82	34	14	37	176	8.80	–	–	12
S.R.Tendulkar	101	98	10	115	3201	36.37	4	22	30
P.S.Vaidya	2	–	–	–	–	–	–	–	2
V.Yadav	19	12	2	34*	118	11.80	–	–	12/7

INDIA

BOWLING

	O	R	W	Avge	Best	4wI
S.A.Ankola	89.3	386	11	35.09	3-33	–
M.Azharuddin	90	468	12	39.00	3-19	–
U.Chatterjee	26.5	117	3	39.00	2-35	–
R.K.Chauhan	168	714	21	34.00	3-29	–
A.D.Jadeja	89	453	8	56.62	2-16	–
V.G.Kambli	0.4	7	1	7.00	1- 7	–
Kapil Dev	1867	6946	253	27.45	5-43	4
A.R.Kapoor	63	234	5	46.80	2-33	–
A.Kumble	644.1	2581	87	29.66	6-12	4
S.V.Manjrekar	0.5	6	1	6.00	1- 2	–
M.Prabhakar	1031	4374	154	28.40	5-33	6
B.K.V.Prasad	158.2	731	19	38.47	3-36	–
S.L.V.Raju	358.5	1498	45	33.28	4-46	2
C.Sharma	472.3	2336	67	34.86	3-22	–
N.S.Sidhu	0.3	2	0	–	–	–
J.Srinath	698	2976	118	25.22	5-24	3
S.R.Tendulkar	377.1	1752	34	51.52	4-34	1
P.S.Vaidya	15.4	77	3	25.66	2-41	–

PAKISTAN

BATTING AND FIELDING

	M	I	NO	HS	Runs	Avge	100	50	Ct/St
Aamer Malik	24	23	1	90	556	25.27	–	5	13
Aamir Hanif	5	4	2	36*	89	44.50	–	–	–
Aamir Nazir	9	3	2	9*	13	13.00	–	–	–
Aamir Sohail	85	84	1	134	2682	32.31	3	17	22
Akram Raza	49	25	14	33*	193	17.54	–	–	19
Aqib Javed	121	36	22	21	144	10.28	–	–	16
Arshad Khan	4	3	2	9*	15	15.00	–	–	3
Asif Mujtaba	65	54	14	113*	1066	26.65	1	6	18
Ata-ur-Rehman	25	9	5	11*	27	6.75	–	–	–
Basit Ali	47	41	6	127*	1225	35.00	1	9	15
Ghulam Ali	2	2	–	38	51	25.50	–	–	–
Ijaz Ahmed	121	107	17	124*	2391	26.56	4	10	42
Inzamam-ul-Haq	96	93	13	137*	3306	41.32	4	24	25
Javed Miandad	228	215	40	119*	7327	41.86	8	50	68/2
Javed Qadir	1	1	–	12	12	12.00	–	–	1
Kabir Khan	2	–	–	–	–	–	–	–	–
Manzoor Elahi	54	46	13	50*	741	22.45	–	1	21
Mehmood Hamid	1	1	–	1	1	1.00	–	–	–
Mohammad Akram	5	3	2	7*	8	8.00	–	–	–
Moin Khan	40	26	7	31	277	14.57	–	–	45/12
Mushtaq Ahmed	90	47	18	26	263	9.06	–	–	19
Nadeem Khan	1	1	–	2	2	2.00	–	–	–
Naeem Ashraf	2	2	1	16	24	24.00	–	–	–

PAKISTAN – BATTING AND FIELDING (continued)

	M	I	NO	HS	Runs	Avge	100	50	Ct/St
Ramiz Raja	170	169	13	119*	5257	33.69	9	29	26
Rashid Latif	70	48	14	39	518	15.23	–	–	68/18
Saeed Anwar	82	81	6	131	2541	33.88	8	7	19
Saeed Azad	1	1	–	19	19	19.00	–	–	1
Salim Elahi	8	8	1	102*	311	44.42	1	2	2
Salim Malik	214	194	28	102	5442	32.78	5	35	64
Saqlain Mushtaq	5	2	–	30	30	15.00	–	–	3
Shakil Ahmed	2	2	–	36	61	30.50	–	–	–
Waqar Younis	112	52	17	37	335	9.57	–	–	10
Wasim Akram	193	148	28	86	1746	14.55	–	2	38
Zafar Iqbal	8	6	–	18	48	8.00	–	–	1
Zahid Fazal	19	18	3	98*	348	23.20	–	2	2

PAKISTAN

BOWLING

	O	R	W	Avge	Best	4wI
Aamer Malik	20	86	3	28.66	2-35	–
Aamir Hanif	21.4	122	4	30.50	3-36	–
Aamir Nazir	69.3	346	11	31.45	3-43	–
Aamir Sohail	478.1	2079	59	35.23	4-22	1
Akram Raza	433.3	1611	38	42.39	3-18	–
Aqib Javed	1018.3	4162	134	31.05	7-37	3
Arshad Khan	32.5	116	2	58.00	1-29	–
Asif Mujtaba	121	631	7	90.14	2-38	–
Ata-ur-Rehman	215.5	980	21	46.66	3-32	–
Basit Ali	5	21	1	21.00	1-17	–
Ijaz Ahmed	63	272	3	90.66	2-31	–
Inzamam-ul-Haq	5.4	42	2	21.00	1- 4	–
Javed Miandad	72.4	297	7	42.42	2-22	–
Kabir Khan	19.2	66	3	22.00	2-32	–
Manzoor Elahi	290.5	1262	29	43.51	3-22	–
Mohammad Akram	40	189	6	31.50	2-36	–
Mushtaq Ahmed	753.3	3295	99	33.28	3-14	–
Nadeem Khan	10	42	0	–	–	–
Naeem Ashraf	7	52	0	–	–	–
Ramiz Raja	1	10	0	–	–	–
Saeed Anwar	25	130	3	43.33	1- 9	–
Salim Malik	368.2	1808	55	32.87	5-35	1
Saqlain Mushtaq	39.5	173	8	21.62	4-47	1
Waqar Younis	926.5	4118	187	22.02	6-26	15
Wasim Akram	1669.4	6281	282	22.27	5-15	15
Zafar Iqbal	33	137	3	45.66	2-37	–

SRI LANKA

BATTING AND FIELDING

	M	*I*	*NO*	*HS*	*Runs*	*Avge*	*100*	*50*	*Ct/St*
M.S.Atapattu	7	7	3	19*	43	10.75	–	–	1
U.U.Chandana	5	3	–	26	46	15.33	–	–	3
P.B.Dassanayake	15	10	2	20*	85	10.62	–	–	9/4
P.A.de Silva	174	170	15	107*	4842	31.23	3	34	49
H.D.P.K.Dharmasena	26	19	9	30*	241	24.10	–	–	3
C.I.Dunusinghe	1	1	–	1	1	1.00	–	–	1/1
J.C.Gamage	4	2	2	7*	8	–	–	–	2
A.P.Gurusinha	128	126	5	117*	3345	27.64	2	18	45
U.C.Hathurusinghe	32	30	1	66	648	22.34	–	4	5
S.T.Jayasuriya	98	92	2	140	1776	19.73	1	9	37
R.S.Kalpage	74	61	27	51	750	22.05	–	1	25
R.S.Kaluwitharana	40	37	3	77	535	15.73	–	3	25/13
R.S.Mahanama	135	132	13	119*	3564	29.94	4	23	72
M.C.Mendis	1	1	1	3*	3	–	–	–	2
M.Munasinghe	5	4	1	8	14	4.33	–	–	–
M.Muralitharan	35	14	8	8	31	5.16	–	–	15
K.R.Pushpakumara	18	6	4	14*	34	17.00	–	–	4
C.P.H.Ramanayake	62	35	14	26	210	10.00	–	–	11
A.Ranatunga	177	169	30	102*	4908	35.30	2	32	39
S.Ranatunga	12	11	–	70	253	23.00	–	2	2
K.J.Silva	1	1	1	1*	1	–	–	–	–
H.P.Tillekeratne	122	107	26	104	2335	28.82	2	8	57/5
E.Upashanta	3	2	1	8*	11	11.00	–	–	1
W.P.U.C.J.Vaas	40	24	13	33	197	17.90	–	–	7
G.P.Wickremasinghe	75	27	10	21*	118	6.94	–	–	15

SRI LANKA

BOWLING

	O	*R*	*W*	*Avge*	*Best*	*4wI*
M.S.Atapattu	0.3	21	0	–	–	–
U.U.Chandana	3	21	0	–	–	–
P.A.de Silva	390.2	1935	45	43.00	3-36	–
H.D.P.K.Dharmasena	212	932	29	32.13	4-37	1
J.C.Gamage	22	104	3	34.66	2-17	–
A.P.Gurusinha	262.1	1337	26	51.42	2-25	–
U.C.Hathurusinghe	140	614	14	43.85	4-57	1
S.T.Jayasuriya	509	2464	71	34.70	6-29	3
R.S.Kalpage	576	2547	66	38.59	4-36	1
R.S.Mahanama	0.2	7	0	–	–	–
M.Munasinghe	36.1	146	4	36.50	3-30	–
M.Muralitharan	309.2	1301	37	35.16	4-23	1
K.R.Pushpakumara	145.2	687	14	49.07	3-25	–
C.P.H.Ramanayake	477.2	2049	68	30.13	4-17	1
A.Ranatunga	746	3536	74	47.78	4-14	1
K.J.Silva	8	55	0	–	–	–
H.P.Tillekeratne	18	70	2	35.00	1- 3	–
E.Upashanta	19	91	3	30.33	2-24	–
W.P.U.C.J.Vaas	333	1303	50	26.06	4-20	1
G.P.Wickremasinghe	543.2	2360	57	41.40	3-28	–

ZIMBABWE

BATTING AND FIELDING

	M	I	NO	HS	Runs	Avge	100	50	Ct/St
D.H.Brain	23	18	4	27	117	8.35	–	–	5
E.A.Brandes	27	20	3	55	188	11.05	–	1	7
M.G.Burmester	8	7	1	39	109	18.16	–	–	2
I.P.Butchart	20	16	2	54	252	18.00	–	1	4
A.D.R.Campbell	31	29	2	131*	613	22.70	1	2	8
S.V.Carlisle	5	5	1	28	66	16.50	–	–	2
S.C.Davies	3	3	–	45	58	19.33	–	–	–
M.H.Dekker	19	18	1	79	339	19.94	–	2	5
C.N.Evans	7	7	–	22	46	6.57	–	–	1
A.Flower	39	38	2	115*	1120	31.11	1	8	34/5
G.W.Flower	29	27	1	84*	725	27.88	–	5	16
D.L.Houghton	47	45	1	142	1280	29.09	1	10	24/2
W.R.James	10	8	1	29	101	14.42	–	–	6
M.P.Jarvis	12	5	3	17	37	18.50	–	–	1
A.C.I.Lock	2	–	–	–	–	–	–	–	1
G.C.Martin	5	4	–	16	31	7.75	–	–	–
H.K.Olonga	2	1	–	6	6	6.00	–	–	–
S.G.Peall	16	13	1	21	82	6.83	–	–	–
J.A.Rennie	9	6	5	20*	47	47.00	–	–	3
B.C.Strang	6	4	3	4*	7	7.00	–	–	3
P.A.Strang	12	11	4	28*	169	24.14	–	–	2
H.H.Streak	21	17	6	36*	202	18.36	–	–	3
A.C.Waller	24	23	3	83*	503	25.15	–	2	8
G.J.Whittall	20	20	2	70	360	20.00	–	2	7

ZIMBABWE

BOWLING

	O	R	W	Avge	Best	4wI
D.H.Brain	181.5	849	21	40.42	3-51	–
E.A.Brandes	224.1	1134	32	35.43	4-21	1
M.G.Burmester	34.5	213	5	42.60	3-36	–
I.P.Butchart	117	640	12	53.33	3-57	–
A.D.R.Campbell	17.3	67	2	33.50	2-22	–
M.H.Dekker	50.5	241	9	26.77	2-16	–
C.N.Evans	2	6	1	6.00	1- 6	–
A.Flower	5	23	0	–	–	–
G.W.Flower	97	506	14	36.14	3-15	–
D.L.Houghton	2	19	1	19.00	1-19	–
M.P.Jarvis	100.1	451	9	50.11	2-37	–
A.C.I.Lock	16.1	78	5	15.60	5-44	1
G.C.Martin	22	95	2	47.50	1-15	–
H.K.Olonga	14	91	1	91.00	1-59	–
S.G.Peall	127	577	7	82.42	3-54	–
J.A.Rennie	63.4	352	4	88.00	2-42	–
B.C.Strang	51.3	208	7	29.71	4-36	1
P.A.Strang	107	456	12	38.00	3-42	–
H.H.Streak	182.1	782	28	27.92	4-25	2
G.J.Whittall	109.2	571	16	35.68	3-46	–

FIRST-CLASS CRICKET RECORDS

To the end of the 1995 season

TEAM RECORDS

HIGHEST INNINGS TOTALS

1107	Victoria v New South Wales	Melbourne	1926-27
1059	Victoria v Tasmania	Melbourne	1922-23
951-7d	Sind v Baluchistan	Karachi	1973-74
944-6d	Hyderabad v Andhra	Secunderabad	1993-94
918	New South Wales v South Australia	Sydney	1900-01
912-8d	Holkar v Mysore	Indore	1945-46
910-6d	Railways v Dera Ismail Khan	Lahore	1964-65
903-7d	England v Australia	The Oval	1938
887	Yorkshire v Warwickshire	Birmingham	1896
863	Lancashire v Surrey	The Oval	1990
860-6d	Tamil Nadu v Goa	Panjim	1988-89

Excluding penalty runs in India, there have been 29 innings totals of 800 runs or more in first-class cricket, the most recent being 802-8d by Karachi Blues v Lahore at Peshawar in 1994-95. Tamil Nadu's total of 860-6d was boosted to 912 by 52 penalty runs.

HIGHEST SECOND INNINGS TOTAL

770	New South Wales v South Australia	Adelaide	1920-21

HIGHEST FOURTH INNINGS TOTAL

654-5	England v South Africa	Durban	1938-39

HIGHEST MATCH AGGREGATE

2376	Maharashtra v Bombay	Poona	1948-49

RECORD MARGIN OF VICTORY

Innings and 851 runs: Railways v Dera Ismail Khan	Lahore	1964-65

MOST RUNS IN A DAY

721	Australians v Essex	Southend	1948

MOST HUNDREDS IN AN INNINGS

6	Holkar v Mysore	Indore	1945-46

LOWEST INNINGS TOTALS

12	†Oxford University v MCC and Ground	Oxford	1877
12	Northamptonshire v Gloucestershire	Gloucester	1907
13	Auckland v Canterbury	Auckland	1877-78
13	Nottinghamshire v Yorkshire	Nottingham	1901
14	Surrey v Essex	Chelmsford	1983
15	MCC v Surrey	Lord's	1839
15	†Victoria v MCC	Melbourne	1903-04
15	†Northamptonshire v Yorkshire	Northampton	1908
15	Hampshire v Warwickshire	Birmingham	1922

† *Batted one man short*

There have been 26 instances of a team being dismissed for under 20, the most recent being by Surrey in 1983 (above).

LOWEST MATCH AGGREGATE BY ONE TEAM

34 (16 and 18)	Border v Natal	East London	1959-60

LOWEST COMPLETED MATCH AGGREGATE BY BOTH TEAMS

105	MCC v Australians	Lord's	1878

FEWEST RUNS IN AN UNINTERRUPTED DAY'S PLAY

95	Australia (80) v Pakistan (15-2)	Karachi	1956-57

TIED MATCHES

Before 1948 a match was considered to be tied if the scores were level after the fourth innings, even if the side batting last had wickets in hand when play ended. Law 22 was amended in 1948 and since then a match has been tied only when the scores are level after the fourth innings has been completed. There have been 53 tied first-class matches, five of which would not have qualified under the current law. The most recent is:

Worcestershire (203/325-8d) v Nottinghamshire (233/295)	Nottingham	1993

BATTING RECORDS

HIGHEST INDIVIDUAL INNINGS

501*	B.C.Lara	Warwickshire v Durham	Birmingham	1994
499	Hanif Mohammad	Karachi v Bahawalpur	Karachi	1958-59
452*	D.G.Bradman	New South Wales v Queensland	Sydney	1929-30
443*	B.B.Nimbalkar	Maharashtra v Kathiawar	Poona	1948-49
437	W.H.Ponsford	Victoria v Queensland	Melbourne	1927-28
429	W.H.Ponsford	Victoria v Tasmania	Melbourne	1922-23
428	Aftab Baloch	Sind v Baluchistan	Karachi	1973-74
424	A.C.MacLaren	Lancashire v Somerset	Taunton	1895
405*	G.A.Hick	Worcestershire v Somerset	Taunton	1988
385	B.Sutcliffe	Otago v Canterbury	Christchurch	1952-53
383	C.W.Gregory	New South Wales v Queensland	Brisbane	1906-07
377	S.V.Manjrekar	Bombay v Hyderabad	Bombay	1990-91
375	B.C.Lara	West Indies v England	St John's	1993-94
369	D.G.Bradman	South Australia v Tasmania	Adelaide	1935-36
366	N.H.Fairbrother	Lancashire v Surrey	The Oval	1990
366	M.V.Sridhar	Hyderabad v Andhra	Secunderabad	1993-94
365*	C.Hill	South Australia v NSW	Adelaide	1900-01
365*	G.St A.Sobers	West Indies v Pakistan	Kingston	1957-58
364	L.Hutton	England v Australia	The Oval	1938
359*	V.M.Merchant	Bombay v Maharashtra	Bombay	1943-44
359	R.B.Simpson	New South Wales v Queensland	Brisbane	1963-64
357*	R.Abel	Surrey v Somerset	The Oval	1899
357	D.G.Bradman	South Australia v Victoria	Melbourne	1935-36
356	B.A.Richards	South Australia v W Australia	Perth	1970-71
355*	G.R.Marsh	W Australia v S Australia	Perth	1989-90
355	B.Sutcliffe	Otago v Auckland	Dunedin	1949-50
352	W.H.Ponsford	Victoria v New South Wales	Melbourne	1926-27
350	Rashid Israr	Habib Bank v National Bank	Lahore	1976-77

There have been 114 triple hundreds in first-class cricket. W.V.Raman (313) and Arjan Kripal Singh (302*) for Tamil Nadu v Goa at Panjim in 1988-89 providing the only instance of two batsmen scoring 300 in the same innings.

MOST HUNDREDS IN SUCCESSIVE INNINGS

6	C.B.Fry	Sussex and Rest of England	1901
6	D.G.Bradman	South Australia and D.G.Bradman's XI	1938-39
6	M.J.Procter	Rhodesia	1970-71

TWO DOUBLE HUNDREDS IN A MATCH

244	202*	A.E.Fagg	Kent v Essex	Colchester	1938

TRIPLE HUNDRED AND HUNDRED IN A MATCH

333	123	G.A.Gooch	England v India	Lord's	1990

DOUBLE HUNDRED AND HUNDRED IN A MATCH MOST TIMES

4	Zaheer Abbas	Gloucestershire	1976-81

TWO HUNDREDS IN A MATCH MOST TIMES

8	Zaheer Abbas	Gloucestershire and PIA	1976-82
7	W.R.Hammond	Gloucestershire, England and MCC	1927-45

MOST HUNDREDS IN A SEASON

18	D.C.S.Compton	1947	16	J.B.Hobbs	1925

MOST HUNDREDS IN A CAREER

	Total		*100th Hundred*	
	Hundreds	***Inns***	***Season***	***Inns***
J.B.Hobbs	197	1315	1923	821
E.H.Hendren	170	1300	1928-29	740
W.R.Hammond	167	1005	1935	679
C.P.Mead	153	1340	1927	892
G.Boycott	151	1014	1977	645
H.Sutcliffe	149	1088	1932	700
F.E.Woolley	145	1532	1929	1031
L.Hutton	129	814	1951	619
W.G Grace	126	1493	1895	1113
D.C.S.Compton	123	839	1952	552
T.W.Graveney	122	1223	1964	940
G.A.Gooch	120	941	1992-93	820
D.G.Bradman	117	338	1947-48	295
I.V.A.Richards	114	796	1988-89	658
Zaheer Abbas	108	768	1982-83	658
A.Sandham	107	1000	1935	871
M.C.Cowdrey	107	1130	1973	1035
T.W.Hayward	104	1138	1913	1076
J.H.Edrich	103	979	1977	945
G.M.Turner	103	792	1982	779
G.E.Tyldesley	102	961	1934	919
L.E.G.Ames	102	951	1950	915
D.L.Amiss	102	1139	1986	1081

MOST 400s: 2 – W.H.Ponsford
MOST 300s or more: 6 – D.G.Bradman
MOST 200s or more: 37 – D.G.Bradman; 36 – W.R.Hammond

MOST RUNS IN A MONTH

1294 (avge 92.42)	L.Hutton	Yorkshire	June 1949

MOST RUNS IN A SEASON

Runs			*I*	*NO*	*HS*	*Avge*	*100*	*Season*
3816	D.C.S.Compton	Middlesex	50	8	246	90.85	18	1947
3539	W.J.Edrich	Middlesex	52	8	267*	80.43	12	1947
3518	T.W.Hayward	Surrey	61	8	219	66.37	13	1906

The feat of scoring 3000 runs in a season has been achieved on 28 occasions, the most recent instance being by W.E.Alley (3019) in 1961. The highest aggregate in a season since 1969, when the number of County Championship matches was substantially reduced, is 2755 by S.J.Cook in 1991.

1000 RUNS IN A SEASON MOST TIMES

28 W.G.Grace (Gloucestershire), F.E.Woolley (Kent)

HIGHEST BATTING AVERAGE IN A SEASON

(Qualification: 12 innings)

Avge			*I*	*NO*	*HS*	*Runs*	*100*	*Season*
115.66	D.G.Bradman	Australians	26	5	278	2429	13	1938
102.53	G.Boycott	Yorkshire	20	5	175*	1538	6	1979
102.00	W.A.Johnston	Australians	17	16	28*	102	–	1953
101.70	G.A.Gooch	Essex	30	3	333	2746	12	1990
100.12	G.Boycott	Yorkshire	30	5	233	2503	13	1971

FASTEST HUNDRED AGAINST AUTHENTIC BOWLING

35 min	P.G.H.Fender	Surrey v Northamptonshire	Northampton	1920

FASTEST DOUBLE HUNDRED

113 min	R.J.Shastri	Bombay v Baroda	Bombay	1984-85

FASTEST TRIPLE HUNDRED

181 min	D.C.S.Compton	MCC v NE Transvaal	Benoni	1948-49

MOST SIXES IN AN INNINGS

16	A.Symonds	Gloucestershire v Glamorgan	Abergavenny	1995

MOST SIXES IN A MATCH

20	A.Symonds	Gloucestershire v Glamorgan	Abergavenny	1995

MOST SIXES IN A SEASON

80	I.T.Botham	Somerset and England	1985

MOST BOUNDARIES IN AN INNINGS

72	B.C.Lara	Warwickshire v Durham	Birmingham	1994

MOST RUNS OFF ONE OVER

36	G.St A.Sobers	Nottinghamshire v Glamorgan	Swansea	1968
36	R.J.Shastri	Bombay v Baroda	Bombay	1984-85

Both batsmen hit for six all six balls of overs bowled by M.A.Nash and Tilak Raj respectively.

MOST RUNS IN A DAY

390*	B.C.Lara	Warwickshire v Durham	Birmingham	1994

There have been 19 instances of a batsman scoring 300 or more runs in a day.

HIGHEST PARTNERSHIPS FOR EACH WICKET

First Wicket

561	Waheed Mirza/Mansoor Akhtar	Karachi W v Quetta	Karachi	1976-77
555	P.Holmes/H.Sutcliffe	Yorkshire v Essex	Leyton	1932
554	J.T.Brown/J.Tunnicliffe	Yorkshire v Derbys	Chesterfield	1898

Second Wicket

475	Zahir Alam/L.S.Rajput	Assam v Tripura	Gauhati	1991-92
465*	J.A.Jameson/R.B.Kanhai	Warwickshire v Glos	Birmingham	1974
455	K.V.Bhandarkar/B.B.Nimbalkar	Maha'tra v Kathiawar	Poona	1948-49

Third Wicket

467	A.H.Jones/M.D.Crowe	N Zealand v Sri Lanka	Wellington	1990-91
456	Khalid Irtiza/Aslam Ali	United Bank v Multan	Karachi	1975-76
451	Mudassar Nazar/Javed Miandad	Pakistan v India	Hyderabad	1982-83
445	P.E.Whitelaw/W.N.Carson	Auckland v Otago	Dunedin	1936-37
434	J.B.Stollmeyer/G.E.Gomez	Trinidad v Br Guiana	Port-of-Spain	1946-47
424*	W.J.Edrich/D.C.S.Compton	Middlesex v Somerset	Lord's	1948

Fourth Wicket

577	V.S.Hazare/Gul Mahomed	Baroda v Holkar	Baroda	1946-47
574*	C.L.Walcott/F.M.M.Worrell	Barbados v Trinidad	Port-of-Spain	1945-46
502*	F.M.M.Worrell/J.D.C.Goddard	Barbados v Trinidad	Bridgetown	1943-44
470	A.I.Kallicharran/G.W.Humpage	Warwickshire v Lancs	Southport	1982

Fifth Wicket

464*	†M.E.Waugh/S.R.Waugh	NSW v W Australia	Perth	1990-91
405	S.G.Barnes/D.G.Bradman	Australia v England	Sydney	1946-47
397	W.Bardsley/C.Kelleway	NSW v S Australia	Sydney	1920-21
393	E.G.Arnold/W.B.Burns	Worcs v Warwickshire	Birmingham	1909

† Includes 20 runs credited under ACB playing conditions for 10 no-balls which, under the Laws of cricket, would have produced 7 runs.

Sixth Wicket

487*	G.A.Headley/C.C.Passailaigue	Jamaica v Tennyson's	Kingston	1931-32
428	W.W.Armstrong/M.A.Noble	Australians v Sussex	Hove	1902
411	R.M.Poore/E.G.Wynyard	Hampshire v Somerset	Taunton	1899

Seventh Wicket

460	Bhupinder Singh jr/P.Dharmani	Punjab v Delhi	Delhi	1994-95
347	D.St E.Atkinson/C.C.Depeiza	W Indies v Australia	Bridgetown	1954-55
344	K.S.Ranjitsinhji/W.Newham	Sussex v Essex	Leyton	1902

Eighth Wicket

433	V.T.Trumper/A.Sims	Australians v C'bury	Christchurch	1913-14
292	R.Peel/Lord Hawke	Yorkshire v Warwicks	Birmingham	1896
270	V.T.Trumper/E.P.Barbour	NSW v Victoria	Sydney	1912-13

Ninth Wicket

283	J.Chapman/A.Warren	Derbys v Warwicks	Blackwell	1910
268	J.B.Commins/N.Boje	SA 'A' v Mashonaland	Harare	1994-95
251	J.W.H.T.Douglas/S.N.Hare	Essex v Derbyshire	Leyton	1921

Tenth Wicket

307	A.F.Kippax/J.E.H.Hooker	NSW v Victoria	Melbourne	1928-29
249	C.T.Sarwate/S.N.Banerjee	Indians v Surrey	The Oval	1946
235	F.E.Woolley/A.Fielder	Kent v Worcs	Stourbridge	1909

MOST RUNS IN A CAREER

	Career	*I*	*NO*	*HS*	**Runs**	*Avge*	*100*
J.B.Hobbs	1905-34	1315	106	316*	**61237**	50.65	197
F.E.Woolley	1906-38	1532	85	305*	**58969**	40.75	145
E.H.Hendren	1907-38	1300	166	301*	**57611**	50.80	170
C.P.Mead	1905-36	1340	185	280*	**55061**	47.67	153
W.G.Grace	1865-1908	1493	105	344	**54896**	39.55	126
W.R.Hammond	1920-51	1005	104	336*	**50551**	56.10	167
H.Sutcliffe	1919-45	1088	123	313	**50138**	51.95	149
G.Boycott	1962-86	1014	162	261*	**48426**	56.83	151
T.W.Graveney	1948-71/72	1223	159	258	**47793**	44.91	122
T.W.Hayward	1893-1914	1138	96	315*	**43551**	41.79	104
D.L.Amiss	1960-87	1139	126	262*	**43423**	42.86	102
M.C.Cowdrey	1950-76	1130	134	307	**42719**	42.89	107
G.A.Gooch	1973-95	941	73	333	**42528**	48.99	120
A.Sandham	1911-37/38	1000	79	325	**41284**	44.82	107
L.Hutton	1934-60	814	91	364	**40140**	55.51	129
M.J.K.Smith	1951-75	1091	139	204	**39832**	41.84	69
W.Rhodes	1898-1930	1528	237	267*	**39802**	30.83	58
J.H.Edrich	1956-78	979	104	310*	**39790**	45.47	103
R.E.S.Wyatt	1923-57	1141	157	232	**39405**	40.04	85
D.C.S.Compton	1936-64	839	88	300	**38942**	51.85	123
G.E.Tyldesley	1909-36	961	106	256*	**38874**	45.46	102
J.T.Tyldesley	1895-1923	994	62	295*	**37897**	40.60	86
K.W.R.Fletcher	1962-88	1167	170	228*	**37665**	37.77	63
C.G.Greenidge	1970-92	889	75	273*	**37354**	45.88	92
J.W.Hearne	1909-36	1025	116	285*	**37252**	40.98	96
L.E.G.Ames	1926-51	951	95	295	**37248**	43.51	102
D.Kenyon	1946-67	1159	59	259	**37002**	33.63	74
W.J.Edrich	1934-58	964	92	267*	**36965**	42.39	86
J.M.Parks	1949-76	1227	172	205*	**36673**	34.76	51
D.Denton	1894-1920	1163	70	221	**36479**	33.37	69
G.H.Hirst	1891-1929	1215	151	341	**36323**	34.13	60
I.V.A.Richards	1971/72-93	796	63	322	**36212**	49.40	114
A.Jones	1957-83	1168	72	204*	**36049**	32.89	56
W.G.Quaife	1894-1928	1203	185	255*	**36012**	35.37	72
R.E.Marshall	1945/46-72	1053	59	228*	**35725**	35.94	68
G.Gunn	1902-32	1061	82	220	**35208**	35.96	62

BOWLING RECORDS

ALL TEN WICKETS IN AN INNINGS

This feat has been achieved on 73 occasions at first-class level.
Three Times: A.P.Freeman (1929, 1930, 1931)
Twice: V.E.Walker (1859, 1865); H.Verity (1931, 1932); J.C.Laker (1956)

Instances since 1945:

W.E.Hollies	Warwickshire v Notts	Birmingham	1946
J.M.Sims	East v West	Kingston on Thames	1948
J.K.R.Graveney	Gloucestershire v Derbyshire	Chesterfield	1949
T.E.Bailey	Essex v Lancashire	Clacton	1949
R.Berry	Lancashire v Worcestershire	Blackpool	1953
S.P.Gupte	President's XI v Combined XI	Bombay	1954-55
J.C.Laker	Surrey v Australians	The Oval	1956
K.Smales	Nottinghamshire v Glos	Stroud	1956
G.A.R.Lock	Surrey v Kent	Blackheath	1956

J.C.Laker	England v Australia	Manchester	1956
P.M.Chatterjee	Bengal v Assam	Jorhat	1956-57
J.D.Bannister	Warwicks v Combined Services	Birmingham (M & B)	1959
A.J.G.Pearson	Cambridge U v Leicestershire	Loughborough	1961
N.I.Thomson	Sussex v Warwickshire	Worthing	1964
P.J.Allan	Queensland v Victoria	Melbourne	1965-66
I.J.Brayshaw	Western Australia v Victoria	Perth	1967-68
Shahid Mahmood	Karachi Whites v Khairpur	Karachi	1969-70
E.E.Hemmings	International XI v W Indians	Kingston	1982-83
P.Sunderam	Rajasthan v Vidarbha	Jodhpur	1985-86
S.T.Jefferies	Western Province v OFS	Cape Town	1987-88
Imran Adil	Bahawalpur v Faisalabad	Faisalabad	1989-90
G.P.Wickremasinghe	Sinhalese v Kalutara	Colombo	1991-92
R.L.Johnson	Middlesex v Derbyshire	Derby	1994

MOST WICKETS IN A MATCH

19	J.C.Laker	England v Australia	Manchester	1956

MOST WICKETS IN A SEASON

Wkts		*Career*	*Matches*	*Overs*	*Mdns*	*Runs*	*Avge*
304	A.P.Freeman	1928	37	1976.1	423	5489	18.05
298	A.P.Freeman	1933	33	2039	651	4549	15.26

The feat of taking 250 wickets in a season has been achieved on 12 occasions, the last instance been by A.P.Freeman in 1933. 200 or more wickets in a season have been taken on 59 occasions, the last being by G.A.R.Lock (212 wickets, average 12.02) in 1957.

The highest aggregates of wickets taken in a season since the reduction of County Championship matches in 1969 are as follows:

Wkts		*Season*	*Matches*	*Overs*	*Mdns*	*Runs*	*Avge*
134	M.D.Marshall	1982	22	822	225	2108	15.73
131	L.R.Gibbs	1971	23	1024.1	295	2475	18.89
125	F.D.Stephenson	1988	22	819.1	196	2289	18.31
121	R.D.Jackman	1980	23	746.2	220	1864	15.40

Since 1969 there have been 47 instances of bowlers taking 100 wickets in a season.

MOST HAT-TRICKS IN A CAREER

7	D.V.P.Wright
6	T.W.J.Goddard, C.W.L.Parker
5	S.Haigh, V.W.C.Jupp, A.E.G.Rhodes, F.A.Tarrant

MOST WICKETS IN A CAREER

	Career	*Runs*	**Wkts**	*Avge*	*100w*
W.Rhodes	1898-1930	69993	**4187**	16.71	23
A.P.Freeman	1914-36	69577	**3776**	18.42	17
C.W.L.Parker	1903-35	63817	**3278**	19.46	16
J.T.Hearne	1888-1923	54352	**3061**	17.75	15
T.W.J.Goddard	1922-52	59116	**2979**	19.84	16
W.G.Grace	1865-1908	51545	**2876**	17.92	10
A.S.Kennedy	1907-36	61034	**2874**	21.23	15
D.Shackleton	1948-69	53303	**2857**	18.65	20
G.A.R.Lock	1946-70/71	54709	**2844**	19.23	14
F.J.Titmus	1949-82	63313	**2830**	22.37	16
M.W.Tate	1912-37	50571	**2784**	18.16	13+1
G.H.Hirst	1891-1929	51282	**2739**	18.72	15
C.Blythe	1899-1914	42136	**2506**	16.81	14

	Career	Runs	Wkts	Avge	100w
D.L.Underwood	1963-87	49993	2465	20.28	10
W.E.Astill	1906-39	57783	2431	23.76	9
J.C.White	1909-37	43759	2356	18.57	14
W.E.Hollies	1932-57	48656	2323	20.94	14
F.S.Trueman	1949-69	42154	2304	18.29	12
J.B.Statham	1950-68	36999	2260	16.37	13
R.T.D.Perks	1930-55	53770	2233	24.07	16
J.Briggs	1879-1900	35431	2221	15.95	12
D.J.Shepherd	1950-72	47302	2218	21.32	12
E.G.Dennett	1903-26	42571	2147	19.82	12
T.Richardson	1892-1905	38794	2104	18.43	10
T.E.Bailey	1945-67	48170	2082	23.13	9
R.Illingworth	1951-83	42023	2072	20.28	10
F.E.Woolley	1906-38	41066	2068	19.85	8
N.Gifford	1960-88	48731	2068	23.56	4
G.Geary	1912-38	41339	2063	20.03	11
D.V.P.Wright	1932-57	49307	2056	23.98	10
J.A.Newman	1906-30	51111	2032	25.15	9
A.Shaw	1864-97	24580	2027+1	12.12	9
S.Haigh	1895-1913	32091	2012	15.94	11

ALL-ROUND RECORDS

THE 'DOUBLE'

3000 runs and 100 wickets: J.H.Parks (1937)
2000 runs and 200 wickets: G.H.Hirst (1906)
2000 runs and 100 wickets: F.E.Woolley (4), J.W.Hearne (3), W.G.Grace (2), G.H.Hirst (2), W.Rhodes (2), T.E.Bailey, D.E.Davies, G.L.Jessop, V.W.C.Jupp, J. Langridge, F.A.Tarrant, C.L.Townsend, L.F.Townsend
1000 runs and 200 wickets: M.W.Tate (3), A.E.Trott (2), A.S.Kennedy

Most Doubles: 16 – W.Rhodes; 14 – G.H.Hirst; 10 – V.W.C.Jupp

Double in Debut Season: D.B.Close (1949) – aged 18, the youngest to achieve this feat.
The feat of scoring 1000 runs and taking 100 wickets in a season has been achieved on 305 occasions, R.J.Hadlee (1984) and F.D.Stephenson (1988) being the only players to complete the 'double' since the reduction of County Championship matches in 1969.

WICKET-KEEPING RECORDS

MOST DISMISSALS IN AN INNINGS

9	(8ct, 1st)	Tahir Rashid	Habib Bank v PACO	Gujranwala	1992-93
8	(8ct)	A.T.W.Grout	Queensland v W Australia	Brisbane	1959-60
8	(8ct)	D.E.East	Essex v Somerset	Taunton	1985
8	(8ct)	S.A.Marsh	Kent v Middlesex	Lord's	1991
8	(6ct, 2st)	T.J.Zoehrer	Australians v Surrey	The Oval	1993

MOST DISMISSALS IN A MATCH

12	(8ct, 4st)	E.Pooley	Surrey v Sussex	The Oval	1868
12	(9ct, 3st)	D.Tallon	Queensland v NSW	Sydney	1938-39
12	(9ct, 3st)	H.B.Taber	NSW v South Australia	Adelaide	1968-69

MOST CATCHES IN A MATCH

11	A.Long	Surrey v Sussex	Hove	1964
11	R.W.Marsh	W Australia v Victoria	Perth	1975-76
11	D.L.Bairstow	Yorkshire v Derbyshire	Scarborough	1982
11	W.K.Hegg	Lancashire v Derbyshire	Chesterfield	1989
11	A.J.Stewart	Surrey v Leicestershire	Leicester	1989
11	T.J.Nielsen	S Australia v W Australia	Perth	1990-91

MOST DISMISSALS IN A SEASON

128 (79ct, 49st) L.E.G.Ames 1929

MOST DISMISSALS IN A CAREER

	Career	**Dismissals**	*Ct*	*St*
R.W.Taylor	1960-88	**1649**	1473	176
J.T.Murray	1952-75	**1527**	1270	257
H.Strudwick	1902-27	**1497**	1242	255
A.P.E.Knott	1964-85	**1344**	1211	133
F.H.Huish	1895-1914	**1310**	933	377
B.Taylor	1949-73	**1294**	1083	211
D.Hunter	1889-1909	**1253**	906	347
H.R.Butt	1890-1912	**1228**	953	275
J.H.Board	1891-1914/15	**1207**	852	355
H.Elliott	1920-47	**1206**	904	302
J.M.Parks	1949-76	**1181**	1088	93
R.Booth	1951-70	**1126**	948	178
L.E.G.Ames	1926-51	**1121**	703	418
D.L.Bairstow	1970-90	**1099**	961	138
G.Duckworth	1923-47	**1096**	753	343
H.W.Stephenson	1948-64	**1082**	748	334
J.G.Binks	1955-75	**1071**	895	176
T.G.Evans	1939-69	**1066**	816	250
A.Long	1960-80	**1046**	922	124
G.O.Dawkes	1937-61	**1043**	895	148
R.W.Tolchard	1965-83	**1037**	912	125
W.L.Cornford	1921-47	**1017**	675	342

FIELDING RECORDS

MOST CATCHES IN AN INNINGS

7	M.J.Stewart	Surrey v Northamptonshire	Northampton	1957
7	A.S.Brown	Gloucestershire v Nottinghamshire	Nottingham	1966

MOST CATCHES IN A MATCH

0	W.R.Hammond	Gloucestershire v Surrey	Cheltenham	1928

MOST CATCHES IN A SEASON

78	W.R.Hammond	1928	77	M.J.Stewart	1957

MOST CATCHES IN A CAREER

1018	F.E.Woolley	1906-38	784	J.G.Langridge	1928-55
887	W.G.Grace	1865-1908	764	W.Rhodes	1898-1930
830	G.A.R.Lock	1946-70/71	758	C.A.Milton	1948-74
819	W.R.Hammond	1920-51	754	E.H.Hendren	1907-38
813	D.B.Close	1949-86			

LIMITED-OVERS INTERNATIONALS RESULTS SUMMARY

1970-71 to 13 February 1996 (prior to World Cup)

	Opponents	*Matches*	*Won by* E	A	SA	WI	NZ	I	P	SL	Z	B	C	EA	UAE	*Tied*	*NR*
England	Australia	57	26	29	–	–	–	–	–	–	–	–	–	–	–	1	1
	South Africa	11	5	–	6	–	–	–	–	–	–	–	–	–	–	–	–
	West Indies	51	22	–	–	27	–	–	–	–	–	–	–	–	–	–	2
	New Zealand	41	21	–	–	–	17	–	–	–	–	–	–	–	–	–	3
	India	29	16	–	–	–	–	13	–	–	–	–	–	–	–	–	–
	Pakistan	36	23	–	–	–	–	–	12	–	–	–	–	–	–	–	1
	Sri Lanka	11	8	–	–	–	–	–	–	3	–	–	–	–	–	–	–
	Zimbabwe	3	1	–	–	–	–	–	–	–	2	–	–	–	–	–	–
	Canada	1	1	–	–	–	–	–	–	–	–	–	0	–	–	–	–
	East Africa	1	1	–	–	–	–	–	–	–	–	–	–	0	–	–	–
Australia	South Africa	20	–	12	8	–	–	–	–	–	–	–	–	–	–	–	–
	West Indies	78	–	30	–	46	–	–	–	–	–	–	–	–	–	1	1
	New Zealand	62	–	43	–	–	17	–	–	–	–	–	–	–	–	–	2
	India	43	–	24	–	–	–	16	–	–	–	–	–	–	–	–	3
	Pakistan	42	–	21	–	–	–	–	18	–	–	–	–	–	–	1	2
	Sri Lanka	32	–	22	–	–	–	–	–	8	–	–	–	–	–	–	2
	Zimbabwe	7	–	6	–	–	–	–	–	–	1	–	–	–	–	–	–
	Bangladesh	1	–	1	–	–	–	–	–	–	–	0	–	–	–	–	–
	Canada	1	–	1	–	–	–	–	–	–	–	–	0	–	–	–	–
S Africa	West Indies	8	–	–	4	4	–	–	–	–	–	–	–	–	–	–	–
	New Zealand	7	–	–	3	–	4	–	–	–	–	–	–	–	–	–	–
	India	14	–	–	8	–	–	6	–	–	–	–	–	–	–	–	–
	Pakistan	11	–	–	4	–	–	–	7	–	–	–	–	–	–	–	–
	Sri Lanka	7	–	–	3	–	–	–	–	3	–	–	–	–	–	–	1
	Zimbabwe	4	–	–	3	–	–	–	–	–	0	–	–	–	–	–	1
W Indies	New Zealand	19	–	–	–	15	2	–	–	–	–	–	–	–	–	–	2
	India	50	–	–	–	32	–	17	–	–	–	–	–	–	–	1	–
	Pakistan	75	–	–	–	51	–	–	22	–	–	–	–	–	–	2	–
	Sri Lanka	26	–	–	–	19	–	–	–	6	–	–	–	–	–	–	1
	Zimbabwe	4	–	–	–	4	–	–	–	–	0	–	–	–	–	–	–
N Zealand	India	41	–	–	–	–	18	23	–	–	–	–	–	–	–	–	–
	Pakistan	40	–	–	–	–	16	–	22	–	–	–	–	–	–	1	1
	Sri Lanka	32	–	–	–	–	22	–	–	8	–	–	–	–	–	–	2
	Zimbabwe	8	–	–	–	–	7	–	–	–	1	–	–	–	–	–	–
	Bangladesh	1	–	–	–	–	1	–	–	–	–	0	–	–	–	–	–
	East Africa	1	–	–	–	–	1	–	–	–	–	–	–	0	–	–	–
India	Pakistan	41	–	–	–	–	–	12	27	–	–	–	–	–	–	–	2
	Sri Lanka	37	–	–	–	–	–	24	–	11	–	–	–	–	–	–	2
	Zimbabwe	10	–	–	–	–	–	9	–	–	0	–	–	–	–	1	–
	Bangladesh	3	–	–	–	–	–	3	–	–	–	0	–	–	–	–	–
	East Africa	1	–	–	–	–	–	1	–	–	–	–	–	0	–	–	–
	U A Emirates	1	–	–	–	–	–	1	–	–	–	–	–	–	0	–	–
Pakistan	Sri Lanka	54	–	–	–	–	–	–	40	13	–	–	–	–	–	–	1
	Zimbabwe	9	–	–	–	–	–	–	7	–	1	–	–	–	–	1	–
	Bangladesh	3	–	–	–	–	–	–	3	–	–	0	–	–	–	–	–
	Canada	1	–	–	–	–	–	–	1	–	–	–	0	–	–	–	–
	U A Emirates	1	–	–	–	–	–	–	1	–	–	–	–	–	0	–	–
Sri Lanka	Zimbabwe	6	–	–	–	–	–	–	–	5	1	–	–	–	–	–	–
	Bangladesh	4	–	–	–	–	–	–	–	4	–	0	–	–	–	–	–
		1046	124	189	39	198	105	125	160	61	6	0	0	0	0	9	30

LEAGUE TABLE OF L-O INTERNATIONALS

	Matches	Won	Lost	Tied	No Result	% Won (exc NR)
West Indies	311	198	103	4	6	64.91
Australia	343	189	140	3	11	56.92
England	241	124	109	1	7	52.99
Pakistan	313	160	141	5	7	52.28
South Africa	82	39	41	–	2	48.75
India	270	125	136	2	7	47.52
New Zealand	252	105	136	1	10	43.38
Sri Lanka	209	61	139	–	9	30.50
Zimbabwe	51	6	42	2	1	12.00
United Arab Emirates	2	–	2	–	–	–
Canada	3	–	3	–	–	–
East Africa	3	–	3	–	–	–
Bangladesh	12	–	12	–	–	–

RECORDS

To 13 February 1996 (prior to World Cup)

TEAM RECORDS

HIGHEST TOTALS

363-7	(55 overs)	England v Pakistan	Nottingham	1992
360-4	(50 overs)	West Indies v Sri Lanka	Karachi	1987-88
348-8	(50 overs)	New Zealand v India	Nagpur	1995-96
338-4	(50 overs)	New Zealand v Bangladesh	Sharjah	1989-90
338-5	(60 overs)	Pakistan v Sri Lanka	Swansea	1983
334-4	(60 overs)	England v India	Lord's	1975
333-7	(50 overs)	West Indies v Sri Lanka	Sharjah	1995-96
333-8	(45 overs)	West Indies v India	Jamshedpur	1983-84
333-9	(60 overs)	England v Sri Lanka	Taunton	1983
332-3	(50 overs)	Australia v Sri Lanka	Sharjah	1989-90
330-6	(60 overs)	Pakistan v Sri Lanka	Nottingham	1975
Highest Totals by other ICC Full Members:				
329	(49.3 overs)	Sri Lanka v West Indies	Sharjah	1995-96
314-7	(50 overs)	South Africa v New Zealand	Verwoerdburg	1994-95
312-4	(50 overs)	Zimbabwe v Sri Lanka	New Plymouth	1991-92
299-4	(40 overs)	India v Sri Lanka	Bombay	1986-87

HIGHEST TOTALS BATTING SECOND

WINNING

313-7	(49.2 overs)	Sri Lanka v Zimbabwe	New Plymouth	1991-92
298-6	(54.5 overs)	New Zealand v England	Leeds	1990
297-6	(48.5 overs)	New Zealand v England	Adelaide	1982-83

LOSING

329	(49.3 overs)	Sri Lanka v West Indies	Sharjah	1995-96
289-7	(40 overs)	Sri Lanka v India	Bombay	1986-87
288-9	(60 overs)	Sri Lanka v Pakistan	Swansea	1983
288-8	(50 overs)	Sri Lanka v Pakistan	Adelaide	1989-90
288-8	(50 overs)	Sri Lanka v Zimbabwe	Harare	1994-95

HIGHEST MATCH AGGREGATES

662-17	(99.3 overs)	West Indies v Sri Lanka	Sharjah	1995-96
626-14	(120 overs)	Pakistan v Sri Lanka	Swansea	1983
625-11	(99.2 overs)	Sri Lanka v Zimbabwe	New Plymouth	1991-92

LARGEST MARGINS OF VICTORY

232 runs	Australia beat Sri Lanka	Adelaide	1984-85
206 runs	New Zealand beat Australia	Adelaide	1985-86
202 runs	England beat India	Lord's	1975
10 wickets	Nine instances		

LOWEST TOTALS†

43	(19.5 overs)	Pakistan v West Indies	Cape Town	1992-93
45	(40.3 overs)	Canada v England	Manchester	1979
55	(28.3 overs)	Sri Lanka v West Indies	Sharjah	1986-87
63	(25.5 overs)	India v Australia	Sydney	1980-81
64	(35.5 overs)	New Zealand v Pakistan	Sharjah	1985-86
69	(28 overs)	South Africa v Australia	Sydney	1993-94
70	(25.2 overs)	Australia v England	Birmingham	1977
70	(26.3 overs)	Australia v New Zealand	Adelaide	1985-86
Lowest Totals by other ICC Full Members:				
87	(29.3 overs)	West Indies v Australia	Sydney	1992-93
93	(36.2 overs)	England v Australia	Leeds	1975
99	(36.3 overs)	Zimbabwe v West Indies	Hyderabad (Ind)	1993-94

† *Excluding instances when the number of overs was reduced after play began.*

LOWEST MATCH AGGREGATE

88-13	(32.2 overs)	West Indies v Pakistan	Cape Town	1992-93

TIED MATCHES

Australia	222-9	(50)	West Indies	222-5	(50)	Melbourne	1983-84
England	226-5	(55)	Australia	226-8	(55)	Nottingham	1989
West Indies	186-5	(39)	Pakistan	186-9	(39)	Lahore	1991-92
India	126	(47.4)	West Indies	126	(41)	Perth	1991-92
Australia	228-7	(50)	Pakistan	228-9	(50)	Hobart	1992-93
Pakistan	244-6	(50)	West Indies	244-5	(50)	Georgetown	1992-93
India	248-5	(50)	Zimbabwe	248	(50)	Indore	1993-94
Pakistan	161-9	(50)	New Zealand	161	(49.4)	Auckland	1993-94

MOST APPEARANCES

		Total	*E*	*A*	*SA*	*WI*	*NZ*	*I*	*P*	*SL*	*Z*	*C*	*B*	*UAE*
A.R.Border	A	**273**	43	–	15	61	52	38	34	23	5	1	1	–
D.L.Haynes	WI	**238**	35	64	8	–	13	36	65	14	3	–	–	–
Javed Miandad	P	**228**	26	35	3	64	23	34	–	35	6	1	1	–
Kapil Dev	I	**224**	23	41	13	42	29	–	32	33	9	–	2	–
R.B.Richardson	WI	**218**	35	49	8	–	11	31	61	21	2	–	–	–
Salim Malik	P	**214**	21	24	11	45	35	28	–	40	8	–	1	1

Most Appearances for other ICC Full Members:

		Total	*E*	*A*	*SA*	*WI*	*NZ*	*I*	*P*	*SL*	*Z*	*C*	*B*	*UAE*
A.Ranatunga	SL	**177**	9	25	7	19	27	33	48	–	6	–	3	–
J.G.Wright	NZ	**149**	30	42	–	11	–	21	18	24	2	–	1	–
G.A.Gooch	E	**125**	–	32	1	32	16	18	16	6	3	1	–	–
W.J.Cronje	SA	**77**	11	20	–	7	7	12	10	6	4	–	–	–
D.J.Richardson	SA	**77**	10	20	–	6	6	14	10	7	4	–	–	–
D.L.Houghton	Z	**47**	2	7	4	4	5	10	9	6	–	–	–	–

BATTING RECORDS

HIGHEST INDIVIDUAL INNINGS

189*	I.V.A.Richards	West Indies v England	Manchester	1984
181	I.V.A.Richards	West Indies v Sri Lanka	Karachi	1987-88
175*	Kapil Dev	India v Zimbabwe	Tunbridge Wells	1983
171*	G.M.Turner	New Zealand v East Africa	Birmingham	1975
169*	D.J.Callaghan	South Africa v New Zealand	Verwoerdburg	1994-95
169	B.C.Lara	West Indies v Sri Lanka	Sharjah	1995-96
167*	R.A.Smith	England v Australia	Birmingham	1993
158	D.I.Gower	England v New Zealand	Brisbane	1982-83
153*	I.V.A.Richards	West Indies v Australia	Melbourne	1979-80
153	B.C.Lara	West Indies v Pakistan	Sharjah	1993-94
152*	D.L.Haynes	West Indies v India	Georgetown	1988-89
Highest individual scores for other ICC Full Members:				
145	D.M.Jones	Australia v England	Brisbane	1990-91
142	D.L.Houghton	Zimbabwe v New Zealand	Hyderabad, India	1987-88
140	S.T.Jayasuriya	Sri Lanka v New Zealand	Bloemfontein	1994-95
137*	Inzamam-ul-Haq	Pakistan v New Zealand	Sharjah	1993-94

HIGHEST PARTNERSHIP FOR EACH WICKET

1st	212	G.R.Marsh/D.C.Boon	Australia v India	Jaipur	1986-87
2nd	263	Aamir Sohail/Inzamam-ul-Haq	Pakistan v New Zealand	Sharjah	1993-94
3rd	224*	D.M.Jones/A.R.Border	Australia v Sri Lanka	Adelaide	1984-85
4th	173	D.M.Jones/S.R.Waugh	Australia v Pakistan	Perth	1986-87
5th	159	R.T.Ponting/M.G.Bevan	Australia v Sri Lanka	Melbourne	1995-96
6th	154	R.B.Richardson/P.J.L.Dujon	West Indies v Pakistan	Sharjah	1991-92
7th	115	P.J.L.Dujon/M.D.Marshall	West Indies v Pakistan	Gujranwala	1986-87
8th	119	P.R.Reiffel/S.K.Warne	Australia v South Africa	Port Elizabeth	1993-94
9th	126*	Kapil Dev/S.M.H.Kirmani	India v Zimbabwe	Tunbridge Wells	1983
10th	106*	I.V.A.Richards/M.A.Holding	West Indies v England	Manchester	1984

MOST RUNS IN CAREER

		LOI	*I*	*NO*	*HS*	**Runs**	*Avge*	*100*	*50*
D.L.Haynes	WI	238	237	28	152*	**8648**	41.37	17	57
Javed Miandad	P	228	215	40	119*	**7327**	41.86	8	50
I.V.A.Richards	WI	187	167	24	189*	**6721**	47.00	11	45
A.R.Border	A	273	252	39	127*	**6524**	30.62	3	39
D.M.Jones	A	164	161	25	145	**6068**	44.61	7	46
R.B.Richardson	WI	218	211	28	122	**6012**	32.85	5	43
D.C.Boon	A	181	177	16	122	**5964**	37.04	5	37
Salim Malik	P	214	194	28	102	**5442**	32.78	5	35
M.Azharuddin	I	199	184	35	108*	**5400**	36.24	3	30
Ramiz Raja	P	170	169	13	119*	**5257**	33.69	9	29
C.G.Greenidge	WI	128	127	13	133*	**5134**	45.03	11	31
A.Ranatunga	SL	177	169	30	102*	**4908**	35.30	2	32
P.A.de Silva	SL	174	170	15	107*	**4842**	31.23	3	34
M.D.Crowe	NZ	143	141	19	107*	**4704**	38.55	4	34
G.R.Marsh	A	117	115	6	126*	**4357**	39.97	9	22
G.A.Gooch	E	125	122	6	142	**4290**	36.98	8	23
K.Srikkanth	I	146	145	4	123	**4092**	29.02	4	27
A.J.Lamb	E	122	118	16	118	**4010**	39.31	4	26
Highest aggregates for other ICC Full Members:									
W.J.Cronje	SA	77	74	11	112	**2263**	35.92	2	12
D.L.Houghton	Z	47	45	1	142	**1280**	29.09	1	10

MOST HUNDREDS IN A CAREER

			Opponents								
		100	*E*	*A*	*WI*	*NZ*	*I*	*P*	*SA*	*SL*	*Z*
D.L.Haynes	WI	17	2	6	–	2	2	4	–	1	–
C.G.Greenidge	WI	11	–	1	–	3	3	2	–	1	1
I.V.A.Richards	WI	11	3	3	–	1	3	–	–	1	–
G.R.Marsh	A	9	1	–	2	2	3	1	–	–	–
Ramiz Raja	P	9	1	–	2	3	–	–	–	3	–
G.A.Gooch	E	8	–	4	1	1	1	1	–	–	–
Javed Miandad	P	8	1	–	1	–	3	–	1	2	–
Saeed Anwar	P	8	–	1	1	1	–	–	–	4	1
D.I.Gower	E	7	–	2	–	3	–	1	–	1	–
D.M.Jones	A	7	3	–	–	2	–	1	–	1	–
Zaheer Abbas	P	7	–	2	–	1	3	–	–	1	–

BOWLING RECORDS

BEST ANALYSES

7-37	Aqib Javed	Pakistan v India	Sharjah	1991-92
7-51	W.W.Davis	West Indies v Australia	Leeds	1983
6-12	A.Kumble	India v West Indies	Calcutta	1993-94
6-14	G.J.Gilmour	Australia v England	Leeds	1975
6-14	Imran Khan	Pakistan v India	Sharjah	1984-85
6-15	C.E.H.Croft	West Indies v England	Arnos Vale	1980-81
6-26	Waqar Younis	Pakistan v Sri Lanka	Sharjah	1989-90
6-29	B.P.Patterson	West Indies v India	Nagpur	1987-88
6-29	S.T.Jayasuriya	Sri Lanka v England	Moratuwa	1992-93
6-30	Waqar Younis	Pakistan v New Zealand	Auckland	1993-94
6-39	K.H.Macleay	Australia v India	Nottingham	1983
6-41	I.V.A.Richards	West Indies v India	Delhi	1989-90
6-50	A.H.Gray	West Indies v Australia	Port-of-Spain	1990-91
Best analyses for other ICC Full Members:				
5-20	V.J.Marks	England v New Zealand	Wellington	1983-84
5-22	M.N.Hart	New Zealand v West Indies	Margao	1994-95
5-29	A.A.Donald	South Africa v India	Calcutta	1991-92
5-44	A.C.I.Lock	Zimbabwe v New Zealand	Napier	1995-96

HAT-TRICKS

Jalaluddin	Pakistan v Australia	Hyderabad	1982-83
B.A.Reid	Australia v New Zealand	Sydney	1985-86
C.Sharma	India v New Zealand	Nagpur	1987-88
Wasim Akram	Pakistan v West Indies	Sharjah	1989-90
Wasim Akram	Pakistan v Australia	Sharjah	1989-90
Kapil Dev	India v Sri Lanka	Calcutta	1990-91
Aqib Javed	Pakistan v India	Sharjah	1991-92
D.K.Morrison	New Zealand v India	Napier	1993-94
Waqar Younis	Pakistan v New Zealand	East London	1994-95

MOST WICKETS IN A CAREER

		LOI	O	R	W	Avge	Best	4w
Wasim Akram	P	193	1669.4	6281	**282**	22.27	5-15	15
Kapil Dev	I	224	1867	6946	**253**	27.45	5-43	4
C.J.McDermott	A	137	1240.3	5006	**202**	24.78	5-44	5
Waqar Younis	P	112	926.5	4118	**187**	22.02	6-26	15
Imran Khan	P	175	1243.3	4845	**182**	26.62	6-14	4
C.A.Walsh	WI	150	1319	5038	**166**	30.34	5- 1	6
C.E.L.Ambrose	WI	122	1083.5	3783	**164**	23.06	5-17	8
S.R.Waugh	A	189	1226	5442	**162**	33.59	4-33	2
R.J.Hadlee	NZ	115	1030.2	3407	**158**	21.56	5-25	6
M.D.Marshall	WI	136	1195.5	4233	**157**	26.96	4-18	6
M.Prabhakar	I	125	1031	4374	**154**	28.40	5-33	6
J.Garner	WI	98	888.2	2752	**146**	18.84	5-31	5
I.T.Botham	E	116	1045.1	4139	**145**	28.54	4-31	3
M.A.Holding	WI	102	912.1	3034	**142**	21.36	5-26	6
E.J.Chatfield	NZ	114	1010.5	3621	**140**	25.86	5-34	4
Aqib Javed	P	121	1018.3	4162	**134**	31.05	7-37	3
Abdul Qadir	P	104	850	3453	**132**	26.15	5-44	6
C.L.Hooper	WI	141	937.4	4107	**129**	31.83	4-34	1
R.J.Shastri	I	150	1102.1	4650	**129**	36.04	5-15	3
I.V.A.Richards	WI	187	940.4	4228	**118**	35.83	6-41	3
J.Srinath	I	82	698	2976	**118**	25.22	5-24	3
M.C.Snedden	NZ	93	753.1	3235	**114**	28.37	4-34	1
D.K.Morrison	NZ	86	696.1	3133	**112**	27.97	5-46	2
Mudassar Nazar	P	122	809.1	3431	**111**	30.90	5-28	2
P.A.J.DeFreitas	E	97	901.5	3553	**109**	32.59	4-35	1
S.P.O'Donnell	A	87	725	3102	**108**	28.72	5-13	6
I.R.Bishop	WI	66	584.1	2441	**106**	23.02	5-25	8
D.K.Lillee	A	63	598.5	2145	**103**	20.82	5-34	6
C.Pringle	NZ	64	552.2	2455	**103**	23.83	5-45	3
W.K.M.Benjamin	WI	85	740.2	3079	**100**	30.79	5-22	1
Highest aggregates for other ICC Full Members:								
J.R.Ratnayeke	SL	78	595.3	2866	**85**	33.71	4-23	1
A.A.Donald	SA	57	510.2	2069	**81**	25.54	5-29	3
E.A.Brandes	Z	27	224.1	1134	**32**	35.43	4-21	1

WICKET-KEEPING RECORDS

MOST DISMISSALS IN AN INNINGS

5 (all ct)	R.W.Marsh	Australia v England	Leeds	1981
5 (all ct)	R.G.de Alwis	Sri Lanka v Australia	Colombo (PSS)	1982-83
5 (all ct)	S.M.H.Kirmani	India v Zimbabwe	Leicester	1983
5 (3ct, 2st)	S.Viswanath	India v England	Sydney	1984-85
5 (3ct, 2st)	K.S.More	India v New Zealand	Sharjah	1987-88
5 (all ct)	H.P.Tillekeratne	Sri Lanka v Pakistan	Sharjah	1990-91
5 (3ct, 2st)	N.R.Mongia	India v New Zealand	Auckland	1993-94
5 (3ct, 2st)	A.C.Parore	New Zealand v West Indies	Margao	1994-95
5 (all ct)	D.J.Richardson	South Africa v Pakistan	Johannesburg	1994-95
5 (all ct)	Moin Khan	Pakistan v Zimbabwe	Harare	1994-95
5 (4ct, 1st)	R.S.Kaluwitharana	Sri Lanka v Pakistan	Sharjah	1994-95
5 (all ct)	D.J.Richardson	South Africa v Zimbabwe	Harare	1995-96
5 (all ct)	A.Flower	Zimbabwe v South Africa	Harare	1995-96
5 (all ct)	C.O.Browne	West Indies v Sri Lanka	Brisbane	1995-96

MOST DISMISSALS IN A CAREER

		LOI	*Ct*	*St*	**Dis**
P.J.L.Dujon	West Indies	169	183	21	204
I.A.Healy	Australia	139	168	29	197
R.W.Marsh	Australia	92	120	4	124
D.J.Richardson	South Africa	77	101	12	113
Salim Yousuf	Pakistan	86	81	22	103
K.S.More	India	94	63	27	90
Rashid Latif	Pakistan	70	68	18	86
I.D.S.Smith	New Zealand	98	81	5	86

FIELDING RECORDS

MOST CATCHES IN AN INNINGS

5	J.N.Rhodes	South Africa v West Indies	Bombay	1993-94
4	Salim Malik	Pakistan v New Zealand	Sialkot	1984-85
4	S.M.Gavaskar	India v Pakistan	Sharjah	1984-85
4	R.B.Richardson	West Indies v England	Birmingham	1991
4	K.C.Wessels	South Africa v West Indies	Kingston	1991-92
4	M.A.Taylor	Australia v West Indies	Sydney	1992-93
4	C.L.Hooper	West Indies v Pakistan	Durban	1992-93
4	K.R.Rutherford	New Zealand v India	Napier	1994-95
4	P.V.Simmons	West Indies v Sri Lanka	Sharjah	1995-96

MOST CATCHES IN A CAREER

		LOI	**Ct**
A.R.Border	Australia	273	127
I.V.A.Richards	West Indies	187	101
M.Azharuddin	India	199	82
R.B.Richardson	West Indies	218	73
R.S.Mahanama	Sri Lanka	135	72
Kapil Dev	India	224	71
C.L.Hooper	West Indies	141	70

ALL-ROUND RECORDS

1000 RUNS AND 100 WICKETS

		LOI	*Runs*	*Wkts*
I.T.Botham	England	116	2113	145
R.J.Hadlee	New Zealand	115	1749	158
C.L.Hooper	West Indies	141	3270	129
Imran Khan	Pakistan	175	3709	182
Kapil Dev	India	224	3783	253
Mudassar Nazar	Pakistan	122	2624	111
S.P.O'Donnell	Australia	87	1242	108
M.Prabhakar	India	125	1844	154
I.V.A.Richards	West Indies	187	6721	118
R.J.Shastri	India	150	3108	129
Wasim Akram	Pakistan	193	1746	282
S.R.Waugh	Australia	189	3980	162

1000 RUNS AND 100 DISMISSALS

		LOI	*Runs*	*Dis*
P.J.L.Dujon	West Indies	169	1945	204
I.A.Healy	Australia	139	1496	197
R.W.Marsh	Australia	92	1225	124

TEST CRICKET RECORDS

To the end of the 1995-96 season (excluding West Indies v New Zealand)

TEAM RECORDS

HIGHEST INNINGS TOTALS

903-7d	England v Australia	The Oval	1938
849	England v West Indies	Kingston	1929-30
790-3d	West Indies v Pakistan	Kingston	1957-58
758-8d	Australia v West Indies	Kingston	1954-55
729-6d	Australia v England	Lord's	1930
708	Pakistan v England	The Oval	1987
701	Australia v England	The Oval	1934
699-5	Pakistan v India	Lahore	1989-90
695	Australia v England	The Oval	1930
692-8d	West Indies v England	The Oval	1995
687-8d	West Indies v England	The Oval	1976
681-8d	West Indies v England	Port-of-Spain	1953-54
676-7	India v Sri Lanka	Kanpur	1986-87
674-6	Pakistan v India	Faisalabad	1984-85
674	Australia v India	Adelaide	1947-48
671-4	New Zealand v Sri Lanka	Wellington	1990-91
668	Australia v West Indies	Bridgetown	1954-55
660-5d	West Indies v New Zealand	Wellington	1994-95
659-8d	Australia v England	Sydney	1946-47
658-8d	England v Australia	Nottingham	1938
657-8d	Pakistan v West Indies	Bridgetown	1957-58
656-8d	Australia v England	Manchester	1964
654-5	England v South Africa	Durban	1938-39
653-4d	England v India	Lord's	1990
653-4d	Australia v England	Leeds	1993
652-7d	England v India	Madras	1984-85
652-8d	West Indies v England	Lord's	1973
652	Pakistan v India	Faisalabad	1982-83
650-6d	Australia v West Indies	Bridgetown	1964-65

The highest innings for other countries are:

622-9d	South Africa v Australia	Durban	1969-70
547-8d	Sri Lanka v Australia	Colombo (SSC)	1992-93
544-4d	Zimbabwe v Pakistan	Harare	1994-95

LOWEST INNINGS TOTALS

26	New Zealand v England	Auckland	1954-55
30	South Africa v England	Port Elizabeth	1895-96
30	South Africa v England	Birmingham	1924
35	South Africa v England	Cape Town	1898-99
36	Australia v England	Birmingham	1902
36	South Africa v Australia	Melbourne	1931-32
42	Australia v England	Sydney	1887-88
42	New Zealand v Australia	Wellington	1945-46
42	India v England	Lord's	1974
43	South Africa v England	Cape Town	1888-89
44	Australia v England	The Oval	1896
45	England v Australia	Sydney	1886-87
45	South Africa v Australia	Melbourne	1931-32

46	England v West Indies	Port-of-Spain	1993-94
47	South Africa v England	Cape Town	1888-89
47	New Zealand v England	Lord's	1958

The lowest innings for other countries are:

53	West Indies v Pakistan	Faisalabad	1986-87
62	Pakistan v Australia	Perth	1981-82
71	Sri Lanka v Pakistan	Kandy	1994-95
134	Zimbabwe v Pakistan	Karachi	1993-94

BATTING RECORDS

HIGHEST INDIVIDUAL INNINGS

375	B.C.Lara	WI v E	St John's	1993-94
365*	G.St A.Sobers	WI v P	Kingston	1957-58
364	L.Hutton	E v A	The Oval	1938
337	Hanif Mohammad	P v WI	Bridgetown	1957-58
336*	W.R.Hammond	E v NZ	Auckland	1932-33
334	D.G.Bradman	A v E	Leeds	1930
333	G.A.Gooch	E v I	Lord's	1990
325	A.Sandham	E v WI	Kingston	1929-30
311	R.B.Simpson	A v E	Manchester	1964
310*	J.H.Edrich	E v NZ	Leeds	1965
307	R.M.Cowper	A v E	Melbourne	1965-66
304	D.G.Bradman	A v E	Leeds	1934
302	L.G.Rowe	WI v E	Bridgetown	1973-74
299*	D.G.Bradman	A v SA	Adelaide	1931-32
299	M.D.Crowe	NZ v SL	Wellington	1990-91
291	I.V.A.Richards	WI v E	The Oval	1976
287	R.E.Foster	E v A	Sydney	1903-04
285*	P.B.H.May	E v WI	Birmingham	1957
280*	Javed Miandad	P v I	Hyderabad	1982-83
278	D.C.S.Compton	E v P	Nottingham	1954
277	B.C.Lara	WI v A	Sydney	1992-93
274	R.G.Pollock	SA v A	Durban	1969-70
274	Zaheer Abbas	P v E	Birmingham	1971
271	Javed Miandad	P v NZ	Auckland	1988-89
270*	G.A.Headley	WI v E	Kingston	1934-35
270	D.G.Bradman	A v E	Melbourne	1936-37
268	G.N.Yallop	A v P	Melbourne	1983-84
267	P.A.de Silva	SL v NZ	Wellington	1990-91
266	W.H.Ponsford	A v E	The Oval	1934
266	D.L.Houghton	Z v SL	Bulawayo	1994-95
262*	D.L.Amiss	E v WI	Kingston	1973-74
261	F.M.M.Worrell	WI v E	Nottingham	1950
260	C.C.Hunte	WI v P	Kingston	1957-58
260	Javed Miandad	P v E	The Oval	1987
259	G.M.Turner	NZ v WI	Georgetown	1971-72
258	T.W.Graveney	E v WI	Nottingham	1957
258	S.M.Nurse	WI v NZ	Christchurch	1968-69
256	R.B.Kanhai	WI v I	Calcutta	1958-59
256	K.F.Barrington	E v A	Manchester	1964
255*	D.J.McGlew	SA v NZ	Wellington	1952-53
254	D.G.Bradman	A v E	Lord's	1930
251	W.R.Hammond	E v A	Sydney	1928-29
250	K.D.Walters	A v NZ	Christchurch	1976-77
250	S.F.A.F.Bacchus	WI v I	Kanpur	1978-79

The highest individual innings for India is:

236*	S.M.Gavaskar	I v WI	Madras	1983-84

MOST RUNS IN A SERIES

Runs			Series	M	I	NO	HS	Avge	100	50
974	D.G.Bradman	A v E	1930	5	7	–	334	139.14	4	–
905	W.R.Hammond	E v A	1928-29	5	9	1	251	113.12	4	–
839	M.A.Taylor	A v E	1989	6	11	1	219	83.90	2	5
834	R.N.Harvey	A v SA	1952-53	5	9	–	205	92.66	4	3
829	I.V.A.Richards	WI v E	1976	4	7	–	291	118.42	3	2
827	C.L.Walcott	WI v A	1954-55	5	10	–	155	82.70	5	2
824	G.St A.Sobers	WI v P	1957-58	5	8	2	365*	137.33	3	3
810	D.G.Bradman	A v E	1936-37	5	9	–	270	90.00	3	1
806	D.G.Bradman	A v SA	1931-32	5	5	1	299*	201.50	4	–
798	B.C.Lara	WI v E	1993-94	5	8	–	375	99.75	2	2
779	E.de C.Weekes	WI v I	1948-49	5	7	–	194	111.28	4	2
774	S.M.Gavaskar	I v WI	1970-71	4	8	3	220	154.80	4	3
765	B.C.Lara	WI v E	1995	6	10	1	179	85.00	3	3
761	Mudassar Nazar	P v I	1982-83	6	8	2	231	126.83	4	1
758	D.G.Bradman	A v E	1934	5	8	–	304	94.75	2	1
753	D.C.S.Compton	E v SA	1947	5	8	–	208	94.12	4	2
752	G.A.Gooch	E v I	1990	3	6	–	333	125.33	3	2

HIGHEST PARTNERSHIP FOR EACH WICKET

1st	413	V.Mankad/Pankaj Roy	I v NZ	Madras	1955-56
2nd	451	W.H.Ponsford/D.G.Bradman	A v E	The Oval	1934
3rd	467	A.H.Jones/M.D.Crowe	NZ v SL	Wellington	1990-91
4th	411	P.B.H.May/M.C.Cowdrey	E v WI	Birmingham	1957
5th	405	S.G.Barnes/D.G.Bradman	A v E	Sydney	1946-47
6th	346	J.H.W.Fingleton/D.G.Bradman	A v E	Melbourne	1936-37
7th	347	D.St E.Atkinson/C.C.Depeiza	WI v A	Bridgetown	1954-55
8th	246	L.E.G.Ames/G.O.B.Allen	E v NZ	Lord's	1931
9th	190	Asif Iqbal/Intikhab Alam	P v E	The Oval	1967
10th	151	B.F.Hastings/R.O.Collinge	NZ v P	Auckland	1972-73

WICKET PARTNERSHIPS OF OVER 350

467	3rd	A.H.Jones/M.D.Crowe	NZ v SL	Wellington	1990-91
451	2nd	W.H.Ponsford/D.G.Bradman	A v E	The Oval	1934
451	3rd	Mudassar Nazar/Javed Miandad	P v I	Hyderabad	1982-83
446	2nd	C.C.Hunte/G.St A.Sobers	WI v P	Kingston	1957-58
413	1st	V.Mankad/Pankaj Roy	I v NZ	Madras	1955-56
411	4th	P.B.H.May/M.C.Cowdrey	E v WI	Birmingham	1957
405	5th	S.G.Barnes/D.G.Bradman	A v E	Sydney	1946-47
399	4th	G.St A.Sobers/F.M.M.Worrell	WI v E	Bridgetown	1959-60
397	3rd	Qasim Omar/Javed Miandad	P v SL	Faisalabad	1985-86
388	4th	W.H.Ponsford/D.G.Bradman	A v E	Leeds	1934
387	1st	G.M.Turner/T.W.Jarvis	NZ v WI	Georgetown	1971-72
382	2nd	L.Hutton/M.Leyland	E v A	The Oval	1938
382	1st	W.M.Lawry/R.B.Simpson	A v WI	Bridgetown	1964-65
370	3rd	W.J.Edrich/D.C.S.Compton	E v SA	Lord's	1947
369	2nd	J.H.Edrich/K.F.Barrington	E v NZ	Leeds	1965
359	1st	L.Hutton/C.Washbrook	E v SA	Jo'burg	1948-49
351	2nd	G.A.Gooch/D.I.Gower	E v A	The Oval	1985
350	4th	Mushtaq Mohammad/Asif Iqbal	P v NZ	Dunedin	1972-73

4000 RUNS IN TESTS

Runs			*M*	*I*	*NO*	*HS*	*Avge*	*100*	*50*
11174	A.R.Border	A	156	265	44	205	50.56	27	63
10122	S.M.Gavaskar	I	125	214	16	236*	51.12	34	45
8900	G.A.Gooch	E	118	215	6	333	42.58	20	46
8832	Javed Miandad	P	124	189	21	280*	52.57	23	43
8540	I.V.A.Richards	WI	121	182	12	291	50.23	24	45
8231	D.I.Gower	E	117	204	18	215	44.25	18	39
8114	G.Boycott	E	108	193	23	246*	47.72	22	42
8032	G.St A.Sobers	WI	93	160	21	365*	57.78	26	30
7624	M.C.Cowdrey	E	114	188	15	182	44.06	22	38
7558	C.G.Greenidge	WI	108	185	16	226	44.72	19	34
7515	C.H.Lloyd	WI	110	175	14	242*	46.67	19	39
7487	D.L.Haynes	WI	116	202	25	184	42.49	18	39
7422	D.C.Boon	A	107	190	20	200	43.65	21	32
7249	W.R.Hammond	E	85	140	16	336*	58.45	22	24
7110	G.S.Chappell	A	87	151	19	247*	53.86	24	31
6996	D.G.Bradman	A	52	80	10	334	99.94	29	13
6971	L.Hutton	E	79	138	15	364	56.67	19	33
6868	D.B.Vengsarkar	I	116	185	22	166	42.13	17	35
6806	K.F.Barrington	E	82	131	15	256	58.67	20	35
6227	R.B.Kanhai	WI	79	137	6	256	47.53	15	28
6149	R.N.Harvey	A	79	137	10	205	48.41	21	24
6080	G.R.Viswanath	I	91	155	10	222	41.93	14	35
5949	R.B.Richardson	WI	86	146	12	194	44.39	16	27
5807	D.C.S.Compton	E	78	131	15	278	50.06	17	28
5502	M.A.Taylor	A	72	129	9	219	45.85	14	33
5444	M.D.Crowe	NZ	77	131	11	299	45.36	17	18
5410	J.B.Hobbs	E	61	102	7	211	56.94	15	28
5357	K.D.Walters	A	74	125	14	250	48.26	15	33
5345	I.M.Chappell	A	75	136	10	196	42.42	14	26
5334	J.G.Wright	NZ	82	148	7	185	37.82	12	23
5248	Kapil Dev	I	131	184	15	163	31.05	8	27
5234	W.M.Lawry	A	67	123	12	210	47.15	13	27
5200	I.T.Botham	E	102	161	6	208	33.54	14	22
5138	J.H.Edrich	E	77	127	9	310*	43.54	12	24
5062	Zaheer Abbas	P	78	124	11	274	44.79	12	20
5002	S.R.Waugh	A	81	125	26	200	50.52	11	28
4906	Salim Malik	P	87	129	19	237	44.60	13	24
4882	T.W.Graveney	E	79	123	13	258	44.38	11	20
4869	R.B.Simpson	A	62	111	7	311	46.81	10	27
4737	I.R.Redpath	A	66	120	11	171	43.45	8	31
4656	A.J.Lamb	E	79	139	10	142	36.09	14	18
4555	H.Sutcliffe	E	54	84	9	194	60.73	16	23
4537	P.B.H.May	E	66	106	9	285*	46.77	13	22
4502	E.R.Dexter	E	62	102	8	205	47.89	9	27
4455	E.de C.Weekes	WI	48	81	5	207	58.61	15	19
4415	K.J.Hughes	A	70	124	6	213	37.41	9	22
4409	M.W.Gatting	E	79	138	14	207	35.55	10	21
4399	A.I.Kallicharran	WI	66	109	10	187	44.43	12	21
4389	A.P.E.Knott	E	95	149	15	135	32.75	5	30
4378	M.Amarnath	I	69	113	10	138	42.50	11	24
4334	R.C.Fredericks	WI	59	109	7	169	42.49	8	26
4320	M.Azharuddin	I	68	96	4	199	46.95	14	15
4236	R.A.Smith	E	62	112	15	175	43.67	9	28
4202	M.A.Atherton	E	56	104	2	185*	41.19	9	27
4114	Mudassar Nazar	P	76	116	8	231	38.09	10	17

The highest aggregates for other countries are:

Runs			*M*	*I*	*NO*	*HS*	*Avge*	*100*	*50*
3471	B.Mitchell	SA	42	80	9	189*	48.88	8	21
3471	A.Ranatunga	SL	61	104	6	135*	35.41	4	23
1113	D.L.Houghton	Z	16	25	2	266	48.39	4	2

MOST HUNDREDS

					Opponents								
			200s	*Inns*	*E*	*A*	*SA*	*WI*	*NZ*	*I*	*P*	*SL*	*Z*
34	S.M.Gavaskar	I	4	214	4	8	–	13	2	–	5	2	–
29	D.G.Bradman	A	12	80	19	–	4	2	–	4	–	–	–
27	A.R.Border	A	2	265	8	–	–	3	5	4	6	1	–
26	G.St A.Sobers	WI	2	160	10	4	–	–	1	8	3	–	–
24	G.S.Chappell	A	4	151	9	–	–	5	3	1	6	–	–
24	I.V.A.Richards	WI	3	182	8	5	–	–	1	8	2	–	–
23	Javed Miandad	P	6	189	2	6	–	2	7	5	–	1	–
22	W.R.Hammond	E	7	140	–	9	6	1	4	2	–	–	–
22	M.C.Cowdrey	E	–	188	–	5	3	6	2	3	3	–	–
22	G.Boycott	E	1	193	–	7	1	5	2	4	3	–	–
21	R.N.Harvey	A	2	137	6	–	8	3	–	4	–	–	–
21	D.C.Boon	A	1	190	7	–	–	3	3	6	1	1	–
20	K.F.Barrington	E	1	131	–	5	2	3	3	3	4	–	–
20	G.A.Gooch	E	2	215	–	4	–	5	4	5	1	1	–

The most hundreds for countries not included above is: South Africa – 9 in 62 innings by A.D.Nourse; New Zealand – 17 in 131 innings by M.D.Crowe; Sri Lanka – 8 in 93 innings by P.A.de Silva; Zimbabwe – 4 in 25 innings by D.L.Houghton. The most double hundreds by batsmen not qualifying for the above list is four by Zaheer Abbas (12 hundreds for Pakistan) and three by R.B.Simpson (12 hundreds for Australia).

BOWLING RECORDS

MOST WICKETS IN AN INNINGS

10- 53	J.C.Laker	E v A	Manchester	1956
9- 28	G.A.Lohmann	E v SA	Johannesburg	1895-96
9- 37	J.C.Laker	E v A	Manchester	1956
9- 52	R.J.Hadlee	NZ v A	Brisbane	1985-86
9- 56	Abdul Qadir	P v E	Lahore	1987-88
9- 57	D.E.Malcolm	E v SA	The Oval	1994
9- 69	J.M.Patel	I v A	Kanpur	1959-60
9- 83	Kapil Dev	I v WI	Ahmedabad	1983-84
9- 86	Sarfraz Nawaz	P v A	Melbourne	1978-79
9- 95	J.M.Noreiga	WI v I	Port-of-Spain	1970-71
9-102	S.P.Gupte	I v WI	Kanpur	1958-59
9-103	S.F.Barnes	E v SA	Johannesburg	1913-14
9-113	H.J.Tayfield	SA v E	Johannesburg	1956-57
9-121	A.A.Mailey	A v E	Melbourne	1920-21

The best innings analyses for other countries are:

8- 83	J.R.Ratnayeke	SL v P	Sialkot	1985-86
6- 90	H.H.Streak	Z v P	Harare	1994-95

MOST WICKETS IN A TEST

19- 90	J.C.Laker	E v A	Manchester	1956
17-159	S.F.Barnes	E v SA	Johannesburg	1913-14
16-136†	N.D.Hirwani	I v WI	Madras	1987-88
16-137†	R.A.L.Massie	A v E	Lord's	1972
15- 28	J.Briggs	E v SA	Cape Town	1888-89
15- 45	G.A.Lohmann	E v SA	Port Elizabeth	1895-96
15- 99	C.Blythe	E v SA	Leeds	1907
15-104	H.Verity	E v A	Lord's	1934
15-123	R.J.Hadlee	NZ v A	Brisbane	1985-86
15-124	W.Rhodes	E v A	Melbourne	1903-04

† *On debut.*

MOST WICKETS IN A SERIES

Wkts			*Series*	*M*	*Balls*	*Runs*	*Avge*	*5 wI*	*10 wM*
49	S.F.Barnes	E v SA	1913-14	4	1356	536	10.93	7	3
46	J.C.Laker	E v A	1956	5	1703	442	9.60	4	2
44	C.V.Grimmett	A v SA	1935-36	5	2077	642	14.59	5	3
42	T.M.Alderman	A v E	1981	6	1950	893	21.26	4	–
41	R.M.Hogg	A v E	1978-79	6	1740	527	12.85	5	2
41	T.M.Alderman	A v E	1989	6	1616	712	17.36	6	1
40	Imran Khan	P v I	1982-83	6	1339	558	13.95	4	2
39	A.V.Bedser	E v A	1953	5	1591	682	17.48	5	1
39	D.K.Lillee	A v E	1981	6	1870	870	22.30	2	1
38	M.W.Tate	E v A	1924-25	5	2528	881	23.18	5	1
37	W.J.Whitty	A v SA	1910-11	5	1395	632	17.08	2	–
37	H.J.Tayfield	SA v E	1956-57	5	2280	636	17.18	4	1
36	A.E.E.Vogler	SA v E	1909-10	5	1349	783	21.75	4	1
36	A.A.Mailey	A v E	1920-21	5	1465	946	26.27	4	2
35	G.A.Lohmann	E v SA	1895-96	3	520	203	5.80	4	2
35	B.S.Chandrasekhar	I v E	1972-73	5	1747	662	18.91	4	–
35	M.D.Marshall	WI v E	1988	5	1219	443	12.65	3	1

200 WICKETS IN TESTS

Wkts			*M*	*Balls*	*Runs*	*Avge*	*5 wI*	*10 wM*
434	Kapil Dev	I	131	27740	12867	29.64	23	2
431	R.J.Hadlee	NZ	86	21918	9611	22.29	36	9
383	I.T.Botham	E	102	21815	10878	28.40	27	4
376	M.D.Marshall	WI	81	17584	7876	20.94	22	4
362	Imran Khan	P	88	19458	8258	22.81	23	6
355	D.K.Lillee	A	70	18467	8493	23.92	23	7
325	R.G.D.Willis	E	90	17357	8190	25.20	16	–
309	L.R.Gibbs	WI	79	27115	8989	29.09	18	2
307	F.S.Trueman	E	67	15178	6625	21.57	17	3
301	C.A.Walsh	WI	80	17093	7534	25.02	11	2
297	D.L.Underwood	E	86	21862	7674	25.83	17	6
291	C.J.McDermott	A	71	16586	8332	28.63	14	2
289	Wasim Akram	P	67	15266	6524	22.57	20	3
266	B.S.Bedi	I	67	21364	7637	28.71	14	1
259	J.Garner	WI	58	13169	5433	20.97	7	–
258	C.E.L.Ambrose	WI	59	13870	5493	21.29	13	3
252	J.B.Statham	E	70	16056	6261	24.84	9	1
249	M.A.Holding	WI	60	12680	5898	23.68	13	2
248	R.Benaud	A	63	19108	6704	27.03	16	1

Wkts			M	Balls	Runs	Avge	5 wI	10 wM
246	G.D.McKenzie	A	60	17681	7328	29.78	16	3
242	B.S.Chandrasekhar	I	58	15963	7199	29.74	16	2
236	A.V.Bedser	E	51	15918	5876	24.89	15	5
236	Abdul Qadir	P	67	17126	7742	32.80	15	5
235	G.St A.Sobers	WI	93	21599	7999	34.03	6	–
228	R.R.Lindwall	A	61	13650	5251	23.03	12	–
216	C.V.Grimmett	A	37	14513	5231	24.21	21	7
212	M.G.Hughes	A	53	12285	6017	28.38	7	1
207	S.K.Warne	A	44	13118	4870	23.52	10	3
202	A.M.E.Roberts	WI	47	11136	5174	25.61	11	2
202	J.A.Snow	E	49	12021	5387	26.66	8	1
200	J.R.Thomson	A	51	10535	5601	28.00	8	–
200	Waqar Younis	P	38	7733	4122	20.61	19	4
The highest aggregates for other countries are:								
170	H.J.Tayfield	SA	37	13568	4405	25.91	14	2
81	M.Muralitharan	SL	23	6099	2745	33.88	5	–
58	H.H.Streak	Z	12	2986	1257	21.67	3	–

HAT-TRICKS

F.R.Spofforth	Australia v England	Melbourne	1878-79
W.Bates	England v Australia	Melbourne	1882-83
J.Briggs	England v Australia	Sydney	1891-92
G.A.Lohmann	England v South Africa	Port Elizabeth	1895-96
J.T.Hearne	England v Australia	Leeds	1899
H.Trumble	Australia v England	Melbourne	1901-02
H.Trumble	Australia v England	Melbourne	1903-04
T.J.Matthews (2)*	Australia v South Africa	Manchester	1912
M.J.C.Allom*†	England v New Zealand	Christchurch	1929-30
T.W.J.Goddard	England v South Africa	Johannesburg	1938-39
P.J.Loader	England v West Indies	Leeds	1957
L.F.Kline	Australia v South Africa	Cape Town	1957-58
W.W.Hall	West Indies v Pakistan	Lahore	1958-59
G.M.Griffin	South Africa v England	Lord's	1960
L.R.Gibbs	West Indies v Australia	Adelaide	1960-61
P.J.Petherick*	New Zealand v Pakistan	Lahore	1976-77
C.A.Walsh‡	West Indies v Australia	Brisbane	1988-89
M.G.Hughes‡	Australia v West Indies	Perth	1988-89
D.W.Fleming*	Australia v Pakistan	Rawalpindi	1994-95
S.K.Warne	Australia v England	Melbourne	1994-95
D.G.Cork	England v West Indies	Manchester	1995

* *On debut. ** Hat-trick in each innings. † Four wickets in five balls. ‡ Involving both innings.*

WICKET-KEEPING RECORDS

MOST DISMISSALS IN AN INNINGS

7	Wasim Bari	Pakistan v New Zealand	Auckland	1978-79
7	R.W.Taylor	England v India	Bombay	1979-80
7	I.D.S.Smith	New Zealand v Sri Lanka	Hamilton	1990-91
6	A.T.W.Grout	Australia v South Africa	Johannesburg	1957-58
6	D.T.Lindsay	South Africa v Australia	Johannesburg	1966-67
6	J.T.Murray	England v India	Lord's	1967
6†	S.M.H.Kirmani	India v New Zealand	Christchurch	1975-76
6	R.W.Marsh	Australia v England	Brisbane	1982-83
6	S.A.R.Silva	Sri Lanka v India	Colombo (SSC)	1985-86
6	R.C.Russell	England v Australia	Melbourne	1990-91

†Including one stumping.

MOST STUMPINGS IN AN INNINGS

5	K.S.More	India v West Indies	Madras	1987-88

MOST DISMISSALS IN A TEST

11	R.C.Russell	England v South Africa	Johannesburg	1995-96
10	R.W.Taylor	England v India	Bombay	1979-80
9†	G.R.A.Langley	Australia v England	Lord's	1956
9	D.A.Murray	West Indies v Australia	Melbourne	1981-82
9	R.W.Marsh	Australia v England	Brisbane	1982-83
9	S.A.R.Silva	Sri Lanka v India	Colombo (SSC)	1985-86
9†	S.A.R.Silva	Sri Lanka v India	Colombo (PSS)	1985-86
9	D.J.Richardson	South Africa v India	Port Elizabeth	1992-93
9	Rashid Latif	Pakistan v New Zealand	Auckland	1993-94
9	I.A.Healy	Australia v England	Brisbane	1994-85
9	C.O.Browne	West Indies v England	Nottingham	1995

† *Including one stumping.*

MOST DISMISSALS IN A SERIES

28	R.W.Marsh	Australia v England	1982-83
27 (inc 2st)	R.C.Russell	England v South Africa	1995-96
26 (inc 3st)	J.H.B.Waite	South Africa v New Zealand	1961-62
26	R.W.Marsh	Australia v West Indies (6 Tests)	1975-76
26 (inc 5st)	I.A.Healy	Australia v England (6 Tests)	1993
25 (inc 2st)	I.A.Healy	Australia v England	1994-95

100 DISMISSALS IN TESTS

Total			*Tests*	*Ct*	*St*
355	R.W.Marsh	Australia	96	343	12
275	I.A.Healy	Australia	79	255	20
272†	P.J.L.Dujon	West Indies	81	267	5
269	A.P.E.Knott	England	95	250	19
228	Wasim Bari	Pakistan	81	201	27
219	T.G.Evans	England	91	173	46
198	S.M.H.Kirmani	India	88	160	38
189	D.L.Murray	West Indies	62	181	8
187	A.T.W.Grout	Australia	51	163	24
176	I.D.S.Smith	New Zealand	63	168	8
174	R.W.Taylor	England	57	167	7
141	J.H.B.Waite	South Africa	50	124	17
135	R.C.Russell	England	44	124	11
130	K.S.More	India	49	110	20
130	W.A.S.Oldfield	Australia	54	78	52
114†	J.M.Parks	England	46	103	11
107	D.J.Richardson	South Africa	28	107	–
104	Salim Yousuf	Pakistan	32	91	13

The most dismissals for other countries are:

41‡	A.Flower	Zimbabwe	16	39	2
34	S.A.E.Silva	Sri Lanka	9	33	1

† *Including two catches taken in the field.*
‡ *Including five catches taken in the field.*

FIELDING RECORDS

MOST CATCHES IN AN INNINGS

5	V.Y.Richardson	Australia v South Africa	Durban	1935-36
5	Yajurvindra Singh	India v England	Bangalore	1976-77
5	M.Azharuddin	India v Pakistan	Karachi	1989-90
5	K.Srikkanth	India v Australia	Perth	1991-92

MOST CATCHES IN A TEST

7	G.S.Chappell	Australia v England	Perth	1974-75
7	Yajurvindra Singh	India v England	Bangalore	1976-77
7	H.P.Tillekeratne	Sri Lanka v New Zealand	Colombo (SSC)	1992-93

MOST CATCHES IN A SERIES

15	J.M.Gregory	Australia v England	1920-21

100 CATCHES IN TESTS

Total			*Tests*
156	A.R.Border	Australia	156
122	G.S.Chappell	Australia	87
122	I.V.A.Richards	West Indies	121
120	I.T.Botham	England	102
120	M.C.Cowdrey	England	114
110	R.B.Simpson	Australia	62
110	W.R.Hammond	England	85
109	G.St A.Sobers	West Indies	93
108	S.M.Gavaskar	India	125
105	M.A.Taylor	Australia	72
105	I.M.Chappell	Australia	75
103	G.A.Gooch	England	118

MOST TEST APPEARANCES FOR EACH COUNTRY

			Opponents								
			E	*A*	*SA*	*WI*	*NZ*	*I*	*P*	*SL*	*Z*
England	118	G.A.Gooch	–	42	3	26	15	19	10	3	–
Australia	156	A.R.Border	47	–	6	31	23	20	22	7	–
South Africa	50	J.H.B.Waite	21	14	–	–	15	–	–	–	–
West Indies	121	I.V.A.Richards	36	34	–	–	7	28	16	–	–
New Zealand	86	R.J.Hadlee	21	23	–	10	–	14	12	6	–
India	131	Kapil Dev	27	20	4	25	10	–	29	14	2
Pakistan	124	Javed Miandad	22	25	–	16	18	28	–	12	3
Sri Lanka	61	A.Ranatunga	4	9	3	1	11	14	16	–	3

The most appearances for Zimbabwe is 16 by A.D.R.Campbell, A.Flower, G.W.Flower and D.L.Houghton.

MOST CONSECUTIVE TEST APPEARANCES

153	A.R.Border	Australia	March 1979 to March 1994
106	S.M.Gavaskar	India	January 1975 to February 1987

MOST MATCHES BETWEEN APPEARANCES

104	Younis Ahmed	Pakistan	November 1969 to February 1987
103	D.Shackleton	England	November 1951 to June 1963

The longest interval between appearances is 22 years 222 days (March 1970 to October 1992) by A.J.Traicos of South Africa and Zimbabwe.

MOST TESTS AS CAPTAIN

93	A.R.Border	Australia	December 1984 to March 1994

MOST UMPIRING APPEARANCES

65	H.D.Bird	July 1973 to December 1995

SUMMARY OF ALL TEST MATCHES

To 18 April 1996

	Opponents	*Tests*	*Won by*									*Tied*	*Drawn*
			E	*A*	*SA*	*WI*	*NZ*	*I*	*P*	*SL*	*Z*		
England	Australia	285	90	111	–	–	–	–	–	–	–	–	84
	South Africa	110	47	–	20	–	–	–	–	–	–	–	43
	West Indies	115	27	–	–	48	–	–	–	–	–	–	40
	New Zealand	75	34	–	–	–	4	–	–	–	–	–	37
	India	81	31	–	–	–	–	14	–	–	–	–	36
	Pakistan	52	14	–	–	–	–	–	7	–	–	–	31
	Sri Lanka	5	3	–	–	–	–	–	–	1	–	–	1
Australia	South Africa	59	–	31	13	–	–	–	–	–	–	–	15
	West Indies	81	–	32	–	27	–	–	–	–	–	1	21
	New Zealand	32	–	13	–	–	7	–	–	–	–	–	12
	India	50	–	24	–	–	–	8	–	–	–	1	17
	Pakistan	40	–	14	–	–	–	–	11	–	–	–	15
	Sri Lanka	10	–	7	–	–	–	–	–	0	–	–	3
South Africa	West Indies	1	–	–	0	1	–	–	–	–	–	–	–
	New Zealand	21	–	–	12	–	3	–	–	–	–	–	6
	India	4	–	–	1	–	–	0	–	–	–	–	3
	Pakistan	1	–	–	1	–	–	–	0	–	–	–	–
	Sri Lanka	3	–	–	1	–	–	–	–	0	–	–	2
	Zimbabwe	1	–	–	1	–	–	–	–	–	0	–	–
West Indies	New Zealand	26	–	–	–	9	4	–	–	–	–	–	13
	India	65	–	–	–	27	–	7	–	–	–	–	31
	Pakistan	31	–	–	–	12	–	–	7	–	–	–	12
	Sri Lanka	1	–	–	–	0	–	–	–	0	–	–	1
New Zealand	India	35	–	–	–	–	6	13	–	–	–	–	16
	Pakistan	37	–	–	–	–	4	–	17	–	–	–	16
	Sri Lanka	13	–	–	–	–	4	–	–	2	–	–	7
	Zimbabwe	4	–	–	–	–	1	–	–	–	0	–	3
India	Pakistan	44	–	–	–	–	–	4	7	–	–	–	33
	Sri Lanka	14	–	–	–	–	–	7	–	1	–	–	6
	Zimbabwe	2	–	–	–	–	–	1	–	–	0	–	1
Pakistan	Sri Lanka	17	–	–	–	–	–	–	9	3	–	–	5
	Zimbabwe	6	–	–	–	–	–	–	4	–	1	–	1
Sri Lanka	Zimbabwe	3	–	–	–	–	–	–	–	0	0	–	3
		1324	246	232	49	124	33	54	62	7	1	2	514

	Tests	*Won*	*Lost*	*Drawn*	*Tied*	*Toss Won*
England	723	246	205	272	–	357
Australia	557	232	156	167	2	277
South Africa	200	49	82	69	–	96
West Indies	320	124	77	118	1	167
New Zealand	243	33	100	110	–	124
India	295	54	97	143	1	148
Pakistan	228	62	53	113	–	114
Sri Lanka	66	7	31	28	–	33
Zimbabwe	16	1	7	8	–	8

ZIMBABWE v PAKISTAN (1st Test)

At Harare Sports Club, on 31 January, 1, 2, 4 February 1995.
Toss: Zimbabwe. Result: ZIMBABWE won by an innings and 64 runs.
Debuts: Zimbabwe – S.V.Carlisle, H.K.Olonga.

ZIMBABWE	
M.H.Dekker c Rashid b Aqib	2
G.W.Flower not out	201
A.D.R.Campbell lbw b Wasim	1
D.L.Houghton c Aamir b Aqib	23
*†A.Flower c Wasim b Kabir	156
G.J.Whittall not out	113
S.V.Carlisle	
P.A.Strang	
H.H.Streak	
D.H.Brain	
H.K.Olonga	
Extras (B4, LB19, W3, NB22)	48
Total (4 wickets declared)	**544**

PAKISTAN				
Aamir Sohail c Houghton b Brain	61		c Campbell b Brain	5
Saeed Anwar c A.Flower b Olonga	8		lbw b Whittall	7
Akram Raza c Whittall b Streak	19	(9)	not out	2
Asif Mujtaba c Carlisle b Streak	2	(3)	b Brain	4
*Salim Malik c Carlisle b Whittall	32	(4)	c A.Flower b Brain	6
Ijaz Ahmed c G.W.Flower b Streak	65	(5)	c Brain b Streak	2
†Rashid Latif c Campbell b Whittall	6		c Houghton b Whittall	38
Inzamam-ul-Haq c G.W.Flower b Streak	71	(6)	c A.Flower b Whittall	65
Wasim Akram c Carlisle b Streak	27	(8)	c Dekker b Strang	19
Kabir Khan not out	2		b Streak	0
Aqib Javed lbw b Streak	0		b Streak	2
Extras (B3, LB4, W9, NB13)	29		(W2, NB6)	8
Total	**322**			**158**

PAKISTAN	*O*	*M*	*R*	*W*		*O*	*M*	*R*	*W*
Wasim	39.5	12	95	1					
Aqib	34.1	8	73	2					
Kabir	35	5	142	1					
Salim	9	0	42	0					
Raza	34	6	112	0					
Asif	7	0	30	0					
Aamir	6	1	27	0					
ZIMBABWE									
Streak	39	11	90	6	(2)	11	5	15	3
Brain	27	4	94	1	(1)	16	4	50	3
Olonga	10	0	27	1					
Whittall	29	10	49	2		16	3	58	3
Strang	15	5	45	0	(3)	19	3	35	1
Dekker	4	1	10	0					

FALL OF WICKETS	*Z*	*P*	*P*
Wkt	*1st*	*1st*	*2nd*
1st	4	36	13
2nd	9	82	16
3rd	42	88	26
4th	311	131	29
5th	–	135	35
6th	–	151	131
7th	–	271	142
8th	–	317	156
9th	–	322	156
10th	–	322	158

Umpires: M.J.Kitchen (*England*) (9) and I.D.Robinson (10).
Referee: J.L.Hendriks *(West Indies)* (4). Test No. 1286/4 (Z 11/P 219)

ZIMBABWE v PAKISTAN (2nd Test)

At Queens Sports Club, Bulawayo, on 7, 8, 9 February 1995.
Toss: Zimbabwe. Result: PAKISTAN won by eight wickets.
Debuts: Zimbabwe – B.C.Strang. ‡ (Moin Khan)

ZIMBABWE

M.H.Dekker c Shakil b Aamir Nazir	0	c Aamir Sohail b Wasim	9
G.W.Flower b Wasim	6	b Manzoor	22
A.D.R.Campbell c Ijaz b Manzoor	60	c Shakil b Wasim	0
D.L.Houghton b Wasim	11	lbw b Wasim	25
*†A.Flower c Ijaz b Kabir	14	lbw b Wasim	8
G.J.Whittall c Aamir Sohail b Manzoor	7	c sub‡ b Aamir Nazir	5
S.V.Carlisle c Kabir b Wasim	1	not out	46
P.A.Strang b Aamir Nazir	32	c Aamir Sohail b Kabir	3
H.H.Streak st Rashid b Aamir Sohail	13	c Manzoor b Kabir	11
D.H.Brain c Rashid b Aamir Sohail	5	b Kabir	0
B.C.Strang not out	0	lbw b Wasim	0
Extras (B1, LB9, NB15)	25	(LB6, NB11)	17
Total	**174**		**146**

PAKISTAN

Aamir Sohail lbw b Streak	26	c Campbell b B.C.Strang	46
Shakil Ahmed lbw b Streak	5	lbw b B.C.Strang	7
†Rashid Latif c A.Flower b Streak	17	not out	1
Basit Ali c B.C.Strang b Streak	0		
*Salim Malik b Streak	44		
Ijaz Ahmed b B.C.Strang	76		
Inzamam-ul-Haq lbw b Whittall	47		
Wasim Akram c Dekker b B.C.Strang	1		
Manzoor Elahi c A.Flower b B.C.Strang	13	(4) not out	1
Kabir Khan not out	8		
Aamir Nazir b Brain	7		
Extras (B2, LB5, W2, NB7)	16	(LB2, W1, NB3)	6
Total	**260**	(2 wickets)	**61**

PAKISTAN	*O*	*M*	*R*	*W*		*O*	*M*	*R*	*W*
Wasim	22	9	40	3		22.3	7	43	5
Aamir Nazir	18	4	36	2		11	1	39	1
Kabir	16	2	45	1	(4)	11	3	26	3
Manzoor	21	8	38	2	(3)	14	6	32	1
Aamir Sohail	2.1	1	5	2					
ZIMBABWE									
Streak	26	5	70	5		6	1	18	0
Brain	15	4	49	1		2	0	35	0
B.C.Strang	23	10	44	3		3.4	2	6	2
Whittall	15	3	42	1					
P.A.Strang	15	4	48	0					

FALL OF WICKETS

	Z	P	Z	P
Wkt	*1st*	*1st*	*2nd*	*2nd*
1st	3	9	14	56
2nd	7	47	16	60
3rd	23	52	58	–
4th	56	63	73	–
5th	73	133	77	–
6th	86	212	93	–
7th	134	226	106	–
8th	167	231	145	–
9th	174	246	145	–
10th	174	260	146	–

Umpires: B.C.Cooray *(Sri Lanka)* (5) and Q.J.Goosen (1).
Referee: J.L.Hendriks *(West Indies)* (5). Test No. 1287/5 (Z 12/P 220)

ZIMBABWE v PAKISTAN (3rd Test)

At Harare Sports Club, on 15, 16, 18, 19 February 1995.
Toss: Pakistan. Result: PAKISTAN won by 99 runs.
Debuts: Zimbabwe – I.P.Butchart.

PAKISTAN				
Aamir Sohail c P.A.Strang b Streak	21	(6)	c G.W.Flower b Whittall	19
Shakil Ahmed c A.Flower b Whittall	29		c A.Flower b B.C.Strang	33
Saeed Anwar c Butchart b Streak	4	(1)	c Carlisle b Streak	26
*Salim Malik c G.W.Flower b Streak	20		c Carlisle b Whittall	5
Ijaz Ahmed lbw b Streak	41		c Whittall b Streak	55
Inzamam-ul-Haq c P.A.Strang b Brain	101	(3)	c G.W.Flower b Whittall	83
†Rashid Latif c P.A.Strang b B.C.Strang	6		c A.Flower b Streak	6
Wasim Akram b B.C.Strang	0		c Campbell b Brain	4
Manzoor Elahi c Streak b B.C.Strang	0		c A.Flower b Streak	0
Aqib Javed run out	0		c A.Flower b Brain	3
Aamir Nazir not out	0		not out	0
Extras (LB3, W3, NB3)	9		(LB3, W3, NB10)	16
Total	**231**			**250**

ZIMBABWE				
G.W.Flower b Aamir Nazir	6		b Aamir Nazir	2
S.V.Carlisle c Salim b Aqib	31		b Aamir Nazir	0
A.D.R.Campbell c Manzoor b Aamir Nazir	14		c Rashid b Aamir Nazir	18
D.L.Houghton c Rashid b Wasim	19	(6)	c Rashid b Aamir Nazir	5
*†A.Flower c Aqib b Manzoor	37	(4)	c Aamir Nazir b Manzoor	35
G.J.Whittall b Aqib	34	(5)	c Shakil b Wasim	2
I.P.Butchart c Inzamam b Wasim	15		c and b Aamir Nazir	8
P.A.Strang c Aamir Sohail b Aamir Nazir	28		c Ijaz b Aqib	5
H.H.Streak lbw b Aqib	0		not out	30
D.H.Brain not out	22		c Inzamam b Wasim	8
B.C.Strang c Inzamam b Aqib	6		c Shakil b Aqib	0
Extras (LB4, W1, NB26)	31		(B5, LB5, NB16)	26
Total	**243**			**139**

ZIMBABWE	*O*	*M*	*R*	*W*		*O*	*M*	*R*	*W*
Streak	18	4	53	4		18	3	52	4
Brain	12.3	1	48	1		16.1	2	61	2
B.C.Strang	32	15	43	3	(4)	26	16	27	1
Whittall	18	3	73	1	(3)	22	3	66	3
Butchart	3	0	11	0					
P.A.Strang					(5)	13	3	41	0
PAKISTAN									
Wasim	28	2	90	2		20	1	45	2
Aqib	25	5	64	4	(3)	17.4	3	26	2
Aamir Nazir	13	3	50	3	(2)	19	3	46	5
Manzoor	10	3	28	1		3	0	12	1
Aamir Sohail	2	0	7	0					

FALL OF WICKETS

	P	*Z*	*P*	*Z*
Wkt	*1st*	*1st*	*2nd*	*2nd*
1st	42	20	58	2
2nd	46	51	72	12
3rd	64	79	88	37
4th	83	94	204	68
5th	159	145	230	72
6th	180	175	233	85
7th	180	193	246	95
8th	183	193	247	95
9th	204	233	250	122
10th	231	243	250	139

Umpires: S.G.Randell *(Australia)* (20) and I.D.Robinson (11).
Referee: J.L.Hendriks *(West Indies)* (6). Test No. 1288/6 (Z 13/P 221)

ZIMBABWE v PAKISTAN 1994-95

ZIMBABWE – BATTING AND FIELDING

	M	I	NO	HS	Runs	Avge	100	50	Ct/St
G.W.Flower	3	5	1	201*	237	59.25	1	–	5
A.Flower	3	5	–	156	250	50.00	1	–	10
G.J.Whittall	3	5	1	113*	161	40.25	–	–	2
S.V.Carlisle	3	4	1	46*	78	26.00	–	–	5
A.D.R.Campbell	3	5	–	60	93	18.60	–	1	4
H.H.Streak	3	4	1	30*	54	18.00	–	–	1
P.A.Strang	3	4	–	32	68	17.00	–	–	3
D.L.Houghton	3	5	–	25	83	16.60	–	–	2
D.H.Brain	3	4	1	22*	35	11.66	–	–	1
M.H.Dekker	2	3	–	9	11	3.66	–	–	2
B.C.Strang	2	4	1	6	6	2.00	–	–	1

Played in one Test: I.P.Butchart 15, 8 (1 ct); H.K.Olonga did not bat.

ZIMBABWE – BOWLING

	O	M	R	W	Avge	Best	5wI	10wM
B.C.Strang	84.4	43	120	9	13.33	3-43	–	–
H.H.Streak	118	29	298	22	13.54	6-90	2	–
G.J.Whittall	100	22	288	10	28.80	3-58	–	–
D.H.Brain	88.4	15	337	8	42.12	3-50	–	–

Also bowled: I.P.Butchart 3-0-11-0; M.H.Dekker 4-1-10-0; H.K.Olonga 10-0-27-1; P.A.Strang 62-15-169-1.

PAKISTAN – BATTING AND FIELDING

	M	I	NO	HS	Runs	Avge	100	50	Ct/St
Inzamam-ul-Haq	3	5	–	101	367	73.40	1	3	3
Ijaz Ahmed	3	5	–	76	239	47.80	–	3	3
Aamir Sohail	3	6	–	61	178	29.66	–	1	5
Salim Malik	3	5	–	44	107	21.40	–	–	1
Shakil Ahmed	2	4	–	33	74	18.50	–	–	4
Rashid Latif	3	6	1	38	74	14.80	–	–	5/1
Saeed Anwar	2	4	–	26	45	11.25	–	–	–
Wasim Akram	3	5	–	27	51	10.20	–	–	1
Kabir Khan	2	3	2	8*	10	10.00	–	–	1
Aamir Nazir	2	3	2	7	7	7.00	–	–	2
Manzoor Elahi	2	4	1	13	14	4.66	–	–	2
Aqib Javed	2	4	–	3	5	1.25	–	–	1

Played in one Test: Akram Raza 19, 2*; Asif Mujtaba 2, 4; Basit Ali 0.

PAKISTAN – BOWLING

	O	M	R	W	Avge	Best	5wI	10wM
Aamir Nazir	61	11	171	11	15.54	5-46	1	–
Aqib Javed	76.5	16	163	8	20.37	4-64	–	–
Manzoor Elahi	48	17	110	5	22.00	2-38	–	–
Wasim Akram	132.2	31	313	13	24.07	5-43	1	–
Kabir Khan	62	10	213	5	42.60	3-26	–	–

Also bowled: Aamir Sohail 10.1-2-39-2; Akram Raza 34-6-112-0; Asif Mujtaba 7-0-30-0; Salim Malik 9-0-42-0.

NEW ZEALAND v WEST INDIES (1st Test)

At Lancaster Park, Christchurch, on 3, 4, 5, 6, 7 February 1995.
Toss: West Indies. Result: MATCH DRAWN.
Debuts: None.

NEW ZEALAND			
B.A.Young c Murray b Walsh	19	c Murray b K.C.G.Benjamin	21
D.J.Murray c Campbell b Ambrose	43	c Murray b Walsh	8
A.H.Jones c Williams b K.C.G.Benjamin	12	not out	10
*K.R.Rutherford c Murray b Ambrose	11	not out	16
S.P.Fleming c Lara b Walsh	56		
S.A.Thomson c W.K.M.Benjamin b K.C.G.Benjamin	20		
†A.C.Parore not out	100		
M.N.Hart c and b W.K.M.Benjamin	45		
D.J.Nash c Campbell b Ambrose	3		
S.B.Doull			
D.K.Morrison			
Extras (B12, LB5, NB15)	32	(LB1, NB5)	6
Total (8 wickets declared)	**341**	(2 wickets)	**61**

WEST INDIES	
S.C.Williams c Parore b Morrison	10
S.L.Campbell lbw b Morrison	51
B.C.Lara b Morrison	2
J.C.Adams c Doull b Morrison	13
K.L.T.Arthurton run out	1
S.Chanderpaul b Thomson	69
†J.R.Murray c Murray b Thomson	28
W.K.M.Benjamin b Doull	85
C.E.L.Ambrose b Morrison	33
*C.A.Walsh not out	0
K.C.G.Benjamin c Parore b Morrison	5
Extras (LB11, NB4)	15
Total	**312**

WEST INDIES	*O*	*M*	*R*	*W*	*O*	*M*	*R*	*W*
Ambrose	31.1	12	57	3	3	0	7	0
Walsh	30	5	69	2	4	1	8	1
W.K.M.Benjamin	33	4	94	1	5	1	12	0
K.C.G.Benjamin	25	7	91	2	6	0	12	1
Chanderpaul	3	1	10	0	2	2	0	0
Arthurton	2	0	3	0	5	1	9	0
Adams					3	1	4	0
Lara					4	0	8	0
NEW ZEALAND								
Morrison	26.2	9	69	6				
Nash	5	2	11	0				
Doull	22	5	85	1				
Hart	25	2	75	0				
Thomson	18	3	61	2				

FALL OF WICKETS

Wkt	*NZ 1st*	*WI 1st*	*NZ 2nd*
1st	32	10	33
2nd	63	21	33
3rd	92	49	–
4th	97	54	–
5th	128	98	–
6th	210	155	–
7th	328	232	–
8th	341	299	–
9th	–	307	–
10th	–	312	–

Umpires: B.L.Aldridge (23) and N.T.Plews *(England)* (9).
Referee: P.L.van der Merwe *(South Africa)* (5). Test No. 1289/25 (NZ 233/WI 309)

NEW ZEALAND v WEST INDIES (2nd Test)

At Basin Reserve, Wellington, on 10, 11, 12, 13 February 1995.
Toss: West Indies. Result: WEST INDIES won by an innings and 322 runs.
Debuts: None.

WEST INDIES	
S.C.Williams c Parore b Doull	26
S.L.Campbell c Su'a b Morrison	88
B.C.Lara lbw Morrison	147
J.C.Adams c Su'a b Doull	151
K.L.T.Arthurton run out	70
S.Chanderpaul not out	61
†J.R.Murray not out	101
C.E.L.Ambrose	
*C.A.Walsh	
K.C.G.Benjamin	
R.Dhanraj	
Extras (LB6, NB10)	16
Total (5 wickets declared)	**660**

NEW ZEALAND			
B.A.Young lbw b Walsh	29	b Walsh	0
D.J.Murray lbw b Ambrose	52	b Walsh	43
A.H.Jones c Murray b Walsh	0	lbw b Benjamin	2
*K.R.Rutherford lbw b Dhanraj	22	lbw b Ambrose	5
S.P.Fleming c Lara b Walsh	47	b Walsh	30
S.A.Thomson b Walsh	6	b Dhanraj	8
†A.C.Parore c Adams b Walsh	32	not out	5
M.N.Hart c Lara b Dhanraj	0	c Ambrose b Dhanraj	1
M.L.Su'a c Murray b Walsh	6	c Arthurton b Walsh	8
S.B.Doull b Walsh	0	lbw b Walsh	0
D.K.Morrison not out	0	c Murray b Walsh	14
Extras (B1, LB14, NB7)	22	(LB2, NB4)	6
Total	**216**		**122**

NEW ZEALAND	*O*	*M*	*R*	*W*		*O*	*M*	*R*	*W*
Morrison	29	5	82	2					
Su'a	44	4	179	0					
Doull	37.2	5	162	2					
Hart	46	4	181	0					
Jones	13	2	50	0					
WEST INDIES									
Ambrose	19	9	32	1	(3)	5	1	17	1
Walsh	20.4	7	37	7	(1)	15.2	8	18	6
Dhanraj	33	6	97	2	(4)	12	2	49	2
Benjamin	12	1	35	0	(2)	8	0	36	1

FALL OF WICKETS	*WI*	*NZ*	*NZ*
Wkt	*1st*	*1st*	*2nd*
1st	85	50	0
2nd	134	52	3
3rd	355	108	15
4th	449	135	70
5th	521	160	93
6th	–	196	93
7th	–	197	97
8th	–	207	106
9th	–	211	106
10th	–	216	122

Umpires: R.S.Dunne (16) and V.K.Ramaswamy *(India)* (16).
Referee: B.N.Jarman *(Australia)* (1). Test No. 1290/26 (NZ 234/WI 310)

NEW ZEALAND v WEST INDIES 1994-95

NEW ZEALAND – BATTING AND FIELDING

	M	I	NO	HS	Runs	Avge	100	50	Ct/St
A.C.Parore	2	3	2	100*	137	137.00	1	–	3
S.P.Fleming	2	3	–	56	133	44.33	–	1	–
D.J.Murray	2	4	–	52	146	36.50	–	1	1
K.R.Rutherford	2	4	1	22	54	18.00	–	–	–
B.A.Young	2	4	–	29	69	17.25	–	–	–
M.N.Hart	2	3	–	45	46	15.33	–	–	–
D.K.Morrison	2	2	1	14	14	14.00	–	–	–
S.A.Thomson	2	3	–	20	34	11.33	–	–	–
A.H.Jones	2	4	1	12	24	8.00	–	–	–
S.B.Doull	2	2	–	0	0	0.00	–	–	1

Played in one Test: D.J.Nash 3; M.L.Su'a 6, 8 (2 ct).

NEW ZEALAND – BOWLING

	O	M	R	W	Avge	Best	5wI	10wM
D.K.Morrison	55.2	14	151	8	18.87	6- 69	1	–
S.A.Thomson	18	3	61	2	30.50	2- 61	–	–
S.B.Doull	59.2	10	247	3	82.33	2-162	–	–

Also bowled: M.N.Hart 71-6-256-0; A.H.Jones 13-2-50-0; D.J.Nash 5-2-11-0; M.L.Su'a 44-4-179-0.

WEST INDIES – BATTING AND FIELDING

	M	I	NO	HS	Runs	Avge	100	50	Ct/St
S.Chanderpaul	2	2	1	69	130	130.00	–	2	–
J.R.Murray	2	2	1	101*	129	129.00	1	–	7
J.C.Adams	2	2	–	151	164	82.00	1	–	1
B.C.Lara	2	2	–	147	149	74.50	1	–	3
S.L.Campbell	2	2	–	88	139	69.50	–	2	2
K.L.T.Arthurton	2	2	–	70	71	35.50	–	1	1
C.E.L.Ambrose	2	1	–	33	33	33.00	–	–	1
S.C.Williams	2	2	–	26	36	18.00	–	–	1
K.C.G.Benjamin	2	1	–	5	5	5.00	–	–	–
C.A.Walsh	2	1	1	0*	0	–	–	–	–

Played in one Test: W.K.M.Benjamin 85 (2 ct); R.Dhanraj did not bat.

WEST INDIES – BOWLING

	O	M	R	W	Avge	Best	5wI	10wM
C.A.Walsh	70	21	132	16	8.25	7-37	2	1
C.E.L.Ambrose	58.1	22	113	5	22.60	3-57	–	–
R.Dhanraj	45	8	146	4	36.50	2-49	–	–
K.C.G.Benjamin	51	8	174	4	43.50	2-91	–	–
W.K.M.Benjamin	38	5	106	1	106.00	1-94	–	–

Also bowled: J.C.Adams 3-1-4-0; K.L.T.Arthurton 7-1-12-0; S.Chanderpaul 5-3-10-0; B.C.Lara 4-0-8-0.

NEW ZEALAND v SOUTH AFRICA (Only Test)

At Eden Park, Auckland, on 4, 5, 6, 7, 8 March 1995.
Toss: South Africa. Result: SOUTH AFRICA won by 93 runs.
Debuts: None.

SOUTH AFRICA				
G.Kirsten b Larsen	16		c Parore b Nash	76
P.J.R.Steyn c Patel b Morrison	46		c Rutherford b Patel	13
A.C.Hudson c Parore b Nash	1		c Young b Patel	64
D.J.Cullinan c Murray b Morrison	96		c Parore b Hart	12
C.E.Eksteen c Fleming b Nash	21			
*W.J.Cronje c Crowe b Morrison	41	(5)	c Hart b Larsen	101
J.N Rhodes c Parore b Nash	0	(6)	b Larsen	28
†D.J.Richardson c Parore b Nash	18	(7)	not out	8
C.R.Matthews c Parore b Larsen	26	(8)	not out	4
P.S.de Villiers c Hart b Larsen	12			
A.A.Donald not out	4			
Extras (LB13)	13		(LB1, NB1)	2
Total	**294**		(6 wickets declared)	**308**

NEW ZEALAND				
B.A.Young c Richardson b Donald	74		c Cullinan b De Villiers	4
D.J.Murray c Kirsten b Cronje	25		c Matthews b De Villiers	24
M.D.Crowe c Hudson b De Villiers	16		c Cullinan b Matthews	14
S.P.Fleming b Matthews	17		c Richardson b Matthews	27
*K.R.Rutherford c Richardson b Cronje	28		c Hudson b De Villiers	56
†A.C.Parore c Richardson b Donald	89		c Cullinan b Eksteen	24
M.N.Hart lbw b Matthews	28	(8)	c Richardson b De Villiers	6
G.R.Larsen not out	26	(9)	c Richardson b Donald	1
D.N.Patel c Richardson b Donald	15	(7)	run out	12
D.J.Nash lbw b De Villiers	1		lbw b Matthews	6
D.K.Morrison c Cullinan b Donald	0		not out	0
Extras (LB5, W1, NB3)	9		(B1, LB4, NB2)	7
Total	**328**			**181**

NEW ZEALAND	*O*	*M*	*R*	*W*	*O*	*M*	*R*	*W*	**FALL OF WICKETS**				
Morrison	26	9	53	3	23	6	78	0		*SA*	*NZ*	*SA*	*NZ*
Nash	27	13	72	4	22	3	67	1	*Wkt*	*1st*	*1st*	*2nd*	*2nd*
Larsen	24.3	17	57	3	18	6	31	2	1st	41	86	41	11
Hart	11	3	45	0	12	3	50	1	2nd	42	108	123	42
Patel	17	2	54	0	30	6	81	2	3rd	145	137	135	50
									4th	168	144	218	114
SOUTH AFRICA									5th	230	226	277	145
Donald	32.4	11	88	4	8	2	44	1	6th	230	268	300	167
De Villiers	36	3	78	2	18	6	42	4	7th	230	303	–	174
Matthews	32	11	66	2	12.5	3	47	3	8th	276	321	–	174
Cronje	17	3	48	2	3	1	18	0	9th	276	322	–	179
Eksteen	23	9	43	0	14	5	25	1	10th	294	328	–	181

Umpires: R.S.Dunne (17) and D.B.Hair *(Australia)* (11).
Referee: B.N.Jarman *(Australia)* (2). Test No. 1291/21 (NZ 235/SA 194)

NEW ZEALAND v SRI LANKA (1st Test)

At McLean Park, Napier, on 11, 12, 13, 14, 15 March 1995.
Toss: New Zealand. Result: SRI LANKA won by 241 runs.
Debuts: None.

SRI LANKA			
A.P.Gurusinha b Walmsley	2	lbw b Larsen	8
D.P.Samaraweera c Young b Walmsley	33	run out	6
S.Ranatunga c Larsen b Nash	12	lbw b Larsen	7
P.A.de Silva c Parore b Nash	0	c Parore b Morrison	62
H.P.Tillekeratne lbw b Morrison	9	c Young b Nash	74
*A.Ranatunga c Young b Walmsley	55	b Morrison	28
†C.I.Dunusinghe c Rutherford b Larsen	11	b Morrison	91
W.P.U.C.J.Vaas not out	33	b Walmsley	36
G.P.Wickremasinghe c Fleming b Morrison	13	c sub (M.N.Hart) b Larsen	16
M.Muralitharan c Nash b Larsen	8	not out	10
K.R.Pushpakumara c Larsen b Morrison	1	c Parore b Morrison	0
Extras (LB6)	6	(B2, LB7, NB5)	14
Total	**183**		**352**

NEW ZEALAND			
B.A.Young c Dunusinghe b Wickremasinghe	2	c Samaraweera b Muralitharan	14
D.J.Murray lbw b Vaas	1	c Dunusinghe b Vaas	36
M.J.Greatbatch lbw b Wickremasinghe	1	c Tillekeratne b Muralitharan	46
S.P.Fleming c S.Ranatunga b Vaas	35	c Tillekeratne b Muralitharan	0
*K.R.Rutherford c Tillekeratne b Pushpakumara	32	c Dunusinghe b Vaas	20
S.A.Thomson c Muralitharan b Vaas	8	c Gurusinha b Muralitharan	4
†A.C.Parore c Dunusinghe b Wickremasinghe	7	c Tillekeratne b Muralitharan	17
G.R.Larsen c Dunusinghe b Vaas	0	not out	21
D.J.Nash lbw b Pushpakumara	0	c Dunusinghe b Vaas	0
D.K.Morrison not out	7	c Gurusinha b Vaas	0
K.P.Walmsley b Vaas	4	c Dunusinghe b Vaas	4
Extras (B5, LB1, W1, NB5)	12	(B6, LB11, NB6)	23
Total	**109**		**185**

NEW ZEALAND	O	M	R	W	O	M	R	W
Morrison	19	5	40	3	25.3	5	61	4
Walmsley	17	3	70	3	38	7	112	1
Nash	16	4	28	2	36	12	87	1
Larsen	17	6	39	2	39	13	73	3
Thomson					6	3	10	0
SRI LANKA								
Wickremasinghe	19	7	33	3	13	2	42	0
Vaas	18.5	3	47	5	26.4	19	43	5
Pushpakumara	5	1	23	2	9	2	19	0
Muralitharan					36	15	64	5

FALL OF WICKETS	SL	NZ	SL	NZ
Wkt	1st	1st	2nd	2nd
1st	15	2	14	37
2nd	40	4	21	108
3rd	40	6	22	108
4th	54	53	121	112
5th	64	65	165	141
6th	88	78	205	141
7th	137	79	294	166
8th	166	94	323	181
9th	178	104	352	181
10th	183	109	352	185

Umpires: D.B.Cowie (1) and S.G.Randell *(Australia)* (21).
Referee: B.N.Jarman *(Australia)* (3). Test No. 1292/12 (NZ 236/SL 59)

NEW ZEALAND v SRI LANKA (2nd Test)

At Carisbrook, Dunedin, on 18, 19, 20, 21, 22 March 1995.
Toss: New Zealand. Result: MATCH DRAWN.
Debuts: None.

SRI LANKA				
A.P.Gurusinha c Patel b Pringle	28		b Su'a	127
D.P.Samaraweera c and b Su'a	33		lbw b Su'a	5
S.Ranatunga c Young b Pringle	22		c Parore b Patel	23
P.A.de Silva c Patel b Walmsley	18		c Murray b Patel	13
*A.Ranatunga c Young b Larsen	0	(6)	c Parore b Larsen	90
H.P.Tillekeratne c Young b Patel	36	(5)	c Murray b Patel	108
†C.I.Dunusinghe lbw b Pringle	0		c Fleming b Patel	11
W.P.U.C.J.Vaas c Fleming b Su'a	51		c Parore b Walmsley	3
G.P.Wickremasinghe c Fleming b Patel	10		c Parore b Walmsley	9
M.Muralitharan c Larsen b Patel	8		run out	7
K.R.Pushpakumara not out	17		not out	1
Extras (LB6, NB4)	10		(B6, LB5, NB3)	14
Total (5 wickets declared)	**233**			**411**

NEW ZEALAND			
B.A.Young c Gurusinha b Vaas	84	not out	0
D.J.Murray c Dunusinghe b Vaas	0	not out	0
M.J.Greatbatch lbw b Vaas	0		
S.P.Fleming run out	66		
†A.C.Parore c De Silva b Vaas	19		
D.N.Patel b Muralitharan	52		
G.R.Larsen c Gurusinha b Muralitharan	16		
M.L.Su'a not out	20		
C.Pringle c S.Ranatunga b Vaas	4		
K.P.Walmsley b Vaas	0		
*K.R.Rutherford absent injured	0		
Extras (B3, LB28, NB15)	46		
Total	**307**	(0 wickets)	**0**

NEW ZEALAND	O	M	R	W	O	M	R	W
Su'a	20.5	5	43	2	26	3	97	2
Walmsley	18	4	41	1	38	8	121	2
Pringle	15	1	51	3	22	8	55	0
Patel	21	3	62	3	57	20	96	4
Larsen	13	2	30	1	25.4	14	31	1
SRI LANKA								
Wickremasinghe	26	5	49	0				
Vaas	40	9	87	6	0.1	0	0	0
Muralitharan	50	20	77	2				
Pushpakumara	16	3	42	0				
De Silva	1	0	11	0				
Gurusinha	6	2	10	0				

FALL OF WICKETS	SL	NZ	SL	NZ
Wkt	1st	1st	2nd	2nd
1st	42	26	11	–
2nd	67	26	63	–
3rd	94	140	81	–
4th	97	196	273	–
5th	122	197	295	–
6th	122	244	344	–
7th	157	291	355	–
8th	178	303	377	–
9th	194	307	405	–
10th	233	–	411	–

Umpires: D.M.Quested (1) and V.K.Ramaswamy *(India)* (17).
Referee: B.N.Jarman *(Australia)* (4). Test No. 1293/13 (NZ 237/SL 60)

NEW ZEALAND v SRI LANKA 1994-95

NEW ZEALAND – BATTING AND FIELDING

	M	I	NO	HS	Runs	Avge	100	50	Ct/St
S.P.Fleming	2	3	–	66	101	33.66	–	1	4
B.A.Young	2	4	1	84	100	33.33	–	1	6
K.R.Rutherford	2	2	–	32	52	26.00	–	–	1
G.R.Larsen	2	3	1	21*	37	18.50	–	–	3
M.J.Greatbatch	2	3	–	46	47	15.66	–	–	–
A.C.Parore	2	3	–	19	43	14.33	–	–	7
D.J.Murray	2	4	1	36	37	12.33	–	–	2
K.P.Walmsley	2	3	–	4	8	2.66	–	–	–

Played in one Test: D.K.Morrison 7*, 0; D.J.Nash 0, 0 (1 ct); D.N.Patel 52 (2 ct); C.Pringle 4; M.L.Su'a 20* (1 ct); S.A.Thomson 8, 4.

NEW ZEALAND – BOWLING

	O	M	R	W	Avge	Best	5wI	10wM
D.K.Morrison	44.3	10	101	7	14.42	4-61	–	–
D.N.Patel	78	23	158	7	22.57	4-96	–	–
G.R.Larsen	94.4	35	173	7	24.71	3-73	–	–
M.L.Su'a	46.5	8	140	4	35.00	2-43	–	–
C.Pringle	37	9	106	3	35.33	3-51	–	–
D.J.Nash	52	16	115	3	38.33	2-28	–	–
K.P.Walmsley	111	22	344	7	49.14	3-70	–	–

Also bowled: S.A.Thomson 6-3-10-0.

SRI LANKA – BATTING AND FIELDING

	M	I	NO	HS	Runs	Avge	100	50	Ct/St
H.P.Tillekeratne	2	4	–	108	227	56.75	1	1	4
A.Ranatunga	2	4	–	90	173	43.25	–	2	–
A.P.Gurusinha	2	4	–	127	165	41.25	1	–	4
W.P.U.C.J.Vaas	2	4	1	51	123	41.00	–	1	–
C.I.Dunusinghe	2	4	–	91	113	28.25	–	1	8
P.A.de Silva	2	4	–	62	93	23.25	–	1	1
D.P.Samaraweera	2	4	–	33	77	19.25	–	–	1
S.Ranatunga	2	4	–	23	64	16.00	–	–	2
G.P.Wickremasinghe	2	4	–	16	48	12.00	–	–	–
M.Muralitharan	2	4	1	10*	33	11.00	–	–	1
K.R.Pushpakumara	2	4	2	17*	19	9.50	–	–	–

SRI LANKA – BOWLING

	O	M	R	W	Avge	Best	5wI	10wM
W.P.U.C.J.Vaas	85.4	22	177	16	11.06	6-87	3	1
M.Muralitharan	86	35	141	7	20.14	5-64	1	–
G.P.Wickremasinghe	58	14	124	3	41.33	3-33	–	–
K.R.Pushpakumara	30	6	84	2	42.00	2-23	–	–

Also bowled: P.A.de Silva 1-0-11-0; A.P.Gurusinha 6-2-10-0.

WEST INDIES v AUSTRALIA (1st Test)

At Kensington Oval, Bridgetown, Barbados, on 31 March, 1, 2 April 1995.
Toss: West Indies. Result: AUSTRALIA won by 10 wickets.
Debuts: None.

WEST INDIES

S.C.Williams c Taylor b Julian	1		c Healy b McGrath	10
S.L.Campbell c Healy b Reiffel	0		c S.R.Waugh b Warne	6
B.C.Lara c S.R.Waugh b Julian	65		c Healy b McGrath	9
*R.B.Richardson c Healy b Julian	0	(5)	b Reiffel	36
C.L.Hooper c Taylor b Julian	60	(4)	c Reiffel b Julian	16
J.C.Adams c Warne b McGrath	16		not out	39
†J.R.Murray c Taylor b McGrath	21		c S.R.Waugh b Warne	23
W.K.M.Benjamin c Taylor b Warne	14		lbw b McGrath	26
C.E.L.Ambrose c Blewett b McGrath	7		c Blewett b McGrath	6
C.A.Walsh c S.R.Waugh b Warne	1		b McGrath	4
K.C.G.Benjamin not out	0		b Warne	5
Extras (B3, W1, NB6)	10		(LB1, NB8)	9
Total	**195**			**189**

AUSTRALIA

M.J.Slater c Williams b W.K.M.Benjamin	18	(2)	not out	20
*M.A.Taylor c Hooper b K.C.G.Benjamin	55	(1)	not out	16
D.C.Boon c W.K.M.Benjamin b Walsh	20			
M.E.Waugh c Murray b Ambrose	40			
S.R.Waugh c Murray b K.C.G.Benjamin	65			
G.S.Blewett c Murray b Ambrose	14			
†I.A.Healy not out	74			
B.P.Julian c K.C.G.Benjamin b Hooper	31			
P.R.Reiffel b W.K.M.Benjamin	1			
S.K.Warne c Adams b Walsh	6			
G.D.McGrath b W.K.M.Benjamin	4			
Extras (LB13, NB5)	18		(NB3)	3
Total	**346**		(0 wickets)	**39**

AUSTRALIA	*O*	*M*	*R*	*W*		*O*	*M*	*R*	*W*
Reiffel	11	4	41	1		11	6	15	1
Julian	12	0	36	4		12	2	41	1
Warne	12	2	57	2		26.3	5	64	3
McGrath	12.1	1	46	3		22	6	68	5
M.E.Waugh	1	0	12	0					
WEST INDIES									
Ambrose	20	7	41	2					
Walsh	25	5	78	2	(1)	3	0	19	0
K.C.G.Benjamin	20	1	84	2	(2)	2.5	1	14	0
W.K.M.Benjamin	23.2	6	71	3					
Hooper	12	0	59	1	(3)	1	0	6	0

FALL OF WICKETS

	WI	*A*	*WI*	*A*
Wkt	*1st*	*1st*	*2nd*	*2nd*
1st	1	27	19	–
2nd	5	72	25	–
3rd	6	121	31	–
4th	130	166	57	–
5th	152	194	91	–
6th	156	230	136	–
7th	184	290	170	–
8th	193	291	176	–
9th	194	331	180	–
10th	195	346	189	–

Umpires: L.H.Barker (21) and S.Venkataraghavan (*India*) (9).
Referee: Majid Khan (*Pakistan*) (1). **Test No. 1294/78 (WI 311/A 548)**

WEST INDIES v AUSTRALIA (2nd Test)

At Recreation Ground, St John's, Antigua, on 8, 9, 10, 12, 13 April 1995.
Toss: West Indies. Result: MATCH DRAWN.
Debuts: None.

AUSTRALIA				
M.J.Slater c Adams b Walsh	41	(2)	c Richardson b Walsh	18
*M.A.Taylor c Walsh b Ambrose	37	(1)	c Murray b Walsh	5
D.C.Boon b Walsh	21		lbw b W.K.M.Benjamin	67
M.E.Waugh c Hooper b Walsh	4		b W.K.M.Benjamin	61
S.R.Waugh b K.C.G.Benjamin	15		not out	65
G.S.Blewett c Murray b W.K.M.Benjamin	11		c Williams b Hooper	19
†I.A.Healy c Walsh b W.K.M.Benjamin	14		c Hooper b Walsh	26
B.P.Julian b Walsh	22		run out	6
P.R.Reiffel not out	22		not out	13
S.K.Warne c Arthurton b Walsh	11			
G.D.McGrath c Murray b Walsh	0			
Extras (LB12, NB6)	18		(B1, LB9, NB10)	20
Total	**216**		(7 wickets declared)	**300**

WEST INDIES			
S.C.Williams c Boon b Warne	16	not out	31
*R.B.Richardson c S.R.Waugh b Julian	37	b Reiffel	2
B.C.Lara c Boon b S.R.Waugh	88	b Julian	43
J.C.Adams lbw b Warne	22	not out	3
C.L.Hooper c Julian b S.R.Waugh	11		
K.L.T.Arthurton c Taylor b Warne	26		
†J.R.Murray lbw b Reiffel	26		
W.K.M.Benjamin c Taylor b McGrath	4		
C.E.L.Ambrose c Taylor b Reiffel	0		
C.A.Walsh b Reiffel	9		
K.C.G.Benjamin not out	5		
Extras (B6, LB3, W1, NB6)	16	(NB1)	1
Total	**260**	(2 wickets)	**80**

WEST INDIES	*O*	*M*	*R*	*W*		*O*	*M*	*R*	*W*
Ambrose	14	5	34	1		19	3	42	0
Walsh	21.3	7	54	6		36	7	92	3
K.C.G.Benjamin	16	3	58	1	(4)	15	1	51	0
W.K.M.Benjamin	15	2	40	2	(3)	24	2	72	2
Hooper	2	0	18	0	(6)	9	3	16	1
Arthurton					(5)	1	0	1	0
Adams						4	0	16	0
AUSTRALIA									
Reiffel	17	3	53	3		6	2	12	1
Julian	10	5	36	1		5	2	15	1
Warne	28	9	83	3		7	0	18	0
McGrath	20.1	5	59	1		6	2	20	0
S.R.Waugh	6	1	20	2					
M.E.Waugh					(5)	6	2	15	0

FALL OF WICKETS

Wkt	*A 1st*	*WI 1st*	*A 2nd*	*WI 2nd*
1st	82	34	22	11
2nd	84	106	43	69
3rd	89	168	149	–
4th	126	186	162	–
5th	126	187	196	–
6th	150	240	254	–
7th	168	240	273	–
8th	188	240	–	–
9th	204	254	–	–
10th	216	260	–	–

Umpires: S.A.Bucknor (17) and D.R.Shepherd (*England*) (24).
Referee: Majid Khan (*Pakistan*) (2). Test No. 1295/79 (WI 312/A 549)

WEST INDIES v AUSTRALIA (3rd Test)

At Queen's Park Oval, Port-of Spain, Trinidad, on 21, 22, 23 April 1995.
Toss: West Indies. Result: WEST INDIES won by nine wickets.
Debuts: None.

AUSTRALIA				
*M.A.Taylor c Adams b Ambrose	2	(2)	c Murray b K.C.G.Benjamin	30
M.J.Slater c Murray b Walsh	0	(1)	c Richardson b Walsh	15
D.C.Boon c Richardson b Ambrose	18		c sub (S.Chanderpaul) b Walsh	9
M.E.Waugh c Murray b Ambrose	2		lbw b Ambrose	7
S.R.Waugh not out	63		c Hooper b K.C.G.Benjamin	21
G.S.Blewett c Murray b W.K.M.Benjamin	17		c Murray b K.C.G.Benjamin	2
†I.A.Healy c Richardson b Walsh	8		b Ambrose	0
B.P.Julian c Adams b K.C.G.Benjamin	0		b Ambrose	0
P.R.Reiffel c Lara b Walsh	11		c Hooper b Ambrose	6
S.K.Warne b Ambrose	0		c Hooper b Walsh	11
G.D.McGrath c Murray b Ambrose	0		not out	0
Extras (LB6, W1)	7		(LB3, NB1)	4
Total	**128**			**105**

WEST INDIES			
S.C.Williams c Taylor b Reiffel	0	c Warne b M.E.Waugh	42
*R.B.Richardson c Healy b McGrath	2	not out	38
B.C.Lara c Taylor b McGrath	24	not out	14
J.C.Adams c M.E.Waugh b Reiffel	42		
C.L.Hooper c Reiffel b S.R.Waugh	21		
K.L.T.Arthurton c M.E.Waugh b McGrath	5		
†J.R.Murray c Healy b McGrath	13		
W.K.M.Benjamin c Slater b Warne	7		
C.E.L.Ambrose c Slater b McGrath	1		
C.A.Walsh c Blewett b McGrath	14		
K.C.G.Benjamin not out	1		
Extras (LB4, NB2)	6	(B4)	4
Total	**136**	(1 wicket)	**98**

WEST INDIES	O	M	R	W		O	M	R	W
Ambrose	16	5	45	5		10.1	1	20	4
Walsh	17	4	50	3		13	4	35	3
W.K.M.Benjamin	6	3	13	1		5	0	15	0
K.C.G.Benjamin	8	2	14	1		8	1	32	3
AUSTRALIA									
McGrath	21.5	11	47	6		6	1	22	0
Reiffel	16	7	26	2		6	2	21	0
Julian	7	1	24	0		3	0	16	0
S.R.Waugh	3	1	19	1					
Warne	12	5	16	1	(4)	3.5	0	26	0
M.E.Waugh					(5)	2	0	9	1

FALL OF WICKETS	A	WI	A	WI
Wkt	1st	1st	2nd	2nd
1st	2	1	26	81
2nd	2	6	52	–
3rd	14	42	56	–
4th	37	87	85	–
5th	62	95	85	–
6th	95	106	85	–
7th	98	113	87	–
8th	121	114	87	–
9th	128	129	105	–
10th	128	136	105	–

Umpires: C.E.Cumberbatch (12) and D.R.Shepherd (*England*) (25).
Referee: Majid Khan (*Pakistan*) (3). Test No. 1296/80 (WI 313/A 550)

WEST INDIES v AUSTRALIA (4th Test)

At Sabina Park, Kingston, Jamaica, on 29, 30 April, 1, 2 May 1995.
Toss: West Indies. Result: AUSTRALIA won by an innings and 53 runs.
Debuts: West Indies – C.O.Browne.

WEST INDIES

S.C.Williams c Blewett b Reiffel	0		b Reiffel	20
*R.B.Richardson lbw b Reiffel	100		c and b Reiffel	14
B.C.Lara c Healy b Warne	65		lbw b Reiffel	0
J.C.Adams c Slater b Julian	20		c S.R.Waugh b McGrath	18
C.L.Hooper c M.E.Waugh b Julian	23	(6)	run out	13
K.L.T.Arthurton c Healy b McGrath	16	(7)	lbw b Warne	14
†C.O.Browne c Boon b Warne	1	(8)	not out	31
W.K.M.Benjamin lbw b S.R.Waugh	7	(5)	lbw b Reiffel	51
C.E.L.Ambrose not out	6		st Healy b Warne	5
C.A.Walsh c Boon b S.R.Waugh	2		c Blewett b Warne	14
K.C.G.Benjamin c Healy b Reiffel	5		c Taylor b Warne	6
Extras (B1, LB9, W1, NB9)	20		(B13, LB8, NB6)	27
Total	**265**			**213**

AUSTRALIA

*M.A.Taylor c Adams b Walsh	8
M.J.Slater c Lara b Walsh	27
D.C.Boon c Browne b Ambrose	17
M.E.Waugh c Adams b Hooper	126
S.R.Waugh c Lara b K.C.G.Benjamin	200
G.S.Blewett c W.K.M.Benjamin b Arthurton	69
†I.A.Healy c Lara b W.K.M.Benjamin	6
B.P.Julian c Adams b Walsh	8
P.R.Reiffel b K.C.G.Benjamin	23
S.K.Warne c Lara b K.C.G.Benjamin	0
G.D.McGrath not out	3
Extras (B11, LB6, W1, NB26)	44
Total	**531**

AUSTRALIA	*O*	*M*	*R*	*W*		*O*	*M*	*R*	*W*
Reiffel	13.4	2	48	3		18	5	47	4
Julian	12	3	31	2		10	2	37	0
McGrath	20	4	79	1	(5)	13	2	28	1
Warne	25	6	72	2	(3)	23.4	8	70	4
S.R.Waugh	11	5	14	2	(6)	4	0	9	0
M.E.Waugh	4	1	11	0	(4)	1	0	1	0
WEST INDIES									
Ambrose	21	4	76	1					
Walsh	33	6	103	3					
K.C.G.Benjamin	23.5	0	106	3					
W.K.M.Benjamin	24	3	80	1					
Hooper	43	9	94	1					
Adams	11	0	38	0					
Arthurton	5	1	17	1					

FALL OF WICKETS

Wkt	*WI 1st*	*A 1st*	*WI 2nd*
1st	0	17	37
2nd	103	50	37
3rd	131	73	46
4th	188	304	98
5th	220	417	134
6th	243	433	140
7th	250	449	166
8th	251	522	172
9th	254	522	204
10th	265	531	213

Umpires: S.A.Bucknor (18) and K.E.Liebenberg (*South Africa*) (7).
Referee: Majid Khan (*Pakistan*) (4). Test No. 1297/81 (WI 314/A 551)

WEST INDIES v AUSTRALIA 1994-95

WEST INDIES – BATTING AND FIELDING

	M	I	NO	HS	Runs	Avge	100	50	Ct/St
B.C.Lara	4	8	1	88	308	44.00	–	3	5
R.B.Richardson	4	8	1	100	229	32.71	1	–	4
J.C.Adams	4	7	2	42	160	32.00	–	–	7
C.L.Hooper	4	6	–	60	144	24.00	–	1	6
J.R.Murray	3	4	–	26	83	20.75	–	–	12
W.K.M.Benjamin	4	6	–	51	109	18.16	–	1	2
S.C.Williams	4	8	1	42	120	17.14	–	–	2
K.L.T.Arthurton	3	4	–	26	61	15.25	–	–	1
C.A.Walsh	4	6	–	14	44	7.33	–	–	2
K.C.G.Benjamin	4	6	3	6	22	7.33	–	–	1
C.E.L.Ambrose	4	6	1	7	25	5.00	–	–	–

Played in one Test: C.O.Browne 1, 31* (1 ct); S.L.Campbell 0, 6.

WEST INDIES – BOWLING

	O	M	R	W	Avge	Best	5wI	10wM
C.E.L.Ambrose	100.1	25	258	13	19.84	5-45	1	–
C.A.Walsh	148.3	33	431	20	21.55	6-54	1	–
W.K.M.Benjamin	97.2	16	291	9	32.33	3-71	–	–
K.C.G.Benjamin	93.4	9	359	10	35.90	3-32	–	–
C.L.Hooper	67	12	193	3	64.33	1-16	–	–

Also bowled: J.C.Adams 15-0-54-0; K.L.T.Arthurton 6-1-18-1.

AUSTRALIA – BATTING AND FIELDING

	M	I	NO	HS	Runs	Avge	100	50	Ct/St
S.R.Waugh	4	6	2	200	429	107.25	1	3	6
M.E.Waugh	4	6	–	126	240	40.00	1	1	3
I.A.Healy	4	6	1	74*	128	25.60	–	1	9/1
M.A.Taylor	4	7	1	55	153	25.50	–	1	10
D.C.Boon	4	6	–	67	152	25.33	–	1	4
M.J.Slater	4	7	1	41	139	23.16	–	–	3
G.S.Blewett	4	6	–	69	132	22.00	–	1	5
P.R.Reiffel	4	6	2	23	76	19.00	–	–	3
B.P.Julian	4	6	–	31	67	11.16	–	–	1
S.K.Warne	4	5	–	11	28	5.60	–	–	2
G.D.McGrath	4	5	2	4	7	2.33	–	–	–

AUSTRALIA – BOWLING

	O	M	R	W	Avge	Best	5wI	10wM
S.R.Waugh	24	7	62	5	12.40	2-14	–	–
P.R.Reiffel	98.4	31	263	15	17.53	4-47	–	–
G.D.McGrath	121.1	32	369	17	21.70	6-47	2	–
B.P.Julian	71	15	236	9	26.22	4-36	–	–
S.K.Warne	138	35	406	15	27.06	4-70	–	–

Also bowled: M.E.Waugh 14-3-48-1.

ENGLAND v WEST INDIES (1st Test)

At Headingley, Leeds on 8, 9, 10, 11 June 1995.
Toss: West Indies. Result: WEST INDIES won by nine wickets.
Debuts: England – P.J.Martin.

ENGLAND			
R.A.Smith c Richardson b Benjamin	16	c Arthurton b Ambrose	6
*M.A.Atherton c Murray b Bishop	81	c Murray b Walsh	17
G.A.Hick c Campbell b Benjamin	18	c Walsh b Bishop	27
G.P.Thorpe lbw b Bishop	20	c Campbell b Walsh	61
†A.J.Stewart c Hooper b Bishop	2	c Murray b Benjamin	4
M.R.Ramprakash c Campbell b Bishop	4	b Walsh	18
P.A.J.DeFreitas c Murray b Benjamin	23	c sub (S.Chanderpaul) b Walsh	1
D.Gough c Ambrose b Bishop	0	c sub (S.C.Williams) b Ambrose	29
P.J.Martin c Murray b Ambrose	2	c Lara b Bishop	19
R.K.Illingworth not out	17	not out	10
D.E.Malcolm b Benjamin	0	b Ambrose	5
Extras (B1, NB15)	16	(B1, LB3, NB7)	11
Total	**199**		**208**

WEST INDIES			
C.L.Hooper c Thorpe b Malcolm	0	not out	73
S.L.Campbell run out	69	c Atherton b Martin	2
B.C.Lara c Hick b Illingworth	53	not out	48
J.C.Adams c Martin b Hick	58		
K.L.T.Arthurton c Stewart b DeFreitas	42		
*R.B.Richardson lbw b Martin	0		
†J.R.Murray c Illingworth b DeFreitas	20		
I.R.Bishop run out	5		
C.E.L.Ambrose c Gough b Malcolm	15		
C.A.Walsh c Stewart b Gough	4		
K.C.G.Benjamin not out	0		
Extras (B4, LB11, NB1)	16	(B1, LB3, NB2)	6
Total	**282**	(1 wicket)	**129**

WEST INDIES	*O*	*M*	*R*	*W*		*O*	*M*	*R*	*W*
Ambrose	17	4	56	1		20.2	6	44	3
Walsh	13	2	50	0		22	4	60	4
Bishop	16	2	32	5		19	3	81	2
Benjamin	13.5	2	60	4		6	1	19	1
ENGLAND									
Malcolm	7.3	0	48	2	(4)	4	0	12	0
Gough	5	1	24	1					
DeFreitas	23	3	82	2	(2)	4	0	33	0
Martin	27	9	48	1	(1)	8	2	49	1
Illingworth	24	9	50	1	(3)	3	0	31	0
Hick	4	0	15	1					

FALL OF WICKETS

Wkt	*E 1st*	*WI 1st*	*E 2nd*	*WI 2nd*
1st	52	0	6	11
2nd	91	95	55	–
3rd	142	141	55	–
4th	148	216	82	–
5th	153	219	130	–
6th	154	243	136	–
7th	154	254	152	–
8th	157	254	193	–
9th	199	275	193	–
10th	199	282	208	–

Umpires: H.D.Bird (62) and S.Venkataraghavan *(India)* (10).
Referee: J.R.Reid *(New Zealand)* (16). Test No. 1298/110 (E 713/WI 315)

ENGLAND v WEST INDIES (2nd Test)

At Lord's, London on 22, 23, 24, 25, 26 June 1995.
Toss: England. Result: ENGLAND won by 72 runs.
Debuts: England – D.G.Cork; West Indies – O.D.Gibson.

ENGLAND			
*M.A.Atherton b Ambrose	21	c Murray b Walsh	9
†A.J.Stewart c Arthurton b Gibson	34	c Murray b Walsh	36
G.A.Hick c Lara b Bishop	13	b Bishop	67
G.P.Thorpe c Lara b Ambrose	52	c Richardson b Ambrose	42
R.A.Smith b Hooper	61	lbw b Ambrose	90
M.R.Ramprakash c Campbell b Hooper	0	c sub (S.C.Williams) b Bishop	0
D.G.Cork b Walsh	30	c Murray b Bishop	23
D.Gough c Campbell b Gibson	11	b Ambrose	20
P.J.Martin b Walsh	29	c Arthurton b Ambrose	1
R.K.Illingworth not out	16	lbw b Walsh	4
A.R.C.Fraser lbw b Walsh	1	not out	2
Extras (B1, LB10, NB4)	15	(B6, LB27, W2, NB7)	42
Total	**283**		**336**

WEST INDIES				
S.L.Campbell c Stewart b Gough	5	(2)	c Stewart b Cork	93
C.L.Hooper b Martin	40	(1)	c Martin b Gough	14
B.C.Lara lbw b Fraser	6		c Stewart b Gough	54
J.C.Adams lbw b Fraser	54		c Hick b Cork	13
*R.B.Richardson c Stewart b Fraser	49		lbw b Cork	0
K.L.T.Arthurton c Gough b Fraser	75		c sub (P.A.Weekes) b Cork	0
†J.R.Murray c and b Martin	16		c sub (P.A.Weekes) b Gough	9
O.D.Gibson lbw b Gough	29		lbw b Cork	14
I.R.Bishop b Cork	8		not out	10
C.E.L.Ambrose c Ramprakash b Fraser	12		c Illingworth b Cork	11
C.A.Walsh not out	11		c Stewart b Cork	0
Extras (B8, LB11)	19		(LB5)	5
Total	**324**			**223**

WEST INDIES	*O*	*M*	*R*	*W*		*O*	*M*	*R*	*W*
Ambrose	26	6	72	2		24	5	70	4
Walsh	22.4	6	50	3		28.1	10	91	3
Gibson	20	2	81	2		14	1	51	0
Bishop	17	4	33	1		22	5	56	3
Hooper	14	3	36	2		9	1	31	0
Adams						2	0	4	0
ENGLAND									
Gough	27	2	84	2	(2)	20	0	79	3
Fraser	33	13	66	5	(1)	25	9	57	0
Cork	22	4	72	1	(5)	19.3	5	43	7
Martin	23	5	65	2		7	0	30	0
Illingworth	7	2	18	0	(3)	7	4	9	0

FALL OF WICKETS	*E*	*WI*	*E*	*WI*
Wkt	*1st*	*1st*	*2nd*	*2nd*
1st	29	6	32	15
2nd	70	23	51	99
3rd	74	88	150	124
4th	185	166	155	130
5th	187	169	240	138
6th	191	197	290	177
7th	205	246	320	198
8th	255	272	329	201
9th	281	305	334	223
10th	283	324	336	223

Umpires: D.R.Shepherd (26) and S.Venkataraghavan *(India)* (11).
Referee: J.R.Reid *(New Zealand)* (17). Test No. 1299/111 (E 714/WI 316)

ENGLAND v WEST INDIES (3rd Test)

At Edgbaston, Birmingham, on 6, 7, 8 July 1995.
Toss: England. Result: WEST INDIES won by an innings and 64 runs.
Debuts: England – J.E.R.Gallian.

ENGLAND				
*M.A.Atherton c Murray b Ambrose	0		b Walsh	4
†A.J.Stewart lbw b Benjamin	37		absent hurt	0
G.A.Hick c Richardson b Walsh	3		c Hooper b Bishop	3
G.P.Thorpe c Campbell b Ambrose	30		c Murray b Bishop	0
R.A.Smith c Arthurton b Bishop	46	(2)	b Bishop	41
J.E.R.Gallian b Benjamin	7	(7)	c Murray b Walsh	0
D.G.Cork lbw b Walsh	4	(5)	c sub (S.C.Williams) b Walsh	16
D.Gough c Arthurton b Bishop	1		c Campbell b Walsh	12
P.J.Martin c sub (S.C.Williams) b Walsh	1	(6)	lbw b Walsh	0
R.K.Illingworth b Bishop	0	(9)	c Hooper b Bishop	0
A.R.C.Fraser not out	0	(10)	not out	1
Extras (LB4, W4, NB10)	18		(NB12)	12
Total	**147**			**89**

WEST INDIES	
C.L.Hooper c Stewart b Cork	40
S.L.Campbell b Cork	79
B.C.Lara lbw b Cork	21
J.C.Adams lbw b Cork	10
*R.B.Richardson b Fraser	69
K.L.T.Arthurton lbw b Fraser	8
†J.R.Murray c Stewart b Martin	26
I.R.Bishop c Martin b Illingworth	16
K.C.G.Benjamin run out	11
C.A.Walsh run out	0
C.E.L.Ambrose not out	4
Extras (B5, LB5, NB6)	16
Total	**300**

WEST INDIES	O	M	R	W		O	M	R	W
Ambrose	7.5	1	26	2					
Walsh	17.1	4	54	3	(1)	15	2	45	5
Bishop	6.2	0	18	3	(2)	13	3	29	4
Benjamin	13	4	45	2	(3)	2	0	15	0
ENGLAND									
Fraser	31	7	93	2					
Gough	18	3	68	0					
Cork	22	5	69	4					
Martin	19	5	49	1					
Illingworth	8	4	11	1					

FALL OF WICKETS	E	WI	E
Wkt	*1st*	*1st*	*2nd*
1st	4	73	17
2nd	9	105	20
3rd	53	141	26
4th	84	156	61
5th	100	171	62
6th	109	198	63
7th	124	260	88
8th	141	292	88
9th	147	292	89
10th	147	300	–

Umpires: M.J.Kitchen (10) and I.D.Robinson *(Zimbabwe)* (12).
Referee: J.R.Reid *(New Zealand)* (18). Test No. 1300/112 (E 715/WI 317)

ENGLAND v WEST INDIES (4th Test)

At Old Trafford, Manchester, on 27, 28, 29, 30 July 1995.
Toss: West Indies. Result: ENGLAND won by six wickets.
Debuts: England – N.V.Knight, M.Watkinson. ‡(S.C.Williams)

WEST INDIES

C.L.Hooper c Crawley b Cork	16	(7)	lbw b Cork	0
S.L.Campbell c Russell b Fraser	10	(1)	c Russell b Watkinson	44
B.C.Lara lbw b Cork	87		c Knight b Fraser	145
J.C.Adams c Knight b Fraser	24		c and b Watkinson	1
*R.B.Richardson c Thorpe b Fraser	2		b Cork	22
K.L.T.Arthurton c Cork b Watkinson	17	(2)	run out	17
†J.R.Murray c Emburey b Watkinson	13	(6)	lbw b Cork	0
I.R.Bishop c Russell b Cork	9		c Crawley b Watkinson	9
C.E.L.Ambrose not out	7	(10)	not out	23
K.C.G.Benjamin b Cork	14	(9)	c Knight b Fraser	15
C.A.Walsh c Knight b Fraser	11		b Cork	16
Extras (LB1, NB5)	6		(B5, LB9, NB8)	22
Total	**216**			**314**

ENGLAND

N.V.Knight b Walsh	17	c sub (S.Chanderpaul) b Bishop	13
*M.A.Atherton c Murray b Ambrose	47	run out	22
J.P.Crawley b Walsh	8	not out	15
G.P.Thorpe c Murray b Bishop	94	c Ambrose b Benjamin	0
R.A.Smith c sub ‡ b Ambrose	44	retired hurt	1
C.White c Murray b Benjamin	23	c sub (S.Chanderpaul) b Benjamin	1
†R.C.Russell run out	35	not out	31
M.Watkinson c sub ‡ b Walsh	37		
D.G.Cork not out	56		
J.E.Emburey b Bishop	8		
A.R.C.Fraser c Adams b Walsh	4		
Extras (B18, LB11, W1, NB34)	64	(LB2, W1, NB8)	11
Total	**437**	(4 wickets)	**94**

ENGLAND	O	M	R	W		O	M	R	W
Fraser	16.2	5	45	4		19	5	53	2
Cork	20	1	86	4		23.5	2	111	4
White	5	0	23	0	(4)	6	0	23	0
Emburey	10	2	33	0	(3)	20	5	49	0
Watkinson	9	2	28	2		23	4	64	3
WEST INDIES									
Ambrose	24	2	91	2		5	1	16	0
Walsh	38	5	92	4		5	0	17	0
Bishop	29	3	103	2		12	6	18	1
Benjamin	28	4	83	1		9	1	29	2
Adams	8	1	21	0	(6)	2	0	7	0
Arthurton	9	2	18	0	(5)	2.5	1	5	0

FALL OF WICKETS

Wkt	WI 1st	E 1st	WI 2nd	E 2nd
1st	21	45	36	39
2nd	35	65	93	41
3rd	86	122	97	45
4th	94	226	161	48
5th	150	264	161	–
6th	166	293	161	–
7th	184	337	191	–
8th	185	378	234	–
9th	205	418	283	–
10th	216	437	314	–

Umpires: H.D.Bird (63) and C.J.Mitchley (8) (*South Africa*).
Referee: J.R.Reid *(New Zealand)* (19). Test No. 1301/113 (E 716/WI 318)

ENGLAND v WEST INDIES (5th Test)

At Trent Bridge, Nottingham, on 10, 11, 12, 13, 14 August 1995.
Toss: England. Result: MATCH DRAWN.
Debuts: None.

ENGLAND

N.V.Knight lbw b Benjamin	57	(7)	c Browne b Benjamin	2
*M.A.Atherton run out	113	(1)	c Browne b Bishop	43
J.P.Crawley c Williams b Benjamin	14	(2)	b Walsh	11
G.P.Thorpe c Browne b Bishop	19		c Browne b Walsh	76
R.K.Illingworth retired hurt	8	(11)	not out	14
G.A.Hick not out	118	(3)	b Benjamin	7
C.White c Browne b Bishop	1	(5)	c Campbell b Bishop	1
†R.C.Russell c Browne b Bishop	35	(6)	c Browne b Benjamin	7
M.Watkinson lbw b Benjamin	24	(8)	not out	82
D.G.Cork c Browne b Benjamin	31	(9)	c Browne b Benjamin	4
A.R.C.Fraser b Benjamin	0	(10)	c Arthurton b Benjamin	4
Extras (B4, LB8, NB8)	20		(LB4, NB14)	18
Total	**440**		**(9 wickets declared)**	**269**

WEST INDIES

S.C.Williams c Atherton b Illingworth	62			
S.L.Campbell c Crawley b Watkinson	47		c Russell b Cork	16
B.C.Lara c Russell b Cork	152	(1)	c Russell b Fraser	20
*R.B.Richardson c Hick b Illingworth	40			
K.L.T.Arthurton b Illingworth	13			
R.Dhanraj c Knight b Cork	3			
S.Chanderpaul c Crawley b Watkinson	18	(3)	not out	5
†C.O.Browne st Russell b Illingworth	34	(4)	not out	1
I.R.Bishop c Hick b Watkinson	4			
K.C.G.Benjamin not out	14			
C.A.Walsh b Fraser	19			
Extras (B2, LB7, NB2)	11			
Total	**417**		**(2 wickets)**	**42**

WEST INDIES	O	M	R	W	O	M	R	W
Walsh	39	5	93	0	30	6	70	2
Bishop	30.1	6	62	3	21	8	50	2
Benjamin	34.3	7	105	5	25	8	69	5
Dhanraj	40	7	137	0	15	1	54	0
Arthurton	9	0	31	0	13	3	22	0
ENGLAND								
Fraser	17.3	6	77	1	6	1	17	1
Cork	36	9	110	2	5	1	25	1
Watkinson	35	12	84	3				
Illingworth	51	21	96	4				
Hick	4	1	11	0				
White	5	0	30	0				

FALL OF WICKETS

Wkt	E 1st	WI 1st	E 2nd	WI 2nd
1st	148	77	17	36
2nd	179	217	36	36
3rd	206	273	117	–
4th	211	319	125	–
5th	239	323	139	–
6th	323	338	148	–
7th	380	366	171	–
8th	440	374	176	–
9th	440	384	189	–
10th	–	417	–	–

Umpires: C.J.Mitchley (9) (*South Africa*) and N.T.Plews (10).
Referee: J.R.Reid *(New Zealand)* (20). Test No. 1302/114 (E 717/WI 319)

ENGLAND v WEST INDIES (6th Test)

At Kennington Oval, London, on 24, 25, 26, 27, 28 August 1995.
Toss: England. Result: MATCH DRAWN.
Debuts: England – A.P.Wells.

ENGLAND			
*M.A.Atherton c Williams b Benjamin	36	(2) c Browne b Bishop	95
J.E.R.Gallian c Hooper b Ambrose	0	(1) c Williams b Ambrose	25
J.P.Crawley c Richardson b Hooper	50	c Browne b Ambrose	2
G.P.Thorpe c Browne b Ambrose	74	c Williams b Walsh	38
G.A.Hick c Williams b Benjamin	96	not out	51
A.P.Wells c Campbell b Ambrose	0	not out	3
†R.C.Russell b Ambrose	91		
M.Watkinson c Browne b Walsh	13		
D.G.Cork b Ambrose	33		
A.R.C.Fraser not out	10		
D.E.Malcolm c Lara b Benjamin	10		
Extras (B15, LB11, NB15)	41	(LB4, NB5)	9
Total	454	(4 wickets)	223

WEST INDIES	
S.C.Williams c Russell b Malcolm	30
S.L.Campbell c Russell b Fraser	89
K.C.G.Benjamin c Atherton b Cork	20
B.C.Lara c Fraser b Malcolm	179
*R.B.Richardson c Hick b Cork	93
C.L.Hooper c Russell b Malcolm	127
S.Chanderpaul c Gallian b Cork	80
†C.O.Browne not out	27
I.R.Bishop run out	10
C.E.L.Ambrose not out	5
C.A.Walsh	
Extras (B5, LB20, W5, NB2)	32
Total (8 wickets declared)	692

WEST INDIES	O	M	R	W		O	M	R	W
Ambrose	42	10	96	5	(2)	19	8	35	2
Walsh	32	6	84	1	(1)	28	7	80	1
Benjamin	27	6	81	3					
Bishop	35	5	111	0	(5)	22	4	56	1
Hooper	23	7	56	1	(3)	22	11	26	0
Chanderpaul					(4)	6	0	22	0
Lara					(6)	1	1	0	0
ENGLAND									
Malcolm	39	7	160	3					
Fraser	40	6	155	1					
Watkinson	26	3	113	0					
Cork	36	3	145	3					
Gallian	12	1	56	0					
Hick	10	3	38	0					

FALL OF WICKETS	E	WI	E
Wkt	1st	1st	2nd
1st	9	40	60
2nd	60	94	64
3rd	149	202	132
4th	192	390	212
5th	192	435	–
6th	336	631	–
7th	372	653	–
8th	419	686	–
9th	443	–	–
10th	454	–	–

Umpires: V.K.Ramaswamy (18) (*India*) and D.R.Shepherd (27).
Referee: J.R.Reid *(New Zealand)* (21). Test No. 1303/115 (E 718/WI 320)

ENGLAND v WEST INDIES 1995

ENGLAND

Batting and Fielding	*M*	*I*	*NO*	*HS*	*Runs*	*Avge*	*100*	*50*	*Ct/St*
M.Watkinson	3	4	1	82*	156	52.00	–	1	1
G.A.Hick	5	10	2	118*	403	50.37	1	3	5
R.C.Russell	3	5	1	91	199	49.75	–	1	9/1
R.A.Smith	4	8	1	90	305	43.57	–	2	–
G.P.Thorpe	6	12	–	94	506	42.16	–	5	2
M.A.Atherton	6	12	–	113	488	40.66	1	2	3
D.G.Cork	5	8	1	56*	197	28.14	–	1	1
R.K.Illingworth	4	8	5	17*	69	23.00	–	–	2
A.J.Stewart	3	5	–	37	113	22.60	–	–	9
N.V.Knight	2	4	–	57	89	22.25	–	1	5
J.P.Crawley	3	6	1	50	100	20.00	–	1	4
D.Gough	3	6	–	29	73	12.16	–	–	2
P.J.Martin	3	6	–	29	52	8.66	–	–	4
J.E.R.Gallian	2	4	–	25	32	8.00	–	–	1
C.White	2	4	–	23	26	6.50	–	–	–
A.R.C.Fraser	5	8	4	10*	22	5.50	–	–	1
M.R.Ramprakash	2	4	–	18	22	5.50	–	–	1
D.E.Malcolm	2	3	–	10	15	5.00	–	–	–

Played in one Test: P.A.J.DeFreitas 23, 1; J.E.Emburey 8 (1 ct); A.P.Wells 0, 3*.

Bowling	*O*	*M*	*R*	*W*	*Avge*	*Best*	*5wI*	*10wM*
D.G.Cork	184.2	30	661	26	25.42	7- 43	1	–
A.R.C.Fraser	187.5	52	563	16	35.18	5- 66	1	–
R.K.Illingworth	100	40	215	6	35.83	4- 96	–	–
M.Watkinson	93	21	289	8	36.12	3- 64	–	–
D.Gough	70	6	255	6	42.50	3- 79	–	–
D.E.Malcolm	50.3	7	220	5	44.00	3-160	–	–
P.J.Martin	84	21	241	5	48.20	2- 65	–	–

Also bowled: P.A.J.DeFreitas 27-3-115-2; J.E.Emburey 30-7-82-0; J.E.R.Gallian 12-1-56-0; G.A.Hick 18-4-64-1; C.White 16-0-76-0.

WEST INDIES

Batting and Fielding	*M*	*I*	*NO*	*HS*	*Runs*	*Avge*	*100*	*50*	*Ct/St*
B.C.Lara	6	10	1	179	765	85.00	3	3	4
C.O.Browne	2	3	2	34	62	62.00	–	–	13
S.Chanderpaul	2	3	1	80	103	51.50	–	1	–
S.C.Williams	2	2	–	62	92	46.00	–	1	5
S.L.Campbell	6	10	–	93	454	45.40	–	4	9
C.L.Hooper	5	8	1	127	310	44.28	1	1	4
R.B.Richardson	6	8	–	93	275	34.37	–	2	4
J.C.Adams	4	6	–	58	160	26.66	–	2	1
C.E.L.Ambrose	5	7	4	23*	77	25.66	–	–	2
K.L.T.Arthurton	5	7	–	75	172	24.57	–	1	6
K.C.G.Benjamin	5	6	2	20	74	18.50	–	–	–
J.R.Murray	4	6	–	26	84	14.00	–	–	14
C.A.Walsh	6	7	1	19	61	10.16	–	–	1
I.R.Bishop	6	8	1	16	71	10.14	–	–	–

Played in one Test: R.Dhanraj 3; O.D.Gibson 29, 14.

Bowling	*O*	*M*	*R*	*W*	*Avge*	*Best*	*5wI*	*10wM*
K.C.G.Benjamin	158.2	33	506	23	22.00	5-69	2	1
I.R.Bishop	242.3	49	649	27	24.03	5-32	1	–
C.E.L.Ambrose	185.1	43	506	21	24.09	5-96	1	–
C.A.Walsh	290	57	786	26	30.23	5-45	1	–

Also bowled: J.C.Adams 12-1-32-0; K.L.T.Arthurton 33.5-6-76-0; S.Chanderpaul 6-0-22-0; R.Dhanraj 55-8-191-0; O.D.Gibson 34-3-132-2; C.L.Hooper 68-22-149-3; B.C.Lara 1-1-0-0.

PAKISTAN v SRI LANKA (1st Test)

At Arbab Niaz Stadium, Peshawar, on 8, 9, 10, 11 September 1995.
Toss: Pakistan. Result: PAKISTAN won by an innings and 40 runs.
Debuts: Pakistan – Ijaz Ahmed II, Saqlain Mushtaq.

PAKISTAN	
Saeed Anwar c A.Ranatunga b Muralitharan	50
Aamir Sohail c Dunusinghe b Vaas	28
*Ramiz Raja c Pushpakumara b Vaas	78
Inzamam-ul-Haq lbw b Vaas	95
Shoaib Mohammad c A.Ranatunga b Vaas	57
Ijaz Ahmed II c Gurusinha b Muralitharan	5
Wasim Akram c and b Muralitharan	36
†Moin Khan c Hathurusinghe b Vaas	51
Waqar Younis c Mahanama b Muralitharan	0
Aqib Javed not out	28
Saqlain Mushtaq not out	8
Extras (B1, LB4, W1, NB17)	23
Total (9 wickets declared)	459

SRI LANKA			
R.S.Mahanama c Moin b Waqar	29	lbw b Aqib	2
U.C.Hathurusinghe c Inzamam b Saqlain	23	c Saeed b Wasim	53
A.P.Gurusinha c Wasim b Saqlain	24	c Saeed b Aamir	10
S.Ranatunga lbw b Wasim	33	c Moin b Aqib	18
*A.Ranatunga lbw b Aqib	8	c Inzamam b Aamir	76
H.P.Tillekeratne not out	44	c Ramiz b Wasim	48
†C.I.Dunusinghe lbw b Wasim	0	c Inzamam b Aamir	0
W.P.U.C.J.Vaas b Wasim	4	c Ramiz b Saqlain	4
G.P.Wickremasinghe b Wasim	0	c Ramiz b Saqlain	6
M.Muralitharan c Saqlain b Wasim	8	st Moin b Aamir	0
K.R.Pushpakumara run out	1	not out	0
Extras (B1, LB6, NB5)	12	(B1, LB6, NB9)	16
Total	186		233

SRI LANKA	O	M	R	W		O	M	R	W
Wickremasinghe	32	5	98	0					
Vaas	29	3	99	5					
Pushpakumara	17	2	89	0					
Muralitharan	50	9	134	4					
Hathurusinghe	18	10	29	0					
Gurusinha	3	1	5	0					
PAKISTAN									
Wasim	20	3	55	5	(6)	10	3	24	2
Waqar	11	2	47	1	(1)	9	1	39	0
Saqlain	18	4	49	2		26	10	58	2
Aqib	11.1	2	27	1	(2)	13	1	50	2
Aamir	2	1	1	0	(4)	21	4	54	4
Ijaz					(5)	1	0	1	0

FALL OF WICKETS

Wkt	P 1st	SL 1st	P 2nd
1st	59	39	8
2nd	102	76	36
3rd	234	83	86
4th	285	102	89
5th	318	132	214
6th	340	134	222
7th	422	142	222
8th	422	143	232
9th	425	184	233
10th	–	186	233

Umpires: B.L.Aldridge (*New Zealand*) (25) and Mahbook Shah (25).
Referee: P.L.van der Merwe (*South Africa*) (6). Test No. 1304/15 (P 222/SL 61)

PAKISTAN v SRI LANKA (2nd Test)

At Iqbal Stadium, Faisalabad, on 15, 16, 17, 18, 19 September 1995.
Toss: Pakistan. Result: SRI LANKA won by 42 runs.
Debuts: Pakistan – Mohammad Akram. ‡ (D.P.Samaraweera)

SRI LANKA				
R.S.Mahanama lbw b Wasim	0		lbw b Mohammad Akram	10
U.C.Hathurusinghe c Saeed b M.Akram	47		c Ijaz b Aqib	83
A.P.Gurusinha c Wasim b Aqib	9		lbw b Aqib	12
P.A.de Silva c and b Saqlain	0		lbw Saqlain	105
*A.Ranatunga c Ijaz b Saqlain	0	(6)	c and b Aamir	2
H.P.Tillekeratne c Moin b Saqlain	115	(5)	lbw b Aqib	0
H.D.P.K.Dharmasena run out	0		c Moin b Mohammad Akram	49
†C.I.Dunusinghe lbw b Wasim	12		c M.Akram b Saqlain	27
W.P.U.C.J.Vaas c Ijaz b Aqib	21		b Aqib	40
G.P.Wickremasinghe c Moin b Aqib	1	(11)	b Aqib	2
M.Muralitharan not out	8	(10)	not out	10
Extras (B3, LB1, NB6)	10		(B4, LB10, NB7)	21
Total	**223**			**361**

PAKISTAN				
Saeed Anwar c De Silva b Muralitharan	54		b Dharmasena	50
Aamir Sohail b Muralitharan	20		lbw b Vaas	0
Saqlain Mushtaq c Mahanama b Muralitharan	34	(9)	c Ranatunga b Vaas	7
*Ramiz Raja c sub‡ b De Silva	75	(3)	c Tillekeratne b Muralitharan	25
Inzamam-ul-Haq b Gurusinha	50	(4)	c and b Muralitharan	26
Shoaib Mohammad run out	12	(5)	lbw b Wickremasinghe	5
Ijaz Ahmed II c Dunusinghe b Wickremasinghe	16	(6)	c Dharmasena b Vaas	8
Wasim Akram c Mahanama b Gurusinha	2		b Dharmasena	26
†Moin Khan st Dunusinghe b Muralitharan	30	(7)	c Muralitharan b Vaas	50
Aqib Javed b Muralitharan	8		not out	1
Mohammad Akram not out	0		c Mahanama b Dharmasena	0
Extras (B4, LB15, NB13)	32		(NB11)	11
Total	**333**			**209**

PAKISTAN	*O*	*M*	*R*	*W*		*O*	*M*	*R*	*W*
Wasim	13	6	31	2					
Mohammad Akram	14	4	42	1		27	5	78	2
Aqib	13	5	34	3	(1)	32.3	6	84	5
Saqlain	20	3	74	3		36	12	84	2
Aamir	7	2	28	0	(3)	44	12	87	1
Shoaib	3	2	10	0		4	2	9	0
Ijaz					(5)	3	0	5	0
SRI LANKA									
Wickremasinghe	23	6	53	1		11	1	23	1
Vaas	14	4	35	0		15	2	45	4
Gurusinha	8	1	30	2					
Dharmasena	30	4	79	0		22.1	6	43	3
Muralitharan	23.3	6	68	5	(3)	20	2	83	2
Hathurusinghe	6	1	10	0					
De Silva	13.3	3	39	1	(5)	4	0	15	0

FALL OF WICKETS

Wkt	*SL 1st*	*P 1st*	*SL 2nd*	*P 2nd*
1st	0	42	11	6
2nd	32	109	24	58
3rd	33	168	200	99
4th	34	213	212	108
5th	117	248	225	119
6th	117	288	240	129
7th	149	288	279	175
8th	213	291	346	206
9th	213	324	354	207
10th	223	333	361	209

Umpires: Khizer Hayat (32) and N.T.Plews (*England*) (11).
Referee: P.L.van der Merwe (*South Africa*) (7). Test No. 1305/16 (P 223/SL 62)

PAKISTAN v SRI LANKA (3rd Test)

At Jinnah Stadium, Sialkot, on 22, 23, 24, 25, 26 September 1995.
Toss: Sri Lanka. Result: SRI LANKA won by 144 runs.
Debuts: None.

SRI LANKA

R.S.Mahanama c Mohammad Akram b Aqib	21		lbw b Aqib	20
U.C.Hathurusinghe c Inzamam b Aamir Nazir	12		c Moin b Aqib	73
A.P.Gurusinha run out	45		c Ramiz b Rehman	18
P.A.de Silva c Shoaib b Rehman	0		lbw b Aamir Nazir	8
*A.Ranatunga b Aamir Sohail	24		c Inzamam b M.Akram	87
H.P.Tillekeratne c Inzamam b M.Akram	24	(7)	b Aamir Sohail	50
H.D.P.K.Dharmasena not out	62	(8)	c Inzamam b M.Akram	7
†C.I.Dunusinghe lbw b Aqib	1	(6)	b Mohammad Akram	7
W.P.U.C.J.Vaas b Aqib	16		run out	27
M.Muralitharan c Aamir Sohail b Aamir Nazir	4		not out	0
G.P.Wickremasinghe run out	1			
Extras (B1, LB12, NB9)	22		(B23, LB10, NB8)	41
Total	**232**		(9 wickets declared)	**338**

PAKISTAN

Aamir Sohail b Dharmasena	48		c Hathu'singhe b Wickr'singhe	5
Shoaib Mohammad lbw b Muralitharan	8		c and b Vaas	1
*Ramiz Raja lbw b Muralitharan	26		c Mahanama b Wickr'singhe	4
Inzamam-ul-Haq b Wickremasinghe	21		c Mahanama b Vaas	0
Basit Ali lbw b Muralitharan	4	(7)	c Dharmasena b Vaas	27
Zahid Fazal st Dunusinghe b De Silva	23	(5)	c Gurusinha b Vaas	1
†Moin Khan c Dunusinghe b Wickremasinghe	26	(6)	not out	117
Aqib Javed c Dunusinghe b Dharmasena	19		run out	6
Ata-ur-Rehman c Mahanama b De Silva	9		c Dunusinghe b Wickr'singhe	4
Mohammad Akram b Muralitharan	5		b Wickremasinghe	2
Aamir Nazir not out	5		c Tillekeratne b De Silva	11
Extras (B3, LB4, NB13)	20		(B13, LB10, NB11)	34
Total	**214**			**212**

PAKISTAN	O	M	R	W		O	M	R	W
Aqib	19.3	6	47	3		24	2	71	2
Mohammad Akram	17	4	37	1	(3)	20	5	39	3
Aamir Nazir	19	6	46	2	(4)	17	2	55	1
Rehman	19	4	42	1	(2)	23	5	66	1
Aamir Sohail	17	4	45	1	(6)	25.3	7	55	1
Shoaib	1	0	2	0	(5)	11	3	19	0
SRI LANKA									
Wickremasinghe	13	2	29	2		18	4	55	4
Vaas	14	0	38	0		24	9	37	4
Gurusinha	1	0	6	0		3	0	16	0
Muralitharan	27.1	6	72	4	(5)	17	3	53	0
De Silva	10	1	29	2	(6)	4	2	5	1
Dharmasena	16	5	33	2	(4)	10	2	23	0

FALL OF WICKETS

Wkt	SL 1st	P 1st	SL 2nd	P 2nd
1st	32	39	37	7
2nd	36	72	71	7
3rd	41	111	97	7
4th	108	119	175	13
5th	118	122	206	15
6th	158	173	265	79
7th	171	173	279	106
8th	216	196	330	132
9th	225	204	330	147
10th	232	214	–	212

Umpires: B.L.Aldridge (*New Zealand*) (26) and Shakil Khan (5).
Referee: P.L.van der Merwe (*South Africa*) (8). Test No. 1306/17 (P 224/SL 63)

PAKISTAN v SRI LANKA 1995-96

PAKISTAN – BATTING AND FIELDING

	M	I	NO	HS	Runs	Avge	100	50	Ct/St
Moin Khan	3	5	1	117*	274	68.50	1	2	6/1
Saeed Anwar	2	3	–	54	154	51.33	–	3	3
Ramiz Raja	3	5	–	78	208	41.60	–	2	4
Inzamam-ul-Haq	3	5	–	95	192	38.40	–	2	7
Saqlain Mushtaq	2	3	1	34	49	24.50	–	–	2
Wasim Akram	2	3	–	36	64	21.33	–	–	2
Aqib Javed	3	5	2	28*	62	20.66	–	–	–
Aamir Sohail	3	5	–	48	101	20.20	–	–	2
Shoaib Mohammad	3	5	–	57	83	16.60	–	1	1
Ijaz Ahmed II	2	3	–	16	29	9.66	–	–	3
Mohammad Akram	2	4	1	5	7	2.33	–	–	2

Played in one Test: Aamir Nazir 5*, 11; Ata-ur-Rehman 9, 4; Basit Ali 4, 27; Waqar Younis 0; Zahid Fazal 23, 1.

PAKISTAN – BOWLING

	O	M	R	W	Avge	Best	5wI	10wM
Wasim Akram	43	12	110	9	12.22	5-55	1	–
Aqib Javed	113.1	22	313	16	19.56	5-84	1	–
Mohammad Akram	78	18	196	7	28.00	3-39	–	–
Saqlain Mushtaq	100	25	265	9	29.44	3-74	–	–
Aamir Sohail	116.3	30	270	7	38.57	4-54	–	–

Also bowled: Aamir Nazir 36-8-101-3; Ata-ur-Rehman 42-9-108-2 Ijaz Ahmed II 4-0-6-0; Shoaib Mohammad 19-7-40-0; Waqar Younis 20-3-86-1.

SRI LANKA – BATTING AND FIELDING

	M	I	NO	HS	Runs	Avge	100	50	Ct/St
H.P.Tillekeratne	3	6	1	115	281	56.20	1	1	2
U.C.Hathurusinghe	3	6	–	83	291	48.50	–	3	2
H.D.P.K.Dharmasena	2	4	1	62*	118	39.33	–	1	2
A.Ranatunga	3	6	–	87	197	32.83	–	2	3
P.A.de Silva	2	4	–	105	113	28.25	1	–	1
A.P.Gurusinha	3	6	–	45	118	19.66	–	–	2
W.P.U.C.J.Vaas	3	6	–	40	112	18.66	–	–	1
R.S.Mahanama	3	6	–	29	82	13.66	–	–	7
M.Muralitharan	3	6	3	10*	30	10.00	–	–	3
C.I.Dunusinghe	3	6	–	27	47	7.83	–	–	5/2
G.P.Wickremasinghe	3	5	–	6	10	2.00	–	–	–

Played in one Test: K.R.Pushpakumara 1, 0* (1 ct); S.Ranatunga 33, 18.

SRI LANKA – BOWLING

	O	M	R	W	Avge	Best	5wI	10wM
W.P.U.C.J.Vaas	96	18	254	13	19.53	5-99	1	–
M.Muralitharan	137.4	26	410	15	27.33	5-68	1	–
G.P.Wickremasinghe	97	18	258	8	32.25	4-55	–	–
H.D.P.K.Dharmasena	78.1	17	178	5	35.60	3-43	–	–

Also bowled: P.A.de Silva 31.3-6-88-4; A.P.Gurusinha 15-2-57-2; U.C.Hathurusinghe 24-11-39-0; K.R.Pushpakumara 17-2-89-0.

ZIMBABWE v SOUTH AFRICA (Only Test)

At Harare Sports Club, on 13, 14, 15, 16 October 1995.
Toss: Zimbabwe. Result: SOUTH AFRICA won by 7 wickets.
Debuts: Zimbabwe – A.C.I.Lock, C.B.Wishart.

ZIMBABWE

M.H.Dekker c Hudson b Donald	1		c Hudson b Schultz	24
G.W.Flower c Richardson b Donald	24		c McMillan b Donald	5
*†A.Flower b Schultz	7	(5)	c Richardson b Donald	63
D.L.Houghton c Richardson b Schultz	5		c Matthews b Donald	30
A.D.R.Campbell c Richardson b Schultz	0	(3)	c Donald b McMillan	28
G.J.Whittall c Richardson b Matthews	29		lbw b Donald	38
C.B.Wishart c Kirsten b Symcox	24		b Donald	13
P.A.Strang b Matthews	0		c Richardson b Donald	37
H.H.Streak c McMillan b Donald	53		c Cronje b Donald	0
B.C.Strang lbw b Schultz	0		not out	25
A.C.I.Lock not out	8		b Donald	0
Extras (LB10, W5, NB4)	19		(LB10, W1, NB9)	20
Total	**170**			**283**

SOUTH AFRICA

A.C.Hudson b B.C.Strang	135	(2)	c B.C.Strang b Lock	4
G.Kirsten lbw b Streak	1	(1)	c A.Flower b Lock	13
*W.J.Cronje c Houghton b Streak	5		not out	56
D.J.Cullinan c Whittall b Lock	11			
C.R.Matthews c G.W.Flower b B.C.Strang	10			
J.N.Rhodes c A.Flower b B.C.Strang	15	(4)	b Streak	6
B.M.McMillan not out	98	(5)	not out	25
†D.J.Richardson c B.C.Strang b Lock	13			
P.L.Symcox c Houghton b Lock	4			
A.A.Donald b B.C.Strang	33			
B.N.Schultz lbw b B.C.Strang	0			
Extras (B9, LB6, W3, NB3)	21		(LB2, W2)	4
Total	**346**		(3 wickets)	**108**

SOUTH AFRICA	*O*	*M*	*R*	*W*		*O*	*M*	*R*	*W*
Donald	17.1	3	42	3		33	12	71	8
Schultz	21	7	54	4		24	7	72	1
Matthews	13	5	30	2	(4)	20	7	52	0
McMillan	3	0	13	0	(5)	15	3	53	1
Symcox	11	5	21	1	(3)	11	3	22	0
Cronje						1	0	3	0
ZIMBABWE									
Streak	26	6	79	2		9	2	24	1
Lock	17	4	68	3		13	1	37	2
B.C.Strang	32	4	101	5		12	6	18	0
P.A.Strang	23	2	58	0		4	0	27	0
Whittall	2	0	11	0					
G.W.Flower	3	1	14	0					

FALL OF WICKETS

Wkt	Z *1st*	SA *1st*	Z *2nd*	SA *2nd*
1st	3	1	13	6
2nd	12	24	64	36
3rd	22	59	71	48
4th	23	85	102	–
5th	71	145	199	–
6th	84	246	206	–
7th	84	261	231	–
8th	122	265	231	–
9th	128	344	279	–
10th	170	346	283	–

Umpires: D.R.Shepherd (*England*) (28) and R.B.Tiffin (1).
Referee: B.N.Jarman *(Australia)* (5). Test No. 1307/1 (Z 14/SA 195)

INDIA v NEW ZEALAND (1st Test)

At Chinnaswamy Stadium, Bangalore, on 18, 19, 20 October 1995.
Toss: New Zealand. Result: INDIA won by 8 wickets.
Debuts: New Zealand – L.K.Germon.

NEW ZEALAND

B.A.Young c Tendulkar b Raju	14	(2)	lbw b Prabhakar	8
M.J.Greatbatch b Srinath	10	(1)	b Prabhakar	16
A.C.Parore lbw b Srinath	2		lbw b Srinath	3
M.D.Crowe c Tendulkar b Kumble	11		lbw b Kumble	24
S.P.Fleming c Mongia b Srinath	16		c and b Kumble	41
S.A.Thomson c Mongia b Chauhan	17		c Mongia b Kumble	6
C.L.Cairns c Manjrekar b Raju	15		b Srinath	23
*†L.K.Germon c Tendulkar b Kumble	48		lbw b Kumble	41
D.J.Nash lbw b Kumble	0		c Kumble b Raju	17
M.N.Hart c Prabhakar b Kumble	1		not out	27
D.K.Morrison not out	1		c Azharuddin b Kumble	9
Extras (B4, LB5, NB1)	10		(B8, LB10)	18
Total	145			233

INDIA

M.Prabhakar c Germon b Morrison	4	c Greatbatch b Hart	43
A.D.Jadeja c Young b Morrison	59	c Parore b Hart	73
S.V.Manjrekar lbw b Nash	15	not out	29
S.R.Tendulkar c Young b Nash	4	not out	0
*M.Azharuddin b Cairns	87		
V.G.Kambli c Parore b Nash	27		
†N.R.Mongia lbw b Cairns	1		
A Kumble not out	6		
J.Srinath b Cairns	0		
R.K.Chauhan c Young b Morrison	1		
S.L.V.Raju c Hart b Cairns	0		
Extras (LB8, W4, NB12)	24	(LB3, NB3)	6
Total	228	(2 wickets)	151

INDIA	*O*	*M*	*R*	*W*		*O*	*M*	*R*	*W*
Prabhakar	6	0	15	0		8	3	23	2
Srinath	14	5	24	3		15	6	41	2
Raju	16	6	47	2	(5)	14	2	43	1
Kumble	18	5	39	4	(3)	27.2	4	81	5
Chauhan	11	7	11	1	(4)	9	1	27	0
NEW ZEALAND									
Morrison	18	5	61	3	(2)	7	1	34	0
Cairns	17.4	5	44	4	(3)	6	1	13	0
Nash	16	3	50	3	(1)	7	1	26	0
Hart	7	1	28	0	(3)	9.5	3	34	2
Thomson	12	3	37	0	(4)	11	1	41	0

FALL OF WICKETS

	NZ	*I*	*NZ*	*I*
Wkt	*1st*	*1st*	*2nd*	*2nd*
1st	14	11	19	101
2nd	22	45	32	145
3rd	30	54	36	–
4th	44	149	58	–
5th	71	211	80	–
6th	71	214	130	–
7th	116	220	134	–
8th	116	220	173	–
9th	144	227	210	–
10th	145	228	233	–

Umpires: S.K.Bansal (4) and M.J.Kitchen (*England*) (11).
Referee: P.J.P.Burge (*Australia*) (15). Test No. 1308/33 (I 293/NZ 238)

INDIA v NEW ZEALAND (2nd Test)

At M.A.Chidambaram Stadium, Madras, on 25, 26‡, 27‡, 28, 29‡ October 1995.
Toss: India. Result: MATCH DRAWN.
Debuts: New Zealand – R.G.Twose. ‡ (no play)

	INDIA
M.Prabhakar not out	41
A.D.Jadeja b Nash	3
N.S.Sidhu c Twose b Cairns	33
S.R.Tendulkar not out	52
*M.Azharuddin	
V.G.Kambli	
†N.R.Mongia	
A Kumble	
J.Srinath	
R.K.Chauhan	
S.L.V.Raju	
Extras (LB1, W1, NB13)	15
Total (2 wickets)	144

NEW ZEALAND

M.J.Greatbatch
R.G.Twose
A.C.Parore
M.D.Crowe
S.P.Fleming
S.A.Thomson
C.L.Cairns
*†L.K.Germon
D.J.Nash
M.J.Haslam
D.K.Morrison

NEW ZEALAND	*O*	*M*	*R*	*W*
Morrison	14	3	34	0
Cairns	16	7	18	1
Nash	15	3	22	1
Haslam	17.1	4	50	0
Thomson	9	0	19	0

FALL OF WICKETS

Wkt	*I* *1st*
1st	18
2nd	73
3rd	–
4th	–
5th	–
6th	–
7th	–
8th	–
9th	–
10th	–

Umpires: K.T.Francis (*Sri Lanka*) (15) and S.Venkataraghavan (12).
Referee: P.J.P.Burge (*Australia*) (16). Test No. 1309/34 (I 294/NZ 239)

INDIA v NEW ZEALAND (3rd Test)

At Barabati Stadium, Cuttack, on 8, 9‡, 10‡, 11, 12 November 1995.
Toss: India. Result: MATCH DRAWN.
Debuts: None. ‡ (no play)

INDIA	
M.Prabhakar c Crowe b Nash	22
A.D.Jadeja c Hart b Cairns	45
N.S.Sidhu c Fleming b Nash	41
S.R.Tendulkar b Cairns	2
*M.Azharuddin lbw b Cairns	35
V.G.Kambli c Germon b Nash	28
†N.R.Mongia not out	45
A.R.Kapoor st Germon b Haslam	42
A Kumble c Greatbatch b Nash	2
J.Srinath not out	21
N.D.Hirwani	
Extras (LB10, NB3)	13
Total (8 wickets declared)	**296**

NEW ZEALAND	
M.J.Greatbatch c Jadeja b Hirwani	50
R.G.Twose lbw b Hirwani	36
A.C.Parore c Mongia b Hirwani	12
M.D.Crowe c Kambli b Hirwani	15
C.L.Cairns c Jadeja b Hirwani	13
*†L.K.Germon run out	2
M.N.Hart c Srinath b Hirwani	8
D.J.Nash not out	10
D.K.Morrison lbw b Kumble	0
M.J.Haslam not out	1
S.P.Fleming	
Extras (B7, LB19, NB2)	28
Total (8 wickets declared)	**175**

NEW ZEALAND	*O*	*M*	*R*	*W*
Morrison	13	0	52	0
Cairns	26.5	4	95	3
Nash	29	4	62	4
Twose	1	0	5	0
Haslam	15	1	42	1
Hart	5	0	30	0
INDIA				
Prabhakar	5	2	10	0
Srinath	8	3	16	0
Kapoor	17	3	32	0
Kumble	27	12	32	1
Hirwani	31	12	59	6

FALL OF WICKETS

	I	*NZ*
Wkt	*1st*	*1st*
1st	69	86
2nd	75	109
3rd	77	130
4th	143	139
5th	172	151
6th	188	155
7th	254	166
8th	267	166
9th	–	–
10th	–	–

Umpires: V.K.Ramaswamy (19) and I.D.Robinson (*Zimbabwe*) (13).
Referee: P.J.P.Burge (*Australia*) (17). Test No. 1310/35 (I 295/NZ 240)

INDIA v NEW ZEALAND 1995-96

INDIA – BATTING AND FIELDING

	M	I	NO	HS	Runs	Avge	100	50	Ct/St
M.Azharuddin	3	2	–	87	122	61.00	–	1	1
N.R.Mongia	3	2	1	45*	46	46.00	–	–	4
A.D.Jadeja	3	4	–	73	180	45.00	–	2	2
N.S.Sidhu	2	2	–	41	74	37.00	–	–	–
M.Prabhakar	3	4	1	43	110	36.66	–	–	1
S.R.Tendulkar	3	4	2	52*	58	29.00	–	1	3
V.G.Kambli	3	2	–	28	55	27.50	–	–	1
J.Srinath	3	2	1	21*	21	21.00	–	–	1
A.Kumble	3	2	1	6*	8	8.00	–	–	2
R.K.Chauhan	2	1	–	1	1	1.00	–	–	–
S.L.V.Raju	2	1	–	0	0	0.00	–	–	–

Played in one Test: N.D.Hirwani did not bat: A.R.Kapoor 42; S.V.Manjrekar 15, 29* (1 ct).

INDIA – BOWLING

	O	M	R	W	Avge	Best	5wI	10wM
N.D.Hirwani	31	12	59	6	9.83	6-59	1	–
A.Kumble	72.2	21	152	10	15.20	5-81	1	–
J.Srinath	37	14	81	5	16.20	3-24	–	–
M.Prabhakar	19	5	48	2	24.00	2-23	–	–
S.L.V.Raju	30	8	90	3	30.00	2-47	–	–

Also bowled. R.K.Chauhan 20-8-38-1; A.R.Kapoor 17-3-32-0.

NEW ZEALAND – BATTING AND FIELDING

	M	I	NO	HS	Runs	Avge	100	50	Ct/St
R.G.Twose	2	1	–	36	36	36.00	–	–	1
L.K.Germon	3	3	–	48	91	30.33	–	–	2/1
S.P.Fleming	3	2	–	41	57	28.50	–	–	1
M.J.Greatbatch	3	3	–	50	76	25.33	–	1	2
M.N.Hart	2	3	1	27*	36	18.00	–	–	2
C.L.Cairns	3	3	–	23	51	17.00	–	–	–
M.D.Crowe	3	3	–	24	50	16.66	–	–	1
D.J.Nash	3	3	1	17	27	13.50	–	–	–
S.A.Thomson	2	2	–	17	23	11.50	–	–	–
A.C.Parore	3	3	–	12	17	5.66	–	–	2
D.K.Morrison	3	3	1	9	10	5.00	–	–	–
M.J.Haslam	2	1	1	1*	1	–	–	–	–

Played in one Test: B.A.Young 14, 8 (3 ct).

NEW ZEALAND – BOWLING

	O	M	R	W	Avge	Best	5wI	10wM
D.J.Nash	67	11	160	8	20.00	4-62	–	–
C.L.Cairns	66.3	17	170	8	21.25	4-44	–	–
M.N.Hart	21.5	4	92	2	46.00	2-34	–	–
D.K.Morrison	52	9	181	3	60.33	3-61	–	–

Also bowled. M.J.Haslam 32.1-5-92-1; S.A.Thomson 32-4-97-0; R.G.Twose 1-0-5-0.

AUSTRALIA v PAKISTAN (1st Test)

At Woolloongabba, Brisbane, on 9, 10, 11, 13 November 1995.
Toss: Australia. Result: AUSTRALIA won by an innings and 126 runs.
Debuts: Pakistan – Salim Elahi. ‡ (Mushtaq Ahmed)

AUSTRALIA	
*M.A.Taylor c Salim Malik b Saqlain	69
M.J.Slater c Mohammad Akram b Wasim	42
D.C.Boon c Inzamam b Wasim	54
M.E.Waugh c Salim Elahi b Saqlain	59
S.R.Waugh not out	112
G.S.Blewett lbw b Waqar	57
†I.A.Healy c sub‡ b Mohammad Akram	18
P.R.Reiffel lbw b Waqar	9
S.K.Warne c Moin b Aamir	5
C.J.McDermott b Waqar	8
G.D.McGrath st Moin b Aamir	5
Extras (B2, LB6, W4, NB13)	25
Total	**463**

PAKISTAN				
Aamir Sohail st Healy b Warne	32		b McGrath	99
Salim Elahi c Taylor b McDermott	11		c Healy b McGrath	2
Ramiz Raja c Taylor b Warne	8		c Healy b McGrath	16
Saqlain Mushtaq lbw b McGrath	0	(9)	not out	2
Inzamam-ul-Haq c S.R.Waugh b Warne	5	(4)	c McDermott b M.E.Waugh	62
Basit Ali c Taylor b Warne	1	(5)	lbw b McGrath	26
†Moin Khan c McDermott b Warne	4	(6)	c Healy b Reiffel	9
*Wasim Akram c Boon b Warne	1	(7)	c Slater b Warne	6
Waqar Younis not out	19	(10)	lbw b Warne	0
Mohammad Akram c Blewett b Warne	1	(11)	lbw b Warne	0
Salim Malik absent hurt	0	(8)	c McDermott b Warne	0
Extras (B4, LB5, NB6)	15		(LB7, NB11)	18
Total	**97**			**240**

PAKISTAN	*O*	*M*	*R*	*W*		*O*	*M*	*R*	*W*
Wasim	38	9	84	2					
Waqar	29.5	7	101	3					
Mohammad Akram	33.1	4	97	1					
Saqlain	44	12	130	2					
Aamir	16.5	2	43	2					
AUSTRALIA									
McDermott	11	4	32	1		11	0	47	0
McGrath	14	3	33	1	(3)	25	7	76	4
Warne	16.1	9	23	7	(4)	27.5	10	54	4
Reiffel					(2)	15	4	47	1
S.R.Waugh						2	1	3	0
M.E.Waugh						5	2	6	1

FALL OF WICKETS	*A*	*P*	*P*
Wkt	*1st*	*1st*	*2nd*
1st	107	20	30
2nd	119	37	88
3rd	213	40	167
4th	250	62	217
5th	385	66	218
6th	411	70	233
7th	434	70	233
8th	441	80	239
9th	452	97	240
10th	463	–	240

Umpires: K.E.Liebenberg (*South Africa*) (8) and S.G.Randell (22).
Referee: R.Subba Row (*England*) (14). Test No. 1311/38 (A 552/P 225)

AUSTRALIA v PAKISTAN (2nd Test)

At Bellerive Oval, Hobart, on 17, 18, 19, 20 November 1995.
Toss: Australia. Result: AUSTRALIA won by 155 runs.
Debuts: None.

AUSTRALIA

M.J.Slater lbw b Wasim	0	(2)	lbw b Mushtaq	73
*M.A.Taylor b Wasim	40	(1)	b Waqar	123
D.C.Boon run out	34		c Waqar b Mushtaq	0
M.E.Waugh c Ramiz b Mushtaq	88		b Wasim	3
S.R.Waugh c Moin b Mushtaq	7		c Moin b Mohammad Akram	29
G.S.Blewett b Mushtaq	0		c Basit b Wasim	11
†I.A.Healy c Basit b Mushtaq	37		c Inzamam b Wasim	24
P.R.Reiffel c Mohammad Akram b Mushtaq	14		b Mushtaq	0
S.K.Warne not out	27		absent hurt	
C.J.McDermott b Waqar	0	(9)	c Wasim b Mushtaq	20
G.D.McGrath b Wasim	3	(10)	not out	2
Extras (B3, LB9, NB5)	17		(B6, LB5, W1, NB9)	21
Total	**267**			**306**

PAKISTAN

Aamir Sohail c Healy b Reiffel	32		c sub (B.P.Julian) b Blewett	57
Salim Elahi b McGrath	13		c Boon b McGrath	17
Mushtaq Ahmed lbw b McGrath	0	(9)	b McGrath	8
Ramiz Raja c and b Reiffel	59	(3)	lbw b Reiffel	25
Inzamam-ul-Haq c Healy b S.R.Waugh	27	(4)	lbw b Reiffel	40
Ijaz Ahmed not out	34	(5)	lbw b Blewett	4
Basit Ali lbw b McGrath	2	(6)	b Reiffel	5
†Moin Khan b McDermott	12	(7)	c M.E.Waugh b McGrath	16
*Wasim Akram c Taylor b McDermott	2	(8)	c Blewett b McGrath	33
Waqar Younis c sub (B.P.Julian) b Reiffel	10		c Blewett b McGrath	4
Mohammad Akram lbw b Reiffel	0		not out	0
Extras (LB1, NB6)	7		(LB11)	11
Total	**198**			**220**

PAKISTAN	*O*	*M*	*R*	*W*		*O*	*M*	*R*	*W*
Wasim	18.3	7	42	3		26.1	7	72	3
Waqar	17	3	54	1		20	4	67	1
Mohammad Akram	10	1	41	0		10	1	58	1
Mushtaq	30	5	115	5		38	8	83	4
Aamir	3	1	3	0		8	2	15	0
AUSTRALIA									
McDermott	18	2	72	2		16	7	38	0
McGrath	19	4	46	3		24.3	7	61	5
Reiffel	15.5	3	38	4		14	6	42	3
M.E.Waugh	8	0	23	0	(5)	12	2	24	0
S.R.Waugh	6	0	18	1	(4)	8	1	19	0
Blewett						10	4	25	2

FALL OF WICKETS

	A	*P*	*A*	*P*
Wkt	*1st*	*1st*	*2nd*	*2nd*
1st	0	24	120	27
2nd	68	24	125	62
3rd	111	79	132	132
4th	156	126	189	142
5th	156	150	233	152
6th	209	155	255	157
7th	235	173	256	205
8th	238	183	296	210
9th	244	198	306	220
10th	267	198	306	220

Umpires: H.D.Bird (*England*) (64) and D.B.Hair (12).
Referee: R.Subba Row (*England*) (15). Test No. 1312/39 (A 553/P 226)

In the second innings Aamir Sohail (0) retired hurt at 6 and resumed at 27.

AUSTRALIA v PAKISTAN (3rd Test)

At Sydney Cricket Ground, on 30 November, 1, 2, 3, 4 December 1995.
Toss: Pakistan. Result: PAKISTAN won by 74 runs.
Debuts: None. ‡ (Moin Khan)

PAKISTAN				
Aamir Sohail c M.E.Waugh b McDermott	4		c Boon b McDermott	9
Ramiz Raja c Slater b Warne	33		c M.E.Waugh b Warne	39
Ijaz Ahmed c McGrath b Warne	137		lbw b Warne	15
Inzamam-ul-Haq c Healy b Warne	39	(6)	c Taylor b McDermott	59
Salim Malik lbw b McGrath	36	(4)	lbw b M.E.Waugh	45
Basit Ali c Slater b McDermott	17	(5)	b Warne	14
†Rashid Latif c Healy b McDermott	1	(8)	lbw b Warne	3
*Wasim Akram c and b McGrath	21	(7)	lbw b McDermott	5
Saqlain Mushtaq run out	0		c M.E.Waugh b McDermott	2
Mushtaq Ahmed c McDermott b Warne	0		lbw b McDermott	2
Waqar Younis not out	0		not out	1
Extras (LB 3, W 2, NB 6)	11		(B 1, LB 5, NB 4)	10
Total	**299**			**204**

AUSTRALIA				
M.J.Slater b Wasim	1	(2)	lbw b Mushtaq	23
*M.A.Taylor c Rashid b Saqlain Mushtaq	47	(1)	st Rashid b Mushtaq Ahmed	59
D.C.Boon c Rashid b Mushtaq Ahmed	16		c sub‡ b Saqlain Mushtaq	6
M.E.Waugh c Mushtaq Ahmed b Wasim	116		c Rashid b Wasim	34
S.R.Waugh st Rashid b Mushtaq Ahmed	38	(6)	b Mushaq Ahmed	14
G.S.Blewett b Mushtaq Ahmed	5	(7)	b Waqar	14
†I.A.Healy c Rashid b Mushtaq Ahmed	6	(5)	c Rashid b Wasim	7
P.R.Reiffel not out	10	(10)	not out	2
S.K.Warne c Rashid b Wasim	2	(8)	c Saqlain b Mushtaq Ahmed	5
C.J.McDermott b Wasim	0	(9)	b Waqar	0
G.D.McGrath c Wasim b Mushtaq Ahmed	0		b Waqar	0
Extras (LB 6, NB 10)	16		(LB 5, NB 3)	8
Total	**257**			**172**

AUSTRALIA	O	M	R	W		O	M	R	W
McDermott	21	6	62	3		15.3	0	49	5
McGrath	22.2	1	79	2		17	3	47	0
Reiffel	22	5	71	0	(4)	8.3	2	15	0
Warne	34	20	55	4	(3)	37	13	66	4
M.E.Waugh	10	4	23	0		14	4	21	1
Blewett	4	2	6	0	(6)	2	2	0	0
PAKISTAN									
Wasim	24	4	50	4		16	5	25	2
Waqar	11	4	26	0		6.1	2	15	3
Mushtaq Ahmed	36.2	7	95	5		30	6	91	4
Saqlain Mushtaq	22	2	62	1		13	5	35	1
Aamir	5	0	18	0		1	0	1	0

FALL OF WICKETS	P	A	P	A
Wkt	1st	1st	2nd	2nd
1st	4	2	18	42
2nd	64	44	58	69
3rd	141	91	82	117
4th	210	174	101	126
5th	263	182	163	146
6th	269	228	185	152
7th	297	240	188	170
8th	299	249	198	170
9th	299	249	203	172
10th	299	257	204	172

Umpires: H.D.Bird (*England*) (65) and S.G.Randell (23).
Referee: R.Subba Row (*England*) (16). Test No. 1313/40 (A 554/P 227)

AUSTRALIA v PAKISTAN 1995-96

AUSTRALIA – BATTING AND FIELDING

	M	I	NO	HS	Runs	Avge	100	50	Ct/St
M.A.Taylor	3	5	–	123	338	67.60	1	2	5
M.E.Waugh	3	5	–	116	300	60.00	1	2	4
S.R.Waugh	3	5	1	112*	200	50.00	1	–	1
M.J.Slater	3	5	–	73	139	27.80	–	1	3
D.C.Boon	3	5	–	54	110	22.00	–	1	3
I.A.Healy	3	5	–	37	92	18.40	–	–	7/1
G.S.Blewett	3	5	–	57	87	17.40	–	1	3
S.K.Warne	3	4	1	27*	39	13.00	–	–	–
P.R.Reiffel	3	5	2	14	35	11.66	–	–	1
C.J.McDermott	3	5	–	20	28	5.60	–	–	4
G.D.McGrath	3	5	1	5	10	2.50	–	–	2

AUSTRALIA – BOWLING

	O	M	R	W	Avge	Best	5wI	10wMM
S.K.Warne	115	52	198	19	10.42	7-23	1	1
G.S.Blewett	16	8	31	2	15.50	2-25	–	–
G.D.McGrath	121.5	25	342	15	22.80	5-61	1	–
P.R.Reiffel	75.2	20	213	8	26.62	4-38	–	–
C.J.McDermott	92.3	19	300	11	27.27	5-49	1	–

Also bowled: M.E.Waugh 49-12-97-2; S.R.Waugh 16-2-40-1.

PAKISTAN – BATTING AND FIELDING

	M	I	NO	HS	Runs	Avge	100	50	Ct/St
Ijaz Ahmed	2	4	1	137	190	63.33	1	–	–
Aamir Sohail	3	6	–	99	233	38.83	–	2	–
Inzamam-ul-Haq	3	6	–	62	232	38.66	–	2	2
Ramiz Raja	3	6	–	59	180	30.00	–	1	1
Salim Malik	2	3	–	45	81	27.00	–	–	1
Wasim Akram	3	6	–	33	68	11.33	–	–	2
Waqar Younis	3	6	3	19*	34	11.33	–	–	1
Basit Ali	3	6	–	26	65	10.83	–	–	2
Salim Elahi	2	4	–	17	43	10.75	–	–	1
Moin Khan	2	4	–	16	41	10.25	–	–	3/1
Mushtaq Ahmed	2	4	–	8	10	2.50	–	–	1
Saqlain Mushtaq	2	4	1	2*	4	1.33	–	–	1
Mohammad Akram	2	4	1	1	1	0.33	–	–	2

Played in one Test: Rashid Latif 1, 3 (6 ct, 2 st).

PAKISTAN – BOWLING

	O	M	R	W	Avge	Best	5wI	10wM
Wasim Akram	122.4	32	273	14	19.50	4- 50	–	–
Mushtaq Ahmed	134.2	26	384	18	21.33	5- 95	2	–
Waqar Younis	84	20	263	8	32.87	3- 15	–	–
Saqlain Mushtaq	79	19	227	4	56.75	2-130	–	–

Also bowled: Aamir Sohail 33.5-5-80-2; Mohammad Akram 53.1-6-196-2.

SOUTH AFRICA v ENGLAND (1st Test)

At Centurion Park, Centurion (Verwoerdburg), on 16, 17, 18‡, 19‡, 20‡ November 1995.
Toss: South Africa. Result: MATCH DRAWN.
Debuts: South Africa – S.M.Pollock. ‡ (no play)

ENGLAND	
*M.A.Atherton c Donald b Pollock	78
A.J.Stewart c Matthews b Schultz	6
M.R.Ramprakash c Richardson b Donald	9
G.P.Thorpe c Richardson b Pollock	13
G.A.Hick lbw b Pollock	141
R.A.Smith b McMillan	43
†R.C.Russell not out	50
D.G.Cork c Matthews b McMillan	13
D.Gough b McMillan	0
R.K.Illingworth b Donald	0
A.R.C.Fraser not out	4
Extras (LB16, W1, NB7)	24
Total (9 wickets declared)	381

SOUTH AFRICA

A.C.Hudson
G.Kirsten
*W.J.Cronje
D.J.Cullinan
J.N.Rhodes
B.M.McMillan
†D.J.Richardson
S.M.Pollock
C.R.Matthews
A.A.Donald
B.N.Schultz

SOUTH AFRICA	O	M	R	W
Donald	33	10	92	2
Schultz	16	5	47	1
Matthews	30	13	63	0
Pollock	29	7	98	3
McMillan	25	10	50	3
Cronje	8	5	14	0
Kirsten	2	1	1	0

FALL OF WICKETS

Wkt	E 1st
1st	14
2nd	36
3rd	64
4th	206
5th	290
6th	320
7th	350
8th	358
9th	359
10th	–

Umpires: C.J.Mitchley (10) and S.Venkataraghavan (*India*) (13).
Referee: C.H.Lloyd (*West Indies*) (9). Test No. 1314/106 (SA 196/E 719)

SOUTH AFRICA v ENGLAND (2nd Test)

At The Wanderers, Johannesburg, on 30 November, 1, 2, 3, 4 December 1995.
Toss: England. Result: MATCH DRAWN.
Debuts: None.

SOUTH AFRICA			
A.C.Hudson c Stewart b Cork	0	c Russell b Fraser	17
G.Kirsten c Russell b Malcolm	110	c Russell b Malcolm	1
*W.J.Cronje c Russell b Cork	35	c Russell b Cork	48
D.J.Cullinan c Russell b Hick	69	c Gough b Cork	61
J.N.Rhodes c Russell b Cork	5	c Russell b Fraser	57
B.M.McMillan lbw b Cork	35	not out	100
†D.J.Richardson c Russell b Malcolm	0	c Ramprakash b Malcolm	23
S.M.Pollock c Smith b Malcolm	33	lbw b Cork	5
C.E.Eksteen c Russell b Cork	13	c Russell b Cork	2
M.W.Pringle not out	10	c Hick b Fraser	2
A.A.Donald b Malcolm	0	not out	9
Extras (B1, LB14, W2, NB5)	22	(B5, LB12, W1, NB3)	21
Total	332	(9 wickets declared)	346

ENGLAND			
*M.A.Atherton b Donald	9	not out	185
A.J.Stewart c Kirsten b Pringle	45	b McMillan	38
M.R.Ramprakash b Donald	4	b McMillan	0
G.P.Thorpe c Kirsten b Eksteen	34	lbw b Pringle	17
G.A.Hick c and b Eksteen	6	c Richardson b Donald	4
R.A.Smith c and b McMillan	52	c Pollock b Donald	44
†R.C.Russell c Rhodes b Eksteen	12	not out	29
D.G.Cork c Cullinan b Pollock	8		
D.Gough c and b Pollock	2		
A.R.C.Fraser lbw b Pollock	0		
D.E.Malcolm not out	0		
Extras (B6, LB1, NB21)	28	(B4, LB7, NB23)	34
Total	200	(5 wickets)	351

ENGLAND	O	M	R	W	O	M	R	W
Cork	32	7	84	5	31.3	6	78	4
Malcolm	22	5	62	4	13	2	65	2
Fraser	20	5	69	0	29	6	84	3
Gough	15	2	64	0	12	2	48	0
Hick	15	1	38	1	15	3	35	0
Ramprakash					4	0	19	0
SOUTH AFRICA								
Donald	15	3	49	2	35	9	95	2
Pringle	17	4	46	1	23	5	52	1
Pollock	15	2	44	3	29	11	65	0
McMillan	10.3	0	42	1	21	0	50	2
Eksteen	11	5	12	3	52	20	76	0
Cronje					3	1	2	0
Kirsten					2	2	0	0

FALL OF WICKETS	SA	E	SA	E
Wkt	1st	1st	2nd	2nd
1st	3	10	7	75
2nd	74	45	29	75
3rd	211	109	116	134
4th	221	116	145	145
5th	260	125	244	232
6th	260	147	296	–
7th	278	178	304	–
8th	314	193	311	–
9th	331	200	314	–
10th	332	200	–	–

Umpires: D.B.Hair (*Australia*) (13) and K.E.Liebenberg (9).
Referee: C.H.Lloyd (*West Indies*) (10). Test No. 1315/107 (SA 197/E 720)

SOUTH AFRICA v ENGLAND (3rd Test)

At Kingsmead, Durban, on 14, 15, 16, 17‡, 18‡ December 1995.
Toss: South Africa. Result: MATCH DRAWN.
Debuts: South Africa – J.H.Kallis. ‡ (no play)

SOUTH AFRICA	
G.Kirsten c Hick b Martin	8
A.C.Hudson c Crawley b Illingworth	45
*W.J.Cronje c Martin b Illingworth	8
D.J.Cullinan c Smith b Martin	10
J.N.Rhodes lbw b Ilott	38
J.H.Kallis c Russell b Martin	1
B.M.McMillan c Russell b Martin	28
†D.J.Richardson c Russell b Ilott	7
S.M.Pollock not out	36
C.R.Matthews lbw b Ilott	0
A.A.Donald b Illingworth	32
Extras (LB11, NB1)	12
Total	**225**

ENGLAND	
*M.A.Atherton c Hudson b Donald	2
A.J.Stewart c Hudson b Matthews	41
G.P.Thorpe c Cullinan b Donald	2
R.A.Smith c McMillan b Matthews	34
G.A.Hick not out	31
†R.C.Russell c Rhodes b Matthews	8
D.G.Cork not out	23
J.P.Crawley	
P.J.Martin	
M.C.Ilott	
R.K.Illingworth	
Extras (LB4, NB7)	11
Total (5 wickets)	**152**

ENGLAND	*O*	*M*	*R*	*W*
Cork	27	12	64	0
Ilott	15	3	48	3
Martin	27	9	60	4
Illingworth	29	12	37	3
Hick	2	0	5	0
SOUTH AFRICA				
Donald	12.1	1	57	2
Pollock	15	2	39	0
Matthews	12	5	31	3
McMillan	9	3	21	0

FALL OF WICKETS

	SA	*E*
Wkt	*1st*	*1st*
1st	54	2
2nd	56	13
3rd	73	83
4th	85	93
5th	89	109
6th	141	–
7th	152	–
8th	153	–
9th	153	–
10th	225	–

Umpires: S.A.Bucknor (*West Indies*) (19) and D.L.Orchard (1).
Referee: C.H.Lloyd (*West Indies*) (11). Test No. 1316/108 (SA 198/E 721)

SOUTH AFRICA v ENGLAND (4th Test)

At St George's Park, Port Elizabeth, on 26, 27, 28, 29, 30 December 1995.
Toss: South Africa. Result: MATCH DRAWN.
Debuts: South Africa – P.R.Adams.

SOUTH AFRICA			
A.C.Hudson c Russell b Cork	31	c Russell b Martin	4
G.Kirsten c Thorpe b Ilott	51	c Illingworth b Martin	69
*W.J.Cronje c Atherton b Martin	4	c Russell b Martin	6
D.J.Cullinan c Russell b Cork	91	st Russell b Illingworth	14
J.N.Rhodes c Smith b Cork	49	lbw b Cork	0
B.M.McMillan c Russell b Illingworth	49	c Hick b Cork	1
†D.J.Richardson c Russell b Illingworth	84	c Russell b Cork	0
S.M.Pollock lbw b Cork	23	c Cork b Illingworth	32
C.R.Matthews st Russell b Illingworth	15	c and b Illingworth	5
A.A.Donald not out	12	not out	12
P.R.Adams run out	0	not out	0
Extras (LB11, NB8)	19	(B8, LB7, W1, NB3)	19
Total	**428**	(9 wickets declared)	**162**

ENGLAND			
*M.A.Atherton c Richardson b Adams	72	lbw b Matthews	34
A.J.Stewart c Richardson b Pollock	4	c Hudson b Donald	81
J.E.R.Gallian c Cullinan b Pollock	14	lbw b Adams	28
G.P.Thorpe c Rhodes b Adams	27	not out	12
G.A.Hick lbw b Donald	62	not out	11
R.A.Smith lbw b McMillan	2		
†R.C.Russell c Cullinan b Donald	30		
D.G.Cork c Richardson b Pollock	1		
R.K.Illingworth c Hudson b Donald	28		
P.J.Martin b Adams	4		
M.C.Ilott not out	0		
Extras (LB9, W1, NB9)	19	(B9, LB8, W1, NB5)	23
Total	**263**	(3 wickets)	**189**

ENGLAND	O	M	R	W		O	M	R	W
Cork	43.2	12	113	4		26.3	5	63	3
Ilott	29.4	7	82	1					
Martin	33	9	79	1	(2)	17	8	39	3
Illingworth	39.5	8	105	3	(3)	22	7	45	3
Hick	12	2	32	0					
Gallian	2	0	6	0					
SOUTH AFRICA									
Donald	25.4	7	49	3	(2)	19	4	60	1
Pollock	22	8	58	3	(1)	10	4	15	0
Adams	37	13	75	3		28	13	51	1
Matthews	20	7	42	0	(5)	19	10	29	1
McMillan	15	6	30	1	(4)	14	6	16	0
Cronje	1	1	0	0					
Kirsten					(6)	2	1	1	0

FALL OF WICKETS	SA	E	SA	E
Wkt	1st	1st	2nd	2nd
1st	57	7	6	84
2nd	85	50	18	157
3rd	89	88	60	167
4th	207	163	65	–
5th	251	168	69	–
6th	326	199	69	–
7th	379	200	135	–
8th	408	258	146	–
9th	426	263	160	–
10th	428	263	–	–

Umpires: S.A.Bucknor (*West Indies*) (20) and C.J.Mitchley (11).
Referee: C.H.Lloyd (*West Indies*) (12). Test No. 1317/109 (SA 199/E 722)

SOUTH AFRICA v ENGLAND (5th Test)

At Newlands, Cape Town, on 2, 3, 4 January 1996.
Toss: England. Result: SOUTH AFRICA won by 10 wickets.
Debuts: None.

ENGLAND				
*M.A.Atherton c Hudson b Donald	0		c Richardson b Donald	10
A.J.Stewart b McMillan	13		c Cullinan b Pollock	7
R.A.Smith b Adams	66	(4)	c Richardson b Adams	13
G.P.Thorpe c McMillan b Donald	20	(5)	run out	59
G.A.Hick c McMillan b Donald	2	(6)	lbw b Pollock	36
†R.C.Russell c McMillan b Pollock	9	(7)	c Hudson b Pollock	2
M.Watkinson lbw b Pollock	11	(8)	lbw b Adams	0
D.G.Cork b Donald	16	(9)	c Kallis b Pollock	8
P.J.Martin c Hudson b Donald	0	(10)	c Adams b Pollock	9
A.R.C.Fraser not out	5	(3)	c Adams b Donald	1
D.E.Malcolm b Adams	1		not out	0
Extras (B4, LB1, W1, NB4)	10		(B2, LB5, NB5)	12
Total	**153**			**157**
SOUTH AFRICA				
G.Kirsten c Atherton b Watkinson	23		not out	41
A.C.Hudson lbw b Cork	0		not out	27
*W.J.Cronje c Russell b Cork	12			
D.J.Cullinan c Russell b Martin	62			
J.N.Rhodes c Russell b Fraser	16			
B.M.McMillan run out	11			
J.H.Kallis lbw b Martin	7			
†D.J.Richardson not out	54			
S.M.Pollock c Smith b Watkinson	4			
A.A.Donald c Russell b Cork	3			
P.R.Adams c Hick b Martin	29			
Extras (LB22, NB1)	23		(LB1, NB1)	2
Total	**244**		(0 wickets)	**70**

SOUTH AFRICA	*O*	*M*	*R*	*W*		*O*	*M*	*R*	*W*
Donald	16	5	46	5		18	6	49	2
Pollock	14	6	26	2		15.5	4	32	5
McMillan	10	2	22	1	(4)	7	3	16	0
Adams	20.1	5	52	2	(3)	22	6	53	2
Kallis	4	2	2	0					
Cronje	4	4	0	0					
ENGLAND									
Cork	25	6	60	3		4	0	23	0
Malcolm	20	6	56	0		2	0	12	0
Martin	24	9	37	3		4	2	3	0
Fraser	17	10	34	1					
Watkinson	15	3	35	2	(4)	4	0	24	0
Hick					(5)	1.4	0	7	0

FALL OF WICKETS

Wkt	*E* *1st*	*SA* *1st*	*E* *2nd*	*SA* *2nd*
1st	0	1	16	–
2nd	24	19	22	–
3rd	58	79	22	–
4th	60	125	66	–
5th	103	125	138	–
6th	115	144	140	–
7th	141	154	140	–
8th	147	163	140	–
9th	151	171	150	–
10th	153	244	157	–

Umpires: D.L.Orchard (2) and S.G.Randell (*Australia*) (24).
Referee: C.H.Lloyd (*West Indies*) (13). Test No. 1318/110 (SA 200/E 723)

SOUTH AFRICA v ENGLAND 1995-96

SOUTH AFRICA – BATTING AND FIELDING

	M	*I*	*NO*	*HS*	*Runs*	*Avge*	*100*	*50*	*Ct/St*
D.J.Cullinan	5	6	–	91	307	51.16	–	4	5
G.Kirsten	5	7	1	110	303	50.50	1	2	2
B.M.McMillan	5	6	1	100*	224	44.80	1	–	5
D.J.Richardson	5	6	1	84	168	33.60	–	2	8
J.N.Rhodes	5	6	–	57	165	27.50	–	1	3
S.M.Pollock	5	6	1	36*	133	26.60	–	–	2
A.A.Donald	5	6	3	32	68	22.66	–	–	1
A.C.Hudson	5	7	1	45	124	20.66	–	–	7
W.J.Cronje	5	6	–	48	113	18.83	–	–	–
P.R.Adams	2	3	1	29	29	14.50	–	–	2
C.R.Matthews	3	3	–	15	20	6.66	–	–	2
J.H.Kallis	2	2	–	7	8	4.00	–	–	1

Played in one Test: C.E.Eksteen 13, 2 (1 ct); M.W.Pringle 10*, 2; B.N.Schultz did not bat.

SOUTH AFRICA – BOWLING

	O	*M*	*R*	*W*	*Avge*	*Best*	*5wI*	*10wM*
S.M.Pollock	149.5	44	377	16	23.56	5-32	1	–
A.A.Donald	173.5	45	497	19	26.15	5-46	1	–
P.R.Adams	107.1	37	231	8	28.87	3-75	–	–
C.E.Eksteen	63	25	88	3	29.33	3-12	–	–
B.M.McMillan	111.3	30	247	8	30.87	3-50	–	–
C.R.Matthews	81	35	165	4	41.25	3-31	–	–

Also bowled: W.J.Cronje 16-11-16-0; J.H.Kallis 4-2-2-0; G.Kirsten 6-4-2-0; M.W.Pringle 40-9-98-2; B.N.Schultz 16-5-47-1.

ENGLAND – BATTING AND FIELDING

	M	*I*	*NO*	*HS*	*Runs*	*Avge*	*100*	*50*	*Ct/St*
M.A.Atherton	5	8	1	185*	390	55.71	1	2	2
G.A.Hick	5	8	2	141	293	48.83	1	1	4
R.A.Smith	5	7	–	66	254	36.28	–	2	4
A.J.Stewart	5	8	–	81	235	29.37	–	1	1
R.C.Russell	5	7	2	50*	140	28.00	–	1	25/2
G.P.Thorpe	5	8	1	59	184	26.28	–	1	1
R.K.Illingworth	3	2	–	28	28	14.00	–	–	2
D.G.Cork	5	6	1	23*	69	13.80	–	–	1
A.R.C.Fraser	3	4	2	5*	10	5.00	–	–	–
M.R.Ramprakash	2	3	–	9	13	4.33	–	–	1
P.J.Martin	3	3	–	9	13	4.33	–	–	1
D.E.Malcolm	2	3	2	1	1	1.00	–	–	–
D.Gough	2	2	–	2	2	1.00	–	–	1
M.C.Ilott	2	1	1	0*	0	–	–	–	–

Played in one Test: J.P.Crawley did not bat (1 ct); J.E.R.Gallian 14, 28; M.Watkinson 11, 0.

ENGLAND – BOWLING

	O	*M*	*R*	*W*	*Avge*	*Best*	*5wI*	*10wM*
P.J.Martin	105	37	218	11	19.81	4-60	–	–
R.K.Illingworth	90.5	27	187	9	20.77	3-37	–	–
D.G.Cork	189.2	48	485	19	25.52	5-84	1	–
M.Watkinson	19	3	59	2	29.50	2-35	–	–
D.E.Malcolm	57	13	195	6	32.50	4-62	–	–
M.C.Ilott	44.4	10	130	4	32.50	3-48	–	–
A.R.C.Fraser	66	21	187	4	46.75	3-84	–	–

Also bowled: J.E.R.Gallian 2-0-6-0; D.Gough 27-4-112-0; G.A.Hick 45.4-6-117-1; M.R.Ramprakash 4-0-19-0.

NEW ZEALAND v PAKISTAN (Only Test)

At Lancaster Park, Christchurch on 8, 9, 10, 11, 12 December 1995.
Toss: New Zealand. Result: PAKISTAN won by 161 runs.
Debuts: New Zealand – C.M.Spearman.

PAKISTAN			
Aamir Sohail hit wicket b Cairns	88	b Patel	30
Ramiz Raja lbw b Cairns	54	lbw b Morrison	62
Ijaz Ahmed c Morrison b Larsen	30	c Germon b Nash	103
Inzamam-ul-Haq lbw b Cairns	0	c Fleming b Nash	82
Salim Malik c Germon b Nash	0	c Germon b Morrison	21
Basit Ali c Germon b Larsen	5	lbw b Cairns	0
†Rashid Latif c Spearman b Morrison	2	c Germon b Cairns	39
*Wasim Akram c Young b Morrison	2	c Fleming b Cairns	19
Mushtaq Ahmed lbw b Nash	5	c Germon b Larsen	24
Waqar Younis not out	12	lbw b Larsen	34
Ata-ur-Rehman c and b Cairns	5	not out	0
Extras (LB1, W1, NB3)	5	(B5, LB6, W4, NB5)	20
Total	**208**		**434**

NEW ZEALAND			
B.A.Young c Rashid b Rehman	16	c Rashid b Mushtaq	18
C.M.Spearman b Mushtaq	40	c Aamir b Mushtaq	33
A.C.Parore c Rashid b Rehman	9	lbw b Mushtaq	5
S.P.Fleming st Rashid b Mushtaq	25	lbw b Rehman	0
R.G.Twose lbw b Wasim	59	not out	51
C.L.Cairns b Wasim	76	c Salim b Mushtaq	8
*†L.K.Germon c Rashid b Wasim	21	run out	12
D.N.Patel c Aamir b Wasim	3	b Mushtaq	15
G.R.Larsen not out	5	c Aamir b Mushtaq	13
D.J.Nash c Rashid b Wasim	11	b Waqar	22
D.K.Morrison b Mushtaq	0	c Salim b Mushtaq	1
Extras (LB4, NB17)	21	(B3, LB9, W1, NB4)	17
Total	**286**		**195**

NEW ZEALAND	O	M	R	W		O	M	R	W
Morrison	14	0	57	2		27	5	99	2
Cairns	11.1	2	51	4	(3)	35	6	114	3
Larsen	15	2	44	2	(5)	29	10	58	2
Nash	11	3	43	2	(2)	30	6	91	2
Patel	3	1	12	0	(4)	24	8	61	1
PAKISTAN									
Wasim	24.5	4	53	5		11	3	31	0
Waqar	16	2	60	0		26	6	73	1
Rehman	17.1	4	47	2		9	1	23	1
Mushtaq	30.4	4	115	3		34.4	13	56	7
Aamir	3	0	7	0					

FALL OF WICKETS	P	NZ	P	NZ
Wkt	1st	1st	2nd	2nd
1st	135	48	55	50
2nd	148	65	195	57
3rd	148	73	224	60
4th	149	119	260	60
5th	177	221	265	75
6th	184	262	339	101
7th	184	265	363	131
8th	187	269	384	163
9th	203	283	425	192
10th	208	286	434	195

Umpires: B.C.Cooray (*Sri Lanka*) (6) and R.S.Dunne (4).
Referee: R.S.Madugalle (*Sri Lanka*) (16). Test No. 1319/37 (NZ 241/P 228)

SECOND XI FIXTURES 1996

Abbreviations: (SEC) Second Eleven Championship Matches (Three days)
(BH) Bain Hogg Trophy (One day)

APRIL			
Mon 15		Southampton	Second XI Champions (Hampshire) v England Under 19
Sun 21	(SEC)	Taunton	Somerset v Nottinghamshire
Mon 22	(SEC)	Bristol	Gloucestershire v Leicestershire
	(SEC)	Canterbury	Kent v Lancashire
	(SEC)	Knowle & Dorridge CC	Warwickshire v Derbyshire
Sun 28	(SEC)	Taunton (King's College)	Somerset v Derbyshire
Mon 29	(SEC)	Bristol	Gloucestershire v Glamorgan
	(SEC)	Uxbridge CC	Middlesex v Worcestershire
	(SEC)	Cheam	Surrey v Leicestershire
	(SEC)	Headingley	Yorkshire v Northamptonshire
Tue 30	(SEC)	Old Trafford	Lancashire v Nottinghamshire
	(SEC)	Hove	Sussex v Kent
MAY			
Thu 2	(BH)	Leicester	Leicestershire v Middlesex
Fri 3	(BH)	Chelmsford	Essex v MCC YCs
	(BH)	Old Trafford	Lancashire v Nottinghamshire
	(BH)	Hove	Sussex v Kent
Sun 5	(SEC)	The Oval	Surrey v Durham
Mon 6	(SEC)	Rocester (Abbotsholme S)	Derbyshire v Yorkshire
	(SEC)	Old Trafford	Lancashire v Worcestershire
	(SEC)	North Perrott	Somerset v Northamptonshire
	(SEC)	Eastbourne	Sussex v Essex
	(BH)	Bristol	Gloucestershire v Hampshire
Tue 7	(SEC)	Bristol	Gloucestershire v Hampshire
Thu 9	(BH)	Derby	Derbyshire v Yorkshire
	(BH)	Chester-le-Street (Riverside)	Durham v Lancashire
	(BH)	Leicester	Leicestershire v Warwickshire
	(BH)	Eastbourne	Sussex v Essex
Fri 10	(BH)	Shenley	MCC YCs v Kent
Mon 13	(SEC)	Chelmsford	Essex v Gloucestershire
	(SEC)	Pontypridd	Glamorgan v Somerset
	(SEC)	Maidstone	Kent v Leicestershire
	(SEC)	Haslingden	Lancashire v Sussex
	(SEC)	Uxbridge CC	Middlesex v Surrey
	(SEC)	Worcester	Worcestershire v Northamptonshire
	(SEC)	Todmorden	Yorkshire v Nottinghamshire
Tue 14	(SEC)	Southampton	Hampshire v Warwickshire
Thu 16	(BH)	Uxbridge CC	Middlesex v Leicestershire
	(BH)	Bradford (Park Ave)	Yorkshire v Nottinghamshire
Fri 17	(BH)	Bishop Auckland	Durham v Nottinghamshire
	(BH)	Worcester	Worcestershire v Somerset
Mon 20	(SEC)	Rocester (Abbotsholme S)	Derbyshire v Essex
	(SEC)	Boldon CC	Durham v Sussex
	(SEC)	Southampton	Hampshire v Glamorgan
	(SEC)	Ashford	Kent v Northamptonshire
	(SEC)	Oakham Town CC	Leicestershire v Lancashire
	(SEC)	Oxted	Surrey v Nottinghamshire
	(SEC)	Worcester	Worcestershire v Gloucestershire
Thu 23	(BH)	Belper Meadows	Derbyshire v Lancashire
	(BH)	Southampton	Hampshire v Glamorgan

	(BH)	Walsall	Minor Counties v Leicestershire
	(BH)	Uxbridge CC	Middlesex v Northamptonshire
Fri 24	(BH)	Maidstone	Kent v MCC YCs
	(BH)	Walsall	Minor Counties v Warwickshire
Mon 27	(SEC)	Chesterfield	Derbyshire v Nottinghamshire
	(SEC)	Swansea	Glamorgan v Lancashire
	(SEC)	Milton Keynes (Campbell Park)	Northamptonshire v Durham
	(SEC)	Harrogate	Yorkshire v Kent
Tue 28	(SEC)	Bournemouth Sports Club	Hampshire v Somerset
	(SEC)	Southgate CC	Middlesex v Essex
	(SEC)	Stratford-upon-Avon	Warwickshire v Sussex
Thu 30	(BH)	Derby	Derbyshire v Nottinghamshire
Fri 31	(BH)	Southampton	Hampshire v Somerset
	(BH)	Shenley	MCC YCs v Surrey
	(BH)	Uxbridge CC	Middlesex v Minor Counties
JUNE			
Mon 3	(SEC)	Chester-le-Street CC	Durham v Warwickshire
	(SEC)	Southend	Essex v Nottinghamshire
	(SEC)	Bristol	Gloucestershire v Lancashire
	(SEC)	Old Northamptonians	Northamptonshire v Middlesex
	(SEC)	Taunton	Somerset v Worcestershire
	(SEC)	York CC	Yorkshire v Surrey
Thu 6	(BH)	Bristol	Gloucestershire v Somerset
	(BH)	Shenley	MCC YCs v Sussex
	(BH)	Northampton	Northamptonshire v Middlesex
	(BH)	Worksop College	Nottinghamshire v Yorkshire
Fri 7	(BH)	Bridgend	Glamorgan v Gloucestershire
	(BH)	Old Trafford	Lancashire v Durham
	(BH)	The Oval	Surrey v Essex
	(BH)	Old Edwardians	Warwickshire v Leicestershire
Mon 10	(SEC)	Pontardulais	Glamorgan v Middlesex
	(SEC)	Portsmouth	Hampshire v Durham
	(SEC)	Maidstone	Kent v Surrey
	(SEC)	Fleetwood CC	Lancashire v Essex
	(SEC)	Milton Keynes (Campbell Park)	Northamptonshire v Leicestershire
	(SEC)	Worksop CC	Nottinghamshire v Warwickshire
	(SEC)	Horsham	Sussex v Somerset
Thu 13	(BH)	Duffield (Eyes Meadow)	Derbyshire v Durham
	(BH)	Southampton	Hampshire v Gloucestershire
	(BH)	Maidstone	Kent v Surrey
	(BH)	Trent Bridge	Nottinghamshire v Lancashire
Fri 14	(BH)	Shenley	MCC YCs v Essex
	(BH)	Milton Keynes (Campbell Park)	Northamptonshire v Minor Counties
	(BH)	Castleford	Yorkshire v Durham
Mon 17	(SEC)	Ashbrooke	Durham v Derbyshire
	(SEC)	Ammanford	Glamorgan v Sussex
	(SEC)	Old Trafford	Lancashire v Yorkshire
	(SEC)	Leicester	Leicestershire v Essex
	(SEC)	Northampton	Northamptonshire v Hampshire
	(SEC)	Ombersley	Worcestershire v Kent
Wed 19	(SEC)	The Oval	Surrey v Gloucestershire
Thu 20	(BH)	Philadelphia CC	Durham v Derbyshire
	(BH)	Old Trafford	Lancashire v Yorkshire
	(BH)	Southgate CC	Middlesex v Warwickshire
	(BH)	Worcester	Worcestershire v Hampshire
Fri 21	(BH)	Brecon (Christ College)	Glamorgan v Somerset
	(BH)	Canterbury	Kent v Sussex

	(BH)	Leicester	Leicestershire v Minor Counties
Mon 24	(SEC)	Darlington	Durham v Essex
	(SEC)	Gloucester (Tuffley Park)	Gloucestershire v Warwickshire
	(SEC)	Canterbury	Kent v Hampshire
	(SEC)	Preston	Lancashire v Somerset
	(SEC)	Hinckley	Leicestershire v Middlesex
	(SEC)	Cheam	Surrey v Sussex
	(SEC)	Barnt Green	Worcestershire v Nottinghamshire
	(SEC)	Sheffield (Abbeydale Park)	Yorkshire v Glamorgan
Thu 27	(BH)	Marlow	Minor Counties v Northamptonshire
	(BH)	The Oval	Surrey v Sussex
	(BH)	Castleford	Yorkshire v Derbyshire
Fri 28	(BH)	Bristol	Gloucestershire v Glamorgan
	(BH)	Marlow	Minor Counties v Middlesex
	(BH)	Taunton	Somerset v Worcestershire
	(BH)	The Oval	Surrey v MCC YCs
JULY			
Mon 1	(SEC)	Coggeshall	Essex v Kent
	(SEC)	Cardiff	Glamorgan v Durham
	(SEC)	Bristol (Optimists CC)	Gloucestershire v Somerset
	(SEC)	Finchampstead	Hampshire v Derbyshire
	(SEC)	Egerton Park CC	Leicestershire v Worcestershire
	(SEC)	Southgate CC	Middlesex v Warwickshire
	(SEC)	Collingham CC	Nottinghamshire v Northamptonshire
Tue 2	(BH)	Bingley	Yorkshire v Lancashire
Thu 4	(BH)	Coggeshall	Essex v Kent
Fri 5	(BH)	Monmouth School	Glamorgan v Hampshire
	(BH)	Urmston	Lancashire v Derbyshire
	(BH)	Bromsgrove CC	Worcestershire v Gloucestershire
	(BH)	Hove	Sussex v MCC YCs
Mon 8	(SEC)	Trent College	Derbyshire v Worcestershire
	(SEC)	Shildon	Durham v Yorkshire
	(SEC)	Saffron Walden	Essex v Surrey
	(SEC)	Usk	Glamorgan v Leicestershire
	(SEC)	Southampton	Hampshire v Lancashire
	(SEC)	Middleton-on-Sea	Sussex v Middlesex
	(SEC)	Coventry & North Warwickshire	Warwickshire v Kent
Tue 9	(SEC)	Northampton	Northamptonshire v Gloucestershire
Thu 11	(BH)	Durham City	Durham v Yorkshire
	(BH)	Saffron Walden	Essex v Surrey
	(BH)	Farnsfield CC	Nottinghamshire v Derbyshire
Fri 12	(BH)	Milton Keynes (Campbell Park)	Northamptonshire v Leicestershire
	(BH)	Taunton	Somerset v Gloucestershire
	(BH)	Hove	Sussex v Surrey
	(BH)	Worcester	Worcestershire v Glamorgan
Mon 15	(SEC)	Swansea	Glamorgan v Derbyshire
	(SEC)	Bristol	Gloucestershire v Middlesex
	(SEC)	Leicester	Leicestershire v Warwickshire
	(SEC)	Wellingborough School	Northamptonshire v Sussex
	(SEC)	Trent Bridge	Nottinghamshire v Durham
	(SEC)	Taunton	Somerset v Kent
	(SEC)	The Oval	Surrey v Lancashire
	(SEC)	Halesowen	Worcestershire v Hampshire
Thu 18	(BH)	Leicester	Leicestershire v Northamptonshire
	(BH)	Welbeck CC	Nottinghamshire v Durham
Fri 19	(BH)	Panteg	Glamorgan v Worcestershire
	(BH)	Maidstone	Kent v Essex

	(BH)	Aston Unity CC	Warwickshire v Minor Counties
Mon 22	(SEC)	Bristol	Gloucestershire v Durham
	(SEC)	Hinckley	Leicestershire v Derbyshire
	(SEC)	Harrow CC	Middlesex v Yorkshire
	(SEC)	Bedford School	Northamptonshire v Lancashire
	(SEC)	Cleethorpes CC	Nottinghamshire v Glamorgan
	(SEC)	The Oval	Surrey v Hampshire
	(SEC)	Hove	Sussex v Worcestershire
	(SEC)	Walmley CC	Warwickshire v Essex
Thu 25	(BH)	Taunton	Somerset v Hampshire
Fri 26	(BH)	Bournemouth Sports Club	Hampshire v Worcestershire
	(BH)	Tring	Northamptonshire v Warwickshire
	(BH)	Taunton	Somerset v Glamorgan
	(BH)	The Oval	Surrey v Kent
Mon 29	(SEC)	Colchester	Essex v Northamptonshire
	(SEC)	Gloucester (King's School)	Gloucestershire v Sussex
	(SEC)	Sittingbourne	Kent v Glamorgan
	(SEC)	Crosby (Northern)	Lancashire v Middlesex
	(SEC)	Kibworth	Leicestershire v Durham
	(SEC)	Clevedon	Somerset v Surrey
	(SEC)	Moseley CC	Warwickshire v Worcestershire
	(SEC)	Marske by Sea	Yorkshire v Hampshire
AUGUST			
Thu 1	(BH)	Chelmsford	Essex v Sussex
	(BH)	Edgbaston	Warwickshire v Middlesex
Fri 2	(BH)	Lydney	Gloucestershire v Worcestershire
	(BH)	Edgbaston	Warwickshire v Northamptonshire
Mon 5	(SEC)	Chesterfield	Derbyshire v Gloucestershire
	(SEC)	Seaton Carew	Durham v Lancashire
	(SEC)	Pontypridd	Glamorgan v Essex
	(SEC)	Bournemouth Sports Club	Hampshire v Sussex
	(SEC)	Harrow CC	Middlesex v Kent
	(SEC)	Nottingham High School	Nottinghamshire v Leicestershire
	(SEC)	The Oval	Surrey v Northamptonshire
	(SEC)	Studley	Warwickshire v Somerset
	(SEC)	Worcester	Worcestershire v Yorkshire
Thu 8	(SEC)	Chester-le-Street (Riverside)	Durham v Somerset
Mon 12	(SEC)	South Shields CC	Durham v Middlesex
	(SEC)	Wickford	Essex v Yorkshire
	(SEC)	Folkestone	Kent v Gloucestershire
	(SEC)	Liverpool CC	Lancashire v Derbyshire
	(SEC)	Oakham School	Leicestershire v Sussex
	(SEC)	Worksop College	Nottinghamshire v Hampshire
	(SEC)	Solihull CC	Warwickshire v Surrey
Thu 15 or Fri 16	(BH)		Bain Hogg Trophy Semi-Finals
Mon 19	(SEC)	Ilford	Essex v Hampshire
	(SEC)	Swansea	Glamorgan v Warwickshire
	(SEC)	Eltham (British Gas plc)	Kent v Durham
	(SEC)	Hinckley	Leicestershire v Somerset
	(SEC)	Lensbury CC	Middlesex v Derbyshire
	(SEC)	Horsham	Sussex v Nottinghamshire
	(SEC)	Kidderminster	Worcestershire v Surrey
	(SEC)	Elland	Yorkshire v Gloucestershire
Mon 26	(SEC)	Felling	Durham v Worcestershire
	(SEC)	Southampton	Hampshire v Middlesex
	(SEC)	Canterbury	Kent v Nottinghamshire

	(SEC)	Haywards Heath	Sussex v Derbyshire
	(SEC)	Bradford (Park Ave)	Yorkshire v Leicestershire
Tue 27	(SEC)	Northampton	Northamptonshire v Warwickshire
SEPTEMBER			
Mon 2	(SEC)	Derby	Derbyshire v Surrey
	(SEC)	Chelmsford	Essex v Worcestershire
	(SEC)	Uxbridge (RAF Vine Lane)	Middlesex v Somerset
Tue 3	(SEC)	Northampton	Northamptonshire v Glamorgan
	(SEC)	Kenilworth Wardens CC	Warwickshire v Yorkshire
Mon 9	(BH)		Bain Hogg Trophy Final (Reserve day Tuesday 10th)
Wed 11	(SEC)	Chesterfield	Derbyshire v Kent
	(SEC)	Southampton	Hampshire v Leicestershire
	(SEC)	Old Trafford	Lancashire v Warwickshire
	(SEC)	Trent Bridge	Nottinghamshire v Middlesex
	(SEC)	Taunton	Somerset v Essex
	(SEC)	The Oval	Surrey v Glamorgan
	(SEC)	Hove	Sussex v Yorkshire
Mon 16	(SEC)	Belper Meadows	Derbyshire v Northamptonshire
	(SEC)	Trent Bridge	Nottinghamshire v Gloucestershire
	(SEC)	Taunton	Somerset v Yorkshire
	(SEC)	Barnt Green	Worcestershire v Glamorgan

MINOR COUNTIES FIXTURES 1996

APRIL		*Benson & Hedges Cup*
Fri 26	Old Trafford	Lancashire v Minor Counties
Sun 28	Jesmond	Minor Counties v Warwickshire
Tue 30	Jesmond	Minor Counties v Leicestershire
MAY		*Benson & Hedges Cup*
Tue 7	Chester-le-Street	Durham v Minor Counties
Tue 14	Derby	Derbyshire v Minor Counties
		MCC Trophy Preliminary Round
Sun 19	Penrith	Cumberland v Cheshire
	Walsall	Staffordshire v Norfolk
	Shenley Park	Hertfordshire v Dorset
	Brockhampton	Herefordshire v Wiltshire
		Bain Hogg Trophy
Thu 23	Walsall	Minor Counties v Leicestershire II
Fri 24	Walsall	Minor Counties v Warwickshire II
		Championship
Sun 26	Budleigh Salterton	(W) Devon v Dorset
	Sleaford	(E) Lincolnshire v Bedfordshire
	Jesmond	(E) Northumberland v Hertfordshire
	Bridgnorth	(W) Shropshire v Herefordshire
Tue 28	Beaconsfield	(E) Buckinghamshire v Suffolk
	Carlisle	(E) Cumberland v Hertfordshire
		Bain Hogg Trophy
Fri 31	Uxbridge	Middlesex II v Minor Counties
JUNE		*Championship*
Sun 2	Colwall	(W) Herefordshire v Dorset
	Bishop's Stortford	(E) Hertfordshire v Suffolk
	Bourne	(E) Lincolnshire v Staffordshire
	Jesmond	(E) Northumberland v Buckinghamshire
	Shrewsbury	(W) Shropshire v Oxfordshire
Tue 4	Neston	(W) Cheshire v Oxfordshire

	Barrow	(E) Cumberland v Buckinghamshire
		MCC Trophy First Round
Sun 9	Barrow or Nantwich	Cumberland or Cheshire v Staffordshire or Norfolk
	Shenley Park or Sherborne School	Hertfordshire or Dorset v Herefordshire or Wiltshire
	Framlingham	Suffolk v Cambridgeshire
	Aylesbury	Buckinghamshire v Devon
	Cleethorpes	Lincolnshire v Northumberland
	Wardown Park	Bedfordshire v Oxfordshire
	St George's	Shropshire v Berkshire
	Panteg, Newport	Wales v Cornwall
		Championship
Mon 10	Millom	(E) Cumberland v Norfolk
Wed 12	Wisbech	(E) Cambridgeshire v Suffolk
	Cannock	(E) Staffordshire v Norfolk
		Bain Hogg Trophy
Fri 14	Milton Keynes	Northamptonshire II v Minor Counties
		Championship
Sun 16	Falkland CC	(W) Berkshire v Herefordshire
	Grimsby CC	(E) Lincolnshire v Northumberland
	Challow & Childrey	(W) Oxfordshire v Wales
	Wellington	(W) Shropshire v Wiltshire
	Ransome's	(E) Suffolk v Bedfordshire
Mon 17	Falmouth	(W) Cornwall v Cheshire
Tue 18	Saffron Walden	(E) Cambridgeshire v Northumberland
Wed 19	Torquay	(W) Devon v Cheshire
		Bain Hogg Trophy
Fri 21	Grace Road	Leicestershire II v Minor Counties
		Championship
Sun 23	Bedford Town	(E) Bedfordshire v Hertfordshire
	Hurst CC	(W) Berkshire v Wales
		Bain Hogg Trophy
Thu 27	Marlow	Minor Counties v Northamptonshire II
Fri 28	Marlow	Minor Counties v Middlesex II
Sun 30		*MCC Trophy Quarter-Finals*
JULY		*Championship*
Wed 3	Fenner's	(E) Cambridgeshire v Staffordshire
Sun 7	Henlow	(E) Bedfordshire v Northumberland
	Reading School	(W) Berkshire v Cornwall
	Hereford City	(W) Herefordshire v Devon
	Lincoln Lindum	(E) Lincolnshire v Cambridgeshire
	Pontypridd	(W) Wales v Shropshire
	South Wilts CC	(W) Wiltshire v Oxfordshire
Tue 9	Thame	(W) Oxfordshire v Cornwall
	Old Hill	(E) Staffordshire v Buckinghamshire
		Tourist Match
Thu 11	Stone	Minor Counties v Pakistanis (One day)
		Championship
Sun 14	Southill Park	(E) Bedfordshire v Norfolk
	Bowdon	(W) Cheshire v Berkshire
	Truro	(W) Cornwall v Dorset
	Brockhampton	(W) Herefordshire v Wiltshire
	Shenley Park	(E) Hertfordshire v Buckinghamshire
Mon 15	Grantham	(E) Lincolnshire v Cumberland
Tue 16	High Wycombe	(E) Buckinghamshire v Norfolk
	Oswestry	(W) Shropshire v Berkshire
		Bain Hogg Trophy

Fri 19	Aston Unity CC	Warwickshire II v Minor Counties
		Championship
Wed 17	Fenner's	(E) Cambridgeshire v Cumberland
Sun 21	Colwyn Bay	*(W) Wales v Devon
		MCC Trophy Semi-Finals
		*This match may be affected by progress in the MCC Trophy and will, in this event, be played one day later.
		Championship
Mon 22	Jesmond	(E) Northumberland v Staffordshire
Wed 24	Kimbolton School	(E) Cambridgeshire v Buckinghamshire
	Askam	(E) Cumberland v Staffordshire
Sun 28	Slough	(E) Buckinghamshire v Bedfordshire
	Weymouth	(W) Dorset v Shropshire
	Lakenham	(E) Norfolk v Lincolnshire
	Thame	(W) Oxfordshire v Devon
	Ipswich School	(E) Suffolk v Northumberland
	Pontarddulais	(W) Wales v Cornwall
	Westbury	(W) Wiltshire v Cheshire
Mon 29	Longton	(E) Staffordshire v Hertfordshire
Tue 30	Reading CC	(W) Berkshire v Devon
	Dorchester	(W) Dorset v Cheshire
	Leominster (Dales)	(W) Herefordshire v Cornwall
	Lakenham	(E) Norfolk v Northumberland
AUGUST		
Thu 1	Lakenham	(E) Norfolk v Cambridgeshire
Sun 4	Chester (Boughton Hall)	(W) Cheshire v Wales
	Camborne	(W) Cornwall v Wiltshire
	Exmouth	(W) Devon v Shropshire
	Dean Park	(W) Dorset v Oxfordshire
Mon 5	Lakenham	(E) Norfolk v Hertfordshire
	Bury St Edmunds	(E) Suffolk v Lincolnshire
Tue 6	Wardown Park	(E) Bedfordshire v Cambridgeshire
	St Austell	(W) Cornwall v Shropshire
	Bovey Tracey	(W) Devon v Wiltshire
Sun 11	Dunstable	(E) Bedfordshire v Cumberland
	Hertford	(E) Hertfordshire v Lincolnshire
	Rover Cowley	(W) Oxfordshire v Herefordshire
	Penarth	(W) Wales v Dorset
	Marlborough CC	(W) Wiltshire v Berkshire
Tue 13	Netherfield	(E) Cumberland v Suffolk
Thu 15	Stone	(E) Staffordshire v Suffolk
Sun 18	New Brighton	(W) Cheshire v Herefordshire
	Dean Park	(W) Dorset v Berkshire
	Trowbridge	(E) Wiltshire v Wales
Tue 20	Kidmore End	(W) Berkshire v Oxfordshire
	Marlow	(E) Buckinghamshire v Lincolnshire
	Toft	(W) Cheshire v Shropshire
	Truro	(W) Cornwall v Devon
	Kington	(W) Herefordshire v Wales
	Long Marston	(E) Hertfordshire v Cambridgeshire
	Jesmond	(E) Northumberland v Cumberland
	Brewood	(E) Staffordshire v Bedfordshire
	Mildenhall	(E) Suffolk v Norfolk
	Trowbridge	(W) Wiltshire v Dorset
Wed 28	Lord's	*MCC Trophy Final*
SEPTEMBER		
Sun 8	tba	*Championship Final (Two days)*

PRINCIPAL FIXTURES 1996

** Includes Sunday play*

Saturday 13 April

The Parks: Oxford U v Leics

Monday 15 April

Southampton: Second XI Champions (Hants) v England Under-19 (Four days)

Wednesday 17 April

Fenner's: Cambridge U v Glam
The Parks: Oxford U v Durham

Thursday 18 April

Old Trafford: Lancs v Yorks (Four days)

Saturday 20 April

Tetley's Shield
*Chelmsford: England 'A' v The Rest (Four days)
Other Matches
*Fenner's: Cambridge U v Derbys
The Parks: Oxford U v Middx

Sunday 21 April

Old Trafford: Lancs v Yorks (One day)

Wednesday 24 April

The Parks: British Us v Warwicks (One day)

Friday 26 April

Benson and Hedges Cup
The Parks: British Us v Kent
Chesterfield: Derbys v Durham
Cardiff: Glam v Essex
Bristol: Glos v Sussex
Southampton: Hants v Ireland
Old Trafford: Lancs v Minor Cos
Lord's: Middx v Somerset
Edgbaston: Warwicks v Leics
Worcester: Worcs v Northants
Headingley: Yorks v Notts

Sunday 28 April

Benson and Hedges Cup
Fenner's: British Us v Glam
Chelmsford: Essex v Middx
Maidstone: Kent v Somerset
Old Trafford: Lancs v Durham
Leicester: Leics v Derbys
Jesmond: Minor Cos v Warwicks
Trent Bridge: Notts v Scotland
The Oval: Surrey v Hants
Hove: Sussex v Ireland
Worcester: Worcs v Yorks

Tuesday 30 April

Benson and Hedges Cup
Chesterfield: Derbys v Lancs
Chester-le-Street (Riverside): Durham v Warwicks
Chelmsford: Essex v British Us
Cardiff: Glam v Somerset
Southampton: Hants v Sussex
Canterbury: Kent v Middx
Jesmond: Minor Cos v Leics
Trent Bridge: Notts v Worcs
Forfar: Scotland v Northants
The Oval: Surrey v Glos

Thursday 2 May

Britannic Assurance Championship
Derby: Derbys v Leics
Chester-le-Street (Riverside): Durham v Northants
Cardiff: Glam v Yorks
Canterbury: Kent v Lancs
Lord's: Middx v Glos
Trent Bridge: Notts v Sussex
Taunton: Somerset v Surrey
Worcester: Worcs v Essex
Other Match
The Parks: Oxford U v Hants

Friday 3 May

*Fenner's: Cambridge U v Warwicks

Sunday 5 May

AXA Equity & Law League
Derby: Derbys v Leics
Chester-le-Street (Riverside): Durham v Northants
Cardiff: Glam v Yorks
Canterbury: Kent v Lancs
Lord's: Middx v Glos
Trent Bridge: Notts v Sussex
Taunton: Somerset v Surrey
Worcester: Worcs v Essex
Tourist Match
Arundel: Duke of Norfolk's XI v Indians (One day)

Monday 6 May

Tourist Match
Uxbridge: England NCA v Indians (One day)

Tuesday 7 May

Benson and Hedges Cup
Chester-le-Street (Riverside): Durham v Minor Cos
Chelmsford: Essex v Kent
Dublin (Clontarf CC): Ireland v Glos
Leicester: Leics v Lancs
Lord's: Middx v Glam
Northampton: Northants v Notts
Taunton: Somerset v British Us
Hove: Sussex v Surrey
Edgbaston: Warwicks v Derbys
Headingley: Yorks v Scotland

Wednesday 8 May

Tetley's Challenge Series
Worcester: Worcs v Indians

Thursday 9 May

Britannic Assurance Championship
Southampton: Hants v Essex
Old Trafford: Lancs v Leics
Lord's: Middx v Durham
Northampton: Northants v Glam
Taunton: Somerset v Notts
The Oval: Surrey v Kent
Hove: Sussex v Warwicks
Sheffield: Yorks v Derbys

Saturday 11 May

Tetley's Challenge Series
*Bristol: Glos v Indians
Other Match
The Parks: Oxford U v Cambridge U (One day)

Sunday 12 May

AXA Equity & Law League
Southampton: Hants v Essex
Old Trafford: Lancs v Leics
Lord's: Middx v Durham
Northampton: Northants v Glam
Taunton: Somerset v Notts
The Oval: Surrey v Kent
Hove: Sussex v Warwicks
Sheffield: Yorks v Derbys

Tuesday 14 May

Benson and Hedges Cup
Fenner's: British Us v Middx
Derby: Derbys v Minor Cos
Bristol: Glos v Hants
Eglinton: Ireland v Surrey
Canterbury: Kent v Glam
Old Trafford: Lancs v Warwicks
Leicester: Leics v Durham
Northampton: Northants v Yorks
Edinburgh (Grange CC): Scotland v Worcs
Taunton: Somerset v Essex

Thursday 16 May

Britannic Assurance Championship
Chester-le-Street (Riverside): Durham v Yorks
Ilford: Essex v Kent
Cardiff: Glam v Derbys
Bristol: Glos v Somerset
Leicester: Leics v Worcs
Trent Bridge: Notts v Lancs
Edgbaston: Warwicks v Hants
Tetley's Challenge Series
Hove: Sussex v Indians
Other Matches
Fenner's: Cambridge U v Middx
The Parks: Oxford U v Northants

Sunday 19 May

AXA Equity & Law League
Chester-le-Street (Riverside): Durham v Yorks
Ilford: Essex v Kent

Cardiff: Glam v Derbys
Bristol: Glos v Somerset
Leicester: Leics v Worcs
Trent Bridge: Notts v Lancs
Edgbaston: Warwicks v Hants
Tourist Match
Lord's: Middx v Indians (One day)

Tuesday 21 May

Tourist Match
Luton: Northants v Indians (One day)

Wednesday 22 May

Britannic Assurance Championship
Horsham: Sussex v Middx

Thursday 23 May

TEXACO TROPHY
The Oval: ENGLAND v INDIA
(First Limited-overs International)
Britannic Assurance Championship
Derby: Derbys v Essex
Abergavenny: Glam v Worcs
Gloucester: Glos v Surrey
Portsmouth: Hants v Durham
Canterbury: Kent v Yorks
Taunton: Somerset v Northants
Edgbaston: Warwicks v Leics
Other Match
The Parks: Oxford U v Notts

Saturday 25 May

TEXACO TROPHY
Headingley: ENGLAND v INDIA
(Second Limited-overs International)

Sunday 26 May

TEXACO TROPHY
Old Trafford: ENGLAND v INDIA
(Third Limited-overs International)
AXA Equity & Law League
Derby: Derbys v Essex
Ebbw Vale: Glam v Worcs
Gloucester: Glos v Surrey
Portsmouth: Hants v Durham
Canterbury: Kent v Yorks
Taunton: Somerset v Northants
Horsham: Sussex v Middx
Edgbaston: Warwicks v Leics

Tuesday 28 May

Benson and Hedges Cup
Quarter-Finals
Tetley's Challenge Series
†Chelmsford or Cardiff: Essex or Glam v Indians
†Somerset to play Indians at Taunton if both Essex and Glamorgan involved in B&H Quarter-Finals

Thursday 30 May

Britannic Assurance Championship
Tunbridge Wells: Kent v Sussex
Old Trafford: Lancs v Glos
Lord's: Middx v Yorks
Northampton: Northants v Warwicks
Trent Bridge: Notts v Durham
The Oval: Surrey v Derbys
Worcester: Worcs v Hants

Saturday 1 June

Tetley's Challenge Series
*Leicester: Leics v Indians
Other Match
The Parks: Oxford U v Glam

Sunday 2 June

AXA Equity & Law League
Tunbridge Wells: Kent v Sussex
Old Trafford: Lancs v Glos
Lord's: Middx v Yorks
Northampton: Northants v Warwicks
Trent Bridge: Notts v Durham
The Oval: Surrey v Derbys
Worcester: Worcs v Hants

Wednesday 5 June

Britannic Assurance Championship
Leicester: Leics v Kent

Thursday 6 June

FIRST CORNHILL INSURANCE TEST MATCH
***Edgbaston: ENGLAND v INDIA**
Britannic Assurance Championship
Chelmsford: Essex v Lancs
Southampton: Hants v Derbys
Lord's: Middx v Glam
Trent Bridge: Notts v Northants
Taunton: Somerset v Warwicks
Hove: Sussex v Durham

Middlesbrough: Yorks v Surrey
Other Match
The Parks: Oxford U v Worcs

Sunday 9 June

AXA Equity & Law League
Chelmsford: Essex v Lancs
Southampton: Hants v Derbys
Leicester: Leics v Kent
Lord's: Middx v Glam
Trent Bridge: Notts v Northants
Taunton: Somerset v Warwicks
Hove: Sussex v Durham
Headingley: Yorks v Surrey

Tuesday 11 June

Benson and Hedges Cup
Semi-Finals

Thursday 13 June

Britannic Assurance Championship
Chester-le-Street (Riverside): Durham v Lancs
Chelmsford: Essex v Northants
Swansea: Glam v Somerset
Bristol: Glos v Sussex
Canterbury: Kent v Middx
The Oval: Surrey v Leics
Worcester: Worcs v Notts
Headingley: Yorks v Warwicks
Tetley's Challenge Series
*Derby: Derbys v Indians (Four days)

Friday 14 June

*Fenner's: Cambridge U v Hants

Sunday 16 June

AXA Equity & Law League
Chester-le-Street (Riverside): Durham v Lancs
Chelmsford: Essex v Northants
Swansea: Glam v Somerset
Bristol: Glos v Sussex
Canterbury: Kent v Middx
The Oval: Surrey v Leics
Worcester: Worcs v Notts
Headingley: Yorks v Warwicks

Wednesday 19 June

Britannic Assurance Championship
Basingstoke: Hants v Northants
Bath: Somerset v Worcs

Thursday 20 June

SECOND CORNHILL INSURANCE TEST MATCH
***Lords: ENGLAND v INDIA**
Britannic Assurance Championship
Derby: Derbys v Middx
Stockton: Durham v Surrey
Trent Bridge: Notts v Glos
Hove: Sussex v Glam
Edgbaston: Warwicks v Kent
Bradford: Yorks v Leics

Friday 21 June

*Fenner's: Cambridge U v Essex

Sunday 23 June

AXA Equity & Law League
Derby: Derbys v Middx
Stockton: Durham v Surrey
Basingstoke: Hants v Northants
Trent Bridge: Notts v Glos
Bath: Somerset v Worcs
Hove: Sussex v Glam
Edgbaston: Warwicks v Kent
Bradford: Yorks v Leics

Tuesday 25 June

NatWest Trophy
First Round
March: Cambs v Kent
St Austell: Cornwall v Warwicks
Carlisle: Cumberland v Middx
Chester-le-Street (Riverside): Durham v Scotland
Chelmsford: Essex v Devon
Cardiff: Glam v Worcs
Southampton: Hants v Norfolk
Belfast (North of Ireland CC): Ireland v Sussex
Leicester: Leics v Berks
Sleaford: Lincs v Glos
Northampton: Northants v Cheshire
Aston Rowant: Oxon v Lancs
Taunton: Somerset v Suffolk
Stone: Staffs v Derbys
The Oval: Surrey v Holland
Headingley: Yorks v Notts

Wednesday 26 June

Tourist Match
Fenner's: British Us v Indians (Three days)

Thursday 27 June

Britannic Assurance Championship
Chester-le-Street (Riverside): Durham v Glos
Southend: Essex v Surrey
Old Trafford: Lancs v Somerset
Lord's: Middx v Warwicks
Northampton: Northants v Derbys
Worcester: Worcs v Yorks
Tourist Match
Trowbridge: England NCA v Pakistanis (One day)

Saturday 29 June

Tetley's Challenge Series
*Pontypridd: Glam v Pakistanis
*Southampton: Hants v Indians
Other Matches
*Canterbury: Kent v Oxford U
*Hove: Sussex v Cambridge U

Sunday 30 June

AXA Equity & Law League
Chester-le-Street (Riverside): Durham v Glos
Southend: Essex v Surrey
Old Trafford: Lancs v Somerset
Lord's: Middx v Warwicks
Northampton: Northants v Derbys
Worcester: Worcs v Yorks

Tuesday 2 July

Lord's: Oxford U v Cambridge U (Varsity Match) (Three days)

Wednesday 3 July

Britannic Assurance Championship
Arundel: Sussex v Hants
Tetley's Challenge Series
Taunton: Somerset v Pakistanis
Tourist Match
Headingley: Yorks v South Africa 'A' (Three days)

Thursday 4 July

THIRD CORNHILL INSURANCE TEST MATCH
†Trent Bridge: ENGLAND v INDIA
Britannic Assurance Championship
Bristol: Glos v Glam
Maidstone: Kent v Durham
Old Trafford: Lancs v Worcs
Leicester: Leics v Essex
The Oval: Surrey v Middx
Edgbaston: Warwicks v Notts
†Rest day on Sunday 7 July

Saturday 6 July

Tetley's Challenge Series
*Northampton: Northants v Pakistanis
Tourist Match
*Chesterfield: Derbys v South Africa 'A' (Three days)

Sunday 7 July

AXA Equity & Law League
Bristol: Glos v Glam
Maidstone: Kent v Durham
Old Trafford: Lancs v Worcs
Leicester: Leics v Essex
The Oval: Surrey v Middx
Arundel: Sussex v Hants
Edgbaston: Warwicks v Notts

Wednesday 10 July

NatWest Trophy
Second Round
Truro or Edgbaston: Cornwall or Warwicks v Surrey or Holland
Chelmsford or Torquay: Essex or Devon v Durham or Scotland
Swansea or Worcester: Glam or Worcs v Hants or Norfolk
Leicester or Reading: Leics or Berks v Ireland or Sussex
Aston Rowant or Old Trafford: Oxon or Lancs v Northants or Cheshire
Taunton or Bury St Edmunds: Somerset or Suffolk v Lincs or Glos
Stone or Derby: Staffs or Derbys v Cambs or Kent
Headingley or Trent Bridge: Yorks or Notts v Cumberland or Middx
Tourist Match
Shenley: MCC v South Africa 'A' (Three days)

Thursday 11 July

Tourist Match
Stone: Minor Cos v Pakistanis (One day)

Saturday 13 July

#Lords: *Benson and Hedges Cup Final*
#Reserve days Sun 14 and Mon 15 July

Sunday 14 July

†*AXA Equity & Law League*
Derby: Derbys v Durham
Chelmsford: Essex v Glam
Moreton-in-Marsh: Glos v Kent
Southampton: Hants v Notts
Leicester: Leics v Middx
Northampton: Northants v Yorks
The Oval: Surrey v Worcs
Hove: Sussex v Somerset
Edgbaston: Warwicks v Lancs
Tourist Matches
TBC: Non-First Class Team (TBC) v Pakistanis (One day)
TBC: Non-First Class Team (TBC) v South Africa 'A' (One day)
†Matches involving B&H Cup Finalists to be played on Tuesday 16 July

Monday 15 July

Harrogate: Costcutter Cup (Three days)

Wednesday 17 July

Britannic Assurance Championship
Guildford: Surrey v Sussex
Tetley's Challenge Series
Edgbaston: Warwicks v Pakistanis
Tourist Match
Cardiff: Glam v South Africa 'A' (Three days)

Thursday 18 July

Britannic Assurance Championship
Chelmsford: Essex v Notts
Cheltenham: Glos v Leics
Old Trafford: Lancs v Derbys
Northampton: Northants v Middx
Worcester: Worcs v Durham
Harrogate: Yorks v Hants
Other Match
Chester-le-Street (Riverside): England Under-19 v New Zealand Under-19 (First Youth Limited-overs International)

Saturday 20 July

Tetley Challenge Series
*Canterbury: Kent v Pakistanis
Tourist Match
*Taunton: Somerset v South Africa 'A' (Three days)
Other Match
Trent Bridge: England Under-19 v New Zealand Under-19 (Second Youth Limited-overs International)

Sunday 21 July

AXA Equity & Law League
Chelmsford: Essex v Notts
Cheltenham: Glos v Leics
Old Trafford: Lancs v Derbys
Northampton: Northants v Middx
Guildford: Surrey v Sussex
Worcester: Worcs v Durham
Headingley: Yorks v Hants

Wednesday 24 July

Britannic Assurance Championship
Kidderminster: Worcs v Northants
Tourist Match
Cheltenham: Glos v South Africa 'A' (One day)

Thursday 25 July

FIRST CORNHILL INSURANCE TEST MATCH
***Lord's: ENGLAND v PAKISTAN**
Britannic Assurance Championship
Derby: Derbys v Kent
Hartlepool: Durham v Essex
Cardiff: Glam v Lancs
Cheltenham: Glos v Warwicks
Southampton: Hants v Surrey
Leicester: Leics v Sussex
Scarborough: Yorks v Somerset

Friday 26 July

Tourist Match
*Trent Bridge: Notts v South Africa 'A' (Four days)

Sunday 28 July

AXA Equity & Law League
Derby: Derbys v Kent
Hartlepool: Durham v Essex

Swansea: Glam v Lancs
Cheltenham: Glos v Warwicks
Southampton: Hants v Surrey
Leicester: Leics v Sussex
Worcester: Worcs v Northants
Scarborough: Yorks v Somerset

Tuesday 30 July

NatWest Trophy
Quarter-Finals

Thursday 1 August

Britannic Assurance Championship
Derby: Derbys v Glos
Canterbury: Kent v Worcs
Leicester: Leics v Northants
Lord's: Middx v Essex
Worksop: Notts v Glam
Taunton: Somerset v Hants
Eastbourne: Sussex v Yorks
Tourist Matches
*The Oval: Surrey v South Africa 'A' (Four days)
Edinburgh (Grange CC): Scotland v Pakistanis (One day)
Other Match
*Old Trafford: England Under-19 v New Zealand Under-19 (First Youth Test Match) (Four days)

Saturday 3 August

Tetley's Challenge Series
*Chester-le-Street (Riverside): Durham v Pakistanis

Sunday 4 August

AXA Equity & Law League
Derby: Derbys v Glos
Canterbury: Kent v Worcs
Leicester: Leics v Northants
Lord's: Middx v Essex
Trent Bridge: Notts v Glam
Taunton: Somerset v Hants
Eastbourne: Sussex v Yorks

Tuesday 6 August

Tourist Match
Chelmsford: Essex v South Africa 'A' (One day)

Wednesday 7 August

Britannic Assurance Championship
Southport: Lancs v Surrey

Thursday 8 August

SECOND CORNHILL INSURANCE TEST MATCH
***Headingley: ENGLAND v PAKISTAN**
Britannic Assurance Championship
Swansea: Glam v Leics
Southampton: Hants v Glos
Northampton: Northants v Kent
Trent Bridge: Notts v Middx
Taunton: Somerset v Essex
Hove: Sussex v Derbys
Edgbaston: Warwicks v Durham

Friday 9 August

Tourist Match
*Worcester: Worcs v South Africa 'A' (Four days)

Sunday 11 August

AXA Equity & Law League
Swansea: Glam v Leics
Southampton: Hants v Glos
Old Trafford: Lancs v Surrey
Northampton: Northants v Kent
Trent Bridge: Notts v Middx
Taunton: Somerset v Essex
Hove: Sussex v Derbys
Edgbaston: Warwicks v Durham

Tuesday 13 August

NatWest Trophy
Semi-Finals

Wednesday 14 August

Tetley's Challenge Series
†Leicester or Hove: Leics or Sussex v Pakistanis
†Depending on outcome of NWT Second Round

Thursday 15 August

Britannic Assurance Championship
Derby: Derbys v Notts
Bristol: Glos v Yorks
Canterbury: Kent v Somerset
Old Trafford: Lancs v Hants
Lord's: Middx v Worcs
Edgbaston: Warwicks v Glam
Tourist Match
*Chester-le-Street (Riverside): TCCB XI v South Africa 'A' (Four days)
Other Match
*Worcester: England Under-19 v New Zealand Under-19 (Second Youth Test Match) (Four days)

Thursday 15 or Friday 16 August

Bain Hogg Trophy
Semi-Finals

Saturday 17 August

Tetley's Challenge Series
*Chelmsford: Essex v Pakistanis
Other Match
*Linlithgow (Boghall CC): Scotland v Ireland (Three days)

Sunday 18 August

AXA Equity & Law League
Derby: Derbys v Notts
Bristol: Glos v Yorks
Canterbury: Kent v Somerset
Old Trafford: Lancs v Hants
Lord's: Middx v Worcs
Edgbaston: Warwicks v Glam

Wednesday 21 August

Britannic Assurance Championship
Weston-super-Mare: Somerset v Durham

Thursday 22 August

THIRD CORNHILL INSURANCE TEST MATCH
***The Oval: ENGLAND v PAKISTAN**
Britannic Assurance Championship
Colchester: Essex v Glos
Cardiff: Glam v Kent
Leicester: Leics v Hants
Northampton: Northants v Sussex
Trent Bridge: Notts v Surrey
Worcester: Worcs v Warwicks
Headingley: Yorks v Lancs
Other Match
*Hove: England Under-19 v New Zealand Under-19 (Third Youth Test Match) (Four days)

Sunday 25 August

AXA Equity & Law League
Colchester: Essex v Glos
Cardiff: Glam v Kent
Leicester: Leics v Hants
Northampton: Northants v Sussex
Trent Bridge: Notts v Surrey
Weston-super-Mare: Somerset v Durham
Edgbaston: Warwicks v Worcs
Headingley: Yorks v Lancs

Wednesday 28 August

Britannic Assurance Championship
Chester-le-Street (Riverside): Durham v Glam
Portsmouth: Hants v Middx

Thursday 29 August

TEXACO TROPHY
Old Trafford: ENGLAND v PAKISTAN (First Limited-overs International)
Britannic Assurance Championship
Chesterfield: Derbys v Worcs
Bristol: Glos v Northants
Tunbridge Wells: Kent v Notts
Leicester: Leics v Somerset
The Oval: Surrey v Warwicks
Hove: Sussex v Lancs
Headingley: Yorks v Essex

Saturday 31 August

TEXACO TROPHY
Edgbaston: ENGLAND v PAKISTAN (Second Limited-overs International)

Sunday 1 September

TEXACO TROPHY
Trent Bridge: ENGLAND v PAKISTAN (Third Limited-overs International)
AXA Equity & Law League
Chesterfield: Derbys v Worcs
Chester-le-Street (Riverside): Durham v Glam
Bristol: Glos v Northants
Portsmouth: Hants v Middx
Tunbridge Wells: Kent v Notts

Leicester: Leics v Somerset
The Oval: Surrey v Warwicks
Hove: Sussex v Lancs
Headingley: Yorks v Essex

Tuesday 3 September

Britannic Assurance Championship
Southampton: Hants v Glam
Old Trafford: Lancs v Middx
Trent Bridge: Notts v Leics
Taunton: Somerset v Derbys
The Oval: Surrey v Northants
Edgbaston: Warwicks v Essex
Worcester: Worcs v Sussex

Friday 6 September

Scarborough: Yorks v Tesco International XI (One day)

Saturday 7 September

#Lord's: *NatWest Trophy Final*
Other Match
Scarborough: Yorks v Durham (Northern Electric Trophy) (One day)
#Reserve days Sunday 8 and Monday 9 September

Sunday 8 September

†*AXA Equity & Law League*
Southampton: Hants v Glam
Old Trafford: Lancs v Middx
Trent Bridge: Notts v Leics
Taunton: Somerset v Derbys
The Oval: Surrey v Northants
Edgbaston: Warwicks v Essex
Worcester: Worcs v Sussex
Other Match
Scarborough: Yorks v Holland (McCain Challenge) (One day)
†Matches involving NWT Finalists to be played on Tuesday 10 September

Monday 9 September

TBC: *Bain Hogg Trophy Final* (One day)
Scarborough: Tetley Bitter Trophy (Three days)

Thursday 12 September

Britannic Assurance Championship
Derby: Derbys v Warwicks
Chester-le-Street (Riverside): Durham v Leics
Chelmsford: Essex v Sussex
Cardiff: Glam v Surrey
Canterbury: Kent v Hants
Uxbridge: Middx v Somerset
Northampton: Northants v Lancs
Worcester: Worcs v Glos
Scarborough: Yorks v Notts

Sunday 15 September

AXA Equity & Law League
Derby: Derbys v Warwicks
Chester-le-Street (Riverside): Durham v Leics
Chelmsford: Essex v Sussex
Cardiff: Glam v Surrey
Canterbury: Kent v Hants
Uxbridge: Middx v Somerset
Northampton: Northants v Lancs
Worcester: Worcs v Glos
Scarborough: Yorks v Notts

Thursday 19 September

Britannic Assurance Championship
*Derby: Derbys v Durham
*Chelmsford: Essex v Glam
*Bristol: Glos v Kent
*Southampton: Hants v Notts
*Leicester: Leics v Middx
*Northampton: Northants v Yorks
*The Oval: Surrey v Worcs
*Hove: Sussex v Somerset
*Edgbaston: Warwicks v Lancs

FIELDING CHART

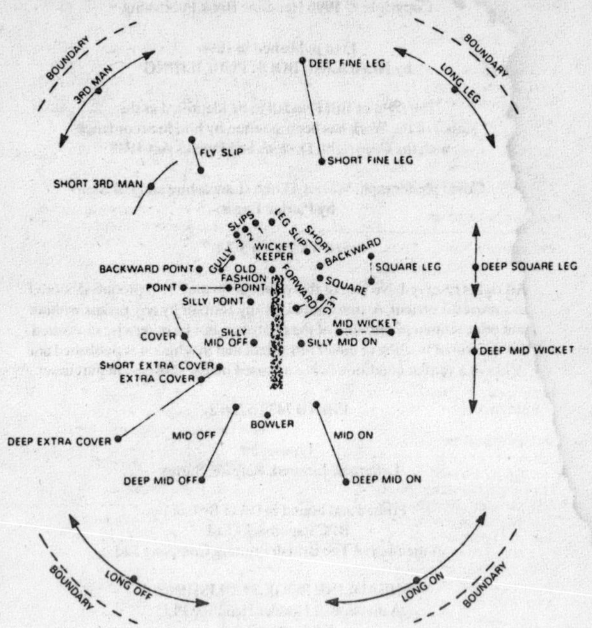

First published in 1996
by HEADLINE BOOK PUBLISHING

Cover photograph: Wasim Akram (Lancashire and Pakistan)
by Patrick Eagar

10 9 8 7 6 5 4 3 2 1

ISBN 0 7472 5226 2

Typeset by
Letterpart Limited, Reigate, Surrey

Printed and bound in Great Britain by
BPC Paperbacks Ltd
A member of The British Printing Company Ltd

HEADLINE BOOK PUBLISHING
A division of Hodder Headline PLC
338 Euston Road
London NW1 3BH